W9-ADR-604

A COMPELLING BOOK . . . details a pattern of misconduct, corporate backstabbing, in-fighting and attempts at cover-up at the highest levels of Prudential's management. There also are tales of wild parties, exotic trips for the sales force, and secret deals with shady characters. —*Miami Herald*

RIVETING . . . in keeping with the tradition of American financial writing that has been emerging since the best-selling story of the takeover of RJR Nabisco, *Barbarians at the Gate.* —*The Economist*

POWERFUL . . . RICH IN DETAIL AND INSIGHT, it is sure to be the definitive book on the scandal. Indeed, it should be required reading for investors, brokers, and brokerage-firm managers. —*Business Week*

ABSORBING AND DEFINITIVE . . . A masterful reconstruction of a substantive financial scandal, one that bears comparison with such landmark exposés as *Barbarians at the Gate, Den of Thieves,* and *The Predators' Ball.* —*Kirkus Reviews*

A SHOCKING STORY OF GREED AND FINANCIAL MANEUVERING. —*Dayton Daily News*

By the time readers finish this well-reported tale, they'll want to string Pru's manager up by their power ties . . . an appalling indictment of the firm's managers, who did dozens of deals with a convicted embezzler, spent millions of investors' dollars on lavish trips to places like Cancun and Maui, and made cozy arrangements with developers to make themselves rich no matter how their clients fared. —*Newsweek*

AN ENTERTAINING AND AN IMPORTANT WORK. —*Publishers Weekly*

FOR A BOOK TO RAISE YOUR BLOOD PRESSURE, READ *SERPENT ON THE ROCK* . . . A STUNNING ACCOUNT. —Jane Bryant Quinn

What are the ingredients to a world class scandal? Abuse of power. A cover-up. Kickbacks. Sleazy characters in nice suits. Innocent victims. Some sex, a few drugs. You name it, the long, sordid tale of Prudential Securities' disastrous foray into the limited partnership business has it . . . a fast paced, skillful rendering . . . engrossing, written in a breezy style and full of revealing details. —*Institutional Investor*

A RIVETING ACCOUNT. —*National Law Journal*

The story would rival a good fictional counterpart in characters, plot, and storytelling. But *Serpent on the Rock* is true. —*San Diego Union Tribune*

A casebook of how not to manage a financial business. —*The Financial Times*

SIZZLES . . . A TELL-ALL BOOK . . . A FANTASTIC PIECE OF WORK. —*South Florida Business Journal*

A MUCKRAKING BOOK. —CNN

Eichenwald goes after Pru-Bache big shots with prosecutorial zeal. He exposes many of them as, variously, liars, bullies, bigots, drunks, cads, and vulgarians. —*USA Today*

AN ELECTRIFYING ACCOUNT . . . don't give this one to your broker. It might give him ideas. —*The American Spectator*

Written in the breathless tradition of *The Predators' Ball*, *Den of Thieves* and *Barbarians at the Gate*. —*Barron's*

AN INCREDIBLE STORY . . . A GRIPPING ACCOUNT . . . The next time someone offers you an investment opportunity too good to refuse, head straight to your library or bookstore for a copy of Kurt Eichenwald's *Serpent on the Rock*, and don't commit a dime until you've read every word. —*The Press Democrat* (Santa Clara, California)

I raved about (*Serpent*) to everyone . . . its narrative unfolds at a breathless pace, and the book is chock-full of richly demonic and quietly heroic characters, lending it a moral vision. —*Insight*

SERPENT ON THE ROCK

SERPENT ON THE ROCK

KURT EICHENWALD

BROADWAY BOOKS
NEW YORK

Visit our website at www.broadwaybooks.com

First Broadway Books trade paperback edition published 2005.

Book design by Lovedog Studio

The Library of Congress Cataloging-in-Publication Data
Eichenwald, Kurt, 1961–
Serpent on the rock / Kurt Eichenwald.
p. cm.
Originally published: New York : HarperBusiness, c1995.
Includes bibliographical references and index.
1. Prudential-Bache Securities, Inc.—Corrupt practices. 2. Securities fraud—United States—Case studies. I. Title.

HV6769.E39 2005
364.16'8—dc22
2005050158

ISBN 0-7679-2384-7 — ISBN 0-7679-2054-6

5 7 9 10 8 6

For my wife, Theresa,

whose love, support, and patience

made it possible

O, that deceit should dwell
In such a gorgeous palace!

> —William Shakespeare,
> *Romeo and Juliet,* Act III, Scene 2

As a firm, we must continuously measure what we do against a barometer that is calibrated in integrity. Our standing should be second to none.

> —George L. Ball, chairman and chief executive,
> Prudential-Bache Securities, July 21, 1988

When we say "Integrity and quality are everything," we mean it.

> —Loren Schechter, general counsel,
> Prudential Securities, June 29, 1992

It is fair to say that Prudential-Bache Securities' reputation within the securities industry is deplorable. . . . [The firm] is well known for its abusive sales practices, lack of adherence to compliance procedures, securities law violations and abusive practices towards its own employees. . . . Prudential-Bache Securities is, quite simply, the author of its own unfortunate reputation.

> —John P. Cione, former lawyer
> with the Securities and Exchange Commission,
> in a sworn statement of July 1990

PREFACE

As long as there is greed, as long as crimes go unpunished, as long as Wall Street can make millions even when clients lose money, the scandal at Prudential will be just another chapter in an ongoing saga of financial fraud . . . if history is any guide, that is a certainty. The only questions are: Who will do it next time? And when?

When I wrote those words in 1996 for the paperback edition of *Serpent on the Rock*, I knew next to nothing about two fast-growing corporate darlings of the 1990s, Enron and WorldCom. About the time the paperback arrived in bookstores, the first of a long series of crimes at Enron—which would collapse in a spectacular scandal in 2001—had begun. WorldCom's first significant crimes were still four years off. But those corporate names, and those dates, were the answer to the rhetorical question I had left with readers. Enron and WorldCom, facilitated by Wall Street investment banks eager to lap up fees, would be the next corporate villains, the next significant culprits in the long line of businesses that have turned to fraud and, in the process, wrecked the lives of untold numbers of Americans.

As I covered the unfolding Enron and WorldCom scandals for the *New York Times*—and later transformed Enron into a book, *Conspiracy of Fools*—at times, I could not help but think that we as a nation were reaping what we sowed. The outrage at Prudential had been just one in a long series of warnings about weaknesses in our financial system, signals that had all too long been ignored. I am something of a fatalist on this issue—as long as big money can be made from fraud, corporate scandals will always be with us. But even I would have thought that the embers from Prudential would have been long cooled before the next fire was lit. For all my pessimism, I was too optimistic.

Why did we learn nothing? Why did corporate America continue down this self-destructive path? To me, the answer is obvious: Despite the vast wreckage caused by Prudential's fraud, no individual was ever held accountable. No one went to jail, no individual was cited by the Securities and Exchange Commission. There were plenty of reasons why—mostly revolving around the statute of limitations. But the limited government action contributed to the full story never being understood by much of the public.

Perhaps the biggest missed lesson was one for business itself. The Prudential scandal demonstrated in myriad different ways the damage inflicted on a corporation when managers fail to pay sufficient attention to protecting the brand name. Rather than simply facing what the firm had done and admitting it, Prudential launched a legal and communications strategy designed to conceal, deny, and mislead. That may have served the firm for a time in the courtroom—although I am hard-pressed to believe that Prudential would have been compelled to pay *more* than the billions it ultimately coughed up. But there is no doubt that this effort forever damaged the name Prudential, leaving it eternally linked to scandal.

The type of obfuscation strategy employed by Prudential—and numerous other institutions wrapped up in such debacles—often backfires. The reason is simple: Regardless of how tainted a corporate culture becomes, most business executives *want* to do the right thing. They want those who do business with them to walk away happy with the experience and eager to return. They want, in short, to be part of an honorable institution, one that gives them pride.

That is why many widespread frauds—particularly those that damage individual customers and investors—often become public. Even if leaders of an institution—whether it be corporate, political, or governmental—decide to cover up, there are always people on the inside who, for a variety of reasons, will try to make sure the wrongs are righted. At both Enron and WorldCom, these types of whistle-blowers played important roles in forcing the scandals to the surface. Sometimes, whistle-blowers work through the system, going up the line of an institution in hopes of finding a remedy. When that fails, they will turn to outsiders—law enforcement, Congress, or sometimes reporters like me.

In the course of my coverage of the Prudential scandal, numerous executives stepped forward on a confidential basis to confirm key pieces of information, details I could never have learned from an outside source. Their motives varied: some were using the press for their own bureaucratic reasons, some were bitter, some were angry. But a surprising number were simply outraged by what Prudential had done, and had come to believe that only the truth would cleanse the company. Many of these executives had seen the destruction of the careers of other Prudential executives who tried to stop what was happening—stories related in these pages—and chose to no longer trust the institution with their concerns. Instead, they went outside the family with their evidence of wrongdoing.

Months into my reporting, there were executives at so many levels of the firm working with me that Prudential's secrets became easy to discover. When the firm was preparing to notify the SEC that subpoenaed records could not be located, a copy of those documents ended up in my possession. When a meeting was held at the highest reaches of the firm to discuss how to keep secret some potential litigation, I was made aware of the meeting, the decision, and the underlying legal claim before the week was out.

Prudential's method of dealing with this was almost funny: Repeatedly, senior executives of the firm would go on the internal squawk box, lambasting my reporting to Prudential's thousands of employees. It was a delightful miscalculation. I could always tell when I had been criticized to the employees; it was as if Prudential was advertising me to potential sources. For days after each squawk box statement, I would receive telephone calls from executives and employees in Prudential offices around the country, offering up leads and tips for stories that I might never have discovered.

The senior executives of Prudential dealing with this scandal never seemed to understand that truth was their ally. If they had simply stopped trying to deny what so many people inside the firm already knew, many of my sources of information would have dried up overnight. If they had stood up and taken responsibility for the horrible things that had happened there, they would have reinforced that the Prudential name still stood for integrity and honor, not obfuscation and deceit.

Moreover, they never would have had to deal with this book. I remember the moment I realized how necessary this book was. Prudential had finally cut a deal with criminal prosecutors, receiving a deferred prosecution agreement. Under that deal, the firm admitted violating the law and defrauding customers, and was put under what is akin to a form of probation.

I returned from that court proceeding eager to hear what Prudential executives had to say, now that the firm had confessed. In a telephone call, one of its senior executives dismissed the admission of guilt: that was just a business decision, the executive said. Everyone inside, he said, still knew that Prudential had done nothing wrong.

I hung up the phone, astounded. Clearly, Prudential planned to continue denying what the evidence showed. That knowledge lit a fire under me. I had to show the world, all in one place, everything that unfolded inside of Prudential.

So as you read the stories of the horrible secrets of Prudential, remember one thing: Many of these tales may well have stayed buried forever, if the firm had simply been honest once it discovered the extent of the wrongdoing inside. To paraphrase an epigraph of this book, Prudential—and Enron, and WorldCom, and all of the other corporations that have become enmeshed in scandal—are truly the authors of these tales. And, sad to say, they and companies like them will keep on writing such stories long into the future.

—Kurt Eichenwald
September, 2005

THE MAIN CHARACTERS

In the late 1970s, as change is sweeping across Wall Street

AT BACHE & COMPANY, NEW YORK
Harry Jacobs, chief executive
Virgil Sherrill, president
Robert Sherman, head of retail for branch group west
Leland B. Paton, head of marketing
Guy Wyser-Pratte, head of arbitrage
Bill Jones, head of security

With the Tax Shelter Department
Stephen Blank, head of division through the summer of 1979
James J. Darr, head of division in the fall of 1979
James Ashworth, regional marketer
David Hayes, regional marketer
Curtis Henry, originator
Dennis Marron, marketer and originator
John D'Elisa, originator
Wally Allen, product manager

The investors in Bache stock
Samuel Belzberg, chief executive, First City Financial
Nelson Bunker Hunt, a Texas billionaire
Lamar Hunt, a Texas billionaire

AT JOSEPHTHAL & COMPANY, NEW YORK
Michael DeMarco, president
Norman Gershman, national sales manager
Neil Sinclair, head of real estate marketing for tax shelters

AT E. F. HUTTON, NEW YORK
Robert Fomon, chairman
George Ball, president
Loren Schechter, deputy general counsel

THE CORPORATE LAWYERS
Martin Lipton, Wachtell, Lipton, Rosen & Katz, New York (counsel for Bache and the Belzbergs)
Clark Clifford of Clifford & Warnke, Washington, D.C. (counsel for Bache)
Alan Gosule of Gaston & Snow, Boston (counsel for Josephthal's tax shelter department)

THE GENERAL PARTNERS
Barry Trupin, head of Rothchild Reserve International, New York
Matthew Antell, president, First Eastern Corporation, Boston
Herb Jacobi, general counsel, First Eastern Corporation, Boston

In the early to mid-1980s, as the partnership business is booming

AT PRUDENTIAL-BACHE SECURITIES, NEW YORK
George Ball, chairman and chief executive
Loren Schechter, general counsel
Robert Sherman, head of retail
Richard Sichenzio, senior vice-president and, later, head of retail

In the Direct Investment Group
James J. Darr, director
William Pittman, product manager and, later, head of all due diligence
Paul Proscia, product manager
David Levine, real estate due diligence
Freddie Kotek, real estate due diligence
Joseph Quinn, real estate due diligence
Douglas Holbrook, energy due diligence
Joseph DeFur, product manager
James Parker, regional marketer
John S. R. Hutchison, product manager
David Wrubel, regional marketer
Frank Giordano, lawyer
Kathy Eastwick, product manager

In the Retail Branches

J. Frederic Storaska, director, Corporate Executive Services, Dallas

Charles Grose, branch manager, Dallas

Carrington Clark, regional director for the Pacific North

John Graner, regional director Southeast and, later, Pacific South

James Trice, regional director Pacific South and, later, Southeast

Richard Saccullo, Atlanta branch manager

AT PRUDENTIAL INSURANCE, NEWARK, NEW JERSEY

Robert Beck, chairman through 1986

Robert Winters, chairman from 1986

Garnett Keith, vice-chairman and supervisor of Prudential-Bache

Matthew Chanin, head of energy investments

AT HARRISON FREEDMAN ASSOCIATES, DALLAS, TEXAS

Clifton S. Harrison, principal

Michael Walters, national sales manager

AT GRAHAM RESOURCES, METAIRIE AND COVINGTON, LOUISIANA

John J. Graham, president and chief executive

Anton Rice III, chief financial officer

Mark Files, vice-president

Paul Grattarola, marketer

Pete Theo, marketer

Alfred Dempsey, executive vice-president

John Corbin, regional wholesaler

Robert Jackson, regional wholesaler

AT THE WATSON & TAYLOR COMPANIES, DALLAS, TEXAS

George Watson, principal

Austin Starke Taylor III, principal

William Petty, national sales manager

AT THE SAVINGS & LOANS

Howard Wiechern, chairman of First South Savings, Pine Bluff, Arkansas

John Roberts Jr., president, Summit Savings, San Antonio, Texas

James Holbrooke, a lawyer for Summit Savings, San Antonio, Texas

In the late 1980s and early 1990s, as the scandal unfolds

AT PRUDENTIAL SECURITIES, NEW YORK

Hardwick Simmons, chief executive

Howard A. "Woody" Knight, president of investment banking and corporate strategy

THE WHISTLE-BLOWERS

William Webb, stockbroker, Fort Myers, Florida

Joseph Siff, stockbroker, Houston

William Creedon, stockbroker, Los Angeles

Eugene Boyle, stockbroker, Wayne, New Jersey

THE PLAINTIFFS' LAWYERS

Charles Cox, partner, Cox & Goudy, Minneapolis, Minnesota

J. Boyd Page, partner, Page & Bacek, Atlanta, Georgia

B. Daryl Bristow, partner, Bristow, Hackerman, Wilson & Peterson, Houston, Texas

Stephen M. Hackerman, partner, Bristow, Hackerman, Wilson & Peterson, Houston, Texas

James R. Moriarty, principal, James R. Moriarty & Associates

AT LOCKE PURNELL RAIN HARRELL, DALLAS, TEXAS

Bud Berry, partner

AT DAVIS, POLK & WARDWELL, NEW YORK AND WASHINGTON, D.C. (COUNSEL FOR PRUDENTIAL SECURITIES)

Gary Lynch, partner

Scott Muller, partner

AT WILMER, CUTLER & PICKERING, WASHINGTON, D.C. (COUNSEL FOR PRUDENTIAL SECURITIES)

Arthur Mathews, partner

AT THE COURTHOUSE

Marcel Livaudais, Federal District Judge, New Orleans

AT THE STATE TASK FORCE

Wayne Klein, chief, Idaho Securities Bureau

Nancy Smith, director, New Mexico Securities Division

Lewis Brothers, director, Virginia Division of Securities

Matthew Neubert, assistant director, Arizona Securities Division

Don Saxon, director, Florida Division of Securities

AT THE SECURITIES AND EXCHANGE COMMISSION, WASHINGTON, D.C.

William McLucas, director of enforcement

Thomas Newkirk, assistant director of enforcement

Joseph Goldstein, associate director of enforcement

Pat Conti, counsel and, later, branch chief, enforcement division

PROLOGUE

JUNE 1991—SCOTTSDALE, ARIZONA

Rhoda Silverman eased her 1984 Chevy Suburban out of the driveway, starting her weekly two-mile trip to her elderly mother's condominium. Saturday had been their day for years, a time when they could chat over breakfast at Smitty's or Luby's Cafeteria. Sometimes, on special days, they even splurged for lunch at Red Lobster.

She flipped on the car's air-conditioning. Summer in Scottsdale had arrived early this year, and this Saturday was particularly sweltering. To beat the heat, they probably would spend the day window shopping at Fashion Square Mall, the newly renovated indoor shopping center. Their visits to department stores had become a Saturday favorite in recent years after Rhoda's mother, Fannie Victor, began to lose her sight to a degenerative eye disease. The eighty-year-old woman loved to sample perfumes, touch the different clothing textures, or just sit in her wheelchair by the fountain, listening to the crowds.

Rhoda looked ahead to the McDowell Mountains as she turned onto Mountain View Road, the carefully landscaped street leading directly to her mother's condo. It was a beautiful drive. But she knew this was one of the last Saturdays she would take it.

Why couldn't I have protected you?

The question almost never left Rhoda's mind. She knew that she and her husband, Bernard, had kept the secret too long, hoping somehow that they would find a solution. But endless tries, sleepless nights, and frequent tears got them nowhere. She was still brooding about it when she reached the parking lot of her mother's retirement community. Maybe, she thought, maybe today would be the day. Maybe, finally, she could tell her mother the truth.

But how do I tell a blind, crippled old woman that she's losing her home?

Rhoda still didn't understand how it happened. Everything had started with such promise. Her mother moved to Arizona in 1985 to be closer to her children. She arrived with about $100,000 from the sale of the small Brooklyn row house she had lived in for decades. It was the first time in her life that Fannie had some money. After all the years of frugality and hard work, of going without vacations or movies or fancy clothes, Fannie finally could live the rest of her life in comfort. All she needed were safe investments.

That was when Bernard met Steve Ziomeck, a young vice-president with Prudential-Bache Securities, at a Scottsdale businessmen's club. Ziomeck's knowledge of finance impressed Bernard, much to Rhoda's delight. After all, she could think of no place safer for her mother's money than with "the Rock," the name that decades of popular advertising helped bestow on the Prudential Insurance Company of America, the company that bought the brokerage in 1981.

When Fannie and her family went to the local Prudential-Bache branch for the first time, Ziomeck put them immediately at ease. A good-looking young broker with a baby face and a calming sales style, he stressed the words that mattered to them: Safety. Security. Income. None of them quite understood the investments Ziomeck recommended. Still, since neither Rhoda nor Bernard had much college or knowledge of finance, they figured that they should trust their broker's selections. Besides, the investments seemed well diversified, in a range of businesses like energy, real estate, airplane leasing, and horse breeding. Ziomeck told them that Fannie could expect $792.67 a month from the investments. Combined with Social Security and money from her children, that was enough to let her live in her own apartment.

With the money tucked away, Rhoda found a spot for her mother at the Villages at McCormick Ranch in Scottsdale. Fannie fell in love with the condo, with its Mexican tile, recessed ceiling, and large bedroom. It was poolside and on the ground level, so she easily could come and go in her wheelchair. Even though her vision was already faltering badly, she still had time to learn her way around before she lost her sight. This was the place, Fannie decided, where she wanted to live out her last days. With Rhoda's help, she took out a mortgage and bought it.

The problems started almost immediately. Checks from Prudential-Bache did not come monthly, as they had thought, but instead every three months. Even then, the money was far less than what Ziomeck told them they could expect. Eventually the checks stopped coming entirely. Rhoda and Bernard, who handled Fannie's bills, began covering her mortgage payments with their own money. But they couldn't keep that up long—

their own business was struggling as the economy slowed, and they just didn't have the cash.

Finally, in November 1990, Rhoda telephoned Ziomeck's assistant, Kelly, exasperated about the investments' poor performance. Why didn't the breeding company make some money by just selling the damn horses? Rhoda asked sharply.

"Didn't anybody tell you?" Kelly responded. "They went out of business."

Rhoda demanded to speak with Ziomeck, and peppered him with questions. She learned that her mother's financial situation was dire. Her mother didn't own stocks, as Rhoda had thought, but something called limited partnerships, a name she did not remember hearing before. The partnerships were performing terribly but couldn't be sold. Unlike stocks and bonds, no real market to buy and sell them existed. All Rhoda's mother could do was hang on, Ziomeck said, and hope that the partnerships' fortunes improved.

But there was no time to wait. Already they were months behind on Fannie's mortgage payments. Rhoda explained the troubles to the mortgage company and offered to turn over the deed to the condo if her mother could stay on as a renter. But the company said foreclosure was the only option. Her mother would have to move out.

Rhoda pulled her car into the space behind her mother's condo. Maybe now was not the right time to tell, she thought. Maybe let her enjoy today.

She went to the door of the condo, swinging it open as she knocked. Fannie was ready, waiting at her kitchen table in a flowered sundress. Rhoda hugged and kissed her mother, and sat down beside her. She launched into some idle chitchat.

Fannie immediately sensed something was wrong. "You're very tense," she said. "You're agitated. What's the matter?"

Rhoda stammered for a moment. Then she blurted it out. "There's a problem," she said, her voice trembling. "I don't know how to go about saying this. I guess the best way is the truth straight out."

For the next few minutes, she rambled about what had happened: the declining income. The partnerships. The mortgage. The failed attempts to find a solution.

Her mother listened quietly. It wasn't sinking in.

Rhoda took a breath. "We've lost the apartment, Mom," she said. "We'll keep trying to get out of this. Maybe business will pick up. I'll try everything I can. But we have to start looking for another place for you to live."

For an instant, the two sat in silence at the table. And then Rhoda heard a throaty, guttural sound like nothing she had ever heard. It was her mother's moan of horror.

"Why would they want to throw an old lady out into the street?" Fannie sobbed, tears streaming down her face. "I don't want to be homeless. I don't want to leave."

Rhoda sank down off her chair and, on her knees, wrapped her arms around her crying mother.

"This is my home," Fannie cried. "I love it here. Oh, please, I don't want to go."

Rhoda could not find the words to calm her mother. Her own guilt and sense of failure overwhelmed her. She began crying, apologizing again and again.

It seemed like they sat there forever. Rhoda held her mother close, rocking her, fruitlessly trying to calm her. Finally, her tears exhausted, Fannie looked up at her daughter.

"Rhoda," she said. "Where did all the money go?"

AUGUST 1993—SAN DIEGO, CALIFORNIA

Mike Piscitelli stared down at the stainless-steel .357 magnum revolver in his hand. The silvery metal of the gun was clean and bright, perfectly reflecting the light of his bedroom. Such was his reward for cleaning the gun every time he fired it and polishing it even if he didn't.

He looked up and saw himself in the bedroom mirror a few feet away. He almost didn't recognize his reflection. Even with his tall, wiry frame, Piscitelli had never seen himself so gaunt. In the last few months, he had lost about two inches from his waist. The dark circles under his eyes from his daily insomnia gave his face a worn, hollowed-out look.

So much had changed. So much had been lost.

Piscitelli watched his reflection as he raised the handgun. Slowly he slid the tip of the six-inch barrel between his teeth. He paused, staring at his image in the mirror as he held the powerful gun in his mouth.

A few years earlier he could never have imagined reaching this point. Piscitelli had been a success. With only a year of college and a career in the wholesale liquor business, he had become a stockbroker in the early 1980s and worked his way up to being a top salesman with Prudential-Bache, the country's third-largest brokerage firm. He earned almost $200,000 a year.

He married a woman he loved. He counted many of his 125 clients as friends.

And then the lies wrecked everything. The lies the firm told him. The lies he repeated to his customers.

The lies helped bring him to Prudential-Bache in 1986. Lewis Jacobsen, the firm's branch manager in Rancho Bernardo, recruited him from Merrill Lynch that year, telling Piscitelli about Pru-Bache's limited partnerships, which pooled small investors' money to buy expensive assets like apartment buildings, oil wells, and airplanes. Pru-Bache had the best partnerships on Wall Street, Jacobsen had said. They gave clients handsome returns and big tax benefits. And, unlike other firms, Prudential-Bache not only paid brokers large commissions for selling the investments but also gave them a share of the cash the partnerships produced later. By selling partnerships, Bache brokers could create their own personal retirement plan, without ever contributing a penny of their own.

It took six months, but Jacobsen sold Piscitelli on Prudential-Bache. It was worth the effort—Piscitelli soon became one of the firm's top salesmen. Using computer programs provided by the brokerage, he recommended how his clients should diversify their investments. The computer almost always said that a chunk of the clients' money should go into Pru-Bache partnerships.

Piscitelli never reviewed the dense, legalistic documents each partnership filed with the Securities and Exchange Commission—he had neither the time nor the desire. That was not his job. Instead, like most stockbrokers, he examined the sales material provided to him by the firm. That was supposed to summarize, in simple English, what the filings said. Then he passed that information on to his clients. The partnerships were safe investments, some as secure as certificates of deposit in the bank. Still, they paid a huge yield, often as much as 13 percent to 19 percent, with some of that money tax-free. Investors could scarcely resist that pitch. By 1988, Piscitelli had sold more than $9 million worth of the partnerships to his clients and friends. The sales material was so convincing that he even bought some for his own portfolio.

But by the late 1980s something terrible started to happen. The Prudential-Bache partnerships began to fall apart, starting with one of the biggest, VMS Mortgage Investment Fund. A real estate partnership, VMS Mortgage had guaranteed high income for three years and then return of the original investment. But instead it simply collapsed. The once-guaranteed income vanished, and most of the principal was lost. Suddenly some of Piscitelli's friends were forced to take out second mortgages on their homes to continue their retirement. Piscitelli called Pru-Bache executives in New York demanding to know what was happening. His was one of hundreds of telephone calls from brokers around the country. Eventually New York stopped answering questions.

Piscitelli's chest pains started soon afterward, followed by intense headaches. He took eight aspirin a day, but the headaches just grew worse. As other partnerships came undone, he spent his days dealing with angry clients while desperately trying to hold his own life together.

Friends filed lawsuits against the firm and Piscitelli. His constant anxiety destroyed his marriage. His annual income dropped to $20,000. A few anonymous telephone callers threatened to kill him. Fearful for his safety, Piscitelli purchased a .25-caliber pistol and a .357 magnum. He loaded them with hollow-point bullets and carried one of the guns at all times, ready to defend himself against his former friends.

By 1993, Piscitelli could no longer function in his job. He couldn't concentrate. He was always irritable. He frequently wept. That May, he went on disability leave. A doctor for Prudential would later diagnose Piscitelli as suffering a major depression caused by anxiety related to the partnership troubles. The broker could not overcome his sense of having betrayed his friends and of having been betrayed by his employer.

Piscitelli looked into the mirror. Tears were streaming down his face and onto the gun in his mouth. He was crying uncontrollably again. He took the barrel out from between his lips and wiped away the tears. Then he turned to put the weapon back into his closet.

He had put the gun in his mouth before. He was sure he would do it again.

Maybe, someday, the time would be right.

But not today. Not today.

※   ※   ※   ※

SLOWLY, ALMOST imperceptibly, the truth settled in as the 1990s began. One at a time, until they numbered in the hundreds, then the thousands, then the hundreds of thousands, people in every state and around the world awoke to realize that they had been victims of the most destructive fraud ever perpetrated on investors by Wall Street.

Although the magnitude of the crime was unparalleled, it was not engineered by the shady penny-stock promoters or crooked savings and loan operators who exist on the underbelly of the financial world. Rather, the scheme emerged full-blown from the New York headquarters of one of the brokerage industry's brightest lights, an investment firm with a name that conveyed the essence of reliability and trust: Prudential-Bache Securities.

The cost of the fraud, in financial and human terms, was so large it surpasses imagination. More than $8 billion worth of risky partnerships packaged by Pru-Bache collapsed after they had been falsely sold as safe and secure. Even after the partnerships lost most of their value, investors had no idea what had happened. Every month, on millions of account statements, Prudential-Bache lied about the true worth of the partnership portfolios, showing them as never having lost a penny in value. And so the damage spread unchecked for more than a decade, like a low-grade fever building slowly toward a fatal disease.

In the end, no single brokerage firm, banker, or trader destroyed the financial security of more people than Prudential-Bache. The losses from the celebrated insider-trading and junk-bond scandals of the 1980s add up to only a small fraction of the damage suffered by investors from the betrayals at Pru-Bache. And yet the hue and outcry that swept the country over the harm inflicted on powerful corporations and institutions by those scandals went unheard for years in the partnership debacle; for too long, the financially unsophisticated victims of Prudential-Bache's crimes did not have powerful lawyers fighting for them or the financial firepower to make their voices heard in Washington. They suffered alone, their scars unseen or ignored for years.

The crime was finally visible when, by the thousands, the firm's clients faced the prospect of losing their homes, their retirements, their children's education. Some investors who carefully pinched pennies for decades wound up in bankruptcy. Scores of Prudential-Bache brokers saw their careers, their health, and their lives fall apart, often because they unwittingly repeated the firm's lies about the investments. Still other brokers, caught up in the greedy revelry of the firm, violated securities laws and common sense by concentrating the portfolios of elderly retirees in the high-commission investments.

The fraud, beginning in the early 1980s, brought in more than a billion dollars in profits to the firm, through the fees and commissions paid by the partnership sales. At the center of the scandal was the Direct Investment Group, the little-known department that propelled Prudential-Bache to the forefront of the partnership business. For executives at the senior reaches of the firm, the flow of cash from the department's business became personal piggy banks, financing profligate corporate spending, regal lifestyles, and even sexual conquest. Limousines, wild parties, and expensive overseas junkets became the order of the day, paid for out of clients' investment dollars.

Overseeing this money machine was a small group of executives who cut corners or ignored problems as they promoted the firm and built personal empires. Alone, none of these men could have created the disaster that emerged from Prudential-Bache; together, their weaknesses and desires combined to push the firm inexorably toward scandal. At the head of the partnership department was James J. Darr, a hard-charging executive who took over in 1979 after his scrupulous predecessor was fired for refusing to sell deals of questionable quality. Darr transformed the department into an organization overwhelmed by charges of corruption.

But the executives who were supposed to watch Darr and rein in rulebreakers simply celebrated the department's financial success, with little attention to how the business was being done. At the top were George L. Ball, a celebrated wunderkind of Wall Street who, as president of E. F. Hutton & Co., oversaw a separate and fatal scandal for that firm before abandoning it to take over as chairman of Prudential-Bache; Loren Schechter, the firm's general counsel and chief law enforcer, who for years failed to notice the evidence of wrongdoing in his midst; and Robert Sherman, the head of retail at the firm, whose taste for liquor, eye for women, and desire for power became ingredients in decisions he made as Darr's supervisor.

The inside story of this massive fraud begins in the dawn of the 1980s at Bache & Company, a struggling third-tier brokerage already mired in scandal. In 1981, the firm was reborn and elevated to a newfound public esteem when it was purchased by Prudential, the respected insurance company. But as Bache's image improved, many of its shoddy practices worsened. By the end, the firm experienced a chain of scandals with connections like an archipelago, visible only beneath the surface. It is only in hindsight that each of those scandals can be seen as warnings—tragically missed, though sounded repeatedly over more than fourteen years—about the terrible secrets at Prudential-Bache Securities.

At its base, this is a cautionary tale about an abuse of the investor faith that is an essential building block of the American economy. That faith has created great industries, from the dawn of the railroad to the age of computers, by allowing huge pools of money to be channeled from individual investors to growing businesses. It has touched almost every American home, helping working people achieve financial independence or reach goals only dreamed of by their parents. At its essence, it is what allows billions of dollars of securities to trade each day based on nothing more than a voice on the telephone. By taking advantage of that faith, Prudential-Bache cracked the foundation of the marketplace. It robbed us of our ability to believe. It betrayed us all.

PART ONE
BEGINNINGS

CHAPTER 1

SOMEBODY AT BACHE & COMPANY was out to get them. The lieutenants in the firm's tax shelter department just knew it. They recognized all the old tricks—the sudden audits of expense statements, the false whispers about misconduct, the unrealistic sales expectations. Probably, they guessed, this was the revenge of that skirt chaser, Bob Sherman. But their boss, Stephen Blank, disregarded the signs. A political war was under way, and Blank would not even arm himself.

It was the spring of 1979, and a quiet power struggle at Bache was coming to a head. Blank, a handsome, dark-haired thirty-three-year-old, won some dangerous enemies at the firm during his six years running the tax shelter department. His tough standards in selecting deals for Bache had stepped on the toes of the executives whose pet projects he rejected. When certain of his decision, Blank refused to yield in his judgment—he often told colleagues that reputations in the business were built not on the successful deals that were sold but on the flops that weren't.

Still, Blank surprised even some admirers when he refused to sell a real estate deal brought in by Sherman, who as the cohead of retail sales stood higher on the Bache corporate ladder. Sherman was a tough, demanding executive who did not like to be turned down. For Blank, the refusal was a fatal move, one that helped set in motion a series of decisions that reshaped the firm forever.

※　※　※　※

STEVE BLANK wound up running the tax shelter division at Bache almost by default. A former high school teacher, he backed his way onto Wall Street in 1970 as a consultant helping brokerage firms manage their paperwork. The timing was perfect—the back offices of brokerages were being crushed by the huge volume of paper they needed to move each day in a booming market. When the back-office problems started clearing up, Blank took a job at Bache sprucing up its training programs.

Two years later, in 1973, Blank's big opportunity arrived. The executive who ran Bache's tiny tax shelter department abruptly resigned, and the firm launched a desperate search for a successor. Blank quickly emerged as the top candidate. He seemed the only one likely to have instant credibility with the sales force—he had already forged strong relationships with brokers and managers from his work in the training program. Until a permanent replacement could be found, Bache turned the business over to Blank. He was twenty-seven years old.

The selection of such a young and relatively inexperienced manager to run a division of a major brokerage firm was met mostly with shrugs. At the time, the tax shelter business was something of an unwanted stepchild on Wall Street. The shelters, also known as limited partnerships or direct investments, raised pools of capital from individuals to invest in business favored by the tax code. Many of those preferences were built in by Congress to encourage investments in certain industries, such as construction and oil exploration. Over years of backroom deals, Congress also granted favorable tax treatment to an array of businesses of less economic value, such as horse breeding, movie production, and even Bible publishing. Any of those businesses could be used in a tax shelter.

The risks of tax shelters were large, since investors sank huge amounts of cash into a single asset. If a big tenant pulled out of an office building owned by a shelter, for example, investors in that deal could well lose their money. But with high risk came the potential for high returns. The shelters usually allowed investors to defer paying or even reduce their taxes. But the shelters also provided income—such as the rents from an apartment building—and the potential of earning a profit when the asset was eventually sold.

The high risks and tax-based rewards attracted only a small cadre of the wealthiest and most sophisticated clients—the people in a high income-tax bracket. With such a specialized and limited clientele, interest among stockbrokers in tax shelters remained fairly low in the early 1970s.

Besides, the obscure real estate and oil deals left Wall Street's stock and bond brokers uneasy. Except to the experts, different pieces of real estate, or different oil wells, all looked pretty much alike. So investors had to trust Wall Street to sift through the available deals and offer the tax shelters with the highest likelihood of eventually producing a capital gain. That meant both the best properties and, equally as important, the most competent and reliable general partner to manage the shelter.

But too often, these general partners, mostly real estate developers and oil wildcatters, impressed stockbrokers as a little too slick, maybe even sleazy. Some general partners sold shelters without knowing much about the business they were promoting—their fortunes were tied to the fat management fees they could charge, not to the growth of their deals. And the deals were complex, with few brokers having the knowledge to explain them properly to their clients. So tax shelters existed largely as a Wall Street footnote, a business that most firms had but did not particularly want.

Then came May 1, 1975. On that day, known ever since on Wall Street as May Day, the securities industry bowed to congressional pressure and abandoned fixed commissions on the sale of stocks and bonds. The competition so often championed by brokerage firms for other industries suddenly romped down Wall Street, setting off a major rate war. Commissions plummeted. No longer could brokerage firms subsidize bloated operations through fat commissions on securities trades. Firms unable to adjust collapsed by the dozens. The industry had to either dramatically cut back expenses or find new products with higher commissions that could be pumped through the sales force. Suddenly tax shelters, which could be sold for higher commissions than stocks and bonds, didn't look so unappealing.

Across Wall Street, firms like E. F. Hutton and Merrill Lynch rapidly built up financial firepower for the tax shelter business. At Bache, Blank had already started expanding slowly. In 1974, he hired Curtis Henry, a tough-talking Texan with a blunt style who had worked as a regional tax shelter marketer at Du Pont-Walston until that firm went under. Henry was given the job of finding and examining tax shelters that Bache could sell. At about the same time, Blank offered a full-time marketing job to David Hayes, a broker in Bache's Washington office who had worked with the department on a part-time basis for years.

With Henry and Hayes as his anchor, Blank aggressively expanded around the country. He hired James Ashworth in San Francisco to market the shelters to Bache brokers in that region of the country. He also brought on John D'Elisa in Smithtown, New York, to perform the close examination, or due diligence, to make sure the deals were good for investors. Legally, Bache had an obligation to its clients to ensure it sold only shelters with the highest potential to succeed. The department had to resist the temptation to sell easily available, lousy deals that could bring huge commissions to the firm but saddle clients with disastrous investments.

By 1978, Blank's temporary assignment had lasted five years. His department now housed twenty professionals and about ten administrative staffers working in the firm's cramped offices at 100 Gold Street in lower Manhattan.

Even with the constant expansion, the department had trouble keeping up with business. Demand for shelters exploded—with high inflation, clients wanted investments like real estate that would likely increase in value at least as fast as consumer prices rose. As more deals were sold, brokers realized the juicy fees available to anyone who could land the lucrative job of general partner.

Suddenly every Bache broker seemed to have a cousin or a friend or a neighbor who wanted to be a general partner in a tax shelter. Their proposals arrived in New York almost every day, some little more than handwritten scrawls on scraps of paper. The department uniformly tossed out those shaky deals, but brokers simply appealed to more senior executives in the firm. Even though the effort was rarely successful, the folks in tax shelters joked that Vince Lombardi, the famed football coach of the Green Bay Packers, didn't invent the power sweep—the end run had come out of Bache.

The biggest political battle over the sale of a shelter began that same year, 1978. One afternoon, Blank received a telephone call from Bob Sherman in San Francisco. Sherman, a hard-driving former stockbroker with an aggressive hunger for profits, ran Bache's retail business in the West and was calling with a pitch: The Robert A. McNeil Corporation was putting together a new partnership investing in California apartment buildings. A buddy of Sherman's who worked for McNeil told him of the deal, and Sherman had promised his friend that Bache would sell it. Now he wanted Blank and his team to give the deal the once-over and get it ready for marketing.

But the proposal left Blank uncomfortable. A number of similar tax shelters were already in the pipeline, and he did not want to offer the same kind of investment over and over. Deals needed sizzle to maintain brokers' attention, and nothing bored the sales force more than repetition. Beyond that, Blank had other concerns about the McNeil Corporation. The company was a polarizing force in the business—some thought it was the greatest, others thought it was the worst—and Blank did not want that kind of headache. As head of the department, he was responsible for accepting each deal, and he always wanted to be untroubled when he did.

He checked with his regional marketers and heard the same negative reaction: Curtis Henry had worked with McNeil after the Du Pont collapse and told Blank he was uneasy about the company. He was also concerned about loans it arranged from the partnerships to other McNeil entities. The loans may have been legal, Henry said, but they sure would be fodder for future lawsuits if the investment went south. Blank's position hardened, and he rejected the proposed deal.

Sherman couldn't believe it. He sent the same proposal back to Blank with instructions for him to look at it again. Blank stood firm. He had no tolerance for political gamesmanship; he wasn't about to let a deal he rejected get shoved down his throat. The marketing staff sensed a dangerous battle in the offing.

"Goddamned Sherman is trying to get me to sell this deal again," Blank grumbled to them in a conference call. To resolve the dispute, he was turning the proposal over to an outside law firm, Kutak, Rock & Huie from Omaha. He would let it check out the matter and decide if Bache should be doing the deal.

At the San Francisco branch, Sherman fumed. *What kind of organization was this that a senior executive couldn't get a perfectly good deal done?*

Sherman directed the brunt of his anger at Jim Ashworth, the tax shelter coordinator for the West who occupied the adjoining office. Time and again, Sherman told Ashworth that he wanted the deal done. It was a good deal. What was the problem? he demanded. But the McNeil deal bothered Ashworth, too, and he said so. As Sherman seethed, Ashworth told him that he did not want to do business with McNeil.

A few weeks later, Kutak, Rock delivered its findings. The lawyers refused to tell anyone in the tax shelter department what they learned. Instead, they insisted on reporting their findings to John Curran, Bache's general counsel. Curran met in his office with the lawyers and listened. In about an hour, he emerged with a judgment: Bache would not be doing McNeil's new partnerships.

The McNeil deal was dead at Bache. The tax shelter boys had won. Sherman couldn't possibly reverse the firm's top lawyer. But they knew the battle was far from over. Their victory could transform the powerful Sherman into a dangerous enemy. The members of the department anxiously awaited any signs of trouble.

———

Jim Ashworth hefted a carry-on bag over his shoulder as he hustled through a terminal at the Phoenix airport. He was looking for a pay phone so that he could call the office. It was early 1979, and Ashworth had just arrived on a flight from San Francisco. As a regional marketer, he spent most of his time on the road, visiting brokers at Bache branches in the West. Over a meal or a drink, he would tell them about upcoming tax shelters. Phoenix was just supposed to be another stop on his busy travel schedule.

To a degree, Ashworth was glad to be getting away from the Bache branch in San Francisco for a while. Since the McNeil blowup, his relationship with Bob Sherman had been strained. Then, just the day before, the two men had bumped into each other at an out-of-town party. Sherman was with a woman who wasn't his wife. And from the look on Sherman's face, Ashworth knew the encounter was only going to cause more trouble.

Ashworth found a bank of pay phones and called to check his messages. Steve Blank had called several times, he was told. His boss wanted to talk to him immediately. Ashworth called him from the airport.

"Jim, you need to get on the next plane for New York," Blank said.

"Why?"

"Take my word for it," Blank replied. "You've got to be here."

Still in the dark, Ashworth booked the next flight to New York. Had he wanted to, Blank could not have shed much light on what was going on—he had been told very little himself. All he knew was that Ashworth, one of his best people, was under investigation by the firm.

Ashworth arrived at the Bache Manhattan headquarters the next morning and was taken to a white, barren room near the firm's security department. Leo McGillicudey, the head of Bache security, came in and sat down. The meeting started off ugly, and quickly grew worse.

"Mr. Ashworth, you are under investigation," McGillicudey announced. "We are accusing you of cheating Bache on expense account items. I want to tell you, this is a very serious matter. You could go to jail. Do you understand?"

Ashworth felt his heart sink. Like every other regional marketer, he submitted dozens of expense reports each year, with some $80,000 in annual charges from around the country. No one had ever questioned them before.

"Do you have financial problems?" McGillicudey asked.

"I don't have any financial problems," Ashworth sputtered. "I didn't do anything wrong. Why do you think I did?"

"I have your records. I have your expense accounts. I want you to tell me about them."

McGillicudey pulled out a pile of Ashworth's expense statements submitted over four years and tossed it on the desk. Then he asked about each statement, day by day, item by item. Why did he spend each penny? On some days, he billed the firm fifty cents for crossing the Bay Bridge. Where were those receipts? The interrogation dragged on for eight hours, with Ashworth struggling to remember why he spent $50 here, $1.25 there. Finally he couldn't take any more.

"Look, I give up," he said. "I can't remember all these. The receipts you have are the ones you have."

"Well, Mr. Ashworth," McGillicudey said as he rose, "then we're done."

Within minutes, Ashworth was told that he was being fired for cheating on his expense account. He was ordered to leave the firm and immediately pick up his personal property at the San Francisco office.

Ashworth stumbled out of the room, destroyed. He was escorted to the lobby and out of the building. He was not permitted to meet with any of his friends in the tax shelter department. The next morning, he flew back to San Francisco and drove his car to the Bache branch on California Street. As he approached the office, he saw a dented cardboard box on the curb outside the building. When he saw what the box contained he felt sick to his stomach.

Someone from Bache had dumped all his personal belongings onto the street.

Blank couldn't believe Ashworth had been fired. He thought Bache had drawn an absurd line in the sand on expense accounts. He doubted anyone—even those who challenged the expenses—could survive the kind of test Ashworth had been put through. Still, Blank naively assumed that the events with Ashworth had no relation to the rest of the department. He felt thankful that the problem ended quickly. At least the tax shelter division could get back to work.

In the spring of 1979, Blank received a telephone call from the security department, asking him to come over to the office right away.

Blank strolled over, unconcerned. Maybe they had learned something new about Ashworth, he thought. But seconds after walking into the security office, Blank was told this meeting was about him: Now the head of the tax shelter department was being investigated. A security officer said he had heard allegations that Blank had received improper gratuities from a general partner doing business with the firm. He wanted to interrogate Blank.

The accusation didn't intimidate Blank; it enraged him. He had worked diligently to build up a reputation as a straight, ethical guy who did deals he thought were right. Taking money from a general partner was probably the worst accusation that could be made against someone in Blank's position. As the gatekeeper between the retail investors and the general partners looking to get rich off the management fees, Wall Street executives making the judgments about which shelters to accept had to be pure. Taking cash from a general partner meant that the gatekeeper was betraying the investors he was supposed to protect.

From what the security officer said, Blank could tell that there was no evidence, just a spurious charge. He'd be damned if he would let his reputation be destroyed in some political game.

"You are making a serious error here," Blank said in a quiet tone of pure anger. "I have done absolutely nothing wrong. And I am not going to let this go past the close of business today."

Instead, Blank said he would immediately take the security officer to his office and let him dig through every file there. Then the two of them would go to his bank and open Blank's safety deposit box and examine all the contents. Finally the two men would go to Blank's home and examine every financial record. The security officer could review whatever he wanted, right away, to make sure that Blank didn't move anything.

Blank paused a moment for effect. Then he issued a warning: If Bache took this step on the basis of just an allegation and found nothing, Blank said, then he would declare war. "Tomorrow I will go out and hire the biggest, meanest law firm I can to take you apart," he said. "And since Bache is letting you do this, I'll go after them, too."

The security officer stared at Blank, expressionless. "Let me get back to you," he said.

Blank stormed out. He never heard from the security officer again.

Tom Huzella and his wife strolled past the swimming pool at the Kahala Hilton in Honolulu, Hawaii, heading toward the hotel's outdoor bar. They were a good-looking, athletic couple, and they exuded self-confidence and success. Huzella, a broker from Bache's Pittsburgh branch, won the 1979 trip to Hawaii in one of the firm's sales contests. About a hundred brokers who had opened the largest number of new accounts were flown to the islands, with Bache picking up the tab.

Although only twenty-nine, Huzella had been a big hitter at Bache for years. He earned his broker's license in 1975, two weeks before his twenty-fifth birthday, and quickly established himself as somebody to watch. During training at the firm, he sat in rapt attention as Steve Blank explained the firm's tax shelter business. Huzella always considered himself good with numbers and saw the tax shelters as more challenging than stocks and bonds. Even better were the commissions: Tax shelters paid as much as 8 percent of a client's investment in commissions, compared to as little as 1 percent for a stock transaction. And since a single unit of a tax shelter almost always sold for several thousand dollars, that meant big money.

With his interest in the shelters, Huzella focused his business on tax lawyers who would easily understand the investments. The success of the first shelters bred more clients for Huzella, as the lawyers referred their colleagues to him. Business came quickly, and almost every week, one or two new clients would give him $100,000 to $1 million to invest. With that kind of volume, Huzella easily qualified for almost every sales-incentive trip sponsored by the firm.

Still, Blank's tax shelter department frustrated him. The demand among Huzella's clients for tax shelters was enormous, but the department just was not churning out enough deals to keep all of his investors satisfied. The department seemed more interested in shooting down deals than in getting them out to the brokers. At times, the problem was embarrassing, such as when Huzella promised some clients that they would get a piece of a particular shelter, only to find the deal sold out. With more and more brokers getting involved in the business, there wasn't enough of the product to go around. By the time of the Hawaiian trip, Huzella was sick of it.

As he approached the bar, Huzella saw Bob Sherman dressed only in a bathing suit and nursing a gin and tonic. Huzella liked Sherman. Because of his big sales, the broker always felt comfortable skipping the normal chain of command and speaking directly with senior executives. Over the years, Sherman had become one of his good friends.

After a few minutes of idle chatting, Sherman asked Huzella about any problems he had with the firm. The broker decided that this would be a good time to dump on Steve Blank. The tax shelter department did not produce enough product, he said, leaving him with lots of angry customers. No matter how many times he complained, nothing changed. Blank just seemed unwilling to whip up lots of deals for the brokers to sell.

Sherman looked down at his drink. "I've had enough of this," he muttered. Then he broke into a smile and looked up at Huzella. "Tommy, watch this."

Still holding his drink, Sherman walked over to a pay phone near the bar and made a call. Huzella couldn't hear what Sherman said but could tell that he was setting something big in motion. He didn't think Sherman could do anything to Blank directly, since the tax shelter department reported to someone else. But Sherman was one of the best at Bache power politics: If there was something he wanted to get done, he knew which buttons to press. Within a few minutes, Sherman hung up the phone and returned to the bar, beaming.

"Well, the problem is solved," he said. "You won't have to worry about Steve Blank anymore. He's gone." Sherman patted Huzella on the shoulder and turned to walk away.

Huzella stared at Sherman in awe. *My God, he did that just to impress me.*

A second thought raced through Huzella's mind, and he turned to his wife. "That man just fired somebody while holding a gin and tonic in his hand," he said. "Now *that's* power."

No one in the tax shelter department ever knew for sure what hit Blank, but they suspected Bob Sherman somehow had been behind it. The word spread fast on June 14, 1979, just after Blank's supervisor, George Meyer, told him he was fired. The reasons sounded hazy—something about not pleasing the brokers and not turning out enough product. The timing was horrible, since Blank had just moved his family to a new house over the Memorial Day weekend. His friends were relieved when he landed on his feet a few days later at Kidder Peabody & Company, a competing investment firm.

Things started changing quickly at the Bache tax shelter department. Executives throughout the firm suddenly began sticking their noses into the department's business and successfully dictating which deals were done. With Blank gone, the buffer that kept the politics at bay and the bad deals from going to market had vanished. Garbage that would not have been given a look was being dressed up and sold with Bache's seal of approval.

Curtis Henry, who originated energy deals at the Dallas branch, couldn't stand it. It seemed like he was beginning to spend more time trying to stop bad deals than promoting good ones. And now, even when he killed a deal, it would not stay dead. Brokers who hoped to earn a finder's fee for bringing in new business just kept the pressure on, and often succeeded. Without Blank there, the Bache end run worked wonders. The worst, Henry thought, was a ridiculous oil deal brought into the firm by Bob McGiboney, one of the top brokers in the Dallas branch office.

Henry had little patience for McGiboney, whose blond, blow-dried hair gave him the looks of the lifeguard he once was. Shortly after Blank was fired, McGiboney came to Henry with an idea—one of his clients, a young man who had graduated a few years before from Baylor University, wanted to sell his own oil-drilling partnership. Henry pored over the proposal and broke out laughing: The guy was only in his twenties, had little net worth, no reputation in the industry, no training in the oil business, and almost no staff. He would have thought McGiboney was kidding if he didn't see the eager look on the broker's face.

"This is absolutely preposterous," Henry said, rejecting the deal with a wave. "There's no way we're going to be involved in this thing."

But a few days later, the deal came back to life. McGiboney had gone over Henry's head. Lee Paton, the firm's head of marketing in New York, heard about the controversy and contacted Henry. "Look, McGiboney is one of our biggest producers, and the Dallas office is one of our best branches," he said. "Unless you can come up with something really wrong with this deal, we are going to have to do the thing."

Henry had no one he could appeal to. The deal was going through.

After reviewing it more closely, Henry was more certain of his original opinion: This shelter was junk. It was composed mostly of little oil wells, which were selling at their highest rates in years because of the oil crisis that year. And the kid from Baylor who was promoting the deal did not make him any more comfortable. In a meeting with Henry and Linda Wertheimer, the Dallas lawyer working on the deal, the kid kept saying all he wanted to do was put together "a good Christian oil deal." Henry and Wertheimer looked at each other and smirked. Apparently their new general partner didn't realize that his lawyer was Jewish.

To make the deal meet the legal requirements of a partnership, Henry ordered a number of changes in the corporate structure. The most important required the client to set up a subsidiary to his main corporation that would serve as the general partner. But only corporations with a strong net worth could legally run partnerships. So, before the deal was sold, Henry ordered the kid to transfer much of his net worth into the subsidiary.

Three months after the deal was sold, Henry received a telephone call from Wertheimer. She wanted to know if he had seen the latest financial statements on the deal. He hadn't.

"Well," Wertheimer said, "I've discovered that the day after you closed that deal, your buddy took all that net worth back out of the subsidiary."

Henry was livid. If investors figured out what had happened, Bache would be on the losing side of a major lawsuit. He fired a letter off to the kid, telling him that he had forty-eight hours to put all the money back. Otherwise, Bache would cancel the deal and give investors all their money back through a process known as a rescission offer.

A few days later, Henry was at the Bache office in Raleigh, North Carolina, shooting the breeze with Roy Akers, the branch manager. Akers's secretary knocked on the door and told Henry that Lee Paton, the head of marketing in New York, was on the telephone and wanted to talk to him.

Paton nearly climbed through the phone in anger. The letter was the final straw, he said. "You know, Curtis, you've pissed off half the people you deal with."

"Lee, my job is to piss people off," Henry said. "When one of our brokers brings a deal in, the only thing we have in common is our name on our business card. I'm on the buyer's side, he's on the seller's side. He's looking for a fee to bring the deal in, I'm looking to see if the deal is any good or not."

"Well, you've really pissed off McGiboney," Paton said. Not only that, but the branch manager in Dallas and the regional director were mad at him, too. The letter had backfired.

Henry never controlled his anger well. This time he did not want to. "Listen, goddamn it!" he snapped. "I'm not worried about what any of those guys think. I'm trying to cover Bache's ass. If this dumb idiot doesn't put the money back, I'm going to proceed with a rescission offer."

Paton started shouting, accusing Henry of being insubordinate. But Henry cut him off.

"Listen, Lee, you don't know what you're talking about. Stop yelling at me."

"I'll yell at you if I want to," Paton screamed. "You work for me!"

"Lee, go fuck yourself!" Henry yelled, and he slammed down the phone.

Things are really starting to fall apart, Henry thought. The shelter department desperately needed somebody in charge before it got worse. And to withstand political pressure like that, Henry knew one thing for sure: It had better be somebody pretty damned ethical.

James Darr, the head of the tax shelter department at Josephthal & Company, burst into his spacious office just two blocks from Wall Street, a look of absolute terror on his face. His cheeks were drained of color, almost matching the lightest shades in his wavy, prematurely graying hair.

Waiting in a chair in front of Darr's desk was Herb Jacobi, the general counsel of First Eastern Corporation, a Josephthal client. Jacobi had arrived earlier that day in the summer of 1978 to speak with Darr about a new tax shelter his company wanted to sell. Darr had been called out of their meeting to speak with his bosses. Now, half an hour later, Jacobi looked up in surprise as Darr rushed into the room.

Their eyes locked. "Herb, you have to help me!" Darr pleaded.

Darr spoke quickly, seeming fearful that his chance to talk might end any second. Some Josephthal executives were about to call Jacobi into another office, Darr said. They might ask some questions about some payments from First Eastern.

"You have to tell them that First Eastern is interested in doing a leveraged lease airplane tax shelter," Darr said.

Jacobi had no idea what Darr was talking about. First Eastern wasn't doing an airplane deal.

"I'll do no such thing," Jacobi replied.

Darr pleaded with Jacobi, begging for him to say there was such a deal in the works.

It was a critical moment for Darr. Josephthal had just caught him improperly taking money from tax shelter promoters. From the people who needed his approval to sell their deals. From people like Matthew Antell, Jacobi's boss at First Eastern.

Someone had slipped Josephthal executives copies of the checks Darr received from First Eastern and another client, Rothchild Reserve International. Lawyers from Josephthal's law firm, Guggenheimer & Untermyer, were investigating. The lawyers had learned that over two months, Darr had deposited $80,000 from clients into his personal account, more than his annual salary. Even the timing seemed suspicious: Within weeks of depositing the checks, Darr purchased a new house in Stamford, Connecticut.*

Already the lawyers had interviewed a number of people connected to Darr. His supervisors and the professional staff members of the tax shel-

* Darr acknowledges receiving the money but denies it was improper. He also denies doing anything unethical during his career. See Notes and Sources.

ter department—Neil Sinclair, Stuart Ober, and David Orr—had been questioned. All of them had been shown copies of the checks and were asked what they knew about them. For the most part, they were simply stunned.

Despite his job as First Eastern's general counsel, Jacobi also knew nothing about the payments. Antell was too clever and was not the type to brag about such things. All Jacobi knew from Antell was that First Eastern, a Massachusetts real estate company, needed Darr's help to sell its tax shelters through Josephthal.

Time was running out. Darr again pleaded with Jacobi to cover for him. Gradually Jacobi came to sense what had happened and became concerned. He didn't care about Darr, but he did worry about First Eastern. Many of the same securities laws that dictated what had to be disclosed about stock offerings also governed tax shelters. Even in private deals, the law required that investors be told about every penny paid to advisers and consultants on the deals. Under the law, even an improper payment had to be disclosed. And no payments to Darr had been revealed in any of the offering documents for partnerships First Eastern sold. Some of the deals already were not doing well. First Eastern could get into trouble, and Josephthal could get dragged into the mess.

Before Darr could finish, Jacobi was asked into another office. Without introducing themselves, two grim-faced lawyers started hammering him with questions. Whom did he work for? What was his job? And what did First Eastern have to do with airplanes?

"Nothing," Jacobi said. "But Matt Antell has always been interested in airplanes." His answer was true. The credenza behind Antell's desk was loaded with airplane brochures. But planes were his love—his business was real estate. Still, Jacobi knew his answer gave Darr just enough confirmation to back up whatever he was trying to pull. No one asked directly about the payments.

The interview dwindled to an end. Jacobi walked out of the room, back to the tax shelter department through Josephthal's marble halls. He walked into Darr's corner office and closed the door. Darr still looked a wreck.

"Herb, I've never done this before," Darr said, still sounding frightened. "I'll never do it again."

Darr looked back down at his desk. "My God, I'm in trouble," he said. Jacobi stared at Darr as he poured out his fears. He doubted that Darr had done it only once. But no matter. Jacobi knew this guy's professional life was at a crossroads. Regardless of what happened, Darr would probably never be in a position to take money from clients again.

※   ※   ※   ※

JAMES J. DARR scratched his way onto Wall Street from modest roots. The only son of Gene and Dottie Darr, he was born in December 1945, just ahead of the first wave of baby boomers. His parents lived a hardscrabble existence, raising their son in the rural, blue-collar country of West Boylston, Massachusetts. In 1948, Gene took a sales job with the Brown Shoe Company, maker of such popular brands as Buster Brown and Naturalizer. The work kept him on the road for days at a time, as he tried to persuade shoe stores to stock his brands. The hefty travel schedule, with Gene clocking as many as a million and a half miles driving from town to town, took its toll on his marriage. Eventually, when Jim Darr was a young man, his parents divorced.

Despite the difficulties at home, Darr excelled academically at West Boylston High School, where he was named a member of the National Honor Society. The ninety-three other students in Darr's class reflected the town's population—working-class whites and mostly second-generation Irish Catholics. Darr was known as a cheerful fellow with an infectious smile and an endless appetite for jokes.

After high school, Darr fit right in at nearby Holy Cross, an all-male college run by the Catholic Jesuits. Most of his classmates were like the blue-collar kids from West Boylston. The student rebellions budding across the country in the late 1960s were still distant static for the students there; many remained committed to military service. The school held an annual military ball, and Darr, who received a scholarship from the Air Force Reserve Officer Training Corps, helped organize the event.

After graduating in 1968, Darr was commissioned a second lieutenant in the air force and within two months was posted as a logistics officer at the Hill Air Force Base in Utah, where parts and maintenance were provided for F-4 jet fighters and other sophisticated weaponry.

In July 1972, Darr was released from active duty. With his education and military service completed, he took his first tentative steps toward a career in business. He accepted a job in Boston as a headhunter for Management Recruiters. Each day, he sat in a close-quarters bull pen, soliciting companies in the hopes of placing midlevel executives in jobs. It was high pressure—Darr was paid mostly on commission, making money only if he was successful. But Darr was good at the job.

Living in Boston, Darr frequently took the short drive to visit his parents. He remained closest with his mother, Dottie, a feisty woman who doted on her only son. Since her divorce, Dottie had made her living as a champion bowler, giving lessons down at West Boylston Bowl. She wrote a column on ten-pin bowling for the *Worcester Telegram & Gazette*. Most Sunday nights, she traveled to Worcester to play in a league at the Lincoln Lanes.

There she met Richard Bailey Sr., a widower and factory worker with New England High Carbon Wire. The two began to bowl together, and after a whirlwind courtship, they married. Richard had three children, and the two youngest, Ginny and Tommy, still lived at home. If Darr approved of the new members of his family, he didn't show it. Although he clearly loved his mother, Darr treated her blue-collar bowling crowd with a haughty contempt. Often for his visits home, he wore a sharp suit and tie; his mother's neighbors could feel the disdain for their blue jeans and work shirts.

At the same time, Darr was developing his own social life outside of West Boylston. He dated Diane Casey, a teacher in the Quincy public schools, and in July 1974, they married. By then, through contacts he developed in business, Darr had grown fascinated with real estate as a great means of making a quick buck. He began pushing investment ideas on his family.

In August 1975, Darr persuaded his new stepfather, a man of Yankee caution who feared financial risk, to invest in a parcel of raw land in Texas. Darr promised his stepfather that the investment would bring huge profits. He said he had a hot tip that the adjoining property was scheduled for development. That, he said, should make the value of the neighboring land skyrocket. If Richard and Dottie bought the land, Darr told them, they would be able to flip it quickly at an inflated price.

Delighted with Darr's hot tip, Richard and Dottie borrowed money to invest in parcel 37 of a property called Deerwood North in Texas. Darr was so confident in the investment that he persuaded them to use the expected profits to buy more land in Wolfeboro, New Hampshire, by taking out more loans. Richard felt uncomfortable—he had never had that much debt in his life. But he figured his stepson knew what he was doing.

Disaster hit almost immediately. Richard's union went on strike; five months later, the wire company shut the factory for good. The development in Texas—the one Darr had promised would bring huge profits—didn't work out. The money needed to pay for the New Hampshire property never materialized.

Richard, dismayed by the mounting financial troubles, clung to the hope that the wire company would reopen. Finally he suffered a nervous breakdown, and his eldest son, Richard Jr., admitted him to the psychiatric ward of St. Vincent's Hospital. Dottie walked out on her new husband that day. On returning from the hospital, Richard Jr. ran into his stepmother heading out the door. She had an armful of her husband's belongings, including his first wife's silver and china sets and a wedding present from his children. Richard Jr. thrust his hands in his pockets out of fear that he would strike Dottie and ordered her to put back everything that was not hers. He watched her until she walked out of the front door for the last time. ·

Dottie soon divorced Richard. In the settlement, they split ownership of the land investments Darr had recommended. Richard senior soon recovered from his breakdown and returned home. He continued to pay off his debt on the land, a small bit at a time, for much of the rest of his life.

In the mid-1970s, Wall Street was a place of turmoil and fear. After an incredible run of huge profits and wild speculation during the 1960s, the securities industry was paying a heavy price. Scores of investment houses that expanded too rapidly in good times simply went bust or merged. The Arab oil embargo in 1973, followed by the deregulation of commission rates two years later, created the harshest business environment for the industry since the Great Depression. The heady confidence and easy money created by rising markets were gone. Many of the young people hoping to make their fortunes on Wall Street were simply a few years too late.

That was the environment in which Darr arrived on Wall Street in June 1976. He got his start by grabbing the industry's lowest professional rung, as a stockbroker trainee with Merrill Lynch & Company. The firm hired him to work in Boston but immediately shipped him to Merrill's New York headquarters for two months of training.

Darr breezed through most of the topics easily by dint of his natural intellect. Although the class had its share of studious trainees, he gravitated toward a group who also caught on quickly. They were the ones itching to head out to a branch and start selling. Evenings among these trainees centered on bar-hopping and occasional marijuana parties. Many in the group struck up long-term friendships, and Darr was no exception.

At one Merrill-sponsored cocktail party, Darr met Wally Allen, a native of Enterprise, Alabama, who had joined the training program after a short career in the real estate mortgage business. The two stayed at the same hotel on Manhattan's East Side and became fast friends.

One night, the two gathered in Allen's room before another evening's carousing and started swapping stories about their backgrounds. Allen mentioned that he served with the army in the Seventh Psychological Operations Group, an intelligence unit based in Okinawa, Japan. The work he did as an analyst was classified, but Allen did not think it was very impressive. His biggest responsibility was acting as custodian of classified documents. But the biggest advantage of the detail, Allen said, was that it kept him out of Vietnam.

Well, Darr said, he *had* served in Vietnam. And like Allen, he worked in the intelligence business. In fact, the entire time he was in Southeast Asia, he always dressed as a civilian. Allen got the picture: Darr worked with some high-level intelligence group, perhaps the Central Intelligence Agency. Allen was surprised someone in that line of work was so open about it but figured Darr was trying to impress him.

It would be several years before Allen realized that everything Darr said that night was a lie. He had never been in Vietnam. He had never even worked with an intelligence division. There weren't many spies handling maintenance detail in Utah. It would prove to be just the first layer in Darr's self-created mythology.

In 1977, after a few months as a broker, Darr tried for the big time. He saw that tax shelters were taking off as a business, and Merrill had one of the biggest departments on Wall Street. That, Darr decided, was the place to be.

After lobbying Jack Loughlin, the head of the department, Darr was hired as a product manager. In that job, he marketed specific types of partnerships.

Product managers never sold investments directly to the public. Instead, they traveled throughout the Merrill retail system, talking up the shelters in the hopes of persuading the brokers to sell them. For Darr, the job was remarkably like his father's. Both traveled around the country representing particular products to retail salesmen. But instead of trying to persuade salesmen to offer Naturalizer shoes, Darr was trying to convince them to sell tax shelters.

Darr proved to be a master at sales. He was not the type to spend much time exploring the deep mechanics of how a particular tax shelter worked, but he always knew enough to persuade brokers to sell a deal. He also was one of the few marketers willing to stand up to arrogant investment bankers. If bankers made a shelter too complicated, he would tell them that they would confuse the brokers.

Darr's style was effective; he worked hard, but never bored his colleagues by poring over the dry details of some business deal. Instead, Darr cracked them up with the latest bawdy joke or his dead-on impersonation of Humphrey Bogart as Captain Queeg. It was a glorious time for Darr. For the first time, big success seemed within his reach.

A few months after joining Merrill's tax shelter department, Darr met Barry Trupin, a prominent and flashy shelter promoter. Trupin left some Wall Street professionals uneasy—his style was a bit too garish, his wealth too prominent. Here was a man who could purchase the old Henry du Pont estate in the wealthy enclave of Southampton, New York, and then undertake a multimillion-dollar effort to transform the Georgian Chestertown house into a French Gothic castle—complete with turrets, towers, and an indoor saltwater pool with its own twenty-foot waterfall.

Trupin loved to give people the impression that he was a financier of high pedigree—he named his company Rothchild Reserve International, making more than a few investors think that it was tied somehow to the Rothschild family, the famous European banking dynasty. Trupin made sure he spelled the name just differently enough—leaving out one *s*—that the real Rothschilds would never bring suit. Even his deals pushed the outer edge of the envelope. The values he ascribed to the assets in his tax shelters always seemed enormous, which, in turn, gave investors even greater tax deductions. But it also would likely attract the attention of the Internal Revenue Service, which could disallow any deductions if the agency found the numbers had been puffed up.*

Trupin fascinated Darr. He was one of the wealthiest men Darr ever knew. They met as competitors over a big computer-lease tax shelter deal that both wanted to sell. In the end, Darr was the victor, but Trupin felt no ill will. He knew that someday he might want to use the fellow who just beat him for another deal.

That day came in mid-1977. Trupin had learned that Mattel, the toymaking company, wanted to lease a large IBM mainframe computer.

---

* Trupin's empire eventually fell apart. The Internal Revenue Service placed tax liens against him, and he moved out of the United States, owing millions to various banks and insurance companies.

Trupin asked Darr if Merrill could help him find the equipment for the deal.

Darr agreed, but on two conditions: first, that Trupin pay $50,000 to Darr personally for finding the equipment, and second, that Merrill be told nothing about the payment. The $50,000 would be a small fraction of what Trupin stood to gain in fees if the deal went through. He readily agreed to both conditions.

For Darr, the chance was slim that anyone at Merrill would ever find out about the money—he had been interviewing for a new job at Josephthal and had an offer in his back pocket. By the time Trupin cut the check, Darr would be out the door. The deal was done in June, and for its work, Merrill Lynch received a 2 percent finder's fee: $11,322—less than a quarter of the cash paid under the table to one of its midlevel employees.

Darr bundled his overcoat tightly around himself as he walked down Broadway. It was January 30, 1978, a bitterly cold Monday in what was already an extremely frigid New York winter. About a block ahead, he could see Trinity Church, which had stood since colonial times like a sentry at the mouth of the downtown financial district. Darr turned onto Wall Street. It was about 3:00 P.M. In an hour, the markets would close and the street would be packed as brokers and traders headed home.

He walked past the thick, gray walls of the New York Stock Exchange and the columns of Federal Hall, where George Washington had once taken the presidential oath of office. He continued for two blocks until he arrived at 45 Wall Street, the offices of the United States Trust Company.

Darr waited for a teller. Finally, at 3:16 P.M., he passed two deposit slips through the teller's window, along with a check he had just received for $50,000. It was the personal payment he had demanded from Trupin for helping him on the Mattel deal. Trupin had successfully sold out the partnership in December, as wealthy investors scooped up shelter deals to help cut their tax liability for the year. True to his word, Trupin wrote Darr the check within weeks.

The teller took the documents from Darr and placed them in an electronic time stamper. Following Darr's written instructions, $45,000 was deposited into checking account number 2551. The remaining $5,000 was deposited in his savings account. In just one transaction, Darr more than doubled the $30,000 he had in the bank.

Darr had been in his job as head of Josephthal's tax shelter department for just over six months. His new firm was no Merrill Lynch—instead of hundreds of offices around the country, it had only about twenty along the East Coast. Until it hired Darr, Josephthal did not even have a tax shelter department. Even his pay was meager by Wall Street standards: about $65,000 a year, plus bonus. But at Josephthal, he was the person in control. He could decide which deals were sold and how much the firm would be paid. Promoters who wanted to sell their shelters through Josephthal had to make sure that Darr was happy.

About a week before receiving his payment from Trupin, Darr took steps that would protect him in case anyone ever heard of the check. At a lunch with Michael DeMarco, the president of Josephthal, Darr tiptoed around the topic of money he expected to be receiving. He had outside business interests, Darr told DeMarco, and would soon be getting income from them. But DeMarco need not worry, he said, because none of those activities conflicted with the interests or businesses of the firm. But in fact, the opposite was true—he was receiving cash from the very types of people whose deals he was supposed to rule on objectively.

The flow of money to Darr soon sped up. Matthew Antell from First Eastern was the next client to pass some cash to Darr. Josephthal sold a limited partnership for First Eastern called King's Court Associates, and three days before the deal was filed with securities regulators, Darr sent Antell a bill for $30,000. The bill did not indicate it was from Josephthal and simply said that First Eastern owed the money for "specialized program structuring and consultation."

A few days later, on March 6, Antell sat down at his desk in Cohasset, Massachusetts, to write a series of $30,000 checks from First Eastern Corporation. After funneling one check through another company he controlled, he wrote a second check, to Rothchild Reserve, the company controlled by Barry Trupin. Antell had never met Trupin.

The check was mailed to Trupin, who deposited it in his account at Citibank. On March 22, after Antell's check cleared, Trupin wrote the fourth $30,000 check in the series, this time to the true recipient, Jim Darr.

Darr was ready to use the money. After starting in New York in a modest apartment in a middle-class neighborhood, Darr had his eye on a $181,500 house in the wealthy suburb of Stamford, Connecticut. Four weeks after receiving his latest check, Darr handed over a down payment of $35,000 in cash for the house. Without the money from clients, he never could have afforded it.

Darr's newfound power and healthy financial shape showed in his strut. He became looser and more arrogant, at times embarrassing some of his professional staff by mistreating potential clients. Stuart Ober, who handled oil and gas deals, bitterly complained to colleagues after he brought one potential shelter promoter into the office to see Darr. Ober liked the promoter and wanted to make a good impression. But Darr treated the client with open contempt. Sitting behind his desk, Darr put his feet up on the table in front of the prospective client's face, lit up a cigar, and leaned back in his chair.

"Tell me about your deal," he said. "*I'll* decide whether it's good or bad."

The client was clearly offended. Within minutes, Darr cut him off and ushered him out. Ober had never seen a performance like that in his life. The client took his business elsewhere.

Darr's antics also made some of his bosses uncomfortable. He was simply too out of step with the collegial atmosphere of a small, old-line firm. He created a huge, separate office for himself, while the heads of most other departments worked in the same room as their staff. Though his department had only four people, Darr hired his own personal secretary. His colleagues could not believe his pomposity—never before had any of them known of a Josephthal executive who would have his secretary call clients, only to put them on hold until her boss picked up the phone.

Still, he showed talent in the job. In negotiations over a deal, no one was tougher. Darr always insisted on the highest fees and the best terms for Josephthal. He even haggled over the commissions that would be paid to the firm's brokers, demanding that each promoter pay as much as was permissible under the securities rules. His colleagues smirked each time they heard Darr push the demand—they knew his bonus was based in part on the amount of commissions his department generated.

And Darr still had his sense of humor, although it started to develop an edge. Once, when spying a homeless person on the street, Darr asked his companion if he recognized the man. His associate said no.

"Well," Darr said, "this guy used to run a tax shelter department a few years back."

The message of Darr's humor was clear: This was a business where anyone's fate could change in an instant.

Norman Gershman, Josephthal's national sales manager, regretted ever hiring Jim Darr. The man's egotistical behavior was bad enough. But by the late spring of 1979, Gershman, Darr's immediate supervisor, was beginning to question his integrity.

Already some of the firm's best clients were refusing to work with Darr. A friend of Gershman's who headed a real estate syndication company called him personally to complain.

"I don't want to do business with the guy," the client said. "He's not being honest."

For Gershman, a quiet, gentlemanly sort from Wall Street's old school, that was enough to make him edgy about his aggressive, arrogant new hire. But then later, Gershman told Darr about a wealthy potential client who was looking to buy a tax shelter. Darr leaned close and lowered his voice.

"I've got a deal we can sell to this guy, but it's not coming through Josephthal," Darr told Gershman. "You know, you and I could make money from this on the side."

Is he seriously suggesting that we pocket the fees that should go to Josephthal? Gershman just stared at him in silence, until Darr turned and walked away. If that was a test, Gershman thought, he was glad to fail.

Before Gershman decided what to do about his suspicions, DeMarco, the head of the firm, called him into his office and shut the door. He wanted to know if Gershman knew anything about payments Darr had been taking from clients.

Even with everything he had heard to that point, the accusation floored Gershman. "I can't believe a professional would do something like that," he said.

But as the two men talked, he began to wonder. DeMarco had copies of the checks. Neil Sinclair, a member of the tax shelter department who handled real estate deals, had somehow obtained the records from Darr's locked desk and turned them over. Both DeMarco and Gershman knew that Darr had purchased a new house in Connecticut and was driving an expensive car. Somebody on Darr's salary could never have afforded it. Until now, everyone just assumed Darr had family money. It was beginning to look like they assumed wrong.

⁂   ⁂   ⁂   ⁂

THE INVESTIGATION dragged on for weeks.

On the books of Josephthal, Darr was still the head of the tax shelter department. But he stopped coming to work every day—many weeks, the other executives in the department had no idea where he was. When they did see him, his face betrayed every fear and every concern. Over a two-month period, he started losing weight, and lots of it. His staff guessed that he had lost more than twenty pounds since the investigation began. Darr looked dreadful.

Finally DeMarco called Gershman aside again. "Listen, we're doing something with the Darr matter," he said. "Stay away from it." Gershman took it as a friendly tip. He never spoke to Darr again.

Even Jacobi, the lawyer from First Eastern, could tell the man was coming apart. Using an assumed name, Darr called Jacobi once at the office and asked for his home number. Then, almost every night, Darr called Jacobi, sometimes in tears, asking the lawyer to figure a way out of the problem. "Please help me, Herb," Darr begged repeatedly.

Jacobi would never know why he did it. He didn't like Darr. He fully believed the only reason Darr called him was to get legal advice without having to pay for it. But the desperate nightly pleadings finally got to him. He told Darr how to resolve his problem: On his next day at work, Darr should go to the cashier's office and write Josephthal a check for some of the client money, saying that he was turning over a fee he earned from First Eastern. He should make sure to mark the check as being for that fee. Turning over some of the money, Jacobi said, would give Josephthal an explanation for the payment in any future litigation and would guarantee that the firm could never turn against Darr. How could they call the money a payoff if they accepted some of it?

On July 17, Darr followed the advice. He wrote a check for $30,000 to Josephthal, saying he was turning over a fee. Then, since he had generated the money, Darr demanded $15,000 back as a finder's fee, and got it. The threat of huge lawsuits for both Josephthal and Darr was effectively eliminated.

Jacobi's advice only solved Darr's potential legal problems; his career was still tenuous. On his days away from Josephthal, Darr hunted for a new job. But he was not looking much for a position on Wall Street—instead, he tried to sell his own tax shelters. He spoke with people he knew in the business, bouncing around possible ideas for an oil deal. He called Jerry Leach, an old colleague from Merrill who now ran the tax shelter division at Smith Barney, Harris Upham & Company.

The two men met for lunch at a restaurant near Wall Street. After a few pleasantries, Darr told Leach that he had gotten together with some associates in the energy business and was putting together a tax shelter with them. Darr would be one of the general partners on the deal. Did Leach think that Smith Barney might be interested in selling the deal?

Leach smiled politely. No, Smith Barney would not be interested in participating in any such deal. *With you*, he thought.

Leach already knew about Darr being caught taking money. The rumors he heard from a buddy at Merrill were that Josephthal essentially had dismissed Darr but was keeping him on staff while he tried to find a new job. That was enough to make Darr radioactive in his eyes. Leach wanted the general partners in his firm's deals to be squeaky clean; there was no way he would do business with Darr. The lunch ended amicably, but with Darr empty-handed.

Darr's meeting with Anton Rice III, another Merrill alumnus, did not go much better. Rice, known to everyone as Tony, had been somewhat of a success off Wall Street—since leaving Merrill, he had plunged headlong into the energy business and was now a senior officer with Graham Resources, a Louisiana oil company. Like Darr, Rice knew the pains of being accused of improprieties. After Rice had left Merrill, executives from the firm investigated allegations that he had held a financial interest in some of the land he helped arrange for sale to various Merrill partnerships. In other words, the deals for public investors might have been benefiting him personally. But after questioning executives, Merrill dropped the investigation.

At the lunch, Darr told Rice that he and a friend wanted to take over as the master salesmen for all of the Graham energy partnerships. Graham would pay them to travel the country and persuade brokers at different firms to sell the deals to their customers. After two hours of haggling, Rice rejected the proposal. Darr wanted too much money; Graham could not possibly afford it.

Darr's luck seemed to have run out. Then, in the fall of 1979, his fortune changed: He received a telephone call from John Holmes, a former investment banker with Oppenheimer & Company who was running a management-consulting firm. There had been a shake-up at the tax shelter department of Bache, Holmes told him. Steve Blank, the longtime head of the department, had been dismissed a few months earlier. The firm was looking for someone with experience in running a tax shelter division. Would Darr be interested in the job?

Darr launched on a series of interviews, and the Bache executives liked what they saw—Lee Paton, the head of marketing, who was assuming reporting responsibility for the department, was particularly impressed. Darr seemed to be the kind of fellow who knew that his job was to sell as much product as possible. All they needed was to conduct the usual background check with former employers. If there were no surprises, Darr had the job.

The telephone call to Josephthal came in November 1979. An investigator from Fidelifacts, a background-checking firm, spoke with Raymond Mando, an executive vice-president with Josephthal. Mando had few ties to the tax shelter division—he headed administrative operations for Josephthal, including personnel. No one had told Mando about the Darr investigation.

A competitor wanted to hire Jim Darr, the Fidelifacts investigator said. What did Mando think of him?

Darr was dependable, cooperative, and reliable, Mando replied. His work performance was excellent. Well, the investigator asked, what about Darr's integrity?

"There was never any reason to question his honesty," Mando said.

"We are pleased to announce that James J. Darr, first vice-president, has joined our firm as Director of our Tax Investment Department."

Bache's small, boxed advertisement, known in the securities business as a tombstone, ran in the *Wall Street Journal* on Friday, November 9, 1979. It was buried near the bottom of page 34, between a tombstone announcing the sale of two egg farms and another ad about the sale of some assets by an electronics company. But, given the attention the Bache ad attracted among the people who knew Darr, it may as well have run on the front page. Josephthal executives who had heard of Darr's troubles could not believe that a firm as big as Bache would hire a man like Darr without doing some intensive investigation.

Herb Jacobi was as stunned as anyone. The Darr investigation had driven First Eastern under. Only Josephthal had sold the company's tax shelters, and since learning of the payments to Darr, it refused to do business with Antell. Jacobi now worked as a lawyer with a regional brokerage firm. Still, after seeing the announcement of Darr's new job, he knew he had a big opportunity. After all, he had helped save Darr; he was sure the man would be grateful. Now he had an executive at a major retail brokerage firm in his debt. This, he thought, was his lucky day.

Jacobi called Bache's main number. An operator transferred him to Darr's line. Apparently his secretary was not in place yet—Darr picked up the phone himself.

"Hey, I saw you in the newspaper today," Jacobi said. "Sounds like a great job. Congratulations."

Darr paused. It was a cold, awkward silence. "It's not nearly as good as you think," he said crisply. "And I can't do anything for your clients."

Without another word, Darr hung up.

After his months of anguish, Darr clearly didn't think he needed Jacobi in his corner anymore. Not when he had landed on his feet at a place like Bache. Now, with a firm that size standing behind him, he really had the power to do some business his way.

CHAPTER 2

HARRY JACOBS, THE CHAIRMAN of the Bache Group, was ready to face the enemy, that interloper who had caused him anguish for so long. That Canadian who hadn't built his career on Wall Street, as he had. Jacobs was sure Sam Belzberg would like nothing more than to raid his firm just to fire him.

After a final check of his notes, Jacobs stepped out of his chauffeur-driven car. As a light snow fell around him in the brisk air, he strode toward the door of the American Airlines terminal at New York's La Guardia Airport. At fifty-nine, he was not much to look at. Bald, thin, and short, Jacobs looked more like a friendly shoe salesman than the man at the top of a major retail brokerage firm.

It was December 16, 1980, a Tuesday, at about 4:00 in the afternoon. Bache's battle with Belzberg, a hard-driving entrepreneur and the firm's largest shareholder, was getting vicious. Belzberg had been buying Bache stock for years and made no secret of his disdain for its managers. In his mind, they had transformed one of Wall Street's prestige names into a joke. Once considered a contender to surpass the size of the giant Merrill Lynch & Company, Bache had tumbled in less than a decade from the country's second-largest brokerage to the eighth. Its past successes lent the firm enormous influence among retail investors, but Wall Street competitors derided it as a "schlock house," good for little more than peddling second-rate securities to naive investors. Belzberg argued that he could turn things around for Bache. He was demanding seats on the firm's board.

Jacobs staunchly opposed the idea. Sure, the firm had a lousy reputation. And yes, it often didn't make much money even when competitors thrived. But now, after thirty-four years with Bache, Jacobs thought he could fix that. He had been named chairman the previous year, after more than a decade of quietly, patiently waiting in the wings. He knew the firm's byzantine workings and its peculiar internal politics. He had won many admirers there through his genial charm and knowledge of the business. He wasn't about to surrender the firm to an outsider now. That meant fighting Belzberg with every bit of ammunition he could find, using the brass-knuckle rules of Bache politics.

Walking past American's ticket counter, Jacobs headed toward the entryway of the Admiral's Club, which offered a comfortable lounge and bar for the airline's best customers. It was here that Jacobs had agreed to meet Belzberg alone, without the usual coterie of lawyers and advisers, in a last-ditch effort at compromise.

The two men shook hands. As they sat down, Belzberg said that he regretted they hadn't met by themselves more often to talk things over.

Belzberg paused. "Mr. Jacobs, I'm embarrassed to ask this, but my lawyer said I should," he said. "Are you wired?"

"I beg your pardon?" Jacobs snapped.

Belzberg held up his hand. "Fine, that's good enough for me," he said. "I assure you I'm not wired. So let's talk."

For the next hour and a half, they discussed Bache, its problems, and Belzberg's ideas for it. Beyond his knowledge and contacts, Belzberg said, Bache would get the benefit of the trading and investment-banking business from his Canadian companies. If they laid aside their anger, everyone would profit. The bitterness between the two sides developed only, Belzberg said, because Bache reneged on promises to him and fought dirty.

"Slowly but surely, you people dug yourself into a hole with confrontation," he said. "The way to end this is to give me two seats on the board. I already own more than fifteen percent of the firm. I'm entitled to the seats."

Belzberg looked Jacobs straight in the eye. "If you refuse me, I will have to look at other avenues at my disposal," he said menacingly. The message was clear: Either Belzberg got his seats, or he would bring in other investors to help buy the whole firm.

Jacobs had listened politely to Belzberg the whole time. Now he stood and extended his hand. "All right, Sam, I'll let you know soon," he said. Belzberg shook his hand and watched Jacobs walk away, confident he had made his point and would get the seats he thought he deserved.

He was wrong. Instead, that airport meeting set in motion the first battle ever for control of a public brokerage firm. When the fight was over, Belzberg learned a secret from a Bache executive that made him realize his confidence at the airport meeting had been a self-deception. There had never been a chance for a deal. After all, compromise requires trust. And that day, Belzberg heard, Harry Jacobs *had* been wired.

If he had known more about the tortuous history of Bache politics, Belzberg might not have been surprised.

*   *   *   *

THE TRADITION of political intrigue that drove Bache's history unofficially took shape at 12:10 A.M. on March 24, 1944, a few months shy of the firm's sixty-fifth anniversary. At that moment, Jules Semon Bache, the eighty-two-year-old Bache patriarch who had transformed a tiny family commodities brokerage into a prominent Wall Street securities firm, died peacefully in his sleep at his winter home in Palm Beach, Florida. He had been bedridden for weeks, the rigors of old age finally slowing his body and mind. His family took shifts standing by him to await the end. In his final minutes, Jules's daughter, Hazel Beckman, and a granddaughter, Muriel Pershing, were at his bedside, quietly holding his hand.

Despite the long expectation of his death, Jules Bache's gentle passing roiled J. S. Bache & Company, the firm he had controlled since 1892. Though the old man had gradually withdrawn from the firm's daily operations over the years, at times threatening to shut the place down, no one had planned for his succession. The competitors for his job eyed each other jealously. The battle for power was engaged.

Succeeding Jules Bache would have been hard for anyone. Throughout his career, he had nurtured a reputation that was almost larger than life. He had the foresight to build his firm with the business of small-time investors—like European Jews in the garment industry—who were ignored by Wall Street's tonier investment houses. Once he saw success, his client roster blossomed to include financial giants like the Rockefellers. He became a prominent New York socialite, known and respected among members of the monied class for his passion for fine art.

None of the candidates seemed capable of stepping into that role. The only blood family member at the firm was Jules's nephew, Harold Bache. But privately, Jules viewed his nephew as an unimaginative lightweight unworthy of the Bache name. Harold didn't have Jules's regal appearance—in fact, he was simply unattractive. At five-four, with a compact, muscular body, jowly face, and large ears, Harold looked nothing like the visionary Jules wanted to have replace him.

The days after his death made that clear. Jules left Harold out of the will, dividing his $10.6 million estate equally among his three daughters and their families. Worse, Jules bypassed his nephew as executor, bestowing the honor on some sons-in-law and grandsons-in-law, including Clifford Michel, a partner at the firm. These four executors received explicit instructions: Liquidate Jules's investment in the firm. He wanted J. S. Bache transformed into a penniless corporate shell.

With that final indignity, Harold the plodder came to life. Most people at the firm knew he had little money of his own. But he was not going to allow his uncle's spite to destroy the family business. Harold sought out customers and friends who were willing to invest a few hundred thousand dollars in the firm in exchange for a partnership role. Unyielding in his search for cash, Harold successfully beat Jules's posthumous effort to kill the firm. In a little more than a year, he had raised more than $4 million in capital from seven new general partners and six new limited partners.

Finally Harold rid the firm of the influence of the man who so mistreated him. In one last flourish, he banished his uncle's name, reorganizing J. S. Bache into Bache & Company. For years to come, the only remnant of Jules Bache would be on incoming mail incorrectly addressed to the old name. Each time one of those letters crossed Harold's desk, he took out his pen and scratched out the offending "J. S."

Harold proved adept at steering the firm. Over the next twenty years, its influence surpassed what it had under his uncle's guidance. He committed himself to a philosophy of constant, unrelenting growth. His dream, recited often to his friends and partners, was to build a brokerage even bigger than Wall Street's giant, Merrill Lynch. He never succeeded, but not for lack of effort—in a little more than two decades, the number of Bache employees grew from 1,800 to almost 6,000.

Every day, Harold awoke at 6:00 A.M. at his duplex apartment on Park Avenue and was whisked downtown forty-five minutes later by the same taxicab. He arrived at his desk by 7:15, long before the 9:30 opening bell of the stock market, a habit that won him the nickname in the newspapers of "the man who opens Wall Street." From his office just off the firm's entryway, Harold kept a steady eye on the stream of Bache executives arriving each morning, greeting them as they walked down the firm's red-carpeted corridor. He frequently wandered about the offices, stopping to ask each man about his job and his life. Sometimes he would relive his days in the marines, rolling up his sleeves to talk battlefield tactics and tell war stories with other veterans.

Such strategizing proved useful in managing Bache, where life grew increasingly treacherous. While Harold's decision to bring in new partners saved the firm, it also created an environment where the intense political maneuvering never ended. With the new capital, his ownership stake in Bache was only about 10 percent. Any of Harold's new partners could throw the firm into disarray by withdrawing their money. Since, for many, that investment composed much of their personal wealth, they wanted as much say in the firm's management as Harold himself.

To keep everyone happy, Harold blurred lines of authority, leaving no one with the power for final decision making. Anyone who gained authority was viewed as a threat by the others and toppled from power. No one could afford to lose any political strength, so no one could gain any. Harold became a master manipulator of Bache's fragile egos. With so much infighting, a strong management team couldn't develop; Bache was transformed into a haven for Wall Street's mediocrities.

Titles became virtually meaningless, as they were transformed into symbols of ego gratification rather than descriptions of responsibility. By the 1960s, more than seventy vice-presidents roamed the halls of Bache, and all of them jealously guarded whatever small power they might have. The thick bureaucracy slowed the firm's responses and destroyed managers unwilling to play Bache's politics of appeasement.

By 1968, Bache was in the same shape it had been in when Jules died: one person in control, and no designated successor. With prodding from his longtime partners, Harold, then seventy-three, finally agreed to name a new Bache president. He picked Harry Jacobs, the head of the firm's syndicate department, and planned to announce his decision in April.

The announcement never came. On March 15, 1968, Harold's driver arrived as always at the Bache Park Avenue home at 6:45 for the morning trip downtown. Unlike most days, Harold was not waiting for him. The driver knocked on the front door, and Harold's wife, Alice, opened it. She did not know what delayed her husband—the two had been sleeping in separate bedrooms for years. She and the driver went to Harold's bedroom. When he didn't answer a knock on the door, they swung it open: Harold was lying in his bed, dead from a heart attack.

For the second time, the death of a Bache threw the firm into chaos. Senior executives launched an endless series of meetings. The squabbling continued for almost a month. Finally, on April 11, the firm made an announcement that reflected its true inner turmoil—no one would be Bache's chief executive. Instead, three rivals for power would share those duties: Jacobs as president; John Leslie, an accountant and lawyer at the firm, as chief administrative officer; and Robert Hall, the firm's treasurer, as chief financial officer.

The arrangement was part of a complex political ploy engineered by Leslie, perhaps the most unlikely candidate to succeed Harold Bache. Leslie had no experience in the firm's moneymaking businesses, having spent all his time on legal and accounting issues since joining the firm in 1955. He had minimal personal interest in the stock market—for years, executives at the firm gossiped that Leslie never owned a single share of common stock. But Leslie craved the power and prestige of running a securities firm.

Born in Vienna, Leslie was aloof and something of a stuffed shirt. Unlike the gregarious Harold Bache, Leslie rarely chatted up his colleagues, who considered him funereal, with cold, clammy hands. Formalities meant a lot to Leslie: He called no one by their first name and demanded that he be referred to as "Mr. Leslie." He advertised his appointment as an honorary consul general for Austria by always wearing the title's ribbons and medals to the firm's formal functions.

In the months after the selection of the new management team, Leslie quickly gathered political strength, bluntly letting executives know that he would remember who didn't support him when he gained control. The tactics worked—in April 1969, Bache named Leslie as chairman. No one opposed him for the job.

With Leslie's stiff personality setting the firm's tone, formalities took hold throughout the firm, even in the men's bathroom, where he posted a sign advising "Please flush." Fortifying his control, Leslie reinforced the old politics of Bache that were the source of his power. A new, complex web of committees diffused the authority of any possible successors for the job and allowed Leslie to play each executive's interests off another's. Success at Bache became a matter of who could be pushed out of the way, as internal politics transformed into guerrilla warfare. Executives launched investigations of one another's expense accounts, looking for problems. If that didn't work, the same tactic would be used on a competing executive's underling. Life at Bache was getting nasty.

Still, fate proved Leslie to be the right man for the job at the time. Within months of his selection, a deep financial funk descended on Wall Street. After years of riding a giddy, rising stock market during the 1960s, the Dow-Jones Industrial Average began sinking mercilessly. Bache lost millions. If it was to survive, its dreams of expansion had to be killed.

Leslie championed a brutal cost-cutting program. He shrank the number of employees from 7,200 to 2,500. He sold whole branch offices, or simply shut them down, and raised $40 million in new capital by selling shares of the firm to the public in 1971. Still, when the market rallied in mid-1971 and competitors began rebuilding, Bache kept cutting back. Its rank on Wall Street slid.

After coming close to the top, Bache deteriorated into a Wall Street also-ran, falling into the ranks of third-tier firms. It seemed almost symbolic in 1971 when, to further reduce expenses, Bache moved from its prestigious Wall Street offices to 100 Gold Street, a drab address near the Brooklyn Bridge, far from the financial district. The dowdy offices were cramped and unremarkable. The luster that had once been at the firm now existed only in its history.

In the mid-1970s, Bache executives tired of Leslie's continuing cutbacks and worried about the firm's slumping position and reputation. Leaning on the chairman, they urged him to relinquish power and name a successor. But, as happened under Harold Bache, all of the rising stars during Leslie's tenure dimmed after gaining modest influence. With no one else in the wings, Leslie turned to Jacobs, who had surrendered much of his own power under Leslie's committee system. Finally, in 1976, after almost a decade of waiting, Jacobs became chief executive of Bache.

It could be argued that Harry Jacobs arrived on Wall Street by plane. Born to a family of architects, he had little interest in stocks and bonds in his youth, instead aspiring to become a pilot. He won his private pilot's license on December 2, 1940, while still a junior at Dartmouth. During the following summer, his flying helped forge a strong tie to Bache that lasted the rest of his life. Jacobs was taking a course in acrobatic flying using a Waco UPF biplane. The equipment was old and the flying school somewhat shoddy, but Jacobs didn't worry. Then, at the end of one practice run, as he came in for a landing, the left strut on his plane collapsed. The plane hit the ground and flipped over. Not knowing he was upside-down, Jacobs unfastened his seat belt and fell, knocking himself unconscious. The hot engine raced, and gas ran over it. The plane seemed ready to explode.

Suddenly a man appeared and grabbed Jacobs, dragging him from the wreckage. It was Jimmy Israel, the brother of Ace Israel, a senior partner at Bache. Jimmy Israel also flew planes and took the same course as Jacobs at the school next door. When he saw Jacobs crash, he ran over to help and saved the young man's life. The two men became fast friends and went on to serve as pilots in World War II. Jacobs survived his stint flying B-25s;

Jimmy Israel died when his B-24 blew up at the end of a runway, killing the crew.

After the war, Jacobs tried unsuccessfully to land work as a commercial airline pilot. In January 1946, he decided to switch careers. Meeting over lunch with Ace Israel, he discussed his various interests and plans. Israel sent Jacobs to the firm, where he was hired in the investment supervisory department. Jacobs's days were filled with menial tasks for other executives, such as looking up stock dividends. But he advanced quickly. By the early 1950s, Jacobs was a member of a group of young institutional salesmen and traders from various firms who were known as the Sandbox Set because of their youth. For Jacobs, Bache became something of a second family for the next several decades.

When Jacobs was tapped as chief executive, Bache's reputation was in tatters. Giants like Merrill and Hutton had moved into new businesses and had grown their sales forces while Bache cut back. The times called for bold and decisive action, but Jacobs dithered. He refused to break up the committee process that created the firm's encrusted bureaucracy. The Bache tradition of indecisiveness and intensive politics was set to continue.

That kind of drift could not continue long at a public company. Bache stock had lost half its value since going public, and its investors were bitter. Anyone with the money and desire could buy Bache and throw out the executives who let it go so badly astray. It was only a matter of time until someone decided to try.

The time arrived in 1978, with a threat from an old friend of Bache. On May 17, Gerald Tsai landed his helicopter on a field in Westchester County to pick up Jacobs for a flight. Tsai was a Shanghai-born stock picker whose success at the Fidelity Capital Fund had helped set off the mutual fund craze in the 1960s. When Tsai split with Fidelity, it had been Bache that had raised the money for his new venture. That had solidified a long, friendly relationship with Jacobs and other senior Bache executives.

Jacobs climbed aboard Tsai's helicopter for what he thought would be a relaxing trip to West Point. But instead, Tsai guided the small helicopter to a New Jersey landing field. There Tsai turned to his friend to tell him the real reason for the day's outing. The recent death of Harold Brady, a large investor and critic of Bache, had opened up an opportunity. With Brady's block of shares possibly up for grabs, Bache seemed vulnerable. Before anything else happened, Tsai had snapped up more than 70,000 shares on the open market and had opened talks about joining forces with two other large Bache investors. Together, they controlled about 8 percent of the firm. Tsai had big plans. He wanted to take over.

Jacobs was aghast. "I want you to fly this helicopter back *right now!*" he growled.

The conversation came to an abrupt halt, as Tsai flew the helicopter through the rain to a field beside Jacobs's home. Jacobs ran into the house and grabbed the kitchen telephone to call John Leslie. The two decided immediately to phone Martin Lipton, a founding partner of Wachtell, Lipton, Rosen & Katz and the country's dean of takeover defense strategy.

The best approach, Lipton advised, would be to offer to buy back the stake controlled by Tsai and the other investors at a price attractive enough to make them agree to go away. Bache offered $10.25 a share for their stock, $2 above what the market was paying. With $1.2 million in free cash on the table, Tsai and the other investors pocketed the money and moved on. Jacobs felt relieved. He successfully fought off a threat to the careers of his friends for a relatively small sum of money. Now he could turn his attention to the firm and mend the scars that years of political intrigue had left behind.

He never had the chance.

The threat from Sam Belzberg emerged slowly from the time of its conception with a single young broker in Toronto.

In the spring of 1978, the broker, John Clark, pored through Bache's balance sheet over and over again. The numbers just didn't add up. Clark, who handled certain investments for the Belzberg family, knew that Bache stock was in the tank, trading at around $8 a share. But the firm's holdings seemed to be worth far more than that. The international division appeared to be particularly misunderstood—Bache had branches and relationships all over the world but assigned no dollar value to that division in its books. Clearly, Clark thought, this was an undervalued stock, weighed down by the market's perception of mismanagement at the firm. It was like finding hidden gold.

Clark had long been responsible for managing the Belzbergs' investment company; called Bel-Fran Investments. He was authorized to purchase as much as $1 million of a single stock without seeking approval. So, on a day in 1978, at his own initiative, Clark purchased more than 100,000 Bache shares for the Belzbergs in the Bel-Fran account.

For years, few outside Canada knew of the Belzbergs, a family of Orthodox Jews who lived in Vancouver. The family immigrated there in

1919 from Poland, where Abraham Belzberg, the family patriarch, had worked as a fishmonger. In Canada, he opened a used furniture business, which became the centerpiece of a vast fortune built on real estate and other investments. After Abraham died in 1976, his three sons, Sam, Hyman, and William, established Bel-Fran as their personal investment company.

Sam Belzberg wanted updates from Clark every three months about Bel-Fran's holdings. At one meeting that year, Clark mentioned his purchase of Bache stock and asked for permission to buy more. Investors were sour on Bache, Clark said, in part because of its history of mismanagement. Still, it had fabulous assets. Over time, the firm's management might improve, he added, and the stock would go up. And even if Bache didn't fix its problems, the Belzbergs wouldn't likely lose much money. A stock can't fall much farther than the gutter.

Clark convinced him, and Belzberg approved the purchase of more Bache shares.

Guy Wyser-Pratte was always among the first at Bache to hear the newest market rumors. As head of the firm's arbitrage department, he spent his days watching the ticker, looking for stock movements and listening for market rumors about potential corporate takeovers. He heavily bought the shares of corporate targets after the announcement of a bid, assuming the risk that a deal would get done. He was good at the job—his group consistently made great profits. By listening so carefully to the market, Wyser-Pratte noticed quickly when big blocks of Bache shares started trading in 1978. He heard that the buyer was the Belzbergs.

The trades set off alarm bells at Bache. Jacobs, who had feared a takeover since the Tsai affair, was telephoned in Munich, where he was attending a business managers' meeting. He instantly feared the Belzbergs wanted control of his firm. At a meeting of the board of directors a few days later, Jacobs approached Wyser-Pratte to ask about the Canadians. The best he knew, Wyser-Pratte said, they were basically a bunch of corporate raiders.

Jacobs blanched. "This is terrible," he muttered. "Terrible."

Over the following weeks, Jacobs became obsessed with the Belzbergs. On March 21, his concern deepened when the Belzbergs filed a Schedule 13-D with the Securities and Exchange Commission, disclosing that they owned 5.1 percent of the firm. Profanity and name-calling weren't in Jacobs's character, so even his mild invective of calling the Belzbergs "that

bunch" shocked his colleagues. Hoping to repeat the success the firm had
with the Tsai threat, Jacobs again sought out Marty Lipton. But this time,
the lawyer begged off the assignment—the Belzbergs were among his roster of clients.

Jacobs racked his brain, convinced that the Belzbergs were an enormous threat. He discussed little else. Wyser-Pratte had seen the reactions
of enough corporate managers in takeover situations to understand what
was happening: Jacobs was hitting the panic button.

Sam Belzberg reached for the telephone on his desk as soon as his secretary told him that Marty Lipton was on the line. Belzberg liked Lipton and
admired his intelligence. He always enjoyed having a chance to talk with
the lawyer.

After exchanging pleasantries, Lipton asked cryptically if they could get
together. Belzberg readily agreed but said he had no plans to travel to New
York anytime soon. Perhaps, Lipton suggested, they might meet in Los
Angeles. Lipton would be traveling there soon, and he knew that Belzberg
frequently visited there. Belzberg agreed.

Days later, Belzberg and Lipton met at the lawyer's bungalow at the
Beverly Hills Hotel. Lipton quickly got down to business.

"What are your intentions with Bache?" he asked.

The question surprised Belzberg. Even though he had kept purchasing
tens of thousands of shares in the firm almost every week, a fact he disclosed in several filings with the SEC, he didn't expect his own lawyer
would be the one asking him about it.

"Marty, I have no intentions," he said. "Why do you ask?"

"They're very worried about your position," Lipton replied. "It's been
very unsettling for them. So they want to know whether you want to bid
for the whole company, whether you want to sell your interest, or whether
you would accept a seat on the board and not buy any more stock."

The offer just fell in his lap. At that point, Belzberg viewed his Bache
investment as just one of many in his portfolio. Maybe someday he might
want to do something with the firm, but at this point, as far as he was
concerned, he was just another passive investor. Now, without raising a
finger or saying anything, he could get a seat on its board. He wouldn't
pass that up.

"Look, Marty, for sure I am not going to buy the company, and for sure
I don't want to sell my shares," Belzberg said. "But yeah, I think I could

be quite happy to sign that I won't buy any more stock and get a seat on the board."

The deal seemed done. Belzberg was pleased. With a seat on the board, he thought, he might be able to help turn this company around and in the process see a tidy profit on his investment. This trip to California definitely had been worth his time.

Only Virgil Sherrill, the recently appointed president of Bache, could have been trusted with the job of officially greeting Sam Belzberg for the firm. If central casting was looking for someone to play a Wall Street chief executive, the search would end when Sherrill walked in the door. Tall, regal, and handsome, with a coiffed white mane of hair and a tanned face that hinted at his love for golf, Sherrill brought a pedigree of mannered diplomacy to the firm. He honed those skills as the chief executive of Shields Model Roland until Bache purchased the investment firm in 1977 for $15 million. With his poise and calm self-control, Sherrill became Bache's new president and the man for sensitive situations.

Sherrill called Belzberg two days after the meeting in Los Angeles.

"Mr. Belzberg, I understand you met with Mr. Lipton," he said. "Thank you very much for agreeing not to buy any more stock. When are you going to be coming to New York? I'd like to get together with you and introduce you to the boys on Gold Street."

Belzberg found Sherrill's ingratiating style flattering but had no idea what the man was talking about. He hadn't researched Bache well enough by that point to know that its headquarters were on Gold Street.

Although he rarely traveled to New York, he told Sherrill, he planned to be there in August. The two men agreed that during that trip, Belzberg would lunch at Gold Street with the boys.

The first night of his August trip to New York, Belzberg arrived at the Regency Hotel on Park Avenue to find a message to call Sherrill. There was a last-minute change, Sherrill told him when he called. Rather than coming all the way downtown to Gold Street, would Belzberg prefer to meet closer to his hotel at the Racquet and Tennis Club?

"Who will be coming from the company?" Belzberg asked.

"Just me," Sherrill replied.

"I thought you wanted me to meet the boys on Gold Street."

"Well," Sherrill said, "we'll see."

Something fishy was going on. Belzberg had no idea what it might be.

The next day, Belzberg walked the ten blocks to the Racquet Club's three-story building on Park Avenue. The club dripped blue-blooded elegance and privilege, with its marble facade and wood-paneled walls. It admitted only men as members, who could buy meals and drinks, play tennis and squash, or lounge in overstuffed chairs beneath the soft light from brass sconces and crystal chandeliers.

Sherrill met Belzberg in the lobby and took him to the club's dining area. Lunch was pleasant, and Sherrill delighted in describing the club's history, from its founding in 1875 to his joining in 1967. The visit was enjoyable, relaxed, and utterly pointless.

By 1:15, Belzberg was restless. His plane back to Vancouver left in less than two hours. His chance to visit the Bache offices had slipped away.

"Mr. Sherrill," he said, "this has been most enjoyable. Unfortunately, I didn't budget sufficient time for our meeting. So, do you have anything else you need to say?"

Sherrill beamed. "I want to thank you very much for not buying any more stock," he said. "I'm sure we are going to find many ways we can work together."

No mention of the board. No mention of a seat.

Belzberg pressed. "Anything else?"

"No," Sherrill said, shaking his head.

Belzberg sat there, numb, his anger building. Apparently, Jacobs or someone could not countenance the idea of bringing Belzberg onto the board and quashed the proposal. *These people take me for a fool*, Belzberg thought.

Finally he stood up from the table. "Well, that's fine, sir," Belzberg said, taking Sherrill's hand. "Thank you very much. It's been very nice to meet you."

Belzberg stormed out of the Racquet Club, seething. He walked the few blocks to the offices of Wachtell, Lipton, arriving unannounced. Lipton ushered the fuming Belzberg into his office.

"What's going on here?" Belzberg demanded. "He didn't offer me anything, and I'm not about to come asking for it."

Lipton looked stunned. "I can't understand it," he said. "That was the deal."

Irritation is not the best motivator. Still, at that moment, Belzberg's anger led him to a decision. He hadn't given Bache much thought before this, but damned if he would let these people humiliate him.

"Marty, this offended me," he said, visibly incensed. "And I have my interests to look out for. So if I don't hear from them in two weeks, the deal is off. I'm going to buy more stock. You tell them that. Two weeks."

The deadline came and went. No word from Bache. Bitter, Belzberg called Clark, his broker. Start loading up on more Bache stock, he ordered.

The takeover threat that Bache tried so long to avoid was starting to be created.

Jacobs felt helpless. By October 1979, the Belzberg problem had escalated from a manageable threat to an absolute crisis. The Canadians bought Bache shares relentlessly, increasing their stake in the firm from 5.1 percent in March to almost 7 percent—a number that would have been higher if Bache hadn't countered by issuing more shares.

Nothing Bache did slowed them—even political pressure, exerted through New York senator Jacob Javits, failed to stop Belzberg. At Bache's request, Javits, who knew Belzberg through his work for Jewish charities, telephoned him in Vancouver to warn that a hostile takeover of Bache would harm the Jewish people. But Belzberg simply denied he planned a takeover, hostile or friendly.

Jacobs and Sherrill agreed to meet their new largest shareholder on September 13 at the Regency Hotel, but all they learned from that tense encounter was that Belzberg intended to purchase as much as 25 percent of the firm. With his rough no-nonsense approach, Belzberg reminded Jacobs of a truck driver.

The time had come to pull out the stops. Jacobs ordered a full-scale investigation of the Belzbergs, in search of damaging information that might be used against them. In late 1979, Bill Jones, a former agent with the Federal Bureau of Investigation who had just been hired as Bache's new head of security, was recruited to dig up dirt. He turned over anything he found to the firm's legal team, including Arthur Liman, a well-known securities lawyer whom Bache had retained, and Clark Clifford, the former secretary of defense and adviser to five presidents who now worked as a Washington lawyer. Despite all that heavy talent, nothing usable was found in the first weeks of investigation.

So Bache stepped up its defense. It retained First Boston to search for a large institutional investor interested in buying a stake in a securities firm. Its annual proxy statement contained a series of bylaw changes, which, if approved by shareholders, would impede a takeover. Still, Jacobs feared that even if the measures were approved, they probably wouldn't stand up in court.

The normally excitable Jacobs was getting even more hyper. He called an endless series of strategy meetings about the Belzbergs—at six in the morning, at ten at night, and every time in between. He buttonholed even junior executives in the hallway, anxiously pressing them for suggestions. But before they could answer, Jacobs would interrupt with the next question. His usual nervous habits worsened: While at his desk listening to someone speak, he would quietly tear a sheet of paper off a pad and slowly rip it into smaller and smaller pieces. After dropping confetti to the floor, he would grab another piece, starting over again.

The agonizing finally produced a decision: Bache needed to line itself up with someone with more money than the Belzbergs. Somebody who could buy Bache shares that came available on the market. Somebody with a long-standing relationship with the firm. Somebody who could be counted on to side with management.

Jacobs thought he knew just the people.

The Hunt family of Texas was the richest in the country. It could buy and sell the Belzbergs before breakfast. The progeny of H. L. Hunt, an Illinois-born wildcatter who reached mythic status after striking it rich in the east Texas oil patch, played in their own multibillion-dollar empire, all of it privately held and veiled in secrecy.

After H. L. Hunt died in 1974, the undisputed head of the clan became Nelson Bunker Hunt, the first son. Weighing in at about three hundred pounds, with thick glasses accentuating the family trait of small eyes, Bunker Hunt was the family's idea man. His brother, W. Herbert, took care of the details. With a fondness for health food and a taste for well-cut suits, Herbert was slimmer and less imposing than Bunker, and he usually deferred to his brother's business judgment.

By 1979, the Hunt brothers had been clients of Bache for almost eight years. The relationship had grown close, particularly when Bache began accepting business from the Hunts on terms other brokerages refused. Bunker and Herbert had been speculating heavily in silver futures contracts, putting up only a small portion of the value of each investment and borrowing the rest. Placing most of their orders through Shearson Loeb Rhoades, the Hunts used millions in borrowed money to buy the contracts, which guarantee delivery of the precious metal at a later date. Most futures traders sell their contracts before that time. But the Hunts started taking delivery of billions of ounces of silver, leaving less of it on the market and in turn driving up prices further.

In September, Sanford Weill, the head of Shearson, demanded some extra insurance from the Hunts: The brothers had to put down $25,000 in cash for each contract rather than the $7,500 they had been paying. That would decrease the risk of the Hunts defaulting on their debts if the price of silver collapsed. But it also would limit the brothers' ability to keep buying, and they chafed at the restriction.

The Hunts transferred their 2,400 contracts from Shearson to Bache, where the delighted executives kept the cash restrictions low. So, when Jacobs needed a rich ally, the Hunts came right to mind. With Bache casting such a strong vote of confidence in the Hunts, surely they might consider helping the firm. Through an intermediary, Jacobs asked if the Hunts would be willing to buy a large stake in Bache.

They gladly obliged. Through a joint account at Bache, the Hunts purchased fifty thousand shares over just five days in October. Bache had found its secret weapon against the Belzbergs. Delighted, Jacobs sent the Hunts an effusive letter, thanking them for being "a tremendous friend of Bache" and adding that their effort would "never be forgotten, regardless of what happened."

The scheduled meeting of Bache's executive committee in February 1980 had a packed agenda. Employee sales production was still too low, and a series of strategies to boost sales were being considered. Bache's training program needed help. And then there was the need to consider a $186 million loan to Bunker Hunt. Since the loan was one of the easiest matters to resolve, it was taken up quickly. Without dissent, the committee approved it after a few minutes of discussion. Years later, executives who attended the meeting would speak in wonder about how a decision that almost destroyed Bache could have been reached so casually.

The Hunts needed money because their silver-buying strategy was collapsing. For months, the brothers had been using their silver hoard as collateral to borrow more money to buy more silver. That, in turn, drove up silver prices, creating more value for their investments, which they used to obtain more loans, and on and on. For everything to work, either the market had to keep going up or the Hunts had to gain control of enough silver to be able to dictate prices. With most of their cash already tied up in the investment, the Hunts needed buckets of borrowed money to keep the cycle going. Otherwise, the market would fall, the value of the collateral would decline, and brokerages would issue margin calls, seeking more cash to cover the Hunts' billions of dollars' worth of purchases.

By January, Bache became the Hunts' favorite choice for one-stop financial shopping. They sent commodities trades through the firm and borrowed hundreds of millions of dollars from it to cover their growing liabilities. The requests were hard to refuse—by that point, the Hunts were Bache's most important customers. Their business increased operating revenues at a critical time and created the potential of billions of dollars in international financing with oil-rich Arab families tied to the Hunts. More important, the Hunts had become large owners of the firm. By January 16, the brothers controlled more than 5 percent of Bache stock. At that level, any investor is required to file a Schedule 13-D with the Securities and Exchange Commission, disclosing the full size of the stake. But the Hunts never bothered. By March 18, they owned 6.5 percent of the stock. And no one knew outside of Bache and the Hunts.

By the end of February, the firm had lent the brothers $233 million. Bache, in turn, borrowed the money for the Hunts from a consortium of banks, including First National of Chicago, Irving Trust, and Bankers Trust. The risk to the firm was enormous: If the silver strategy collapsed and the brothers defaulted, Bache would be on the hook for almost a quarter of a billion dollars, nearly all of its total capital.

Even as Bache took the audacious gamble, the Hunts' silver game was on the verge of being shut down. On January 18, silver prices hit an all-time high of $50.35 an ounce, up from $6.50 an ounce twelve months earlier. That increase of more than 800 percent alarmed executives at the Commodity Exchange Inc., or Comex, where silver trades. For months, they anxiously watched the Hunts' buying spree, convinced that the brothers had created a speculative bubble. When it burst, banks and brokerages that loaned money for silver purchases would be caught short. Some might fail. The Hunts had to be reined in.

The next day of trading, January 21, the exchange announced it would only accept orders to liquidate positions. By the next day, silver dropped $10 in one trading session. Brokerage firms sent out margin calls to the Hunts, demanding millions of dollars. The brothers faced a critical cash squeeze. They turned to Bache, which agreed to lend them more money.

The Hunts' silver strategy finally imploded in March. In just the first two weeks of the month, silver prices dove by more than $14, to $21 an ounce. The Hunts' silver lost some $2 billion in value; their collateral evaporated in the marketplace. The stream of margin calls became a flood. From Bache alone, the margin calls to the Hunts hit $10 million a day.

On March 19, Harry Jacobs was traveling in Austria when he received a panicked telephone call from Virgil Sherrill in New York. The Hunt brothers just met their latest margin call, Sherrill told Jacobs, by turning over silver instead of cash. It was like paying the minimum on a huge credit card balance by turning over shirts they bought on the card the prior month—it was a sure sign of financial trouble. Jacobs canceled his trip and immediately booked a flight back to New York.

After fruitlessly trying to raise money, on March 25, Bunker Hunt gave up. The brothers could not meet their margin calls. Through an assistant, he sent a three-word message to his brother, Lamar, to convey to Herbert: "Shut it down."

That afternoon, Jacobs telephoned Herbert Hunt to tell him that the brothers' latest margin call required delivery of $135 million by the following morning.

"We can't make it," Herbert replied calmly.

America's wealthiest family, and the most important client in Bache's history, had run out of cash. Astounded executives at Bache decided to liquidate the Hunts' account. The next day, Bache sold $100 million worth of the silver. The Hunts were still almost $36 million in the hole. The support under the inflated silver market had vanished. Financial disaster loomed.

Jacobs hit the phones, imploring regulators in Washington and New York to shut down the silver market. Once the Hunts' default became known, he argued, silver prices would collapse further, potentially crippling Bache. He and Sherrill traveled to the Comex in downtown Manhattan and waited outside the exchange's boardroom as its senior officers met in emergency session. But the effort was a waste of time—the exchange and federal regulators refused to shut down the market. If they did, they feared the market's credibility would be destroyed for years.

By morning, the Hunts joined Bache's lobbying effort. At 8:00 A.M., Herbert Hunt telephoned the Commodity Futures Trading Commission, the market regulator. He said investors should be forced to liquidate their contracts at the previous day's closing price. Otherwise, if the market opened, Hunt warned, the consequences would be bleak.

"The Hunt family will be washed out," he said. "We will go broke."

Within minutes of that call, a lawyer from Bache called from a pay telephone at the Comex to again urge the CFTC to close the market. For the first time, the lawyer revealed that Bache had extended $233 million in loans to finance the Hunts' silver speculation. If the silver market kept falling, the lawyer implied, Bache might go out of business.

But the decision was final. The government would not close an entire financial market to save one foolish brokerage firm.

That day, March 27, 1980, the silver market collapsed. After opening at $15.80 an ounce, the market was swamped with rumors that the Hunts couldn't meet a $1 billion margin call and that Bache was going under. Silver lost almost a third of its value, plunging to $10.80 an ounce. The chaos cascaded through the financial markets.

The silver meltdown shook some of the highest reaches of government. G. William Miller, the Treasury secretary, was readying himself for a speech at the National Press Club when he heard of the unfolding disaster. He placed an emergency telephone call to Paul Volcker, the chairman of the Federal Reserve, but accomplished little. Miller arrived late for his speech, badly shaken. He showed the strain while talking, at one point referring to *Face the Nation* as "Face the Naked."

The situation at Bache was dire. Silver delivered by the Hunts began to be piled in stacks in a back hallway by the firm's metals department. The SEC had halted trading in the firm's stock. Examiners from the New York Stock Exchange had swooped down in the morning to pore through the firm's books to see if it still met the minimum capital rules to stay in business. By midday, officials from the SEC began telephoning Bache competitors, asking whether they would be willing to take over some of the firm's branch offices. The planned dismantling of Bache had begun.

That night, Bache held the most critical board meeting in its history. Depending on the price of silver the next day, Bache could go out of business. Jacobs looked haggard as he watched executives calculate to the penny how far silver could fall without killing the firm. The answer was grim—Bache would be in violation of the minimum capital rules if silver dropped another $2.80 an ounce. If it fell $4, all its capital would be wiped out. In disbelief, the board members discussed plans for shutting Bache's doors for good.

As the talks dragged on, a secretary called Wyser-Pratte, the head of arbitrage, out of the meeting. A Belgian investment-banking firm was calling him. The Belgian firm represented a large film company, Wyser-Pratte was told, which needed silver for its business. Would Bache be interested in selling the entire Hunt silver inventory to that company? Wyser-Pratte caught his breath—the bid they offered was high enough to let Bache stay open the next day.

Wyser-Pratte sprinted back to the boardroom, exclaiming, "Hey, we got a bid on the whole block."

Everyone visibly relaxed. Demand was returning to the silver market. The metal's price had hit its floor. Rejuvenated, the board rejected the Belgian bid and decided to seek higher offers. The silver market would not be putting Bache out of business.

But the firm was still in danger. After several weeks, the banks returned to Bache. They wanted more assets pledged to their loans. In an all-night session, the bankers and Bache lawyers hammered out an agreement for additional collateral. Under the deal, Bache would pledge a large portion of its own capital to secure the loans. In effect, the bankers would have the power to potentially take over the firm. The lawyers sent for a Bache executive to sign the deal.

Virgil Sherrill walked into the conference room and sat down at the table to read the documents. The disheveled bankers and lawyers, with a day's beard growth on their faces and their ties askew, watched as the meticulously clad Sherrill calmly examined each of the pieces of paper that would endanger the firm's independence.

Finally Sherrill put the documents back on the table and stood up. "Gentlemen, when you made these loans, you received collateral, and that collateral was in silver bullion," he said. "It was the only collateral you received on these loans and it will be the only collateral you will ever receive on these loans. Have a wonderful day."

With that, Sherrill strode out of the room, leaving behind the stunned army of bankers and lawyers.

Bache survived the silver crisis. Miraculously, it escaped without losing any money, largely because of the skills of Frederick Horn, an unflappable, chain-smoking commodities trader who liquidated the Hunts' silver. By the time he was done, Bache could actually report a small profit in the quarter of the silver crisis.

For the Hunts, the silver crisis ended the family's decades of financial secrecy. To make good on some obligations, the brothers shed assets, such as an interest in some Canadian oil properties. As collateral for more than $1 billion in loans, the Hunts put much of their personal fortune in hock, mortgaging oil and gas leases, coal leases, real estate, cattle, and antiques— even a Rolex watch and a Mercedes-Benz were put up.

But what would happen with their huge stake in Bache? For months, Jacobs and other executives endlessly discussed theories about where the

6.5 percent of the firm would go. In late November, they knew the answer. A filing with the SEC disclosed that the Hunts had sold much of their stake to an outfit called First City Financial. Bache executives knew the name well: First City was the centerpiece of the Belzberg empire.

The enemy had returned. Now the Belzbergs controlled 15.5 percent of Bache. Sam Belzberg rattled his saber a little louder, demanding to see Jacobs. His secret weapon gone, Jacobs agreed to the meeting with Belzberg at La Guardia. The firm stood almost defenseless. If the Belzbergs launched a takeover, the chances Jacobs would prevail were slim.

The last thing Bache could afford at that moment was the disclosure of another scandal.

CHAPTER 3

JOHN D'ELISA PUT HIS right leg forward and leaned into it, pushing his body as low to the ground as he could. He breathed out as he held the position for an instant, feeling his hamstrings stretch. D'Elisa always spent a lot of time limbering up before he ran, scrupulously following each step of the little routine he developed years before. It was a great time of solitude, one that made him feel relaxed and ready to run.

As he stretched in the cool evening air, D'Elisa absentmindedly watched some of the hundreds of people standing with him on Liberty Street in the shadow of the World Trade Center. Normally, by 6:30 in the evening, the financial district in downtown Manhattan would be mostly deserted. But on this night, September 23, 1980, that small part of the city surrounding Wall Street teemed with life. Hundreds of runners from more than sixty brokerage firms and investment banks were there, preparing for the second annual five-kilometer Securities Industry/United Way Challenge Race. Some of them were engrossed in their own warm-up exercises. Others just walked about eager to start the race.

Even though this was only the second year the race had been held, the competition was intense: The team with the best time won the right to keep the Challenge Cup until next year's race. D'Elisa ran for Bache, where he worked in the tax shelter department. He wore a white T-shirt with the firm's name emblazoned on the front in stark, blue lettering.

Nearby, D'Elisa saw Bill Pittman limbering up. Pittman, a volatile former stockbroker, had been hired by Steve Blank years before to handle the department's administrative duties, from organizing paperwork to keeping the supply cabinet stocked. But since Darr had taken over ten months earlier, Pittman's fortunes had changed. Darr gave him the chance to work as a tax shelter marketer. Few members of the department could understand why Darr did it. Pittman was barely qualified for the job: He seemed to know little about tax shelters and had received his undergraduate degree from a night school only a few years before.

Still, there was no doubt that Pittman was a hell of a runner. With him in the race, D'Elisa thought, Bache might actually have a chance of doing well this year.

D'Elisa kept stretching as he watched a tall, thin man walk through the crowd. During the day, no one would have noticed the man; nothing about him would have seemed remarkable. But on this evening, he seemed oddly out of place. He was dressed in a suit, white shirt, and tie with his dark hair slicked back. Among the runners in their brightly colored shorts and shirts, he looked almost shadowy. The man's eyes locked on D'Elisa, and he strode purposefully toward him. D'Elisa stood up as the man came to a stop directly in front of him.

"Hi," the man said. "I'm Neil Sinclair."

D'Elisa nodded a greeting. He had never heard the name before.

"I used to work with Jim Darr at Josephthal," Sinclair said. "I understand that Jim is now with you at Bache, running your department."

"Yes?"

"I just want to tell you to watch yourself," Sinclair said. "Jim is on the take."

D'Elisa just stared at Sinclair. He didn't quite know how to respond. "All right," he finally said. "I appreciate the information."

Sinclair nodded and turned away. D'Elisa watched as the stranger walked off, disappearing again into the crowd, then returned to his stretching, without mentioning the odd encounter to his teammates. At 7:00 P.M. sharp, the race began. D'Elisa's encounter with Sinclair did not throw off his running performance—he ran all five kilometers in twenty-six minutes, placing eighth on the Bache team.

But the whole time, and for days afterward, Sinclair's words rang in D'Elisa's head. It wasn't what he'd heard that disturbed him the most. After working with Darr for almost a year, D'Elisa was more bothered by his own reaction.

He wasn't shocked at all.

Jerry Leach, the head of Smith Barney's partnership division, peered across a conference table in the squat Oklahoma City headquarters of Seneca Oil Company. Never before had he seen Curtis Henry, his old friend from Bache, appear closer to bursting a blood vessel. Henry wanted to strike a deal so that Bache and Smith Barney could jointly sell Seneca's next tax shelter. But as Seneca managers looked on at the September 1980 meeting,

Leach gave no ground. Repeatedly he dismissed Henry's proposals with a wave, saying that Smith Barney did not need a partner.

This type of cautious mating dance between two brokerage firms was standard fare in the business. Almost every corporation has multiple Wall Street relationships, and eventually, those different firms can come together on a deal too large for just one to handle. That spreads the fees and gives the client assurance that the deal will get done. Seneca's planned $15 million partnership seemed perfect for such a combination between Smith Barney and Bache. Both firms had relationships with the company, with Smith Barney selling its past partnerships and Bache handling other investment-banking work. But Smith Barney had never handled a tax shelter this large; Henry could not understand Leach's refusal to let Bache sell half the deal. He kept telling Leach that Smith Barney could never sell the deal by itself.

Leach knew Henry was right. He doubted his brokers would be able to move even one-third of the deal alone. To get it sold, he would have to bring in another brokerage firm. But he would never allow Smith Barney to work with Bache. Not anymore. Not since the firm hired Jim Darr, his old colleague from Merrill. Leach had heard about what had happened at Josephthal and thought Darr was dirty.

More than a year earlier, Leach had rejected Darr's proposal to have Smith Barney sell an oil deal he was packaging. If Bache was foolish enough to put a person like that in charge, Leach thought, so be it. But he would not bend his position: No department he controlled would do business with Darr.

Leach didn't want to embarrass Henry, so he refused to cite his real objections to Bache in front of Seneca's management. He hoped Henry would recognize that stubbornness was not his style and back down. But Henry didn't understand the unspoken message. Leach's chorus of nos made him too angry to think.

Finally Leach pushed his chair back from the conference table. "Curtis," he said, "why don't you and I go take a walk outside, and just talk by ourselves a little bit."

Henry liked the suggestion. Now they could talk turkey without worrying about what the client thought. By the time they got back, he figured he would have half the deal in his back pocket. Both men stood up and told the Seneca executives they would be right back. With Henry following, Leach left the conference room and headed out the company's front door. He didn't stop until he reached a street corner, where Henry sidled up beside him. They both stood silently for an instant, watching the cars drive by. Leach seemed to be gathering his thoughts.

At last, he turned to Henry. "I've got problems, Curtis. I can't do a joint deal with you."

Henry felt flustered. Finally he sputtered, "Well, why not?"

"I can't do a joint deal with you as long as Jim Darr is in charge of your department at Bache."

Confused, Henry looked at Leach. He himself disliked Darr and made no effort to hide his contempt for his boss's arrogance and bullying behavior. But Leach's reaction seemed extreme.

"Well," he replied, "he's kind of rough to get along with, but why does that mean you can't do business with us?"

Leach looked around. No one was there. He decided to stop dancing around the topic and asked Henry if he knew what had happened to Darr at Josephthal. Henry shook his head.

"He got caught with his hand in the cookie jar," Leach said. Darr, he said, got caught taking money from clients.

Somewhere in his heart, Henry knew he should have felt stunned. But he didn't. "That wouldn't surprise me," he said.

"I don't know how Darr got out of it," Leach said. "But you need to be very, very leery of your new boss."

Henry muttered something. Everything was happening too fast.

"I cannot and will not recommend doing any joint business as long as that guy is your boss," Leach continued. "Now this conversation is at an end. I can either go in there and withdraw, or you can. Which one of us is going to be the gentleman?"

Henry's head was spinning. He wanted this deal badly, but he knew the right answer. "I'll go in and withdraw," he said, defeated. "I'll be the gentleman."

Leach thanked him, and they returned to the conference room. Henry wound it down quickly, muttering that it looked like Smith Barney might be able to handle the deal alone after all. Everyone stood up and shook hands. Henry left the room and walked out the building's front door, still feeling unnerved.

He had never simply walked away from a deal before. He had no idea how he would explain what had just happened back at Bache. How could he say that Smith Barney shunned the firm because Leach thought the new boss was crooked? Nobody would believe him—everyone knew he didn't like Darr. If he said anything, he could be out on the street looking for a job, with his former boss a sworn enemy. But if he kept quiet, and Leach was right, there was no telling what might happen at Bache. No matter what he decided to do, Henry knew it wouldn't be the right choice. There wasn't one.

Oh, my God, he thought. *What am I going to do now?*

When Jim Darr first arrived at Bache's tax shelter department, his reputation among his new staff was already sour. For some, it was the things he said during the job interviews that did it. For others, it was the conditions they knew he must have accepted to get hired.

Early on, Henry felt uncomfortable about whoever Blank's potential replacement would be after someone he respected walked away from the job. Henry had recommended an old associate, Lee Roeder, who established himself in tax shelters at Paine Webber. But shortly after his interview with Lee Paton at Bache, Roeder called Henry to say thanks, but no thanks.

"I can tell you right now, I'm not interested in the job, and I doubt very seriously if they are going to offer it to me," Roeder said.

"Why?" Henry asked.

"Their idea of the size of that department and the growth they want out of it are crazy," he replied. "In no uncertain terms I told them that there were not enough quality deals available to get the department to the size they wanted." There was only one way, Roeder said, to reach Bache's goal: start selling lots of junk deals.

Great, Henry thought in disgust. Paton and all those others had no idea what the tax shelter business was about. You couldn't just create good deals out of thin air—quality properties managed by quality general partners were tough to find. But in typical Wall Street fashion, these guys saw a business booming and wanted to push it further. All they considered, Henry suspected, was that E. F. Hutton had been building its tax shelter business exponentially in the past year. Under the leadership of George Ball, Hutton's go-go president, the firm was hiring new staff and selling tax shelters at a rapid clip. But already, the quality of some Hutton deals was being viewed on the Street as suspect. Too many lousy shelters were being sold too fast. Just because Hutton and Ball wanted to risk their clients' money to build an empire didn't mean Bache had to follow them into the gutter. Whoever accepted the job on those terms, Henry felt sure, was not going to be someone he liked.

Months later, the first person in the department to meet Darr was David Hayes, the longest-surviving member of Bache's tax shelter business. Over the years, Hayes had cultivated a reputation for honesty, at times going so far as criticizing Bache deals to brokers. By 1979, he had more credibility with brokers than anyone else in the department. So, in selecting a new boss for the department, it made political sense to try to win Hayes's support. Paton telephoned him in Washington, asking him to come to New York to meet a candidate for the job named Jim Darr. Hayes agreed; he had never heard the name before.

Hayes almost immediately took a dislike to Darr. Everything about Darr's manner screamed that he was obsessed with control and had a self-important air of superiority. More times than Hayes could count, Darr started his comments with the phrase "I'll tell you how to do it." The entire time they spoke, Darr stared directly at Hayes, never moving his eyes. *He's trying to intimidate me*, Hayes thought.

The meeting came to an end, and after shaking hands, Hayes headed out the door, feeling enormously uneasy. From the way Paton acted, it was clear to Hayes that Darr already had the job in his back pocket. Hayes could not believe he would be working with the guy.

The next month, Darr hit the department like a hurricane. Since Steve Blank's dismissal, things had been drifting. Open positions went unfilled. Follow-up on some deals was missed. Morale suffered, and Paton made it worse by holding back some bonuses he thought were too high, even though they had been promised by Blank.

Darr tackled all those problems with gusto. He had enormous energy and spoke forcefully about the need to transform the department into one of the biggest and best on Wall Street. Darr described, in military detail, his strategy: He had learned the game plan at Merrill Lynch. Their structure of product managers and other marketing specialists was the one to emulate.

From almost his first day on the job, Darr's new hires were given jobs prescribed in the Merrill playbook. One of his first hires was Wally Allen, his old friend from his training days at Merrill. Allen had since left Wall Street and was working at a southern coal company. But Darr thought he would be the perfect person to help bring a little bit of Merrill into the department. Within months of Darr's arrival, Allen was working at Bache in the new job of product manager.

In his first months, Darr also pushed Paton to turn over all the bonuses that were being withheld. Bonuses for both John D'Elisa and Curtis Henry had accrued over the past year, based almost exclusively on the number of deals done by the department. Even if the bonuses were too high, Darr argued, Bache had to keep its word. He persuaded Paton, and early in 1980, he told D'Elisa the news.

"Since you're going to work here, they should honor their commitments," Darr said. "But there's no guarantee we're going to continue paying you the way you have been paid. It's important to reorganize the department in a way that makes us more efficient in the way we do business."

D'Elisa said that would be fine, and Darr handed him his check.

"You know, I worked real hard to get you this bonus," he said, staring straight at D'Elisa. "I think I deserve a piece of it."

Is he testing me? For an instant, D'Elisa was speechless. "OK, Jim," he finally replied. "I'll take you out to dinner."

Darr smiled and walked away. D'Elisa still felt a little shaken. Maybe Darr had been kidding. But it sure didn't sound like it.*

That same week, Darr called Henry to talk with him about his bonus. He told Henry that he had persuaded Paton to pay the accrued bonus. It was more than $80,000, the most Henry had ever received.

"You know," Darr said, "this is an awful lot of money. More than you deserve." Henry said nothing. For this much money, he could take a few insults.

"But I got it for you," Darr continued. "So the least you can do is give me $5,000 of it."

There was not a hint in his voice that Darr was joking. Besides, Henry was already sure that Darr was not the kind of person who joked about money. Henry felt disgusted by the request. The only way he could think to respond was pretend nothing had happened.

"Well, thank you very much for getting me my money," Henry said. "I really appreciate it."

They wound up their conversation. Darr never mentioned the $5,000 again.

Darr quickly revised the way his troops were paid, trying to make it in everyone's financial interest to sell more deals. Product managers and regional marketers would be paid on what Darr called "gross marketed equity," a fancy term that simply stood for the dollar volume of deals sold. The more the marketers sold, the more money they made. The origina-

---

*Darr denies ever having asked any of his employees for part of a bonus.

tors, D'Elisa and Henry, didn't sell deals, so they would receive special compensation. Darr helped set up a special partnership, called Trace Management, which took a one percent interest in every transaction they assembled. Henry and D'Elisa each took a one-third interest in Trace. Darr took the last third for himself, even though he was not originating deals.

By early 1980, Darr had his first opportunity to speak to all of his troops in person at the department's quarterly meeting in New York. All of the marketers and originators came to town and gathered in Darr's office at Bache's headquarters. Darr started a speech, letting them know that things were going to change.

"We are going to do more business than we have ever done," Darr said. "We are going to have bigger deals, and newer sponsors. We are going to have a well-run department, and we are going to become a leader on the street."

For the most part, his hour-long presentation sounded like the typical pep talk. But then Darr shifted gears. His department was not going to be like others on Wall Street, he said. His shop was going to be clean.

"I know all the other heads of the departments on the street," Darr said. "I know which ones of them have secret bank accounts in the Bahamas and in Switzerland. I know the ones that are getting side deals. And we are not going to do anything like that."

Several members of the department listened in amazement. None of them had heard about people in the business having secret bank accounts or taking payoffs.

Darr changed the subject again and soon brought his talk to a close by emphasizing one last point. "And don't any of you forget," he said, pointing a finger at his staff, "your job is to make me look good."

Nothing about working together. Nothing about teamwork. *Make me look good.* The meeting broke up, and everyone headed out of the crowded room. No one was talking. Finally, the silence broke.

"Great motivation speech," someone muttered caustically. Everybody cracked up.

As the weeks wore on, the discomfort with the new boss grew. There was no question that Darr was smart—he understood the dynamics of the tax shelter business and had a clear plan of how to change the department. But his behavior veered at times into the realm of the bizarre. Darr's talk about his military background was particularly troubling. He loved to brag about his exploits during the war, but he rarely told the same story twice about where he served and what he did.

The first time he discussed his military background with his new colleagues, he said that he flew F-4 Phantom jet fighters for the air force in Vietnam. At another meeting, Darr suddenly changed course, describing in detail his experiences as a helicopter pilot in the war. He told how he and other pilots used to fly low over Vietnamese rivers, trying to make the wheels of their helicopters spin by touching the water. On some days, he said he was in Special Forces, on others, he said he was a Green Beret. Then he changed his story again, saying that he had not served in Vietnam at all—instead, he told them, during the war years he was stationed by the Central Intelligence Agency in Iran to help support the shah. He had been selected, he said, because he spoke Farsi fluently. Nobody was likely to be able to challenge the claim. The ayatollah wasn't buying tax shelters.

By then, nobody believed a word Darr said about his past. They couldn't understand why the man lied so frequently, and so obviously. But it put them on guard, worried about what other falsehoods Darr might be telling. Finally, at a quarterly meeting, David Hayes had enough of the lies. Darr was discussing his experience in some branch of the armed forces when Hayes broke in.

"I thought you served in the air force," Hayes said, leaning against a wall.

Darr glared at Hayes and walked toward him, placing the palms of his hands on Hayes's chest, as if in one more step he would go for the throat. Then Darr just stood there, glowering. Hayes stared right back. *He doesn't know what to do next,* Hayes thought. Finally, Darr smiled and took his hands away. The confrontation ended.

Darr's bullying style extended into every facet of the department, transforming even the weekly conference call for marketers. Established by Blank, the call had been designed to give everyone a chance to discuss problems they might have with particular deals or to learn about offerings in the pipeline or to offer suggestions about possible sponsors. But Darr had no tolerance for marketers raising perceived problems with a deal or suggesting changes. In the calls, Darr pounded one theme: sell. New York would put the deals together. Their job was to sell the shelters—without question.

"If you don't sell out this project, then you are going to be out of the firm," Darr barked at his marketing staff in one conference call. "I'll find people who can do your job if you can't handle it."

Other times, if some marketers felt uneasy about the quality of a particular tax shelter, Darr threatened not to pay the bonuses they had already earned unless the new deal sold out.

With Darr leading the charge, new and previously unknown promoters suddenly appeared at Bache. Among the first was a group of men whose biggest qualification seemed to be their personal ties to Darr. The group included John Holmes, the headhunter who helped Darr get his job at Bache and who now was one of his good friends. Their oil tax shelter, called Integrated Energy, Inc., or I.E.I., struck many in the department as odd. For one thing, neither Holmes nor another chief principal, Gene Mason, worked in the oil patch. While some oil professionals were brought into the deal, Mason, a Philadelphia lawyer, would be president and chairman. Holmes's background was limited to Wall Street. Also, the company would not invest in oil wells—instead, it would be a roll-up, purchasing stakes in other energy partnerships and throwing them together into what would become a publicly traded entity.

Curtis Henry, who handled the due diligence for energy deals, grew more uncomfortable after he reviewed the plans for I.E.I. *This is a perfect Wall Street deal*, he thought. *They're creating net worth out of thin air.*

I.E.I. at that point had no office space. No accounting procedures. No full-time employees. No systems to evaluate the value of the oil reserves coming into the company. No capital. None of the normal elements of a regular business. "This isn't a company," Henry told colleagues. "It's an idea."

I.E.I. quickly became the butt of jokes, with executives referring to it derisively as "E.I.E.I.O." But Darr was passionate about the deal, talking it up to his superiors as a fabulous transaction that would make Bache lots of money. Other members of the department didn't understand his excitement; they began to gossip that maybe Darr was so agog about the deal because of his friendship with Holmes.

Finally, Darr told Dennis Marron, who worked for the department in New York, one of the reasons he was so fired up about the deal: If I.E.I. went through, Darr himself stood to make a lot of money. He told Marron that the idea for I.E.I. had, in fact, been his and that he had been working on the deal when Bache hired him. So, as part of his pay package, he said, Bache promised that if he sold the deal, the firm would pay him a special bonus equal to the amount he would have made for his interest in the new oil company. I.E.I. went public at $10 a unit. Its price immediately collapsed, with the units losing more than half their value. While the deal blew up for investors, Bache walked away with huge fees.

No one could argue that Darr failed to bring money into the firm. Sales had picked up since he arrived. The department kept expanding, with Darr scouring for new hires. His staff might not trust him, but Darr could run the business.

Despite his lies, his bullying, and his arrogance, he seemed to be at Bache to stay. Then the word spread about Darr's past at Josephthal, and the plots against him began to be hatched.

Curtis Henry walked across a Manhattan parking lot to David Hayes's car. The two men had come to town for meetings at Bache's New York headquarters in September 1980. A few minutes earlier, Hayes had asked Henry to come on a trip to a Bache branch in New Jersey. The branch had scheduled Hayes for a presentation to brokers about a new tax shelter. It was a deal Henry knew something about, and he agreed to tag along and help out.

The two men chatted amiably as Hayes drove the car through the Midtown Tunnel, crossing the New York State line to New Jersey. It had been weeks since Henry had heard the allegations from Leach about Darr taking money. He still hadn't decided what to do about it. But in his mind he kept replaying the events that occurred since Darr came to Bache: Darr's pronouncements about how everyone in the business was taking money but him. Darr hitting him up for part of his bonus. The strange deals. Now it all was starting to make sense. As Hayes drove into New Jersey, Henry decided that the moment had finally arrived to tell someone in the department what he knew.

"David, I'm going to tell you a story that you are not going to believe," Henry said. "But nevertheless, it's the truth." For the next few minutes, he described what Leach had said. Hayes kept his eyes on the road, listening quietly until Henry finished.

"Jesus," Hayes said. "Well, this is not good news."

For the rest of the trip, the two men discussed nothing else. When they finally arrived at the Bache branch, they stayed out in the parking lot another twenty minutes, hashing through what they should do.

The bottom line, Hayes said, was that they simply didn't have enough information to make a decision. "If this is a true story, if we can find out if there is somebody else who can confirm this story to us, maybe we should begin to think about doing something," Hayes said. "For now, this is just a rumor."

"Yeah," Henry said. "But it's a scary one."

John D'Elisa's concern about Darr's history gradually began to border on obsession. After his encounter with Sinclair at the footrace, D'Elisa made inquiries with people he knew in the business. Among those he called was Alan Gosule, a lawyer in Boston with Gaston & Snow who had done work with Josephthal's tax shelter department.

After discussing some pending deals, D'Elisa asked what Gosule knew about Darr.

"Darr's got a reputation," Gosule replied. "He's a really bad guy."

D'Elisa pressed the lawyer for more information, but he refused to explain further. D'Elisa thanked Gosule for his help and hung up more anxious than before. He knew Gosule well; he wasn't the kind to traffic in rumors. If Gosule was worried about someone's integrity, D'Elisa knew he should worry, too.

D'Elisa decided to tell someone else in the department what he had heard. He telephoned David Hayes, who just days earlier had returned from his trip to New Jersey. He'd been sitting on some information, D'Elisa said, and wanted to talk with Hayes about it. He'd heard stories about Darr taking payoffs at Josephthal. Did Hayes think he should do anything?

"Oh, shit," Hayes said. Without even trying, the confirmation he wanted was coming in.

Hayes telephoned Henry in Dallas immediately. More people knew this Darr story than just Leach, he said. Now D'Elisa had heard it coming straight out of Josephthal. For the next few hours, Hayes, D'Elisa, and Henry telephoned back and forth. They didn't learn anything new but ruminated endlessly about what to do. If this became a scandal, they knew Bache wouldn't handle it well—the firm was already smarting from the silver crisis and the rounds of criticism from an angry Congress and the press. The Belzbergs were making new rumblings about going after Bache. The three feared that the Darr problem might make Bache executives panic and shut the whole department down to keep this new scandal secret. All of their jobs could be on the line.

But keeping things quiet was not going to be an option. Within days, Douglas Kemmerer, a Bache tax shelter marketer in San Francisco, caught wind of the internal rumors and started calling around to ask others what they knew. Kemmerer worried Hayes—he thought the guy loved corporate intrigue far too much and wouldn't keep his mouth shut. He called Henry and D'Elisa and said they had to meet.

With Henry in Dallas, Hayes in Washington, and D'Elisa in Smithtown, Long Island, the only chance to meet face-to-face would be at the department's next quarterly meeting in Manhattan, scheduled in two weeks. But they agreed that they would say nothing about their suspicions at Bache headquarters; the risk of detection was too great. Instead, they had to meet somewhere they could speak privately.

Henry called Dennis Marron, who worked for the department in New York, to see if he could find a meeting place. When Marron asked why, Henry told him what was going on. The story confirmed Marron's worst fears. He had listened to Darr for months, spinning lie upon lie about his military career, and had grown more uncomfortable with his boss as each new version emerged.

"The guy is pathological," Marron muttered. Henry pushed Marron again about a meeting place. After thinking for a moment, Marron had an idea.

"What about Wally Allen's apartment?" he asked.

Allen, Darr's old friend from his Merrill days, rented an apartment just two blocks from the firm after Darr hired him. It was the perfect place, Marron said. It was close enough that everyone could go there during the lunch break and be back in an hour without anyone the wiser. But the idea left Henry wary. After all, Allen knew Darr longer than he knew any of them. How could they know that he could be trusted?

"I don't think Wally will be a problem," Marron replied. "He may have been hired by Darr, but he's not a big Darr fan."

Marron was right. Allen agreed to let everyone meet in his apartment and said he would not tell anybody about what was happening.

By October, the plans were set. The staff of the Bache tax shelter department arrived in Manhattan for the quarterly meeting. Nothing seemed unusual. They listened as Darr spoke about the sales performance of the prior quarter, they took notes during presentations about new deals scheduled to be sold. At the lunch break on the first day, everyone streamed out of the building, headed toward nearby restaurants. Amid the hubbub, Hayes, D'Elisa, Henry, Marron, and Allen politely rejected any lunch invitations. They had other plans.

The five men left separately from Bache's headquarters at 100 Gold Street and slowly walked the two blocks south to Allen's apartment at the old Excelsior Power Company. The Excelsior, built in 1888, was the first coal-generated electric power–generating station in Manhattan. In 1979, the brick building was transformed by a historic rehabilitation, giving somebody, somewhere a tax shelter. One at a time, the men followed as Allen led the way to his apartment. Through the nondescript lobby of the Excelsior, down a long hallway to the small, new elevator, up to the fifth floor, left, down the carpeted hall, into the apartment at the end.

Allen, whose tastes ran to contemporary, simple designs, had decorated his apartment almost exclusively with futons. Everyone started trying to fashion chairs out of them. Grabbing a few beers out of Allen's refrigerator, the men chatted nervously in the living room as they waited for everyone to arrive. They commented on the apartment's gorgeous view of the Brooklyn Bridge and kidded Allen about his taste in furniture. At some point, the suggestion was made that the group take a name in honor of their meeting place. From then on, the gathering would be known within Bache as the first official meeting of "the Futon Five."

No one ran the meeting. It just flowed, like a group therapy session without a therapist. D'Elisa opened the conversation, describing what he had heard from Sinclair and Gosule. Then he turned the floor over to Henry, who told of his experience with Leach in Oklahoma. Despite the repetitive nature of the information, all of them knew it was still too thin. They needed something more.

D'Elisa turned to Allen. "Look, you've known Jim longer than anybody," he said. "What do you know about the guy? Have you ever heard of anything like this?"

Allen shrugged. It seemed like he knew less than everybody else.

For almost an hour, the five men debated what to do. They talked about the silver crisis and how they all might lose their jobs if this was mishandled. They had to have a solution in place if Darr got fired. Among themselves, they agreed that they would turn the department over to Hayes, who would run it either permanently or until a new manager could be found. More important, they decided that they had to keep investigating. D'Elisa was assigned to contact Gosule again and pump him for information. Everyone else was told to make quiet inquiries about Darr among their contacts in the business. Hayes suggested that he find out which employees conducted investigations of crooked brokers for Bache and turn the matter over to them.

As the meeting broke up, no one realized that the messages had been mixed in their conversations. Hayes thought he was supposed to contact a

Bache investigator immediately; everyone else thought he would be waiting until they amassed more information. It would prove to be a critical miscommunication.

On returning to Washington, Hayes called a lawyer he knew in the Bache legal department, saying that there was a problem with an employee suspected of illegalities. He said the employee's supervisor had not yet been told about the problems because no one was sure yet if they were true. The lawyer told Hayes he had done the right thing and said that the person who handled such matters would contact him soon. Two days later, he received a telephone call from Bill Jones, the former FBI agent who headed Bache's security department. Hayes said that members of the tax shelter department had reason to believe that their boss had been involved in illegal activities at his former firm. For the next few hours, Jones questioned Hayes in detail about everything he knew: the rumors about Josephthal. The questionable deals being sold at Bache. Darr's lies about his background.

By the time it ended, Hayes had exhausted everything he knew about Darr. Jones thanked him and said he would get back to him later. Hayes hung up, pleased that, with all the ways this could have been potentially mishandled, the right people seemed to be onto the case.

Jones dug into the Darr investigation with relish. After interviewing Hayes, he contacted other members of the Futon Five. He also called Douglas Kemmerer in San Francisco, who had been trading stories with some members of the group about what he heard was happening.

When D'Elisa heard from Jones, he couldn't believe it. *It's too soon for this.* Somebody must have spilled the beans, probably Kemmerer, he thought. He didn't have all the information he needed. So D'Elisa started pressing Gosule hard, demanding in a telephone call that the lawyer open up.

"You have got to let me know what's going on," D'Elisa pleaded. "You have to get involved in this. If you don't, this whole thing is going to get mixed up and everyone is going to get hurt here."

"Look, John, this is a tough one," Gosule said. "I'm trying to build a relationship with Bache. I don't want to jeopardize that."

"Damn it, Alan, if you know something, you have an obligation to stand up and say it," D'Elisa snapped.

Gosule struggled for a moment with his conscience. He wanted desperately to help D'Elisa but feared that doing so would eventually backfire on him. He weighed his options as D'Elisa pressed him. *Oh, the hell with it.*

"All right, John, listen," Gosule said. "I'm going to tell you what I know. But I want you to know, I'm doing this for you, I'm doing this for Bache, and I'm doing this for our industry."

With that, Gosule launched into his story. He knew nothing firsthand, the lawyer cautioned, but had heard enough to be sure that D'Elisa was on the right track. He had close contacts within Josephthal and already heard about what had happened there. Darr had received checks from at least two real estate syndicators who did business with Josephthal, and deposited the money directly into his personal bank account. Gosule said he knew people who had seen copies of both the checks and the deposit slips.

D'Elisa listened carefully, surprised that Darr would have left such an obvious trail. He had thought Darr would have been more clever.

There was more, Gosule said. After speaking with D'Elisa a few weeks ago, Gosule had mentioned Bache's interest in Darr's background to some of his friends. One of them was a client who had sold some real estate deals through Josephthal. Gosule had thought little of the conversation—his client had nothing to do with the general partners who gave Darr checks.

"Yes?" D'Elisa asked.

"Well, this client told me that he has information that could be helpful to your case," Gosule said. "Jim tried to put the squeeze on him, too." The client had told Gosule that Darr had approached him for money when he was trying to sell a tax shelter deal through Josephthal.*

But Darr didn't make the demand at the height of his power, Gosule said. He sought the payment long after Josephthal had discovered the others, after that firm's investigation had ended, just weeks before he started at Bache.

D'Elisa couldn't believe it. He had found the smoking gun. *Jim Darr is history.*

Darr knew nothing of the secret investigation under way, and every member of the Futon Five made sure not to act suspiciously. They knew it would take weeks for everything to be wrapped up. So, the department plugged along as always. The product managers marketed deals. Darr held his weekly conference calls. The origination team searched for new general partners. And D'Elisa had found one in Texas he thought was particularly intriguing: a real estate man named Clifton Harrison.

Shortly after hearing about Harrison, D'Elisa took a trip to Dallas to

---

* Through his lawyers, Darr denied ever demanding money from Gosule's client.

visit Harrison at his company, Harrison Freedman Associates. Harrison gave D'Elisa a tour around the small company's operations, speaking effusively about all of his deals. D'Elisa was impressed. This new potential client was nothing like the gruff real estate developers and packagers with whom he usually did business. Harrison was just the opposite. He had no rough edges. His style and mannerisms had more of a delicate, Continental flavor. He was extremely deferential; when they went to a restaurant, he ordered D'Elisa's food for him. Harrison wore his hair to his shoulders, with a European cut, and dressed in expensive imported suits. D'Elisa thought Harrison's fabulous image could help promote deals he sponsored.

Better still was the nature of Harrison's business. He was not just a developer who built buildings or a syndicator who packaged existing properties. Harrison bragged about managing money for Phillips N.V., a Dutch institutional investor. The Dutch money had been the key to Harrison's success in the real estate business, helping him finance a number of lucrative deals. D'Elisa knew that kind of relationship in real estate was fairly uncommon and could help Bache make some contacts to improve its European business as well. Pleased with what he saw in Harrison, D'Elisa boarded a jet back to New York and briefed Darr on this new potential sponsor. Harrison should speak with Darr soon, D'Elisa said.

Harrison made the trip from Dallas a few weeks later. The meeting went well, and Darr seemed intrigued with Harrison's jet-setter lifestyle and his experiences and contacts in Europe. Darr gave D'Elisa the go-ahead to start exploring possible deals with this flamboyant real estate man from Texas.

Harrison started doing some business with Bache's European branches, which reported to the international division. Darr and D'Elisa were eager to put together some American deals for the tax shelter department. Even though D'Elisa usually reviewed the real estate deals, for the Harrison partnerships he passed that responsibility on to Curtis Henry. Since Henry was based in Dallas, the decision to put him in charge seemed obvious.

One afternoon, Darr and D'Elisa placed a call by speakerphone to Henry at the branch office. "Curtis, we've had this sponsor who has been doing some things with our European offices," Darr said. "Now, we've decided that this guy has a good reputation and we are going to do some American deals with him."

Henry grabbed a pen and paper to start taking notes. "OK, so what do I do?"

"He's down in Dallas, so I am putting you in charge of putting the due diligence together," Darr said.

"OK, that's fine," Henry said. "Who's the sponsor?"

"Clifton Harrison."

Henry paused for an instant. "Well," he drawled. "OK."

Henry wrote the name "Clifton Harrison" across the notepad on his desk. Then he put down his pen. "Before you tell me about this deal, I've got one serious question. When did our policy change?"

"When did what policy change?" Darr asked.

Henry paused, wishing he could see Darr's face at that moment.

"About doing business with convicted felons," he replied.

※   ※   ※   ※

CLIFTON STONE Harrison was the most successful ex-convict in Texas real estate. Born in 1938 in a small farming town in east Texas, Harrison had already seen the fortunes of his life rise and fall many times. He was raised in Amarillo, a west Texas town where his family moved after his father found a job at a bomb factory during the war. A severe dyslexic, Harrison was unable to read or write until he was fourteen years old. Many of the people who knew him, including his teachers, decided that he was mentally retarded. But, under pressure from his mother, Harrison was kept in school.

Harrison became a quiet little boy who often pulled back from the crowd, choosing instead to live mostly within himself. At school, he always sat in the back of the room, saying nothing. He heard the remarks of pity, like "Clifton's such a nice boy. But he sure is dumb." They cut him deeply.

For his mother, the criticism fueled constant battle with the school. She insisted that the teachers pass him. When they refused, she stood her ground and turned up the pressure. Finally, they just threw up their hands and agreed to move Harrison on rather than fight his mother again.

When Harrison turned thirteen, his parents sent him to Ponca Military Academy, in the hopes that smaller classes, more attention, and discipline might help him overcome his disabilities. While he was there, Harrison successfully learned to read and write. But his hold on the skill was thin— he always remained terrified of reading aloud. He grew to fear going to church, out of concern that the preacher might ask him to read a selection from the Bible.

His shaky grasp of literacy slowed Harrison down in college. The classes were very difficult for him; he excelled at nothing. He jumped from school to school, never clicking with one institution and never doing well enough to graduate.

With little going Harrison's way, an uncle got him a training-level job at the First National Bank in Dallas in February 1963. There Harrison found a talent. He did well analyzing loans and proved adept at selling himself. Harrison was selected to join the national accounts division, where he would be an assistant cashier in the bank's lending activities around the country.

For the first time in his life, the boy from west Texas began enjoying success. He became boisterous and glad-handing, with a taste for expensive clothes and fast cars. He wanted to be accepted among the wealthy elite of Dallas but did not have the income to travel in that circle. To accomplish what he wanted, he needed more money.

So he started stealing. The scheme began simply in 1964, when he falsely reported stock certificates he owned as missing. When he received the new certificates, he sold them. Then he pledged the worthless originals as collateral for loans from Wynewood State Bank & Central Finance Company. He did not intend to repay the debts.

In 1966, when he received lending authority at First National, his crimes worsened. He filled out all the necessary paperwork to support bogus loans. In some cases, he made up names for the supposed borrowers; in others, he used the names of famous people in Dallas. Then he took that money from the bogus loans and deposited it in his own bank account under the name B&J Investment Co.

Harrison was drunk on the thrills of money. He borrowed some money to pay other loans back. He bought stocks and bonds in the hopes that a rising market would pay off all his debts. Harrison did not see any harm in what he was doing; it was all just one big, giddy game.

Eventually, the senior officers at First National realized that their junior executive spent more money than he earned. They decided to investigate. Following up on their suspicions, Roy Lambert, an auditor for First National, confronted Harrison about his lavish spending. Harrison grew indignant, denying that he had done anything improper. But within days, Lambert had pieced together Harrison's scheme. The bank contacted federal prosecutors in Dallas. That weekend, Harrison traveled to Las Vegas for a few days of gambling. On Sunday afternoon, when he returned home, he was met at Love Field by agents of the Federal Bureau of Investigation and taken to jail.

On September 6, 1967, Harrison pleaded guilty to multiple counts of embezzlement, bank fraud, and mail fraud. The case was assigned to Federal District Judge W. M. Taylor Jr., which Harrison found almost amusing—one of the people whose names he improperly used for the bogus loans was that of the judge's nephew. Judge Taylor sent Harrison to a federal mental institution for three months of psychiatric evaluation. After being found sane, Harrison appeared again before Judge Taylor, who sentenced him to three years in prison in Texarkana, Texas.

For the first time in his life, Harrison was in an environment where he could read and write better than most of the people around him. He met big-time criminals, including members of the Mafia being held in protective custody. Some, impressed with Harrison, asked him to work with them when he got out. But the offers frightened Harrison, and he declined.

Prison life proved difficult for Harrison, who at times ran into the very circle of people he had tried to impress with his stolen money. Once he attended a speech at the prison that was being given by an executive with a local savings and loan. After he arrived, Harrison realized that he had done business with the executive while at the bank.

"Clifton!" the executive called out. "What are you doing here?"

Harrison was humiliated.

I have to educate myself, he decided. *Education is the only way you can get out of this ghetto.*

Harrison pleaded with the prison officials in Texarkana and persuaded them to send him to a rehabilitation program. Eventually they agreed, and Harrison was transferred to a minimum security prison in Dallas. He applied and was accepted at Southern Methodist University. So, every day beginning the next semester, Harrison, wearing his prison-issue clothes, boarded a bus at the prison and headed to SMU. He arrived at 6:00 A.M. and spent his mornings in the cafeteria, waiting for classes to begin.

He began studying real estate, and did well. After his first year at SMU, Harrison was paroled. He received his bachelor's degree, then went on to earn an MBA with a concentration in real estate. But Harrison's hope for a job in the business seemed limited. Not too many people in the real estate business wanted to take on an ex-convict.

With the help of an admiring professor, Harrison found a job selling limited partnerships for Irving Klein, a scrappy local real estate investor. Soon Harrison was rubbing elbows with the Dallas elite he admired, selling them Klein's successful deals. Harrison bragged that even Stanley Marcus, whose Neiman-Marcus department stores were legend, was one of his satisfied customers.

When Klein died in the early 1970s, Harrison already had a fat Rolodex and a good reputation. He persuaded two of his investors, Raymond Freedman and Herman Ulevitch, to back him in a new company, Harrison Freedman Associates. Through his connections, he started doing business with the Strauss family of Dallas, who were related to Bob Strauss, a politically prominent lawyer who was in line to be the next chairman of the Democratic Party. Harrison even hired Strauss's law firm, Akin, Gump, Strauss, Hauer & Feld, to handle some of his business dealings.

Bolstered by his success, Harrison launched a drive to win a presidential pardon. A number of his high-profile investors wrote recommendations to the Justice Department. In later years, Harrison would brag to friends that Bob Strauss himself helped lobby for the pardon. With such high-profile support, Harrison pulled it off. President Gerald R. Ford signed Harrison's pardon on October 9, 1974, one month after his pardon of Richard Nixon. Everything was finally in place for Clifton Harrison to start his life over.

But by 1980, as Bache began knocking on Harrison's door, troubles started emerging in his real estate empire. His investors, Freedman and Ulevitch, felt that Harrison had become carried away with money. There was a feeling of being lavish—extra lavish. There were too many fancy cars, too much expensive jewelry, too many unpaid bills. Freedman thought it was obvious that Harrison spent more money than he made. He just had no idea how Harrison did it.

Worse, some of the deals Harrison put together were collapsing, and in some instances, he was leaving his partners on the hook for the mess. An office park in Dallas was foreclosed on, and shopping centers in Bowie and Lewisville, Texas, defaulted. Harrison failed to pay $434,000 owed on a note he arranged and signed; Freedman and Ulevitch paid the debt. Finally Freedman decided that Harrison's claims of rehabilitation were bunk. Something about the way Harrison did business just didn't seem kosher. He wanted out. Harrison agreed to buy Freedman's shares in Harrison Freedman and signed an IOU for $100,000. More than fifteen years later, that debt would remain unpaid.

When Bache started looking into doing business with Harrison, nobody asked Freedman's opinion of his partner. But years later, when asked what he would have said if asked, Freedman's response was blunt: "Hell no. Do not invest with this man."

※   ※   ※   ※

D'ELISA FIGURED the deal was dead the minute he and Darr heard about Harrison's criminal record. As soon as Henry told them about it, Darr went ballistic.

"What are we doing?" Darr demanded. "D'Elisa, why are we talking to this guy?"

Well, that's that, D'Elisa thought. Darr took the matter to the security department, asking that Harrison's background be investigated. But soon, before D'Elisa knew what was happening, Darr started changing his tune about Harrison. Maybe, he said, the criminal record wasn't an impossible problem. The man did have a presidential pardon, after all.

"This is something we should take up with counsel," Darr said, "to see whether we can do business with this guy."

D'Elisa couldn't understand why they were even trying. There was no actual deal on the launching pad, just the idea of doing one. They could cut their losses now and walk away clean. Even E. F. Hutton, with its aggressive push into market share, had taken a look at Harrison just a few months earlier and turned up its nose. Why did Bache have to chase this business?

The biggest problem, of course, would be disclosure. Under the federal securities laws, material information about a general partner had to be told to investors. D'Elisa could not imagine what investors would think after finding out that the man Bache recommended to look out for their savings had stolen money from a bank.

Darr checked with Peter Fass, who served as one of the department's outside lawyers. Word started coming back to the department that Darr was pushing the lawyers to get Harrison approved. At one meeting on another topic, Fass took D'Elisa aside to talk to him about what was happening.

"What do you need this for?" he asked. "Darr is putting a lot of pressure on me to get a resolution on this guy."

Later, D'Elisa spoke to Derek Wittner, a lawyer who worked under Fass. He was appalled. "What, are you guys fucking crazy?" he asked. "We don't need this."

Finally Fass approached the attorney general for the state of New York for an opinion. If a general partner was convicted of a felony but received a presidential pardon, did the partnership have to disclose the criminal record to investors? After some review, the attorney general decided that the answer was no. Investors could be kept in the dark.

Harrison was delighted with the outcome. To celebrate, on October 31, he went to Schumer's Wine & Liquors at 59 East Fifty-fourth Street and ordered three magnums of Dom Perignon for $388.04. He sent the expensive champagne to the lawyers who had played so critical a role in getting him approved to sell tax shelters through Bache.

About that time, Darr called Curtis Henry to talk to him about Harrison. Henry was stunned. He thought that the deal had been killed during their earlier telephone call.

"I'm going to have Clifton come and see you," Darr said. "We need to talk about his previous life. We're proceeding to do some due diligence on him."

Henry could not imagine that a Harrison deal would get done. Bache would be the laughingstock of the business if it used a convicted felon as a general partner. With so many possible real estate promoters available, he could not think of any reason why the firm should waste its time on Harrison.

He also had another concern. At that point, the Bache investigation of Darr was secretly in full swing. The whole thing could become a horrible scandal. Harrison already seemed to be trying to get close to Darr. With his record, Harrison might get unfairly tarred by the association, once the whole story came out. It would be best for everybody, Henry thought, to tell Harrison to stay away.

Harrison came to Bache's Dallas branch a few days later, nattily dressed in an expensive suit and tie. He told Henry the whole story, circling again and again back to President Ford. "I have a full presidential pardon," he drawled repeatedly.

Henry wanted none of it. "I don't know how we can do anything with you," he said. "I don't know how people will react to it. The fact that you have a pardon from Gerald Ford doesn't mean that you haven't been in prison and these events didn't occur."

"But the president of the United States . . ." Harrison began.

"Look, Clifton, let me tell you something," Henry said. "I know you have become associated with Darr in the last few months, and he is your new maven here."

Henry leaned closer and lowered his voice. "But if I were you, I would take a low profile right now. I will tell you right now, Darr is under investigation for some things he did at his last firm, and there is a pretty strong belief that he will not be here soon. With all your problems, I really think you should get yourself some distance from him."

Harrison looked at Henry, his poker face not registering the slightest surprise. He bantered halfheartedly with Henry for a few seconds and then stood up. The meeting was over. "Well, thank you very much, sir," Harrison said, shaking Henry's hand. "Hope to see you soon."

Henry watched Harrison walk toward the branch office door. He was sure that after his blunt honesty, this would be the last time he would have to speak to Clifton Harrison. He was right, but for reasons far different from what he imagined.

None of the Futon Five could believe it: Somehow, some way, Darr found out about the Bache investigation. Somebody must have told him. Besides Jones and Gosule, no one outside the department was supposed to know. And they knew that none of them had an interest in giving Darr a chance to protect himself.

But there was no doubt Darr had found out. His terror was palpable. His cocksure attitude vanished; now he walked around the department like a zombie. His face seemed heavily lined, and he stopped talking to his staff. Even executives who knew nothing about the investigation could tell something was wrong with their boss. Whenever Darr left a meeting, the gossip flowed. *Jim looks worried. What's the matter? Is he getting fired?* The Futon Five listened to their colleagues in silence. Too many people knew what was happening already.

Soon, though, the word spread everywhere. Bill Pittman, whom Darr had promoted from administrative manager to marketer, became Darr's biggest defender.

"How could you be so disloyal?" Pittman snapped at Dennis Marron. "How could you turn on the man who signs your checks?"

"As far as I know, my checks come from Bache, not from him," Marron replied coldly. "My loyalty is to the firm."

Pittman challenged almost every member of the Futon Five, but no one took him seriously. He was not a senior member of the department. His uncontrollable temper made him the butt of jokes. Many were still laughing about how, a few weeks earlier, Pittman lost control in a restaurant when Kemmerer played a joke on him. In response, Pittman picked up a plateful of strawberry shortcake and heaved it at his tormentor's head. The plate missed its target but flew across the restaurant, shattering into tiny pieces. If this was the best defender Darr could find, the Futon Five quipped, then he must be sunk.

Jones's investigation was going very badly for Darr. He had tracked down Alan Gosule, who in recent weeks had obtained more damning information about Darr. A friend at Josephthal had given Gosule an envelope containing copies of checks and deposit slips from Darr's transactions with clients. He agreed to turn the documents over to Jones.

Gosule and Jones agreed to meet on November 13 at the Plaza Hotel in midtown Manhattan. At the appointed time, Jones took the elevator to a suite where Gosule was waiting. Jones lightly tapped on the door, and Gosule let him in. They spent no time with small talk—Gosule handed Jones the envelope and suggested that he examine the contents. Then Gosule told Jones he had someone for him to meet. The lawyer brought out his client, who had claimed that Darr had put the squeeze on him before moving to Bache. Gosule introduced the two men and walked out of earshot as the client answered Jones's questions. After about twenty minutes, Jones stood up and thanked both men. Gosule escorted the investigator to the suite's door.

Before opening the door, Jones turned to him. "I want you to know," he said, "Darr is as good as dead."

Jones spoke with John D'Elisa that same day. "We've got him nailed," the investigator said. Jones was ready to let senior Bache executives know what he had found. His report would be done in a day or so. D'Elisa called the other members of the Futon Five. Hayes had heard the same thing from Jones. They needed to start getting ready for a transition of leadership. It would be tough for the firm, particularly for Lee Paton—he had just been named a director a few months before. Now one of his first big hires was about to be labeled a crook.

Darr's mood blackened. He began to seek out other senior executives in hopes of finding an ally. He visited George McGough, the head of Bache corporate resources, and poured out his fears. These rumors were swirling around and they just weren't true, Darr said. He didn't know what to do about it.

"Look, if you're innocent, and these rumors are untrue, take a polygraph," McGough said. "We'll give you the questions in advance, or you can help formulate the questions. Then everyone will know what the results are, and it'll be over with."

Darr looked pensive. "Yeah, that would probably be the best way," he said softly. "Who would see the record?"

"It would be whoever is heading this thing up. Who do you think should see it?"

The two men chatted another few moments about Darr taking the test. Then Darr got up to leave, saying he would get back to McGough.

McGough heard nothing back from Darr about the test. But soon after he received a telephone call from John Curran, Bache's general counsel.

"Did you try to convince Jim Darr to take a polygraph?" Curran asked.

"Yeah," McGough said. "I think he is going to take it, too."

"Well, we don't want him to take it," Curran said. "Just forget about it."

It sounded to McGough like Bache was getting ready to resolve the Darr matter somehow. "OK, John, that's fine," he said.

In mid-November, Douglas Kemmerer called Dennis Marron at home on the weekend. The calls had become almost a daily ritual. Kemmerer seemed to have become the most plugged in on the developments in the Darr investigation. This time, his information seemed too incredible to be believed.

"Darr's going to beat the rap," Kemmerer said.

"Oh, come on, Doug, that's crazy," Marron replied. "How could he beat the rap? The firm is not going to keep a guy around that does that kind of stuff."

"I'll bet you a dinner."

"Fine," Marron said. "You're on."

But in the office that Monday, it began to sound as if Kemmerer might be right. Word started getting around that Darr had appealed to one of his bosses, who were just learning of the investigation. Darr promised that he had done nothing improper, saying that the money he received was for work he had done on an airplane lease deal and other consulting. The members of the Futon Five started to fear that the investigation might be on the verge of backfiring.

Gosule arrived in the office that day after a weekend of relishing victory. He was sure he'd put a dirty player out of the business and solidified his relationship with the tax shelter department. It thrilled him to think that his contribution to the investigation could well lead to more business for Gaston & Snow from a thankful Bache.

That morning, he received a telephone call from John D'Elisa. "I can't believe it!" D'Elisa sputtered. "Darr beat the rap!"

"That's impossible!" Gosule replied.

But when Darr arrived that day, everyone could tell he had won. His fearful look gone, Darr strutted into the office with his chest out and his head high. He took obvious delight in his sudden comeback.

A number of executives in the department, including all of the Futon Five, were called to an emergency meeting at Bache a few days later. They gathered in a conference room, where Darr was sitting quietly, glaring at them. Someone started discussing a new deal that was in the works. As a speaker droned on, Lee Paton's secretary came into the room. Darr's eyes locked on her as she walked around a table to where David Hayes sat. She tapped him on the shoulder.

"Lee would like to see you," she said.

Darr smirked as Hayes walked out of the room. Hayes had heard the rumors but couldn't believe Darr was getting cleared. He walked apprehensively into Paton's office a few minutes later and shut the door.

"All right, David," Paton said, his tone of voice betraying deep anger. "This little investigation is finished. Darr has checked out. He's clean as a whistle."

Hayes felt light-headed, blown away. He knew about the checks. He knew about Gosule's client. Jones himself had told him that everything he suspected was true.

This is a total political cover-up, Hayes thought. Maybe it was because of the silver crisis a few months before. Maybe Paton didn't want to admit a mistake. Either way, it was clear to Hayes that somebody at Bache was trying to avoid a scandal.

"How could you be involved in something like this?" Paton asked sharply.

Hayes didn't know what to say.

"David, how could you be involved in something like this?"

Hayes sat there, numb, silent.

"David, *how could you be involved in something like this?*" Paton demanded.

Hayes finally mumbled something about doing what he thought was right. He staggered to his feet and headed to the door. He couldn't wait to get out of Paton's office. Back in the conference room, he slumped into his chair. Paton's secretary then returned and tapped Wally Allen on the shoulder.

"Lee would like to see you," she said.

One by one, Paton spoke to almost everyone who had been involved in the investigation of Darr. Later, he announced to other senior officers in the department that Darr had been cleared, so as to dispel any rumors.

Only Dennis Marron did not hear the news that day. He was out of town on business and wasn't expected to catch up with anyone in the department for more than a week, when all of them were supposed to travel to Puerto Rico for an oil and gas conference.

For some of the Futon Five, Paton inadvertently signaled that their careers at Bache were over. In his meeting with Henry, Paton produced a document pertaining to Trace Management, the entity that provided a participation for him, D'Elisa, and Darr in some tax shelters. Paton said Trace angered the brokers, who wanted to share in the profits, too. So he wanted Henry to sign the document, which would liquidate his ownership stake and, Paton said, let Bache dissolve Trace.

Well, this is certainly a blatant, bald-faced lie, Henry thought. He was sure Paton was trying to get him to surrender his stake in Trace so they wouldn't have to pay him anything after he was fired. He told Paton that he would review the document with his accountant and get back to him the next week.

He never had the chance. On Monday, Darr called D'Elisa into his office for a moment. "I want you to see something."

Darr turned on the speakerphone and telephoned Henry in Dallas. No one could find him at the branch. But just then, Henry called in from a pay telephone in the men's restroom at a French restaurant in Dallas's Quadrangle shopping center. He was having lunch there with his sister, Kay. His secretary told him to call Darr immediately.

"I'm sitting here with D'Elisa, and I want you to know we are reconsidering the way the department is organized," Darr said, staring at D'Elisa as he spoke. "There is no longer any room for you here. You're fired."

Henry wasn't surprised. "All right, Jim," he said.

"Well, I'm going to put this down as termination for insufficient production."

"Darr, you're going to put down whatever you're going to put down," Henry replied. "But you know that's not the reason and I know that's not the reason. But I don't care. I'm having lunch with my sister right now, and I'm going back to that." Henry slammed down the telephone.

As the days passed, the casualties spread. Darr fired Kemmerer, who didn't attend the Futon Five meeting but was one of the biggest talkers. Gosule's firm, Gaston & Snow, was never offered another assignment from the department. If the firm fired all of the Futon Five, the department would have collapsed from lack of manpower. So, for the time being, Darr just confronted the others but allowed them to stay. He talked to Marron in Puerto Rico at the oil and gas conference.

"Looks like you owe Kemmerer that dinner," Darr told him. Marron was stunned. Not only did Darr survive; somehow he found out about his private conversations. Darr smiled and walked out to the tennis court, with an obviously delighted Bill Pittman following him. At that moment, Marron realized that, because of Pittman's loyalty, the guy whom they all belittled was now Darr's new favorite.

In the days that followed, it became clear that Darr emerged from the investigation more powerful than before. Paton gave Darr an accelerated promotion to senior vice-president—a symbol of regret, Darr bragged, for the aggravation he suffered because of the investigation. Questions disappeared about I.E.I., the energy roll-up, and the deal was put on the fast track. Clifton Harrison reemerged and began dropping by the office more often. Darr became his champion, pushing the department to pursue deals with him. Within weeks, the department's first deal with Harrison was being put together.

Finally, when everything settled down, Darr called a meeting in his office of the department's executives, including the surviving members of the Futon Five.

"I am now the most investigated person in this firm," Darr declared. "I have been given a completely clean bill of health." To some listeners, the meaning was obvious. Darr's ethics were now above question at Bache. No one could challenge him.

"Some of you tried to destroy me," he said, "and I won't tolerate it. So I want this clear: If any of you ever attempt to do anything again that could harm me or my family, I'll take decisive action."

Darr looked slowly around the room, checking to see that everyone was listening.

"I'll kill you."

CHAPTER 4

HARRY JACOBS FLIPPED THROUGH the secret investigative file on his desk, reading each page carefully. The findings clinched it: Bache couldn't possibly be involved with someone tied to illegal activities. It didn't matter that no one had ever brought charges. Bache might cripple its already soiled reputation by associating with such people. Jacobs finished reading with renewed certainty: The Belzbergs had to be stopped.

It was January 1981, and Bache's massive, worldwide investigation of the Belzbergs was finally getting results. For months, the firm's investigators had dug into the Belzbergs' background, poring through corporate records, chasing down rumors in the Canadian business community, and leaning on friends in the government.

Finally, paydirt: Buried in a file cabinet at the Bureau of Customs was a report linking the Belzbergs, albeit tenuously, to the Mafia. The report had been written by customs agents, who, along with the FBI and Canadian Mounties, secretly watched a February 1970 meeting of American and Canadian mobsters at the Acapulco Hilton. All of the kingpins were there, including Meyer Lansky, the infamous underworld financier. As undercover agents dutifully took notes, Lansky got chummy with a man later identified as Hyman Belzberg, Sam's brother. For the next few days, Hyman Belzberg was seen in the company of Lansky and Benny Kaufman, a reputed member of the Canadian Mafia.

The report was thin gruel. It had no information on Hyman Belzberg's conversations with the mobsters. Bache tried to follow up leads, without success. Still, for Jacobs, the secret report was more than enough; he wasn't going to let his firm be overrun by gangsters.

In mid-January, Bache's nominating committee met to consider Belzberg's request for board seats. Jacobs took his information with him to the meeting. He told the five members that, based on the shocking facts uncovered by the firm, he could not and would not accept any of Belzberg's board nominees. His implicit threat wasn't missed: The board was choosing between Belzberg and Jacobs. If they voted against him, Jacobs would resign. With little debate, the committee sided unanimously with Bache's chairman and rejected Belzberg's demand.

After the board's decision, Jacobs called a meeting of senior executives and advisers. He knew that something more had to be done to stop the Belzbergs from buying Bache shares. Once they owned enough to control the firm, they could name their own board. Almost certainly, the executives who opposed the Belzbergs so aggressively would then all be fired.

Unless, suggested Clark Clifford, the former defense secretary who was advising the firm, Bache could scare the Belzbergs away. Why not sit down with Sam Belzberg and let him know the information that Bache had uncovered? Belzberg might be so shocked and scared of exposure that he'd turn tail and run. And to make sure the message had the highest impact possible, Clifford volunteered to carry it to the Belzbergs personally.

Jacobs was delighted. Clifford's reputation among Washington's power elite dazzled him; he felt sure Belzberg would be thunderstruck when such an important man delivered such a dangerous threat. Jacobs said he would contact Belzberg to tell him that Clifford would be calling.

He made the telephone call a few days later. Belzberg felt certain Jacobs was going to tell him that the demand he made at the La Guardia meeting had been approved. So he was surprised when he called back and Jacobs sounded so distant. In a tone of obvious pride, Jacobs told him that he should expect a telephone call from Clark Clifford.

Belzberg paused for an instant, perplexed. "Who's that?"

The first stage of the Bache new strategy had flopped. Although many American businessmen might have been impressed to receive a call from a former defense secretary, the Bache strategists forgot something about their adversary: He lived in Canada. He had never heard of Clark Clifford.

A few minutes later, Clifford telephoned Belzberg, suggesting that they get together to talk. "Could you come down to Washington to see me?" Clifford asked.

Belzberg had never heard such arrogance. *They* were the ones who wanted to see *him*. Why should he go to Washington? "Look, if you want to talk to me, why don't you come to Vancouver?"

Clifford paused. "Do you know who I am?"

"I'm really sorry. I don't. And I really don't know where this conversation is going to take us."

Clifford again asked Belzberg to come to Washington and gave him his private telephone number. Belzberg hung up the phone and instantly dialed Jacobs again. "Harry, I left you at that meeting with a very simple situation," he said. "I want two seats on the board. So why is this Clark Clifford fellow calling? Who is he?"

Jacobs hesitated for an instant. "Well, something very terrible came up, out of nowhere, as we were discussing your nomination to the board," he replied. "Mr. Clifford has been retained by us to talk to you about it. It's very important that you go to Washington and see him."

Whatever came up, Belzberg responded, it couldn't be that terrible. He wasn't going to Washington, he said, and would proceed with his plans for the firm.

A few weeks later, Belzberg was flying from Denver to eastern Canada. With a simple rerouting, he would be able to take his private plane to Washington. He telephoned Clifford, and the two men agreed to meet at Dulles International Airport in the first-class lounge of Air France. A few hours later, Belzberg was sitting across from Clifford, a tall man with patrician good looks and white hair. The meeting grew rancorous quickly.

Bache had considered putting him on the board, Clifford said, but had voted it down. He pulled a stack of papers out of a briefcase and showed them to Belzberg. "The firm is simply too concerned about the terrible thing your brother did," he said, motioning toward the papers.

For an instant, Belzberg could not imagine what Clifford was talking about. Then it hit him: *Hymie's trip to Acapulco.*

For years, the time his brother unwittingly had palled around with the Mafia during a vacation had been a big family joke. While in Acapulco, Hymie, who ran the family's furniture business, had bumped into Benny Kaufman, who owned a Canadian rug dealership. The two had done business before. Hymie had no idea that Kaufman was a reputed mobster. It was Kaufman who introduced him to Lansky. Hymie didn't recognize the name; he just assumed he was meeting some businessman. When Hymie returned home, the Mounties came calling to investigate. Hymie was dumbstruck. He said he had no clue that his friends from the Acapulco Hilton were reputed mobsters. The Mounties wrapped up the investigation quickly, and Hymie, while a little embarrassed, was none the worse for wear.

"You couldn't be talking about that crazy thing in Acapulco, could you?" Belzberg asked.

"Oh, we don't think it's crazy at all, Mr. Belzberg," Clifford responded.

For the next few minutes, Belzberg explained what happened. He told Clifford that the Mounties had investigated and cleared the matter up years earlier. "You don't know Hymie," he said. "Only he could walk down the beach with gangsters and not know it."

Belzberg offered to have the Canadian attorney general telephone Clifford the next day to confirm everything, but Clifford demurred. The board had already voted, he said, so such a phone call would be unnecessary. The meeting reached an impasse. After a few minutes, Belzberg left, frustrated and angry.

On the plane headed to Toronto, Belzberg stewed. He kept running through his mind how mistreated he felt. He never had intended to take over Bache. But they kept pushing him and pushing him. And now this, from someone like Clifford, whom he now understood had been an adviser to presidents. By the time his plane arrived, Belzberg had put away a few drinks, and he was boiling. Despite the late hour, he picked up a telephone and called Clifford's private line.

"Mr. Clifford, I'm really surprised at you, a man of your stature, trying to intimidate me with this kind of dirt," Belzberg said. "You've worked with presidents, and here you are wallowing in the mud. I'm not just going to take this sitting down."

"Are you threatening me?" Clifford snapped.

"I'm not threatening you. I'm saying that I gave Mr. Jacobs a proposal, and what you have brought up here means nothing to me. You're not interested in finding out the truth, so I'm not worried about it."

"Well, Mr. Belzberg," Clifford responded, "if you don't stop buying stock in Bache, this is all going to be in the papers in the next week or so."

Belzberg's soft voice betrayed his absolute anger. "I have been threatened with my life before, sir," he said. "And you don't frighten me."

He slammed the phone down in its cradle.

It didn't take long for Bache to realize that its latest tactic had been a disastrous miscalculation. Belzberg opened up the throttle on buying Bache stock. In just two trading sessions, a few days after meeting with Clifford, he purchased more than 20,000 shares. By February 9, a few weeks after their meeting, the Belzbergs had snapped up another 200,000 shares. No longer were Sam Belzberg's investment decisions based on strictly financial considerations; now he was being driven by pure anger. He wanted to teach Bache a lesson. Even when Bache made good on its threat, turning the information about Hymie and the Mafia over to the *Wall Street Journal*, Belzberg just bought more shares. Soon he controlled close to one-quarter of the firm's publicly traded shares.

"Is there nothing that will stop these people?" Jacobs moaned at a Bache executive committee meeting that month.

On March 2, 1981, he decided he had had enough. He called Robert Bayliss, an investment banker with the First Boston Corporation. Bayliss was a longtime friend of the firm—he was the banker who helped take Bache public in 1971.

Jacobs told Bayliss that he had a new assignment for him: He wanted to put Bache on the block. After a hundred years of independence, the firm had to be sold to the highest bidder. It was the only way left to stop Belzberg.

Bayliss hopped on the assignment and called back the next day with tantalizing news: First Boston had received a nibble of interest from the Prudential Insurance Company of America, the financial giant based in Newark, New Jersey. The company was already looking to get into the brokerage industry but had not found the right situation yet. If they moved quickly, Bayliss said, a deal could be wrapped up in a matter of days. Jacobs was skeptical. He knew that Prudential was a mutual company, meaning that it was owned by its policyholders. He doubted whether it could legally buy a securities firm.

Still, a company like Prudential could be the answer to Bache's problems. If nothing else, it brought something to the table that Bache desperately needed: undeniable, unwavering integrity. Prudential's reputation had been built over more than a hundred years, since being founded by an obscure life insurance agent named John Dryden. Its image as a company dedicated to helping working people find financial security could wrap Bache in a new blanket of respectability. The firm's scandals and missteps might finally be washed away. With a simple stroke of a pen on a merger agreement, Bache's sullied past could be subsumed into the glorious history of the Prudential.

※   ※   ※   ※

JOHN FAIRFIELD Dryden, a bookish, gangly thirty-four-year-old, arrived in Newark in 1873 with a wife, two children, and a history of failure. Dryden's career had centered on fruitless attempts to build a life insurance company for the poor and working class. He wanted to model his company on the Prudential of England, which had already succeeded in that line of the business. But Dryden's contemporaries scoffed. In an era when American insurance was a privilege of the wealthy, the idea seemed too radical. Worse, few of them believed the poor could afford the premiums. Dryden was told repeatedly that his business plan was only so much social dreaming, destined to go belly-up. When Dryden replied that he could sell his policies for as little as three cents a week, he was dismissed with a laugh.

Newark was Dryden's last chance to build his company. Then the nation's third-largest industrial city, Newark built a reputation in trade and manufacturing on the strength of its leather making, metalwork, and jewelry manufacturing. Across the country, beer drinkers knew the local Feigenspan's brand as P.O.N., for Pride of Newark. The scores of mills, ironworks, and factories dotting the waterfront attracted hundreds of new immigrants and working-class Americans to Newark. It was among these people that Dryden hoped to find his customers.

Dryden cut an impressive figure for the people of Lincoln Avenue in Newark, where he took up residence. With his thin, long legs and piercing blue eyes, he stood out as a man to reckon with. Each day, he tried without success to persuade members of Newark society to invest in his idea. Finally, Dryden met Allen Bassett, a big-talking former military captain who made his money in real estate after the Civil War. Dryden persuaded Bassett to let him have some desk space at no charge so that he could organize the Widows and Orphans Friendly Society, a nonprofit organization that would sell insurance to its members. This, Dryden hoped, could be the foundation of the profit-making insurance company he hoped to establish.

With Bassett opening the doors, Dryden's new society attracted the support of some prominent Newark citizens, some of whom took unpaid positions as the foundation's senior officers; Dryden assumed the lowly title of secretary. After a few months, with its leadership helping the society to gain great respect in Newark, the group converted into a full insurance company. That allowed it to sell policies to anyone, not just its members. The name was changed to the Prudential Friendly Society, in a tip of the hat to the Prudential of England. Dryden approached new investors and won more support for his ideas. Within a short time, he had raised the $30,000 in capital his company needed.

The Prudential had been born.

In 1876, while running an errand for his mother, fifteen-year-old William Digannard was struck by a train and killed. He was the eldest son of a poor family, and his death may have gone unnoticed in history but for one thing: Digannard's parents were among the first to collect on a Prudential life insurance policy. Their decision to take out the policy on their son's life allowed them to bury him without destroying the family's meager finances. "What my poor desolate household would have done without this policy I do not know," William's father wrote in a letter to the company. "God bless and prosper the Prudential Company."

Just a year after opening its doors, Prudential had earned a reputation as a company on the side of the needy. Its life insurance policies proved to be an enormous hit. The company paid claims within twenty-four hours, as promised. It charged as little as three cents a week, as promised. And it made life better for the struggling people of Newark, as promised.

Within a few months, Dryden was a fixture at factory yards during lunch. Standing on a box amid gatherings of soot-covered workers, he peddled his peculiar little policies as protection for their wives and children. He found few takers at lunchtime, but once the day was done, Prudential's office filled with rugged men toting lunch pails and searching for more information. Money—a few pennies at a time, collected door-to-door—began pouring into the new company.

By 1883, Prudential found itself in the strongest financial position in its history; it had 200,000 policyholders, and that number was expanding at a rapid clip. Just two years later, on May 13, 1885, Prudential issued its policy number 1,000,000 to its newest insurance client, and new president, John Dryden.

With business booming, the company attracted New York advertising agencies that saw Prudential as a potential client. Mortimer Remington, a young account executive with J. Walter Thompson Advertising Agency, got his foot in the door through his father-in-law, a friend of Dryden. Remington persuaded the Prudential president that the company needed a national advertising strategy, complete with a trademark recognizable to any prospective client. Once hired, Remington pored through books and magazines in search of inspiration.

The truth of how Remington found his trademark idea has been a source of some mythmaking within the company. But it doesn't matter whether, as some have it, Remington's brainstorm hit when he saw a large, rocky hill in New Jersey or while thumbing through a library book containing pictures of geological formations. Either way, within a few weeks, Remington returned to Dryden with his suggestion: The trademark should be a likeness of the Rock of Gibraltar, with the legend "Prudential has the strength of Gibraltar." Dryden was delighted. For years to come, Prudential would be known as "the Rock."

By the late nineteenth century, Prudential's rich cash hoard came to be coveted by its own shareholders. A huge surplus had grown at the company, largely the result of better-than-predicted mortality rates. Dryden divvied up the kitty among policyholders, reasoning that his company had essentially overbilled. But, as the shareholders saw it, the money belonged to them—after all, the policyholders had received exactly the insurance they wanted for the price they agreed to pay.

As the years passed, Dryden's split with his shareholders grew deeper. A group of dissidents sued the company, demanding that it be prohibited from distributing its surplus capital to policyholders and be ordered to turn $2.5 million over to the shareholders. The court split the difference—it upheld the company's right to make the concessions but agreed that the shareholders should receive the millions they wanted.

For Dryden, the problem had become untenable. Aggressive stock speculators were snatching up shares, with an eye toward the cash surplus. Dryden feared that his company would be torn apart by short-term greed and left with too little cash to honor claims. He decided Prudential had to rid itself of shareholders and turn the ownership over to its policyholders, a process known as mutualization. Dryden set the complex process in motion, and by 1915, after intense lobbying, the New Jersey state legislature authorized Prudential to repurchase its shares and transfer ownership of the company to the policyholders. When the effort succeeded, years later, Prudential was left answerable to almost no one.

But Dryden did not live to see the battle through. Shortly after the push toward mutualization began, he slipped into a coma during a minor operation. In a matter of days, on November 24, 1911, John Dryden died at his home. Born into poverty, he left behind an estate valued at more than $50 million.

As the years passed, the responsibility for running the Prudential fell on a series of unimaginative homegrown favorites. For decades, none of these bland executives wanted to tinker much with the company's recipe for success. Prudential grew almost unavoidably, with its national reservoir of goodwill expanding with each policy it sold.

Heavy advertising polished that image, burning the name Prudential into the national psyche as a synonym for duty and honor. The ads, imprinted with the company's increasingly familiar trademark, used slice-of-life vignettes that went for the jugular. Any uninsured reader who put down the ads without guilt wasn't paying attention.

Typical was an ad that ran in 1925, captioned "The Little Grey Lady." It showed a sad picture of an elderly woman, looking forlornly out of a closed window as she worked at a seamstress table.

"Toil—toil—a merciless cycle of toil is all she knows," the ad read. "Daily, those slender, needle-scarred fingers tremble more and more. Someone is responsible for this—glaringly responsible. A husband, a brother, a son has failed in his imperative duty." The duty, the ad said, was to purchase life insurance. With it, the old lady would have been allowed to live her final years in comfort.

By the time of the Great Depression, the company's advertising was re-shaped as many policyholders, strapped for cash, allowed their policies to lapse. It was a potentially devastating trend for any insurance company, one that the ads tried to stanch.

One ad in late 1929 featured a middle-aged woman with her young daughter, sitting anxiously in a darkened room. Hanging over their heads was a newspaper announcing a mortgagee's sale. "The life insurance pol-icy that would have saved their home was permitted to lapse," the copy read. Similar ads were used to raise policyholders' concerns about their children's education, all with great success.

The subtext of these messages reinforced the image of trust: By doing business with Prudential, your mother won't have to work in her old age, your family home will be protected, and your children will be educated. It was all the more comforting because, for many, the message was true.

By 1946, Prudential had become fat, cautious, and unimaginative. Risk taking was shunned. Its executives were comfortable, pampered, and prissy. But in that year, everything changed when the board elected Car-rol Shanks as the company's seventh president. Unlike his predecessors, Shanks was not a dyed-in-the-wool insurance man; he made his reputation in the wilder, more aggressive world of Wall Street. Shanks stirred mixed emotions among his followers; some saw him as cold and calculating, but he engendered excitement and inspiration in others. Everyone knew him as tough, decisive, and, when he needed to be, ruthless.

Shanks moved quickly to bust up Prudential's lazy, parochial ways. He forced out the deadwood at the top, a shock in a culture that had not seen a high-level dismissal in decades. Ignoring seniority, he brought in his own team of managers loyal to him. Within months, Prudential had a new general counsel and new heads of several departments. The moves shot fear through Prudential's executive workforce, but they also served as a wake-up call throughout the ranks of the lumbering insurance giant.

In 1948, after shattering the cozy relationships in the executive suites, Shanks turned his eye to the rest of the company. He worried that by keeping all the senior management talent in Newark, Prudential wasn't going to find and develop talent around the country. So Shanks broke Prudential into pieces, scattering essentially separate companies, known as regional home offices, throughout the United States and Canada. He established the first regional home office in Los Angeles in 1948, quickly following in Toronto, Houston, Jacksonville, and across the country. Decentralization sped up sales coverage, built local prestige, and quickened service. It proved an enormous success.

Shanks then shook up the company's investment strategy. Until then, Prudential had been happy to sink its money only into huge blocks of blue-chip stocks and bonds. Instead, Shanks wanted Prudential to embrace risk. He pushed the investing department to loan money to strong, growing companies that might have trouble finding bank credit. That way, Prudential could charge higher rates. He developed the company's group health insurance program, convinced that if the private insurance companies didn't start offering such products, the federal government would. Prudential was no longer just an insurance company. It was a powerhouse, expanding rapidly into every aspect of the financial services world.

The Pru, as reshaped by Shanks, was a stronger, more aggressive company than it had been at any time in its history. Shanks could have left with the reputation as the company's greatest leader since Dryden. Then Shanks got tripped up by a tax shelter.

In 1960, the *Wall Street Journal* reported on its front page that Shanks had personally borrowed money to set up a tax shelter that purchased a lumber company. An hour after closing on the deal, Shanks sold 13,000 acres of timber to a subsidiary of Georgia-Pacific, the paper company. That sale gave Shanks enough money to repay his loans and saved him close to $400,000 in taxes. The *Journal* article pointed out a few facts that made the deal seem smarmy: Shanks served on Georgia-Pacific's board of directors, while Owen Cheatham, the chairman of Georgia-Pacific, was a director of Prudential. At the time of the deal, Georgia-Pacific owed close to $65 million to Prudential. The *Journal* article heavily implied that the timber transactions were unethical sweetheart deals.

The board of directors was incensed. In all its years, neither the company nor any of its senior officers had ever been singled out with an accusation of an ethical lapse. The stench of scandal was new to Prudential, and the board of directors didn't like it. By December, Shanks resigned under pressure, so angry that he refused to even visit the company for more than a decade.

By 1973, the Prudential had again fallen into another rut of complacency. Little had changed at the company since Shanks's resignation, even though the 1960s had been a decade of enormous transformation in the financial world. Although the company had become the largest insurance company in the world in 1966, it had reached the goal by plodding along without much innovation.

Then, that year, the company named Robert Beck as president. Beck was the first man since John Dryden to rise from the job of insurance agent to Prudential president. He started his career working as a financial analyst for the Ford Motor Company, as one of Robert McNamara's famous "Whiz Kids." But Beck was restless. He wanted to get into sales. In college, he had worked part-time with Prudential, and he loved insurance. He spoke of it with the fervor and earnestness of a crusader. So he left the automobile industry and took a job as a Prudential insurance agent, working his way up over the years.

As the youngest president ever to work at Prudential, Beck felt in close contact with the trends of the time, particularly the focus on consumerism that was sweeping the nation. Consumers wanted their worlds easier and services more readily accessible. To Beck, it made perfect sense for a financial company the size of Prudential to offer its customers the full range of financial services, from insurance to stocks to tax shelters.

The idea took hold in the mid-1970s when Donald Regan, then the chairman of Merrill Lynch, pushed his company into offering "womb-to-tomb" financial services. Merrill established the Cash Management Account, which allowed customers to write checks against their investment portfolios, and pushed its franchise in stocks and bonds into everything from insurance to credit cards. Beck felt sure that this was the future of the industry, with brokerage firms providing the cash management and lending services of banks. He wanted his insurance company on the cutting edge.

So Beck, after taking over the newly powerful position of chairman of Prudential, adopted long-range plans of transforming the insurance company into the nation's first financial supermarket. He wanted to wade into the business slowly—he knew that another insurance company, INA of Philadelphia, had stumbled badly when it invested in Blyth Eastman Dillon and lost a lot of money. Beck's team looked first at smaller, regional brokerage firms and mutual fund families. The right property at the right price didn't seem to be available.

Then, on March 5, 1981, Beck was vacationing at Ocean Reef, Florida, when he received a telephone call from David Sherwood, the president of Prudential. Sherwood said he had heard from First Boston that Bache had put itself up for sale. The firm seemed to fit perfectly into Prudential's plans. Its planning group had already begun sizing up Bache months earlier. Sherwood asked Beck what he thought the company should do.

Tell the planning group to start digging deeper, Beck replied. In a few days, he would return to Newark to be briefed on the matter. Maybe, Beck thought, Prudential's search was over.

* * * *

MARCH 17, 1981, was the kind of day that couldn't make up its mind. It was gray. It was sunny. It was windy. Then the snow flurries fell. Despite the lousy weather, more than 100,000 people packed Fifth Avenue to watch the marching bands play in the city's 219th annual St. Patrick's Day parade. Manhattan was virtually transformed into an urban canyon of green, as revelers laughed and drank, in a celebration not so much of Ireland's patron saint as of themselves.

Downtown, few in the offices of Bache took notice of the merrymaking. Burned out and exhausted, Bache executives had been struggling for eight days and nights to finalize a merger deal with Prudential. A team of executives from the insurance company had effectively commandeered the senior management of Bache, demanding information to help them analyze everything about the brokerage firm. When Beck returned from Florida, he called in specialists with knowledge in computers, law, and marketing and ordered them to dig into the bowels of the Bache ship to make sure there were no leaks.

Jacobs had told Bache's board of Prudential's interest about a week earlier and had assigned Clark Clifford part of the responsibility for negotiating a deal. The Bache directors had asked few questions, but Jacobs had told them that Prudential seemed serious. "I think everybody needs to be standing by," he said.

So far, Jacobs liked what he saw. On March 9, he and Virgil Sherrill met with Sherwood, Prudential's president, and Frank Hoenemeyer, its top investment strategist. The Prudential executives clearly had already done a lot of homework. They said that Prudential wanted to tap into a wealthier customer base. Although Bache was at the lower end of that scale for Wall Street, its customers still had a higher average income than Prudential's customers. They knocked aside Jacob's original concerns that a mutual company couldn't purchase a securities firm, saying that Prudential lawyers had already thoroughly researched the issue and that it presented no problem. They wanted a deal wrapped up quickly. Speed and secrecy were of the essence.

By St. Patrick's Day, everything was in high gear. That morning, personnel reports on senior Bache executives were delivered to Prudential. The reports, ranging in length from two to four pages, included a full biographical sketch and a picture of each executive. They were reviewed both by senior executives of Prudential and its board. A report on Jim Darr, the man who would play the most significant role in Prudential's investment, was not included in the stack.

After an eight-hour summit meeting, Beck and a group of Prudential executives voted to recommend the purchase of Bache to the insurance company's directors. The next morning, after a two-and-a-half-hour meeting, the board voted unanimously in favor of purchasing Bache at a price of $32 a share, or about $385 million.

Given the green light, a retinue of Prudential executives trooped over to the offices of Sullivan & Cromwell to meet with Jacobs and his advisers. The deal was approved, they said, at $32 a share. Jacobs felt a little shocked—that price was only slightly above the market value. The $385 million equaled Bache's cash flow for only about three weeks. He conferred with Clifford for a moment, and the lawyer then approached the Prudential executives. Everyone was pleased with Prudential's offer, Clifford said, but Bache was interested in a higher price.

Beck cut the suggestion down instantly. "Listen," he said. "If you don't want this deal to fall apart, you'd better take what we're giving you." The price was $32 a share, and no more.

Clifford backed down, and within a matter of minutes, there were handshakes and smiles all around. Jacobs called an emergency meeting of Bache senior executives at 4:00 P.M. to let them know about the deal. That evening, Beck and Hoenemeyer arrived at Bache headquarters to meet with the firm's directors. After a short and friendly introduction, the two men left the room for a few minutes. The proposed offer sailed through Bache's board with unanimous approval. Beck and Jacobs, starving after their nonstop work, celebrated the victory with salami sandwiches.

About that time, Sam Belzberg was on a plane landing in the Edmonton airport. He was flying with his wife to London, and the only available flight from Vancouver required the short stopover. Belzberg expected the stop to be uneventful. Because the time on the ground was so short, none of the passengers was permitted to get off the plane.

So it surprised Belzberg when a Canadian Mountie boarded the plane in Edmonton and walked directly toward him.

"Mr. Belzberg?" the Mountie said after reaching Belzberg's seat. "You have a telephone call."

Belzberg was told he could get off the plane as long as he was accompanied by the Mountie. Within a few minutes, he was in the airport, speaking with one of his close aides. They had heard some critical information: Bache was being sold to Prudential Insurance.

Belzberg stood in the airport for several minutes, almost speechless. His quarry of several years had suddenly slipped his grasp. The whole ugly battle was coming to an end.

Harry Jacobs bounded out to a helicopter pad in downtown Manhattan and scrambled aboard for the short flight to Newark. It was early in the day on March 19. Already, midlevel executives and brokers at Bache were learning about the merger, although they had heard nothing yet from their chairman. The front page of that morning's *New York Times* carried an article headlined "A Prudential Offer for Bache Accepted" that provided numerous details of the deal.

After arriving at Prudential's headquarters, Jacobs was whisked to Beck's office, where he was presented with piles of documents to review. Then, with little fanfare, the executives signed the contract, agreeing to convert Bache into a private subsidiary of the Prudential.

Later that day, the news was officially announced to the wire services. As Bache brokers watched the headline cross the tape, the mood at the firm became one of absolute delight. After months of scandal and stumbling, Bache had found a parent with pockets so deep that they seemed to reach down into Fort Knox. Calculators appeared on Bache desktops across the country as the employees with stakes in the firm counted the money they would make from the deal. Not only were their futures more secure, but many of them stood to receive a financial windfall.

Prudential managers began touring the firm almost immediately. In New York, Beck, Sherwood, and Garnett Keith, the executive vice-

president responsible for overseeing Prudential's newest acquisition, arrived at Bache for a walk-around. Meeting with groups at a time, Beck extended his hand to as many of the employees as possible.

"We're looking forward to working with all of you," Beck said repeatedly. "We think that this is a great match." Prudential was committed to
the firm's success, Beck said. They planned to do whatever it took to make
Bache into the finest brokerage firm in the world.

Over the coming weeks, despite all of the excitement, little changed in
the day-to-day business of the brokerage firm. Beck paid little attention to
the goings-on at Bache, handing off responsibilities for direct oversight to
Garnett Keith. The only significant change seemed to be that, for the first
time in years, Harry Jacobs felt safe again. "We have a feeling of relief,"
Jacobs told a reporter shortly after the deal was completed. "After the Prudential merger, we felt more secure in our jobs."

With huge capital and a rock-solid reputation standing behind the firm,
Bache was ready to expand its business across America. Soon every division of the firm, including tax shelters, would be able to reach millions of
potential new customers.

CHAPTER 5

"PITTMAN, PICK UP, GODDAMNIT!" Darr screamed into the office intercom. "Pick up! Pittman! Don't you hurt her!"

It was a Friday night in 1981. The sounds of Bill Pittman screaming and cursing at Kathy Eastwick, a compliance administrator, were thundering through the fifth-floor hallways in Bache's tax shelter department. He sounded frighteningly close to beating her.

Pittman was already well known in the department as a man with an irrational temper. At times, he would look up in the middle of a meeting and inexplicably threaten a colleague. He frightened coworkers by walking the hallways with a baseball bat, periodically smacking it into his palm. It was the kind of behavior, colleagues whispered, that, combined with Pittman's relative lack of talent or education, would get him bounced out of almost any Wall Street firm.

But not Bache. Since the Futon Five debacle, when Pittman threw his complete support behind Darr, his career had taken off. No one had shown Darr more unquestioning loyalty. As an apparent reward, Darr greatly increased Pittman's influence. His responsibilities as a product manager grew, he was included in more top-level meetings, and he gained greater access to Darr than almost anyone else. But even as Pittman's authority increased, the job stress seemed to dig at him more and more. His blowups became more frequent. This time, as members of the department listened to Pittman scream at Eastwick, some wondered whether he was losing his mind.

The run-in started because of demands Pittman had made of a secretary an hour or so earlier. He had told her that he wanted some marketing materials for a new partnership printed up that night. The secretary had gone to the firm's print shop to ask if they could do an emergency rush job, but as soon as the printers found out it was for Pittman, they had refused. They weren't going to put themselves out for a man they disliked. As the joke went at Bache, with his temper tantrums, Bill Pittman had burned more bridges than the atomic bomb at Hiroshima.

When the secretary told Pittman he would have to wait, he screamed at her and threw a cup of coffee on her desk. The secretary burst into tears and ran away. Eastwick, who supervised the secretaries, found the woman crying a few minutes later and tried to calm her down. Eastwick couldn't believe how nasty Pittman had been. A few minutes later, she stormed into Pittman's office.

"What have you done to this poor woman?" she asked. "Look, Bill, there's no reason to get so upset. I'll make sure the printing gets done by early next week."

Pittman looked up from his desk, his eyes blazing in absolute fury. "No!" he screamed. "I want it done tonight! I want it done right now!"

"Bill, it's Friday night," Eastwick said. "Everybody's going home."

"Don't you undermine me! Goddamn you! You work for me!"

With that, Pittman stood up and pounded his fist on his desk.

"I'm just telling you that you're being too tough on the girl," Eastwick yelled back.

"Don't you talk to me like that!" Pittman yelled, slamming his fist onto the desk again. "Who the hell do you think you are?"

Pittman seemed to lose control as his screaming grew louder. He repeatedly banged his fist into the desk. Then, with a wild look in his eye, he leaned over and slid his hands under his desk. Even though the desk appeared to weigh more than a hundred pounds, Pittman started to lift it.

Oh, my God, Eastwick thought. *He's trying to throw his desk at me.*

Darr heard the ruckus in the next office and buzzed the intercom, demanding that Pittman pick up. Finally, as Eastwick broke into hysterical tears, Darr burst into Pittman's office.

"Pittman, are you nuts?" he yelled. "Leave her alone!"

Darr grabbed Eastwick, pulling her into his office and shutting the door. Then he headed back to Pittman's office. As Eastwick cried, Darr screamed at Pittman, telling him he had to learn to control himself. Darr would later claim to colleagues that he had grabbed Pittman by the shirt and thrown him against the wall.

Other members of the department who witnessed the exchange couldn't believe what they had seen. It wasn't just unprofessional, it was *scary*. After all, Pittman wasn't some inconsequential administrator anymore. He was a decision maker, one of the most powerful people in the tax shelter department, someone who would help set its agenda over the coming years. And he acted like a madman.

————————

Another winner from the undoing of the Futon Five was Paul Proscia. A man of average height with dark, receding hair, Proscia had been bouncing around Bache since graduating from St. John's University in 1968. He spent most of his years at the firm as Pittman had, primarily handling administrative duties. The job was distant from the business of assembling and selling securities—largely, Proscia spent his days making sure that stock certificates weren't lost or stolen. But in the late 1970s, he got his big break when Harry Jacobs selected him as assistant to the chairman. The job lasted two years, and by all accounts, the genial Jacobs thought highly of Proscia. But when Proscia left the chairman's office to take a job as the assistant manager in a commodities department in downtown Manhattan, things didn't go quite as well. He was out of the job in a few months, and ready for a new assignment.

Shortly after the announcement that he had been cleared of allegations from the Futon Five, Darr brought Proscia into the tax shelter department as a product manager. Although the department needed the help, few of his new colleagues could understand this particular hire—Proscia didn't seem to have much knowledge about the business. And it didn't help that when Proscia felt pressured in some sales presentations, he started stuttering. Other members of the department whispered that Darr must have been trying to put himself in good stead with Harry Jacobs by hiring the chairman's former assistant. Even though Darr had been cleared by Bache, they reasoned, it never hurt to try to counter the stench of the allegation. Besides, given time, they knew Proscia would figure out how to do his job.

Then, just a few months later, Darr made an announcement: He was promoting Proscia to senior product manager. The other New York marketers were livid—they couldn't believe that they would have to report to someone who was still learning some of the basics. Worse, sometimes his behavior was totally unprofessional. At one quarterly meeting at the Drake Hotel in Manhattan, Proscia got rip-roaring drunk. About midnight, the meeting broke up and a group of inebriated Bache executives and partnership sponsors left through the hotel lobby. Proscia, who was having one for the road, stumbled and spilled his tequila on a girl about seventeen years old. His colleagues watched in horror as the department's newest executive got down on his hands and knees and licked the alcohol off the teenager's leg.

The person who was the angriest about Proscia's promotion was Wally Allen. As one of the only experienced product managers in the department, Allen not only didn't respect Proscia but at times had to pick up the slack caused by his new boss's lack of experience. Repeatedly, Darr called Allen in to help out on deals that Proscia couldn't handle. The worst came in early 1981 with Montford Place, a real estate deal sponsored by a young general partner named Rick Strauss. The deal itself, involving apartments in Texas, was average at best, and Strauss did not have much experience yet. But Darr treated the deal like it was the keys to the kingdom: Strauss's father was Bob Strauss, the former chairman of the Democratic Party, and his uncle was Theodore Strauss, a prominent Dallas businessman. If Darr could get to them, he predicted that the firm would land a lot of new business.

"This relationship is going to be a stepping-stone to big things," Darr said of the deal at one staff meeting. "Ultimately, we'll develop something with his father and with all the vast connections his family has."

It sounded like a great idea until Darr turned the deal over to Proscia to sell to brokers. After several months, the Strauss deal languished, unsold, on the shelf. Darr did everything he could to push it along, including threatening the jobs of all the regional marketers if they didn't flog it. But nothing worked. Investors were not interested. Finally, Darr called Allen in and asked if he would help out.

"Fine, I'll be glad to do it," Allen said. "But I want to have complete control of the deal."

"OK, Wally," Darr replied. "But try and humor Paul a little bit."

The response just made Allen angry. "Look, Jim, if I'm going to do it, then I'm going to do it. I'm not going to play games."

Darr agreed, and Allen went into high gear. He organized a meeting with Rick Strauss for some brokers he knew in Dallas. Then he took the brokers to tour the property. It was a tough sell—the deal had been around so long, it had the musty, stale air of an investment in trouble. But after a few weeks of hard work, the sales started coming in.

One afternoon Allen was at his desk, reviewing some of the materials from the Strauss deal, when his telephone rang. It was Proscia, calling from outside the office. He wanted Allen to update him on what was happening with the Montford deal.

"Paul, just stay out," Allen said. "Either I'm going to do the deal, or you're going to do the deal. But it's not going to be both of us."

Proscia seemed taken aback by Allen's condescending tone. "Hey, Wally," he yelled. "I'm the top guy here. So we do what I say."

"Fine," Allen snapped. "Then you go sell this fucking deal." He hung up.

At that moment, Allen realized that he couldn't stay at Bache. Working for Darr had been bad enough. Now he had to report to somebody he couldn't respect. *The next chance I get,* he thought, *I'm out of here.*

He sat back and shook his head. Business for the department was just taking off. Demand for tax shelters was growing around the country. Darr was hiring new marketers and due diligence executives almost every day. But now, at this important juncture, the New York marketing effort of Bache's tax shelter division was falling into the hands of Paul Proscia and Bill Pittman. Two guys, Allen thought, who a year or so earlier were little more than flunkies.

Ellen Schachter slipped on her dress shoes and walked to the mirror in her bedroom. She gave herself one last lookover: Her clothes were attractive but not flashy, her brown hair was in a conservative business cut. It was just the right image for her interview with Jim Darr. The meeting in March 1981 was the last hurdle for her to get a job in Bache's tax shelter department. She did not want to blow it. The job was the best she had ever tried to get.

Schachter was amazed that she had gotten this far in the process. As much as the possibility of getting the job intrigued her, it also worried her deeply. Although she was an MBA and had worked as an accountant for years, she didn't know much about tax shelters. She had never even worked on Wall Street before. Her application for this job had been a fluke. Schachter had been a bored accountant when her father suggested she approach a stockbroker he knew at Bache about opportunities there. The broker had agreed to shop her résumé around the firm, and the tax shelter department was the first to approach her about a job examining the quality of deals to make sure they were safe investments. She was amazed that the firm thought she was qualified. She said as much in one of her first interviews with Dennis Marron, a surviving member of the Futon Five.

"Don't worry," Marron replied. "We'll train you as you go."

At the time, Bache desperately needed more bodies in the department. The year 1981 was developing into the most important one in the department's history. A tax revolt was spreading across the country. As the year began, Ronald Reagan was inaugurated as the nation's fortieth president, raising hopes for a more probusiness mind-set in Washington. Inflation was still rampant, pushing taxpayers into higher tax brackets even though their spending power remained unchanged. The shelters lost most of their smarmy tinge—no longer were they looked down on as a means of helping the rich escape their obligations; instead, they were sold as a financial necessity, a hedge against inflation in an era of high taxation. They were quickly becoming one of Wall Street's most popular products.

At Bache, Darr worked fast to meet the surging demand. On the marketing side, he had already established several tiers of executives. In New York, there were product managers responsible for answering broker questions about a deal and helping to usher it through the system. At the next level were the regional marketers, spread across the country. They told brokers about new deals and conducted seminars. In coordination with the product managers, they also arranged meetings with the developers and oil executives who wanted the lucrative general partner's role in the shelters. The regional marketers, in turn, had help from the marketers who worked for the general partners. These marketers, called wholesalers, sold only one sponsor's products and met with the firm's regional marketers and product managers to plan ways to bombard brokers with educational material and sales literature. Although wholesalers did not work for Bache, they were given extremely wide latitude to travel throughout the branch offices, helping the department persuade the brokers to sell the latest deal.

Outside of marketing, the other important division of the tax shelter department was due diligence. On Wall Street, due diligence is one of those five-dollar financial terms with a very simple meaning. When brokerage executives say they performed due diligence on a deal, it means that they examined it closely to make sure there were no glaring problems that might put investors at risk. In Bache's tax shelter division, the due diligence team was broken down into two groups, one for real estate deals and the other for energy deals. Deals involving equipment leasing or esoteric assets like horse-breeding farms were handled by both groups.

By the spring of 1981, executives with long backgrounds in the shelter business had been shunted aside or were losing influence for having opposed Darr. The announced acquisition of Bache by Prudential had bolstered confidence in the firm's once-sickly capital base. Darr knew he would have the resources available for a massive expansion in both marketing and due diligence. Prudential's backing made the firm a more attractive employer, and Darr could attract a number of high-profile, well-qualified marketers. But his sights were set lower in selecting due diligence executives. Rather than seeking out executives with a background in the business, Darr loaded up the department with inexperienced young people, most of whom were fresh out of business school. Then he turned over much of the responsibility for ferreting out potential problems with a tax shelter to them. Ellen Schachter was the first of this new breed for the due diligence team.

Her interviews with the department began in February, when she met with Marron and D'Elisa, who still ran due diligence for real estate. Schachter heard from Marron that she had done well. But he said she would have to pass one more interview with the head of the department, Jim Darr.

"What's he like?" Schachter asked.

Marron shrugged. "Judge for yourself."

A few days later, Schachter took the trip from her apartment to 100 Gold Street to meet with Darr. She arrived a few minutes early and waited outside Darr's office. He kept her waiting past the appointed time, until finally he came to the door and asked her in. Schachter felt almost immediately uncomfortable. Darr never looked her in the eye. He made her horribly uneasy. To Schachter, Darr looked spooky.

The meeting was short and unpleasant. Darr had almost no questions for Schachter. Instead, the interview was mostly a pep talk, delivered in a tone of pure arrogance. "This is going to be a great department," Darr said. "You'll be making lots of money with us."

The meeting came to an end, and Schachter stood up to shake Darr's hand. She had said almost nothing the entire time. A day or so later, Marron called her. She had passed the last test with flying colors. Ellen Schachter was the newest due diligence officer for the Bache tax shelter department.

A few weeks later, in April 1981, Schachter was visiting the home of a friend who worked as a stockbroker at Josephthal. She told him she had found a new job, which would be starting on May 1, with Bache. The friend asked her what department she would be in. When she told him tax shelters, his face fell.

"Oh, my gosh," the broker said. "Be careful of your boss."

"Who, Darr?" Schachter asked. "What's the matter with him?"

"He's a bad guy. Keep your distance."

Schachter pressed for details. Her friend told her that Darr had been caught taking money from clients at Josephthal. And, he said, Josephthal had allowed him to leave without pressing charges, just to rid itself of the problem.

Schachter didn't know what to think. She had just been presented with the best job opportunity of her life. Now, before her first day, trouble had been dumped in her lap. Even worse, on her employment application she had mentioned that she maintained a brokerage account at Josephthal. She worried that if Darr saw that, he might think she knew something. Her job might be over before it started. A few weeks later, on one of her first days on the job, she went to Marron and pulled him aside into a private office. At that point, Schachter had never heard of the Futon Five and had no idea she was speaking to one of its original members.

"I've heard some bad stuff about Darr," Schachter said.

Marron looked stunned. "How did you . . ." He paused. "What are you talking about?"

Schachter quickly outlined what she had been told by her friend from Josephthal and mentioned her concerns about her employment application. Marron seemed to visibly relax, as if he'd heard it all before.

"Well, it might be tough for you," Marron said, "because if Darr looks at the employment application and sees the name 'Josephthal,' he's not going to like it. But you just do your job and mind your business, and there's really no reason why you have to deal with Darr."

Marron spent a few more moments trying to reassure Schachter and then stood up to leave. Schachter still felt concerned.

"But, Dennis," she asked. "Don't you think we need to tell somebody else at the firm about what I heard?"

Marron stopped in the doorway of the office and looked back at Schachter.

"The firm already knows," he said. Then he turned to walk away.

By June 1981, D'Elisa's briefcase was stuffed with résumés from young MBAs, all of them eager to join the department's due diligence team. He and Wally Allen interviewed a number of candidates but were most impressed with David Levine, a recent business school graduate from the University of Pennsylvania. Although there was competition for Levine from other firms, he had been won over by D'Elisa and Allen. Levine liked the chemistry of the place.

Like Schachter, Levine also had to clear the final interview with Darr. But Levine came away from that meeting with a different feeling from Schachter. Even though Darr seemed somewhat arrogant, he displayed a level of charm that Levine enjoyed. To a degree, he felt flattered by Darr's attention. The department had little in the way of any business school talent, and Darr seemed to want it badly. Levine decided that at Bache he would be permitted a fair degree of autonomy. So, when D'Elisa came back with a competitive offer, he snapped it up.

In his first few days, D'Elisa told Levine to start a six- to nine-month study to explore the possibility of the department developing a more active business in public tax shelters. Its business to date had been founded mostly on private deals. Such deals had some advantages—for example, a private partnership did not have to register with the Securities and Exchange Commission or publicly file financial information, both of which cost money. But the disadvantages were far larger: The firm still had to send each buyer an investment memorandum describing the deal and disclosing all of the relevant facts. Under the rules at that point, an unregistered security could be sold only to a maximum of a hundred buyers, sharply restricting the amount of money that could be raised. All buyers had to meet certain income and asset standards to ensure that they had the financial wherewithal to handle the risk of the tax shelters.

Still, in the department, it was well known that the high commissions paid by tax shelters encouraged some brokers to fudge their clients' true financial condition in order to get them approved to invest. As the joke went, Bache's files held the names of more people making at least $250,000 than actually existed in the world.

Public deals would solve that problem. Partnerships could be registered with the SEC, then sold to thousands of investors across the country, almost as if they were stocks. All the partnerships would have to do was file prospectuses that disclosed all the risks. Then, for the most part, the law would shift responsibility for assuming that risk onto the investors themselves. If such a market could develop, it would increase the amount of money that partnerships could raise by an exponential factor. And with public deals, the stringent rules restricting which types of investors could purchase the deals would no longer apply.

Levine tore into his assignment with zeal. Working with public filings and contacting people in the industry, he found the competition in the public market and what products they were selling. By the time he finished his analysis, he had assembled a huge matrix of the sale and performance of every public tax shelter available. There seemed to be enormous room for growth. Levine thought that Bache could do great business by selling more public deals.

But Levine's increasing excitement about the prospects for the business was being offset by a growing distaste for Darr. The more he got to know him, the more Levine thought that his initial impression of Darr had been off base. For some reason, Darr seemed to delight in publicly humiliating the people who worked for him, usually by picking their weakest point. Even though Pittman and Proscia were Darr's biggest supporters, he would belittle them at department meetings by saying that they were lucky he existed because they would never be able to find another good job on Wall Street. Sometimes, when it was time for the meetings to break for lunch, Darr would start shaking all over, crudely mimicking a low-blood-sugar attack. Then he would announce that a marketer who was known to have diabetes needed to eat.

With due diligence executives like Levine, Darr's attempts at humiliation in business discussions were more veiled. He would ask technical questions about particular deals that were virtually impossible to answer, such as obscure financial data that might be buried in a footnote of an offering memorandum. If the executive stumbled in answering, Darr would aggressively pursue follow-up questions, sometimes to the point where the executive could no longer speak. Once the executive left the room, Darr would burst into peals of laughter. "I really had him going that time," Darr said, laughing after one particularly ghastly encounter.

D'Elisa had taken a liking to Levine and couldn't stand it when Darr played his games with him. So he quietly found out what questions Darr was planning to ask. Then, before the interrogation began, he took Levine aside and slipped him the answers. By doing so, D'Elisa figured, he wasn't harming Levine's education; he was just robbing Darr of some cruel pleasure.

Levine's understanding of Darr was solidified in the fall of 1981 at one of the department's quarterly meetings in New York. A number of Bache's general partners attended, making presentations about future projects. Levine sat with his colleagues from around the country in an auditorium at the Gold Street headquarters. Darr sat in the back of the room, occasionally interrupting with his own observations.

Suddenly, a movement in the aisle attracted Levine's attention. It was Darr, signaling that he wanted Levine to come out of the row. Levine stood and pushed past his colleagues. He knew what this was about: It was time for the quarterly bonuses. During these meetings, Darr loved taking people aside, one at a time, to deliver bonus checks. Levine was curious to find out how much he would be making.

He reached the end of the row, and Darr escorted him toward the back with an envelope in his hand. They stopped as they reached the back wall, and Darr turned to look at Levine.

"David, you're a sharp guy," Darr said. "And you'll have a choice, very soon, to either stay here and have a tremendous amount of power, or join another firm where you could earn a lot more money."

Levine felt somewhat uncomfortable. He had expected to hear something about his performance. Darr's line of conversation seemed out of context.

"So, that's the choice, money or power," Darr continued as he handed Levine his bonus of about $4,000. "For me the answer has been easy. That's why I stay here. I like power."

For what he wanted, Darr was in the right job at the right time. A new administration in Washington was pushing historic revisions in the country's fiscal policies, changes that would alter the American economy. And in an unintended ripple effect, they would transform Jim Darr into one of the most powerful people in the retail brokerage business.

It dawned foggy and damp on August 13, 1981, in California's scenic Santa Ynez Mountains. By late morning, troops of reporters and photographers took the white-knuckle drive up the winding road to the mountaintop. They gathered in front of the stucco house, built in 1872, that was now part of President Reagan's Rancho del Cielo. For weeks, the news media had been wagging a collective finger at Reagan for vacationing during the entire month of August. There was much going on in the world—the air-traffic controllers' strike and Moscow's criticisms of the new administration's Soviet policies. But on this day, the reporters awaited Reagan's arrival for a historic ceremony. He was about to sign into law the package of tax and budget reductions that had come to symbolize his administration. It was the defining moment in the eight-month-old Reagan presidency.

The Reagan bill, called the Economic Recovery Tax Act, promised to cut personal income-tax rates by 25 percent over three years and sharply cut business taxes to encourage new investment in plants, equipment, and real estate. After presenting the plan less than a month into his administration, Reagan, as well as his supporters, expressed confidence that the proposal would effectively kill the burgeoning tax shelter industry. On its face, the argument seemed to make sense. After all, shelters were largely a response to high tax rates, and the Reagan plan was expected to cut personal income-tax rates by an average of 25 percent over three years. But there was a critical flaw in their argument: Rather than kill the shelter business, the Reagan bill would spur their growth by making them more attractive investments.

The heart of his business tax-cut plan was a program known by the acronym ACRS, which stood for Accelerated Cost Recovery System. Under that proposal, assets such as real estate and equipment could be depreciated far faster than they had been in the past. Essentially, where the tax code once declared that a building would run itself down in twenty-five years, giving investors depreciation deductions throughout the entire period, under ACRS the time was reduced to fifteen years. That made investments in real estate and other depreciable assets far more attractive. It sharply boosted the amount of deduction bang an individual could get for each investment buck. Never had there been any legislation so significant to the growth of the tax shelter industry.

At noon, Reagan finally appeared, wearing faded jeans, a denim jacket, and cowboy boots. He grinned broadly, looking relaxed and tanned and projecting the image of a man enjoying victory. He sat down at a table as he apologized for the fog. Then, using twenty-four pens, Reagan signed the bill.

"This is only the beginning," he promised.

From that instant, Wall Street's shelter gurus were scrambling. They understood that the new law would greatly increase the already growing demand for tax shelters. The possibility of a real public market developing in shelters seemed all the more likely.

Within days, before Wall Street barely got out of the gate, the tax shelter business got another boost. A second radical change was announced on August 18 in the staid and solemn pages of the *Federal Register*. A publication of the United States government, the *Register* carries all proposed regulation and regulatory changes, and it is hot reading among lawyers and lobbyists. On that August day, it carried a proposal from the Securities and Exchange Commission that was read widely across the financial world: The government securities regulator wanted to change the rules for selling unregistered securities like private partnerships.

The proposal, known as Regulation D, reduced some of the restrictions on such sales. It eliminated the ceiling that restricted the sales of unregistered securities to just a hundred people, loosened the definitions of what kind of investors could participate in such offerings, and raised the dollar amount of securities that could be sold to such investors. The intent of the change was to make it easier for small businesses to sell stock to the public, opening up new ways to raise capital. But it also had a mammoth effect on private offerings in the tax shelter world—now such offerings could be bigger, broader, and sold to more people than ever before.

By itself, Regulation D would have rapidly expanded the tax shelter business on Wall Street. Combined with the Reagan tax changes, it served as a turbocharger. Almost any firm that wasn't already in the business launched its own tax shelter division. Firms that already had them, from Hutton to Merrill to Bache, expanded their operations even faster.

One of the biggest investment fiascoes in history had been set in motion.

The deals at Bache were coming fast and furious. Whatever demand the tax shelter department had seen earlier paled to what happened after the tax act and Regulation D. No one could keep up with the work. Even with all the new hires, the department's staff was still skeletal compared with the number of people it actually needed. David Levine was pulled off his project exploring the public marketplace to handle more real estate due diligence work with John D'Elisa. Ellen Schachter still helped Dennis Marron on energy deals, but was also assigned the job of putting together a brochure to explain the new tax bill to brokers. The more the salespeople understood about the changes in the law, the more likely they would be able to convince their clients to buy the next tax shelter.

The department threw all the bodies that could be found into the effort. Schachter sought some support from Lauren McNenney, an office temp who helped copy documents and answer telephones. McNenney, who in 1981 was working the first of two summers as a temp in Bache's tax shelter division, had no business background—she had last worked as a lifeguard at a day camp. She attended Barnard College, where she majored in English. But her writing skills gave her a big break: Schachter asked McNenney to help edit and proofread the tax bill brochure. Soon McNenney was allowed to write some material on her own.

With the work piling up, McNenney was a godsend. People in the department turned to her more and more, gradually allowing her to pick up assignments that were slipping by the wayside for lack of manpower.

The due diligence team was overwhelmed not just from the number of new deals they had to approve—they also had to keep tabs on the old deals that had already been sold. Darr had negotiated for Bache to be paid a monitoring fee from some tax shelters it sold in exchange for reviewing their financial performance. Supposedly, this was designed to make sure that the general partners managing the deals did things right and took care of their investors. It was a key selling point for Bache brokers: In sales pitches, they painted a picture of top Bache financiers in green eyeshades peering over the shoulders of the general partners, watching everything that was done. The image of financial professionals crunching numbers late into the night to make sure investors were protected was a persuasive marketing tool.

But asset monitoring paid only a small fraction of the fees that Bache received from selling new deals. So the job of keeping an eye on the performance of the old shelters quickly became viewed as simply a headache, an obligation that slowed down the whole process of churning out deals without enough juice from fees to make up for the effort. The monitoring assignment became a hot potato, passed from executives to subordinates, and from them on down the line.

By the summer of 1981, dozens of complex tax shelters from around the country were mailing records to New York every three months so that Bache could monitor their performance. Each day, the scores of financial documents were carried from the Bache mail room to the tax shelter department for sorting. Then financial statements from a number of Bache energy deals were delivered to the desk of Lauren McNenney. The responsibility for reviewing, analyzing, and logging that financial data had fallen on her shoulders.

The monitoring process that Bache brokers bragged about to clients as an example of the firm's new, rock-solid stability was largely in the hands of a part-time temp.

Fred Fiandaca, Prudential's liaison to Bache, popped open the back door of the dark, chauffeur-driven sedan and clambered inside. In an instant, George McGough, the head of Bache corporate resources, slid in beside him. It was March 1982, and the two men had just finished a luncheon meeting. They were heading back to Bache to finish up some work. Fiandaca liked McGough—the two had been working closely for months trying to coordinate Bache's purchasing operations with Prudential's. The payoff had been enormous. The combined purchasing power allowed Bache to receive enormous discounts on merchandise—the savings it received on furniture alone had climbed from 25 percent off list price to as much as 60 percent.

But Fiandaca knew the success in that one area was dwarfed by stumbling throughout the rest of the firm. Even though the merger had been completed almost nine months earlier, Bache's missteps continued. The firm had embarrassed itself by proudly touting an agreement in principle to purchase Bateman Eichler Hill Richards Inc., a large West Coast securities firm, without first securing a large stake in the firm. The announcement signaled to the marketplace that Bateman Eichler was for sale, and two weeks later, a humiliated Bache announced that the deal was off. Kemper Insurance took advantage of Bache's foolishness, rushed in with a better offer, and snapped the prize away.

Bache even fumbled the mailings announcing the introduction of its first important new product since it had been acquired by Prudential. Known as the Command Account, the product combined money market accounts with checking and debit cards. It was supposed to be in direct competition with Merrill's Cash Management Account, a product envied by senior Prudential executives. But the thousands of Bache announcements became simply another embarrassment. The mailings about the Command Account were sent to the wrong locations around the country. A prospective customer in Norwich, Connecticut, for example, received a letter telling him that if he wanted to open a Command Account, he should contact the nearest Bache branch—in Scottsdale, Arizona. The mailing made Bache look like a bunch of bumblers, which, to a degree, it was.

As far as Fiandaca could tell, the only Bache department that was doing well was Darr's tax shelter division. In that regard, Prudential executives knew they had been very lucky. They had wanted to get into the retail tax shelter business in a big way, but even they did not expect the impact that the Reagan tax bill and Regulation D would have on partnership sales.

Still, that one department's success was not enough to overcome Bache's mediocrity. The firm's total financial performance continued to be dismal. For 1981, it earned only about $5 million on more than $730 million in revenue. The first months of 1982 were even worse, with Bache stacking up millions in losses. Although some of that could be attributed to the lagging stock and bond markets, Bache's performance was worse than that of any of its big competitors. After years of success, Prudential uncomfortably watched its name associated more and more with a firm that seemed to symbolize failure.

Fiandaca never mentioned his concerns to McGough, but the Bache executive could tell that the time for Jacobs and Sherrill was running out. He saw the firm plow ahead, making important decisions without consulting Prudential. It seemed like once the Belzbergs were out of the picture, Jacobs settled back in the comfort of Bache's bloated bureaucracy, seeking consensus and running the firm in its old, slipshod way. He felt like shak-

ing Jacobs and telling him to wake up. Prudential was not going to be ignored.

As Fiandaca and McGough rode through the crowded streets of Manhattan back to Bache, they chatted about their meeting and the most recent results from the purchasing program. McGough decided to find out
what Fiandaca knew.

"But I guess it's not working so well on the higher levels," McGough
said.

"Yeah, obviously not."

McGough paused for an instant. "How long do you think it will last?"

"By summer," Fiandaca said. "Harry just doesn't understand what this is
all about."

"So what's going to happen?"

"Knowing the way they do it," Fiandaca said, "I think they will probably go out and try to get the best guy on the Street to run the firm."

McGough thought about that for an instant. A list like that couldn't be
too long. Wall Street is not a place overrun with good managers. The only
two choices he could imagine were the chairman of Shearson Loeb
Rhoades, which had just been purchased by American Express, or else the
president of E. F. Hutton, who had built up that firm's huge retail force in
a matter of years.

"Well," McGough said, "then it's either going to be Sandy Weill or
George Ball."

Inside the Bache cafeteria that warm June morning, some two hundred
executives munched on toast and eggs as they waited in anticipation. It was
the one-year anniversary of Bache's merger with Prudential, and Jacobs
had organized this special ceremonial breakfast to commemorate the day.
Everyone wanted to be there—this was one of the few meetings attended
not only by every senior member of the firm but by a phalanx of Prudential executives, including Bob Beck himself. Word started circulating days
before that Jacobs had special plans for his presentation, which probably
had something to do with the television monitors that had been set up
around the cafeteria.

By the time they had finished eating, Jacobs stood up. He was never
much at public speaking, and this morning was no different. Working off
his prepared text, he described what had happened to the firm since the
merger. The lights dimmed and a video began, showing Bache employees
working hard. Jacobs described the firm's performance in glowing terms,

from the number of people working to the new opportunities created by the Prudential merger. The tax shelter department was doing particularly well.

Some executives shifted uncomfortably in their seats. They knew that these highlights were ignoring the truth about the disasters at Bache. Since the firm was no longer a public company, the numbers were not out, but most executives knew that Bache had lost close to $50 million in the first six months of the year. It was hardly a performance to celebrate.

The video rolled to an end. Then Jacobs, sounding slightly nervous, said he wanted to show a movie clip that he thought summed up the relationship that had grown over the year between Prudential and Bache.

The television monitors lit up again. The executives watched, astonished, as they saw a film of a large bald man in a tuxedo, looking something like a classy Telly Savalas, dancing down a long, circular staircase. Thin wisps of violin music played, joined by an oboe and then a swelling orchestra. A short, redheaded girl joined the tuxedoed man on the staircase. Slowly, the two began to dance across the screen. By now, most of the executives realized that they were watching a scene from the just-released movie version of *Annie*, the musical. The bald man was Albert Finney, playing Daddy Warbucks and singing a duet with Aileen Quinn as the spunky orphan.

Bache executives were mortified as they began to understand Jacobs's message: Prudential was Daddy Warbucks, and Annie was Bache. It seemed a bit sophomoric and horribly out of place. A number of executives snuck a peek at Prudential's chairman to see his reaction. If Bob Beck could have let his mouth fall open in shock without attracting attention, he looked mortified enough to do it.

Daddy Warbucks and Annie then burst into the song "I Don't Need Anything but You." The discomfort in the room worsened as the executives listened to the words.

Together at last, together forever
We're tying a knot they never can sever.
I don't need sunshine now to turn my skies to blue.

Harry Jacobs approached the microphone and sang the last line, revised especially for the breakfast:

I don't need anything but Pru.

Throughout the room, Bache and Pru executives sat, staring in amazement. It was so out of character for Jacobs. Worse, it was so embarrassing. Guy Wyser-Pratte, the head of arbitrage, was sitting next to Howard Elisofon, a lawyer who worked with Bob Sherman in the retail group. The two men looked at each other, and Elisofon leaned over to whisper in Wyser-Pratte's ear. "Well, *he's* gonna be fired tomorrow."

In the executive offices of Prudential's Newark headquarters in June 1982, Garnett Keith picked up the packet of materials gathered in the hunt for Jacobs's replacement. The search had been going full-steam for months—in February, Prudential had retained Russell Reynolds Associates, the corporate headhunting firm, to look across Wall Street for the very best candidate. Prudential couldn't stand Bache's troubles any more. Its continued blunders were sapping whatever remnants of morale remained in the retail system. The firm was losing scores of top brokers. Bache's history of feudal bickering continued unabated, and Prudential's investment was already beginning to look like a disastrous mistake. Somebody needed to go in and shake up the place.

The people at Prudential knew that Jacobs would be devastated by the news. No one had yet hinted to him that his job was in jeopardy. In recent months, Keith had even praised Jacobs, saying how the people in Newark still stood behind him. Keith apparently did not think there was any reason to create problems before it was necessary.

Keith looked over the report from Reynolds. The headhunters were aggressively pushing one candidate, George Ball from Hutton. Keith knew Ball's reputation well; Virgil Sherrill from Bache had tried to woo him to the firm a year or so earlier by offering him the chance to run the retail division. Ball had rejected the offer out of hand. But the headhunters said that he seemed very interested in the opportunity to run the whole place. They said he had the right attitude: Every time he found a new difficulty at Bache—and there were many—he'd act delighted about having another problem to fix.

Ball sounded like the perfect candidate to salvage Prudential's investment. He had transformed Hutton's weak sales force into a Wall Street monolith and pushed the firm into building huge new business lines. His aggressive pursuit of the tax shelter business had been particularly impressive. Hutton emerged from the ranks of the also-rans to become one of Wall Street's undisputed leaders. If Ball could repeat that kind of performance with Bache, particularly given the strength in tax shelters already, the firm might turn around.

But even as Keith was giving the go-ahead to pursue Ball more aggressively, the facade of Hutton was starting to crack. A series of bad decisions was setting Hutton on the path to its own destruction. Keith did not know it, but if Ball was to save his reputation, he needed to get out of Hutton— and soon.

CHAPTER 6

THE MIDDLE-AGED BUTLER walked into the executive kitchen at E. F. Hutton. He picked up a silver tray laden with a heavy tea set and ambled toward the office of the firm's president. Without a word, he stepped into the office and placed a white Ginori china cup on the table in front of Bradford Ryland, a Hutton broker. Ryland watched as the tuxedo-clad butler picked up the matching pot and carefully filled the cup with tea. The aroma permeated the air as a second cup, filled with coffee, was set in front of Ryland's host, George Ball.

Ryland smiled as he leaned forward to pick up the cup. *I'll say this for him*, he thought. *Ball's got style.*

That had always been Ball's talent, going back to when he and Ryland were undergraduates together at Brown University. No one was better at projecting the right image or making people feel at ease. Who else would have taken the time to hunt down the Ryland family's coat of arms and send it to him? If Ball had not worked on Wall Street, he almost certainly would have headed into politics. Sometimes Ball even spoke wistfully of using his skills to seek office, maybe as a governor or perhaps a senator.

Ball was chatting amiably, asking Ryland about his family. They had no particular agenda that morning in September 1981. Ryland, who worked at a Hutton branch in California, had been vacationing in East Hampton, Long Island. While he was there, he decided to travel into Manhattan and drop by Ball's office. Ryland loved talking with him. Whenever Ball asked for input, he always seemed to take Ryland's suggestions seriously. Probably, Ryland thought, it was because he was not afraid to be blunt.

Ball picked up his coffee and blew on it slightly, to cool it down. There were some really exciting things going on at the firm, he said. The firm had figured out an idea that was making it lots of money. All Hutton had to do, Ball said, was fiddle with the "float"—the vast amounts of uncollected checks in transit between its various bank accounts. Usually banks would take advantage of the float by keeping the interest on deposited money while checks cleared. For an individual bank customer, the amount of money was piddling. But for Hutton, with hundreds of bank accounts and thousands of checks deposited each day, it was in the millions. With this idea, Ball said, Hutton simply overdrew its accounts against uncollected funds. By purposely writing checks for money not in the accounts, Hutton could take back the float and earn money on what amounted to interest-free loans. The idea was working out fabulously for the firm, he said.

Ryland sipped his tea as he listened to Ball's description. As excited as Ball was about this overdrafting idea, it left Ryland uneasy. He could not imagine that banks—and regulators—would look kindly on a company writing checks for money it didn't have. The whole thing struck Ryland as awfully illegal.

"George," he said, "that sounds like kiting a check."

Ball smiled. "Brad," he said, setting down his cup, "don't be so negative."

The answer was pure Ball: always seeing the bright side, always confident, always plowing straight ahead. But Ryland was right, as Ball would soon find out. The great idea was about to backfire and destroy everything Ball had worked for.

※　※　※　※

THE REAL George Ball had always been something of a puzzle. The people who worked for him inevitably described him as friendly, open, and a fabulous communicator. He engendered loyalty and a drive to perform. But in truth, Ball struggled to create that image. Boyish looking, with light red hair, Ball's effusiveness was a mask he developed to cover his painful shyness. At times, his nervousness seemed too close to the surface; whenever excited or stressed, his childhood stuttering problem reemerged. But in the gleam of his intense blue eyes and his eagerness to please, Ball's obsession with success was palpable. His frantic energy was almost boundless. This charming, handsome man, with his willingness to work punishing hours, struck almost everyone who met him as someone who would go a long way.

The son of a college professor, George Ball was born in the Chicago suburb of Evanston, Illinois. When young George was about ten, his father, Lester, took a job as superintendent of schools in Millburn Township in New Jersey's horse country. With that change, the Ball family began living in Short Hills, a wealthy suburban enclave popular among financial executives. It would be where George Ball would spend most of his life.

Ball lived a pleasant suburban childhood in New Jersey. Early on, in playing baseball, tennis, and ice hockey, Ball developed a fierce sense of competition and a desire to participate. He was never a particularly good loser, but he always preferred to play—even when he lost—rather than sit on the sidelines.

Later in his childhood, Ball met Captain R. Claude Robinson, a former member of the Bengal Lancers, the British cavalry regiment. Robinson would prove to have an enormous influence on Ball's life. He founded Adventures Camp for Boys in northern Wisconsin, and young George Ball attended every summer. The camp was spartan, with no water, no electricity, and no flushing toilets. Robinson demanded much from his boys, always urging them to run faster, jump higher, and push themselves past the point of exhaustion. To underscore his philosophy, Robinson told tales of endurance with the Bengal Lancers: He described officers jumping horses bareback with their arms crossed and told of his own experience being buried alive for days in a common grave after his company had been wiped out by artillery fire.

Although perhaps fanciful, the stories made a mark on Ball. Combined with Robinson's demands for rigorous performance, they led Ball to believe that no one ever reaches his full potential. He thought anyone could always push harder and get further. The philosophy launched Ball on his lifetime pursuit of self-improvement.

Ball's first taste of Wall Street came in the summer after his freshman year at Brown. Hoping to find a job, he spoke with Les Talbot, a boyhood friend's father who worked as a floor broker with Edwards & Hanley. Talbot was a mannerly, thoughtful sort from a gentlemanly generation on Wall Street. He often told young Ball about his days at the New York Stock Exchange. The culture in the financial world seemed foreign to Ball. That summer, Ball asked Talbot for help in finding a job in the business. Edwards & Hanley had a business relationship with E. F. Hutton, a more prominent and faster-growing brokerage firm. Talbot pulled a few strings and found Ball a job there. He was hired as a quote clerk, assigned to track down prices of stocks for brokers in an era before desktop computers made those readily accessible.

The job was far from prestigious. Only a few people worked alongside Ball as quote clerks, including a retarded man and a renowned thief. Still, Ball was fascinated by the business. The excitement of watching the harried brokers barking orders into their telephones, the frenetic energy of the traders on the floor of the exchange thrilled him. Here was the heartbeat of American capitalism, and Ball was right there to hear it. He could see himself remaining in the business for the rest of his life. For the next few years, he returned to Hutton, taking a different type of clerking job each summer. By his senior year, Ball had a strong knowledge of the sales business from his work at Hutton.

In 1960, Ball graduated from Brown with a degree in economics and signed up for a two-year stint in officers' training with the navy. Stationed in Maryland, he proposed to Mary Frank, whose family was from the New York City suburbs. While Ball was still in the navy, Frank became his first wife.

When Ball was released from active service, Wall Street beckoned. He immediately returned to Hutton in hopes of finding full-time work. The timing could not have been better: Arthur Goldberg, a young and methodical Hutton broker, had recently been given responsibility for creating a broker training program. Goldberg set up a branch at 61 Broadway in Manhattan, staffed entirely by trainees. The hopes were that the specialized branch would create a flow of young talent. Ball landed a spot as a trainee. The job paid $135 a month, enough to let Ball and his young wife scrape by.

Despite the vast knowledge he built up during his summers at Hutton, Ball's skills as a broker were not the best. But because of his work experience, Ball's fellow trainees began to turn to him with questions and problems. Soon Goldberg noticed that the trainees seemed to flock around the desk of the intense young redheaded man who knew all the answers. That gave Goldberg an idea. If people turned to Ball as a leader, he may as well be trained as one.

Ball became Goldberg's protégé, following him up the corporate ladder through a succession of rapid promotions. In the fall of 1967, Ball was asked to open up a new Hutton office in Newark, just a few short blocks from the offices of Prudential Insurance.

The assignment was a tremendous challenge. The branch would be the first business to open its doors in Newark since the race riots a few months earlier. The atmosphere was frightening, and Ball feared that he would have great trouble attracting brokers to the new office. But eventually he decided to turn that fear to his advantage. He told his evening sales staff that he would pick up the cab fare to the train station for every broker who opened a new account. Brokers who preferred not to walk through the tense streets of Newark opened new accounts quickly.

The Newark office flourished, and its profitability increased each year. With Goldberg's support, Ball was winning some attention from the firm's senior executives. In 1969, he was promoted to regional vice-president, with responsibilities for supervising all of the branches in the New York area. A year later, after some vicious internal fighting that led to Goldberg's resignation, Hutton named Bob Fomon, the former head of corporate finance on the West Coast, as the firm's chairman.

The turn of events looked bad for Ball at first. Not only had he lost Goldberg, his mentor, but Ball had openly thrown his support to the losing candidate for the job. He expected to suffer serious consequences as a result of backing the wrong horse. And at first, he did; some of his responsibilities were transferred to another regional vice-president who had supported Fomon. But the new chairman was smart enough to know that he needed Ball's skills with brokers. So Fomon sought out Ball and grew to like his style. Within a matter of months, in 1970, Fomon promoted Ball to the post of Hutton's national sales manager. Seven years later, Ball was named president.

Ball's relationship with brokers was almost magic. He traveled around the country, visiting every branch and speaking personally with every big producer. He knew virtually thousands of brokers and stunned most of them with his uncanny ability to recognize them on sight. But Ball took that one step further, asking each manager and big producer detailed questions that showed an astonishing knowledge about their personal lives. Rare was the broker who was not flattered to hear Ball ask about each of his children—by name and age. But the personal attention Ball lavished on his team was not spontaneous; it required a lot of rehearsal. Before visiting any branch, he ordered up reports on the managers and their top producers. For days, he studied their names and the names of their family members, their birth dates, their alma maters, and their interests. As Ball scurried about his office, readying himself to leave, his secretaries would hold up pictures of brokers, and he would call out their names and backgrounds. What seemed like familiarity at times was little more than the result of an old-fashioned cramming session.

Even if it was rehearsed, Ball's apparent chumminess was an effective managing tool. He built up a personal following among the brokers, for whom Ball was their biggest cheerleader. To them, he was always "George." Big producers knew that they could call him personally with any problems, something they would never have dared do with more aloof executives like Fomon. When not speaking to them in person, Ball was churning out rambling, personal memos to the firm. These memos, called "Ballgrams," reflected Ball's quirky mind-set, complete with made-up words affectionately known as "Ballisms." In the world of the Ballgram, a pitched internal battle was "Starwarsian" and the *New York Times* was "the Great Grey Blab." Ball turned himself into one of the most prolific memo writers in Wall Street's history, covering topics from new business to old deals to his daughter's horseback riding. Sometimes they were educational, sometimes they were entertaining. But almost always they were strange.

Brokers who weren't won over by Ball's effusiveness could not help but be captivated by his eagerness to open the firm's wallet. Promising big signing bonuses and huge commissions, Ball recruited heavily for Hutton among all the top producers on Wall Street. The large payments—including as much as 30 percent of a broker's annual commission up front—pushed Hutton's compensation costs into the stratosphere and led to a massive growth in its size. By 1980, the firm had ballooned beyond anyone's wildest expectations. It had grown from 1,450 brokers in 1972 to 6,600. And almost all of them were loyal to Ball, the man who had brought them on board.

※　　※　　※　　※

IN 1980, sitting in his plush office on the top floor of Hutton headquarters on the southernmost tip of Manhattan, Ball reviewed the numbers showing that his firm was in trouble. Profits had peaked that year, and the operating performance was deteriorating. So were relations in the executive suites. Despite Ball's proximity to Fomon—whose cavernous office, with its rubberized floor, was directly opposite his own—the two men had begun drifting apart. Fomon was pulling away from the business, as if he were uninterested in the nitty-gritty of the firm's workaday tasks.

As Ball looked out his office window at a view of the East River and the seaport, he knew that he faced a deep business challenge. With costs still climbing, revenues were harder to come by. The deregulation of commission rates five years earlier was still creating intense pricing competition. And high interest rates made investors reluctant to go into the stock market. He had repeatedly called executives into his office to discuss ways to boost revenues, but without much success. Ball knew how to spend money, but he seemed unable to decide on how to cut back. With the meager business unable to cover those costs, Hutton's profitability sank. Ball had created an unwieldy expense monster. He had to find a way to boost earnings.

Bank account overdrafting came to the rescue. Like every brokerage firm, Hutton needed millions of dollars each day to finance its operations. The idea had started in 1978, with Hutton branches writing perfectly legal checks against funds that had not yet cleared. It took away float from the banks, but those institutions were still paid for their services. Then, in 1980, Hutton pushed the aggressive idea over the line. Rather than just using small overdrafts to recapture float that the banks would have taken, the firm began writing huge, multimillion-dollar overdrafts to create float for Hutton. In effect, Hutton was stealing millions of dollars out of the nation's banking system.

Writing bad checks allowed it to borrow a lot of the money interest-free. In 1980 alone, overdrafting its bank accounts helped Hutton cut its bank borrowings to $192 million a day from $383 million a year earlier—a change that would save it tens of millions of dollars in interest payments. And profits from interest earned climbed, too—reaching $95.9 million in 1980, almost double the previous year's performance.

With such a performance, Ball aggressively pushed his team to overdraft the bank accounts. Managers who brought in huge sums from overdrafting received big bonuses. Those who did not were admonished. Ball encouraged regional managers to give the slackers Monopoly money, sealed in plastic, along with their regular bonuses to show how much they might have made had they overdrafted their bank accounts more aggressively.

He used the Ballgrams to egg on managers and account executives, known as AEs, to do more overdrafting. In a May 12, 1981, memo to the firm entitled "Interest," Ball described a branch that had been earning "a consistent $30,000 per month in interest just by overdrafting of the bank account." But after changing cashiers, the branch's interest income from overdrafting dropped to less than $10,000 a month. The conclusion? "A good branch cashier is worth as much as an AE," he wrote.

By October 1981, Ball felt compelled to point out to the firm that it was hooked on overdrafting; the sales of securities no longer covered its huge expenses. "Without gigantic interest profits," he wrote, "the bottom line would have been a dismal one, as I know you are aware."

Shortly after he wrote those words, a discovery would be made at a small bank in upstate New York that would obliterate those profits forever.

––––––––

John Lounsbury, the chief auditor of Security New York State Corporation, picked up the telephone in his office in Rochester, New York, on almost the first ring. It was Steve Milne, the control officer at the holding company's subsidiary, Genessee Country Bank. Lounsbury heard several times a day from staff members he had stationed at the company's nine banks. But rarely did they sound as concerned as Milne did this day in December 1981.

"We had an account opened recently by E. F. Hutton," Milne said. "And we're just getting burned with activity."

Lounsbury couldn't help but be amused. Bank auditors always keep their eyes open for rapid series of transactions in new accounts. Such fast business was usually a clear sign that some scam artist was trying to write as many bad checks as possible before getting caught. But Lounsbury knew Genessee was a small bank that had not seen much business from brokerage firms. The account from Hutton's branch in Batavia had been opened only a few days earlier. Perhaps, he suggested gently, Milne was just seeing the results of a good business day at a branch of a prominent brokerage firm.

"You don't understand," Milne replied with deep concern in his voice. "There are millions of dollars of transactions in this account, and they don't have the money for it."

Lounsbury shifted in his seat. It didn't take much knowledge to realize that a Hutton branch in upstate New York couldn't be doing that much daily business. "I don't understand," he said, and asked for all the details Milne could provide.

With a little digging, Lounsbury and Milne learned that, except for a few customer checks, almost every transaction in the Hutton account involved checks from United Penn Bank in Wilkes-Barre, Pennsylvania, and another bank in Reading. The latest check was for $8 million, drawn on United Penn. Lounsbury decided to telephone United Penn to see if the check was any good. He explained the situation and asked a banker there if Hutton had good funds to back up its check.

"Oh, hell," the banker replied. "This is E. F. Hutton. They never have good funds."

The banker said that that account was backed by still another uncollected check that would not clear for days. That check was drawn on a third Hutton account with a New York City bank. Lounsbury hung up the telephone. He knew exactly what he was looking at, and it shocked him: This financial giant was trying to rip off a tiny little local bank. Hutton was passing bad checks from one account to the next in what is known as a pinwheel, creating float for the firm. If some con man had been trying it, the sheriff would be knocking on his door before nightfall.

Well, the hell with this, Lounsbury thought. He telephoned Milne and told him to bounce the Hutton check. Genessee would not pay any Hutton checks that were not covered by cash on deposit. It took days for Hutton to figure it out, during which time it bounced $22 million worth of checks at Genessee.

Lounsbury then telephoned the local branch manager of Hutton to demand an explanation. But the manager said that he was simply following orders from New York. His contact, he said, was a regional operations manager with the firm. Lounsbury hung up and immediately telephoned that executive.

"What are you people doing?" he demanded after describing what he had learned.

The operations manager sounded panicked. Lounsbury shouldn't blame him, he said. He was just a middle manager, taking orders from above. "I'm just a pawn in all this," he said.

Then the operations manager made a suggestion. To make up for any troubles caused to Genessee, Hutton would wire more than $30 million in cash to the bank. Lounsbury agreed, and the money arrived an hour later. Still, the auditor was angry, and on December 11, he shut down the Hutton account, retaining the $30 million for three months.

Mulling it over, Lounsbury decided that Hutton was willfully breaking the law in an attempt to defraud the banks. On December 29, he wrote letters to the state and federal banking regulators, the FBI, and the Secret Service describing everything Hutton had done. A few days earlier, United Penn had notified the Federal Deposit Insurance Corporation, a federal banking regulator. As the complaints flowed in, the banking regulators realized they had a potentially significant problem on their hands. They had to investigate.

By January 1982, the FDIC had examined enough of Hutton's practices to know something improper was up. "At first glance, it could appear that Hutton was 'playing the float,'" wrote Gerald Korn, an FDIC examiner. "But further investigation revealed evidence of an apparent, deliberate kiting operation almost 'textbook' in form."

As the regulators fanned out, some of Hutton's best banking relationships started suffering. John McGillicuddy, the chairman of Manufacturers

Hanover, assured the regulators that he was satisfied with his bank's relationship with Hutton, but shortly after being questioned, his bank imposed new rules restricting Hutton's cash management business. So Hutton took its money to another bank.

The time had come, the regulators decided, to confront Hutton.

Loren Schechter, Hutton's deputy general counsel, could not imagine what the problem was. In February 1982, state banking regulators called Hutton, asking to meet with representatives of the firm to discuss its banking practices. As far as Schechter was concerned, this meeting would be a nonevent with a lowly bureaucrat, sitting at a government-issued metal desk.

At six-two and more than two hundred pounds, Schechter had the look of a retired football player and the demeanor of a professional wrestler. A man with thick black hair touched with gray, Schechter had always wanted to be a lawyer. As a child growing up in Queens, New York, he was an avid reader of every Perry Mason mystery and dreamed of courtroom battles. Even though he drifted instead into securities law, he became a legal brawler all the same. In his ten years as a Hutton lawyer, he chiseled a reputation as one of the biggest defenders of the firm's actions, even those that pushed close to the line. This time was no different. Although Schechter could not imagine what the regulators wanted, he was sure Hutton had done nothing wrong.

Schechter arrived at the state banking department's offices in the World Trade Center in downtown Manhattan on February 10, at 10:00 A.M. Rather than meeting with a single bureaucrat in the bowels of the building, as he had expected, he was taken to the department's boardroom. There he was confronted by a small battalion of federal and state bank examiners. There were few pleasantries. Ernest Patrikis, deputy general counsel of the New York Federal Reserve, asked Schechter if he knew that Hutton had bounced $22 million in checks at the Genessee Country Bank in LeRoy, New York.

"I've never even heard of LeRoy," Schechter replied. "Why is this important?"

Because, Patrikis replied, the $22 million in checks appeared to be part of a larger pinwheel.

"What's a pinwheel?" Schechter asked.

"That's when you move money for no other purpose than to create float."

The regulators said that they had found massive evidence of pinwheeling and overdrafting by Hutton, specifically in its accounts at Manufacturers Hanover and Chemical. They demanded that Hutton look into the matter, and Schechter, shaken by the confrontation, readily agreed.

After the tense meeting ended, Schechter scurried back to Hutton. He tracked down the firm's general counsel, Tom Rae, and filled him in on what the regulators had to say. Rae agreed that Schechter would be in charge of the in-house investigation. The lawyers then called an emergency meeting with their accountants from Arthur Andersen. The accountants could not have been surprised: In 1980, five accountants from the firm had warned Hutton executives, including Rae, that the overdrafting policies might not be legal. Those concerns had been dismissed by Rae and others, who said that the banks were fully aware of the nature of the transactions. But if the accountants expected Hutton to switch opinions after hearing from regulators, they were disappointed.

Rae, with the backing of Schechter and other Hutton executives, again asserted that their banking strategies were perfectly proper. "There's nothing illegal here," he said to the accountants, with the agreement of the other Hutton executives. "The banks knew all about it." No one, Rae concluded, could be defrauded if they walked into a transaction with their eyes open. Besides, the Hutton executives argued, banking regulators had no authority to do anything to a brokerage firm.

And Genessee, Rae said, would be no problem. The bank wanted to continue doing business with Hutton. It didn't even want to charge Hutton a penny in interest on the overdrawn balances, he claimed. In truth, Genessee had already shut down Hutton's accounts months earlier and refused to do any more business with the firm.

The only thing the firm had to worry about, the executives said, was potential negative publicity if reporters learned of the banking problems. That might hurt Hutton's image. But no one, they said, could accuse Hutton of participating in illegal conduct.

Stephen Hammerman, the general counsel of Merrill Lynch, poked his head into the firm's compliance department. He had been walking down the hallway at Merrill's headquarters one day in April 1982 when he heard some members of his staff talking urgently about a problem that had developed. It seemed a good time to investigate.

"What's going on, guys?" Hammerman said to the lawyers and investigators gathered in the office.

Over the next few minutes, they told Hammerman of a brokerage account that had been opened at the firm in the name of Traex Corporation.
Someone named Franco Della Torre had begun making cash deposits into
the account totaling more than $4.9 million. As required under a law de-
signed to deter money laundering, the firm was reporting all cash deposits
greater than $10,000 to the government. Still, the compliance team was
uncomfortable. Della Torre brought the cash in suitcases from ritzy hotels
like the Waldorf and the Parker Meridien. Although the deposits were
made at the firm's headquarters in Manhattan, the account was based in
Lugano, Switzerland, and the money was sent there. It had all the earmarks
of a crime, probably laundering drug money.

"What are the size of the bills we're talking about?" Hammerman asked.

"Mostly tens and twenties," said Louis Brown, a member of the firm's
security team.

"Well, what does this person do for a living?"

"He said he's in the real estate business."

Hammerman cracked a smile. "That's a hell of a lot of rent somebody's
paying," he said.

Hammerman prided himself on running a tight ship. It didn't take
J. Edgar Hoover to figure out that, whatever this client was up to, Hammerman didn't want Merrill involved in it.

"Let's throw the account out of here," he said to the group. "Shut it
down."

Hammerman turned around and continued down the hall, glad to have
rid the firm of a potentially devastating problem.

A few days later, Arnold Phelan, the head of commodities at Hutton,
approached Loren Schechter with big news: He had just snagged a major
account from Merrill Lynch. It was a big-time company, represented by an
Italian named Franco Della Torre. The new client wanted to maintain his
account in Lugano, Switzerland, but Della Torre would be making huge
cash deposits in New York City. Phelan asked if the setup was acceptable.

Schechter said he couldn't see why not. He told Phelan to make sure
that all deposits of more than $10,000 were reported, as the law required.
Still, Schechter decided it would be better to double-check about this potential new client, so he kicked the matter upstairs to find out what Ball
thought. Hutton's president was delighted—he loved nothing more than
hearing about his firm winning a major new account from a competitor.
As long as Hutton followed the rules, he didn't see anything wrong with
accepting the money.

Della Torre began dropping off his suitcases full of cash at Hutton's front door. Executives with the firm carefully monitored the deposits, making sure that they filled out all of the necessary forms. Over the next few months, Della Torre deposited $15.5 million in small bills at E. F. Hutton.

The next time bomb for Hutton had been planted. By the time it went off, Hutton would already be the subject of a massive federal criminal investigation for its check-kiting scheme.

Like the original complaint that came from the tiny Genessee bank, the criminal investigation of Hutton's check-kiting scheme started in a most unlikely spot. Al Murray was one of the hundreds of young assistant U.S. attorneys who worked for the Justice Department. Murray was an aggressive sort working in the small outpost in Scranton, Pennsylvania, a place that almost never became involved in large-scale securities cases. Still, it would be Murray, the son of a Brooklyn criminal court judge, who would launch the criminal investigation of E. F. Hutton.

On a day in April 1982, Murray sat at his desk studying a curious FDIC memorandum about Hutton. For some reason, the firm had been overdrafting its bank accounts. The details in the memo sent to criminal investigators in New York and Pennsylvania amazed him. To Murray, Hutton's banking practices seemed like the stuff of a great criminal case: a firm with a household name involved in huge money transfers that appeared to siphon off cash from the nation's banking system. Murray decided to dig deeper.

He subpoenaed the full FDIC report in May. It detailed what happened at Genessee Country Bank and United Penn and laid out other information about the practices Hutton used in its bank overdrafts. Murray also found copies of the letters that Lounsbury, the bank auditor, had sent to the government months before. He contacted John Holland, a postal inspector, and the two started working on the case. Holland decided he should speak with Lounsbury to see if the small-town bank auditor might have some information that could help them.

So one morning in the spring of 1982, Holland drove across two states, toward the city of Rochester, New York, on the shore of Lake Ontario. Lounsbury was delighted to hear from somebody in the government. As months of silence had followed his letter-writing campaign, he had just assumed that his complaints had been dropped into some bureaucrat's garbage can.

The meeting started with Holland showing Lounsbury the FDIC memo, saying, "I don't really know what I have here."

Lounsbury got up from his desk and walked over to his file cabinet. He had planned ahead and saved every scrap of paper relating to the Hutton transactions. "I've got a whole file drawer full of information here that might help you."

Over the next two hours, they reviewed the records, with Lounsbury walking Holland through each step slowly. He showed how Hutton had used the system to loot the banks.

Eventually, Holland concluded, "Based on this, I think these folks have been committing a fraud by using the United States mail. That's a crime. I think I can get them."

Holland returned to Scranton and reported what he had learned to Murray. Lounsbury's information emboldened them to press on. Grand jury subpoenas were issued to Fomon, Hutton's chairman, and two other senior Hutton executives. Throughout the top ranks of the brokerage, word spread quickly that a criminal probe of Hutton's checking practices had begun.

Despite all his typical public enthusiasm that summer, Ball had his private, undisclosed anguish. Fomon had become more erratic, clinging desperately to power while backing away from critical decisions. With the overdrafting on hold as the firm's lawyers investigated, Hutton was stumbling and its profits were eroding. The criminal investigation was unnerving the firm's senior ranks.

With all the firm's problems, Ball began thinking about leaving. The planning began in April when he received a telephone call from Leland Getz, an executive with Russell Reynolds Associates, the headhunting firm. His first conversation with Getz had been cryptic.

"I'd like to meet with you about something very important," Getz said.

"What about?" Ball asked.

"It's about you."

That was mysterious enough, so Ball agreed to meet secretly with Getz. Over lunch at a Manhattan restaurant, Getz quickly got to the point. "Would you be interested in running Bache?"

Ball sat back and thought. He had never before considered working anywhere else but Hutton. Just one year earlier, he had rebuffed an offer to take a senior job at Bache.

But with all of Hutton's unfolding problems, the timing was perfect for an exit. It seemed as good a time as any to bail out. He leaned up to the table.

"Tell me more."

Bob Fomon's vengeful anger at George Ball poured out to the crowd of Hutton brokers assembled in Denver, Colorado, in August 1982. "That fucking little redheaded wimp jumped ship," the Hutton chairman growled in an angry, drunken voice. "That son of a bitch."

It had been a few weeks since Ball's surprise announcement of July 19 that he was leaving Hutton to take over Bache. Fomon at first had taken the news like a bewildered parent abandoned by his child. But on this night, as the realization sunk in that his protégé was now his competitor, Fomon tore into the man. He couldn't believe Ball would desert his team for a place like Bache.

"Bache, for God's sake!" he growled. "The biggest fucking joke on the Street! They've never known how to make money. And that's what *George* used to say! He ridiculed them more than anybody!"

Fomon had good reason for his anger. Since Ball announced his resignation, he had already made it known within Hutton's ranks that he was willing to cherry-pick the firm's best people for Bache. It should have been no surprise to Fomon—after all, Ball had made his name on Wall Street in part through his talents at raiding other brokerage houses for their top producers. In short order, Ball launched the same war, but this time his beachhead was Bache and the enemy was Hutton: He lured Greg Smith, a close friend who headed Hutton's equity division, as well as a number of the stock analysts who worked for him. He also recruited Hutton's top stock strategist, its chief economist, and a number of its top brokers. Soon Ball would start raiding the firm's legal department.

While Ball was busy building his new team at Bache, a Customs Service agent was making a discovery that would eventually speak volumes about one of the new recruits—and about the future direction of Ball's new firm.

In October 1982, Mike Fahy sat at a desk in the World Trade Center offices of the United States Customs Service, just a few blocks from Hutton headquarters. His eyes barely moved as he stared at the computer screen in front of him, waiting on the system to finish cross-checking some names. Suddenly a single name popped up on the screen: Franco Della Torre, a customer of E. F. Hutton. Fahy jumped up from his seat.

"I've got a hit!" he shouted.

Fahy had found something that might be the big break in the yearlong investigation of what law enforcement officials thought was the largest international money-laundering and heroin ring ever uncovered. Fahy had found Della Torre by running all the names from the address book of another suspected money launderer through the computer to see if any had been reported making large cash deposits at an American financial institution. Della Torre was the only match. Fahy typed a few commands into the computer and a six-foot-long list of Della Torre's transactions with the brokerage firm began to print out.

Fahy called Robert Paquette, a special agent with the FBI who was in charge of the case, and told him about Della Torre. Paquette was elated. Finally they had a critical lead. If they could follow Della Torre, or even eventually turn him into a government witness, they might crack the entire ring.

Paquette decided to contact Merrill and Hutton, which had both filed forms documenting Della Torre's large deposits. He called Merrill first, which quickly agreed to cooperate with the government investigation. Then Paquette called the security department at Hutton, which passed him on to Loren Schechter in the law department. Paquette explained the government's interest in the Della Torre account. He asked Schechter for Hutton's cooperation, requesting that the firm keep the account open. He wanted Hutton to notify the FBI the next time Della Torre made a cash deposit. That way the government could start monitoring his actions.

"This is a very intense ongoing investigation," Paquette said. "We need to make sure it's not compromised."

"Don't worry about it," Schechter said. Hutton would be glad to cooperate. The firm would need a subpoena to turn over the account information, Schechter said, but he would make sure that Paquette was notified of the next deposit.

Over the next few days, Paquette did some background checks on Della Torre. He contacted Louis Freeh, the assistant United States attorney general in charge of the case, to brief him on the developments. Freeh prepared subpoenas for the account information at both Merrill and Hutton. Paquette served Merrill first and quickly received the information he wanted. Then he walked across the financial district toward Hutton's offices. It was a bitterly cold day, and as he walked along the narrow Manhattan streets, Paquette bundled his heavy coat around himself. He took off his gloves only after arriving in Hutton's lobby. A security guard directed him to Schechter's office.

Something immediately seemed to be wrong. Schechter wouldn't look Paquette in the eyes. Paquette had interviewed enough guilty people to know that Schechter was acting like he had something to hide.

"I've got all the subpoenas you asked for," Paquette said. "Has Della Torre surfaced yet?"

Schechter stared down at his desk. "We've got a problem," he said. "I don't think we are going to be able to help you now."

"Why?" Paquette asked, growing increasingly uneasy. "What's happened?"

"The accounts have been closed," Schechter replied.

Paquette couldn't believe it. Somebody had to have been tipped off. "How could that happen?"

"We notified the clients in Switzerland."

Paquette slumped in his chair. "What?" His mind started racing, thinking of some way to salvage the operation. "Has it been a definitive announcement, or an insinuation?" he asked. "Is there any chance of regenerating contact?"

"You've got to speak about it with our general counsel, Mr. Rae," Schechter said as he stood up from his desk and escorted Paquette down the hall.

Over the next few minutes, Paquette heard Tom Rae explain how Hutton had decided to notify the clients of the government investigation and shut down the accounts out of fear for the lives of the firm's employees. He told Paquette it would be impossible to reconstruct the relationship.

Paquette left Hutton in a fury. *Schechter stabbed us all in the back!* he thought. It was Schechter who had made the commitment to cooperate and then turned around and breached the government's trust. Paquette couldn't believe that the lawyer hadn't notified him of a problem at Hutton. If Schechter had just given him a courtesy call, Paquette thought, everything could have been salvaged. Schechter had obviously been faced with a choice between doing what was right and doing what was safe. And, Paquette thought, he had made the wrong choice.

Paquette immediately went to the offices of the U.S. attorney at Foley Square, where he found Louis Freeh and told him what had happened. Paquette's anger paled next to Freeh's. More than a year's worth of investigation had been thrown into the toilet by one of America's premier brokerage firms. Freeh launched into an endless tirade against Hutton. The government had to start all over again.

Two years of investigations ensued that otherwise would have been unnecessary. Dozens of FBI agents were used to monitor thousands of hours of wiretaps, running twenty-four hours a day. The cost ran into the millions of dollars. In the end, Freeh and the FBI were able to reconstruct the case and break up the billion-dollar pipeline that funneled heroin to the United States for distribution through pizza parlors and cafés. The case, dubbed the Pizza Connection, would be the largest in the history of law enforcement, and it helped to propel Louis Freeh to the post of director of the FBI. But almost to the end, Freeh never let an opportunity slip to criticize Hutton for its acts.

None of that criticism much affected Schechter. Within a few months of his encounter with Paquette, he had called George Ball about getting a new job. Soon afterward, Loren Schechter was tapped to be the chief law enforcer and top watchdog of the firm that had been renamed Prudential-Bache Securities.

"Average sucks," George Ball announced in November 1982 to a group of sixty-one top Prudential-Bache brokers assembled at a get-together in Phoenix. "Like Zeus on Mount Olympus, we're going to stand above the others."

Ball broke into a wide smile as the group of successful stockbrokers erupted into wild cheers. After years of embarrassment from working for a Wall Street also-ran, the brokers finally had someone in charge who made them proud. In just a few months, Ball had invigorated the firm, pushing it endlessly into new, unexplored directions. Almost unbelievably, he had transformed it into one of the hot brokerages on Wall Street. Ball was more than just another boss; for the firm's brokers, his arrival was something more akin to the Second Coming. As they watched Ball push his host of reforms, the brokers whispered their secret hope that he would be able to do for Bache what he had done for Hutton.

On his first day as Bache's new chief executive in mid-August, Ball had hit the firm like a whirlwind. At 7:00 A.M. that morning, he stepped out of the chauffeured sedan that had driven him to 100 Gold Street from his posh home in northern New Jersey. He headed through the revolving door into Bache's lobby. A look of disgust came over his face. Shabby was the best word for the place. The entryway was drab and lifeless; the closest thing to decoration was a series of smudged, handwritten signs warning visitors that security guards could search their packages.

Ball shook his head. The lobby was an embarrassment. It looked like a warehouse. This was no image for a brokerage firm to project if it wanted to be successful. He went up to his office and ordered changes. The next morning, Bache's dreary entryway was refurbished. The amateurish signs were stripped away; potted plants and a small garden of flowers appeared. If he wanted employees to be proud of the firm, Ball reasoned, then they had to start taking pride in its image. The time had come to put a new face on a firm known throughout Wall Street as a schlock house. In its place, he told friends, he planned to build "something majestic."

Bit by bit, Ball transformed the grimy, shopworn world of Bache into something more polished. No detail was too small: The "please flush" sign hung in the executive restroom by John Leslie, the former chairman, was taken down and placed in Ball's office—an implicit ridicule of Bache's stodgy old ways. Free coffee and Danish appeared some mornings by order of the new boss; on one holiday, all employees received a box of expensive chocolates. A nice fall weekend provided Ball with an excuse to order flowers for every woman in the building. Even top executives shared in Ball's largesse. During one tedious meeting where poor financial results were being discussed, Ball suddenly flipped on a tape recorder. The conference room filled with the sounds of the country and western song "Cowboys in the Continental Suit" by Marty Robbins. Jumping up, Ball announced, "All right, everybody, over to Paul Stuart and get fitted for a new suit!" Thrilled, the group of executives headed out to the nearby men's clothing store and started snapping up suits and ties. Ball stood by at the cash register, approving and picking up the tab for each purchase.

But the cheery new boss with the Boy Scout looks also let it be known that he was no softy. Performance counted, and anyone who wasn't up to the task was shown the door. "We have to be brutal about getting rid of second-raters," Ball told *Fortune* magazine during his first six months on the job.

Ball swung the ax at Bache's plodding management with relish. He stripped the power from the chairman and vice-chairman, Harry Jacobs and Virgil Sherrill, although he allowed them to retain their titles. Ball abolished one of Bache's two boards of directors, dismissing the second as "superfluous." Then he launched what amounted to an all-out purge of other top managers. Even John Curran, the general counsel, was eased out. Within a few months, Ball had fired five senior executives and fifteen of their subordinates, including almost every member of the firm's executive committee.

In the world Ball was creating, there was no room for sentiment. Ball was touched when one of Bache's regional directors gave him a military officer's sword mounted in a frame and complete with an inscribed plaque. The director was encouraging Ball to lead the Bache troops into battle. It made Ball feel all the worse when he fired the executive a few days later. Although he kept the sword and hung it in his office for years, he removed the plaque, which had the name of the regional director on it, to keep from feeling guilty.

By tossing out so many senior executives, Ball tore apart allegiances and relationships carefully constructed throughout Bache over the years. Thus, he shattered the usual Bache network for career advancement. In its place, he was bringing in new recruits from Hutton, like Schechter. Resentments started building up against this new clique. Bache veterans who had hoped to climb further up the ranks watched in dismay as a newer, younger group of executives moved to the top.

"Ball's bringing in his own team here," Bob Sherman, now the head of retail, told his staff that fall. "And there's going to be nothing in it for any of the rest of us." Sherman made it clear that, despite Ball's efforts to create a new spirit of cooperation, he was not going to join the team.

The bitterness toward Hutton executives rarely broke into the open in any significant way. In large part that was because even as the Bache veterans saw their future options shrink, Ball increased their power exponentially. Ball tossed aside the committee process that had so hobbled Bache over the years, pushing the decision making down to lower levels. The division managers were big boys, he reasoned, and could decide what to do without interference from above.

Under Ball's direction, Sherman's division rapidly gained prominence. Ball ordered a massive recruiting program for brokers, aimed at bringing thousands of the biggest producers on Wall Street into Bache. He did it the same way he had at Hutton—by promising huge up-front bonuses and commissions. The deal not only was lucrative for the brokers, it locked them into Bache—the bonus was provided in the form of a loan, forgivable over two to three years. If they left Bache before that, the firm could hit them up for the remainder of the money. Within the first year and a half, the program brought in an astonishing 1,100 new brokers. The firm's reach expanded far beyond anything it had ever been.

And now Bache had dozens of new products available to its vast cadre of clients. Ball saw great prospects in particular for the firm's tax shelter division, which had been beefed up significantly since the Prudential takeover. Tax shelters needed to be a bigger part of the retail sales effort, Ball thought, and he shifted responsibility for such products from Lee Paton to Bob Sherman. Ball liked what he saw in the division, particularly its heavy sales and the can-do attitude of its boss, Jim Darr.

Ball had big plans for Darr's department. He thought its focus on tax shelters missed not only the point but also the huge potential market for the business. Rather than focusing exclusively on the tax benefits—which would restrict the customer base to only the wealthiest clients—Ball instead wanted to put more emphasis on deals that would provide a hedge against inflation while producing investment income. More investors would be interested in having a piece of an apartment building's monthly rent, or the profits from a producing oil well, than would want the tax deductions for those investments.

Under Ball, tax shelters would still be sold. But so would other limited partnerships that were less tax related and more resembled traditional income investments. Ball ordered that the name of the tax investment department be changed to the Direct Investment Group to reflect this new focus on deals that could be sold to a wider range of customers.

Ball's most important change for tax shelters was unveiled in September 1982, a few weeks after he joined Bache. In a September 16 memo to every stockbroker in the firm, Ball announced that the firm was instituting a new policy "which will allow Bache account executives, their clients and the firm to share in the future together." The program offered new financial incentives for stockbrokers to sell limited partnerships in which a Bache subsidiary served as a co–general partner. In addition to the usual hefty commission, brokers who sold more than $25,000 of any such deal would share in half of the cash Bache received from the partnerships.

Essentially, brokers would receive a windfall, potentially worth tens of thousands of dollars a year. From then on, every broker in the retail system had an enormous self-interest in selling Bache's tax shelters, whether their clients needed them or not. Stockbrokers would get a cut of the kitty for sales of more than $25,000 worth of partnerships even if it was to elderly investors who couldn't bear the risk. It was a policy that, on its face, was a prescription for disaster.

"We believe that Bache is the only firm to have, as a matter of policy, this type of sharing arrangement," Ball wrote in his memo. "As a part of this, we hope to provide a wide variety of superbly crafted Bachepartnered tax directed investments. . . . It will make us the unquestioned leader in our industry."

What Ball left unsaid was what would happen to the other half of the money that went into the Bache entities. Most Bache brokers reasonably assumed that the cash would just go to the firm. But, in fact, under a separate compensation system, a hefty chunk of the money would instead go to selected executives within the tax shelter department. That compensation would come on top of the executives' salary and bonuses.

Darr would be the recipient of the largest share of that cash. But for the money to come in, the department had to find a stable of relatively weak tax shelter promoters who would be willing to split the general partner's role with Bache. The more of those deals the department sold—at times, regardless of quality—the more money Darr and his allies stood to make.

Days after the new shelter payment program started, Ball announced that the firm was changing its name to Prudential-Bache, a move that would tap the goodwill associated with the Prudential name. Almost simultaneously, Bache's old advertising agency was shunted aside, and the ads it created featuring the Bache broker as a hard-boiled hustler working twenty-four hours a day were shelved, as was the tag line "The winning attitude of Bache. Put it to work for you." Instead, Ball sought out a more visionary motto, one that appealed to the needs and insecurities of individual investors.

By November, television viewers around the country saw the seductive new ads that portrayed a dawn in finance. A red sun rose with unusual haste behind a city skyline, as a voice-over described a "bright new world of financial opportunity" that could be explored with the investment experts at Prudential-Bache, who were "part of Prudential, the Rock."

The ad closed on a single line: "Bring us your future."

Over the next few years, hundreds of thousands of investors would do just that.

PART TWO
BETRAYAL

CHAPTER 7

CLIFTON HARRISON BOUNDED OFF the elevator into the offices of the Prudential-Bache Direct Investment Group. He bantered for a moment with a receptionist, who allowed him to walk past without checking to see if he was expected, then headed briskly toward Darr's office. "Good morning, Vawn," Harrison drawled as he reached a desk outside the executive suite. "How are you this fine day?"

Darr's secretary, Vawn Major-Hazell, looked up at Harrison and smiled. By late 1982, Harrison was a frequent visitor to the department, using its offices as almost his personal New York headquarters. With his polish, expensive clothes and unflagging good manners, Harrison charmed many of the women in the department. He came off as a friendly—if hyperactive—senior executive. And with good reason. With Darr as his chief backer, Harrison had been catapulted from being just a convicted felon hustling for attention on Wall Street to a top sponsor of partnerships sold by Prudential-Bache.

As Major-Hazell and Harrison chatted, Darr emerged from his office, beaming. He and Harrison had grown especially close; Harrison was one of the few general partners Darr would meet alone, behind closed doors. Harrison, who loved to tell tales about his playboy exploits, bragged about escorting Darr to swank parties hosted by Manhattan's jet set, including Steve Rubell, the flamboyant cofounder of Studio 54, and Roy Cohn, the feared Manhattan lawyer and former sidekick to Senator Joseph McCarthy. Darr seemed giddy with excitement anytime Harrison planned to take him out for a night on the town.

On this day, Harrison wanted to take one of his victory laps around the department to thank the people who worked on his most recent deal. Shortly after he arrived, he and Darr headed toward the cramped cubicles in the due diligence area. Harrison popped his head into each and thanked everyone. Finally he arrived at the cubicle of David Levine, who handled much of the work on Harrison's deals.

"David," Harrison said as he shook Levine's hand, "I want to thank you. You've done a marvelous job." Harrison prattled a bit about his next deal, saying how it would be the best one yet, then he said good-bye.

As Levine watched Harrison stroll away with Darr, his polite smile dissolved into a scowl. *Why the hell are we doing business with this guy?*

No one in due diligence was happy about Harrison's prominence in the small camp of general partners that Darr was forming for the Direct Investment Group. His criminal record—and the decision to keep it secret from both brokers and investors—was only part of the problem. Even D'Elisa, the man who found Harrison, finally had decided that the man was little more than a fake.

"I am very uncomfortable with this guy," D'Elisa had told Levine while reviewing a Harrison deal. "He's got no expertise. He brings nothing to the table. And he's a felon."

D'Elisa knew that the success of a partnership often hinged on the integrity, knowledge, and experience of the deal's sponsor. Harrison came up deficient on all counts. His financial condition was far riskier than D'Elisa might have imagined when they first met; his debts left him with a negative net worth.

Worse, Harrison never lost the heavy spending habits he picked up in his days as an embezzler. He spent tens of thousands of dollars a month on dinners at fancy restaurants, nights at elegant hotels, limousines, furs, expensive wines, and flowers for his wife and girlfriends. The spending was so reckless that in 1981 Diners Club had threatened to cancel his account for failing to pay his balance of $14,597.43. Months later, he cracked the spending ceiling on his MasterCard. The man held up by Prudential-Bache as a top financial professional could not even manage his own credit cards.

Making matters more troublesome for the due diligence team, Harrison's knowledge about real estate was woefully thin. He rarely could answer their detailed questions about his deals. Instead, Harrison often just dismissed his questioners with a wave and a claim that he only dealt with the finest properties. But in truth, the deals Harrison championed were never his own real estate developments. Instead, he used his reputation as having an "in" at Prudential-Bache to persuade other developers to allow him to raise money for projects with a tax shelter. If the developer agreed, Prudential-Bache sold the shelter to its retail investors. The developer would then receive money to help finish construction. For his part, Harrison would be named the shelter's general partner, allowing him to charge investors huge annual management fees. Harrison, the developer, and Prudential-Bache all made money from the arrangement.

As far as D'Elisa was concerned, all Harrison deserved for that sort of effort was a one-time finder's fee, not the right to manage the properties. But Darr not only insisted that Harrison be named general partner, he also helped make sure those deals received only light due diligence. If D'Elisa or Levine asked too many questions, Harrison went over their heads to Darr. If due diligence did not want the deal approved, Darr simply took it to the department's investment committee, which rarely ignored his opinion. If there were five votes on the committee, the joke went, then Darr had four of them. After all, he played the largest role in deciding how everyone on the committee was paid. It was in no one's self-interest to cross him.

What made Darr's embrace of the Harrison deals all the more inexplicable was the fact that the department didn't need the business. Scores of reputable corporations, developers, and syndicators were knocking at the firm's door with partnerships to sell. The list of potential general partners included a number of high-profile, high-quality groups, such as Lincoln Properties, a large real estate company in Chicago. Although the firm did business with such groups, the volume never equaled that of the Harrison deals.

It all seemed very suspicious. From D'Elisa, the real estate due diligence team knew that Darr took money at Josephthal and that Harrison had been imprisoned for embezzlement. Put two people like that together, the reasoning went, and sparks had to fly. It became an article of faith among many in the department—despite a lack of evidence—that Harrison was paying Darr to sell his shelters. When Harrison's huge fees were calculated, executives would joke about what percentage would line Darr's pockets. Even a trip Darr and Harrison took to Europe was fodder for black humor.

"They've got to go check out their Swiss bank accounts sometime," Levine said when he heard about the trip.*

Even with all their scorn, the due diligence team knew that Harrison

---

*Harrison admitted that he gave Darr expensive gifts, including a $9,000 painting— a charge Darr denied. Both men denied that Darr ever received improper cash payments. Also, although Darr told the government that he had an interest in an account at Swiss Canto Bank as part of another investment, he said he did not control a Swiss account. See Notes and Sources.

could market the hell out of himself and his deals. That was largely because Harrison had no qualms about putting the deals together in a way that ensured the highest tax breaks possible for investors—either by pouring tax-deductible debt onto the building project or by relentlessly pushing up the appraisals of the properties. Of course, that aggressiveness also raised the risk that the partnerships might anger the Internal Revenue Service, but few brokers or investors seemed to worry about that.

There was so much focus on the tax benefits of the deals that few investors noticed the many fees that had been lathered on by Harrison and the Direct Investment Group. The charges were so thick that the chances of obtaining a capital gain on the investments were virtually obliterated. Through the endless assortment of fees, more than 20 cents out of every dollar invested by clients immediately went into the pockets of Harrison and Prudential-Bache.

To bring more fees into Prudential-Bache, Darr set up a complex web of corporations, such as Bache Properties and Bache-Harrison Associates. Though the arrangement was not disclosed to investors, those corporations allowed Darr and other executives he chose to share in some of the cash flow from the partnerships.

Darr often played hardball in negotiations on how much money those corporations would receive—once going so far as refusing to hand over investor cash that had already been raised unless Harrison agreed to pay higher fees to the firm and to Bache Properties. By directing the fees to the shell companies, Darr sidestepped the restrictions imposed by the National Association of Securities Dealers on the amount a brokerage firm could charge in selling a security. The Bache subsidiaries were not selling securities—they were monitoring, consulting, and advising.

"It was ridiculous. If we could have figured out a way to charge a fee for breathing, we would have done it," one member of the department said years later.

By 1982, the money was rolling in from the huge fees tacked onto the Harrison partnerships. But, unknown to Darr, Harrison had planted a time bomb—in one of their very first deals. That partnership, called Bessemer–Key West L.P., raised about $4.4 million. The partnership was designed to tap into Harrison's European contacts. It raised the money exclusively from investors in West Germany, where Bache had a strong presence. But the partnership was a tough sell—it invested in two shopping centers based in Bessemer, Alabama, and Key West, Florida, hardly the places where a German investor would be inclined to put his money.

So Harrison made his investors a promise. On May 20, 1981, he wrote letters to all of the potential foreign investors and guaranteed that the deal would be a success. If, by 1986, they were dissatisfied with the investment, Harrison said he would repurchase their partnership stake for 150 percent of the original cost—putting himself on the hook for $6.6 million. To the investors, the promise was even more attractive because it came on the letterhead of Bache-Harrison, the corporation set up as a device for charging fees. With a commitment for guaranteed profits, apparently backed by a large American brokerage firm, foreign investors snapped up the deal.

Harrison didn't tell any senior Pru-Bache executive in New York about his guarantee, including Darr. Worse, he didn't have anything close to the money he needed to live up to his promise. At the time he sent out the letters, Harrison's net worth was in the deficit column, at a total of negative $350,000. If he ever had to make good on his commitment, he would be wiped out. Under federal securities laws, it was the kind of fact that had to be disclosed to investors in every subsequent Harrison deal. But since Harrison didn't tell Bache, the firm raised millions of dollars for him over the next few years without revealing his financial guarantee in the deal for the German investors.

The first big Harrison deal in the United States came that same year with a partnership called Barbizon New York Ltd. The partnership invested in the Barbizon, a twenty-four-story hotel in the heart of Manhattan. With Harrison as the general partner, the deal raised $6 million for refurbishing the hotel. Investors expected tax deductions and hoped to enjoy the cash flow the hotel received from guests.

The deal was immensely profitable to Bache and Harrison. Harrison was paid $100,000 a year in the first year—and $150,000 each year afterward— as a "servicing fee." Metro-Housing, a Harrison affiliate set up for the Barbizon deal, tacked on an "incentive management fee" of at least 4 percent of the deal's cash flow.

Still, Harrison was more than generous to Bache with his investors' money. The firm was paid $540,000 in commissions and expenses. In other words, 9 percent of the money contributed by the investors immediately went into the firm's pockets. Bache-Harrison, the jointly owned corporation, slapped on another $78,000 in fees for finding a loan. Then Bache International, another affiliate, received $25,000 for arranging the same loan. And although the arrangement was not disclosed to investors, Bache Properties would also receive 20 percent of certain money received by Metro-Housing. In the end, at least 17 percent of the money invested in the deal went into the pockets of the brokerage, its executives, and Harrison.

Although the firm didn't tell any of the investors that Harrison was a convicted felon, it became a point of great importance almost immediately after the deal closed. Every luxury hotel needs to be able to sell alcohol in its restaurants and through room service. But that requires a liquor license from the state. In 1982, Harrison decided to apply for a license and picked up all the necessary forms from the New York State Liquor Authority. He went down the application, answering no to each question on such matters as whether he had been known by another name or had ever filed for bankruptcy.

He turned to the second page. There, in the middle of the document, was the question: "Have you ever been convicted of any felony or of any other crime?" Harrison scribbled the answer "yes, misappropriation of bank funds." Then he studied the other requirements: He would have to submit his fingerprints to the government, and his filing would become a matter of public record. Harrison tossed aside the form. He refused to complete it, even when bankers who lent money to the deal begged him. Harrison would not create a new public document that would disclose his criminal record.

Clifton Harrison, whose felony conviction wasn't viewed by Darr as sufficient reason to prevent him from raising millions from retail clients, could not legally sell any of those same people a glass of wine.

Peter Archbold, the manager of Pru-Bache's Dallas branch, leaned back in his chair as he listened to one of his fellow branch managers who had just called with a question: Why hadn't the Dallas branch done more sales in a Clifton Harrison deal involving a Texas property?

Archbold had figured someone would ask him that at some point. The Dallas office was one of the firm's jewels and was a huge seller. Archbold had earned the reputation as a team player from the time he was an assistant manager in Binghamton, New York, in 1972. By 1982, Dallas had one of the best collections of prospective clients for tax shelters—booming oil in Houston and rising real estate prices in Dallas produced a surplus of wealthy investors with no idea what to do with their money. Because Harrison was a Texan, it seemed likely that the branch would sell out the deal all by itself. But the Dallas brokers knew something the rest of the firm hadn't been told.

"Well, Harrison is pretty well known here," Archbold said. "He's a convicted felon."

"You're kidding."

"No, I'm not," Archbold said.

The two managers talked for a bit and then hung up. A few minutes later, Archbold's telephone rang again. It was Bob Sherman, the head of retail, and Jim Darr. Both men sounded absolutely livid. The other branch manager had just called New York in a rage, wanting to know why he had never been told that the firm was doing business with a felon.

"What are you doing putting down our deals?" Sherman demanded.

Archbold was taken aback. He hadn't done anything except tell another manager the truth. Obviously, this was a touchy point in New York. So before he got into any more trouble, he agreed that he wouldn't say anything again that would put down the deal.

A few days later, Archbold received a telephone call from another branch manager, again asking why the Dallas office wasn't selling the Harrison deals. Did the brokers in Dallas know something that other people in the firm should know?

"No comment," Archbold replied.

The other manager tried again to finagle an answer, but Archbold refused to budge. He wouldn't tell his colleague anything. Within a few minutes of the frustrating call coming to an end, his telephone rang. It was Darr and Sherman on the line again.

"What the hell are you doing saying 'no comment'?" Sherman asked.

"Well, what do you want me to say?" Archbold replied. "You don't want me to answer their questions. Tell me what I should say and I'll say it."

Darr and Sherman mumbled a response. They told Archbold to be more careful but never told him what to say. Archbold hung up with the uncomfortable feeling that New York was trying too hard to keep Harrison's background a secret.

Tom Huzella, the biggest-selling partnership broker in Pittsburgh, was flattered to hear that Clifton Harrison was on the phone. "Tommy, thank you for selling the Barbizon," Harrison said, drawling Huzella's name out so it sounded like "Tah-may."

"You are one of my key people," Harrison said. "Now, you help me with my next deal, and I'll send you and that lovely Carol of yours to Monte Carlo."

The ego stroking had its intended effect. Huzella, along with a number of other top brokers, became a huge fan of the Texas developer. It wasn't just that his deals had enormous tax breaks, or that Harrison knew how to flatter brokers. Probably the biggest selling point was Darr. Whenever he spoke to the brokers, he made it clear that the full resources of his department were behind Harrison.

Huzella had been impressed by that when Darr first introduced Harrison to him in late 1980. While Huzella was visiting New York on other business, Darr called him into his office, where he saw an impeccably dressed man with long, flowing hair.

"Tom, this is Clifton Harrison," Darr said. "He's a world-renowned real estate investment banker. He's been very successful in the Dallas real estate market and knows the New York market. We're going to be doing a lot of things with him." He was someone with almost a Midas touch, Darr said.

As Darr spoke, Harrison reached into his pocket and produced an oversized business card that carried a European address. He offered it to Huzella. As they spoke, Huzella noticed that Harrison could not maintain eye contact. Instead, Harrison was always looking around the room, as if he feared missing something. It struck Huzella as odd. But, if Darr recommended Harrison so strongly, Huzella figured he must be a first-class general partner. So, when Harrison's deals started coming out, Huzella eagerly told his clients about them.

"We have this wonderful investment with a New York City property called the Barbizon," he told prospective clients. "It's being put together by Bache with Harrison Freedman Associates, an internationally known real estate developer."

Eventually in his pitch, Huzella, like every broker in the system, assured potential clients of the investment's safety.

"This has the full blessing of the firm," he said. "We spend a lot of money on due diligence to make sure everything is done right."

D'Elisa stormed into his office in Smithtown, New York, and called in his secretary for some dictation. He had finally had it with Clifton Harrison. The man refused to cooperate with any of the requests from the due diligence department. If Levine or D'Elisa asked for financial records to back something up, Harrison would just refuse, or instead would go over their heads to Darr. Harrison failed to show up for appointments to review his deals. Even when he did come, he never had done his homework—he couldn't answer some of the simplest questions. On this day in 1982,

D'Elisa decided to throw down the gauntlet. If he couldn't get Harrison under control, maybe some memos in the file might make Darr do it.

After his secretary sat down, D'Elisa dictated a memo to Harrison. "I fail to understand why we have so many problems in the deals we do with you," D'Elisa said. "We require adherence to procedures that we have gone over again and again with you in Dallas and New York. These continued problems may require us to reevaluate future programs with you."

Then D'Elisa told his secretary to take another memo, this time to Darr. "Clifton seems to feel that he has leverage in dealing with me through his close relationship with you. I am sure you will agree that he, like any other sponsor, including some of our proprietary sponsors, must follow strict offering and submission procedures." He added bluntly, "I refuse to have myself or my staff antagonized by someone who is not part of this organization."

Once his secretary finished typing the memos, D'Elisa reviewed them and shipped copies to Darr, Proscia, and Peter Fass, the outside lawyer who worked on Harrison deals. That, D'Elisa thought, might shake things up a little. The head of real estate due diligence had put a memo in the file saying that a sponsor was using his influence over the head of the department to avoid following standard procedures. It was the kind of document that might cripple any defense if the firm was sued over a Harrison partnership. The memos had the intended effect—for a short time. Darr called to assure D'Elisa that Harrison would start cooperating. And he did, for about three weeks. But then Harrison again started refusing to cooperate with the due diligence department.

If D'Elisa expected that his protests would slow down Darr's appetite for Harrison deals, he was disappointed. The department soon started marketing one of the biggest real estate deals in its history, called the Archives New York Limited Partnership. The deal, with Harrison as the general partner, was a $16.5 million offering—an astonishing sum at the time.

Proscia handled the marketing out of New York. In consultation with Darr and Harrison, he developed an aggressive strategy: Branch offices were canvassed to find brokers who would want to sell the product; regional marketers for the tax shelter department were telephoned and ordered to include discussions of Harrison in any future meetings; and plans were drawn up for training brokers about the tax shelter deals. On Harrison's tab, ten of the firm's top brokers were flown to Manhattan for a dinner hosted by Darr and Harrison at the expensive 21 Club.

Amid all the hoopla, no one noticed the deal's fatal flaws. It needed at least $40 million in financing but had access to only $30 million in loans at any one time. In other words, from the first day the partnership was formed, the Archives deal was already short $10 million in cash. Even the loans it had were dicey—they were conditioned on the completion of a construction budget. The offering documents implied a budget existed; in fact, there was none.

The biggest, most public deal in the history of the department was doomed from the start.

The sounds of a raucous party spilled out from a private room on the second floor of Smith & Wollensky. Prudential-Bache's entire partnership department—from Darr to the regional marketers to the secretaries—was at the Manhattan steakhouse celebrating the successful completion of the Archives deal, one so large that it would mean big bonuses for the department's professionals. So, on this night in the fall of 1982, Harrison hosted the dinner at one of Darr's favorite restaurants. It was becoming a tradition that general partners would buy the department dinner at Smith & Wollensky once every three months.

The dinners had all the subtlety of a Roman orgy. They were nothing like the staid, civilized, and professional closing dinners that sometimes accompany the completion of a successful deal on Wall Street. "The Smith & Wollensky dinners were epic in their grossness and expense," one department executive who worked at a number of Wall Street firms said years later. "To this day, I've never seen anything else like it. And the fact that we were making somebody outside the department pay for it was disgusting."

In the days leading up to the Harrison dinner, Darr wandered about the department, speaking to female employees.

"What are you going to be wearing at Smith & Wollensky?" he asked. "Are you going to wear a nice dress?"

By the night of the dinner, the excitement was overflowing. Some members of the department purchased new clothes just for the occasion. At the appointed time, everyone ambled into the banquet room and found a seat around the long tables arranged in a C shape.

Then the heavy drinking started. As master of ceremonies, Darr wandered about the room with a knife in his hand, cutting off the tie of any executive who didn't turn away fast enough. Later, he stood up and gave a speech, hurling insults at Harrison, the host, as well as at members of the department.

With the cost on someone else's tab, executives, secretaries, and other staff members ordered enough food for several meals. Giant five- and six-pound lobsters were delivered to the table in front of a single person, along with huge steaks and side dishes. At the end of dinner, they loaded the extra food into doggy bags and took it home. Everyone knew that after a Smith & Wollensky party, they could expect free dinners at home for days.

Even the due diligence executives were ordering with abandon, although not for the free food. Instead, the evening at Smith & Wollensky was their one opportunity to get back at Harrison. If they couldn't stop his deals, at least they could run up his tab. During the meal, a secretary leaned over to David Levine. She showed him the wine list and asked if it would be all right to order a particularly expensive bottle of wine. Levine looked at the list and saw the bottle cost close to $150.

"Oh, yeah," he said. "A $150 bottle of wine? No problem."

The drinking and revelry went on for hours. The marketing executives started a competition of trying to drink more of the expensive wine than anyone else. Darr, who told everyone he was something of a wine buff, always had his own favorite brand and year—even if it was not on the wine list—brought in special in a crystal decanter. Pittman also liked wine and begged Darr for a taste of the good stuff, but Darr refused.

During the meal, two executives, who by then were completely drunk, slid under the table and began crawling around the room, looking up the women's dresses. One marketer picked up an extremely expensive brand of champagne and downed it straight out of the bottle. When he finished, he hurled the bottle across the room. It whizzed past Freddie Kotek, a member of the due diligence department, barely missing his head before hitting the wall.

Following the after-dinner drinks, the drunken and sated ordered cigars all around. Executives stood, stumbling out of the room, cigars in hand. A waiter walked into the room carrying a leather case with the bill, which he placed in front of Harrison.

Kotek and other members of the department were walking past Harrison as he opened the case and looked at the bill. Harrison looked positively stunned.

"I don't believe it," Harrison muttered to no one in particular. "Six thousand dollars for a dinner, and I didn't get no pussy."

The due diligence executives looked at each other and rolled their eyes. *Boy, this is a class act we're working with,* Kotek thought.

They strolled out of the room as Harrison put down his American Express card to pay the bill. They felt satisfied that they had at least been able to stick it a little bit to Darr's friend.

But in truth, the dinner didn't cost Harrison a penny. Like all of the Smith & Wollensky dinners, held four times a year for much of the rest of the decade, the general partner simply submitted the bill to the partnership he ran. It was, after all, a legitimate business expense. So the cost of the dinners didn't come out of the pocket of Harrison, or Darr, or any of the people who gorged themselves on those nights.

Instead, the bills for the department's drunken revelry were paid out of the savings that small retail clients had entrusted to Prudential-Bache.

Later that same year, on a sultry Texas Sunday in October 1982, the relationship between Harrison and Darr reached a high point, in front of about 150 spectators.

They gathered at St. Michael and All Angels Episcopal Church, a place so well known for its wealthy parishioners that Dallas wags call it "St. Mink's and All Cadillacs." In the elaborate church, Harrison waited that day to marry his fourth wife, Alexandra, less than a year after divorcing his third wife. Joining him in the front of the church as one of his two best men was Darr, who had flown down from New York specially. Executives in the department marveled that, over so short a period of time, Darr had apparently become Harrison's best friend.

Harrison liked to brag that this time he was marrying into money: His new wife's family, he told friends, controlled a major international company. Wealth showed in the apparent cost of the wedding—between the service at St. Michael and the reception at the tony Northwood Country Club, some guests estimated that the price tag for the day must have reached as high as $60,000.

A few weeks later, Harrison returned from his honeymoon and immediately headed to the Direct Investment Group. He was roaming about the department when he stopped at the desk of Kathy Eastwick, the former compliance administrator who now worked as a product manager. Eastwick congratulated Harrison on his new bride. After thanking her, he cracked a smile.

"You won't believe what Mr. Darr did to me," Harrison said.

"What did he do to you now?" Eastwick asked.

"Well, you know I've told you he never spends a penny," Harrison said. "But do you believe that man made me pay for his airline tickets for him to come to my wedding?"

D'Elisa set his portfolio briefcase on the kitchen table, opened its flap, and carefully slid a tape recorder inside. He plugged a microphone wire into the recorder and slowly laid the wire up the inside of the briefcase and over its opening at the top. Then he tore off a piece of electrical tape and attached the tiny, sensitive microphone to the outside of the briefcase. He closed the flap over the microphone; it was hidden, but pointed toward an opening between the flap and the briefcase. D'Elisa turned on the recorder and checked it out. It picked up his voice perfectly.

He stood back and examined his handiwork one more time. No one would be able to see the microphone was there. Finally he was ready to go tell Darr he was quitting. Whatever tricks Darr decided to play in response would be captured on tape. It was the only way D'Elisa could think of to protect himself from Darr's manipulative tactics.

By May 1983, Darr was one of the most powerful people at Prudential-Bache. Despite the initial promise when Ball took over, the firm was still struggling with heavy losses. The Direct Investment Group was one of the rare divisions in the firm that was actually making money. And Ball believed in feeding success. Whatever resources Darr wanted had been given to the department. In speeches to brokers, Ball had almost always thrown in a line of support for the partnership effort. Ball frequently invited Darr to make presentations to senior executives. No one could have missed Ball's seal of approval for Darr and the Direct Investment Group.

That particularly delighted Bob Sherman, the head of retail and Darr's boss. To him, Darr's partnerships appeared the way to almost limitless revenues—and fat bonuses for all of the executives involved.

"Darr's producing a lot of money," Sherman told a group of senior retail executives at the time. "He's going to be making a big contribution to retail." To some executives, Sherman also said that Darr had secretly confided that he had once worked with the Central Intelligence Agency. That, Sherman said, was particularly exciting.

Even with the support that the department was receiving from the firm, D'Elisa did not think he could work there anymore. He thought the department was doing bad business. He had watched all the quality people either get forced out or simply abandon the firm in disgust. Of the Futon Five, only he and Dennis Marron still survived. Too many of the executives who remained were concerned about the wrong things. In D'Elisa's mind, Darr had corrupted people with the easy money that his department was bringing in. Too many of them had seemed to forget that this business wasn't about living the highest life.

Despite his frustration, D'Elisa had stayed with the firm because he worked out on Long Island, some forty miles away from Darr. But weeks earlier, Darr had called to say that D'Elisa would have to start working in Manhattan. D'Elisa immediately had started looking for another job and had found one at Bear Stearns & Company. He didn't want to work alongside Darr; D'Elisa didn't want to risk being corrupted, too.

After setting up his tape recorder, D'Elisa traveled to Prudential-Bache headquarters and went to Darr's office. Before walking in, he turned on the recorder.

"Relax, John," Darr said as D'Elisa sat down. "I know why you're here. I know you've got a job offer from another firm and I know you're seriously considering it."

There it is again, D'Elisa thought. Ever since the Futon Five fiasco, Darr delighted in telling members of the department that he knew everything they did and said. Dennis Marron theorized that Darr somehow was listening in on their telephone calls. Others thought it more likely that there were spies in the department.

"So, what would it take to make you happy here?" Darr asked.

For you to leave, D'Elisa thought. He said the Bear Stearns offer was too good to pass up. It was making him a partner, which Prudential-Bache couldn't do, since it was not a partnership. Plus, he said, Bear Stearns was paying him a lot more money.

"Look," Darr replied. "I can't make you a partner, but this is what I can do. I'll make you a senior VP. I'll give you a $50,000 raise. And I'll vest you immediately."

The offer was unbelievable. The raise was enormous. But the vesting offer was more important: That would guarantee D'Elisa a share in the fees and cash flow pouring into the corporations, like Bache Properties, that Darr set up for the partnerships. Each day, he was establishing new corporations, such as Prudential-Bache Energy and Prudential-Bache Minerals, among others, and they were bringing in millions of dollars a year. Darr's offer could easily have been worth $2 million. Still, it wasn't good enough.

"Jim, I don't want to commute into the city every day."

A look of anger flashed across Darr's face. "You're willing to commute into the city every day for Bear Stearns, aren't you? Why aren't you willing to commute into the city for me?"

"Well, I just would prefer not to."

Finally Darr caved. D'Elisa could stay on Long Island, as long as he shipped one of his staff members to Manhattan. Then Darr would live up to all the other financial promises. The offer was too sweet to simply reject out of hand.

"All right, Jim, I'll consider doing the deal," he said.

"Come back to me tomorrow, and I'll talk with the necessary people," Darr replied. "But it's a done deal."

The next afternoon, D'Elisa couldn't bring himself to make the final commitment. He needed more time to think about it. Even with all that Darr had put on the table, he still was not convinced that it was worth it. He felt as if he were selling his soul.

After a sleepless night with his head spinning, D'Elisa decided to take the deal. He went into Manhattan the next morning and walked into Darr's office.

"All right, Jim, if we're going to do this, I want it in writing," he said. "I want a contract."

"OK, I'll give you a contract," Darr replied. "But forget about the Long Island office. You could have had it yesterday. But you're a day late. You can't have it today."

D'Elisa stood up and shook Darr's hand. "Thanks a lot," he said, and he turned to walk out of the office. That was the end. He quit his job.

If Darr had been so quick to back out on the Long Island commitment, D'Elisa knew that everything else would vanish, too. He was tired of playing Darr's games. He just wanted out.

D'Elisa took the elevator downstairs, pushed through the building's revolving door, and began walking briskly down the street. With each step he took, he felt an enormous weight lifting off his shoulders. It was over. After the years of battling and intrigue, it finally had come to an end.

He didn't even want to guess how long the people he left behind would survive.

Clifton Harrison grabbed a chair in a conference room at Prudential-Bache and threw it against the wall.

"Goddamn it, you asshole!" he screamed at David Levine. "What's the matter with you? This is a great deal!"

Levine stood his ground. He wasn't going to pass on the latest partnership that Harrison brought into the firm in June 1983. By then, Levine was far along on the due diligence learning curve. He knew that Darr and Harrison were pushing bad deals through the department. This latest one, called Exchange Center Limited Partnership, was the worst. Levine decided that, this time, he was going to stick with his analysis, regardless of the pressure.

The $32 million Exchange Center deal made little sense to anyone on the due diligence team. It was an awful transaction for investors. The deal would build a thirty-nine-story red-granite office tower on South Lasalle Street in the heart of Chicago's financial district. The fees and expenses were so heavy that Levine did not see how any investor could make a penny on the deal. All told, Harrison, Prudential-Bache, and the Direct Investment Group would pocket more than 20 percent of the money that was raised.

When the Chicago deal first came in the door, Levine decided to pass it to Jeff Talbert, a new, young member of the due diligence group. He wanted to see how Talbert would react. After all, Talbert knew nothing about Harrison's criminal background or the troubles that his other deals had experienced. It was the best way to get an honest response. Levine dropped the documents on Talbert's desk without telling him any of the details.

"Let me know what you think of this one," Levine said.

Talbert started reviewing the documents and, after just a few minutes, decided that Levine must be kidding. The deal was ridiculous: It assumed it could charge rent of $32 a square foot by 1985, when the best estimates for the rental costs in that year averaged around $27. Nobody would pay the extra $5. With such unrealistically positive assumptions, the deal had to flop. Talbert carried the documents back over to Levine's cubicle. Freddie Kotek and some other members of the department were there talking with him.

"I've gone over this, and I was surprised," Talbert said. "There are lots of problems. I can't even figure out why we're looking at this deal."

"It's a Cliffy deal," Levine replied.

Talbert looked perplexed. "Who's Cliffy?"

Kotek spoke up. "Cliffy, Clifton Harrison. Cliffy's a guy we do deals with, a friend of Darr's."

Talbert could see the disgust on his colleagues' faces. "Well, what's wrong with the Cliffy deals?"

"They're all like that one," one of his coworkers replied. "They suck."

"And he's a convicted felon," Levine added.

The four talked about what should be done with the Chicago deal. Talbert said that if these Harrison deals were as bad as everyone said, he was worried about them. What would happen when they blew up? Brokers would get mad, and then the department wouldn't be able to sell anything. It seemed like an incredibly risky way to run the business.

Then it came up that there was one other Harrison deal in the pipeline, Fountain Square Limited Partnership, which would raise a little more than $6 million for a building in downtown Cincinnati. Maybe, someone joked, they should appease Darr by letting the Cincinnati deal through while killing the $32 million Chicago deal. At least that way, less money would be on the line.

Levine looked back at the documents, steaming. D'Elisa was not there anymore to fight for them. But, Levine thought, if the newest person in the department could throw aside the Chicago deal that quickly, he was not going to let it through. This one he was going to take to the mat. He rejected the deal out of hand.

But Darr refused to accept Levine's opinion. He and Harrison called Levine into a meeting in a conference room and double-teamed him. Levine refused to change his decision.

Later, Darr told Levine that since there was such a split opinion, the matter would be taken to the department's investment committee for a decision. Levine knew what that meant: Unless he could think of something, the deal would go through. Darr completely controlled those investment committee meetings.

Levine walked back to his desk with a new resolve. If Darr wanted to present the deal to the committee, fine. But Levine was going to make sure they knew, in a written memo, about the deal's problems. Word spread that Levine was going all out in his effort to kill the deal.

The investment committee met soon after. On that day, Joseph Quinn, a former official with Chase Manhattan Bank, took over D'Elisa's job as the new head of due diligence. Shortly before the meeting, Levine spoke with Quinn and told him about what was happening with the Chicago deal.

The meeting started later that morning in the department's boardroom. Senior executives, including Darr, gathered around the conference table as Levine distributed copies of his two-page memorandum on the Exchange Place deal. For the next half hour, Levine went through his memo, point by point: The deal was one-sided, in favor of the general partners over the investors; the rents were above market; the real estate market was soft. He supplied a stream of data to support his position.

Finally Levine finished his presentation. With such a massive criticism on paper, he figured the meeting was over. He couldn't see how it would be possible for even Darr to push this deal through. Levine started gathering his things.

"Now, wait a minute," Darr said. "We have an interesting problem. We've had two people who did the due diligence here, and they don't agree."

Levine looked up, stunned. "What?" He couldn't understand what Darr was talking about. He ran due diligence for real estate private placements. And everyone in his department agreed with his analysis.

Darr motioned toward someone sitting at the table. "Ralph, why don't you tell us what you found," he said.

One of the department's appraisers stood up and began passing out copies of a second memo. Levine couldn't believe it. Appraisers figured out fair values of purchase prices for buildings. They never reviewed deals for their investment quality on their own. They didn't have the background to do it.

This is a total setup, Levine thought.

For the next few minutes, the appraiser described the benefits of the Exchange Place deal. He trembled as he spoke, obviously very nervous and uncomfortable. In Levine's mind, the report made no sense. But Darr had managed to regain control. The appraiser finished his report and sat back down.

"Well, thank you very much, Ralph," Darr said. "Obviously, David, you need to go back and take another look at this." The investment committee gave the go-ahead for the department to proceed with the deal.

Levine and Quinn headed out of the meeting room to Quinn's office, where Levine slumped into a chair, pale and wiped out. The stress from trying to do his job properly was overwhelming.

"I'm living in the Soviet Union, trying to fight the KGB," Levine muttered.

Quinn looked nervous. "This is a nightmare," he said. "I don't want to do this deal."

Finally Quinn came up with a suggestion: They would proceed with the deal, but they would question it to death. Darr couldn't stop them from demanding more information from the developer and general partner. So they would just keep demanding more and more financial records until the developer Harrison had found walked away out of frustration. Levine agreed.

As the due diligence team learned of what had happened in the conference room, most of them began to say the same thing: Darr was creating a monster. He didn't have any interest in their judgment about deal quality—he just wanted to keep the products coming. There was only so much Quinn, Levine, and everyone else could do to hold him off. Someday, the deals he pushed through would start falling apart. When that happened, there would be hell to pay. A lot of careers were going to be ruined, potentially even their own.

Dennis Marron closed a bound report filled with financial data from NRM Energy Company. He looked out of his office window at a view of the Brooklyn Bridge and sighed. Marron knew he had to block Prudential-Bache from doing its next big oil partnership with NRM. Nothing was particularly terrible about NRM—Pru-Bache had already sold a number of the oil company's partnerships. But Darr seemed very close to the NRM executives, talked about them frequently, even traveled to their Dallas headquarters a few times to visit. That was enough to make Marron suspicious. He saw the havoc that Darr's friendships were causing for the due diligence team in real estate. Marron wasn't going to allow another Clifton Harrison problem to develop with the oil and gas partnerships.

Marron was frustrated—handling due diligence for Darr had an Alice-in-Wonderland quality about it. The numbers, the experts, the market all said one thing. But each morning, the due diligence team stepped through the looking glass into the Direct Investment Group, and everything turned on its head. The old standards didn't matter. If Darr wanted to do a particular deal, it was almost impossible to stop him.

This time, the deal was too important. For months, Marron and Douglas Holbrook, a specialist on energy financing who recently had been hired out of the firm's corporate finance division, had been trying to put together a unique energy deal with Prudential Insurance. It would be an energy income deal, in which investors' money is used to purchase oil reserves that had already been discovered and proven. Then, if the partnership is well managed, it makes money for investors by pumping the oil out of the ground and selling it at a profit.

The idea was attracting attention at the highest levels. Ball himself was involved in discussing some of the terms of the deal. He had explored selling a similar partnership at Hutton, and it interested him. As this would be the first major product involving Prudential Insurance, Ball wanted to make sure everything was handled just right.

If Prudential Insurance agreed to invest, the deal would be enormously appealing to retail investors. What client wouldn't want to invest money alongside one of the world's largest companies? Making it even better, Holbrook was insisting that some of the money paid to general partners up front—known as the promote—be held back until clients received their original investment back from partnership distributions. That would help put more investor cash to work and improve the chances for success.

The partnership would also have big benefits for Prudential-Bache. One of the Direct Investment Group's subsidiary corporations, called Prudential-Bache Energy Production, would serve as a co–general partner in the energy income deals. Then it could charge management fees and snap up a piece of the cash flow. It could be enormously lucrative for the firm, and also for select members of the Direct Investment Group, such as Darr, who would share in the money flowing into the subsidiary company.

Darr liked the idea as soon as he heard it, and he immediately told Marron that he wanted NRM brought into it as the managing general partner. "They're the best guys for this," he said.

Marron objected. As far as he knew, NRM had little involvement with institutional investors like Prudential Insurance. Other companies had stronger financial positions. He did not mention his most serious concern: Darr's relationship with NRM.

"Go see NRM," Darr commanded.

A short time later, Marron and Holbrook were on the plane to Dallas to meet with NRM executives. After about an hour of speaking with them, neither Marron nor Holbrook was much impressed. They struck Holbrook as having more knowledge about partnership sales than they did about the oil and gas business.

As the last stop on their due diligence trip, Marron and Holbrook visited the bank that was financing much of NRM's operations. The banker in charge of the account praised NRM as a fast-growing company with strong finances.

"Would you lend NRM more money if they needed it?" Marron asked.

"Oh, absolutely," the banker replied.

Wait a minute, Holbrook thought. *We're leaving something out of this equation.* "If Prudential–Bache stopped raising capital for NRM, would you still lend them money?" he asked.

The banker looked shocked by the question. "Well," he said, "no, we wouldn't."

The conclusion was obvious: NRM was getting bigger because

Prudential-Bache was raising money for it. If the firm stopped, the growth could stop as well. Marron and Holbrook were trying to judge the wave height in the ocean by examining the wake from their own boat.

"Man," Holbrook said after they left the bank. "We've got to figure out a way to get these guys out of this deal."

On the three-hour flight home, Marron and Holbrook plotted how to ditch NRM. If they found another oil company that Prudential Insurance liked, Darr could never stop it. But unless they stumbled on a solid company soon, they knew that, no matter what their objections, NRM was going to do the deal. They needed to move fast.

Holbrook was sure he was having lunch with executives from Crawford Energy. That was what he remembered hearing from Ed Devereaux, the partnership marketer in the New York region. He barely knew Crawford but figured there would be no harm in meeting them. Even if he didn't strike up any business, at least he would get a free meal.

So in early 1983, Holbrook and Devereaux went to the City Midday Club at 140 Broadway, just a short walk from Wall Street. As they got off the elevator, Holbrook recognized Rich Gilman, a former insurance company executive he had met over some deals years before. Holbrook had immense respect for Gilman and strode quickly toward him to say hello.

Holbrook was surprised to find out that Gilman was one of the two people he was meeting. Gilman introduced the other man as Anton Rice III, known to everyone as Tony. Holbrook took almost an immediate dislike to Rice. A tall man with graying temples, blow-dried hair, and French cuffs, Rice struck Holbrook as striving too hard to hit some Wall Street image. He had a little too much of a salesman's smell to him, all polish and gentility.

As the four men followed the maître d' to a table, Holbrook thought fast. Gilman had introduced Rice as the chief financial officer of Graham Resources, not Crawford Energy. Gilman apparently worked with Graham, too. Holbrook had heard of that company before. Headquartered in Metairie, Louisiana, Graham had been founded in 1975 by Ford Graham, a sharp and crusty oilman who started in the business in 1938, and his son, John, a Princeton graduate and lawyer.

Holbrook remembered that he had seen a tombstone advertisement in the *Wall Street Journal* in 1980 announcing that the St. Paul Fire and Marine Insurance Company had committed to investing close to $90 million with Graham in an energy property acquisition deal. If Graham was good enough to attract St. Paul, he thought, and employed quality people like Gilman, maybe it would be the right choice for the energy income deal.

As the men dined on fresh salmon and beef tenderloin, Rice laid out the purpose for the meeting: Graham had been raising money for drilling partnerships with Merrill Lynch but now wanted to do business with Pru-Bache. Rice mentioned that he once worked for Merrill and knew Darr from there. He left out the fact that Darr had tried to get a job at Graham while still working at Josephthal. It didn't strike Rice as important.

Holbrook listened politely, then shook his head.

"We're not interested in a drilling deal," he said. "We're looking at doing an income fund. Maybe if you're interested in something like that we might be able to talk."

The conversation was all very sketchy, without any hard proposals. After more than an hour, the meal came to an end, and everyone stood up from the table. "Well, it was great seeing you, Rich," Holbrook said. "Let's not lose track of each other. Maybe we have something we can work on here."

Holbrook and Devereaux said good-bye to their hosts and hustled back to the firm. Holbrook strode into Marron's office immediately.

"I may have found an option to NRM," he said.

Marron listened as Holbrook excitedly described his meeting. He spoke highly of Gilman, adding that if Graham had sent only Rice, he never would have thought about doing business with them. Graham had done transactions and was a company of real substance. Marron liked what he had heard. He told Holbrook to call Prudential Insurance and see what they thought. Maybe they had found a way to beat Darr at his own game.

Darr stopped Marron in the hallway as he was about to walk past.

"Dennis, I want you to get control of Holbrook. He's yours. Control him." Then he walked away.

Marron knew that Darr was angry at his team. Holbrook had no qualms about speaking his mind on a deal and never seemed afraid to tell Darr when he disagreed with him. Marron knew that alone would be enough to infuriate Darr. But now, he and Holbrook had displaced NRM with Graham in the energy income deals. Darr could never reverse the decision even if he wanted to—it had the full backing of Prudential Insurance. The company had agreed to invest in the Graham deals.

Still, Darr made Marron's job as difficult as possible. Even though the Direct Investment Group had already started putting together more than $100 million worth of Graham partnerships, Darr refused to meet with executives from Graham Resources, saying he was too busy. So Marron and Holbrook handled the negotiations almost by themselves, frequently flying down to the company's headquarters in the unfashionable outskirts of New Orleans. It was there, during one negotiating session with John Graham, that the story of Darr's past came up yet again.

"I've heard some information about Jim Darr," Graham said. "As I understand it, he's not totally aboveboard, and I'm concerned about that. Is that something I have to worry about?"

Marron couldn't believe it. *Everyone* seemed to know Darr's reputation.

"Well, I have to admit that I've heard some things about him, too," Marron said. "But the transaction we're doing here is a good one. We've got Prudential Insurance in it. Jim Darr, whatever his problems are, shouldn't affect it at all."

Graham pursed his lips for a moment. "All right, fine," he said.

The Prudential-Bache Energy Income Fund was ready to go in June 1983.

Both Holbrook and Marron were immensely proud of what they had accomplished. They had conceived of the idea, brought it to the table, and found the managing general partner. Because of their work, Prudential-Bache was in one of its first huge ventures with Prudential Insurance, its new parent. Holbrook figured that with his and Marron's success, they would soon have more authority to pursue other quality deals.

Holbrook forgot that the coin of the realm in the Prudential-Bache Direct Investment Group was not success in deals, it was loyalty to Jim Darr. By that standard, both he and Marron were penniless.

In the summer of 1983, Holbrook sat at his desk, feeling almost numb from shock. Rumors had been circulating for weeks that Darr wanted someone new in charge of due diligence for energy deals. Marron and Holbrook would soon have a new boss. But Holbrook could not believe that even Darr would select the person whose name was in the rumor mill: Bill Pittman, the volatile product manager who, not much earlier, was handling the department's paperwork.

Holbrook shook his head in disbelief. Pittman had absolutely no qualifications for the job. He knew nothing about oil and gas and hadn't been to business school. He was Darr's yes-man. Holbrook scrambled down to Marron's office as soon as he heard the news.

"I just heard that Pittman got promoted over you," he said. "You're not going to take this, are you?"

Marron seemed resigned, almost tired of the battles. "Well, what can I do about it?" He wanted to move out to Denver and work out of an office there, and at least Darr had given him permission for that.

"But, Dennis, my God! Bill Pittman?"

Marron shrugged. There was no undoing Darr's decision. Marron went to Denver. A few weeks after Pittman started in his job, he walked into Holbrook's office and told him they were not going to be able to work together. Holbrook left and accepted a standing offer he had with A. G. Becker, a competing firm. The men Darr could not control were off Prudential-Bache's energy due diligence team. After his one defeat over NRM, Darr had reasserted his power.

A few months later, members of the department attended a meeting of the Direct Investment Group. Darr stood before members of his staff, as well as Matthew Chanin, an energy expert from Prudential Insurance who was deeply involved in the Graham deals. Darr described some recent successes and took special note of the work his department performed in finding and assembling the Prudential-Bache Energy Income Fund.

"I'd like to congratulate the person who really carried the ball on energy income and is largely responsible for its success," Darr said. "And that's Bill Pittman."

Pittman, who played absolutely no role in putting the deal together originally, raised his arm from the audience to accept Darr's praise.

The meeting broke up, and Chanin wandered over toward Marron, looking a little disturbed.

"Boy, Dennis," he said. "You just got screwed."

Three executives from Graham Resources walked into a cocktail party at a hotel near Fort Lauderdale, Florida. They were scheduled to meet a group of thirty Prudential-Bache brokers and managers who were attending a sales conference in the late summer of 1983. It was Graham Resources' first opportunity to size up the types of people who would be selling the new Energy Income Fund.

The Graham executives—Rich Gilman, Paul Grattarola, and Rusty Renaudin—fanned out in the massive marble room. They walked among the Prudential-Bache brokers and managers, who were busily munching on shrimp hors d'oeuvres and downing free drinks. Waiters in white gloves walked through the crowd, whisking away the empty plates and glasses that the brokers scattered about the room.

James Parker, the Direct Investment Group's chief marketer for Florida, introduced the Graham executives to as many brokers as he could. After about half an hour, the crowd moved to a conference room. There the Graham executives were scheduled to make a presentation describing the new energy income partnership.

Before leaving Louisiana, the three executives had plotted how to handle this group from Prudential-Bache. This, they decided, would be the best opportunity to get some intelligence on the firm's brokers and managers. Graham had done business with Merrill Lynch in the past and knew the high level of training that those brokers received. Renaudin and Grattarola, both regional marketers for Graham, were former Merrill Lynch stockbrokers and felt they understood the sales staff's mentality.

The best pitch, the group had decided, was to treat the Prudential-Bache brokers as if they were from Merrill Lynch. That meant making a sophisticated marketing presentation about the way the Energy Income Fund worked and how it might perform. This would not be like hocking shoes; instead, Graham would provide an educational lecture that would help the brokers understand the product and see where it might fit with their clients' investing needs. If the presentation went over the heads of the crowd, then Graham, in coordination with Prudential's marketing team, could dumb it down a little the next time.

The task of making the presentation at the Florida meeting was given to Gilman. As all the brokers and managers found their places, Gilman sat down at the head table, reviewing his notes. Finally he was introduced and stood up before the assembled group.

"I'm here today to introduce you to an exciting new product that will provide your clients with a unique way to participate in the oil and gas industry," Gilman began. "It is called the Prudential-Bache Energy Income Fund."

As planned, Gilman launched into a sophisticated description of how the partnerships worked. Although the presentation was technical, it was not financially complex. He described how the partnerships would use investor money to buy oil in the ground, then pump it and sell it. The cash from sales—minus expenses—would be returned to the investors in distributions. Included in each distribution was the original cash used to buy oil plus the profit from its sale. It was like investing in a car for $1,000, souping it up, and selling it for $1,500—the money received included $500 in profit and $1,000 in original investment.

Finally Gilman explained that determining the value of the oil in the ground was somewhat complex. Although a reserve was purchased all at once, it would be pumped out over decades, with the price of oil always changing. He described how values are assigned to the reserves, using the parlance of the industry, mentioning the "present value" of the reserves and the "internal rate of return" of the partnership.

Gilman paused and looked up. A sea of blank, uncomprehending eyes looked back at him. The brokers and managers had absolutely no idea what he was talking about. Nor did anyone look like they much cared.

A hand went up, and Gilman pointed toward the man. "Do you have a question?"

"Yeah," the Prudential-Bache broker said. "What are you guys going to pay in commissions?"

As complex as the Energy Income Fund was to understand, the first thing that the brokers cared about was how much money was in it for them.

For the next few minutes, Gilman fielded question after question about the commission structure of the partnerships, from how much would be paid overall to how much would end up in the brokers' pockets.

Grattarola sat back in disgust. *Great*, he thought. *We've got a bunch of guys here interested in just three things: commissions, commissions, and commissions.*

Eventually, the brokers started asking some questions about the oil business. But the queries were either pointless or so idiotic that Gilman seemed to have trouble keeping a straight face.

"Is oil going to $100 a barrel?" The Graham executives did not know.

"Well, how long do you think it would take for it to go that high?" Again, they said they did not know if it ever would.

Near the end, they called on a broker who was eagerly waving his hand. "Is it true that the oil is in huge underground lakes?" Grattarola took that question. After pausing for a minute to catch his breath, he answered. No, it was not true.

The meeting drew to a close, and a number of branch managers walked to the front of the room. Several of them looked extremely angry. One short, overweight manager pushed himself into the Graham executives' faces.

"What the hell were you people talking about?" the manager demanded angrily. "Present values? Internal rates of return? We don't want to hear any of this fancy stuff. You just talk about yield. How much money would somebody who put $10,000 in an oil partnership get each year?"

The Graham executives could not believe what they were hearing.

Yield was the return on investment—for most retail clients, it usually referred to the amount of fixed interest they were paid on a bond. Even in the sloppy parlance of Wall Street, telling investors that the partnership's cash distributions were a yield would not only be misleading, it would be fraudulent. Perhaps part of the money—the difference between the costs of purchasing and selling the oil—might be referred to loosely as "yield." But as Gilman had just explained, the distributions also included a return of the original capital that was used to buy the oil in the first place. Describing the distributions as "yield" would be like telling bank customers that all cash withdrawals from their own accounts were interest payments. It was simply false.

"Calling this 'yield' does not tell the whole story," Gilman answered. "It would be very misleading."

"Well, then it's too damn complicated," the manager replied. "If you guys can't break this down and make it simple, then nobody at this firm is going to sell it. Let me tell you, if your sales pitch is longer than three minutes, then I don't want you talking to my brokers. They've got better things to do."

After a few more tense minutes, the meeting broke up. The three Graham executives hustled out of the room. They were supposed to drive a rental car to the airport, where they were scheduled to fly to another meeting of Prudential-Bache brokers. But they decided to take a limousine. They needed the driving time to start preparing a much slower, less sophisticated presentation. They hired a car and piled into the back.

"Well," Gilman said. "What do you think?"

"I think we're in deep shit, guys," Grattarola said. "These are the dumbest bastards I've ever run into. We've got managers who don't understand and are a bunch of hustlers. We've got brokers who are stupid and not well trained."

Renaudin agreed. "These guys don't know their ass from a hole in the ground."

The three discussed whether it was possible that the ignorance they were seeing was just in Florida, or if it was throughout the firm.

"I'll tell you, we don't need sales material for this bunch," Grattarola said. "We're going to need educational material. We've got to keep it real simple for these guys and go back to the very, very basic stuff."

Some questions were raised about whether educational material alone would help the brokers sell the partnerships. But Grattarola was insistent.

"These guys don't understand investments," he said. "They don't understand the terminology of the Street. And they sure as hell don't understand oil and gas. We could end up with some serious compliance problems."

All of them knew what Grattarola was saying. These brokers could easily fall out of compliance with the securities laws requiring them to accurately describe investments to their clients. How could they be accurate if they didn't understand what they were selling?

Getting the brokers educated was the top priority. Otherwise, they might start breaking the law.

"Today I want to tell you about an investment opportunity with potential high cash flow, a superior structure, a unique sharing arrangement, and low risk."

By the late summer of 1983, hundreds of Prudential-Bache brokers across the country heard those words in the opening seconds of the first marketing video for the Energy Income Fund. The video, put together by the Direct Investment Group, began with a shot of Ron Gwozdz, the department's first product manager for the energy partnerships. As he recited the opening line, he walked to an office door and grabbed a hard hat. He threw open the door, and the scene dissolved to an oil field setting. For the next few minutes, Gwozdz talked about the experience of Prudential Insurance and Graham Resources in the oil business. He introduced John Graham, who discussed how low oil prices made the timing for the investment perfect.

"Ron, I've never seen a better time to buy products in the ground at distressed prices," Graham said.

Graham dismissed the idea that there might be a long-term glut of oil and natural gas. "That's somewhat misleading," he said. "This should not be the case."

When Grattarola saw the video, he thought it was a disaster. It didn't explain the partnerships—if anything, it oversimplified them. It made them seem safer than they actually were. It didn't discuss the risks. It didn't raise any of the important compliance issues. It offered none of the education that was so critically needed. But few people in the senior ranks of Graham or the Direct Investment Group seemed to care. The video was simple. It would get the partnerships sold.

The video ended with Gwozdz walking in an oil field, praising the partnership. "Prudential-Bache Energy Income Fund 1 is a limited partnership that is projected to give you high cash flow, appreciation, and low risk," he said. He added that the partnership "has a projected return on investment of from 16 percent to 19 percent."

By the fall of 1983, those marketing lines had been used to raise $26.7 million from 2,328 investors for the first Graham energy income partnership sold by Prudential-Bache. The investors all heard about the high returns and the low risks.

The largest criminal fraud to come out of the Direct Investment Group was under way.

CHAPTER 8

DAVID LEVINE WALKED ACROSS the lobby of the Drake Hotel toward a bank of pay telephones. After watching a long presentation at one of the department's quarterly meetings in late 1983, he needed to stretch his legs. He smiled as he saw Lauren McNenney just ahead. A few months earlier, McNenney had joined the department as a full-time analyst, following two summers working as a temp. She and Levine became fast friends who shared an admiration for each other and a distaste for the Direct Investment Group.

On this day, the two of them had something to celebrate: Levine had successfully killed a bad deal. Usually there were huge battles with Darr, as he tried to wheedle, cajole, or compel the due diligence team to approve the deals for sale. But earlier that week, when VMS, the Chicago real estate company, brought in a partnership syndication of an apartment building in Greenwich Village, Darr had not flinched when Levine rejected it. Levine argued that the deal's success relied on converting the property from a rental building into a cooperative. Although it might be profitable if the conversion worked, Levine thought it was far too risky. Besides, it was a small deal, and VMS had another firm lined up to sell it.

As Levine and McNenney chatted about his recent victory, Darr spotted them from across the lobby and strolled toward them. He signaled Levine that he wanted to talk.

"David," Darr said, "I want you to call VMS about that Greenwich Village building. Bob Sherman needs an apartment in the city. I want you to have VMS get him one there."

Levine stared at Darr, a look of incomprehension on his face. He couldn't believe that Darr wanted him to hit up a sponsor for an inside deal on an apartment. Darr asked what the rentals were in the building, and Levine rattled the prices he remembered off the top of his head.

"Yeah, that sounds about right," Darr said. "Call them today."

Darr strolled away, evidently confident that Levine would follow up on his instructions. For much of the day, Levine agonized about what to do. Finally, that afternoon he telephoned Mitchell Hochberg, a friend who worked at VMS, and relayed the request.

"David, come on," Hochberg replied. "You're really putting me on the spot. I mean, you guys just rejected this deal, and now you want us to get you an *apartment*?"

Still, VMS came through and agreed to provide a nine-hundred-square-foot apartment for the use of the Prudential-Bache executive. About a week later, Levine received a telephone call from Bob Sherman, complimenting him on the job he had done.

"I really like the apartment," Sherman said. "But there are a couple of things I want you to get done." Sherman instructed Levine to have VMS redo the kitchen cabinets, install a new refrigerator, and perhaps put in a stall shower.*

"Oh, and also," Sherman said, "see if you can do anything about the rent."

Disgusted, Levine hung up. He thought what Darr and Sherman were doing was completely unprofessional, not to mention unethical. He wasn't even sure if it was legal. A clever plaintiff's lawyer could certainly argue that the apartment was a form of compensation that needed to be disclosed to investors. But Levine was sure this little side deal with VMS would never find its way into the real estate company's prospectuses.

Levine wanted nothing more to do with it. He called Hochberg and told him that VMS needed to speak to Sherman. Then he stepped out of it. Later, he found McNenney, who had witnessed the original conversation with Darr, and told her what happened. She couldn't believe how open Darr and Sherman were about something that, in her mind, was clearly a corrupt act.

"If they don't think this is sleazy enough to hide from us," McNenney said, "what else must be going on that we don't even know about?"

More than they could imagine.

William Petty, an executive vice-president with Watson & Taylor Investments in Dallas, was surprised when his secretary told him that Jim Darr from Prudential-Bache was on the line. It was an afternoon in the second week of November 1983, a few months after Watson & Taylor had sold its

---

*Sherman's lawyer acknowledged that his client obtained an apartment in a VMS building, and, although VMS did renovate the apartment, he said his client received no special breaks and no special benefits.

first public real estate limited partnership through Darr's department. Even though Petty frequently heard from the Direct Investment Group, usually it was Freddie Kotek in due diligence or one of the marketing people. Darr never called him.

"Yeah, hi, Bill," Darr said, sounding somewhat frustrated. "I'm looking for George."

Immediately, the call made sense. Darr had developed a close relationship with George Watson, a named principal in the real estate company, and the two men spoke frequently. Watson, a thin, bald man with a quiet demeanor and a toothy grin, seemed to consider keeping Darr on his good side to be a central part of the job. Often he told Petty to take care of selling the deals, and Watson would take care of Darr. But on this day, Watson was not in the office. Darr had only asked for Petty as a second choice.

"George isn't in," Petty said. "Is there anything I can do for you?"

"Yeah, tell me where I should send my $20,000 check."

Petty paused for an instant. "Jim, I'm sorry, I don't know what you're talking about."

"You know," Darr replied. "For that land deal, over there on Stemmons Freeway."

Petty sat back in his chair. He had never heard of the deal. "Jim, I'm sorry, I still don't know what you mean. Let me talk to George and I'll have him get back to you."

He hung up the phone, perplexed. What was Darr doing investing in some land deal with Watson & Taylor? The company made huge profits buying and selling land in its private deals with its own money. Petty could not imagine that Darr was being allowed to invest in those lucrative private deals, too. He made a mental note to speak with Watson as soon as possible.

Later that day, after Watson returned, Petty walked down the hallway to his boss's wood-paneled office. "George, Jim Darr called about sending a check on a land deal," he said. "I didn't know anything about it. What should I tell him?"

Watson looked up from his desk and smiled. "I'll take care of that, Bill," he said in his smooth Texas twang. "Don't pay any further attention to it."

A couple of days later, Watson came to Petty's office and knocked on the door. He said he wanted to talk to Petty about an investment.

"I've got this land deal that's a laydown," Watson said. Petty perked up his ears. He knew that Watson used that word only when he had found something that was really good.

"Well, what is it?"

"It's over on Stemmons Freeway," Watson said. "It's a done deal."

Petty looked at Watson, confused. "What do you mean?"

"The land has already been sold," Watson said.

Already been sold. Petty could not believe his good fortune. In Texas in the early 1980s, the land business was wild, with developers and speculators making millions of dollars from buying and selling properties like stocks. It was possible to sell some land, with the final transfer of ownership simply awaiting zoning changes or other delays. From what Watson said, Petty figured that was the situation here—although the closing had not yet taken place, Watson had a buyer and a profit already sewed up. Now he was selling participations in the guaranteed profit. Watson's offer to let him buy a piece of this property was like a gift, Petty thought. For every dollar he could invest, he would receive a proportionate share of whatever profits Watson had locked in. The more money he could invest, the more money he would make.

"Gee, how much can I put in?"

"Well, $5,000," Watson said.

That didn't sound like much. "You sure there's not any more available?" Petty asked. He was feeling a trifle greedy. If he could have put everything he owned in this investment, he probably would have.

"No, just $5,000."

"All right," Petty said. Before he could reach for his checkbook, a thought crossed his mind. This was the second time in just a few days he had heard about a Watson land deal over on Stemmons. "Is this the deal Darr called about?" he asked.

"Yes, it is," Watson said.*

So Darr is putting in $20,000, and I'm restricted to $5,000, Petty thought. Watson was right—he *did* take care of Darr. When Petty later saw the list of investors in the deal, which was called Lombardi Number Three, he realized that the only other people from Watson & Taylor allowed to invest were two executives who would see the transaction's paperwork. Petty was sure the only reason he had been offered a stake was that he had heard about Darr's involvement.

The Lombardi deal proved a big winner. Within a matter of months, the payback on the deal came out, with Darr netting about $45,000. Petty did

*Petty described this conversation in secret sworn testimony to government investigators. In an interview, Watson denied it ever occurred and denied that the Lombardi deal had been presold. See Notes and Sources.

not know it, but this was Darr's second investment with a Watson & Taylor deal. George Watson had offered Darr the first opportunity in February, on almost the exact same day that the prospectus was filed with the Securities and Exchange Commission for the first Watson & Taylor public partnership sold through the Direct Investment Group. That deal, which was not disclosed in any of the public partnership's filings, netted Darr a profit of $46,258 in less than one month.

Even with what little Petty knew, Darr's financial ties with Watson bothered him. Darr was accepting rich investment opportunities from Watson at the same time he was judging the general partner's deals for public investors. It all seemed too ugly, too smarmy. But Petty could understand why Watson would want to keep the Prudential-Bache executive happy. At that point, almost no one was more important to George Watson's financial future than Jim Darr.

A fourth-generation Texan, Watson had come from a long line of wealthy Texas real estate men. At the age of sixteen, he was infected by his family's real estate bug following his success at selling some of his grandmother's land for $1.5 million. After receiving his business degree from the University of Texas in 1965, he dabbled some more in real estate but went through some tough times. Then, in 1974, he teamed up with Austin Starke Taylor III, a serious man known to everyone as Tracy. A former insurance agent, Taylor brought something to the business: connections in politics and business. His father, a wealthy cotton exporter and real estate investor, was a premier player on the Dallas axis of politics and business, and would be elected mayor during the 1980s. Through his father, Taylor had access to people who could make zoning changes or decide highway routes. Those were the sorts of decisions that could inflate the value of a land investment overnight.

Watson & Taylor expanded rapidly in its early years. Through a series of different entities, grouped under the name "the Watson & Taylor Companies," the two men assembled and managed real estate properties both for the company's account and for outside investors. They were particularly attracted to deals involving mini-warehouses, a niche of the business that had less glamour—and far less risk—than developing office towers. In the late 1970s, their track record attracted the attention of Steve Blank's tax shelter department. Soon Watson & Taylor was selling real estate limited partnerships through Bache. The deals were not huge moneymakers for Bache, but they were solid performers.

By 1983, Watson & Taylor had been successful enough with earlier deals to sell its first big public partnership through Prudential-Bache. It took a little more than thirty days for the firm's brokers to sell the entire $14.4 million deal to 1,961 clients.

Better still for the Direct Investment Group, Watson agreed to allow a subsidiary of the brokerage, called Prudential-Bache Properties, to share the role of general partner. On top of the huge 8 percent commissions it received for selling the deal, the firm received a percentage of the cash flow from the partnership. And a chunk of that money went to select executives in the Direct Investment Group, including Darr.

Even as Watson & Taylor were raising millions thanks to Darr's ability to tap the huge network of retail brokers, the economics of Texas real estate were vastly changing. In 1982, Congress and the Reagan administration deregulated the multibillion-dollar savings and loan industry, allowing the institutions to invest directly in assets such as real estate. Suddenly huge thrift deposits were searching out real estate investments, helping to drive the prices of properties sky-high. Developers around the country immediately struck up deals with S&Ls or bought them outright for the purpose of using the deposits to finance real estate projects.

George Watson and Tracy Taylor forged a business relationship with a savings and loan just months after Prudential-Bache sold their first public partnership. Their effort began in 1982 when Taylor met Howard Wiechern, the chairman of First South, a small S&L in Pine Bluff, Arkansas. On a sweltering Saturday afternoon, Taylor flew to Pine Bluff to discuss a proposed land development project with Wiechern. The two men spoke about the background of Watson & Taylor, as well as about its recent business and future prospects.

"The Texas market is hot," Taylor said. "There will be lots of opportunities to make money."

Wiechern seemed suitably impressed. He listened as Taylor proposed that, if First South financed Watson & Taylor's developments, the company would share 25 percent of the profit. Wiechern shook his head.

"No, the way we do deals here in Arkansas is we're fifty-fifty partners," he said. "We put up the money and you put up the work and find the projects and make them happen."

After some negotiations, the men struck a deal. By May 1983, the floodgates had opened. That month, without approval from its lending committee, First South loaned Watson & Taylor $20 million. Over the next few weeks, First South loaned millions more to Watson & Taylor so that the company could pay the interest on other loans. Later, Wiechern and First South's president, Rod Reed, would backdate documents to make the loan appear properly approved and legitimate. The First South loans came so fast and steadily that by August 1983, three months after its first transaction with Watson & Taylor, Wiechern's thrift went in violation of federal regulations that restrict the amount of money that could be loaned to a single borrower. First South would remain in violation of those rules for years.

The ready financing from First South and Prudential-Bache not only further enriched George Watson and Tracy Taylor. It also freed up capital that allowed them to make even larger profits investing in raw land for their own account. Some of the deals were phenomenally profitable in less than twenty-four hours. On one day, Watson & Taylor purchased about ninety-three acres of land in the morning and, thanks to some rezoning arranged through political connections, resold it that same afternoon for a pretax return of 4,771 percent. Another property of almost eight acres gave them a 12,463 percent pretax return. And a large parcel of about 130 acres snapped up and sold in one day brought a 68 percent return. Those were the wild, woolly days of Texas real estate, and profits were virtually guaranteed, so long as the market held up.

It was in this atmosphere that Watson approached Darr about investing with his company in the raw land deals. The first involved a 15.6-acre property called Trinity Mills, which Watson & Taylor purchased on February 1, 1983. Although the property was fully financed, Watson allowed Darr to invest $107,274 in exchange for 10 percent of the profits. That money was used to pay down part of a bank loan, even though no principal payments were due until November. Darr's investment did little to decrease the interest costs—twenty-eight days later, or about two weeks after Darr's check would have cleared, Watson & Taylor signed a contract to sell the property. Darr made $46,539. With that success under their belt, on October 3, Watson met with Darr in his office at the Direct Investment Group in New York and told him about the Lombardi deal on Stemmons Freeway, offering him a stake of more than 3 percent. Watson showed him nothing but some newspaper articles that mentioned the property, but Darr quickly agreed to invest.

Darr mentioned the Watson & Taylor deals both to Bob Sherman, his boss, and to Loren Schechter, the general counsel. Years later, Schechter would have no memory of ever hearing about the investments. But at the time, based on whatever Darr told him, he did not see any problem with a senior officer at the firm investing in lucrative private deals with a general partner.

Weeks after the Lombardi deal closed, Watson gave friends another tip: First South, the Arkansas savings and loan that financed so much of Watson & Taylor's business, was about to go public. Watson was sure the stock would be a fabulous buy.

"This stock is going to go up right away," Watson said one day to Bill Petty. "I'll see if I can get you some."

In the end, Watson did not get Petty any of the stock, but it was not for lack of shares. Both he and Taylor loaded up on First South stock when the thrift went public in November 1983. They had decided to become the biggest investors in the institution that they owed tens of millions of dollars. Both men purchased just below 5 percent of the company's stock in their own names. If they purchased any more for their own accounts, they would have to disclose their stake in a Schedule 13-D, filed with the SEC. This document is extremely important because it lets investors know when a takeover might be under way or when a single investor might bear a degree of control over a company's direction. But even though both George Watson and Tracy Taylor kept buying First South stock, they sidestepped the disclosure requirements. Instead of buying the stock in their own names, shares were purchased for their children or by close business associates. Eventually, the government would determine that, through these various accounts, Watson & Taylor secretly controlled more than 26 percent of the total shares in First South. The rest was purchased by the public.

Darr now had a friend with access to close to a billion federally insured dollars. That would quickly come in very handy.

Alan Warrick, a First South executive who handled its investments, looked up from his desk when he heard the knock at his door. It was the secretary for his boss, Howard Wiechern. She had just come from her desk outside the executive office and was standing in the doorway.

"Alan," she said, "Howard would like to see you for a moment."

It was early 1984. Warrick set down the papers he was reviewing. Wiechern was friendly enough, but Warrick knew that when he asked to see someone, he wanted them right away. Warrick adjusted his tie and followed Wiechern's secretary back to the chairman's office, knocked on the door, and was invited in.

Wiechern was meeting with three businessmen and seemed delighted to be entertaining his guests. Warrick recognized two of the men as George Watson and Tracy Taylor, whom he knew were First South's biggest shareholders and biggest borrowers. He figured something important was up, because Watson and Taylor usually came to Pine Bluff only to work on big deals with First South. Warrick did not recognize the third guest in the room, a white-haired man whose expensive clothes signaled his affluence.

"Alan, come in, come in," Wiechern said. "You know George and Tracy. I'd like to introduce Jim Darr. He's an executive at Prudential-Bache Securities and a close friend and business associate of George and Tracy."

Warrick nodded to Watson and Taylor and shook hands with Darr. He had never heard of him. But since he was from Prudential-Bache, Warrick figured that Darr was there to discuss some investment opportunities for First South. That was right up Warrick's alley.

"Alan, sit down for a minute," Wiechern said. "Look. First South's going to be making a home loan to Jim Darr. I want you to get somebody in lending to help work out this deal for him."

Warrick agreed but felt puzzled. He didn't handle mortgages; he was much higher up in the organization than any loan officer. Clearly, this was a loan that meant a lot to Wiechern. And if Wiechern wanted the loan approved, it would be.

As they discussed the terms of the proposed loan, Warrick began to understand why Wiechern was involved. This was no ordinary mortgage: Darr wanted $1.8 million to buy a mansion in one of the wealthiest sections of Greenwich, Connecticut. The loan would cover the entire purchase price—on closing, Darr would not put any cash into his new home at all. But despite the huge risks for First South, they would charge him a relatively low interest rate—the prime rate plus one point.

It was an incredible deal. As far as Warrick knew, this would be the single largest home loan ever granted by First South. Now he understood why Darr had flown all the way to Arkansas to finance a home in Connecticut. It certainly paid to have friends in the thrift business.

The meeting broke up, and Warrick stood. Darr shook his hand.

"I look forward to working with you guys here at First South," Darr said. "Looks like you have a great organization."

Warrick walked out of Wiechern's office. This was going to be a loan of great value to First South. Just by stretching a bit to let Darr buy his mansion, First South now had an ally in one of the most powerful depart-

ments of one of the biggest brokerages on Wall Street. Warrick was sure
that First South and Darr would do business again.

"Goddamn it, Virg!" George Ball snapped. "Have you got anything specific or not?"

Ball felt exasperated. Yet another person, this time Virgil Sherrill, had
come to him with more bad rumors about Jim Darr. By 1984, Ball had
been besieged by whispers that there was something crooked about Darr,
something wrong with his Direct Investment Group, something that could
harm the firm. But the more Ball heard, the more frustrated he became.
Even though the rumors were rampant, no one was able to tell him exactly what Darr had done. Ball knew Darr was one of the best-paid people at Prudential-Bache. For all he could tell, what he was hearing was the
jealous backblow from the usual Wall Street compensation envy.

The conversation with the patrician Sherrill was typical. Sherrill had
strolled into Ball's office minutes earlier, saying that they needed to speak
privately. Then, with the door closed, Sherrill said that he had been hearing things, horrible things, about the head of the Direct Investment Group.
He felt obliged to let Ball know.

"From what I hear, Jim Darr is a bad man," Sherrill said. "We need to
be careful."

But when Ball pressed Sherrill for details, he had none to give. Ball
asked who the source of the information was. Sherrill demurred, saying "I
gave my word that I would keep that confidential."

Ball threw up his hands in despair. What was he supposed to do with
this? Ball respected Sherrill immensely, but he didn't think he could make
any judgments on such thin information. It wasn't something he could just
dismiss out of hand—Peter Bernard, a dapper head of corporate finance,
had told him that he thought Darr was dishonest. He even heard the rumors from Alan Hogan, the short, brash executive whom Ball selected as
his chief administrator. But none of them would give him anything con-
crete.

"All right, Virg, thank you for telling me."

After Sherrill left, Ball sat at his desk, pondering his next move. He
didn't have the time to waste playing Twenty Questions. Prudential-Bache
had ended up being a much bigger disaster area than he had ever anticipated. The firm had its share of incompetents, but Ball was shocked at the
huge trove of sleazy executives who had roosted over the years in middle
and senior management. The bumblers were easy to spot and boot out, but

no one walked the halls with name tags saying "Sleazebag." Ball had too much else on his plate to hunt them all down. Very little at the firm seemed to be managed well. About the only departments Ball did not worry about was the Direct Investment Group. It was one of the few that ran on all cylinders. Left to its own devices, the department brought in as much as $40 million in annual profits. Ball thought Darr deserved the lion's share of the credit. Although Darr struck him as a shameless self-promoter with lousy people skills, there was no arguing that he knew how to sell partnerships.

Still, if people as disparate as the patrician Sherrill and the street-smart Hogan thought there was a problem, Ball could not ignore it. He picked up the telephone and called Schechter's law department. He had decided to have Darr secretly investigated. For what, Ball wasn't sure. But he felt confident that once someone looked into Darr's activities, the man would either be cleared or be sent packing.

How could anybody run up an $1,800 hotel bill in just one weekend? Bill Petty was so stunned by the bill on his desk from Dallas's elite Mansion Hotel that he reviewed it again and again. He could not decide what was more outrageous: that Jim Darr and his wife ran up a bill that high in just two days or that Darr expected the Watson & Taylor partnership to pay it for him. Why was it partnership business to host a Prudential-Bache executive and his wife to a lavish weekend on the town?

Petty first heard about the bill from Paul Proscia, the senior product manager with the Direct Investment Group, who told him that Darr's bill was on its way to Watson & Taylor.

"Why?" Petty asked, astonished.

"Because Darr and his wife had dinner with George and his wife," Proscia said. "And this is the way Jim wanted to handle it."

Petty was not going to stand for it. There was no way the retail investors in the public Watson & Taylor partnership should pick up the tab for Darr's extravagance. Petty picked up his telephone and called down to Watson's office. He wanted him to hear what Darr was pulling.

"George, I've got this $1,800 bill here for Darr and his wife, and Paul Proscia wants us to pay it," Petty said.

"Yeah, OK," Watson said. "Go ahead and pay it."

Petty sat back in his chair, stunned. "You've got to be kidding. George, this is $1,800 *for one weekend*."

"That's OK," Watson said. "Pay it."

Petty hung up. He could not believe how cavalier Watson was about throwing the money away. Particularly since it was money that belonged to his investors.

Loren Schechter read Darr's contract several times on a day in early 1984. He had never seen anything like it. As far as Schechter was concerned, Darr's deal with Prudential-Bache had to be one of the most amazing in the history of Wall Street.

The contract showed that Darr was getting a huge share of the cash flow going through the subsidiary corporations that were serving as co–general partners. Other executives in the Direct Investment Group had similar contracts, but none anywhere as lucrative as Darr's. Essentially, without having to put a penny into the deals, Darr was the largest single recipient in the world of partnership cash distributions. Even if a single partnership distributed only a few thousand dollars, that had to be multiplied by scores and scores of others sold by the firm. Darr's bank account was like an ocean fed by endless little raindrops of cash.

Some of the other terms of the contract were even more unbelievable. The way the contract read, Darr could well keep being paid even if he left Prudential-Bache to work for a competitor. Schechter had never seen an agreement that more thoroughly divorced the interests of an executive from the interests of the firm. But there was nothing he could do about it. The contract had been signed and delivered long before he started handling the firm's legal work.

Besides, even if Schechter wanted to change the contract, he would probably meet stiff resistance. Darr was bringing in huge amounts of cash to the firm. And cash was Ball's bottom line. So Darr could operate his department as his own personal fiefdom and demand most anything he wanted. Unless Schechter caught him doing something heinous, Darr was probably untouchable.

The prospectus for Prudential-Bache/Watson & Taylor Ltd. 2 arrived at the Securities and Exchange Commission on March 16, 1984. A clerk in the commission's Office of Applications and Report Services picked up the document, stamped it "Received," and placed it in a box for filing by a coworker. There was nothing unusual about the four-inch prospectus, nothing that made it stand out from the other records stacked around the office.

In fact, the document was immensely important, mostly for what it did *not* disclose. The prospectus was the first to be filed since George Watson started giving Darr the opportunity to invest in the private land deals, investments that had reaped Darr a return of more than 100 percent. But nothing about those side deals was disclosed to the 3,764 investors who poured $25.6 million into the second public deal for Watson & Taylor sold by Prudential-Bache. Even the section "Conflicts of Interest" was silent about Darr's investments.

Perhaps Darr's investments in Trinity Mills and Lombardi had somehow slipped everyone's mind. After all, it had been many months since those deals had closed. But it was not likely that his third and latest transaction with Watson & Taylor had been missed—Darr's personal investment of $43,398 in a deal called Northwest Highway/California Crossing Joint Venture was negotiated even as the prospectus for the public partnership was being written. He was admitted to the joint venture on March 1, one day before the completion of the prospectus. Darr's personal finances were on the table at literally the same time decisions were made about the new public partnership.

When stockbrokers called up their clients to peddle the newest Watson & Taylor product, none of them would know about Darr's conflicts of interest. Instead, they repeated the assurances from the marketing material provided by Darr's Direct Investment Group that the partnership was safe. "These partnerships will exhibit our philosophy of risk aversion," brokers throughout the country said, reading off the sales script. The investment had three objectives: income, growth, and perhaps most important, safety.

It would not be until years later, after losing almost 70 percent of their money, that Prudential-Bache clients would find out about Darr's conflicts. Only then could they ask whether the Direct Investment Group approved the deals because of their perceived quality or because of undisclosed investing opportunities offered to Darr by the general partner.

It was a question that could have been raised in those years about a number of strange partnership offerings emerging with increased frequency from the Direct Investment Group. But no one at Prudential-Bache—not even Darr's superiors whom he soon started inviting to join in his side deals—thought to ask.

Back in New York in late 1983, Joe Quinn, the new head of real estate due diligence for the Direct Investment Group, focused on a growing problem: Could he keep Clifton Harrison's deals, and perhaps Harrison himself, from going bankrupt? And could it be done without investors finding out?

The lack of care in the department's due diligence for the Harrison deals became evident over the summer, as their financial problems mushroomed. Both the Barbizon and the Archives partnerships, two of the first big Harrison deals sold through Prudential-Bache, were on the verge of going belly-up. All of the flaws that had been overlooked when the deals were first sold—from the missing construction budgets to the inadequate bank financing—had come home to roost. The Direct Investment Group faced potential catastrophe. If the Harrison deals went under so soon after being sold, Pru-Bache brokers would never trust the department again. Darr dropped the problem into Quinn's lap, while shutting Harrison out of bringing in any more partnerships until the troubled deals were fixed.

For weeks, Quinn thrashed over the problems with Harrison in Prudential-Bache's offices. At times other members of the due diligence department were called in to explain facets of the deals. Quinn, whose stiff, fastidious demeanor showed up in his penchant for frequently combing his hair, stood like a high school teacher at an easel in his office, writing down each element of the deals while his staff explained them. Some due diligence team members looked on Quinn's easel as a form of torture, as he forced them to explain the same concepts over and over again. But for Quinn, the easel was a crutch that helped him to understand. Unlike some of the dive-bombers of Wall Street, who would rush in with a solution without understanding the problem, Quinn always wanted to be sure he was fully prepared.

Quinn did not like the answers the easel gave him about the Barbizon. It needed a cash infusion of about $1.5 million. Without that money, redevelopment of the hotel would soon stop, and the banks could well foreclose. That would be a disaster for investors—under federal law, a foreclosure could result in the government recapturing all of the tax deductions they had taken so far. Worse for Darr and the department, a number of Pru-Bache executives, including Darr himself, had been so persuaded by the sales pitch that they purchased their own interests in the Barbizon partnership. Failure of the deal would not only burn the department with the brokers, it would cost Darr and his bosses money.

Quinn had to think of someplace to find a loan. Apparently, going to the bank was out of the question—even though Prudential-Bache investors were assured of Harrison's financial stability, the banks might balk at his creditworthiness. The firm itself could not give the loan without assuming huge new liabilities for the partnership. So Quinn came up with an idea: He would hit up one of the department's growing stable of general partners for a loan to Harrison. Then Harrison could lend the money to the Barbizon and salvage the deal.

After discussing the idea with Harrison, Quinn decided that Barry Breeman, a tough-talking, chain-smoking New Yorker, would be the perfect general partner to ask. Breeman had been Quinn's last employer and was instrumental in helping him get his job at the Direct Investment Group. When John D'Elisa resigned, Breeman recommended Quinn to Clifton Harrison, who was well known for having the inside track in the department. Harrison carried the recommendation on to Darr, who hired Quinn almost immediately.

Breeman, a high school graduate with one year of college, ran a real estate syndication company called Carnegie Realty Capital that he formed in 1983 with three partners: Anthony Viglietta, Fred Manko, and Jon Edelman. As Quinn knew, Carnegie would have strong reasons to keep Harrison out of bankruptcy court. Before Harrison was restricted from doing new deals, he was brought in to help Carnegie market a partnership called 680 Fifth Avenue Associates to Prudential-Bache brokers. Carnegie would be as eager as anyone to make sure that Harrison kept his good name with the sales force.

In November, Quinn telephoned Breeman and quickly got to the point. "Clifton Harrison needs $1.5 million to put into the Barbizon," he said. "Could Carnegie lend him the money?"

"I have to speak to my partners," Breeman said. If they agreed to the loan, then Harrison would get the money. He told Quinn he would call back soon with their answer.

That day, at Carnegie's offices at One Exchange Plaza, Breeman told his partners about Prudential-Bache's request. Without much discussion, the partners agreed to lend Harrison the money. But Jon Edelman insisted that they extract as much as possible from Harrison for security on the loan. Edelman disliked Harrison from their dealings on the 680 Fifth Avenue deal; at one point, he walked away from a conversation convinced that Harrison had insulted him. Now, with Harrison in desperate shape so soon afterward, Edelman saw an opportunity for a payback. To assuage Edelman, the partners agreed to impose the strict terms he wanted.

Soon Breeman called Quinn with their answer. "All right, Joe," he said.

"We're willing to provide Clifton with the loan. But we're going to need some significant collateral."

"That's understandable," Quinn said. "Did you have anything in mind?"

"Yeah," Breeman said. "Everything he owns."

It was no joke. For Harrison to get his money, he had to put every one of his belongings in hock. His home. His general partnership interests. His cars. Even his Cartier watch. If Harrison defaulted, Carnegie would take it all.

When told of the demands, Harrison swallowed hard but accepted. He had little choice. In November 1983, when he signed the agreement, his finances could scarcely be more precarious. He was effectively insolvent. No one would be willing to buy a partnership sponsored by someone in such sorry financial shape. And no one could argue it was immaterial—a general partner's financial health was among the most important of disclosure items. If he didn't find a way to bail himself out, Harrison would never sell another partnership. But apparently for Darr, Harrison's dilemma seemed like a remarkable opportunity to make money. In a few weeks, he would convert the Carnegie loan into a centerpiece not only of his own personal finances but those of other Prudential-Bache executives as well.

On February 27, 1984, Darr thumbed through the fourteen-page brochure for a new $1.67 million real estate partnership offering that Clifton Harrison wanted to sell. Clearly, Harrison hoped that the money from this deal would get him out from under the Carnegie loan. But Darr did not like what he saw. He thought Harrison was trying to charge investors in the new partnership too much. He decided to tell Harrison that the asking price had to be lowered. It was a rare instance where Darr demanded a decrease in the amount of money partnership investors had to pay. Then again, in this deal, all of the investors would be Prudential-Bache executives, including Darr himself.

Darr sat down at his desk and wrote a brusque letter to Michael Walters, the head of marketing for Harrison Freedman Associates. "Dear Mike," he began. "We intend to pay no more than $1.2 million total for this offering, if it is to be purchased by Prudential-Bache executives." He added sharply, "I would suggest you restructure your numbers or sell it elsewhere."

Harrison had little choice but to lower his asking price. Selling the partnership, which held his interest in the Barbizon and a neighboring brown-

stone, was the fastest way to pay off the Carnegie loan. And the partnership could scarcely be sold through Pru-Bache brokers. If it was, all of
them would see his financial troubles and probably would never sell one
of his deals. He needed to get back into the partnership business desperately, so that he could start charging some new fees. Despite his tight finances, he still spent money with abandon. In the weeks after he obtained
the Carnegie loan, Harrison purchased a roomful of nineteenth-century
English antique furniture, including a satinwood table for $3,800 and a
George IV mahogany clock for $5,500. In one month alone, Harrison rang
up $12,000 in bills on his credit cards and, on top of that, purchased an
$11,000 stereo system.

Darr held all the cards. To keep up his wild spending, Harrison needed
to get out from under his Carnegie debt quickly. So Darr negotiated the
most lucrative investment possible: None of the Pru-Bache executives
would have to put up a dime to buy the partnership. Instead, they would
simply assume a piece of Harrison's debt to Carnegie, which they would
then pay off over the years. That made the deal a no-brainer. Though they
would have no money at risk, the Pru-Bache executives would be able to
obtain immediate tax credits. Even better, they stood a good chance of
making a significant profit on the deal, as Darr was virtually dictating
the price and refusing to allow Harrison to charge any fees for managing
the partnership. In essence, Darr was not allowing Harrison to do to
Prudential-Bache executives what he routinely did to hundreds of
Prudential-Bache clients.

Within a few weeks, Harrison and Darr agreed to set the value of the
deal at $1.25 million. Darr contacted senior executives throughout
Prudential-Bache, including George Ball, and told them about the great
investment opportunity he had created for them. Apparently, no one questioned the propriety of Darr striking personal deals with the same people
whose partnerships were being sold by his department.

Ball declined to participate in the deal, but three other executives outside the department—Virgil Sherrill, the vice-chairman; Bob Sherman,
the head of retail; and Richard Sichenzio, a senior vice-president in the retail group—agreed to invest. In the Direct Investment Group, only Paul
Proscia, Bill Pittman, and Joe Quinn were offered the opportunity. Quinn
opted out; Darr, Pittman, and Proscia invested. All of the executives assumed $125,000 of Harrison's debt to Carnegie, except for Darr and Sher-
rill, who each assumed $375,000.

The Carnegie partners were delighted with the outcome. Not only had the risk of the loan been spread among many more people, but Harrison still owed Carnegie for the debt that the Prudential-Bache executives left on the table. And until the executives' partnership closed, Carnegie continued to retain all of Harrison's belongings as collateral.

The inequity of the deal was obvious to Harrison's staff. Mike Walters of Harrison Freedman wrote a letter on March 26 to Howard Feinsand, a lawyer for Harrison, describing the terms for the deal that had been forced down Harrison's throat. "Enclosed please find the final edition of Barbizon '84," he wrote. "This deal has been carefully structured for the investing pleasure of Jim Darr and his merry men."

But the deal achieved Harrison and Darr's original purpose: Harrison's financial statements had been prettied up, to the monetary benefit of Pru-Bache executives. The Direct Investment Group lifted its ban on Harrison deals. Although no investors would ever be told, the side deal also gave Harrison enough appearance of financial strength that he would soon be used to salvage an important private placement. By the completion of that deal, called Madison Plaza, Darr's own interests and those of Carnegie, Harrison, Watson & Taylor, and First South would converge. This time, they would be in deep conflict with the interests not only of investors but also of banking regulators.

It seemed like almost nobody wanted to buy the Madison Plaza partnership. The $52 million offering in 1984 was the most important real estate partnership Pru-Bache ever sold. As the largest private placement in the history of the firm, it would pay at minimum more than $7 million in fees and expenses. The partnership also involved some high-profile property: a full square block in the heart of midtown Manhattan, near Grand Central Station on Madison Avenue. But the deal, sponsored by Carnegie, was inordinately complex, involving multiple mortgages and two partnerships, one that owned the buildings and another that owned the land.

The deal's complexity scared off brokers. Few were willing to sell their customers a deal they could not explain. That made Madison Plaza enormously frustrating for Darr—unlike some other deals, the partnership was an "all-or-nothing" deal. If the full $52 million was not raised by May 31, 1984, the deal would be canceled and Prudential-Bache would not be paid. In turn, all of the investors who had already signed up to purchase it would receive their money back. It was a requirement designed to make early investors comfortable that, if the marketplace rejected the partnership, they would not be left holding the bag. Such market discipline was rarely applied in the Direct Investment Group, and it was chafing Darr badly.

With so much at stake, Darr launched a direct, personal effort to sell the deal. He reviewed a marketing video for brokers called *Miracle on Madison Avenue* and ordered a series of editing changes to snazz it up. Still, sales did not improve. He ordered Proscia and other executives to shelve competing deals so everyone could focus their selling effort exclusively on Madison Plaza. That didn't work. So on February 29, Darr dictated a series of intimidating wires to his regional sales staff to pressure them into pushing Madison Plaza out the door.

"I fully expect you to take the lead in this transaction nationally," Darr dictated in one typical internal memorandum to Ed Devereaux, a marketer for the New York region. "I also expect you to have sold $10,000,000 by the end of the production month in March."

Darr then added, "Whatever it takes, do it."

Even that failed to improve the sales. In early May, with the deadline for closing fast approaching, slightly more than half of the Madison Plaza deal had been sold. The market had decisively rejected the deal. Under the terms of the offering memorandum, Madison Plaza should have been canceled and investors' money returned. But the prospect of losing the huge fees and having to return the clients' money was too embarrassing. So, contrary to the terms of the partnership and without the approval of investors, the Direct Investment Group extended the deadline. As Darr had encouraged, the department did whatever it took. They turned to Clifton Harrison.

In May, Harrison called Carnegie, sounding confident and flush. He had just finished negotiating the deal with Prudential-Bache executives that would help bail him out of his Carnegie loan. And he recently had found new partners with access to millions of dollars.

"I know you're having trouble selling the Madison units," Harrison said. "I have some money, and some partners, and we should get together to see if we can work out a solution to close this transaction." But Harrison imposed conditions: He would have to be named a co–general partner on the deal, and Carnegie had to release its claim to the collateral he had put up for his loan.

Harrison's newfound negotiating power came from the business relationship he had just struck up with John Roberts Jr., the president and sole shareholder of Summit Savings Association, a high-flying savings and loan in Plainview, Texas. Harrison and Roberts met weeks earlier, as they were separately looking at a Florida hotel called the Brazilian Court that both considered a spectacular property for a partnership. As they chatted about real estate, they decided that they would make a fabulous team. Roberts thought Harrison, with his Prudential-Bache connections, was a premier real estate investor.

Meanwhile, Harrison knew that his new friend had huge sums of cash from Summit at his disposal. Roberts, whose only banking experience had been as a borrower before he purchased Summit in 1983, reveled in his sudden ability to invest millions of dollars in big-time transactions. After taking control of Summit, he started throwing money around while sniffing out huge deals. He attracted a lot of attention: He lived a high-flying lifestyle, jetting on private planes between New York, Palm Beach, and Plainview. He insisted on expensive dinners, top-rate caviar, the best champagnes, and first-class hotels. While his wife remained at home, Roberts would fly with his girlfriends around the country on a regular basis. To a large degree, Roberts and Harrison were soul mates—they both lived to spend money.

"I don't need a salary," Roberts told a colleague at Summit. "Just pay my expenses."

At times, Roberts paid for his expensive tastes by illegally helping himself to Summit's money. When he decided that he wanted a new Gulfstream II jet aircraft, he arranged for a fraudulent $4.5 million loan to a borrower who was simply a front for Roberts himself. The borrowed money was then illegally used to buy Roberts his plane.

With Roberts's easy-money ways, his small S&L quickly gained the reputation among financiers as a ready source of cash. Roberts began rubbing elbows with the likes of Adnan Kashoggi, who would later gain fame in the Iran-contra affair for his help in financing weapons deliveries to Iran. But Harrison seemed most likely to be able to catapult Roberts into the big leagues. First, Harrison introduced him to senior Pru-Bache executives. Then Roberts met other members of the firm's stable of general partners, including John Holmes, the headhunter who helped Darr get his job. The message from all the feting was clear: Roberts could be a player at Prudential-Bache as long as he came to the table with his thrift's money. If he helped on the Madison Plaza deal, he would win the gratitude of some powerful people.

The proposal to use Harrison and Roberts was as complex as Madison Plaza itself. About $15 million worth of the deal still had to be sold for it to close. So, rather than wait for Pru-Bache brokers to track down retail investors, Summit would lend the $15 million to the deal. Carnegie would then transfer that money to a Cayman Islands bank account and use it to purchase the unsold units for the benefit of the ACP/CRC trust, a company managed by Harrison and Roberts. Then, as Prudential-Bache continued to sell interests in Madison Plaza, the money raised from retail investors would be transferred back to Summit to pay the loan. The proposal sidestepped the "all-or-nothing" requirement and ensured that Pru-Bache would be paid its hefty fees.

That proposal was finalized on May 25, 1984. Without even asking for a loan application, Roberts agreed to lend the $15 million. The only strict term of the loan was that Summit had to be repaid before any general partners' fees went to either Harrison or Carnegie.

Darr was delighted. He wanted to meet Roberts, the man who had rescued the deal and saved his department from an embarrassing failure. So on June 1, while on a trip to New York with James Holbrook, a lawyer for Summit, Roberts made a pilgrimage to the Direct Investment Group accompanied by John Holmes, Darr's old friend.

They met on that warm and sunny Friday afternoon in Darr's new office. Weeks earlier, Prudential-Bache had moved to a shiny thirty-two-story office building off the East River called One Seaport Plaza. The meeting was amiable, and Darr was positively gracious to Roberts.

"I'm really pleased that you're doing the Madison project," Darr said. "I want you to know, I will personally make phone calls to Prudential-Bache brokers and see to it that the project is sold out quickly."

Roberts thanked Darr, feeling dazzled. Here he was, a former real estate broker, being told that the awesome retail network of Prudential-Bache Securities was about to be set in motion for his benefit. Roberts started laying out the details of the next acquisition he wanted to pursue. He had been examining First American Financial, a title insurance company he wanted to buy out of the American Century Corporation, another company he controlled. Darr's eyes seemed to light up as the details of the possible inside deal were described.

"That sounds like an incredible deal," Darr said. "If Prudential-Bache doesn't get involved in the deal, I'd like to invest in that personally."

Holmes then took the floor, telling Darr and Roberts about an oil and gas venture he and a partner were pursuing called American Completion. Darr beamed. That sounded like another great deal, he said. Turning to Roberts, Darr suggested that he should not let Holmes's deal pass him by.

"I think you ought to give John Holmes a million dollars or so," Darr said.

Roberts nodded in agreement. He would lend Holmes the money once he returned to Texas. Roberts was rapidly becoming another Darr disciple.

Days later, after a week of marathon negotiations, Roberts returned to Texas. Holbrook, the Summit lawyer, met one last time with Harrison and Steven Davis, a senior vice-president for acquisitions at Harrison Freedman, at La Guardia Airport in the American Airlines Admiral's Club. They relaxed over drinks while munching on free pretzels and crackers. At one point, Harrison excused himself, leaving Holbrook and Davis alone. Davis seemed to feel a little boozy, and the conversation became fairly loose.

"You know, Clifton needed this Madison Plaza deal," Davis said. "He's really overextended."

"Really?"

"Yeah, Clifton lives from deal to deal," Davis said. "He needs the next deal to pay for the expenses he didn't pay in the last deal. So every deal becomes very critical. He lives from hand to mouth on a daily basis."

Holbrook sat back in his chair. What he was hearing sounded awfully dangerous. At some point, Harrison would be unable to sell the next deal; then the whole house of cards would come tumbling down. When that happened, it would burn Harrison's investors, including the newest ones in the huge Madison Plaza deal. But worrying about the investors was Prudential-Bache's job, not his. As long as Summit was paid back its $15 million, Holbrook didn't much care what happened to retail investors.

John Roberts picked up the telephone in his office at Summit Savings Association and dialed Darr's direct number at Pru-Bache. It was Roberts's second call on the morning of Thursday, August 30, and he was excited. He had just finished speaking with Clifton Harrison, who offered some positive news about several deals they were working on together. While they spoke, Darr had called and left a message.

Roberts's call was put right through, and the two men chatted about various deal ideas of Darr's. The merger business was starting to boom, and Darr was dropping the names of companies he thought could be ripe for takeover, such as the Weyerhaeuser Company, the Seattle timber concern. Later, Roberts mentioned a deal involving some Aspen real estate that he hoped to sell through Prudential-Bache.

"Well, if you bring it here, you should hire Clifton Harrison as a consultant to put the book together," Darr said, again trying to insert Harrison into someone else's deal. "He knows how to do it and knows his way around the firm."

At the end of the conversation, Darr brought up another matter. He said that Watson & Taylor, one of Pru-Bache's general partners, had some loans with an Arkansas thrift called First South. Would Summit be willing to swap some of its own loans for $50 million worth of First South's loans to Watson & Taylor? Roberts said he would be happy to look into it.

Roberts could not have known, but at that moment, First South was desperately trying to get one step ahead of banking regulators. Two weeks earlier, on the same day that Darr purchased his new $1.8 million house with money supplied by the Arkansas S&L, First South's independent auditors from Deloitte, Haskins & Sells finished a devastating report. The auditors said that First South had loaned $55 million more to Watson & Taylor than was legally permitted to go to a single borrower. As required, they sent a copy of the audit report to the Federal Home Loan Bank Board, then the chief regulator for the savings and loan industry.

The report petrified Howard Wiechern, First South's chairman. He fretted that federal regulators would soon be breathing down his neck about his relationship with Watson & Taylor. That could present a major problem. Just months earlier, First South and Watson & Taylor launched a criminal conspiracy to hide the true nature of their financial relationship from the thrift's auditors. A company called Watson & Taylor Management, which had a total worth of $25 million, had borrowed $40 million from First South. When the auditors objected, Watson signed guarantees for the loan. But in a secret scheme, Wiechern agreed in writing that the guarantees would never be enforced. In effect, nothing about the problem loans would change except that a few fraudulent documents would be stuffed into the files at First South. If the government figured out what had happened, somebody was going to go to jail.

Wiechern had to eliminate the government's interest in the loans to Watson & Taylor by getting them off the books. That required finding another S&L willing to trade loans so First South could hide the magnitude of its problems from regulators. Apparently, either directly or through Watson & Taylor, First South turned for help to its largest mortgage borrower, Darr, who in turn spoke to Roberts at Summit.[*]

For months after their August conversation, Darr heard no develop-

[*]Darr denies having discussed loan swaps between Summit and First South. See Notes and Sources.

ments on the loan-swap proposal from Roberts, and apparently he assumed everything had been handled. But, in fact, Roberts was severely distracted by his own growing troubles. Regulators had begun to question him about the propriety of his management at Summit. Both First South and Summit were getting caught up in the first wave of the savings and loan scandal that would unfold across the Southwest for much of the rest of the decade. Eventually, Texas state regulators swooped down on Summit and demanded that, because of his wild spending, Roberts remove himself from the S&L. That same day, federal regulators contacted Wiechern in Arkansas to say that they would be arriving soon to start a complete audit of First South. All of the problem loans to Watson & Taylor were still on First South's books.

Soon Darr was phoning Summit again, demanding to speak with Roberts. He reached Holbrook, the S&L's lawyer. Holbrook was surprised to hear from Darr—over several months, he had left messages for Darr at the Direct Investment Group, saying that he wanted to know why Summit had not been repaid its $15 million from the Madison Plaza deal. Darr never called him back. At first, Holbrook assumed that was the purpose of the call, but he quickly realized that Darr had other matters to discuss.

"Listen, I've had some conversations with John Roberts, and he made a commitment to have Summit buy some loans from First South," Darr said. "Why isn't that being done? I want it taken care of quickly."

Holbrook could not believe what he was hearing. Darr's tone put him on edge. *He's talking to me like he's the president of a bank and I'm some loan officer*, Holbrook thought.

"I have no knowledge of any of this," Holbrook said. "Roberts is no longer involved with the savings and loan and can't make these commitments. We certainly aren't going to be making these commitments."

Darr sounded nearly apoplectic. "But John promised me. So I think you need to do this." Suddenly his tone of voice became more menacing. "And if not, I have done a lot of things for John and Summit and you in New York," he said cryptically. "We've done things that were supposed to be paid back, and this is one of the things you were supposed to do for me."

Holbrook had no idea what favors Darr was talking about and did not want to know. And he did not take well to being threatened.

"I'm sorry," he said. "John is no longer involved here, nor can he make a commitment. And, I apologize, but to this extent, I am not going to help you."

Then he hung up the phone.

Holbrook did not know it, but at that instant, he helped to set in motion a series of events that would damage First South, Watson & Taylor, and eventually Darr himself. But it would be years before anyone at Prudential-Bache knew anything about it.

George Ball felt a little virtuous. He had not allowed himself to be unduly swayed by the rumors about Jim Darr's ethics. And now, in late 1984, months after Ball ordered the investigation of Darr, lawyers for Prudential-Bache reported that they had found no evidence of impropriety. The lawyers chased down every rumor they heard and repeatedly hit dead ends. Although there were widespread stories that Darr was dirty, none of the people they interviewed had any details. To a degree, the investigation had been hampered by Ball's instructions: He wanted it conducted as quietly as possible, to avoid feeding the Darr rumors. The investigators did not even question Darr himself. From all the lawyers could tell, Darr might not be the most pleasant fellow in the world, but they found nothing to prove that he was dishonest.

What was most telling about the second investigation of Jim Darr is what the lawyers left out in their oral report to Ball: They did not mention that Darr had already been investigated by the firm once before, or that the five men who reported specific allegations of wrongdoing against him had been fired or eased out. The lawyers did not find out about Darr's demands for an apartment from VMS for Sherman or about Darr's private investment deals with Watson & Taylor. They also missed his $1.8 million sweetheart mortgage loan from First South and his efforts to coordinate loan swaps out of that troubled S&L for the benefit of Watson & Taylor. In short, the investigators learned nothing about what was actually going on in one of the firm's biggest departments.

Once the lawyers finished their report, Ball felt pleased. He had prevented an innocent man from being maligned by jealous tongues, he thought. Better still, he could now take comfort in Darr's honesty. After all, Darr had just been investigated. Regardless of whatever bad rumors he heard about Darr in the future, Ball felt confident that he would not have to take them seriously.

CHAPTER 9

BOB SHERMAN STEPPED OFF an American Airlines jet into the bright sunshine at the Cancún International Airport. His flight to Mexico on the afternoon of February 19, 1984, had arrived right on time. The small airport was bustling with tourists, buzzing excitedly about having escaped the frigid North American winter. Sherman, dressed in a sport shirt and sport coat, headed onto the tarmac and walked briskly toward the airport's baggage pickup.

Sherman entered the terminal, looking around expectantly. Not a single senior executive from Direct Investment Group was there to meet him. In fact, no one from Pru-Bache was waiting for him. An expression of sheer anger crossed his face. At the very least, Sherman expected that as the head of the firm's retail division, he would be treated with a degree of respect. He set down his carry-on bag and stood inside the terminal gate, furious.

He continued to scowl as a bald, heavyset man walked toward him. "Mr. Sherman?" the man said. "I'm Paul Grattarola, the national sales manager for Graham. We're the sponsors of this trip. I'm here to take you to the hotel."

Sherman looked at Grattarola, visibly upset. "Where's Jim Darr?" he demanded. "Where are the other people from Direct Investments? Why aren't they here?"

Oh, boy, Grattarola thought, realizing he had another Prudential-Bache prima donna on his hands. He would have to handle this delicately.

"Well, I apologize for that," he told Sherman. "We've got some activities going on back at the hotel, and everyone is there."

Sherman scowled and looked away. Clearly, the explanation had not soothed his bruised ego.

Grattarola picked up Sherman's bags and escorted him to the waiting car. He was dreading the ride back to the hotel. Ever since Graham had assigned Grattarola the responsibility for planning this trip for hundreds of brokers and managers from Pru-Bache, his encounters with the firm's executives had been an endless headache.

The trip was billed as the energy income fund's due diligence trip. In itself, the name was a laugh. If the Prudential-Bache brokers and managers wanted to perform due diligence on the energy income fund, they needed to fly out to one of the partnerships' oil fields in Wyoming or Texas, or maybe to Graham headquarters in Louisiana. Not too many oil wells were likely to be drilled on the beaches of luxury hotels in Mexican resort towns. But then, not many of the 183 Pru-Bache executives who came on the trip, many accompanied by their spouses, were there to learn anything about oil wells.

In truth, the trip was little more than a legal bribe to induce the firm's brokers and managers to sell the energy income partnerships. Any broker who sold $200,000 or more of the energy partnerships won a spot on the trip. Managers who pushed their troops to sell $500,000 worth were also included. All of the qualifying executives won two round-trip air fares to Cancún, four nights at one of the city's finest hotels, plus free meals and drinks. The cost of the entire trip was on Graham, which in turn passed the bills on to the public partnerships. Somehow Graham viewed providing luxurious entertainment for the people who sold the partnerships as an appropriate use of clients' money.

But none of the clients would know anything about it. The trips were never specifically disclosed in the two-inch-thick prospectus for the first series of the Prudential-Bache Energy Income Fund. So none of those clients would ever question whether their broker sold them the partnership because of an honest belief that it was a good investment, or because the broker needed another $10,000 in sales to win a luxurious holiday.

There was little question that the trips succeeded in persuading brokers to sell partnerships. When the Prudential-Bache Energy Income Fund was first offered eight months earlier, John Graham told colleagues that he would be surprised if more than $30 million of partnerships were sold. By the time of the trip to Cancún, Prudential-Bache brokers had persuaded 8,090 clients to invest $91 million in the deals.

Not that Graham was unique in providing the trips; its trips were just among the best. All of the big partnership sponsors did the same thing, although Pru-Bache had the reputation of expecting the most trips with the highest expense. By 1984, the sales force expected the free vacations. Brokers who once only asked "What's the commission?" had added another question to their list: "What's the trip?"

The Direct Investment Group soon was demanding that general partners package the most elegant, expensive, and perk-laden trips possible—to England, Sardinia, Amsterdam, Hawaii, or other luxurious travel spots.

Grattarola had learned about that imperious attitude firsthand in planning the Cancún trip, particularly when it came to the care and feeding of Jim Darr. Grattarola was given specific instructions from the Direct Investment Group: While in Cancún, Darr would have a limousine available for him at all times. He also wanted a large hotel suite.

Darr even refused to accept spending restrictions placed on other Prudential-Bache executives. Although the brokers and managers were allowed to order as much champagne as they wanted, Grattarola limited each of them to four bottles of Dom Perignon. In Mexico, that top-of-the-line champagne easily cost more than $100 a bottle. But four bottles were not enough for Darr. He wanted—and would order—far more than the limit. After all, the money wasn't his.

As the demands flowed into Graham's headquarters, Grattarola, a blunt Italian American with a long background in the brokerage business, grew uncomfortable. Darr alone might well push the trip over budget. Grattarola sought out Tony Rice, Graham's chief financial officer, and explained the problem.

"Whatever Jim wants, give it to him," Rice said. "Without question."

Even with free rein, Grattarola had trouble meeting all of Darr's demands. After all, Cancún was not Manhattan—some of the things Darr wanted were difficult to obtain. At first, Grattarola could not locate a single available limousine there. He finally tracked one down in Mexico City. But the limousine company refused to send one of its cars hundreds of miles for just a five-day stay. So, billing the cost to the public partnerships, Graham paid for the limousine for two weeks, even though it would be sent back after five days. Delighted, the Mexican company had the limousine driven down to Cancún for Darr and his wife.

Rice instructed Grattarola to give Darr a presidential suite in Cancún. The suite was gigantic, at about five thousand square feet, with multiple levels, a huge bathtub, and its own swimming pool. It was literally the presidential suite: Before they agreed to let Darr stay there, hotel officials checked with the aides to Mexico's president to make sure he was not coming that week. Afterward, Grattarola had to agree that Darr would move if the president changed his mind.

Encouraged by Rice and John Graham, Grattarola went all-out on the kingly treatment for Darr. He arranged for Darr and his wife to be ticketed separately from the others at the airport. On the other end of the trip, Darr's group was met by a mariachi band. While other Prudential-Bache executives waited in line for their luggage to be examined at customs, the Darrs were taken to a special room. There they were offered champagne while their luggage was specially handled. Grattarola also asked the mayor of Cancún to send a representative to greet Darr and to thank him for bringing such a large contingent of American businessmen to the resort.

It had all come off without a hitch earlier that day. Now Grattarola could see that his failure to create a similar reception for Sherman had left him seething. Grattarola figured that Sherman had his own spies on the trip, who must have told him about Darr's majestic welcome. Apparently, Sherman had expected the same treatment. But instead, Sherman waited in line at customs just like any other tourist. Grattarola tried striking up a conversation, but Sherman just muttered at him irritably. Finally they were ready to go, and Grattarola took Sherman out to a waiting car.

As the drive began, Sherman asked where he would be staying. Grattarola said that he had arranged for Sherman to stay in a suite at the Sheraton.

"Is it as good as Darr's?" Sherman asked.

Here we go, Grattarola thought. "I don't believe so," he said. "There's only one suite in town that size."

"Well, why don't you kick Darr out of it and put me in? I'm senior to Darr. He reports to me."

Grattarola spoke carefully, measuring his words. "I don't handle politics, Mr. Sherman," he said. "I worked these things out through the people in Direct Investments. I've done what they asked me to do. We did the best we could. I've looked all over town, and there is no other suite like that."

Sherman snorted. "Well, you don't do a very good job. I'm not impressed with you, and I'm certainly not impressed with your organization."

For the next few minutes, Sherman was mostly silent, with an occasional cutting remark about how little he thought of Graham. Grattarola felt enormously uncomfortable. He had never met a Pru-Bache executive more senior than Sherman. And the man clearly hated him.

Finally, as the car drove along the streets of Cancún, Sherman broke the silence.

"Look, you're in charge of this thing," he said. "Well, I want unlimited expenses for room service. I'll probably want to have a party, and I don't want any restrictions. I don't want to have to deal with a bunch of rules. Understand?"

Apparently, all these senior Prudential-Bache executives were satisfied with the same things. If they would buy peace for Graham, Sherman's demands were cheap.

"That's fine," Grattarola said. "We'll take care of that."

"And one more thing," Sherman said. "I'd like some girls in my suite tonight."*

What the hell? Grattarola was shocked. He had just met Sherman. The man had no idea how Grattarola would react to such a request. And the truth was, although Grattarola would do everything within the rules to make brokerage executives happy, he would not cross his own self-imposed line.

"I don't do things like that," he replied caustically. "I don't buy sex and I don't give cash."

Grattarola could almost see the rage in Sherman's eyes.

"Do you know who I am?" Sherman snarled. "I'm one of the highest guys at Prudential-Bache. And I want entertainment. I want to throw a party, and I want girls. I want you to get girls."

"I won't do that," Grattarola said.

For the next few seconds, Sherman raged at Grattarola. He was an important executive, he said, and was Graham's guest. He expected to have his demands met. He expected Graham to pay for everything.

Finally Grattarola pushed back. "Look," he said. "If you feel that strongly about it, when we go back to the hotel, you write up the request on Prudential-Bache stationery. Say that you want me to get four ladies to your suite this evening. You sign it, and I'll do it."

Sherman's eyes narrowed into slits. "You dago son of a bitch," he hissed. "This is war."

Not another word was spoken during the ride. When they pulled up to the hotel ten minutes later, Sherman stormed out of the car. Just as he reached the lobby door, he turned and looked daggers at Grattarola.

"Do you think you can handle the luggage?" he snapped. He marched away, leaving Grattarola responsible for moving his bags up to his suite. Grattarola arranged for a bellhop to handle the suitcases. Then he got back into the car and headed for his own hotel.

Oh, my God, Grattarola thought. *Am I going to be fired?*

He hurried to his room as soon as he arrived at his hotel. Then he grabbed the telephone and dialed the room number for Joseph DeFur, a

---

* Sherman denied asking anyone to procure women for him while he was in Cancún.

product manager with the Direct Investment Group. A few months before, DeFur had taken over the responsibility for the Energy Income partnerships. Grattarola reached him immediately and told DeFur about his run-in with Sherman.

"I'll tell you, Joe," he said. "Sherman is livid. I am in deep trouble."

DeFur thought the whole thing was amusing. As he listened to Grattarola, he couldn't stop laughing. DeFur said he would make some calls. Within twenty minutes, Darr called Grattarola.

"What's the matter?" Darr said, laughing. "You didn't get along with Bobby?"

"Hey," Grattarola said. "I'm in a lot of trouble here, and you guys are all making a big joke."

Darr's tone of voice grew serious. "You're not in trouble," he said. "Sherman can't do anything to you, and he can't do anything to me. He's just a lot of noise. So don't worry about it."

To a large degree, Darr was right. In the year and a half since Ball's arrival, Sherman's star at Prudential-Bache had waned. The hopes he once had of taking over the firm had vanished; without that aspiration, Sherman had settled into playing intense political games. He called meetings of his senior staff to plot means of undermining other executives. Sherman's insular approach and obvious selfishness bothered Ball, but he was not yet ready to make a change in the department. Still, it was obvious to everyone that Sherman was losing power.

As Darr wrapped up the conversation with Grattarola, he told the Graham executive that no matter how Sherman felt, there would be no repercussions from the matter. Grattarola thanked him.

"One thing would help take care of this," Darr added.

"Yeah?"

"Don't put a limit on Sherman's bar tab," he said. "Just let him get drunk."

John Corbin, the top marketer from Graham, stared across the crowded lobby of the El Camino Royale Hotel in Cancún. The place was packed with dozens of Prudential-Bache brokers and managers. Most of them had just arrived with Corbin on the last plane from California on February 19. Corbin, who handled Graham's West Coast marketing of the energy income partnerships, baby-sat them as they checked in. He had just spent about twenty minutes greeting everyone at the door. Now he was relaxing against the wall, holding a drink and keeping an eye on his charges.

As Corbin sipped his drink, he spotted Laurel Vass, a broker from the

Stockton, California, office. She was headed toward him with a woman whom Corbin didn't recognize. Apparently, Vass had given one of her two tickets for the trip to a friend.

"Hey, John," Vass said. "We've got a problem."

"What's the matter?"

"We're supposed to be in this hotel, and there's something wrong with our reservation," she said. "They don't have room for us, and they say they want to put us in another hotel."

This was just the kind of problem that wholesalers were handed all the time on these trips. Corbin figured that he would have to start looking around to find another marketer who could be thrown out of a room. Then the free room could go to the broker and her friend. But all that would take a while and certainly would not be finished that night.

"I'll see what I can do," Corbin said. "But give me some time."

Before the women could reply, Corbin spotted Bob Sherman. He was making a beeline directly toward the two women.

"Is there a problem here?" Sherman asked.

"Well, evidently we've got too many people booked into this hotel," Corbin replied. "And these two ladies were hoping to stay here. But now, I've got to get them over to another hotel."

Sherman beamed. "Well, ladies," he said graciously. "Why don't I give you a ride over to your hotel?"

As Sherman escorted the women out the door, Corbin helped move their bags outside. Within a few minutes, Sherman and the women were driving away. Corbin felt relieved that the problem had been taken care of so easily.

The next day, Corbin ran into the two women again on the beach. They started talking. They were all young, single, and attractive, and soon they and some of Corbin's friends began to spend time together. They walked to the beach for some snorkeling and swimming. By evening, Corbin had found the women a room at the El Camino, where he was staying. They decided to have dinner together, along with Rich Gilman from Graham, and headed back to the hotel to get ready.

Waiting for Vass was a message from Sherman and Carrington Clark, a West Coast regional director for Prudential-Bache and a close friend of Sherman's. They wanted to know if the two ladies would join them for dinner. Vass telephoned them back immediately.

"Thank you for the invitation," she said. "But we've already got something else going on tonight with John Corbin."

The next night, Corbin and a few friends planned a dinner party at a Mexican restaurant. Vass and her friend were invited. Before they left, Vass received another message from Carrington Clark. Again, he wanted to know if the two ladies would have dinner with him and Sherman. Vass again declined, telling Clark that she was going to a party with Corbin.

About twenty minutes later, a Pru–Bache executive took Corbin aside. Sherman and Clark were angry at him, the executive said. They felt hurt that he was having a party and had not invited them. Corbin called Clark immediately.

"Hi, Carrington," he said. "Listen, a bunch of us are going out tonight to a Mexican restaurant for dinner. Do you and Bob Sherman want to come along."

"No thank you, John," Clark said coldly. "We'd rather not."

They said their good-byes, and Corbin hung up the telephone. Whatever was happening, it sure sounded to him as though Clark and Sherman were a bit peeved at him.

Corbin had no idea that the events of the last two days could well cost him his job.

Paul Grattarola ran toward the man-made lake by the El Camino Royale. The mariachi band he had hired to perform had just fallen into the water. The group had been standing on a small boat, playing for one of the Prudential-Bache dinner parties, when it capsized. It was the second night of the Cancún trip. Until the band lost its balance, the trip had been marred only when one broker's wife physically assaulted her husband's branch manager. Besides that, everything had been running like clockwork. Grattarola stood by as the musicians were fished out of the water.

Once that problem was out of the way, Grattarola went back to supervising the party. He took his responsibilities for arranging the trip very seriously and hated for anything to go wrong. As his gaze wandered over the crowd, his eyes locked with Bob Sherman's, who was staring directly at him. Sherman moved forcefully toward Grattarola. He obviously wanted to talk.

"Well, you were right about the suites," Sherman said. "I called Rand Araskog, the chairman of ITT, to see if the Sheraton had something larger than Darr's suite. They don't. He's got the largest suite in the city."

Grattarola just looked at him. He knew that Sherman was trying to awe him with his easy access to the chairman of ITT, which owned the Sher-

aton hotel chain. But he was not impressed. With Sherman the head of retail at a national brokerage firm, Grattarola would have been shocked if he
hadn't been close to someone like Araskog.

"Well," Grattarola finally said, "I guess that's the answer then."

"No, that's not the answer," Sherman said. "I want Darr out of that
room. I want it. I'm his boss. Hell, I'm everybody's boss here. I want you
to fix it. Tonight."

Grattarola tried hard not to grit his teeth. "Look," he said. "I can't go
around throwing senior guys out of their rooms. If you can work this out
with Darr, that's fine. I'll help get you moved over there. But I'm not going to just throw him out."

The scowl descended over Sherman's face again. "Son of a bitch," he
muttered. Then he turned and walked away, disappearing into the crowd
of merrymakers.

Two nights later, about four hundred brokers, managers, and their spouses
milled about a courtyard at the El Camino Royale. It was the last full night
that the group from Prudential-Bache would be staying in Cancún, and it
was meant to be something special. At other dinners that week, there had
been singers, fireworks, and elegant food. But this time, Graham went all-
out. The hotel's man-made lake had been partially drained to create a big
private beach. A special awards ceremony had been arranged to honor the
brokers who had sold the most energy income partnerships. A representative from the president of Mexico had even been invited to extend his
greeting.

Darr had agreed to make a rare talk to all of the firm's brokers, during
which he would present the awards. Darr asked for a Graham executive to
write the speech but refused to describe what he wanted to say. So, with
no input from Prudential-Bache, a speech was written about the great sales
performance that year by the firm's brokers in the Energy Income Fund.

The Pru-Bache managers and brokers had started gathering early in the
courtyard. On the stage, Darr and other executives hobnobbed with the
Mexican official.

The crowd quieted down as Darr walked to a podium on the stage.
With a tone of respect, he introduced the special guest. The Mexican official, a man of average height dressed in a light suit, stepped up to the
podium amid polite applause. His heavy accent made his English difficult
to comprehend. But almost everyone understood the gist of his words: On

behalf of the Mexican president, he thanked them for coming, extended his hopes that they had enjoyed their stay, and invited them to return in the future.

Suddenly, from the back of the courtyard, there was a loud noise.

"Come on!" Bob Sherman yelled. "Let's get this show on the road!"

Everyone turned and looked as Sherman staggered in, accompanied by two attractive women in their twenties who were not part of the Prudential-Bache group. Everyone could tell that Sherman was rip-roaring drunk. Some thought that if he didn't have the women to lean on, he'd fall down.

The Mexican official continued speaking.

"What's with this?" Sherman shouted. "Doesn't this guy speak English?"

Sherman and the women wandered through the crowds. Some wives of brokers shot their husbands dirty looks as Sherman walked by with the young women under his arms. More than a few seemed to be wondering what their husbands had done on other trips they had attended by themselves.

"Come on!" Sherman shouted. "Let's get it over with. Let's party!"

Suddenly Sherman started pointing at Darr, who was visibly upset by his boss's behavior. "Holy shit! Look at that old man up on the stage with the white hair," he shouted. "He is fucking ugly!"

The Mexican official sat down. Then Sherman spun around, yelling at the assembled brokers. "You guys think you're so fucking great! But you might not even be at this fucking firm next year! We don't need you!"

Grattarola, who was up on the stage to help hand out the awards, began to think that it might not have been a good idea to pull the restrictions on Sherman's bar tab. He leaned over to speak with Darr.

"We've got to do something," Grattarola said. "We've got to get him out of here. Do you want to take care of it, or should I call the hotel people?"

"I'll take care of it," Darr replied. He stood up and walked down from the stage, signaling one of his regional marketers to come with him over to Sherman. For about thirty seconds, Darr spoke with Sherman, trying to calm him down. Darr wrapped his arm around him, as the marketing executive got on his other side. They turned Sherman around and, walking as if in a chorus line, headed for the exit.

"Come on, Bob," Darr said softly. "Let's go."

A few minutes passed by, and Darr returned. He walked briskly to the stage, hopped up on it, and headed back toward the podium.

"Well, I'd like to apologize to everyone, and particularly the wives here tonight, for the language," he said. "Bob's not always like that. Obviously, he had too tall a beer."

His audience tittered. Darr was putting them all back at ease.

"All right," he said. "It's time to start presenting the awards for some really great work."

Nothing more was said about Sherman, but as the evening wore on, a heavy pall settled over the crowd. Sherman's performance had left many of them uncomfortable. He was the highest-ranking executive there that night. He was one of the people responsible for making the decisions that directed the huge sales force of the giant brokerage firm. Investors around the country were affected by what he decided to change and what he chose to ignore.

It was hard to believe someone that important could be such a public embarrassment.

Carrington Clark called John Corbin as soon as everyone returned from Cancún.

"I have never been treated so shabbily in my entire life, John," Clark said. "I want you to know that I hold you personally accountable for ruining my trip to Cancún."

Corbin didn't know what to say. He had no idea what Clark was talking about. But he did know that Clark could make his life miserable. Not only was Clark the director for the West Coast region that Corbin covered for Graham, but he was also one of Sherman's best friends. If Corbin didn't smooth the problem over, there might be hell to pay.

"I'm sorry if you had a bad time, Carrington," he said. "What is it that happened?"

"Don't give me that," Clark snapped. "You kept taking out that girl when you knew I was interested in her. You ruined my trip."

Corbin paused. Now he understood. Clark and Sherman had kept asking out Vass and her friend. Each time, the two women went out with Corbin and his friends instead.

He knew Clark had a reputation among the female brokers at Pru-Bache. More than a few of them had talked about sexual harassment problems at the firm involving Clark, and Sherman as well.[*] But apparently,

---

[*] Clark and Sherman were later accused by a Prudential-Bache broker of sexual harassment in a suit against Prudential Securities before the National Association of Securities Dealers (NASD). See Notes and Sources.

Clark thought that his position entitled him to go out with whomever he pleased and to tell Corbin whom he could take out. Corbin shook his head. He didn't need the permission of Clark or Sherman to go out on a date. But there was no saying that to Clark. He was too angry.

"I'll tell you how things are going to be from now on," Clark said. "I don't want you offering anything to my brokers that isn't offered to me. Not one meal, not one drink. And I want to know everything you're doing in my region, anytime."

"All right, Carrington," Corbin said. "That's fine."

Corbin hung up and sighed. Having dinner with those women had brought a heavy price. Now Clark—and probably Sherman—didn't like him at all.

Tony Rice, the chief financial officer of Graham, eased into a chair by the telephone at his comfortable home in Stamford, Connecticut. He didn't like what he was about to do. But the instructions had come from Jim Darr himself. John Corbin, the biggest-selling wholesaler at Graham, had to be fired.

While there had been some complaints that Corbin exaggerated the performance and safety of the Energy Income Funds, that was not Darr's concern. Apparently, Corbin had offended Bob Sherman and Carrington Clark in Cancún—something to do with some woman. Now, to appease them, Prudential-Bache wanted Graham to get rid of him.

For Rice, the relationship with Pru-Bache was too important to argue about the matter. He had always lived in Connecticut, far from Graham's Louisiana headquarters, so he could keep a finger on the pulse of Wall Street. It had been his job to make sure Darr was happy. At first the two men had had a strained relationship. Then Rice did Darr a few favors, like pulling some strings to get him accepted at the Greenwich Country Club. Since then, the two had developed a good rapport. Rice was not about to blow it over John Corbin.

Rice started calling around, trying to find Paul Grattarola, who as Graham's national sales manager was Corbin's boss. Rice eventually tracked him down in San Francisco, where Grattarola was visiting with his son.

"I've got to talk to you," Rice said. "It's an emergency."

"What's up, Tony?"

"You've got to fire John Corbin."

The request was greeted by a few seconds of total silence.

"And why is it we need to fire our number-one salesman?" Grattarola finally said, his tone disbelieving.

"You're not listening to me," Rice replied. "Corbin's got to be fired. Right away."

"Tony, whether you agree or disagree with the way John sells, he's still our number-one guy," Grattarola said. "I mean, what do we tell the managers in the Prudential-Bache system in California? That we reward our best people by firing them?"

Rice sighed. "Well, all right, here's the story. Darr called me. Sherman wants him fired. So we've got to fire him."

"Sherman?" Grattarola asked. "What the hell happened with Sherman? What's going on?"

Rice said that he didn't know the details, but it had something to do with some women at Prudential-Bache who interested Sherman and a friend of his. But the women went out with Corbin instead.

The information struck Grattarola cold. The whole conversation seemed absurd. He couldn't believe that Rice was willing to disrupt the entire company's business simply because some Prudential-Bache executives had their egos hurt. He told Rice that before they did anything, they needed to get more information. Otherwise, if they were wrong, Graham could be facing a huge lawsuit for wrongful termination. And if they were right, then the company could have a sexual harassment problem.

"Let me see if I can talk to Darr about this," Grattarola said. "I'll try and do some damage control."

Grattarola had been scheduled to fly to Hawaii in a day or so for a seminar for Prudential-Bache brokers. He picked up the telephone and canceled those plans. Instead, he arranged to fly to New York to meet with Darr. Within a few days, he was at the offices of the Direct Investment Group. For the first time, Darr agreed to meet with Grattarola in his office, behind closed doors. Even though Darr obviously thought the issue was serious, he couldn't help laughing about it every so often.

"But we do have a problem, because Sherman does want Corbin fired," Darr said.

Grattarola went through the same litany he laid out to Rice, about the problems that would be created within the Prudential-Bache system if the top wholesaler for Graham was fired for little reason. Darr sat back in his chair.

"You know, you're right," he said. "But what can we do to prevent it from happening again?"

The question hit Grattarola like a sock in the stomach. His temper flared up.

"How can we prevent it?" he snapped. "I don't know how I can prevent a guy from picking up some girl. If she wants to go, she'll go. What do you want me to do?"

Darr paused, thinking for a moment. "Well, somebody's got to pay a price here," he said. "Do a favor for Carrington Clark. Some marketing thing. Pay for a seminar in his region. If Carrington feels better, I'm sure I can pawn the whole thing off."

"OK, that's fine. But what about Sherman?"

"I'll take care of Sherman," Darr said. "Don't worry about it."

Relieved, Grattarola left Darr's office and called Clark out on the West Coast to schedule a meeting. Clark told him that he was just about to leave for two weeks on the road, but he agreed to meet Grattarola at the airport where he would be the next day. Grattarola arrived at the meeting tired and angry. It was the first time he had ever met with Clark without being surrounded by brokers. Clark sat with a scowl on his face.

"Carrington, this whole thing is really ridiculous," Grattarola said.

Clark looked taken aback. "I am really offended by that," he said. "We've got a serious problem here, and I don't know how we can straighten it out."

What bullshit, Grattarola thought. The implied threat to Graham's business seemed unmistakable. It infuriated him.

"Look, Carrington, we don't have a serious problem here at all," he said. "If you want to make it serious, then we can make it serious."

Grattarola leaned forward in his chair and lowered his voice. He was ready to bore in. "All we're really talking about here is some married man who wanted to date a single woman who instead went out with a single guy. I don't want to get into moralities here, and I couldn't care less who you shack up with or don't shack up with, or who you pimp for or who you don't pimp for."

He leaned back. "I was told by Darr to straighten this out with you, and that's what I'm here to do," Grattarola said. "Let's get it over with. What do you want from me?"

Clark, apparently stunned, backed down slightly. Although his tone was still angry, he began discussing some ways that the problem could be solved. The two men agreed that, as appeasement, Graham would pay for some sort of event in Clark's region. Clark said that he wanted Graham to sponsor a full training seminar, plus a cocktail party, for all of the big producers in the region.

Son of a bitch is trying to blackmail me, Grattarola thought. He knew the total cost of the request would be close to $9,000.

"No, I'm not going to do that," he said.

Instead, he suggested hiring a speaker he knew who lectured about telephone techniques for brokers. Grattarola figured that would cost about $1,000 for each speech, and he offered to pay for two. Clark agreed.

As the two men stood up to leave, Clark said, "But listen. If Corbin ever comes back into my region again and fools around with any of my brokers, I'll see to it that he's taken care of."

Fine, Grattarola said. Clark continued on his trip, and Grattarola flew back to New Orleans. He felt angry for days afterward. He had flown all over the country and dropped out of his trip to Hawaii just to deal with a bunch of pampered egos.

The Corbin affair had drawn to a close. The total cost to resolve it—between the lectures for brokers, the last-minute airplane flights, the hotels, and the rental cars—was close to $15,000. Those bills were handed off to the energy income partnerships, to be paid for out of the investment dollars of Prudential-Bache clients. And all because Bob Sherman and Carrington Clark, two married men, couldn't get a date.

The prospectus for the second series of energy income partnerships was completed on March 9, 1984, just a few weeks after the Cancún trip. It was the first to be put together since Bill Pittman took over the due diligence for energy deals, and it contained a number of changes from the earlier prospectus.

One difference involved Pittman himself. Although his name did not appear in the first prospectus, in the new one, Pittman was listed as the second-highest-ranking officer—subordinate only to Darr—with Prudential-Bache Energy Production, Graham's co–general partner. With that change, Pittman was among the group in line to receive a share of the cash flow from the energy partnerships.

Buried on page 50 of the prospectus was another change: A few paragraphs, written in dense language, explained how Graham partnerships that had already been sold were having financial trouble. The partnerships had difficulty making their quarterly distributions, the document said. But $120,000 in cash was distributed anyway—much of it a return of investors' own capital. Graham simply loaned millions of dollars to the partnerships to help cover the distributions, as well as pay operating expenses and interest costs on the debt.

Few of the 17,925 Prudential-Bache clients who would purchase $200 million worth of the second series of energy partnerships likely read the prospectus. But the message buried in the thick, complex document was unmistakable: The energy income partnerships weren't working. Because of high expenses and falling energy prices, the partnerships did not have enough cash flow from the sale of oil to make the promised distributions. By quietly advancing the cash, Graham pumped up the distributions, making the partnerships look like strong performers. That assured brokers and clients that the partnerships were good investments.

The sales material distributed to Pru-Bache brokers throughout the spring and summer of 1984 emphasized the supposed quality of the latest income partnerships. Any attempts to tell investors that the partnership distributions included return of their own original investment had been abandoned. Instead, the new sales literature falsely referred to those distributions as the partnerships' "yield." The Pru-Bache brokers who just months earlier struck Graham executives as too unsophisticated to understand the energy income partnerships were being fed a pack of lies by the Direct Investment Group.

The first lie blared off the front page of a nine-page fact sheet about Series II: "Last year was great. 1984 should be even BETTER." The fact sheet never mentioned the financial problems that were forcing Graham to lend money to the partnerships.

Other documents distributed to brokers were even more blatant in their falsehoods. The extremely risky investments were repeatedly labeled as safe and conservative. "This is a low-risk investment in oil and gas, offering high yield," said a July 16, 1984, sales sheet about the partnerships. "Safety" and "low risk" were listed as the top sales points in other marketing materials.

Any brokers or investors who compared this prospectus with the one distributed almost a year earlier for the first series of energy income partnerships might have been confused. The earlier document provided harsh warnings about the partnerships' riskiness, with no attempts to play those warnings down. On the front cover, in bold and capital letters, the document read: "THESE SECURITIES INVOLVE A HIGH DEGREE OF RISK."

But the second prospectus, assembled under Pittman's watch, eliminated the obvious contradiction. The cover made no mention of the partnerships as risky. Instead, it simply referred investors to another part of the prospectus: "FOR A DISCUSSION OF RISK FACTORS CONCERNING THIS INVESTMENT, SEE 'Risk Factors.'"

The simple, easy-to-understand statement about the partnerships' true risk had simply been removed from the second prospectus. It appeared nowhere else in the document.

Pittman sauntered toward David Levine's office in the Direct Investment Group. As usual, he was dressed in one of the expensive European suits that he loved, and he was in good spirits. He had returned a few weeks earlier from the trip to Cancún. He was looking tanned and healthy.

Pittman rarely dealt with the executives in real estate due diligence anymore. Ever since he had been promoted from his job as a product manager, he had little reason to speak with them. But today, in the spring of 1984, he had a question to ask Levine. He never hid the fact that he was somewhat contemptuous of Levine and his colleagues. All of them were far younger than Pittman, who was now forty-one. Most of them had business degrees; Pittman only had an undergraduate degree from night school. And Darr had a habit of heaping praise on the young MBAs at meetings with brokers, saying how they were the group making sure that the firm sold only the best partnerships. The attention they received seemed to dig at Pittman.

He arrived at Levine's office and stuck his head in. The young executive was speaking with Freddie Kotek, one of his colleagues in real estate due diligence. Pittman interrupted and began raising his questions for Levine in a demanding tone. Kotek slouched in his chair. He wasn't interested in the conversation as it droned on.

Suddenly Pittman turned sharply toward Kotek, staring at him with an expression of anger.

"Don't give me that wise-ass college smile!" Pittman snapped. Then he turned back to Levine and finished his conversation. A few minutes later, after Pittman walked away, Levine and Kotek both cracked up.

"Boy," Kotek said, "if I ever had to work for that guy, I'd be out of here."

Darr announced the restructuring of the real estate due diligence department at a meeting of the Direct Investment Group in September 1984. He arrived in the conference room looking confident. There were going to be some changes in the department, he said. Some people needed to be moved around to take advantage of everyone's own individual skills.

"The end of the year is coming up," Darr said, "and we need to get some deals done."

The executives in the room listened fearfully. They knew that Darr had been frustrated with the pace of due diligence under Joe Quinn. A number of deals were being held up by questions from the due diligence department. Quinn liked to take matters slowly and deliberately, to make sure that he did not make a mistake. But there was no place for that kind of approach in the Direct Investment Group. Some members of the department had heard Darr complain about Quinn noodling the deals to death. David Levine had also made himself very unpopular with the marketing staff by aggressively pointing out the problems that he found in the real estate deals. So now, as they listened to Darr talk about the need to get deals done, the due diligence executives started worrying about their jobs.

"I'm going to make some changes," Darr continued. "I'm going to move Joe over to be in charge of asset management, to make sure these investments perform."

There was no mistaking the fact that Quinn was being demoted. Quinn already was responsible for asset management—that department reported to him. With this change, he was losing almost all of his responsibility.

"Now, to take Joe's place, I'm naming someone who in the last year has proven his skills in due diligence and origination," Darr said. "Bill Pittman."

The room was completely silent.

Later that same day, Pittman called David Levine into his office for a talk. Levine stepped in and shut the door behind him before taking a seat.

"David," Pittman said, "I'm taking you off real estate."

Instead, Pittman told him, he wanted Levine to handle some of the more esoteric partnerships, which for the department were far less lucrative. Levine was being pushed out of the business he knew so that he could begin reviewing deals involving businesses like horse breeding, about which he knew nothing.

Levine just looked at Pittman, trying to contain his contempt. He thought the man was an idiot. And now he had to work for him. *You couldn't find your asshole with both hands*, he thought. *You're just some fucking marketing guy.*

"All right," Levine said, and he got up to leave.

To a degree, Levine had seen it coming for months. Ever since he successfully killed Harrison's deal in Chicago, Levine had allowed himself to become increasingly vocal in his objections to the low-quality deals that were flying through the department. He threw up roadblocks every time he saw a problem and refused to back down. In doing his job, he knew he was putting his career in jeopardy.

Levine tried handling the esoteric deals. Keith Fell, the due diligence executive who had been reviewing partnerships such as horse-breeding deals, was moved over to cover real estate.

In October, Levine went to the office of Peter Fass, an outside lawyer who worked with the partnership division, to review a horse-breeding deal that was being readied for sale. Levine was told to help draft the prospectus on the partnership.

After a few minutes, Levine excused himself and went to call Fell, who was back at Prudential-Bache. Maybe Fell could explain the horse deal to him. But a quick conversation with Fell reinforced how little he knew. When Fell started talking about mares, Levine had no idea that was the word for a female horse.

As Fell finished his explanation, Levine felt frustrated with how little he knew. "What the hell am I doing here?" he asked.

Levine knew the answer to his question even as he asked it. When he had been hired to handle due diligence for the department, he knew very little, and so had been considered harmless. Back then, he couldn't slow down Darr's aspirations for huge sales by objecting to bad deals. But once he understood his job, he was simply in the way. By having Levine and Fell switch jobs, Pittman had successfully put them all back to square one. Neither of them knew enough now to consistently sift the bad deals from the good.

Freddie Kotek and David Levine had never seen someone looking so anguished. Dick Anastasio, an appraiser for the Direct Investment Group, had come to speak with his two colleagues a few minutes earlier on this day in October 1984. His face looked ashen.

"What the hell am I supposed to do?" Anastasio asked. "This deal is terrible. I'm really being pressured by Pittman to change my numbers. I just don't think I can do it."

Anastasio had been a respected member of the due diligence team since he started working for the department a few years before. His job was to examine the real estate properties that sponsors wanted their limited partnerships to purchase. The job was incredibly important: When the proposed partnerships came into the Direct Investment Group, the general partners already knew what price they would have to pay for the property they wanted. If the property appraisal came back lower than the purchase price, the deal had a significant problem. Clients who put money in the deal would be overpaying and would be virtually guaranteed that much of their investment would be lost. Anastasio was known as an appraiser who was thorough, reliable, and totally independent.

His latest appraisal had been for a partnership sponsored by the Related Companies, a New York real estate group. Anastasio's values for the property had come back far below what Related had proposed to pay. A few weeks earlier, when real estate due diligence was handled by Joe Quinn, that would have killed the deal.

But now Bill Pittman was in charge. He sent Anastasio's appraisal back and asked him to try again. Perhaps, he suggested, he could increase his numbers. Appraisals are flexible; there are often honest disagreements about values. Anastasio took another look and raised the value slightly, but the values still were nowhere near the purchase price. Pittman was not pleased. He sent the appraisal back again.

That was a few days before Anastasio came to speak with Levine and Kotek. "Pittman keeps sending the numbers back to me, again and again. He keeps asking me to push it up higher. I can't raise it much more."

Both Levine and Kotek looked uncomfortably at Anastasio. They both felt bad for him. They knew he was under enormous pressure. He had a family, a mortgage, and could not afford to lose his job. But he also could not bring himself to give Pittman the appraisal he wanted. There would have been no rational justification for it, other than self-preservation.

"Dick," Levine finally said. "Do whatever you feel you have to do."

The agony that Levine and Kotek saw in Anastasio's face angered them both. They hated Bill Pittman. Hated his willingness to cut corners. Hated his willingness to get deals sold at almost any cost.

A few days later, Kotek and Anastasio were speaking with Pittman when the topic of Anastasio's latest appraisal on the Related deal came up. Still millions less than the sale price, it was the best he could do within the parameters of an honest appraisal.

"Well, look," Pittman said. "Now we're within ten percent of the price. That's fine. We can write ten percent off as the margin of error." He smiled. "We're going to do the deal."

Anastasio blanched. Kotek looked at Pittman with disgust.

Levine kept in close contact with Fell over the next few weeks. He explained all of the problems he had with the real estate deals that were in the pipeline and let him know all of the dirty secrets about the Harrison partnerships. And he continued being vocal in his objections to the low-quality deals coming out of real estate.

But he never had the opportunity to do much more work on the horse-breeding deals. About thirty days after Levine was told of the job switch, Pittman's secretary showed up at his office door. Pittman again wanted to speak with him. Levine headed over to Pittman's office right away.

"David," Pittman said as Levine sat down. "It's very obvious to us that you're not happy here. We think you should resign today."

In his heart, Levine knew it had been coming. Still, Pittman's statement hit him hard. He sat in front of Pittman's desk, momentarily unable to speak.

"Either you can resign," Pittman said, "or you're fired, as of now."

Levine halfheartedly mumbled a few objections. He was too discouraged to put up much of an argument. That day, he typed up his letter of resignation and handed it to Pittman. Fifteen minutes later, he headed out the front door of Prudential-Bache's office by the East River, feeling depressed and defeated. His two-year career in the Direct Investment Group was over.

"Bruce, we've got to find another deal," Pittman said. "Have you got another deal?"

Bruce Manley, the national sales manager from Franklin Realty, listened with amusement in late 1984 as Pittman begged him to come up with another partnership to sell. Franklin, a real estate company, had never been a big partnership sponsor at Prudential-Bache. For years, the company had sold only small private deals through the firm. But Manley had enough exposure to know that the firm's due diligence operation was deteriorating. When D'Elisa ran things, there had been tough questions. Although Quinn asked a lot of questions, he did not have D'Elisa's real estate savvy.

Manley's opinion of the due diligence operation had hit an all-time low a few months earlier. Franklin had presented a deal to the firm for consideration, sending a copy of a proposed prospectus. Weeks later, Manley heard that he would be receiving a telephone call from Direct Investment Group's due diligence team. He assembled all the necessary paperwork and waited by the telephone.

About ten minutes later, the call arrived. A woman from due diligence got on the line. She asked one question: Where were the commissions for the firm listed in the prospectus? After Manley told her the page number, she thanked him, then hung up.

From that point on, Manley had lost his respect for the due diligence at Prudential-Bache. Now, on this day, he had Pittman on the phone, practically pleading for Franklin to come up with an offering. Franklin had just offered a deal through the Pru-Bache system, and it had sold out in about five days. Pittman wanted desperately to pull off a repeat performance as fast as possible.

Manley thought for a moment. The only deal that the company had ready was one that had been shown to Prudential-Bache a few weeks earlier. The due diligence team had rejected the deal, saying that the real estate market in the area looked weak and that it appeared Franklin was overpaying for the property.

"The only one I can think of that's available was the one you guys rejected a short time back," Manley said.

"Well, that's fine," Pittman said excitedly. "We need to have another deal. So why don't we take a look at that one again. Maybe we can futz with it and make it a little more acceptable and revive it."

Manley agreed and spoke with some of Pittman's team about changes that could be made. After reviewing the numbers for a few weeks, Pittman came back and said that the deal had been made acceptable. It was scheduled for marketing through the Prudential-Bache system.

That day, Manley sat in the chair at his desk, making a final review of the prospectus. It was almost identical to the original deal that had been sent to Pru-Bache, the one that had been rejected for being too risky for investors. The price of the apartment building was the same. The projections for performance were the same. The market conditions in California were the same. In fact, only one change was made in the entire prospectus that made the deal acceptable to Pittman:

Prudential-Bache's fees were increased.

The deal sold out in about ninety days. Investors eventually lost most of their money.

George Ball laughed at the large, ugly statue of a mother suckling her child. It was being presented to him as a joke at the November 1984 retirement party of David Sherwood, the outgoing president of Prudential Insurance. Traditionally, the statue was given to the worst-performing company in the Prudential family, symbolizing the struggling company's need to feed on mother Pru. For losing a bundle of money, Prudential-Bache was the statue's new home.

After two years of running the firm, Ball was beginning to feel some heat for its lousy performance. The firm had been hemorrhaging cash— for the first nine months of 1984 alone, it lost about $105 million. Prudential Insurance had been compelled to invest another $100 million into Pru-Bache on October 22 to help keep the firm going. The high hopes that followed Ball's arrival had all been dashed.

Ball desperately wanted to turn things around. Somehow, he needed most of the firm to start generating huge profits. Only a few departments seemed able to make any money at all, with the Direct Investment Group being one of the standouts. If every department could run as efficiently as that one, Ball felt sure that Prudential-Bache could start making some consistent profits.

So Ball decided to use the presentation of the statue as an opportunity to urge his troops to start bringing in the profits. On November 26, he wrote up a Ballgram, describing how the firm had been given the statue and what it symbolized. It was something that no member of the Prudential family wanted.

"I also want to unload the statue as soon as possible—to pass it, flowing on a sea of profits, to another Prudential company," he wrote. "Accomplishing that, quickly and loudly, is one of our primary goals."

At the end of the memo, Ball included a new rallying cry for the firm: "Shed the statue. Losses suck."

To make sure no one would miss the point, Ball sent out thousands of buttons that featured a picture of the statue. Surrounding the picture, in bright red lettering, were the words "Losses Suck."

Within six months of Bill Pittman taking over real estate due diligence, the group's makeup was almost totally changed. Levine had been asked to leave. Freddie Kotek, Lauren McNenney, and Jeff Talbert had all found other jobs. It was the same thing that had happened a year earlier when Darr gave Pittman the responsibility for energy due diligence: Everyone who had done their jobs and raised questions that slowed down the limited partnership money machine had been driven out of the firm.

By late 1984, the transformation of the Direct Investment Group was complete. It was run by Darr, a former broker. Due diligence was handled by Pittman, a former broker. It reported to Sherman, a former broker. And the firm was controlled by Ball, a former broker. Everyone in an important supervisory position for the department came from a background based purely on sales. For them, the proof of success was the dollar volume of the partnerships that could be stuffed into accounts of Prudential-Bache clients.

Only one person with supervisory authority over the Direct Investment Group was not a broker. But by then, that executive, Loren Schechter, had a number of other issues on his plate. Even as the general counsel, he could not pay much attention to what was happening in the firm's partnership division.

In that year, Schechter was too busy negotiating with the Securities and Exchange Commission on behalf of Prudential-Bache. He was desperately trying to stop the regulatory agency from filing one of the largest complaints in its history against a national brokerage firm.

CHAPTER 10

WARM AIR FILLED THE conference room at the SEC's Atlanta regional office. Someone had turned the thermostat up too high. Even though it was just 9:45 on the frosty morning of February 21, 1985, the heat made all five people in the room shift in their seats from discomfort. But Richard Saccullo, head of Prudential-Bache's largest branch in Atlanta, was probably the most uncomfortable of all.

It was the beginning of Saccullo's second day of interrogation by two SEC lawyers from Washington, D.C. With each pointed question, it grew more evident that the investigators doubted the professed zeal of Saccullo and Prudential-Bache for enforcing securities rules on brokers.

The SEC lawyers, Jared Kopel and Karen Shapiro, sat across a conference table from Saccullo and Patrick Finley, an associate general counsel for Prudential-Bache. A court reporter sat nearby. Kopel, the senior SEC lawyer on the case, watched Saccullo closely as he answered questions. Saccullo, a heavyset, jovial-looking man with thinning brown hair, was a star in the Pru-Bache system. Even though he had already been cited once by the commission for failing in his supervisory duties, Saccullo remained one of Sherman's favorites. He projected the image of a man who knew he was untouchable at the firm.

But Saccullo would have trouble emerging from this new investigation unscathed. By following a trail of documents, Kopel had uncovered a web of connections between Saccullo's branch and Joseph Lugo, a shady penny-stock trader from Florida. From all appearances, the Prudential-Bache Atlanta branch had been involved in a complex scheme with Lugo to illegally manipulate the price of a penny stock.

The stock was in a Florida restaurant chain called Capt. Crab's Take-Away. By studying trading records, Kopel had discovered large purchases of the stock coming from the Atlanta branch in the summer of 1983. That heavy buying drove up the price of Capt. Crab shares. At the same time, insiders at Capt. Crab, along with a handful of stockbrokers associated with

Lugo, had been selling shares. The purchases by the Pru-Bache Atlanta branch looked like the classic manipulation, designed to temporarily increase the share price so that the sellers could make huge profits. Making it all the more suspicious were the identities of the two young brokers whose clients were the biggest buyers of the shares: Robert Scarmazzo and his close friend David Scharps, the son of Capt. Crab's president.

Somehow, Prudential-Bache had become tied up in a sleazy scheme. Now, with the deposition of Saccullo, Kopel thought he had the best chance to find out why that happened. Saccullo had been the manager of the Atlanta branch during the manipulation. At the time, the firm's compliance officers found the trading in Capt. Crab suspicious. They ordered Saccullo to restrict the purchases by only accepting unsolicited orders, meaning trades requested by customers without being suggested by the brokers. Saccullo disregarded those instructions for some time. Later he ignored orders from compliance to stop trading in Capt. Crab shares altogether.

SEC lawyer Shapiro paused for an instant as she studied a document in preparation for her next question. It was one of the wires from compliance that had been sent to Saccullo. It said that six clients of the young broker named Scarmazzo had purchased 14,200 shares in Capt. Crab on one day. All of the order tickets described the sales as unsolicited. Because the compliance department had trouble believing that so many customers decided to buy the same obscure stock on the same day, the wire asked Saccullo to investigate.

Shapiro held the Scarmazzo wire in her hand as she read it to Saccullo. "Do you recall receiving this wire?"

"In general terms, yes," Saccullo said.

"What, if anything, did you do to ascertain whether the shares were, in fact, unsolicited?"

Saccullo almost shrugged. "I spoke with Scarmazzo and was told by Scarmazzo that the shares were, in fact, unsolicited."

Kopel kept staring at Saccullo, unflinching. *My broker told me he didn't break the rules, so I believed him.* The basic point of the compliance department's concern was that they feared Scarmazzo was *lying.*

"Did he give an explanation as to why so many accounts decided to make purchases on the same day?" Kopel asked.

"I called the man and we had a conversation," Saccullo replied. "He assured me the trades were unsolicited, and I had no reason to think he was telling me anything but the truth."

It was like a game of cat and mouse. No matter how the SEC investigators asked the questions, Saccullo fell back on the same answer. But by this point, it didn't much matter what Saccullo had to say in his defense. Already the SEC investigators believed that he had not done his job as a manager. That was enough for a regulatory sanction.

Still, the SEC needed to know more about Joseph Lugo, the Florida penny-stock trader involved in the manipulation. After asking about David Scharps, the son of Capt. Crab's president, the investigators brought up Lugo's firm, Rooney Pace.

"Did you have any discussions with Mr. Scharps about Rooney Pace's activity in the stock?" Shapiro asked.

"Mr. Scharps periodically had conversations with someone by the name of Joe Lugo," Saccullo replied.

"How frequently did you hear Mr. Scharps having conversations with Mr. Lugo?" Shapiro asked.

"Probably half a dozen times."

"Prior to your hearing any conversations between Mr. Scharps and Mr. Lugo," Shapiro asked, "had you otherwise heard of Mr. Lugo in any other context?"

"No," Saccullo said. "Mr. Lugo at some point in time opened up an account in my office to buy a tax shelter." The deal, Saccullo said, was an airplane leasing deal with a company called Polaris.

"Who did he open that account with?"

"With David Scharps."

No one in the room realized the significance of what Saccullo had just said. Some of the money Lugo earned on the Capt. Crab manipulation had been sucked into the partnership fraud. The Polaris deal that Lugo had purchased had been sold by the Prudential-Bache system as safe and secure. Within ten years, it would lose 90 percent of its value. But Pru-Bache and its brokers would receive large fees and commissions.

Prudential-Bache had defrauded one of its accomplices in a major stock scam.

The crowd in the courtroom of Florida state judge Nelson Harris stared silently at the dark-haired man sitting at the defendant's table. Many in the audience knew the man and had once been his clients. He was Sam Kalil Jr., the former assistant manager in Prudential-Bache's Jacksonville branch. And he was in the courtroom on this day in February 1985 to find out how much jail time he would have to serve for looting his customers' accounts at the firm.

Just two years earlier, Kalil had been among the elite at Pru-Bache. He had been a member of the Chairman's Council, the organization for the top ninety brokers at the firm. Even George Ball had thought that Kalil was the kind of salesman everyone else should emulate. Kalil had projected an image of a convincing, energetic, and engaging broker.

"Sam is a model of what I want this firm to be," Ball had told an associate after watching Kalil at a meeting.

A few months later, in December 1983, Kalil was arrested on charges of grand theft, forgery, and securities fraud. The broker's success had been founded on crime. He created huge commissions by buying and selling securities without customer approval and by pushing his unsophisticated clients into complex, unsuitable investments. They lost millions of dollars. To hide his crimes, Kalil stole close to $2 million out of profitable customer accounts and transferred the money into the accounts with losses. Kalil had contested the charges until January 1985, when he agreed to plead guilty to felony charges.

Judge Harris asked Kalil if he had any statement before he passed sentence.

"I'm so sorry for what happened," Kalil said. "I'm deeply ashamed for what I've done."

But Judge Harris was not moved. He sentenced Kalil to serve twenty-six months in prison, four months in a halfway house, and ten years' probation.

The sentence did not bring an end to the Kalil matter for the SEC. The agency had launched an investigation of Prudential-Bache's Jacksonville branch at the time of Kalil's arrest. By the sentencing, the SEC investigation had raised troubling concerns about the firm's management: A branch executive had notarized a signature that Kalil had forged. And Kalil's suspicious cash transfers all were approved unquestioningly by his manager.

The Kalil and Capt. Crab investigations moved simultaneously up the pipes in the SEC—by 1985, a consensus emerged at the commission to consolidate the investigations into a single case. The violations in Atlanta and Jacksonville signaled systemic problems at Prudential-Bache. Since 1976, the firm had been sanctioned for problems in its branches four times—more than any other major firm. Nothing made the firm straighten out. Somehow it had wandered off the path of investor protection.

This time would be different. The SEC lawyers wanted to set an example with Prudential-Bache. The punishments meted out would have to be severe. That way, the lawyers felt sure that the firm would not be able to simply ignore the SEC again.

In the spring of 1985, a group of lawyers sat in a narrow conference room on the fourth floor of the SEC's Washington headquarters. Several had lined yellow legal notepads in front of them, ready for use. On one side of the table sat Loren Schechter, the Prudential-Bache general counsel, looking confident and calm. With him was Arthur Mathews, a wiry, red-bearded partner from the prestigious law firm of Wilmer, Cutler & Pickering. Mathews, a former deputy associate director of enforcement for the SEC, was widely regarded as one of the country's top experts on securities laws.

Across from the two men sat a small group of staff lawyers from the SEC enforcement division. They were there to listen to the Pru-Bache lawyers argue why the commission should not take any action against the firm in the Kalil and Capt. Crab matters.

"A lot of this goes back to the spring and summer of 1983," Schechter said. "We were just taking over from the old guard at Bache. We've solved the problems since then. We've beefed up compliance. Everything you're talking about is just ancient history."

The SEC lawyers seemed unimpressed. Over the years, they had heard various executives from Bache protesting the same thing every time regulators caught the firm violating securities laws. This time, the regulators felt compelled to take serious action.

"Look, I'm in charge now," Schechter said. "The compliance department has direct access to me. I will enforce their directives. I'm there to make sure that this firm follows the letter of the law."

Again, Schechter's sentiments were met with shrugs. The enforcement division had heard this all before, one of the lawyers said.

"But that was different," Schechter said. "You don't need to worry about us. We know how to clean up the messes from the Bache bunch. We're the real professionals from E. F. Hutton."

Reporters and television cameras packed the Justice Department briefing room on May 2, 1985. They were there for a rare event: Edwin Meese, the attorney general of the United States, was personally going to announce a development in a major criminal case. At 2:00 P.M. sharp, Meese stepped up to a podium, scowling slightly from the bright lights. He began to read a prepared statement.

"The Department of Justice today filed a criminal information charging E. F. Hutton & Company, one of the nation's largest securities dealers, with two thousand counts of mail and wire fraud," Meese said. "The essence of the charges was that Hutton obtained the interest-free use of millions of dollars by intentionally writing checks in excess of the funds it had on deposit."

Hutton was pleading guilty to the charges, Meese said, and would pay the maximum criminal fines allowable of $2 million.

The four-year investigation of Hutton's elaborate bank fraud by prosecutors in Pennsylvania had finally hit its target. With the charge led by Al Murray, the assistant U.S. attorney in Scranton, the government had unwound the complex scheme that between July 1, 1980, and February 28, 1982, had defrauded some four hundred banks of up to $8 million. As part of the settlement, the department agreed to grant immunity to as many as fifty Hutton executives. No one from the firm would ever go to jail for the crimes.

The meetings between the SEC and the Prudential-Bache lawyers continued throughout the summer of 1985. By the fall, serious negotiations for a settlement began.

The talks were tense, and Schechter took a hard-line position. But after Hutton's guilty plea, he never again spoke of how the regulators could rest comfortably knowing that compliance at Pru-Bache was in the hands of the team from Hutton.

"Mr. Ball, you have the right to have counsel assist you in the course of this morning's proceedings," said Congressman William Hughes. "Are you accompanied by counsel?"

It was 10:25 on the morning of October 31. Hughes, a New Jersey Democrat, had just struck his gavel to its base, silencing the crowd in room 2237 of the Sam Rayburn House Office Building. The ten-member House Judiciary Subcommittee on Crime was ready to hear from Ball in its investigation of the crimes of E. F. Hutton.

Ball introduced his lawyer, Lloyd Cutler, the former White House counsel in the Carter administration.

"Thank you," Hughes said. "Mr. Ball, I am going to place you under oath at this time. Will you please raise your right hand?"

A few minutes later, Ball began his testimony. He said he knew that

Hutton had a cash management system in place to minimize the loss of interest on the float to banks. But that was as far as his knowledge went.

"I was not aware of the procedures or specific methods used," Ball said. "I was certainly not aware that some regions and branches were abusing the system in order to generate additional interest income by excessive overdrafting."

Subcommittee members produced Ball's memos from his Hutton years urging the retail sales force to do more overdrafting. But Ball's resolve was unshaken. He insisted that he knew nothing about any improper activities.

"One should not mistake a search for improvement as a willingness to cut corners," Ball said. "Exhorting branches to increase their interest profits or their stock sales or cost-effectiveness was in no way a call for sharp practices."

More important, Ball protested, he was not Hutton's top executive. He had no responsibility for the cash management system. No one in that department reported to him. He could not, he said, be held accountable for actions taken in divisions of the firm for which he was not responsible.

"Just out of curiosity," asked Congressman Romano Mazzoli, a Democrat from Kentucky, "at Prudential-Bache, do you do any of this sort of thing now?"

"No, we do not."

"You do not do excessive overdrafting?"

Ball explained that Prudential-Bache maintained an agreement with the banks that specified the amount of money the institutions could make off the firm's float each year. He added that he was not sure how much money that was.

"You don't know what's going on in your company now?" Mazzoli asked.

"No, what I'm saying—"

"Because you said you didn't understand, apparently, what was going on over at E. F. Hutton."

"I was not responsible for the practices at Hutton," Ball protested. "At Pru-Bache, I'm chief executive officer. And number two, being somebody who is not totally stupid—"

Mazzoli smiled. "So," he said, interrupting Ball. "You do know what's going on now?"

Ball never answered the question.

Bob Sherman sat on the edge of a couch in George Ball's office, staring intently across a coffee table into his boss's blue eyes. "We just can't fire Rick Saccullo," Sherman implored. "He's a good guy. We've got to let him stay with the firm."

Ball nodded.

"Listen," Sherman said, "Saccullo was duped in this Capt. Crab thing. He may have been negligent, but he's effective. We can't just cut him loose."

By the fall of 1985, Ball had heard the same impassioned plea from Sherman several times. When Ball first heard about the Capt. Crab investigation, he could not imagine it would go as far as it had. Based on what he had learned from Loren Schechter, the SEC case sounded to Ball like just a small-time problem at a local branch. That was why he had said nothing when Sherman promoted Saccullo to the all-important position of regional director for the Southeast even while the investigation was still going on.

But in the last few months, everything had changed. Schechter had told Ball that the SEC was consolidating the Capt. Crab case with the Kalil matter and looking at both incidents as a sign of a systemic breakdown in compliance at the firm. The agency clearly wanted to make a big splash with the case.

The SEC lawyers had entered into settlement negotiations with the firm but were demanding a heavy price. The enforcement staff wanted to appoint an outside expert to review Prudential-Bache's compliance procedures and remake them from the ground up. For a major brokerage firm, it was a humiliating requirement.

But on top of that, there was the problem with Saccullo. For the regulators, Saccullo had come to personify the cowboy atmosphere at Pru-Bache. He was a manager who had already been nailed once by regulators for failing to supervise. In most cases, there would be no question. Saccullo would be fired. But Sherman was putting everything on the line for him.

Ball stood up. "All right, Bob," he said. "I hear you. I understand what you're saying. We'll see what we can do."

Sherman thanked Ball and got up to leave. Ball wasn't quite sure what would be done with Saccullo. He figured that Saccullo could probably continue at the firm only as a broker. Once the SEC filed their complaint, he thought, there would be no way for Saccullo to continue in a management role at Prudential-Bache.

———

The day broke bitterly cold on January 2, 1986. The New Year's festivities had just ended. After a day of rest, the nation's stockbrokers and traders were coming back to life. It was a slow, easy day. Most businesses were not yet back up to full speed. In the nation's newsrooms, the first working day of the New Year was widely known as one of the dullest.

But in the press room at the Securities and Exchange Commission, excitement was brewing. The commission was releasing a thick pile of documents in what officials promised would be a major securities case. By early afternoon, copies of release number 34-22755 were dropped off to the reporters. At the top of the document, the case citation read "In the Matter of Prudential-Bache Securities Inc."

After almost two years of investigation, the firm had settled both the Capt. Crab and Kalil investigations with the SEC. In the Capt. Crab case, the SEC brought charges against Saccullo. In their announcement, the SEC said that Saccullo had settled the charges and accepted a censure and an eighteen-month bar from serving in any managerial role at a brokerage firm. Kalil's former manager in Jacksonville also accepted a censure and a bar of one year. Prudential-Bache agreed to hire the outside consultant to review the firm's supervisory procedures.

The order itself would have been an embarrassment to most brokerages. But the firm's spin on the sanctions was highly unusual, if not downright dishonest: The settlement showed the high esteem the SEC had for Prudential-Bache.

"We appreciate the SEC acceptance of this approach as a reflection of our continuing determination to conduct business as a leader should," said Peter Costiglio, a firm spokesman.

Still, in speaking with reporters, Gary Lynch, the enforcement division chief, made clear that the commission considered the problems at Pru-Bache to be widespread. "The two cases demonstrate that there were very serious supervisory problems at Bache," Lynch said. "It's time for a very hard look, an extensive reevaluation of their procedures."

Few investors or regulators would have guessed that, at that very moment, the firm's abusive sales practices were continuing—and getting worse.

Ball tapped on the large, wooden door in the Dallas branch office. J. Frederic Storaska, one of the firm's biggest-producing brokers, stood up with an expression of absolute delight on his face.

"George, how wonderful to see you," Storaska said. "Welcome to Corporate Executive Services."

It was January 24 at eleven o'clock in the morning, just a few weeks after the Capt. Crab settlement. Ball had arrived to meet with the man he
considered to be one of his best hires for the retail system. The two had
met in Ball's last years at E. F. Hutton, where Storaska had been a stand-
out broker. In 1984, Ball had personally recruited Storaska to join the Pru-
Bache team.

Storaska, a hulking, heavyset man with thick, dark hair and a seemingly
boundless ego, was not like most brokers. Instead of spending his days toil-
ing on the telephone, cold-calling potential clients, Storaska focused only
on the cream of the investment world. He hunted down newly wealthy
entrepreneurs, such as businessmen who had recently sold their companies.
Storaska knew that no matter how much these people understood the line
of business that brought them their wealth, they were most likely novices
when it came to investing. Over the years, he perfected the pitch that they
would run their businesses while he protected their money. It had been a
fabulously successful strategy for Storaska at Hutton and later at Kidder
Peabody. When Ball saw the millions of dollars that Storaska was bringing
in, he knew he wanted that for Prudential-Bache.

Even with Ball's reputation for showering big brokers with money and
goodies, the deal he struck with Storaska raised eyebrows throughout the
firm. Storaska was offered what was essentially his own department within
the Dallas branch, called Corporate Executive Services, or CES. He had his
own sales staff and clerks. For every $750,000 in revenues he generated, the
firm would pay for another CES staff member. Storaska traveled by limousine and would soon have his own airplane. As the final sweetener, Ball offered Storaska almost a quarter of a million dollars up front. By this
morning in early 1986, it seemed like money well spent. Little more than a
year after CES opened, Storaska was one of the top ten brokers in the firm.

"So, Fred, is everything else here to your satisfaction?" Ball asked.

Storaska nodded. His branch manager, Charles Grose, and his regional
director, Bill Hayes, had been extremely helpful, he said.

"Good," Ball replied. "I told Bill to make sure he took care of you."

After some idle talk about Storaska's family, the forty-five-minute meeting came to an end, and Ball stood up to leave.

"Keep up the good work," Ball said. "You're setting an excellent example for others to follow."

Ball might not have known it, but he had set in motion what would become a major compliance problem for the firm. Within a month of
Storaska's hiring, the firm was notified that he was under investigation by

the Chicago Board Options Exchange for allegations of improper trading before he was terminated by Kidder.[*]

It would only be a matter of months before the first customer complaint arrived at Prudential-Bache, charging that Storaska was improperly making trades at his own discretion without written approval. It was the kind of complaint that should have sent up red flares throughout the compliance department of Prudential-Bache.

But the letter of complaint was just filed away. With Storaska anointed by none other than George Ball himself, it would take a lot more than an exchange investigation and a few customer complaints for Prudential-Bache to do something about him. A lot more.

In Jacksonville, Rick Harris, the new manager of the local Pru-Bache branch, was slogging through the last leg of the Kalil affair. The SEC settlement rekindled a flurry of bad publicity for the branch, and Harris worked hard to keep his brokers focused on their business. He walked about the office, complimenting his best brokers on their latest sales, while offering weaker ones suggestions on how to improve.

But each day it was getting harder for Harris to stay upbeat. Since being assigned to clean up Jacksonville a few months before, he had developed a direct pipeline into the New York rumor mill. Lawyers for the firm contacted him every day, and he frequently heard stories about problems in New York that horrified him. Then, over drinks, an executive for VMS, a partnership sponsor, had told him an amazing story about the company getting Bob Sherman an apartment. The VMS executive anguished about it, and Harris was appalled.

Still, he tried to keep his mind off the horror stories. Within a few days of the SEC settlement, Harris saw a prospectus for a new real estate deal that he thought might be a good investment for his branch's clients. Unlike some other products, the deal was not a proprietary deal at Prudential-Bache but was being offered at firms all over Wall Street. Harris had reviewed the prospectus for the deal as soon as it arrived in the office and immediately went out to speak to his brokers.

"Hey, I want everybody to take a look at this," he said. "It looks like it's properly structured, and the prospectus is pretty straightforward. This is probably the kind of investment that is worthy of a small percentage of some client's portfolio."

[*] Storaska's industry records do not show any action ever being taken as a result of the Options Exchange investigation.

The brokers liked the deal, and within a few days, they had sold a huge amount of it to their clients. Harris was pleased. His brokers were showing that the Jacksonville branch was still alive and kicking, despite all the bad press.

A few weeks later, in early February, an offering of a similar real estate deal, called Duke Realty Investments, came out from Prudential-Bache in New York. Even though this deal was proprietary, Harris didn't give the prospectus a second look. He figured any professional in the business would know that clients had to keep their portfolios diversified. Almost every client of the branch who could consider such a real estate investment had already been approached with something comparable.

Worse, the deal was also the latest Clifton Harrison offering. Harris had already heard the scuttlebutt about Harrison being a convicted felon and was not comfortable selling his products. So, even though this deal was sponsored by his firm, the branch was not selling any of it.

Within a few days, the first phone call came from New York. "Why aren't you guys selling Duke Realty?" the New York product manager asked.

"Look," Harris said. "We just sold one of these. The branch doesn't have an appetite for another one. The customers don't need it, and the brokers aren't interested."

The explanation did nothing to quell the anger in New York. As far as the marketers there were concerned, if a branch sold a lot of a product weeks earlier, then it should be able to sell even more of the same thing later. Harris's arguments about the need for portfolio diversification fell on deaf ears. The calls with complaints from New York kept coming for days.

Harris did not know it, but the pressure for sales was coming from Darr himself. Darr had pushed Sherman heavily into promoting the Duke deal, and Sherman, in turn, had begun pressuring the people who worked for him in ways he never had before. The push to sell was going on across the country, and would be unrelenting until the deal was closed.

Finally, Harris called a special meeting of the Jacksonville brokers.

"Guys, New York and the region are putting particular pressure on us to sell this Duke product," he said. "It's a proprietary offering, so I can appreciate that they want to do a good job. So if for whatever reason you had four or five people who were out of town when that first deal came through, or if you had people who said no, contact them all and offer this."

Harris thought for a second and added something to make sure none of his brokers misunderstood. The last thing he wanted was his brokers getting into a hard sell of a deal clients didn't want, just days after the SEC settlement.

"If your clients say no, don't worry about it," he said. "I'll take the heat."

A few days later, Harris checked around. His brokers had sold only about five hundred shares of the Harrison deal. They had checked with their clients. Nobody wanted it.

Those results angered the firm's senior executives even more. Finally, the regional sales manager called Harris, demanding that his branch push their clients harder.

"Look, I don't care what they want to do in New York," Harris said. "What they're asking us to do is not appropriate. I'm not going to do it."

Harris had never seen so much pressure to sell a deal that clients did not want. He assumed that by throwing down the gauntlet with the sales manager, maybe now they would leave him alone.

The next day, Harris was walking through the branch when his secretary called out for him. Peter Archbold, the regional manager in Florida and Harris's boss, was on the line. He wanted to speak with Harris immediately. Harris walked back to his office, shut the door, and picked up the telephone.

"Hey, Peter," he said. "What's up?"

"I want to talk to you about this Duke Realty deal," Archbold said. "You're going to sell a lot of it. And if you don't, you're fired."

Harris was floored. He'd heard war stories about managers' jobs being threatened for not cramming enough of a particular deal down clients' throats, but he always took those stories with a grain of salt. He never believed anyone could do something so unprofessional.

"Peter," he asked after he collected himself. "Are you telling me that my job is in jeopardy if we don't sell a lot of this offering?"

"That's right."

Harris hung up the phone. At that moment, he couldn't afford to lose his job. He stroked his temple as he thought about what to do. He could not believe the firm was pushing him to do something so improper after the SEC settlement.

Finally Harris reached a decision. He would put together some sort of incentive, like a cash prize or some sort of brownie points, for his brokers to sell the Duke deal. Essentially, he would offer them a bribe. Harris walked out into the branch to tell his brokers about it.

"I'm not proud of this," he said after explaining some of the situation, "but if you can find a way to get it done, then do it."

This is disgusting as hell, Harris thought. He was ashamed of himself.

Harris took a deep breath. He needed to make some preparations and to get things lined up. It would take him a few weeks, he knew, but he was going to get the hell out of the place. The dirt at the firm seemed everywhere.

The dark sedan pulled into the basement garage at Prudential headquarters in Newark. James Trice, a regional administrator for Prudential-Bache on the West Coast, hopped out of the backseat. An escort immediately whisked him upstairs to an anteroom outside the company's boardroom. As he entered the room, Trice saw George Ball sitting in an overstuffed chair.

"Jim," Ball said as he stood up. "How are you? How's your son?"

Trice smiled and told Ball about his family. Then Ball got to the point.

"Listen, Bob Sherman spoke to me and he really wants you to go to the Southeast as regional director," Ball said. "He really feels strongly about it."

Of that, Trice had no doubt. More than a year earlier, Sherman had tried to get him to swap jobs with Jack Graner, who was the regional director during the Capt. Crab disaster. Graner, another Sherman favorite, had been subpoenaed by the SEC in the investigation. Graner was petrified and wanted to get out of Atlanta. Sherman had suggested that Trice would take his place. But Trice liked California and had refused. Graner came to California anyway, taking a demotion to be regional sales manager. Sherman had replaced him in Atlanta with Saccullo, the manager who was a target of the SEC investigation.

Now that Saccullo had been barred from holding a supervisory position, Sherman had launched a full-court press to again try to persuade Trice to take the Southeast job. Just before the meeting with Ball, Trice had met with Sherman in a private dining room at Prudential-Bache headquarters. Sherman had offered him a raise, a company car, and a slot on the Pru-Bache board if Trice would agree to go. Then he had said that Ball wanted to speak with him out at Prudential Insurance, where he was attending a meeting with the company's board.

Despite the royal treatment, Trice didn't want the job. He told Ball that it was not a good time for him to be leaving California because of some family problems.

"Well," Ball said, "you can go back whenever you want to, if you need to. That's not a problem. We'll take care of it. It won't be any cost to you."

Trice raised an eyebrow. They were offering him free airfare back and forth across the country. This package was really getting rich.

"Jim, we'd greatly appreciate this," Ball said. "We realize it's an imposition on you, but we really would appreciate it. We'll remember it."

Trice sat back in his chair. "I want to ask you a question," he said. "If I refuse to do this, do you want my resignation?"

Ball smiled. "Oh, absolutely not. That's not the intention of this. We want you to go down there because we need you."

Less than a week later, Trice called Sherman and told him he'd take the job. Jack Graner was promoted to Trice's old job, giving him supervisory responsibility for the firm's golden branches on the West Coast.

That left open Graner's job as California's regional sales manager. Sherman thought he knew the perfect person: He selected Rick Saccullo, the former Atlanta branch manager who had just been sanctioned by the SEC. Once his eighteen-month bar from supervision was over, Saccullo would be more influential than ever.

The day the firm announced Saccullo's selection for the job, Carrington Clark, the regional director, received a telephone call from Robert Leecox, the manager of Prudential-Bache's St. Louis branch.

"Hey, is it true that we're getting Saccullo as the regional sales manager?" Leecox asked.

"That's the word, Doc," Clark said.

"Well, why don't we just hire Al Capone?" Leecox asked. "I mean, if we're going to use somebody in trouble with the government, at least Capone's a more visible guy."

On February 27, 1986, Jim Trice and his assistant, Marvin Coble, caught the red-eye from Los Angeles to Atlanta. They were ready to get started running the troubled Southeast region of Prudential-Bache. For the first time, they would get a firsthand look at the mess left behind by Rick Saccullo and Jack Graner.

Within a few days of arriving in Atlanta, both Trice and Coble thought that the region was far worse than they had imagined. It was a hotbed of sloppy broker activity, with little to no discipline imposed from above. Many of the brokers just went about doing their own thing without worrying about their higher-ups.

"This place is running like a country club," Trice told Coble.

On his first full week in the job, Trice toured the region to meet his branch managers. On Tuesday, March 4, Trice held a dinner meeting in Richmond, Virginia, with all of the branch managers in that state. He chatted with each manager, and the evening seemed to be going well. Finally he struck up a conversation with Joseph Schwerer, manager of the firm's Norfolk branch. Schwerer told Trice he had a problem.

"What's the matter?"

"I've got two problem brokers in my branch who seem to be getting into some trouble," Schwerer said. Schwerer told Trice that the two brokers had been violating numerous rules. They had even set up their own dummy company that engaged in bogus trades with some of their own clients.

Trice's good mood gave way to shock. This sounded horrible.

"Well, my God," Trice said. "Why don't we just get rid of these guys?"

"That's the problem," Schwerer said. "The legal department told me I can't."

Trice assured Schwerer that he would take care of the problem as soon as he returned to Atlanta. A few days later, he telephoned a lawyer in the legal department. He laid out everything he had just heard about the two brokers in Norfolk.

"Why haven't we fired them?" he asked. "They sound like a major problem."

"We can't," the lawyer replied. "We're already in the soup with these guys, and we have some pending litigation. If we fire them, we'll have them as adverse witnesses against us. We can't afford to do it. So we'll just have to sit with it and hope it will just work itself out."

"So we're keeping these characters around to make sure we don't lose a couple of lawsuits?" Trice asked. "That just isn't right."

Trice hung up, called another lawyer, and then called Bob Sherman. Each time, he was told the same thing: Regardless of the allegations, the brokers had to be kept on at the firm. The potential liability from them was just too large.

As far as Trice could tell, Prudential-Bache had learned absolutely nothing from its humiliating settlement with the SEC. If what he was seeing kept up, he knew it wouldn't be long until the regulators came back and slammed the firm with sanctions all over again.

Jared Kopel settled comfortably into his chair at his new office in Palo Alto, California. The Capt. Crab investigation, which he had supervised at the SEC for almost three years, had been his last case as a government regulator. Within months of the filing, Kopel had taken a job with the law firm of Wilson, Sonsini, Goodrich & Rosati. After all his years in government service, private practice looked pretty good.

On this day, an old acquaintance told him a bit of news. Rick Saccullo, the former branch manager and one of the men Kopel had investigated and helped charge, had been transferred to California to work as a regional sales manager. To Kopel, it certainly sounded like a promotion for the man who was largely responsible for Prudential-Bache's recent regulatory troubles. His acquaintance asked what he thought of the outcome.

Kopel just shrugged. "It's not really surprising, given what I've come to expect from Prudential-Bache," he said. "But it certainly doesn't augur well for their future."

Charles Grose charged across the Dallas branch office toward Fred Storaska's Corporate Executive Services Department. In his hand, he held another letter of complaint about Storaska, one of several to have arrived at the branch by mid-1986. This time the letter came from the accountant for some customers. The accountant wrote that her clients, Lawrence and Virginia Heiner, were deeply distressed to be receiving confirmations in the mail of trades that they had never authorized. The issue about the Heiners' account had come up before, and Storaska had assured Grose that the husband had authorized all purchases. Now, with this letter, Grose was worried. He had been in the business long enough to know that repeated complaints of unauthorized trading were a red flag for potentially major securities law violations.

"Fred, I've got to talk to you about the Heiners again," Grose said as he walked into Storaska's office. "I've got a letter here, and they're upset. I don't understand why, when you're telling me that Mr. Heiner authorized these purchases."

"Well," Storaska said, "their accountant actually authorized the purchases."

"Well, that's funny," Grose said, thrusting the letter toward Storaska, "because the accountant is the one writing the letter of complaint!"

Storaska looked down at the letter in Grose's hands and then calmly looked back up. The expression of confidence never left his face.

"She's not a very smart person," he said.

Grose felt like he was going to explode. "How the hell do you take an order for $1.2 million worth of bonds for someone you don't think is very smart? Secondly, how could you take that order from an accountant who doesn't have power of attorney?"

Storaska stared back at Grose, still serene and unruffled by the confrontation. "Lawrence Heiner told me I could take orders from the accountant."

Grose wanted to scream. Taking on Storaska was like trying to grab smoke. No matter what Grose did, Storaska always had another line. But this one made no sense: Anytime a customer passes trading authorization to another party, the broker has to obtain it in writing. Most brokers knew that after their first day of training.

"You *can't* use verbal authorization for a power of attorney," Grose boomed. "The *law* says that you've used discretion. Fred, this is the type of trading that could cause you many serious legal problems."

Grose cut off the conversation and left. Any other broker probably would have been fired at that moment, but Grose felt powerless. He knew Storaska was untouchable. He was protected from above by George Ball himself.

He headed back to his office, grabbed a sheet of interoffice memo paper, and quickly typed up a version of the events that had just happened for his files. Grose was sure that, someday, Storaska would blow himself up by running roughshod over securities laws. The SEC would be swarming all over the branch. If Grose couldn't punish Storaska, at least he could protect himself. He finished typing the memo, then opened his credenza and stuffed the memo into his rapidly growing secret file about regulatory problems that no one wanted to stop.

On Monday, May 12, 1986, the SEC disclosed the most significant enforcement action in the agency's history. After almost a year of investigation, it had cracked an insider-trading scandal emanating from Nassau, the Bahamas, out of the modest offices of Bank Leu International Ltd., a subsidiary of Switzerland's oldest private bank. That morning, lawyers for the commission rushed into the courtroom of Federal District Judge Richard Owen in New York. They were seeking an injunction to prevent the transfer of $10 million out of a Bank Leu account controlled by Dennis B. Levine, an investment banker with Drexel.

Shortly after 7:30 that night, prosecutors with the U.S. attorney's office in Manhattan arrested Levine for insider trading. In hopes of cutting a deal, Levine offered the government information about his insider-trading accomplices. The names included one of Wall Street's biggest fish, Ivan Boesky, the wealthy arbitrageur. For the next five years, prosecutors and the SEC, starting with Levine's information, aggressively pursued a trail of evidence that led them to some of Wall Street's most powerful financiers. By the time they were done, a number of prominent executives, including Michael Milken, Drexel's junk-bond wizard, would go to jail. It would be one of the greatest successes in the history of securities law enforcement.

The huge investigations of Wall Street insider trading and market manipulations consumed the working days of almost every top official in the SEC enforcement division. With so much manpower delegated to pursuing the high-profile lawbreakers, few aggressive inquiries were made into whether Prudential-Bache was following the terms of the 1986 settlement. It would be seven years later, after the Boesky and Drexel investigations were finished, before the government finally learned that Pru-Bache had ignored the strict compliance requirements of its settlement and engaged in a series of even more serious violations.

Even as the SEC and prosecutors were striking fear all over Wall Street, one of America's top brokerage firms was a renegade.

CHAPTER 11

SOON AFTER DAYBREAK, a phalanx of hunters checked their shotguns as they waited near the main lodge at Longleaf Plantation. The men, many wearing bright orange baseball caps emblazoned with the Longleaf name, had just finished a hearty breakfast at the commercial hunting reserve near Lumberton, Mississippi. In a few minutes, professional guides would drive them by Jeep to their designated courses. There the hunters would begin their daylong pursuit of fattened, pen-raised bobwhite quail. The morning sky was clear on this day in January 1985. A light rain that fell during the night gave the brisk air an especially crisp scent. It was the perfect weather for Longleaf's classic hunt, a blend of Old South traditions and European courtliness.

John Graham, the head of Graham Resources, walked past the crowd of hunters as he carried his bags to his car. A slender, round-faced man with well-groomed dark hair, Graham was a familiar face at Longleaf. A born hunter, Graham began visiting the reserve in the late 1970s and had loved it from the start. To him, it was the perfect mix of outdoors and elegance. After a day's hunt, the evenings at Longleaf featured sumptuous dinners of roast quail in wine sauce and southern cuisine, served by tuxedo-clad waiters.

It was a lifestyle Graham craved, one he enjoyed even more since becoming the most important general partner working with the Direct Investment Group. In just a year and a half, Graham had raised more than $170 million from 15,477 investors for the Prudential-Bache Energy Income partnerships. Now he often hobnobbed with his new friends at Pru-Bache and had personally introduced them to Longleaf. Darr himself had become an avid hunter since being taught to shoot by Tony Rice, Graham's chief financial officer. Now Darr, as well as Pittman, Joseph DeFur, and other Prudential-Bache executives, could truly appreciate what Longleaf had to offer. The trips were expensive, costing more than $250 per person for the day; an overnight stay added about another $200 per person to the bill. But none of the Prudential-Bache executives paid a dime. Instead, after each trip, Longleaf shipped the huge bill to Graham Resources' headquarters in Louisiana, where the cost was passed along to the energy income partnerships. Investors were picking up the tab for the newest hobby at the Direct Investment Group.

Graham walked to the back of his car, popped open the trunk, and threw in his bags. Before he could turn around, Mark Files, a senior vice-president at Graham Resources, sidled up alongside him and tossed his bags into the trunk as well. The men had just finished a wonderful two-day hunt at Longleaf. They had bagged near the limit on quail and were ready to head home. Files, an owlish-looking version of Graham himself, had agreed to share a car ride home with his boss so that they could have a private talk. They needed to discuss some problems facing the energy income partnerships. Problems that investors didn't know about.

In a matter of minutes, Files and Graham were on their way. They both knew this would be a serious conversation. The partnerships hadn't been producing enough cash to keep distributions high. All the assurances investors received about the safety and high returns of the partnerships had been just so much false advertising. If investors found out how poorly the deals were faring, sales of new partnerships would flounder. Without new sales, the fat fees that Graham Resources and Prudential-Bache received from the deals would level off. So Graham Resources had quietly advanced more than $2 million to the partnerships, which was used for expenses and distributions, making it appear as if investors were receiving hefty returns.

The men turned south on Interstate 59 as they talked about what the distribution rate should be for the recently completed quarter for the first energy income partnership, called P-1. Files suggested that they arrange for a 15 percent distribution. Graham agreed. Fifteen percent sounded reasonable to him.

Still, distributions that high might require another cash advance from Graham Resources. All these advances were starting to concern him, Graham said. The subsidies were getting too large. Even though the subsidies had a long-term benefit to the oil company, they tied up an enormous amount of its capital. So Graham had another idea.

"I want you to arrange for bank lines of credit to those partnerships," he said.

Files nodded.

"And you should camouflage, to the extent you can, the purpose of it," Graham said.

Keeping the truth hidden was important. It was unlikely that investors in the partnerships would be happy to learn that the cash they were receiving was borrowed money. Particularly since the prospectus, as well as the sales material for the energy income partnerships, said that Graham would not borrow money to pay for distributions.

"All right, John," Files said.

This was a tricky problem. Files could tell that Graham felt trapped by the advertised distributions the partnerships were supposed to have and wanted a better alternative than telling investors the truth about the partnerships' performance.

Graham said he didn't want to tell Prudential-Bache about the plans. In his estimation, it wasn't right to talk with the firm about the difference between the actual cash-flow distributions and the amount brokers were projecting in their sales pitches.

"And if they see through the borrowing plan," Graham said, "we should just ask for their forgiveness, rather than their permission."*

Graham seemed to be angry with Prudential-Bache, and, in his mind, with good reason. Even with all the money the Direct Investment Group was pouring into Graham Resources, relations between Darr and the oil company were tense. Darr insisted on piling huge fees for Pru-Bache onto the partnerships. He even demanded for Pru-Bache a piece of some fees Graham Resources charged. In recent months, Darr had tacked on a new one percent acquisition fee for Prudential-Bache. That money came out of the so-called organization and offering expenses, or O&O, that Graham charged for putting the partnership together and selling it. That fee went toward anything that was considered a cost of putting the deal together, no matter how loosely related it was. Even the multimillion-dollar trips to induce brokers to sell the energy income fund were counted against the O&O.

But Darr had taken so much money out of the O&O that it left Graham Resources without enough to cover those actual costs. With securities rules limiting the amount of investors' money that could be spent on costs, Graham itself was stuck with paying the rest of the bill out of its own

---

* Graham has denied making some of these comments. In addition, former Graham executives contend that no borrowings were ever used to inflate distributions. Money was borrowed only for other purposes. See Notes and Sources.

pocket. Essentially, Graham Resources was paying the acquisition fee to Prudential-Bache, a fact that enraged John Graham. During their drive from Longleaf, his anger at Darr's piggishness boiled over.

"I want to get the one percent back on our O&O," he said. He clearly thought he was getting screwed by Darr.

That almost sounds like an ultimatum, Files thought. "I know it's a serious matter," he said. It made no sense for Graham Resources to keep eating those expenses all on its own.

Graham suggested that if the Direct Investment Group wanted to take so much of the money allocated for those expenses, perhaps the energy company should negotiate turning the responsibility for paying all of the O&O over to Prudential-Bache. At least in that way, the brokerage firm would be carrying the risk for making up any losses.

Files didn't like the idea at all. After all, it wasn't just the Direct Investment Group that could push off some of its costs onto the partnerships as organization and offering expenses. Graham Resources could do it, too, charging some of its own overhead off as a partnership expense and bolstering the energy company's profitability.

The best way to recover the O&O was to push higher sales. That would mean more fees for Graham Resources from all the other fees it charged to the partnerships. Selling the energy income partnerships was becoming a volume business.

While they were on the subject of the Direct Investment Group, Files said he had something he wanted to mention: Darr was champing at the bit to go hunting again.

"I can sense that Jim Darr wants to visit Longleaf again this quail season," Files said. He had already checked into a number of dates that would be available in February and March. But there would be some restrictions on the number of people who could come, and they would not be guaranteed their favorite lodge.

"If we have an interest in the turkey season, though, the dates are fairly open," Files added. "But I'd judge that Darr wouldn't enjoy turkey hunting as much. There's little shooting and a great deal of waiting." Darr was a guy who liked action. He had no patience for waiting.

The two men discussed one last possibility: bringing Darr out to Longleaf on a hunt with executives from Prudential Insurance and First City National Bank of Houston. But Files shook his head.

"I think it would be a mistake to bring Darr on that hunt," he said. "We already have a number of kings to take care of there."

———————

Charles Dawson sauntered out of the Prudential-Bache branch in north Dallas and headed toward his brown Chrysler LeBaron. He was ready to drive back to his one-man branch in the tiny Texas town of Sulphur Springs, eighty miles east of Dallas. At six-four with gray hair and a friendly face, the forty-five-year-old Dawson looked like the country broker that he was. He was probably the only employee at Prudential-Bache who ran a dairy farm on the side. But on that day in April 1985, he was the firm's top salesman.

Minutes earlier, Dawson had dropped off orders for $1.4 million worth of energy income partnerships with the Dallas branch's wire operator. It was the largest amount of the partnership ever sold by one broker on a single day. Then, without a word, Dawson turned around and headed out on his way back to Sulphur Springs.

Dawson pulled his car out of the Pru-Bache parking lot and drove south on Central Expressway. He should have been feeling delighted. After all, with an 8 percent commission, he had just grossed more than $110,000. But he was too worried to celebrate. He hadn't sold an energy partnership for two years, ever since the bad experience he'd had while working at a small regional brokerage. An energy partnership he sold at that firm had been a disaster. His clients lost most of their money.

When he arrived in Dallas earlier that week, he had raised his concerns about the Graham partnerships to Charles Grose, the branch manager. But Grose just waved his worries away.

"Look, this is Prudential-Bache," Grose had said. "This whole program is being looked over by Prudential Insurance itself. You can't ask for better."

Dawson's car approached the twin gold towers that stood alongside Central Expressway. They were the first of a cluster of glass structures built in Dallas in recent years. A huge construction boom, driven by easy cash from S&Ls and limited partnerships, had pushed up prices to astronomical levels throughout much of Texas.

He turned on the air conditioner. It didn't work too well in the used car he drove, but at least it was something. Dawson came to Dallas every so often. Some of his biggest clients lived there, and somehow they felt better doing business with a broker from Sulphur Springs than with one from the Dallas branch. All that week, he had been going to their homes, one at a time, to present the latest energy income fund. Sitting at their kitchen tables, he told his clients about the advantages spelled out in the sales material. Even though the material said that the investors could expect returns in the range of 15 to 20 percent, Dawson undersold those figures, telling his clients that they might receive returns in the range of 13 to 15 percent. Dawson didn't like his clients to be overoptimistic.

Most important in his sales pitch was Prudential Insurance itself. Repeatedly Dawson stressed that the Rock was investing its own money in the energy income partnerships. That was good enough for his clients: One invested $800,000 in the partnership, and three others purchased $200,000 of it.

Dawson drove past Fair Park, home of the Texas State Fair. As he finally hooked up with Interstate 30, he was feeling a bit better. He thought again about how Prudential Insurance invested in the deal itself. There couldn't be anything to worry about.

Tony Rice walked into the conference room in the offices of the Direct Investment Group. The room was full of a bustling crowd of executives. Rice, the chief financial officer of Graham Resources, had an expression of relaxed friendliness on his face. To a large degree, it was a front. He didn't particularly like Darr, and had it not been for their business relationship, their country club chats and hunting trips never would have happened. For sure, Rice would not have always paid for their activities by sending the bills to the partnerships. But for this meeting on May 30, 1985, he needed to be at his most charming. That was the only way he could hammer out a truce between Graham Resources and Darr.

Rice, as always, was dressed impeccably in a well-cut European pin-striped suit with elegant cuff links. His clothing looked all the more fashionable compared with that of the rumpled man accompanying him. Alfred Dempsey, a heavyset Graham executive, was not much concerned with sartorial splendor. Someone just walking into the room would not likely guess that Dempsey was the man responsible for overseeing Graham Resources' marketing, legal, and financial planning.

On the other side of the table were the Direct Investment Group's top executives, including Darr, Pittman, and Proscia. They were joined by Joe DeFur, a product manager for the energy income partnerships; Tony Hertl, an accountant hired by Darr two years earlier to handle the finances for all of the Prudential-Bache co–general partners, such as Prudential-Bache Energy Production; and Jim Sweeney, who was there to take notes on the meeting.

The executives swapped a few jokes, complete with affected laughter.

But the pretense didn't cover the thick tension in the air. Everyone knew what they were there for: John Graham was demanding that his company receive more money to pay for the organization and offering expenses, as well as for other costs. Darr, in turn, wanted to keep his hands on as much of the cash as possible. The dispute had reached a stalemate and was starting to threaten the men's relationship.

Rice opened the conversation by discussing the fact that all of the competitors with energy income partnerships seemed to be disappearing.

Perhaps, Rice said, the market was saying that energy income partnerships were a product of the past. The future seemed to be in so-called roll-ups, which take all the oil wells and other energy assets out of a group of limited partnerships and roll them up together into a single publicly traded company. Traditionally, roll-ups were disastrous for investors. But the general partners—in this case, Graham Resources and Prudential-Bache—received fat fees for assembling a roll-up.

Darr shook his head. "I don't like it," he said. "A roll-up could kill the future sales of the income funds."

One big problem was that investors had paid more than 15 percent of their initial capital to purchase these partnerships. If, a few years later, the partnerships were rolled up into a stock they could have purchased for a 3 percent commission, they would be livid. Plus, then the old partnerships would be gone. There would be no track record for brokers to refer to when they tried to sell new partnerships.

Then perhaps, Rice suggested, they could find a way just to roll up the oldest income partnerships. That way, the track record of the recently sold partnerships could still be used in the sales materials for new deals.

The twisted logic seemed to escape everyone in the room. Essentially, Rice was suggesting a deal that would likely cost the early investors much of their remaining capital.

The Direct Investment Group executives said that they would think about the idea.

Rice proceeded to the next topic: The partnerships needed to borrow some money.

"From time to time, there has been insufficient cash on hand for purposes such as developmental drilling costs, taxes, et cetera," Rice said. "We've been advancing cash to the partnerships interest-free to meet those needs. But now we'd like to arrange for a loan from Citibank for that cash."

Just as John Graham had instructed Mark Files in the car ride from Long-leaf, the true purpose for the money was being camouflaged. But it was a flimsy explanation. It was like someone who spent money on a movie every night saying he needed to borrow cash to buy food. That loan was not financing the necessary food expense—instead, the money for food had been blown at the movies. In the same way, Graham was taking money away from necessary expenses, such as paying taxes, to make distributions. But the distributions were supposed to be the cash left over *after expenses*.

Bill Pittman looked quizzically at Rice. This sounded fishy to him.

"If the partnerships are borrowing money to meet present needs, doesn't that mean that the returns being paid to investors are inflated?" he asked.

Bull's-eye. Even Pittman, with his limited background in the energy industry, had seen through the ruse. But the moment just slipped away under Rice's smooth assurances.

"No, no, no," Rice said. He could see how Pittman might think that, he said, but it wasn't so. The accounting treatment of the developmental drilling was different from the accounting for distributions, he said. On top of that, the loans were only for a few million, so the interest payments should not affect the returns. The money they were making from energy production was enough to support the distributions, he said.

"All right," Darr said. "Under the circumstances, it seems reasonable to obtain the credit commitment from Citibank."

The joviality left Rice's face and was replaced with an expression of gravity. "That leads us to the organization and offering expenses," he said.

Rice said that the partnerships had about $1 million worth of O&O expenses that Graham Resources had simply absorbed. The only way to make up for it would be to boost sales with more aggressive marketing. But in the first few months of the year, sales had been dropping off. In the latest partnership, the money allocated for O&O was not even going to cover all of the legal and accounting costs.

"We were able to recover all of the O&O on the first energy income program," Rice said. "But that's changed in the current program because of Prudential-Bache's one percent acquisition fee that's considered part of the O&O."

Darr visibly stiffened. He had fought hard to get that extra money coming into his department. He wasn't about to give it up simply because it was creating financial trouble for the biggest general partner working with the Direct Investment Group.

Still, Rice said, sales had started picking up recently. "If sales remain strong, the problem is going to diminish," he said.

The executives from the Direct Investment Group seemed to nod their heads almost in unison. Darr signaled he wasn't willing to budge on the 1 percent acquisition fee. John Graham, through Tony Rice, was making it clear that his company would not keep financing Darr's greed. The only way that Graham Resources and the Direct Investment Group could keep dipping into the pockets of Prudential-Bache clients would be to step up sales on the next group of partnerships.

Everyone knew what he had to do.

The image of an elderly couple, nearing retirement age, beamed out from the video screens set up in a conference room. A group of about thirty Prudential-Bache brokers watched silently. The couple stood in the doorway of their modest white house, happily receiving a letter from their mailman. It was, the video implied, another fat distribution check from their investment in the energy income partnerships. The image dissolved into a picture of a working oil well.

"Prudential-Bache Energy Income Partnerships II: A means to profit from the energy market both today and in the future," a disembodied voice intoned as orchestra music swelled. "It's an investment we're proud to put our name on."

The lights came up in the conference room. Pete Theo, a top marketer for Graham Resources, hung his jacket on a chair and strode in his shirtsleeves to the front of the after-work crowd of brokers. They had gathered on an evening in late June 1985 to hear Theo's latest pitch about the energy income partnerships. The new marketing video was just the first part of Theo's sales effort.

Theo, a trim, broad-shouldered man with straight, dark hair and a narrow face, said he wanted to talk about a few features of the investments. He walked away from a podium to a nearby paper flip chart. Picking up a black marker, he wrote "SAFETY" in big, capital letters on the chart.

"How safe is the investment income?" Theo asked as a number of the assembled brokers wrote the word "safety" on their notepads.

Plenty safe, indeed, Theo said. A lot of oil companies borrowed heavily in the late 1970s, when energy prices were high, he said. Now they needed to raise cash and were selling their oil wells at rock-bottom prices to earn the money to pay down the loans. So, the energy income partnerships were buying those oil wells at distressed, fire-sale prices. This "loan payoff" theory was the latest rationale behind the energy income partnerships. It had never been used to justify the sales of the earlier partnerships.

"Next item: income," Theo said, as he wrote the word on the flip chart. A number of brokers dutifully wrote that word in their notebooks.

He turned away from the flip chart, tapping the back of the marker on his hand. "Why are we buying these properties?" he asked. "What does it do for us?"

Theo turned back to the flip chart. "It produces substantial income by buying at the prices we're able to buy when these oil companies are forced to sell," he said. "We can produce income in the fifteen to twenty percent range."

In big numbers, Theo wrote "15–20%" on the flip chart. Some of the Prudential-Bache brokers copied these numbers onto their notepads.

"The first year, with the start-up costs and the lag time of making these acquisitions, the income will only be in the twelve to fourteen percent range," Theo said. In smaller numbers, he wrote "12–14%" as the brokers copied it down.

Theo didn't mention that in more than two years of operation, the Prudential-Bache Energy Income partnerships had *never* produced an actual return in that range. The only way they even appeared to do so was through the return of investors' original capital and the advances from Graham.

"Now, at this point, let me jump down to tax benefits," Theo said, writing the words "tax benefits" on the flip chart. "Even though we are only producing twelve to fourteen percent in the first year, the vast majority of this income is tax-free, and in subsequent years, you will see about one-third to one-half being tax-free."

Some brokers nodded at the familiar refrain. The videotape had just mentioned all of the tax benefits reaped from investing in the energy income fund. They'd read in the sales material about how the tax code's oil depletion allowance sheltered as much as half of the partnership cash flow. It was a major selling point to investors, who were delighted to hear that they could receive such high returns on tax-free income.

But repetition never made it true. There was little, if any, tax benefit from investing in the energy income partnerships. In reality, as much as 50 percent of the distributions clients received in the early years was just a return of the original cash they invested. They owed no taxes on it because none of it was income. The sales point was a heinous and seductive lie.

By that time in Theo's speech, many of the brokers were convinced: Their customers could be paid a high return for purchasing a safe investment. But Theo topped it all off with the most persuasive bit of information in his whole presentation.

"In addition to this, I think it's worthy to take a look at who's buying," Theo said. "Prudential Insurance is the biggest investor in this program."

There was no better recommendation than that, many of the brokers thought. The people at Prudential Insurance were the best in the business. If they liked this deal, it had to be good.

Matthew Chanin, one of the top energy experts at Prudential Insurance, finished reviewing a letter from Graham Resources as he sat at his desk. Chanin was concerned. He didn't like what he was hearing about Graham's huge expenses. And now, in this letter from Al Dempsey dated July 2, 1985, Graham Resources was letting Chanin know that their large distributions seemed unsustainable.

Chanin wasn't alone in his discomfort. His colleague, Michael Resanovich, felt uneasy about the Direct Investment Group. The styles of Darr and the Prudential Insurance executives were just too different. Darr was more volume oriented than either Chanin or Resanovich had anticipated. No matter what the topic, Darr saw it through the prism of boosting sales. As far as Resanovich was concerned, the energy income partnerships were a smoldering problem that could flare up at any time. He thought Darr was a loose cannon who accepted weak due diligence.

Chanin knew Resanovich's concerns and shared some of them. The two men attempted to raise some red flags, but in truth, they could do little. They were midlevel executives at the giant insurance company. Darr was one of the most powerful executives at another firm that just happened to be owned by Prudential Insurance. If George Ball was happy with Darr, so be it.

Still, they could do everything in their power to rein in any excesses in the energy income partnerships. Now Graham Resources seemed to be in enough financial trouble to allow Chanin to impose some new, stricter terms on the way they did business.

The letter Chanin had just received from Al Dempsey presented the first opportunity to spell out those terms. The letter made clear that the partnerships were not making enough money to sustain 15 percent distributions. But Dempsey feared that if the distributions were cut, investors would not want to purchase the new partnerships as they were rolled out. Reality didn't make a good sales pitch.

So Dempsey had a suggestion: Deceive the investors.

"In an effort to allow us the forty-five to sixty days necessary to 'condition' the marketplace for a decline in distributions with the least possible impact on our current marketing effort, we suggest maintaining the 15 percent distribution level," he wrote.

By doing so, "I believe that the adverse impact on sales can be moderated and will result in a sustainable sales level over the balance of the year which proves profitable to all parties." Except, of course, for the investors who were tricked by the phony track record into buying the next partnerships.

The option of telling the truth, Dempsey implied, would be disastrous to the profits for Prudential-Bache and Graham Resources.

"Reducing the second quarter distributions to the sustainable 12–12.5 percent level will, in my judgment, make future marketing of our programs at profitable levels impossible," he wrote.

In a few days, a second request came from Graham through Tony Rice, asking for permission to borrow $5.7 million from the bank. After thinking about his options, Chanin decided to allow the loan. But only if Graham accepted certain conditions to improve partnership performance.

On July 16, Chanin dictated a memo to Tony Rice. Chanin said that he would allow the partnerships to borrow the $5.7 million. To make sure that sales stayed healthy, he also would permit them to continue paying the inflated 15 percent distributions by allowing Graham to advance cash to the partnerships for now.

But Chanin's agreement came with conditions. Graham Resources had to reduce the bloated administrative expenses that it was charging to the partnerships. Prudential regarded that expense reduction "as an issue of utmost importance," Chanin wrote.

He was satisfied with the terms. If Graham Resouces cut expenses, fewer partnership revenues would be going toward maintaining the lifestyle of Graham executives. If he was successful, the energy income partnerships stood a much better chance of turning a profit.

Exactly one week after Matt Chanin dictated his memo, the new agreement seemed ready to fall apart. Rice and Mark Files had asked Dempsey to review the cash flow of all of the existing partnerships, called P-1 through P-6. He was instructed to determine if the additional cash that Graham Resources had agreed to advance the partnerships would be enough to maintain the bogus 15 percent distributions for the next half a year.

It wasn't. By Dempsey's calculations, the partnerships were still $500,000 short, despite the $1.5 million that Chanin had allowed them to advance to the partnerships. Dempsey was concerned. If they didn't make the 15 percent distribution, he felt sure that sales would fall.

Dempsey had to let his bosses know. He sat down at a typewriter. "STRICTLY CONFIDENTIAL," he typed at the top of the memo addressed to Rice and Files. He then told them about his findings about the $500,000 deficit.

"If we were dealing with anyone but Matt, I would not feel uncomfortable finessing the $0.5 million shortfall," he typed. "What do you think?"

Dempsey hit the return key twice and typed a final sentence.

"Please destroy this memorandum after reading," it said.

"$uperbroker" arrived on the desks of Prudential-Bache brokers in July 1985. He was the main character in a poorly drawn, cheesy comic book. The superhero himself appeared to be bursting through the cover. He was unlikely to win fans: $uperbroker looked like a self-absorbed yuppie with a dollar sign emblazoned on his chest.

The comic book was being used to advertise two upcoming sales trips sponsored by Graham. The first was to Oktoberfest in Munich, West Germany, and the second was to a Caribbean island. On the back cover, the mild-mannered version of $uperbroker explained that brokers only had to sell between $250,000 and $600,000 worth of the energy income partnerships to qualify for various versions of the trips. The more the brokers sold, the better the trip.

The first page of the comic book featured Clark Barr, a stockbroker who made a good business selling stocks and bonds. In the first panel, he wisely instructs an elderly client named Mrs. Grimsley to invest $5,000 in relatively safe municipal bonds. But the next day, he reads about the energy income funds and their sales contest for the trip to Munich. Images of large-breasted women offering steins of German beer pop into his head. From then on, every time the broker hears the word "contest," he becomes $uperbroker, selling the energy income fund to all his clients. By the last panel, $uperbroker is—foolishly—telling the elderly Mrs. Grimsley to forget about those municipal bonds and advising her to put the money into the much riskier energy income fund instead.

The comic book was just the first part of a concerted effort to encourage more sales with the two free trips. At the same time, Graham also sponsored a "limerick contest" with brokers, with beer steins as a prize. Throughout Prudential-Bache, dozens of brokers turned away from their stock quote machines to start writing limericks. Alan Myers, a broker from

Philadelphia who was one of the contest winners, wrote a limerick that celebrated the Munich trip and reflected the deeply held but false beliefs about the partnerships' tax advantages. He wrote:

Income that's sheltered from "Sam,"
Is the product of Pru-Bache and Graham,
If you sell enough
(And that's not too tough)
You'll travel to Munich and "jam."

Not all the brokers enjoyed the fun and games. A number of Pru-Bache's female brokers were particularly offended by the $uperbroker comic book, with its sexist portrayal of women. The whole thing seemed horribly unprofessional. In late July, a copy of the $uperbroker comic book, complete with a short note of complaint, arrived on George Ball's desk from Barbara Gutherie, a broker from Paramus, New Jersey.

"Mr. Ball," Gutherie wrote, "if we wish to lose our image as a 'schlock house,' we should stop acting like one."

As far as Matt Chanin was concerned, the energy income partnerships were just not viable in the long term. He had looked at the numbers over and over again, and they just weren't working. By October 17, 1985, he was ready to take a drastic step.

"If Graham doesn't make some significant changes," Chanin told a group of executives in a conference room at Prudential-Bache headquarters, "I'm going to have to consider whether I should keep investing Pru's money in this."

The words hit the room like an atomic bomb. The investment of Prudential Insurance in the energy income partnerships had been the big selling point. How would they explain it to the brokers if the Rock decided that it had to drop out?

The first step needed for renewed support from Prudential Insurance, Chanin said, was for the high expenses at the partnerships to be cut. Despite the terms Chanin had put in place months earlier, Graham's bloated expenditures still ate into profits.

"This issue has to be addressed and resolved before I agree to participate in another offering," he said. For the first time, the future of the energy income partnerships was in question. The expenses had to come down if Prudential was going to stay on as an investor.

Darr watched the thick group of bare trees pass by as he rode in Tony Rice's car through the winding roads in Stamford, Connecticut. They were on their way to a shoot at a nearby range. Their shared interest in hunting and guns had become a passion. Already, by late 1985, they had hunted prairie dogs in Wyoming, wild boars in south Texas, and, of course, quail at Longleaf. Now Rice was planning a real treat for Darr in the next few months: a bear hunt in Alaska. The cost of the hunts was tens of thousands of dollars, all paid by the partnerships. With all the expenses the partnerships had, Rice figured that a $20,000 or $30,000 bill for a hunting trip was just a drop in the bucket. Keeping Darr happy was a necessary cost of business.

But by constantly paying for Darr, Rice had created expectations that sometimes proved embarrassing. When he invited Darr to hunt prairie dogs, Rice said that he would need a .22 Winchester magnum. The rifle could be ordered at any gun shop, but Darr apparently did not want to be bothered. He called Rice and asked him to take care of getting the gun for him. So Rice ordered the gun, had the sights adjusted, and put on a scope. In total, it cost about $900. A few days after it was ready, Rice took the gun with him to a party at Darr's house. After arriving, he set the gun in a closet and later told Darr it was there. When Darr asked how much he owed, Rice just shook his head. After the hunt, he said, he would just take it back. Using partnership money, Graham Resources was just entering into a hunting lease with a ranch in west Texas. Rice said he would use the Winchester down there.

But after the hunt, Darr kept the rifle, and Rice avoided the embarrassment of asking for it back. It must have been, Rice assumed, just an honest misunderstanding.

Rice headed toward Interstate 95. As they often did, he and Darr discussed their personal finances. Darr mentioned that he had borrowed $1.8 million from First South.

Rice seemed a bit taken aback. "That sounds like a big mortgage to me," he said.

It also didn't sound particularly wise. Rice knew from earlier conversations that First South was largely controlled by George Watson and Tracy Taylor, the principals of Watson & Taylor. Owing that much money to a savings and loan might give those men an inordinate amount of power over Darr.

"Jim, considering you have a mortgage with people you've got another business relationship with, you might want to have a larger cushion," Rice said. Perhaps, he was suggesting, Darr should have more equity in his house.

The conversation rambled on, until Darr returned to the topic of First South. Rice didn't know it, but Darr himself was now a huge shareholder in the financial institution. Federal regulators had recently finished examining First South and were preparing a report on the loans to its biggest shareholders, Watson & Taylor. In that environment, First South executives had contacted Darr and told him they had a huge block of more than eight thousand shares in the S&L for sale. They did not tell him who the seller was. Darr agreed to buy, but on the condition that First South lend him another $345,000 for the purchase, through a second mortgage on his house. The deal was quickly struck, and Darr bought the block of stock. By now the loans on his house exceeded the price he had paid for it a little more than a year before.

Darr had been so persuaded by the pitch on First South that he thought Rice might be interested in buying some of the stock himself. It was a fabulous investment, Darr said. "Would you be interested in buying some First South shares?"

Rice shook his head. The ties among Darr, First South, and Watson & Taylor already struck him as strange. He didn't want to bet his savings on it.

Mark Files tapped a few numbers into his calculator as he looked at some records on his desk at Graham Resources. The results were horrible. Just a few months before, Al Dempsey had estimated that the partnerships' profits, plus maximum borrowings, would leave them short $500,000 for the last two quarters of 1985. To deal with that problem, Graham Resources agreed to advance the money, even though Files didn't think the energy company had the financial wherewithal to do it.

Now, in the first week of January 1986, the final numbers for the year were coming in. And they were far worse than anyone ever imagined. The partnerships were short another $800,000 in the fourth quarter alone. Graham had to figure out how to bring the bad news to Prudential Insurance and Prudential-Bache. Maybe they could help out.

After all, Graham Resources had a lot of financial demands coming up. The company was planning to move in a few months from suburban New Orleans to Covington, Louisiana, on the north shore of Lake Pontchartrain. There would be no more of the modest office space in Metairie. Instead, they wanted to lease a tony, $11 million building. Their new office was a virtual palace, looking out on acres of man-made ponds, waterfalls, and streams, complete with a row of fountains marking the entrance. And all of it had been designed to the strict specifications of John Graham's wife, Suzy.

At that point, poor distributions would be a disaster. If sales fell off now, they couldn't pay for their new, regal digs.

On Monday, January 23, 1986, the oil market cracked. Almost thirteen years after the Arab oil embargo, the oil ministers for the Organization of Petroleum Exporting Companies were split. They were unable to curb the production of oil by their members. Oil prices dropped below $20 a barrel for the first time in years. Everyone, from New York commodities brokers to Texas oil barons, was stunned. In Washington, the White House celebrated the price drop, saying that the lower prices were good for consumers. The slide would continue relentlessly for months—eventually, for a fleeting moment, pushing oil prices below $10 a barrel.

The possibility that a rising oil market would cover up the mismanagement of the Prudential-Bache Energy Income partnerships was obliterated.

That same day, Matt Chanin called Jim Sweeney at the Direct Investment Group and lowered the boom: Prudential Insurance wanted out of the energy income partnerships.

"With the recent developments in the oil markets, it's time for all of the partners to reassess their positions," Chanin said. "There's no stability in the market now."

Prices could go in any direction, he said. Any assumptions he made to help him decide what to do would be only so much guesswork.

"In view of this," Chanin said, "I can't at this time recommend to the Prudential board that they authorize participation in Energy Income Fund III."

Sweeney took a breath. The new series was slated for marketing in a matter of months. The department was still selling some partnerships out of Series II. Chanin's decision could change everything.

"Well, in light of this, do you think that sales of the current income fund should be halted?" Sweeney asked.

"I never try to tell marketing people what to do, Jim," Chanin replied. "But I think it's in everyone's best interest to take a step back and reassess the situation."

Resigned, Sweeney told Chanin that he would arrange a meeting between him and other executives in the department to discuss future plans. In all likelihood, that would be the death knell for the energy income partnerships.

Al Dempsey hung up from his conference call with executives from the Direct Investment Group. He was feeling pretty good. Just a few days before, Matt Chanin's decision about pulling out seemed to threaten the future sales of the energy income partnerships. But now, after hearing the word come back from the Direct Investment Group's quarterly meeting, Dempsey knew everything was under control.

Earlier that day, he had spoken with Darr, Pittman, and Sweeney about the ramifications of Chanin's decision. The executives had been debating whether it would be better for Prudential Insurance simply to cut its investment substantially or to withdraw from the program. They spoke with all their top marketers during the conference, and the opinion was relatively uniform: It would be hard to explain why Prudential Insurance was cutting its investment. But if the company withdrew completely, the executives would be able to find the right marketing spin to persuade the firm's brokers to keep selling. Given all the regulations on insurance company investments, the executives agreed that Prudential Insurance's disappearance could be made more "believable" than its cutback.

Within months, the announcement of Prudential Insurance's decision went out on the internal communication system at Prudential-Bache branches around the country. It stressed that California regulations limited insurance companies to 10 percent of their assets in a single investment and that the Pru was bumping up against that limit. Apparently, nobody realized that the assets of Prudential Insurance grew massively each year, meaning that it could always invest more and still be below 10 percent.

As the announcement came across the internal computer, executives throughout the firm immediately smelled something fishy.

In Florida, Jim Parker, who had been the regional marketer there for partnerships since shortly after Darr arrived, looked at the announcement with disbelief. He picked up the telephone and called Bob Jackson, a slender, sandy-haired man who worked as the Florida regional marketer for Graham Resources.

"Hey, Bob," Parker said. "What's this about Prudential backing out of putting money into this deal because of some California regulation?"

"I just heard about that," Jackson said. "Doesn't sound like any rule I've ever heard of. I'm going to call New Orleans and see if I can get an explanation."

A few hours later, Jackson called back. He had received little information from his bosses.

"Bob, I can't put my finger on it, but something here doesn't jibe," Parker said. "I guess I'm having a hard time believing that the national investing policy of Prudential Insurance is being determined by some rule in California."

"It does sound strange."

"Well," Parker said, "how do we go about finding out if it's true or not?"

Jackson thought for a moment. He didn't have any idea.

"I don't know who the hell I could go to here," Parker said. "One thing I've learned over the years is you don't question what's happening in New York."

The conversation came to an end. Parker still felt enormously uneasy, but he wasn't about to raise a ruckus about it. He knew what had happened to the Futon Five. If he challenged the propriety of what was being done by the Direct Investment Group in New York, Parker was sure he'd lose his job. He decided to keep his mouth shut about his suspicions and just keep selling.

In early 1986, the first sales materials for the Prudential-Bache Energy Income Partnerships Series III were completed by the firm's marketers in New York.

One of the first documents most brokers saw was a fact sheet written by the Direct Investment Group. On the cover, beneath the name of the partnership, were three words: "A Proven Producer." The statement was a pure deception.

Few of the brokers concerned about risk in the oil and gas markets could have withstood the barrage of misleading, and sometimes outright fraudulent, information they received in the sales literature. The brokers were told that the partnerships were an ideal substitute for certificates of deposit, one of the safest investments possible.

The Direct Investment Group even coated the prospectus with marketing material designed to soothe any concerns about the quality and safety of the partnerships. The prospectuses arrived in the branches covered in "wrappers" containing slick, full-color graphics and photographs and descriptions of the supposed high quality and safety of the investments. The wrappers were far from subtle: For Series III, they featured a trim older couple walking barefoot down the beach. Above their photograph was the caption "For Investors Planning Their Retirement."

Throughout Prudential-Bache, on the advice of their brokers, elderly clients of the firm sunk their retirement accounts into this supposedly high-yielding, safe investment.

Over the next four years, using similar sales material, Prudential-Bache brokers would persuade another 98,484 clients to sink more than $1 billion of their savings into the energy income partnerships. Many of them were relying on that money for their retirement. All of them would live to regret the day they trusted the word of Prudential-Bache.

The two life-size elephants, each hand carved out of three thousand pounds of monkeypod wood, loomed over the crowd of Prudential-Bache executives. The group was gathered in the Hindustani Pavilion on the ground floor of the elegant Loew's Anatole Hotel in Dallas. The hotel is a city unto itself, with 1,620 rooms, eleven restaurants, and atriums so large that they can handle rodeos as easily as theater productions. It seemed the perfect place for this meeting in early 1986, Prudential-Bache's huge national forum for publicly placed limited partnerships. With so many partnerships secretly struggling, the meeting's name was almost laughable: "A Commitment to Excellence."

The list of almost three hundred expected attendees read like a who's who at Prudential-Bache and the Direct Investment Group. George Ball was there, along with Darr. Mingling alongside were representatives from almost every general partner for the large public deals promoted by the Direct Investment Group. Graham Resources alone sent more than a dozen executives to the meeting.

On one side of the pavilion, George Watson and Tracy Taylor from Watson & Taylor swapped jokes with a small group of the brokers. Nearby, Joel Stone, the president of VMS, was enjoying a deep belly-laugh about something he'd just heard. In the middle of the group, Merv Adelson, the chairman of Lorimar, the film production company that sold movie partnerships through Prudential-Bache, was talking with a few other brokers. Clifton Harrison was nowhere to be seen—after all, this was a meeting for public partnerships, and Harrison almost exclusively sold private deals. But word among the brokers was that as long as the Pru-Bache executives were in Dallas, Harrison would be dropping by unofficially over the next few days.

Wandering through the crowd of boisterous brokers and managers was Charles Dawson, the country broker from Sulphur Springs, Texas, who had hit the jackpot in 1985 by selling $1.4 million worth of the energy income partnerships in one day. Even though he had sold only a small number of partnerships since then, Dawson's accomplishment still awed his colleagues. Many of them worked in big cities, at some of the busiest branches in Prudential-Bache, but had never had a day like that. After his accomplishment had been written up in one of the Graham Resources newsletters, Dawson's success had entered the realm of legend.

Still, Dawson felt out of place at the meeting. So many of the Pru-Bache managers and general partners seemed dressed to the hilt. Dawson felt a little conspicuous in his off-the-rack $100 suit from a local department store. The jewelry, the extravagance of the hotel, the rich food there for the taking—to Dawson, all of it seemed a bit excessive for people who were simply supposed to be helping their clients buy and sell investments.

"Excuse me, Mr. Dawson?"

Dawson turned toward the female voice. Hallie Jennings, an assistant vice-president with the Direct Investment Group in New York, was looking at him.

"Yes, ma'am?" he replied.

"I was wondering if you would like to meet Jim Darr?" Jennings asked.

Dawson shrugged. Working out of a one-man office in a small Texas town, he never had much opportunity to meet his Prudential-Bache colleagues. He basically ignored and was untouched by the interoffice politics of the firm. Dawson had no idea who this Darr fellow was, but he liked meeting new people.

"Sure," he said.

Jennings turned and walked through the crowd toward a tall man with prematurely white hair. On sight, the man left Dawson uncomfortable. Amid all the expensive clothing, his suit stood out. Dawson figured it had to be worth a couple of thousand dollars.

"Mr. Dawson," Jennings said, "this is Jim Darr."

Dawson extended his hand, and Darr, unsmiling, took it.

"Hi," Dawson said as he pumped Darr's hand. "What branch do you work out of?"

Darr's grip went limp and he released Dawson's hand. His face turned beet red in anger. Dawson had never seen someone become so enraged so quickly.

"Don't you know who I am?" Darr spluttered.

"No, sir, I'm sorry. I don't."

"You work for me. I'm the head of the Direct Investment Group. When you sell partnerships, you're my employee."

Dawson didn't quite know what to say. "Well, sir, I'm sorry, I just don't mix much with the folks from New York."

"Well, let me tell you," Darr growled. "I'm the one who selects the partnerships. I'm the one who decides which ones get sold and which ones don't. When you sell your customers a partnership, it's only because I approved it first. That's who I am." Darr turned away and stomped into the crowd.

Jennings burst into laughter. "I would have paid a thousand dollars just to see Darr's face like that," she said. "Not knowing who he was really put him down."

"Well, why should I know?" Dawson shrugged. "I don't deal with these folks."

The whole encounter left Dawson with a distinctly uneasy feeling. If this arrogant executive was the one who decided which partnerships were sold, Dawson was not as comfortable with them as he had been before.

The next evening, Dawson arrived for an awards ceremony in the Chantilly West Ballroom on the ground floor of the Anatole, a few yards from the Hindustani Pavilion. Light from the crystal chandeliers on the light peach fabric that covered the walls bathed the room in elegance. Dozens of tables covered in white linen dotted the room. As Dawson approached his table, he felt his stomach drop. He was seated with Darr.

Dawson greeted Darr as he took his seat. Darr looked at him and an odd smile came across his face; it was almost as if he knew he was about to even a score.

"Well, Charlie, welcome," Darr said pleasantly.

The other members of the table spoke among themselves. Then Darr, speaking loudly enough so that almost everyone at the table could hear, turned to Dawson.

"So, I hear you run a dairy farm," Darr said, his voice dripping with sarcasm. "That sounds *real* interesting."

Dawson felt his face flush. He loved his dairy farm. He had been raised on one. He didn't like the fact that this fancy-suited New York executive thought it was an object of ridicule.

After some speeches during dinner, the awards ceremony began. Darr made the presentations. Eventually, he reached an award for Dawson, given for having the best performance on a single day.

"Well, this award is for Charlie Dawson, but I think I better hand it out quickly," Darr said with a smile. "I'm sure Charlie will want to go home early so he can take care of his cows."

Brokers around the room tittered. Dawson stood up to accept his award, feeling a slow burn. He took it without a word and returned to his table. He didn't like the fact that Darr was trying to put him down in front of his colleagues. He had only had two experiences with Darr, but already he hated him. Darr's actions and arrogance spoke volumes to Dawson.

If that's the way you feel, you son of a bitch, Dawson thought, *I'll never sell your partnerships again.*

If Darr had suspected what Dawson thought, he likely would not have cared. By 1986, brokers throughout the country had to sell his products. Their managers pushed them to do so, and the regional directors pushed the managers. The regional directors felt pressure from New York, all seeming to emanate from Ball's office. With the losses stacking up at the firm, Ball needed to keep up the performances of strong departments, such as the Direct Investment Group.

Darr had big plans to transform his influence into more power. In just a matter of years, or maybe just months, he felt sure he could take Bob Sherman's job. And that would be the first step on the way to his plan to succeed Ball. Darr didn't need the good graces of some country broker who didn't even know who he was. He had come to expect far better treatment than that.

CHAPTER 12

THE SLEEK, BLACK LIMOUSINE drove past the Prudential-Bache headquarters in lower Manhattan, continued for about a block, then pulled up to the front of 170 John Street. Decades before, the granite building had been a ship's chandlery, selling supplies to the schooners, barks, and transatlantic packets that tossed their lines and heaved their loads onto the docks at the East River. But after the sea traffic dwindled, the seaport had fallen into disrepair. It was not until the 1980s that the area was rebuilt into a popular tourist attraction and Wall Street hangout called South Street Seaport. Now the John Street building housed the Yankee Clipper Restaurant. Where once the astonishing sight of a limousine on the seaport's narrow streets and alleys might have brought dock work to a halt, by the late spring of 1986, it was a common sight.

After pulling to a stop, the driver settled in for a wait. The car had been dispatched not long before from Smith Limousine Company to make a pickup for one of its corporate accounts. Whenever the customers were not paying for the limousine out of their own pockets, they never seemed to mind letting the bill run up.

Finally the door from the Yankee Clipper opened, and the driver saw a familiar face walking toward the limousine. He stepped out of the car, walked around to the back door on the passenger side, and opened it. Jim Darr nodded as he climbed in. The driver hopped inside and drove off, headed toward Darr's home in Greenwich.

Darr loved limousines. He boasted about his frequent limo rides to his colleagues, seeming to view them as a measure of his success. His trips were not even charged to his company, Prudential-Bache. Instead, Darr often relied on the general partners whose deals he sold to let him use their corporate accounts. Then they would just pass on the cost for Darr's indulgence to their investors.

This time, Clifton Harrison's corporate account was being charged for Darr's trip. Darr had used Harrison's limousine service before to shuttle him from his home to the office. Other times, he used it to travel the short distance from Prudential-Bache to the River Café, just under the nearby Brooklyn Bridge. Even if Darr could not bring himself to use a taxi, that short hop using a car service would cost less than $15. But since he was not paying for the limousine, he kept it waiting outside that restaurant. The total tab for three and a quarter hours was $136.50.

The trip from the Yankee Clipper would be even more expensive. With all the waiting and traveling, seven hours passed between the time the limousine arrived at the restaurant until it dropped Darr off at his house. It cost $297.50, with the entire bill paid by the investors who did business with Clifton Harrison.

It was one of the last times Darr would be able to enjoy his friend's largesse. Harrison's freewheeling spending of partnership money—for Darr, for brokers, and for himself—was on the verge of coming to an end. But not until after one last extravagant blowout.

The stately *Queen Elizabeth 2*, the world's most famous luxury ship, was docked in its berth at Manhattan's West Side passenger terminal. Thousands of people stood along the pier on the Saturday morning of April 20, 1986, watching as the pride of the Cunard line was readied for the boarding of its excited and wealthy customers.

Amid the crowds, about a dozen Prudential-Bache brokers waited patiently. The brokers—all men—happily talked with their wives about the exhilarating five-day trip they were all about to take. In a short time, their transatlantic cruise to Southampton, England, would begin. Along the way, they were planning to shop on board at Harrods, gamble at the Players Club Casino, and enjoy the "Golden Door Spa at Sea" program. Then, after visiting London, they would be flown back to America on the Concorde. The extravagant trip would cost them nothing. The entire bill was being footed by Clifton Harrison.

As they waited in line, several of the brokers noticed there was something wrong with their host. His usual jovial demeanor was gone—in its place, he seemed tense and worried. They knew that Darr was supposed to be on this trip, but for some reason he had canceled at the last minute. Instead, Harrison brought along Howard Feinsand, his lawyer. That alone struck the brokers as odd.

As the days on the cruise passed by, the brokers' concern about Harrison grew. He spent almost no time with them—instead, he seemed to be in continual consultation with Feinsand. Whatever was going on, it seemed serious.

Unknown to the brokers, Harrison was facing dangerous legal troubles. A Minneapolis investor named John McNulty had filed a lawsuit against him and Prudential-Bache months earlier. McNulty, a lawyer, had purchased an interest in the Archives partnership in 1982. When the investment fell apart, he contacted Harrison, who indicated that the fault for the trouble lay with the banks. But after conducting an investigation, McNulty believed that Harrison had mismanaged the partnership. Now his lawyer, Charles Cox, was trying to get Harrison under oath. Harrison didn't like the idea.

Harrison's legal problem with an investor would not have surprised the brokers he was hosting. For even as they feasted on sumptuous meals, at times ordering expensive entrées not included on the ship's lavish menus, they spoke bitterly of their host. Despite all the praise that Darr and the Direct Investment Group showered on Harrison, his deals were turning into debacles. Their performance projections had almost uniformly been worthless; the brokers' best customers flooded them with an endless stream of complaining telephone calls. Already the brokers were shying away from Harrison's deals.

"I'll tell you one thing," Agostino Zolezzi, a top-selling Prudential-Bache broker, told a colleague as he relaxed on a lounge chair on the QE2. "I am never going to do another one of Clifton's deals. They've been unmitigated disasters."

Finally, after a few days on board, Harrison contacted the brokers. He wanted to hold a twenty- or thirty-minute sales conference to discuss his plans for future deals. They gathered that day in one of the QE2's private lounges. Most of the brokers on board showed up. Without his usual exuberance, Harrison described his plans for new deal structures in the wake of the government's growing interest in tax reform.

"We can't ignore what's happening in Washington," Harrison said. "I'm going to be turning away from tax shelters. My future deals are all going to be driven by the economics of the property. I'm going to be spending much more time looking at cash flow instead of tax implications."

The brokers wanted to hear none of it. "Forget the next deal, Clifton," one of them barked. "What went wrong with the projections on Madison Plaza?"

Another broker interrupted. "Your Brazilian Court deal doesn't look like it's doing too well either. What's happening?"

The pointed questions came one after another. It was clear that the angry brokers were just a few steps shy of becoming an ugly mob. Harrison stood in front of them, looking tired. In a flat voice, he sloughed off the questions with vague assurances.

"There have been some problems, we're all aware of that," he said. "But my future deals are all going to be driven by economics, and that's a whole new ball game. I think we need to focus on that."

Harrison stumbled through a few details about the deals he expected to be offering soon, but no one in the room cared. If any of the Pru-Bache brokers had doubts whether they planned to sell any of Harrison's future deals, they were resolved in that lounge on the QE2. Harrison could not offer them a simple explanation about what was going wrong. They began to feel like fools. How had the people in New York been so confident about Harrison's partnerships? Had anyone been doing any due diligence at all?

It was too late to be asking those questions. The brokers didn't know it, but there would be no next deal. Harrison's financial troubles were already mounting, his real estate empire on the verge of collapse. He had no secret deals to strike with Prudential-Bache executives; his friends in the S&L industry had all been booted out of the business. For the first time since he began selling partnerships through Pru-Bache, Harrison was standing on his own. He would not even be able to afford the QE2 trip and would have to negotiate an installment plan to pay for it.

All he needed was one more push, and everything could fall apart.

Two weeks later, he was pushed.

It began on May 15 in the small village of Massing-Rott, West Germany, at the office of a respected general practitioner named Dr. Herbert Schieffer. After rummaging through some of his files, Schieffer found the document he had received six years before, when his stockbroker was attempting to persuade him to invest the deutsche mark equivalent of $20,000 in a particular partnership. The deal would pool the investor capital to help purchase two shopping centers based in Bessemer, Alabama, and Key West, Florida. Like most of his fellow investors, Schieffer had known little about either location and at first felt uncertain about the investment.

Then Schieffer received an astonishing document from Clifton Harrison, the proposed general partner for the deal. In that 1981 letter, Harrison guaranteed that in 1986 he would repurchase the partnership units from him for 150 percent of the original investment, or $30,000. If Schieffer did not want to sell, he could simply hold on to his investment. The letterhead had the Bache name in it. Schieffer believed what it said.

Now it was 1986, and Schieffer was certain he wanted to sell. The partnership had done poorly, and he was awfully glad that he had retained Harrison's guarantee in his files. After locating the document, he stamped his name on the bottom of the letter, acknowledging that he wanted his money back. All he had to do, he thought, was send the letter back to Harrison, and he would have his money in a matter of weeks.

For the next three weeks, all across West Germany—in Stuttgart, Sauerlach, Offenburg—as well as in Austria and Greece, dozens of Harrison's investors repeated Schieffer's action, hunting down their guarantee, signing it, and mailing it to Dallas.

The letters poured into Harrison's office. The man who needed an installment plan to pay for the prior month's trip on the *QE2* was suddenly facing a debt of more than $1.9 million. And he had no way to pay for it.

Tillie Tillman, one of the biggest sellers of Harrison's partnerships, was in a virtual panic. On that day in the summer of 1986, a colleague who worked with him at the Prudential-Bache branch in Long Beach, California, had told him of an unbelievable rumor about Harrison. As someone who had sold close to $1.5 million worth of Harrison's partnerships in 1985 alone, Tillman was sure that someone—someone at Prudential-Bache, he hoped—would have given him the information if there was any truth to it. But no matter. He wanted to get to the bottom of this immediately. He called Harrison Freedman Associates in Dallas and asked to speak with Mike Walters, the chief marketer.

"Mike, I've got to talk to you," Tillman said, his words pouring out. "Is Clifton a convicted felon?"

Walters muttered something, sounding distinctly uncomfortable. "I don't want to talk about this on the telephone, Tillie," he said. "Can you come to my office?"

"Next flight, I'll be there."

Tillman grabbed some clothes from home and rushed to the airport. His head was swimming. For as long as he had been at Prudential-Bache, he had been pushing his clients into Harrison deals. He repeatedly vouched for the man, relying on the assurances of his bosses at the firm. And now he found out that Harrison might be a common criminal—reformed, perhaps, but a criminal nonetheless.

He took the next flight to Dallas. He could barely sit still during the flight. His agitation about what he had heard just kept growing. How could Prudential-Bache have expected to hide something like this? he wondered. With all the general partners in the world, why in the hell would they do business with one who went to jail?

He arrived at Dallas–Fort Worth Airport in the late afternoon and took a taxi to Harrison Freedman Associates. When he arrived, he was immediately whisked in to see Mike Walters. Before Tillman could say anything, the heavyset Walters beat him to the punch.

"Yes, Tillie, it's true."

The words hit like a dagger in Tillman's heart. He felt almost woozy as he sank into a chair in Walters's office. Rage welled up inside him.

"How in the hell could we have not heard about this until now?" he exploded.

Walters hustled over to his door and shut it. He looked upset that he had not done so sooner. Then he walked back and slumped into the chair at his desk, sighing.

"Well, it's just been a big cover-up all this time," he said. "Otherwise, it would have been a mess."

"Damn right it would!" Tillman barked. "Who the hell wants to get in bed with a convicted felon?"

Walters looked on impassively as Tillman got control of himself. Finally Tillman looked up, with his eyes almost pleading for an explanation. "Mike, what the hell happened?"

"It goes all the way back, Tillie," Walters said. "All the way to the beginning."

Walters told Tillman that years before, he had witnessed Jim Darr arguing with the lawyers about whether deals from Harrison should be sold by the firm. He said the lawyers had thought the idea was crazy. But Darr had argued forcefully that Harrison should be approved, Walters said, saying that the presidential pardon had expunged his record.

Tillman listened, feeling numb. He almost wanted to cry. He had decided recently not to sell any more of Harrison's deals because of their poor performance. But he knew now it was too late. His clients couldn't sell the illiquid partnerships. Suddenly he knew they were trapped. Millions of dollars of their money rested on the reliability of a man he would never have recommended had he known the truth.

"Oh, my God, Mike," Tillman said. "The people I put into these deals are some of my best friends in the world. What the hell do I tell them? What do I say?"

Tillman swallowed hard. He might not know what to tell his clients, but he knew what he would tell his colleagues. He was ready to make enough commotion that by the time he was done, brokers throughout Prudential-Bache—including all of the biggest sellers of Harrison's deals—would know the truth. The same questions would start to be asked again and again. How could something like this have been kept secret? And where were the people who were supposed to be watching the Direct Investment Group?

Kristi Mandt, a broker with Prudential-Bache's Seattle office, woke gradually on the morning of July 9, 1986. Her head pounded a bit, and her mouth felt dry. Before she opened her eyes, Mandt knew she had drunk too much the night before. That was bad. Mandt had been struggling with alcoholism since 1983. She knew if she kept drinking, her job was on the line.

Mandt slowly opened her eyes. She was in a hotel room. She looked over to the side of the bed and felt a rush of shock. Lying next to her was Bob Sherman, the head of retail for Prudential-Bache. She looked under the sheets. Both of them were naked. She could tell that Sherman had had sex with her.

Mandt stood up, looking for her clothes scattered around the room. She needed to dress and get out. Slowly it all started to come back to her. She was in Denver, Colorado, at a sales conference. A few weeks earlier, Carrington Clark, the Prudential-Bache regional administrator in charge of her office, had told Mandt that her drinking had put her job in jeopardy. Clark said he had kept her from being fired. Now, he said, she was in debt to him. He could fire her at will. The speech frightened her. She needed her job.

Then Clark told Mandt that he wanted her to fly to Denver for the sales conference, where she would meet up with him and Sherman. Mandt did as she was told. On arriving the night before, Sherman and Clark took her to a bar. There they all drank heavily. They did nothing related to business. Mandt remembered very little else. She felt ashamed. Sherman, and maybe even Clark, had sex with her while she was drunk, she thought.*

As Mandt gathered her things, she noticed her airline ticket and scooped it up. She needed to keep it for later. When Clark told her to travel to

---

* Sherman denied ever sexually harassing Mandt or doing anything improper with her. Clark refused to comment on the record. These events are described by Mandt in an NASD arbitration she filed in 1992 against Prudential Securities.

Denver, he said all expenses would be paid; all she had to do was send him her ticket receipt for reimbursement. As she packed to leave, she remembered precisely what Clark had said about the bill.

"We'll just charge it to a limited partnership promoted by Prudential-Bache."

Garnett Keith, a vice-chairman of the Prudential Insurance Company, dabbed a linen napkin to his mouth as he ate his lunch. He was eating alone with Jim Darr for the first time. In recent years, Darr's Direct Investment Group made up such a huge portion of Prudential-Bache's revenues—and was one of the few departments in the whole firm that showed a profit—that the senior officers of Prudential Insurance could not help but notice. George Ball himself had nothing but praise for Darr, and often singled out the Direct Investment Group in his presentations to the board of directors of Prudential Insurance. With Darr's unquestionable success, he might be someone on the way up in the Prudential organization. So Keith, a bone-thin man with graying hair, was more than happy to host Darr for lunch in the fall of 1986.

Things went poorly almost from the start. Even though Keith had a Wall Street background, he was used to dealing with insurance executives and sophisticated investment bankers. Darr was nothing but a pure salesman, and one who was far too ham-fisted in his self-promotion.

As Keith listened, Darr expounded on the huge volume his department was doing in partnerships and the great success he saw for the future. Darr's naked ambition was too close to the surface. His crude attempts to portray himself as the person who should run Prudential-Bache's retail division, or perhaps even take over for Ball someday, left Keith uneasy. This was Darr's big opportunity with Prudential Insurance, but he was taking a wrecking ball to his own reputation. By the time the lunch came to an end, Keith felt a strong distaste for the executive so responsible for bringing in revenues to the firm.

"Well, Jim," Keith said as he stood up. "That was a most enjoyable lunch. We'll have to do it again sometime."

Smiling, Keith headed toward the exit with Darr. Despite his attempt to project enthusiasm, he was glad the lunch was over. Darr unsettled him. But Keith never shared his concerns about Darr with George Ball, the man most responsible for the business of Prudential-Bache.

————

In Frankfurt, West Germany, Guenter Hoffstaedterr, an executive with the Bache office there, prepared a cable for transmission to Clifton Harrison. Hoffstaedterr had developed a relatively close relationship with Harrison over the years, although most of their conversations were by cable and telephone. Hoffstaedterr had believed in Harrison, particularly given the strong backing that the Texan received from the New York headquarters. That was why Hoffstaedterr had so strongly pushed the Bessemer–Key West deal among German citizens.

But the customers had grown angry about their investment in recent years. First, they stopped receiving distributions. Hoffstaedterr begged Harrison to figure out a way to make them, but to no avail. He didn't know that Harrison had kept all the money that could have been distributed as a fee. Now almost all the customers were demanding their money back, plus 50 percent. They came in waving some piece of paper Harrison had signed committing himself to make the huge payoff. Hoffstaedterr knew that Harrison didn't have the money on hand to buy back the interests. Worse, he knew that Harrison had told no one in New York what was happening. With each new demand from a customer, Hoffstaedterr's concerns grew. He had to reveal to his bosses in America what was happening.

At 6:15 P.M., Frankfurt time, Hoffstaedterr sent off his cable over the RCA Global Communications network. In it, he told Harrison about a few new customers who wanted their money back and added up the new total debt for him. Near the end, he delicately told Harrison that as far as New York went, the jig was finally up.

"Clifton, please remember that whatever happens in respect to your repurchase obligations, I have to report to my senior officers in New York," he wrote. "I hope that this is understood and doesn't upset you."

The news would greatly upset the executives at Prudential-Bache in New York.

"Tough shit. It's Harrison's problem. We're not paying it."

The lawyer from the New York legal department could not have been more vehement when talking to the firm's executives in Frankfurt. Almost as soon as Hoffstaedterr informed his bosses in New York, the matter had been turned over to the firm's lawyers. After just a little research, they were well aware that Harrison did not have the means to shell out almost $2 million to his investors. He already was swimming in personal debt— finding a bank to take care of this problem would be almost impossible.

But the lawyers took a hard line. In their conversations with the Frankfurt executives, they repeatedly stressed that Prudential-Bache would not shell out a penny to any of the German investors. Harrison had been the one who signed the commitment letter; Bache had just been the selling agent. It was not responsible.

That aggressive position did not last for long. Some of the German investors became angry with the repeated refusals from Harrison and the firm to honor the commitment. By Harrison's agreement, they were supposed to have been paid their money by September 30, and yet by October, they were still waiting with no end in sight. Some of them contacted German regulators. Within a matter of days, officials from the West German government called Pru-Bache in New York, demanding to know why it was not honoring the commitment.

When the lawyers argued that the commitment had been Harrison's and not theirs, the German officials were not impressed. After all, the letterhead Harrison had used was for a company called "Bache-Harrison Associates." That, the officials said, was enough to put Prudential-Bache on the hook. The Germans did not know, nor would they likely have cared, that Bache-Harrison had simply been a contrivance intended to be nothing more than a means of gathering fees.

After some back-and-forth, the officials implied heavily that if Prudential-Bache chose not to live up to its commitments, the firm would be facing trouble. It might even lose its right to sell securities in West Germany.

That changed the lawyers' minds. They realized this was a problem that the firm would have to help resolve. Prudential-Bache would have to bail Harrison out of trouble again.

At precisely forty-five seconds after eleven o'clock on the morning of October 22, 1986, the Marine Corps band assembled on the south lawn of the White House struck up "Hail to the Chief." President Ronald Reagan, wearing a lightweight brown suit, strode briskly from the White House toward a specially erected platform. It was a glorious, Indian-summer day. Behind Reagan, the Truman Balcony of the White House was decorated with rows of yellow chrysanthemums. Reagan bounded up to the platform and smiled out to a crowd of more than fifteen hundred people. It was the largest audience ever gathered during the Reagan administration for the signing of legislation. But it wasn't every day that the federal tax code was revised from top to bottom.

As the crowd applauded, Reagan passed by a desk and walked to a podium that held the presidential seal.

"Well, thank you, and welcome to the White House," Reagan said. "In a moment, I'll be sitting at that desk, taking up a pen, and signing the most sweeping overhaul of the tax code in our nation's history. To all of you here today who've worked so long and hard to see this day come, my thanks and the thanks of the nation go out to you."

It had been an incredible journey to this day, beginning in 1982 when Senator Bill Bradley and Representative Richard Gephardt proposed the Democratic version of tax reform. In 1984, Don Regan, the secretary of the Treasury, had unveiled his own version, and in 1985, Reagan had adopted tax reform as the central piece of domestic legislation in his second term.

The legislation was shockingly simple. It replaced more than a dozen tax brackets, ranging from 11 percent to 50 percent, with two basic brackets. The top bracket was just 28 percent. In exchange, the legislation wiped away hundreds of deductions that taxpayers had used over the years to cut their tax bills. The new legislation would almost completely gut the tax shelter business, which had been fueled by the rules in Reagan's first tax bill.

"I feel like we just played the World Series of tax reform," Reagan said to the laughter of the crowd. "And the American people won."

"Tax reform should be a wash," Darr told the executive committee of Prudential-Bache. "It shouldn't affect our partnership sales at all."

Ball listened impassively as Darr made his presentation. For months, Pru-Bache's senior executives had watched anxiously as the tax reform legislation moved slowly through Congress. Some had felt elated each time the legislation seemed to be teetering on the precipice of failure; they had felt dismayed when, time after time, the bill survived, only to move the next step toward becoming law. By the summer of 1986, when tax reform had begun to seem much more of a real possibility, Ball had begun asking Darr about whether the Direct Investment Group could survive. Darr had assured him repeatedly that it not only would survive, it would flourish. So, now that the bill had become law, Darr was presenting his upbeat viewpoint to the executive committee of the firm.

To a large degree, the department's survival was a testament to the planning of Ball and Darr. By redirecting their energies in 1982 away from just tax-driven deals, focusing their attention instead on economic deals like the energy income partnerships, they had created a special niche in the industry. They believed that business could survive whatever tax changes Washington wanted to put in place.

Of course, the potential tax deductions of an asset such as real estate make up a portion of the price any buyer would be willing to pay. A property without tax deductions would be worth less than a similar property that offered such benefits. But Darr told the committee that Washington's removal of that tax value was meaningless for the future of the department.

"If we're looking at a building worth $20 million last month, it should be worth $12 million today," Darr said. "The price adjustment should be instantaneous. This is a sophisticated market. We just buy at the lower price and ride the profits up from there."

The argument was sheer lunacy—every lobbyist for the Realtors, syndicators, and builders had argued all through the drafting of tax reform that it would send real estate into a prolonged recession. An apartment building was not like a stock—it didn't have an instantaneous quote adjustment on the floor of some exchange. Instead, because real estate was illiquid, prices would have to drop slowly, over many years, as sellers and buyers struggled to find the true value of the assets. It was a process no one in the real estate industry had ever been through before.

But Ball felt soothed and delighted by Darr's breezy assurances. Partnership departments around Wall Street were shutting down, but Ball just shrugged that off as bad planning on their part. He felt sure that he had the best people in the partnership business. Ball could trust their judgment. Prudential-Bache's advertising didn't just describe the firm as "market wise" for nothing. The Direct Investment Group could keep growing strong. With so many firms dropping out of the business, now was the time to try to step up Prudential-Bache's sales and start profiting from their experience.

"All right, Jim," Ball said with a smile. "Go get 'em."

Clifton Harrison stood in his home in Dallas, holding the telephone slightly away from his ear. On the other end of the line, Joel Davidson, a lawyer from Prudential-Bache, was screaming at him.

"Sir, I honestly don't believe this is my obligation," Harrison said. "Perhaps Mr. Hoffstaedterr said some things to the German investors that I didn't understand. I don't speak German."

Davidson was apoplectic. The commitment to the German investors was written in *English*. It was signed by Harrison. This was Harrison's obligation. He had to make good on it. The stakes were too high.

Finally, after days of negotiation, Harrison agreed to Prudential-Bache's demands: He would accept the responsibility for repaying the Bessemer–Key West investors their money but would use loans from the firm to do so.

By early November 1986, Davidson was writing up the outlines of a deal between Harrison and Prudential-Bache. Under their agreement, Pru-Bache would loan Harrison about $1.9 million in exchange for two promissory notes from him. Interest payments on the notes would be due quarterly. As security, Harrison would take out a second mortgage on the Bessemer Shopping Center in Alabama, granted in favor of Prudential-Bache. Harrison would not be permitted to sell the Bessemer property, and all of the cash flow from it would be applied to paying the new mortgage interest.

Harrison accepted the terms. Under the highly restrictive agreement, he waived all his rights to the Bessemer property until he paid Prudential-Bache back the $1.9 million. The property effectively belonged to Pru-Bache.

The lawyers for Prudential-Bache felt comfortable that they had protected the firm's interests. But there was one big problem: Whenever a mortgage is created, it must be recorded for public files. If Pru-Bache did that, a public record would be created, one that would be accessible to every investor in the Harrison partnerships—as well as their lawyers. Recording the mortgage would be direct proof of Harrison's financial problems. It also could lead to the disclosure of the huge commitment Harrison made in 1980 to the Bessemer–Key West investors. More than $250 million in Harrison partnerships had been sold by the firm since then, and not one of the disclosure documents revealed the commitment to the Germans. Any investor who found out about it could sue.

Prudential-Bache sidestepped the problem, and the mortgage was never recorded. No public document was created. Investors would never be told of this financial crisis.

Prudential-Bache, as a firm, was now effectively a secret investor with Clifton Harrison. It would soon learn the grim reality of that position: Despite the written assurances, Harrison would soon renege on every term of the agreement. Within a few months, he skipped the first quarterly payment he owed on the loan. Soon he was declared in default.

Prudential-Bache lawyers threatened to take legal action against Harrison but never did so. They had outsmarted themselves and handed Harrison a weapon: If they sued, the firm would create a public document showing all of the information it had failed to disclose to investors. Harrison had them over a barrel.

Harrison's control of the situation was so complete that, later, when he sold the Bessemer property and pocketed the proceeds, Prudential-Bache didn't raise a single objection. Years later, when asked why Harrison had been allowed to walk away with millions of dollars of the firm's money, Loren Schechter offered an incredible explanation.

"It was an administrative oversight."

"Mr. Harrison, would you raise your right hand and repeat after me, please."

Harrison, seated at a conference table in his lawyer's office on East Fifty-second Street in Manhattan, raised his hand and swore to tell the truth. It was ten o'clock in the morning on March 23, 1987. The lawsuit brought by John McNulty, the angry investor in the Archives deal, had finally reached Harrison's doorstep. Charles Cox, McNulty's amiable but aggressive Minneapolis lawyer, was ready to start the deposition. It would be the first time that any investor with Harrison would be able to ask him questions under oath.

The stakes were enormous. Almost without fail, every deposition begins with a short questioning about the witness's background. Depending on the questions Cox asked, Harrison might be compelled to reveal the secret of his criminal background that he and Prudential-Bache had tried so long to keep hidden.

Cox reviewed some notes. After asking Harrison to state his name and place of residence, Cox started with an open-ended, catch-all question.

"I notice in the private placement memorandum your background is set out in some length," Cox said. "Is there anything that you feel should be added to what's set out in there?"

His hands folded in front of him, Harrison looked at Cox placidly. "I don't recall what's set out in the memorandum."

"Well, let's start this way, then," Cox said, as he led into a series of questions about Harrison's early background. He asked about Harrison's education and his first job. Harrison said he had worked at a bank, which he left in 1966.

"After 1966 and the bank, what did you do?"

Harrison's eyes shifted over to his lawyer, then back to Cox. "Can I talk to my counsel?"

"Sure." Cox shrugged.

Cox watched, puzzled, as Harrison conferred in whispers with his lawyer, Steven Kaplan. After a few moments, they finished, and Kaplan looked at Cox.

"Charlie," Kaplan said, "Mr. Harrison will answer, you know, questions regarding his educational background and work experience, and that's what you're asking about."

Cox didn't understand what was going on. "You say he won't?"

"He will."

"All right."

"Is that what you're asking about, you want to know the sequence of his education and what his work experience is?"

Cox's antennae went up. Kaplan wanted him to limit the scope of his questions. His lawyer's sense told him he was circling around something important. He wasn't about to agree to restrict his inquiry.

"How he got where he is," Cox replied. He was keeping his options open.

Cox went back to the questioning and again asked what Harrison had done after leaving the bank in 1966. At first, Harrison said he attended Southern Methodist University in 1967. Cox raised an eyebrow. Harrison was skipping a period of time between the bank and college.

"Did you do anything in the interval?" Cox asked.

"I was a carpenter," Harrison replied without flinching. He left out that he did his woodworking as a prison inmate.

"Was that your first real introduction to construction?"

"Unfortunately, I think, yes."

Cox shrugged. He couldn't understand what all the fuss was about. "Good place to start, really," he said.

"It was difficult being a carpenter."

Cox looked back at his notes. There was something here, and he was missing it. He decided to try again. "Why did you leave the bank?"

"We had major disagreements."

"By 'we' you mean you and your—"

"Me and my direct supervisor."

Cox asked a few questions about the supervisor and then decided he wasn't getting anywhere. He moved on to questions about Harrison's time at SMU. Cox asked no more questions about Harrison's life during the years he spent in prison.

His criminal background could continue to remain a secret. All it took was for Harrison to avoid telling the full truth while under oath. And all in front of a lawyer for Prudential-Bache.

Tillie Tillman was raging again at his branch manager, Dave Diestel.

"It's unbelievable the crap they've been piling onto us! Darr and that crowd should be shot!"

From the time Tillman had told his friend Diestel about Harrison's felony conviction, both men had been stunned. They talked about it constantly. Even now, in early 1987, neither could offer an explanation of how Darr and his team betrayed the trust of so many of their own brokers. Whatever their reasoning, it impressed them both as the most cynical of deceptions.

What Tillman had learned about Harrison had gotten around the firm quickly. With massive telecommunication systems, complete with thousands of telephones connecting the brokers, retail brokerages are tiny places. The details of a shouting match in a San Diego branch can be known within the hour in Bangor, Maine. Tillman was the first person to publicly roar about Harrison's criminal conviction. He didn't care who heard him—in fact, he hoped as many people as possible did.

Almost daily, another broker heard the news. *The firm had been representing a convicted felon.* Some brokers were anguished to learn the news.

But most other brokers felt lucky, as if they had sidestepped an oncoming train. Their clients had not been interested in the kind of pure tax shelters Harrison peddled, so they had stayed away from the deals. Instead, most of them had focused on selling partnerships with the potential for real economic returns, like the energy income deals. The brokers were sure that those deals were legitimate. They could see the high cash distributions their clients were receiving each quarter. So when they started to hear that Graham Resources was preparing a whole new type of partnership for sale, the brokers at Prudential-Bache awaited it eagerly.

CHAPTER 13

IN THE CONFERENCE ROOM just down the hall from his office, Darr was giving a pep talk. Executives from the Direct Investment Group, along with Tony Rice from Graham Resources, listened closely as Darr spoke. He sounded like a football coach before the biggest game of the year.

"We're going to clear the decks for this one and put all our muscle behind it," Darr said. "We've never marketed a product this aggressively."

The meeting on November 11, 1986, followed months of discussion about assembling a new type of partnership with Graham to take advantage of the horrific collapse in oil prices. All the talk was paying off. Pru-Bache was days from launching its latest product with Graham, a partnership called the Prudential-Bache Energy Growth Fund.

"The Energy Growth Fund is extremely important to Prudential-Bache," Darr said. "Direct Investment due diligence is on the line."

The idea behind the growth fund was simple. With the collapse of oil prices, banks throughout the Southwest were struggling with loans to energy companies that had been secured by oil reserves. The banks had written down the loans, assigning them a value that was a fraction of the original amount. Under the theory of Graham and the Direct Investment Group, a loan of $100 million, for example, was being carried by a bank at a value of $40 million. That meant that the growth fund could purchase half of that loan for $20 million. But the good part was that the loan was secured by oil reserves that were still worth $80 million. The growth fund could either receive huge profits when the borrower paid off the entire $100 million, or it could seize the $80 million worth of reserves if the borrower defaulted. Either way, it sounded like a no-lose deal.

On top of that, the new partnerships would be extremely lucrative for both Graham Resources and Prudential-Bache. The exorbitant fees charged to other partnerships would look downright tiny compared with those of the growth fund. Prudential-Bache and Graham would extract 15 percent of investors' capital up front. Then they would take another 15 percent of every partnership distribution. Whenever a client received back a dollar of the original cash, at least thirty cents would be missing.

Darr feared the growth fund would be so envied that Wall Street's premier firms, such as Goldman Sachs and Salomon Brothers, would rapidly put together their own copycat products. So he wanted the growth fund marketed as quickly as possible.

Probably that was the reason why none of them had bothered to find out whether the growth funds might actually work. Graham had held substantive discussions with only one bank, First City National Bank of Houston, which had been one of its primary lenders. On top of that, no one had performed anything but the most cursory due diligence.

So at this meeting three days before sales began, Darr demanded that someone put together some last-minute financial information on the growth fund. After all, the marketers couldn't sell the deal without some numbers to back up the theories.

"We've got no solid projections or case studies, and we're already working on the marketing guide," he said. "The guide has to be available in six days. So let me tell you what we need for success here."

Darr rattled off what he wanted the numbers to prove: First-year distributions would equal 15 to 20 percent, and investors would receive all their money back within five years. He seemed to have no basis for pulling those numbers out of the air, other than the fact that they sounded good.

In the end, the rushing proved to be unnecessary. Prudential-Bache had nothing to fear from Salomon Brothers and Goldman Sachs. Competitors don't copy failure. If anyone had checked before offering $500 million worth of growth funds to clients, they would have learned a very salient fact: The loans they wanted to purchase didn't exist for sale. They were figments of some marketer's imagination.

Tony Rice smiled as he briefed twenty Prudential-Bache branch managers about the energy growth fund. The crowd was getting pumped up. Ed Devereaux, a regional marketer for the Direct Investment Group, felt especially excited as he listened to the description of the growth fund. The product sounded brilliant. He was proud that his firm would be the first one on the market buying these discounted, overcollateralized loans.

As Rice made his presentation, Darr sat nearby, hanging on every word. At times, Darr would interrupt Rice, telling him to describe some complex element of the growth fund in simpler terms. Once he finished his presentation, Rice asked if anyone had any questions.

"Why would the banks give you guys this special opportunity to cherry-pick their loans?" a manager asked incredulously.

"Well, let me explain that to you," Rice began. As he discussed the rules surrounding write-downs of loans and what that meant in banking, brokers exchanged furtive glances. What Rice was saying didn't make any sense.

Darr walked to the front of the room, saying he would take over the question himself. But even Darr's answer seemed to leave the manager puzzled. He asked another question about why the partnership worked the way it did. Darr scowled. He could barely contain his growing anger.

"Because that's the way it is," Darr barked. "That's what happens. It's not your place to challenge the products we put together. We handle the due diligence on the deals, and you make sure they're sold."

Darr moved on to other questions. Even with his belligerent attitude, the pointed questions kept coming. Finally Darr looked exasperated.

"Look," he said, "if all you do is find fault, how are we gonna generate the revenue to keep you guys in business and pay your bonuses?"

The response fell on a silent crowd. Devereaux was no longer excited about the product. At that moment, he decided to avoid selling the growth fund as much as possible. The way Darr was acting, there had to be something wrong with it.

John Hutchison, a Prudential-Bache product manager for all Graham partnerships, looked over the sales material for the growth fund in late 1986 with a sense of delight. Hutchison was a veteran of the Direct Investment Group. He had already proved his skill handling the energy income partnerships. The growth fund looked like a breeze.

Hutchison was not the kind of person to invest his money recklessly. But the more he read about the growth fund, the more it seemed like a no-lose investment. Buying portions of these overcollateralized, discounted bank loans was perfect. He set down the sales material and took out his checkbook. He wanted to invest in this deal himself. Later he suggested to some of his colleagues, including Kathy Eastwick, a product manager and former compliance administrator, that they should invest their money in the growth fund, as well.

They had a lot of company. The Prudential-Bache Energy Growth Fund started to be sold on November 17, 1986. Within weeks, it was raising $1.2 million a day from clients. It was a total success.

"Harding's Highlights," the partnership marketing material shipped out to all of the Prudential-Bache brokers in the Southwest, offered tips on the growth fund in early 1987. Linda Harding, a marketer in the region who wrote the material, seemed truly excited about this investment. She repeated the statements about how the fund would be purchasing overcollateralized, discounted loans from banks.

"It's like buying a bond at twenty-five cents on the dollar," she wrote. But when this bond matured, she added, the investor would receive at least the whole dollar.

"This should be considered every bit as safe as the energy income fund, with tremendous upside potential!!!" she wrote.

In Florida, the reaction among brokers and managers to the growth fund concept was one of almost pure ecstasy. Jim Parker, the regional marketer for the Direct Investment Group in Florida, had never seen a partnership accepted by the field so quickly. For years, Parker had attempted in vain to persuade Ernie Higbee, the manager of the firm's branch in Gainesville, to sell a lot of partnerships. But as soon as Parker described the idea behind the growth fund, he could see Higbee's eyes light up.

"This could really be a home run for clients," Higbee said excitedly.

Higbee was so enthralled with the idea that he agreed to make a presentation on the growth fund at an upcoming seminar for all of the brokers and managers in Prudential-Bache's Southeast region. The executives all gathered on the morning of February 7, 1987, at the Sheraton Premier hotel in Tysons Corner, Virginia. As Higbee gave his presentation, his excitement about the growth fund's potential seemed to infect the crowd.

"I put up $20 million and I've got $80 million in proven, producing reserves" as collateral, he said. "I'm number one in the pecking order in this loan. I get the first $20 million no matter what."

Higbee broke into a huge smile. "Now, where's the risk?" he asked the crowd.

With what they were planning to do, Higbee said, investors could expect three to five times their money back in just five to seven years.

Of course, the prospectus said no such thing. In fact, little of what was in the sales material was broadcast in those terms in the public filing. Instead, it warned that the investment was extremely risky. But Higbee assured the brokers that the prospectus was largely worthless.

"Read the prospectus and chuck it," he said. "There are so many caveats that you can't make a simple presentation."

Charles Patterson, a senior officer with First City National Bank of Houston, pored through documents analyzing some of the loans that his bank had just sold to the Prudential-Bache Energy Growth Fund. He looked down the sheets of engineering reports and financial data that estimated the value of the loans.

And then Patterson smiled.

Ten million dollars, he thought. For reasons he could not understand, Graham had agreed to pay $10 million more for the loans than First City thought they were worth. In an open bid, the bank never could have received the $57 million Graham Resources was willing to pay out of its growth fund. Whatever the rationale, Patterson didn't much care. First City had been struggling with serious problems stemming from too many bad loans. For a change, Patterson had some good news to report to the bank's board. Better still, he could tell them that Graham wanted to buy more loans for the growth fund as soon as possible.

Patterson didn't know it, but he was looking at the evidence of one of the most blatant deceptions ever to emerge out of the Direct Investment Group. He had never heard the false promises the firm had made about how the growth fund would buy discounted loans secured by oil reserves worth four times the investment. And he never could have suspected such commitments existed, because none of the loans purchased by the growth fund was anything like that. Many of them had no discount at all. The only one with a significant discount was secured by oil reserves worth only slightly more than the purchase price. Graham Resources appeared to be doing nothing more than just taking problem loans off the books of its onetime bankers.

Had anyone from Prudential-Bache or Graham Resources asked Patterson before the marketing of the growth fund started, he might have told them that their idea made no sense. If a bank had a loan on its books like the one described in the growth fund sales material, it wouldn't be sold. Banks aren't in the business of generating losses.

But, at least for their investors, the energy growth funds were. With 15 percent fees for investing and another 15 percent for distributions, the investments in loans that carried no discount were guaranteed to be losers. That didn't stop Graham Resources and the Direct Investment Group from characterizing huge losses for investors in the first growth fund as enormous gains. After all, the second growth fund partnership was ready for sale almost immediately. To help sales, the first growth fund needed the appearance of strong performance. Even though the fund had not made a penny, it distributed money anyway through a complex deception that simultaneously fattened the pockets of Graham Resources and Prudential-Bache.

First, the fund took $4.7 million of customer money. Fifteen percent, or $700,000, came off the top for fees to Graham Resources and Pru-Bache. With the remaining $4 million, they purchased a participation in a loan to a company called HRB Rig. The loan had no discount—the $4 million participation had an original value of $4 million. It was as if the growth fund had lent the money to HRB itself.

The beauty of the investment was that HRB owed a payment of about $4 million in just weeks. When the cash arrived, the growth fund had money that could be distributed to investors. But first, Graham and Pru-Bache took out about $600,000 to cover the 15 percent back-end fee. The remaining $3.5 million was distributed to investors.

It was the perfect deception. In weeks, Prudential-Bache and Graham Resources had shunted investor cash through a number of companies, converting $4.7 million into $3.5 million. Graham and Pru-Bache pocketed the $1.2 million difference.

When they received their bogus distribution, investors were not told they had just suffered a $1.2 million loss. Instead, their brokers held up the distribution as evidence of the growth fund's success. After all, it was already showing double-digit returns.

Within days, that lie would spread to every broker in the firm.

The summer 1987 edition of *Energy Digest*, a newsletter for Prudential-Bache all about the energy partnerships, featured a cover photograph of a fish.

"There were no scales on your eyes last fall," the caption announced on the cover. "Thanks to you, this is the one that didn't get away."

Inside, the first page featured a picture of brokers standing on a ship, holding huge fish in the air, along with a sign proclaiming "Growth Fund: 17% annual distributions."

A huge portion of that distribution came from the secret $4 million shuffle of cash in the HRB Rig loan that had actually produced a $1.2 million loss. Nothing was said of that.

"Congratulations to all of you for helping to make the growth fund such an enormous success!" the newsletter said. It also added that the high returns meant brokers could sell even more of the next growth fund, called G-2.

"You'll find it much easier netting new accounts for G-2," it said. "Big and little fish alike will respond to the allure of high returns, and you'll be hoisting your sales higher!"

The purported success of G-1 had its effect. After raising just $89 million from about six thousand Prudential-Bache investors for the first growth fund, the fictitious performance brought in many new investors. More than nine thousand people, mostly small investors including many in retirement, sank $118 million into G-2.

It, too, would prove to be a loser.

John Hutchison walked out of his office on the thirty-third floor at Prudential-Bache and headed down the hallway. Hutchison felt pretty good about the work he had been doing in marketing the growth fund. With this latest 17 percent return, the growth fund really seemed to be proving itself. Lingering doubts among the brokers about the deal had held down the sales of G-1 somewhat, but now the performance was proving the naysayers wrong. Hutchison was getting ready to make a new pitch for G-2 and wanted to check a few things out with Brian Martin, an executive in the due diligence department who had been assigned the job of reviewing the growth fund's performance.

Hutchison reached Martin's office and tapped on the door as he walked in.

"Hey, Brian," Hutchison said in his thick North Carolina accent. "How's the deal doing?"

The instant Hutchison saw Martin's face, he knew something was terribly wrong. Martin was pale, looking almost panicked. He signaled for Hutchison to close the door.

"God, Hutch, you're not going to believe this," Martin said. "I've been reviewing the loan portfolio we purchased from First City."

Martin paused, then swallowed. "Hutch," he said, "there's not a single investment inside that portfolio that's anything close to what we've been saying."

"What?" Hutchison spluttered.

"None," Martin said, shaking his head. "Absolutely none."

Hutchison felt the blood rush from his face. His head was spinning. At that instant, an odd thought flashed through his mind. This was one of those "Kennedy assassination" experiences. He would never forget where he was when he realized that the Direct Investment Group had engineered a multimillion-dollar fraud with the first growth fund.

"Linda, could you please tell me how many of Fred Storaska's orders are real?"

Hutchison was on the telephone with Linda Harding, a regional marketer for the Southwest. It was June 1987.

"They're all real, John," Harding said, laughing.

"Right." Hutchison snorted. "Tell me that when he calls back in to cancel half of them."

Despite what Hutchison knew about the fraud in the first growth fund, it was still his job to help market the second one. To do that, he had to keep an eye on purchase orders submitted by Storaska, the director of Corporate Executive Services in Dallas.

In the time since he had been hired by George Ball, Storaska had increased his business each year. His CES department had been doing well in its focus on the investment needs of newly wealthy entrepreneurs. By 1987, Storaska had accounts that were the kind other brokers built entire careers on. Part of the Onassis family money was invested with Fred Storaska. Some of the wealthiest oilmen in Texas trusted their savings to him. The reach of CES had become so broad that almost every entrepreneur who became rich by selling a company eventually received a cold call from Storaska or a member of his staff.

On top of that, Storaska had rapidly become the most important Prudential-Bache broker for the Direct Investment Group. Once he discovered limited partnerships about a year before, it seemed he could not sell enough of them.

But to midlevel executives like Hutchison, Storaska's big business was largely a joke. The huge orders frequently arrived all on one day. Sometimes it would be on the last day that was counted toward monthly commission payments. Other times it was the last day that a particular partnership was for sale. Invariably, after the huge orders were in and the commissions were paid, Storaska would cancel them. No one watching closely in the Direct Investment Group could believe that so many of his clients could order the partnerships on the same day and all change their minds a few weeks later. It appeared as if Storaska was doing nothing more than lending himself huge amounts of the firm's money interest-free each month by abusing the commission system.[*]

On June 12, 1987, Storaska placed at least $1 million in orders for part-

[*] Through his lawyer, Storaska has denied doing anything improper at Prudential-Bache. See Notes and Sources.

nerships, including $500,000 worth of the second energy growth fund. All of it went into just five customer accounts. Every customer ordered the exact same thing: $100,000 worth of the growth fund and $100,000 worth of a partnership called Summit Insured Equity. The mass order, entered on the last day of the commission month, had attracted Hutchison's attention. That was exactly the kind of order Storaska would later cancel. On seeing it, he had immediately called Harding to find out how much of the order was going to be canceled.

Despite Harding's confidence that Storaska's orders were real, in a few weeks they were all canceled. Grose, the Dallas branch manager, sent an angry memo to Storaska, the latest in a series he had written accusing his top broker of improprieties.

"It is unacceptable for you to place a trade in a customer's account [if] you have not previously discussed the trade," Grose wrote. "In addition, it is unacceptable to place a trade in a customer's account with intentions to move the trade to the appropriate customer at a later date. These actions are a major breach of internal policies and regulatory rules."

Grose ended his memo with a threat. "Under no circumstances should this ever be done in the future. Trades must be placed where they belong with the customer's full and prior knowledge. Any deviation will force me to take serious action."

The threat meant nothing to Storaska. Three days later, he did it again, purchasing $50,000 worth of the energy growth fund for one of his clients. The trade was later canceled, with the customer claiming he had never been consulted. The purchases of partnerships—both canceled and kept—continued throughout the year. As always, Grose took no action out of fear of alienating his superiors, including George Ball. Storaska's abuses continued unabated, pushing up the total sales of partnerships. He became one of the biggest winners of sales trips in all of Prudential-Bache.

The helicopter sat silently at the Kahului Airport in Maui as the first evening stars came into view. The pilot had been waiting several hours, ready to transport Darr and his party to their hotel on the Hawaiian island. They were the only ones on the Graham Resources' 1987 sales trip to Maui who had demanded a helicopter flight to the Kapalua Bay Hotel and Villas. Darr did not want to endure the forty-five-minute drive over rough terrain. Besides, the cost of the helicopter would just be billed to the energy partnerships.

But that night, Darr's plane arrived late. It was too dark for the helicopter ride. He seemed angry after hearing that he would have to travel to the hotel by car, just like everyone else. Within minutes, the car was loaded, and Darr was on his way. The partnerships still paid for the helicopter time.

By 1987, the Graham partnerships had become the most important product sold out of the entire Prudential-Bache system. Series II of the energy income program had been completed, and Series III was well under way, with more than $200 million in sales. The growth fund, of course, had been selling at a rapid clip. For all of 1987, Graham was projecting that it would sell $450 million worth of both partnerships. This trip to Maui was the perfect capper, a celebration of another year of big sales.

John Hutchison, the Pru-Bache product manager who helped arrange the trip, arrived in Maui exhausted. He was the one who had been assigned to arrange Darr's helicopter. Darr had also demanded that several cases of expensive wines be waiting for him in his room, and Hutchison had spent hours on the telephone in search of his boss's favorites. It was such a common demand that Hutchison kept Darr's usual choices—Jordan '77 and '78, and Château St. Jean '83—scribbled in his Rolodex for easy access. After finding enough of the wines, Hutchison then had arranged to have them shipped from the mainland to Hawaii.

A day or so into the trip, Hutchison wandered by the swimming pool at the hotel when he noticed his wife, Robin, sitting next to a Houston broker named Joe Siff. Hutchison slumped into a neighboring lounge chair and ordered a drink from a passing waiter. Siff was delighted. He liked Hutchison and always knew he would be good for another amazing tale about Darr's excesses.

"Hey, John," Siff said. "What's the latest story on Darr?"

Hutchison sighed deeply. "You're not going to believe this one, Joe."

For the next few minutes, Hutchison told his rapt audience about the helicopter Darr had demanded and the long search for cases of his favorite wines.

"But that's not the worst of it," Hutchison said. "He demanded about two or three times the amount of wine that he could conceivably consume, even with a party. I don't know what he's up to."

A few weeks later, Hutchison was back in New York. He needed to settle a few final issues on the recently completed trip. He telephoned Valerie Lee, a vice-president of the Wernli Group, the travel agency for Graham. Before Hutchison could get two words out, Lee interrupted.

"So, John, you know what happened with all that wine shipped out to Darr's hotel?"

At first, Hutchison wasn't sure he wanted to know. "No, what happened?" he asked cautiously.

"He had it all boxed up and shipped back to his home in Connecticut."

This sounded like too much, even for Darr. "You're kidding me," Hutchison said.

"No, really. We were originally going to ship it UPS, but somebody at the hotel told the UPS man it was alcohol, and they refused to ship it. So they had to box it up and send it Federal Express."

Hutchison finished his conversation and hung up the telephone, disgusted. From what he heard, the partnerships appeared to be spending money to stock Darr's wine cellar.

He stood up, wandered down the hallway, and walked into Joe DeFur's office. Everything he heard made Hutchison so anxious that he felt compelled to tell someone else about it. So he described everything he knew about the helicopter and the wine.

DeFur looked on, seeming nonplussed. But Hutchison was looking for an answer.

"Joe," he asked, "why does Darr do this?"

"Because he's the chairman of the department," DeFur replied casually. "That's the prerogative of the chairman."

That summer, Darr latched onto a whole new idea about how he could make himself some money off the energy partnerships: unload Prudential-Bache's interest in the energy income partnerships.

Clients and brokers were already beginning to see the first signs that the income partnerships didn't work. The oldest of those partnerships, P-1 through P-4, no longer had the inflated distributions that investors had received early on. Their distributions dropped to 3 percent or less, a far cry from the 15 to 20 percent investors were told to expect. Investors with passbook accounts were earning more.

Each quarter, brokers called the Direct Investment Group and Graham Resources to find out why the distributions were so low. Every time, they heard a new excuse: A well had caught fire. There had been a tornado. There was a lag time between pumping the oil and seeing the profits. For a while, those stories had seemed to satisfy the brokers, but sales of the partnerships were starting to suffer.

In that atmosphere, Darr approached Tony Rice with a whole new idea. He had been reviewing his personal contract, which provided him with a piece of the money from the Prudential-Bache subsidiaries that served as general partners. Bearing that in mind, Darr told Rice that he wanted Graham Resources to strike a new deal to buy Prudential-Bache's interest in the income funds.

"If I could sell Pru-Bache's interest in these partnerships, I could make a lot of money by virtue of my contract," Darr said. "I want Graham to make a tender offer for the Pru-Bache interest."

Rice agreed to look into the idea, but it did not go over well with Graham executives. Rice came back to Darr and told him the idea would not fly. Graham Resources could not get the financing to pay for the deal. Darr said nothing, but he looked angry. He clearly wanted to make that money.

Darr came back, again and again, with new ideas about how he could make money by changing the way the energy partnerships did business. On July 23, 1987, Darr was in California when he called in to the office. He heard that Pittman and DeFur were meeting with Al Dempsey from Graham. Darr was immediately patched into the meeting through a conference call. He had an idea he wanted to explore with Dempsey, he said.

"How much cash is available in the income and growth funds for investment?" Darr asked.

"Basically, we've got about $275 million of the energy income fund and about $275 million of the energy growth fund," Dempsey replied.

Darr asked a few more questions, then explained why he was interested.

"Prudential-Bache is changing our compensation," he said. More of it would be based on the dollar volume of transactions filed. "So it would be better for all of us in the Direct Investment Group if you guys registered and became effective with any proposed transactions before December 31."

Dempsey and Darr talked about the terms for a few minutes. Finally Dempsey agreed that Graham would work to ensure that the next $500 million worth of energy growth funds and energy income partnerships would be put together quickly. They could be ready for sale as soon as November.

Huge decisions about the future of partnerships involving thousands of investors were being based on the financial interests of senior executives in the Direct Investment Group.

The management committee of Graham Resources met on October 27, 1987, in a conference room at the company's new headquarters in Covington, Louisiana. They faced a serious problem: Just nine months after the sale of the first growth fund was finished, the partnership was in desperate financial trouble. One Graham executive said that the growth fund only had enough money to pay an 8 percent distribution, but the market was expecting a distribution of 15 percent to 17 percent, which had to be paid in about two months. Investors were already jittery because the stock market had crashed eight days before. If the growth funds failed to perform, sales for every one of the Graham products might collapse.

There was only one significant deal in the pipeline for the growth fund, involving a transaction with Maple Gulf Coast Properties, a company partially owned by a consultant to Prudential. That transaction had been recommended about two weeks before but would not provide cash returns quickly enough to boost the upcoming distribution.

Within a week of the management committee meeting, the deal with Maple was changed. The growth fund agreed to purchase $6 million worth of preferred stock from Maple, although the true cost to the investors was closer to $7 million. About $1 million of their investment had been taken off the top for fees to Pru-Bache and Graham. The remaining money was handed over to Maple in November.

Of course, for there to be a distribution, the growth fund had to transform its investments into cash. So a few weeks after it handed Maple the $6 million to buy the preferred stock, Maple handed the same cash—from the same bank account—right back. The money paid part of a loan Maple had received from the growth fund. Effectively, the investors in the growth fund had paid off the Maple loan themselves. Then another 15 percent was sliced off the $6 million for the back-end fees to Graham Resources and Prudential-Bache. The remaining $5.1 million was distributed to the growth fund investors.

The growth fund celebrated its 14 percent distribution as a sign of its strength. No investors were told that they had just suffered a $1.9 million loss.

David Wrubel, a bearded young executive with a long history in the partnership business, sat in an anteroom outside of Darr's office. He had been scheduled to meet with Darr at 2:00 P.M. and had been waiting for almost half an hour. He was supposed to be interviewed by Darr as the last step in getting hired as a marketer in the Direct Investment Group. He didn't like the idea, but he needed the job and tried to be philosophical about it. If his father could survive World War II, Wrubel figured, then he could survive Prudential-Bache.

In a wave of cutbacks following the stock market crash a few weeks before, Wrubel had just lost a job marketing partnerships for Drexel. The timing was dreadful. He and his wife were expecting their first child in a matter of weeks, and at that moment, throughout Wall Street, thousands of people like him were being shown the door.

He had heard from some friends at Prudential-Bache that there was an opening as a regional marketer in the Northeast. He feared it would be nothing like his last job. Despite all the investigations of Drexel's junk-bond department, he thought the firm was a great place to work. Everyone there seemed concerned about turning out high-quality partnerships. But Prudential-Bache had the reputation of being a schlock house that attracted lightweights. During his years in the partnership business, he had heard too much about Darr's ego and bizarre behavior to think that the Direct Investment Group might somehow be an exception.

He had already had a taste of the department's peculiarities. The previous night, he had received a call at home from Barron Clancy, one of the senior executives in the Direct Investment Group. Clancy said he had terrible news: Darr didn't like beards.

Wrubel was floored. He'd had a beard throughout his entire Wall Street career. No one had ever objected before. He told Clancy that if he shaved that night he would look terrible at the interview. Clancy warned him to be prepared for Darr's reaction.

As Wrubel waited outside Darr's office, he tried not to be self-conscious about his beard. Finally, at about 2:30 P.M., he was shown into Darr's office.

Wrubel had never seen Darr before, but he lived up to his image. He was dressed in the standard-issue outfit for Wall Street in the 1980s: pinstripe suit, suspenders, yellow tie, cuff links, and a light blue monogrammed shirt with a spread collar. Wrubel looked about the huge office, trying to find something he could admire that might help break the ice. But as soon as he took a seat, he realized it didn't matter. Darr was not a man for small talk.

"So," Darr said, "what the hell makes you think you can be successful at Prudential-Bache?"

What the hell kind of question is that? Wrubel thought. *No small talk? No coffee?* But he needed the job too much to say any of those things. He swallowed his pride and gave Darr a quick, snappy answer.

"Because I was successful at Drexel with a bunch of brokers with a similar mind-set to the ones here," he said. "I was able to develop a sense in their minds of my own personal credibility. I kept at it, I worked real hard, and I can do the same thing here."

Darr raised his hand to his chin and sat back in his chair. He seemed to like the answer.

For the next half an hour, Darr drilled Wrubel with questions. Finally Darr placed his hands down on his desk and started to get up.

"Well," he said. "Welcome aboard."

Darr walked around his desk, shook Wrubel's hand, and patted him on the back. As he started to escort him out of the office toward the elevators, he stopped suddenly.

"Oh, by the way," Darr said, chucking Wrubel under the chin. "Nice beard."

Darr turned to walk away, a devilish smile on his face. Wrubel stood there, thinking he had just spoken with one of the oddest people he had ever met.

A few weeks later, on January 25, 1988, Wrubel headed up the steps at the Smith & Wollensky steakhouse for his first quarterly dinner with the Direct Investment Group. The weather was terrible, and Wrubel was soaking wet. As he walked into the restaurant's private dining area on the second floor, he saw Darr across the room, sitting on a bar stool. He looked angry.

By this point, Wrubel had already had his fill of the oddities from Prudential-Bache and the Direct Investment Group. He was one of the very few executives in the department who had not developed a career at Prudential-Bache or with some general partner affiliated with the firm. He knew the partnership business. He knew what Wall Street could be like. And this wasn't it.

Already, he had been warned by other regional marketers to watch himself around the department. If anything ever went wrong, he heard, Darr and his supporters would rationalize it away. They looked for any reason to throw their weight around and cared nothing about the quality of the partnerships. All that the senior officers of the Direct Investment Group wanted was heavy, continual sales of partnerships. Another acquaintance told Wrubel that he might have some trouble with the senior executives of the department because he was Jewish. The Direct Investment Group, he was warned, was laced with anti-Semitism. All this was not the kind of information that endeared his bosses to Wrubel.

As Wrubel checked his coat and umbrella, Darr signaled from his bar stool for him to come over. This would be their first conversation since the job interview. When Wrubel walked over and said hello, Darr glared at him angrily.

"I have a real problem with you," Darr said.

Here we go again, Wrubel thought. *Aren't you going to offer me a drink?*

"What's the problem?" he said.

"I told you to shave off your beard. And it's still there."

The beard again. This was getting to be ridiculous.

"Jim, you didn't tell me to shave off the beard. When I left your office the day you hired me, you said 'Nice beard.' Don't you remember?"

"Yeah, but I told Barron Clancy to tell you to shave it off. Didn't he tell you?"

Wrubel didn't want to get Clancy in trouble. But he had never passed a direct order that Darr wanted it shaved off. He'd only told him that Darr didn't like beards. It would be a few days until Wrubel found out that Darr had never asked Clancy to tell him anything.

"No, he didn't tell me."

Darr picked up his drink and squinted at Wrubel. "What if I told you right now, shave off your beard or you're fired. What would you tell me?"

Somehow, perhaps because the beard had come up so often, Wrubel had a ready response.

"I'd tell you that you ought to give me three months with it," he replied. "These are the months that I am going to be meeting with brokers and branch managers and establishing who I am. They're used to somebody else. But, when I leave the office, they will remember the new guy. They might not remember my name. But they'll remember me as the guy with the beard."

Darr roared, "That's a great answer." He finally chuckled. "Keep the damn beard."

Later that night, everyone took a seat at the table for dinner. Waiters were walking about the room, bringing wine or refilling the drinks. A clinking noise cut through the conversation. Darr was tapping his glass with his knife as he stood up.

"Welcome to the first quarterly meeting of 1988," he said with a smile. "Since we are blessed with a new regional coordinator, and we have never heard him speak before, I think it would be particularly appropriate for our new Jewish friend to say grace over the meal."

Amid some laughter, all eyes turned toward Wrubel. He was furious and offended. He had never experienced such disgusting behavior during his years on Wall Street. Another time, in another situation, he would have quit on the spot. But he had a family to support. He swallowed his pride and stood up, a wineglass in hand.

"Dear God," Wrubel said. "You've got better things to do than pay attention to a group of people like us tonight."

The crowd of Direct Investment Group executives laughed and clapped as Wrubel sat back down. He smiled as he looked at Darr, trying to control his hatred.

This place was worse than anything he could imagine.

The next day, it got worse. At about 7:30 in the morning, the executives from the Direct Investment Group gathered in a large auditorium to hear the latest about partnerships being planned for the future. Darr would not arrive until later, so the opening speech was handled by Paul Proscia. He impressed a number of executives in the room as a terrible speaker.

About an hour after the meeting began, Darr came in and took over. Before he went through the production reports for the year, he wanted to mention a few promotions and new hires.

"I would like to introduce our new regional coordinator for the metropolitan region," Darr said. "He comes to us from Drexel Burnham, where he essentially had the same role. David Wrubel."

Darr looked up and nodded toward Wrubel. "David, would you please stand up."

Wrubel stood and looked about the room. "Jim, thanks a lot," he said. "I'm really excited to be here at the best direct investment firm on the Street. It's going to be a real challenge, and I look forward to getting to know all of you."

As he sat down, Wrubel noticed a deathly silence descending on the room. It was as if the birds in the jungle were quaking in fear at the arrival of the lion. In the front of the room, Darr was staring at him, looking like he wanted to teach Wrubel a very rough lesson.

"Who told you to say that?" Darr snapped.

Wrubel muttered an apology. He was starting to learn the rules of the game in Darr's domain. No one was permitted to speak unless he asked them. Wrubel wouldn't make that mistake again.

His first temptation to speak out of turn came later in the meeting. Darr was describing his new pet project, a super real estate partnership that would purchase distressed properties at rock-bottom prices. The idea would bring together three general partners in real estate: the Related Companies, A. G. Spanos, and Fogelman Properties. All of the general partners had already sold a number of deals through the Direct Investment Group, many of which were struggling.

As Wrubel listened, he realized that what Darr was describing was similar to a deal that Drexel had already put together. That one involved Lincoln Properties, a general partner that at the time had one of the best reputations in the business. But even with all that quality, the Drexel deal was not working. Lincoln had not been able to find enough good-quality real estate at bargain prices, and it wasn't about to buy lousy properties just to generate some fees for itself. Instead, the investor money sat in the partnership, doing nothing. That was the primary sign of a deal that should never have been done.

Wrubel started to say something, but held himself back. By this point, he knew the truth of the Direct Investment Group. Substantive discussions were not welcome. Darr did whatever he wanted. At a Drexel meeting, Wrubel would never have hesitated to bring up his point, and the deal would likely have been shelved. But disagreements with Darr were not permitted.

As Wrubel sank lower into his chair, Darr finished his presentation and asked if there were any questions. An executive in the back of the room responded.

"I don't know how the brokers are going to feel about a deal like this," the executive shouted. "I mean jeez. Maybe we should call it the Prudential-Bache Jewish General Partners deal."

Darr cracked up. "You know, you have a good point," he said. "On the other hand, because the deal is all Jewish general partners, it'll probably be a good thing in the minds of our brokers."

Wrubel was shell-shocked. It was the most amazing thing he had ever heard in a business meeting.

Fred Storaska strode toward the podium at a partnership sales meeting in Vancouver, British Columbia. He had just been introduced as the number-one broker in the firm in direct investments for 1987. In that one year, he had sold $22 million of the partnerships to his clients. If Storaska were a branch, he would be the fifth most productive in the country, an emcee had said in an introduction. Now Storaska was going to share the secrets of his success.

Storaska arrived at the podium amid a smattering of applause. He looked up sharply and began speaking quickly in a rambling, disjointed manner. After talking about some of his strategies, Storaska began to discuss himself and his style.

"I make it a point to work 105 hours a week," he said. "I'm up at 4:00 A.M. I go to the office and I'm at the office on Monday morning at 5:30.

I usually don't leave the office until about either Tuesday night or Wednesday night. I usually catch a couple of hours sleep on my couch on Monday night and Tuesday night."

A few members of the audience started whispering. Many of them had heard stories about Storaska walking down hallways in the Dallas branch some mornings dressed only in his underwear and bathing in the men's room sink. Now, it seemed, those stories might be true.

"When people talk about hard work, they say, 'Well, you know I've got a family and I've got this commitment and I've got that commitment,' " Storaska said. He paused a moment for effect and looked at the crowd.

"There are no excuses permitted!" he barked.

His speech meandered into various topics, until finally he settled on the concept of personal control.

"You need to totally take control," he said. "Realize you work for yourself. You don't work for anybody else. You're your own business."

Taking control meant pushing other advisers to the client out of the way when it came time to talk investments.

"Take the accountant out of the picture," he said. "Get rid of him. Cripple him. You psychophysiologically cripple the accountant in the first meeting."

To illustrate his opinion about keeping control, Storaska related a story about when he was called in to visit his son's high school principal. He said that he listened while the principal laid out some concerns about the boy's behavior. While still sitting in front of the principal, Storaska said, he turned to look his son in the eye.

"And I said, 'Don't you ever let a son of a bitch like this tell you if you can go to school,' " he said. " 'He's simply a high school principal. If you ever let somebody like this set your goals in life, you'll end up being like him.' "

Finally Storaska told of a time he was flying in his CES corporate plane when he received an emergency telephone call. A client needed to speak with him immediately in Seattle. So his pilot made an emergency landing at the city's airport. Rather than going to the terminal for private planes, he pulled up to a gate meant for a Pan American Airlines 747—the quickest way to stop. A policeman arrived and stopped them. But Storaska said that he told the officer that his police chief might know him because he once taught self-defense. As Storaska told the story, the officer called his boss, who instantly recognized Storaska's name and ordered him released. They then offered Storaska a police escort, he said.

"And I asked the officer, I said, 'Could we have really caused any harm?' He said, 'Yeah, there's a Northwest flight and another flight circling because there was a security problem on the ground.' "

Storaska stood up straight and tall. "And I said, 'Well, they'll just have to circle,' " he boomed. " 'I have important business down here.' "

When the speech came to an end and Storaska walked off the stage, the Prudential-Bache brokers watched in astonishment. As they filed out of the room, a few of them talked among themselves and found they all agreed: The biggest seller of limited partnerships at Prudential-Bache sounded like a nutcase.

At 10:00 A.M. on April 28, 1988, shareholders from E. F. Hutton gathered in an auditorium at 33 Maiden Lane to officially declare that brokerage firm dead. Hutton had never recovered from its guilty plea to two thousand felony counts stemming from its banking practices under George Ball in the early 1980s. Since then, some clients had been rattled about doing business with a felon. The market crash of October 19, 1987, had been the capper. Hutton could no longer survive. The firm was sold to Shearson Lehman Brothers. But few on Wall Street doubted that the sale was a result of the firm's check-kiting scandal.

That same week, Ball's new firm, Prudential-Bache, quietly reached its own milestone: Its sales of the energy income partnerships surpassed $1 billion, making it the biggest-selling partnership for small investors in the history of Wall Street. It was also the single largest deception emanating out of the Direct Investment Group. But it was not the most blatant.

The quarterly meeting of Prudential-Bache's California brokers in early 1988 had all the subtleties of a Turkish bazaar. Brokers wandered about the hotel in Palm Springs as marketers from the firm and from outside companies tried to lure them with the glory of their wares. Some described closed-end funds that they said every client should own. Others pitched complex trading instruments that they said could earn money from interest rate movements. But as all the brokers had come to expect, the biggest merchants in the bazaar offered limited partnerships. With oil wells, airplanes, and real estate, the partnership marketers had more than enough merchandise in stock.

A new deal, being pitched by a marketer named John Macejka from the Direct Investment Group, was attracting the most attention at the meeting. Called the VMS Mortgage Investors Fund, it sounded simply too good to be true.

Macejka told the brokers that, unlike other partnerships, the fund would trade on a stock exchange. That way, investors could bail out at any time, or, if they wanted, buy more of the deal. On top of that, investors would be guaranteed a 12 percent annual return for three years. It couldn't have sounded safer. A number of brokers decided, then and there, that they would sell the VMS product to their most safety-conscious customers.

It was a decision that would destroy many of their careers.

Bill Creedon, a broker in the firm's Los Angeles office, hung up the telephone just as the branch manager walked into his thirteenth-floor office. Creedon respected his manager, John Eisle. It was Eisle who had recruited him to Prudential-Bache a few months after the death of his last firm, E. F. Hutton. Creedon, a former navy officer, was also a man who believed in the chain of command. This day in February 1988 would be no different.

"Hey, Bill," Eisle said as he sat down in front of Creedon's desk. "I've got something I want to show you. We've got a deal coming up that I think would be perfect for your conservative clients transferring over from Hutton. Take a look at this."

Eisle tossed a piece of paper on Creedon's desk, and the broker picked it up. It was a photocopy of some handwritten marketing material for the VMS Mortgage Investment Fund. Creedon read it through and was impressed. The deal had lots of guarantees, and the marketing material stressed that it was a safe investment designed for the most cautious investors.

"The firm is going to be selling this in a few weeks," Eisle said. "I'm really excited about it. It's a slam dunk. It's the right thing for retirees. It's a great investment for all your widows and orphans," he said, joking about the cautious nature of Creedon's clients.

"It does look interesting," Creedon said. "I'd like to look more carefully at it."

"Fine, go ahead," Eisle said. "I think you'll like what you see."

A short time later, Creedon reviewed the prospectus. Another superior, Jack Graner, the Prudential-Bache director for the Pacific South region, had also dropped by to encourage him to sell the deal. But in the end, Creedon still had doubts. He telephoned New York to speak with John Macejka, the assistant product manager on the deal. The conversation lasted more than an hour. Creedon's main interest was whether these so-called guarantees were real. Too often on Wall Street, he said, guarantees can be empty promises.

"We are very comfortable with the guarantee," Macejka said. "It's a real guarantee."

Macejka stressed that the firm had done extensive due diligence, both on the investors' fund and on VMS itself. "This is one of our best sponsors, with one of their best deals," Macejka said.

Near the end of the hour, Creedon circled back to the guarantees again. He had seen guarantees at Hutton that, in reality, applied to the investors' money only after fees and expenses. Were these guarantees like that, or did they actually protect 100 percent of the cash put in?

Macejka huffed, clearly offended. "Of course it covers all their money. What kind of people do you think we are?"

The VMS Mortgage Investment Fund was an out-and-out fraud. What the brokers were told was the finest product ever offered by one of the firm's strongest sponsors was little more than a desperate attempt to bail out the floundering real estate empire of VMS. The guarantees, which made the deal so attractive to elderly, risk-averse clients, were meaningless.

The guarantees were only as strong as VMS itself. And VMS was falling apart. Even as the Direct Investment Group was praising the financial skill of VMS, the company was in such a cash bind that it was putting a hold on paying forty-two of its mortgage loans. The same month that the prospectus was filed for the new product, VMS's executive committee was projecting that the company would have a deficit of more than $140 million for the year. About that time, VMS compiled a huge list of troubled properties, with the total at risk in those investments reaching more than $700 million. One investment called the Buckeye Properties was months away from defaulting. VMS itself had advanced huge sums to Buckeye to keep it afloat. If the property stopped payments, VMS could be wiped out, and the entire real estate empire financed by Darr's Direct Investment Group would collapse.

In reality, the mortgage investment fund, sold as one of the safest and most secure deals ever to emerge from Prudential-Bache, was probably the riskiest investment ever produced by the Direct Investment Group. It could survive only with a major boom in the prices of real estate. If that didn't happen, tens of thousands of the firm's safety-conscious investors could lose everything.

But this time, the Direct Investment Group had made a fatal error. Although Prudential-Bache might lie, the stock market does not. And this deal was meant to be listed on a stock exchange. As soon as the shares of the fund started trading, Pru-Bache clients would finally find out how risky these supposedly safe investments were. But trading was not scheduled to start until early 1989. Until then, many of the deceptions from Prudential-Bache would continue unchecked.

Darr strolled beneath two elegant chandeliers as he headed toward the men's hairdresser just off the lobby of the Berkeley Hotel in London, England. He pushed open the solid wood door at the front of the salon and walked in. Soon he was seated in one of the three styling chairs, looking out at the picture-window view of Hyde Park. Outside, it was a lovely Tuesday in May 1988. The bright shopping districts of central London and Knightsbridge were chockablock as always with late-afternoon crowds shopping in elegant stores, bustling toward the theaters, or visiting some of the area's finest museums.

A stylist came up behind Darr and began snipping his curly white hair. Darr had been busy during his few days in London, where he had traveled with his wife, young daughter, and her nanny. In just a few days, he had toured the city in a hired car and had purchased $1,200 in tickets for the Chelsea Flower Show. His family often ordered room service and ran up huge bills for restaurants. He and his wife stayed in the Pavilion Suite, one of the largest rooms at the hotel, for $1,056 a night, about three times the cost of one of the hotel's standard rooms. His daughter and her nanny each had her own room. All of them flew to London on the Concorde at a cost of $22,324.66. All told, their trip cost more than $50,000. With the costs picked up by the investors in the energy income and energy growth partnerships, Darr probably thought little about tacking on another $30 to make sure his hair looked nice.

The trip, held during a week in late May, was the latest and most extravagant of the sales awards sponsored by Graham Resources. It began in London and later moved on to Scotland. Almost every big seller of the Graham partnerships was there. Fred Storaska, who won the trip by selling more of the energy partnerships than all but one of his colleagues during the qualifying period, didn't come. He was too busy. But Charles Grose, the branch manager so angered by Storaska's violations of the rules, did get to go, since Storaska's sales helped qualify him for the trip.

He joined about 120 other brokers and managers, accompanied by senior executives from the Direct Investment Group and Graham. By that time, any effort to contain costs and protect investors' savings had been completely abandoned. Darr set the standard. He demanded to stay at the Berkeley, separated from all the other brokers and executives at the prestigious—but far cheaper—London Hilton.

Paul Proscia insisted on limousine service around the city. Al Dempsey's wife also hired limousines, at one point using one to go sightseeing at Stonehenge. Dempsey himself spent more than $6,000 on items labeled in the bills as "incidentals." Pete Theo, the head of Graham's marketing effort, spent close to $4,000 on tickets for the musical *Phantom of the Opera.* More than $750 worth of Dom Perignon was consumed in one day. And, on a night in Edinburgh, Scotland, John Graham and other executives spent close to $800 in partnership money to rent kilts for a Highland party.

Prudential-Bache clients unknowingly lost more than $1 million of their savings as their brokers, led by Darr, spent a week drinking, dancing, and having fun. All as a reward for investing their clients' capital in partnerships that were secretly falling apart.

Years later, some of the brokers who went on the trip would reflect that somehow it seemed fitting that this huge, self-indulgent bash would be Darr's last big waste of partnership money. For as Darr was shuttling about London, senior executives at Prudential-Bache were reviewing a secret, three-volume report about him. Unknown to almost anyone in the Direct Investment Group, some of Darr's secrets had surfaced months before. The third investigation of his ethics by Prudential-Bache had been launched. But unlike the others, this inquiry had finally hit pay dirt.

PART THREE
DISCOVERY

CHAPTER 14

LOREN SCHECHTER GLANCED AT his watch before pushing himself back from his desk. The time had come for his big performance. In a few minutes on this day in January 1988, Schechter would be playing the bad cop to the good cop portrayal by Frank Giordano, a lawyer in the Direct Investment Group. Schechter was not sure how it would all come off, but he was positive what the results would be: George Watson, whose Watson & Taylor Companies were one of Darr's favorite general partners, would be stripped of control of his public partnerships sold by the firm.

Schechter threw on his suit jacket as he headed to the thirty-third floor. Giordano had begun meeting with Watson in a conference room there sometime before. By then, Giordano was supposed to have already laid out the problems they had discovered: From what they saw, Watson had charged too high a price to sell a shopping mall his company owned to one of the public partnerships. Worse, the sale appeared to have bailed Watson out of his personal liability on the property. Even to some of Watson's own executives, it looked as if he had used money from Prudential-Bache clients for his own benefit.

On top of that, Watson & Taylor seemed likely to get into deep trouble with federal banking regulators. Lending improprieties at First South had attracted government attention. The regulators had already determined that George Watson and Tracy Taylor secretly controlled more than a quarter of the institution's publicly traded shares. Watson & Taylor, along with First South, looked like they were about to be slapped with fraud suits by the federal regulators. The prospect of Watson & Taylor's trouble with the government already worried Darr enough that he had asked Giordano to renegotiate his personal investments in Watson's private land deals. Originally Darr had personal liability in some of those deals, so if they went bad, he could be on the hook for more money. But the renegotiated deals absolved Darr of any personal liability and just gave him a share of the investment profits. Usually such a change would cost an investor money, since unloading the liability had enormous value. Watson usually let Darr do it for free. In some instances, Darr did not put cash in the deals as required under the new arrangement. Instead, Watson did it for him.

But Schechter knew nothing about this intrigue involving Darr's personal finances. As he stepped off the elevator and headed toward the Direct Investment Group, all he cared about was the federal inquiry and the shopping center deal that benefited Watson. In a way, Schechter was looking forward to confronting Watson. He loved the back-and-forth of legal battles. He tapped on the door of the conference room and stepped inside. Schechter had no idea that the next few minutes would redefine the future of his career and of Prudential-Bache.

Watson sat opposite Giordano, accompanied by Bruce Manley, who had recently been hired from Franklin Realty to be Watson & Taylor's national sales manager.

Watson's eyes were blazing. Apparently he was putting up a hell of a fight. He did not want to lose control of his partnerships or the fat fees his company received from them. He was in mid-argument as Schechter sauntered up to the table.

"There was nothing wrong with that property," Watson said. "It was a good price, a fair price. There is no reason for anyone to be upset about it."

Giordano started to make a reply, but Watson interrupted.

"I told you, Darr himself approved of this deal. How can you say there's something wrong with it if the head of the department approves it?"

In fact, Darr had signed off on the deal in December 1986. After Joe Quinn, the head of asset management for the department, rejected the proposal, Watson had taken it directly to Darr. Despite the opinion of his senior staff, Darr sided with Watson.

Schechter listened to Watson for a few moments. Giordano made some arguments, but Watson was not listening. It looked to Schechter as if he were going to be needed. As he saw his job, he had to get the point across to Watson, in the most obnoxious way possible. Watson started to speak again, but Schechter, standing over the conference table, broke in.

"This issue is not open for discussion," he thundered. "This property is being taken out of the partnership, and you are losing the ability to take any more money out of it."

Watson looked up at Schechter, his face contorted with controlled rage. "We did everything in this properly, and—"

"I don't much care," Schechter said brusquely. "This is the way we're going to do it. No discussion. No debate. This is it. You've got no choice."

Watson sat in his chair, steaming. He locked his fingers together and rested his chin on his hands for an instant. Then he dropped his hands and looked Schechter dead in the eye.

"This is pretty shabby treatment for someone who has been as nice to one of your senior officers as I have," he said. "Here I've been covering this fellow's capital investments in our private deals, and now this. Well, I think we all should start being careful about rattling cages."

Schechter's eyebrows raised in astonishment. He had no doubt about what he had just heard or whom Watson was talking about: Darr was using Watson's money for his personal investing. This could be devastating. Schechter felt sure that nothing like that had been disclosed in the prospectuses for the Watson & Taylor deals. If there was anything to this allegation, then, at best, Darr had received compensation that had not been revealed to investors. It could well have been illegal. If investors found out about it, the lawsuits against Prudential-Bache would be massive.

Schechter stood up. "This meeting has come to an end," he said. "I think we have made our position clear. That's how it stands."

He turned and walked out of the room. Watson stood up and stormed down the hallway toward Darr's office. Darr met with him immediately. Within seconds, the sounds of the two men screaming at each other echoed throughout the thirty-third floor of Prudential-Bache. The noise could even be heard back in the conference room. Manley, Watson's national sales manager, could not make out the words. But he felt convinced that the fight almost certainly had something to do with the secret that Watson had just spilled to the top legal officer of Prudential-Bache.

At that moment, Schechter was walking back into his office. He was thinking about speaking to Joel Davidson, another member of the law department. They had to decide quickly which law firm to hire for the investigation into Darr's relationship with Watson & Taylor.

As 1988 began, the Dallas law firm of Locke Purnell Rain Harrell had just weathered a few months of chaos. In June, it had become the largest law firm in the city following a merger with a smaller firm. With the combination, Locke Purnell occupied more than six floors in the tall silver tower at First Republicbank Center downtown.

Locke Purnell had a long history in corporate law and a stellar reputation for its financial and corporate practice. It had handled a range of tax and securities matters for the corporate giants on its client list. But the latest assignment from Prudential-Bache was perhaps the law firm's most unusual: Schechter wanted Locke Purnell to investigate the financial relationship between a Pru-Bache executive and Watson & Taylor, a prominent real estate company well known to the Dallas lawyers.

The lawyers running the investigation were Bud Berry and Chris Allison. Berry knew George Watson. The two men traveled in the same social circles and their daughters attended the same school.

Shortly after being assigned to conduct the investigation, the Locke Purnell lawyers contacted executives at Watson & Taylor, saying they wanted to review all of the company's documents pertaining to Darr's investments. Lawyers at Watson & Taylor walked around the company, telling a number of department directors that they should cooperate with the investigation. But apparently no one bothered to tell George Watson about the lawyers poring through the documents in his office, looking for evidence of impropriety.

Bruce Manley watched all the comings and goings of the Locke Purnell lawyers with interest. From his perspective, by investigationg Darr, they were looking at the right person but weren't asking all the right questions. Unknown to most of the executives within Watson & Taylor, Manley probably knew more about the allegations surrounding Darr than anyone at the company. When Manley worked for Franklin Realty, he'd developed a close relationship with a number of executives in the partnership department. He had heard all of their stories about Darr hitting up general partners for personal benefits. He knew about Darr's mortgage with First South. He had been told about Darr taking money from general partners when he worked at Josephthal. He even knew the full story of the Futon Five, the small group of Bache executives who tried to turn in Darr but instead saw their own careers collapse.

Manley wanted to tell the Locke Purnell investigators everything he had heard, but he was afraid he would lose his job. To report what he knew without facing any trouble himself, Manley figured he had to be sneaky. He decided that he needed to find a go-between, someone who could call Locke Purnell and report the information for him. It only took a second for Manley to know the perfect person to call.

Manley dialed the number of one of his close friends and sailing buddies. He had no doubt that this man would want to help. After all, his friend had once worked for Darr; he was the one who'd heard from a competitor that Darr took payoffs. But after trying to report the information, he had lost his job as the senior tax shelter executive in the Southwest. To Manley, it seemed a bit of ironic justice that Curtis Henry, one of the original members of the Futon Five, was about to be offered the opportunity to finish what he had helped start more than seven years before.

The phone rang. "Hello," Henry drawled.

"Hey, Curtis, it's Bruce," Manley said softly. "We have to talk."

A few days later, in the afternoon of January 21, 1988, Curtis Henry sat in his office in San Diego, California, reviewing some notes from his talk with Manley. He was with one of his business partners, Charles Humphrey Jr. The two men were extraordinarily close. They had met years before, when Henry still worked for Bache and Humphrey was a lawyer in the tax shelter business. Sometime after Henry left Bache, the two, along with another Futon Five member, David Hayes, had become partners in a franchise of video stores called Major Video.

Because Humphrey was a lawyer, Henry consulted him about all the information he'd heard from Manley. Manley's story had left Henry dumbstruck. Although he thought Darr was dirty, Henry had never considered him stupid. He couldn't believe that Darr would so blatantly intertwine his financial interests with those of his general partners after so narrowly escaping the Futon Five investigation. It struck Henry as almost pathological.

Humphrey agreed that Manley's information should be shared with Locke Purnell, but on a few conditions. First, Humphrey should make the call to put a layer between Henry and Locke Purnell. And second, the call should be anonymous. Humphrey wanted to make sure that Henry wasn't dragged into another confrontation with Darr. It seemed the perfect way to get the information across without risk.

After a few minutes, Henry finished reviewing the Manley information with Humphrey and looked up from his notes.

"So that's it. You ready, Chuck?"

Humphrey nodded his head. "Yup."

"Then let's do it."

Humphrey picked up the telephone and dialed the number for Locke Purnell in Dallas. Henry stood beside him so he could hear every word. It took a while for anyone at Locke Purnell to answer the telephone. It was past 6:00 P.M. in Dallas. The switchboard had shut down for the night.

Finally Richard Colella, a Locke Purnell lawyer, picked up the phone. Humphrey asked whom he was speaking with, and Colella identified himself.

"Mr. Colella, I'm not at liberty to give you my name," Humphrey said. "I am an attorney and a member of the bar. Are you working on the investigation being conducted by Locke Purnell involving Watson & Taylor?"

Every lawyer is trained on how to handle approaches like that. Anyone—from a rival lawyer to the subject of the investigation himself—could call up and ask such a question. Colella was appropriately noncommittal.

"I don't know what you're talking about," he said. "Why don't you tell me why you're calling?"

"I wouldn't expect you to answer that question," Humphrey said. "But I want you to give a message to whoever is working on the investigation at your office."

Colella grabbed a pen. He listened silently, ready to take notes.

"One of my clients has informed me that the Locke Purnell attorneys examining the relationship between Watson & Taylor and James Darr should investigate the financing of Darr's personal residence, specifically with respect to the terms and conditions of that loan, as well as the identity of the lender and the lender's principal shareholders."

Colella scribbled down the information. Humphrey never mentioned First South, but he and Henry felt sure that Locke Purnell would figure it out.

"Also," Humphrey continued, "my client believes that William Petty, a former employee of Watson & Taylor, would confirm that Darr acquired an interest in some of Watson's private partnerships only after the profitability had been assured. The documents you are reviewing have been backdated to conceal this."

Colella wrote that down as well. He waited a second for more, but then it became apparent that Humphrey was finished.

"Well, again, sir, I don't know what investigation you're talking about, but I'll pass this message on to see if someone might be interested in the information," Colella stated.

"Thank you, Mr. Colella," Humphrey said. Then, without another word, he hung up.

Humphrey and Henry sat in the office for a moment in silence. Henry felt sure that what they had just done would set in motion events that not even Darr could control. But in that instant, he didn't feel elated, or fearful, or happy. Instead, he was resigned, as if what had just happened had been determined by fate.

We had to do it, Henry thought. *Darr had to be stopped.*

Bill Petty was walking past the kitchen in his Austin home when the telephone rang. It was a morning in mid-January, days after Humphrey had given Petty's name to Locke Purnell. He strode over to the phone and picked it up.

"Mr. Petty," the caller said. "My name is Bud Berry, and I'm a lawyer with the Dallas law firm of Locke Purnell Rain Harrell. Our firm has been retained by Prudential-Bache to conduct an investigation involving Watson & Taylor."

Petty listened, intrigued. At this point, he was not quite sure whether Berry was legitimate, but he thought the lawyer sounded fairly convincing. Petty was a cautious man who played his cards close to the vest. He had no idea if this investigation might lead to some liability for him. For now, he was going to let Berry do most of the talking.

"All right," he said. "So why are you calling me?"

"We've received an anonymous telephone call that you would have information that might be of interest to us."

"Well, what are you investigating?"

"We've been asked to look into the financial relationship between James Darr and Watson & Taylor," Berry said. "Would you know something about that?"

For an instant, Petty felt astonished. It had been four years since Darr had accidentally tipped him off about the investment he had with George Watson in a private partnership called Lombardi Number Three. He remembered how amazed he had felt when Watson had told him the land in the partnership had been presold and the profits guaranteed. He remembered how Watson had allowed Darr to invest $20,000 in the deal but let him put in only $5,000. This topic that so interested the Dallas lawyer on the phone was definitely something Petty could help him with.

"I know about that relationship," Petty replied.

Berry mentioned that Locke Purnell was aware that he had invested with Darr in the Lombardi deal and also knew that he was the former national sales manager for Watson & Taylor. Those were some of the areas Berry wanted to discuss.

"Would you mind meeting and talking with me?" Berry said. "I can fly down to Austin, meet you anyplace you'd like."

Petty was willing to talk, but he still wasn't completely sure that Berry was who he claimed to be. He couldn't think of who else might want this information, but Petty wanted to be safe.

"Tell you what," Petty said. "You write me a letter on your firm's letterhead confirming everything you've just told me. I'll take a look at it, and if everything's OK, I'll meet with you."

Berry agreed and contacted his colleague, Chris Allison. Allison dictated the letter right away for Bill Petty. At the top of the letter was a single line:

"Re: James Darr investigation."

Berry relaxed on a sofa chair near the lobby of the Marriott Austin Airport Hotel, off the intersection of Interstate 35 and Highway 290. Petty had selected the hotel as the location for their meeting on the morning of January 28, and Berry was the first to arrive.

Within a few minutes, Petty walked into the lobby. He noticed Berry almost immediately, but at first wasn't sure if that was the man he was looking for. Berry didn't look much like a lawyer to Petty. Most lawyers he knew always seemed intense and pensive. But Berry seemed relaxed, almost laid-back. He was wearing a sport coat instead of one of the standard-issue pin-striped suits. For a second, Petty hesitated. Then he realized that any lawyer who went by the name "Bud" was probably going to look a little more at ease than the typical corporate lawyer. Petty walked up to Berry and introduced himself. The two men wandered to the back of the hotel lobby, where they found a table in a bar area. They both ordered something to drink, and Berry took out a pen and a legal pad. They talked for a few minutes, with Berry trying to help Petty relax.

"I want to take this one step at a time," Petty said.

"I understand that," Berry said. "We can take everything real slow."

He gradually began asking questions. Berry was a skilled interviewer. He started by leading Petty through his personal and professional background, letting him handle softball questions that would put him more at ease. Petty described being hired to work for Watson & Taylor and his eventual departure from the company in 1985. He had been working as a financial consultant to real estate companies since then, he said.

Berry started pushing into more sensitive areas. He asked about the Lombardi Number Three deal. Petty relayed the story of how Darr had called him in the office, looking for George Watson and wanting to know where he could send his money. He described how a day or so after he told Watson about the call, Watson offered him the chance to invest $5,000 in the same deal.

"George told me that the property involved had already been sold and that the profit was assured," Petty said. "And sure enough, my five thousand dollars was returned to me a month or so later, and sometime after that, I made another eleven or twelve thousand dollars."

"Do you have a copy of the check you invested in Lombardi?" Berry asked.

"I'm sure I do."

"I'd like to see it, if I could."

Petty shrugged. "I don't see any reason why not."

Berry asked if Petty or any other midlevel officers had been allowed to invest in deals other than Lombardi. Petty shook his head and said that, to his knowledge, the Lombardi deal had been the only time anyone at his level had been offered the opportunity.

Berry flipped a page in his legal pad. "Do you know anything about the financing Darr received on his house in Connecticut?"

"Well, I'm aware that Watson & Taylor arranged a million-dollar loan from First South Savings and Loan to Darr so he could buy that house," Petty said. "Both Watson and Taylor are big shareholders in First South."*

As he scribbled that information in the legal pad, Berry asked if Petty had any other information of interest. Petty nodded, describing how Watson had paid a $1,800 hotel bill for Darr and his wife in Dallas, even though Petty questioned the amount.

"There was also a time when we had a sales incentive trip to Switzerland," Petty said. "Darr called up and said he wanted to fly on the Concorde. He insisted on it. I told George, and really questioned that expense. But George gave the go-ahead, so we bought the tickets."

Berry finished writing that on his notepad and looked up. "Anything else?"

Petty shifted in his seat, looking uncomfortable. "Yeah," he said. "I could name four other Pru-Bache sponsors who would say that Darr put the touch on them in return for Pru-Bache cosponsoring their deals."

Berry asked for details, but Petty made it clear that at this point he had gone as far as he was ready to go.

---

*Petty was mistaken about the size of the mortgage. The first mortgage, covering 100 percent of the purchase price, was for $1.8 million. The second mortgage was for $345,000.

"I'm not comfortable about saying too much now," he said. "I'm worried about my own liability here and the downside of speaking up. I've lived with these secrets for years. I'm willing to talk, but I want to be careful."

"All right, sir, I understand that," Berry said. "I want to thank you for all your help. At this point, either someone from my firm or Joel Davidson from the Prudential-Bache law department will get back to you on this."

Petty nodded his head. The two men shook hands and headed out the door. Their meeting had lasted almost two hours. It was about lunchtime, and the crowds were already gathering down the street at the popular Nighthawk steakhouse. Petty hopped into his car and drove away.

Bud Berry and Joel Davidson turned their rental car into Petty's driveway on the chilly Monday morning of February 8, 1988. It had been a little more than a week since the meeting at the Marriott. Berry had told Prudential-Bache's lawyers in New York about what he had learned, and almost immediately Davidson asked to see Petty personally. Petty's oblique reference to other general partners was too intriguing to ignore. Berry arranged to meet with Petty at his home, and Davidson flew down from New York.

The three men gathered in Petty's living room that morning. This time, Petty seemed more at ease, and the lawyers got right to the point. They asked if Petty could provide them with more information about Darr's dealings with other general partners.

Petty thought for a moment, then leaned back in his chair. After a few seconds of reflection, he looked at both lawyers. He was ready to talk.

"You need to speak with some of the people who used to work for Darr," Petty said. "They're the ones who could tell you a lot of information about Darr getting personal benefits out of the partnerships."

Petty started spilling some names as Berry took notes. He suggested that they call Wally Allen and John D'Elisa, two of the original members of the Futon Five, and told the lawyers where the men could be found. He also suggested that they contact Curtis Henry, although he didn't know where Henry was. No one knew that, through an intermediary, they had already been in contact with him.

The lawyers asked Petty for whatever details he knew about Darr's personal involvement with general partners.

"I can't offer any details," Petty said, "but I've heard about a lot of instances where Darr got something in exchange for decisions he made." Then he paused again, apparently thinking about how he wanted to phrase what he was about to say.

"You want to take a look at his dealings with Clifton Harrison from Dallas," Petty said. "Darr received about $200,000 in benefits from him in connection with real estate syndications Harrison did through Pru-Bache."

Petty said he had heard that Darr had also profited from personal dealings with a real estate syndicator from Birmingham, Alabama, and had received financial favors in conjunction with horse syndications sold by the firm and sponsored by a company in Lexington, Kentucky.

"Also, you need to look at Darr's limousines," Petty said. "A company called VMS regularly provided limousines for Darr's use."

Berry wrote down that information, too. Then he asked Petty to tell Davidson about the Lombardi Number Three deal. Petty repeated all the information he had passed on more than a week before at the Marriott.

"Another thing you need to be aware of," Petty said. "There was something wrong with the due diligence in that department. The entire time I was at Watson & Taylor, nobody other than Darr ever even bothered to take a look at the properties the public partnerships invested in."

Berry nodded and wrote that down, too. After about two hours, their meeting wound down.

Petty looked over at Davidson. "I assume that something is going to be done about all this."

"We'll keep you informed," Davidson said, his face a blank slate.

The lawyers left. Petty never heard from them again.

On the evening of February 16, the telephone rang at Locke Purnell. Richard Colella answered it.

"Mr. Colella," said Charles Humphrey, with Curtis Henry standing by his side. "This is the lawyer who recently spoke to you anonymously. I'm again calling on behalf of my client."

"Yes?"

"There's some other information that I believe you should know about," Humphrey said. Henry had picked up another story about Darr and wanted to make sure that Locke Purnell had heard it.

Humphrey said that during the mid-1980s, Darr and a group of other Prudential-Bache executives purchased foals of horses owned by a breeding partnership. The purchases were made individually, or through a partnership, he said.

"The offering documents for the breeding partnerships said that the foals were supposed to have been sold at auction to the highest bidder," Humphrey said. "Each of the partnerships has the word 'Amherst' in its name."*

Colella took down everything Humphrey said. "All right, I'll pass this on and see if anyone is interested."

"Thank you, Mr. Colella," Humphrey said, and hung up the phone. It was the last time he fed a tip about Darr to Locke Purnell.

Loren Schechter sat in his office, carefully reviewing the nine-page summary of the final report by Locke Purnell. Dated February 23, 1988, it was a rather dry recitation of facts, without any attempt to reach a conclusion about the propriety of Darr's actions. The law firm had reviewed documents on six of Darr's investments with Watson & Taylor and interviewed principals about one other investment. All of the records they had found were included in a massive, three-volume set that had been sent to the Prudential-Bache law department.

What Schechter read made him enormously uncomfortable. In one partnership, Darr invested no money at all, although Watson & Taylor contributed almost $6,000 for him. In another, the land in a partnership was sold before Darr was admitted to the deal. In a few more, Darr transformed a joint venture interest, which had some liability for him, into a net profit interest without paying any money for the change. The signs that these deals were far from arm's-length transactions went on and on.

At the end of the summary, Schechter read about the anonymous caller and his contact with Richard Colella. Then he closed the last page of the summary and began reviewing the notes Berry had typed up from his meetings with Bill Petty. Locke Purnell had not followed up with any of the people mentioned by Petty, such as Wally Allen and John D'Elisa. Even so, the information was devastating, if only because of the number of major general partners whose names turned up in the document. Clifton Harrison. VMS. Watson & Taylor.

Schechter finished the last page of Berry's notes. He didn't need to bother reading the hundreds of documents in the three-volume set. The summary was enough for him to make a conclusion: Darr was involved in improper dealings. There could be no place for him at the firm. He was a liability and a growing danger each day he stayed at Prudential-Bache.

---

* Darr and other executives purchased a horse from an Almahurst Bloodstock partnership. They named it Sherman Almahurst. Darr said that the purchase was made at auction, as required by the partnership prospectus.

Schechter knew that the decision to fire such a high-ranking executive would have to come from George Ball. He stood up and headed toward Ball's office. Schechter had to speak to the firm's chairman immediately.

George Ball finished reading the summary to the Locke Purnell report shortly after Schechter handed it to him. Schechter had been fairly clear about how he thought the matter should be handled. And from what he had read, Ball had to agree. He didn't know if the information he was reading described illegal conduct, but he was certain that it was improper. Darr had to go.

But then again, maybe not right away. Ball realized that this report gave him the perfect opportunity to rearrange the senior management of Prudential-Bache in a manner more to his liking. He had tried for years to bring Bob Sherman on to the team, to persuade him to work with the other departments for the greater good of the firm, but to no avail. Ball thought Sherman was just too much out of the old Bache mold of turf-fighting and byzantine intrigue. Sherman didn't fit in with the firm Ball wanted Pru-Bache to become.

The perfect thing to do, Ball decided, was make a clean sweep of it. Sherman had to go, and Darr desperately wanted his job. But Darr had to go, too. The easiest way to avoid any problem would be to toss them both out on the same day. Replacing two top managers was not something that could be done overnight. It would take months of planning and corporate games-playing by Ball. He told Schechter that he would get rid of Darr, but he wanted to take some time to ensure that all the changes were handled as smoothly as possible. He had to brace other senior managers and let them know what was going to happen. He also had to find a replacement for Sherman and build this person up to the troops. Once all was ready, Ball said, Darr would be fired.

That was how Darr was able to continue at Prudential-Bache for almost nine months after the general counsel and chairman of the firm came to believe he was up to no good. During that time, more than half a billion dollars of new partnerships were sold. In every one of those partnerships cosponsored by the firm, Darr's name appeared as the chairman of the Prudential-Bache subsidiary acting as general partner. None of those documents disclosed the Locke Purnell findings or the concerns of the two top officers of Pru-Bache about Darr's honesty. Investors would not be told.

But by now Prudential-Bache had far too many secrets to keep hidden. Some of them were about to be uncovered.

Cartons of documents about the Archives partnership were piled around a conference room in the midtown Manhattan offices of Manufacturers Hanover Trust. The records about the partnership sponsored by Clifton Harrison had been produced in early 1988 after the bank received a discovery request in the McNulty lawsuit.

Charles Cox, the Minneapolis lawyer who represented McNulty, had flown up to New York to pore through the documents with a legal assistant. Neither Cox nor his assistant, Nancy Trimbo, knew exactly what they were looking for. But Cox felt sure that somewhere in the morass of paper were the documents that would help his case.

The minutes slid into hours. Cox reviewed the lending documents, construction budget records, and appraisal materials. The information seemed good. It was clear that Prudential-Bache and Clifton Harrison had been irresponsible in the management of the Archives partnership. But with what he had so far, it would be a very hard-fought case.

Cox stretched as Trimbo passed him another file folder from the boxes. He opened it and dug through the various records. One document, which had the word "Confidential" stamped across the top, attracted his attention. It was some sort of security report, written many years earlier about Harrison.

Cox set the document on the table, flipped open the cover page, and started reading. Before he finished the first page, his eyes opened wide.

"In 1967, Clifton S. Harrison pled guilty to federal charges of misappropriation of bank funds and mail fraud as a result of which he was sentenced to serve three years," the report read.

The more Cox read, the more amazing it became. Harrison's embezzlement had involved a securities fraud as well. The report said he had been caught embezzling only because the bank officers realized he was spending more money than he made. Whenever he ended up short, he just figured out a way to defraud the bank and finance his high living. *This* was exactly the reason that the disclosure rules in the federal securities laws had been written.

Cox jumped up. "Jackpot!" he called to Trimbo. "Take a look at this!"

As she read the file, he watched with enjoyment as the shock registered on her face.

We've got them now, Cox thought. *We've got them.*

Clifton Harrison needed some money. Even with the millions of dollars in fees he received from his huge deals sold through Prudential-Bache, by the spring of 1988, he was still spending more money than he made. Despite his years of financial trouble, Harrison had never cut back on the elegant restaurants, valuable antiques, rental homes for the summer, and other indulgences. Until now, whenever he ran out of money, his friends at Pru-Bache always bailed him out.

This time was different. Since the Bessemer–Key West disaster, Harrison's relationship with Prudential-Bache had been in tatters. Even his old friend Darr seemed to be avoiding Harrison now. The Direct Investment Group would not sell any more of his deals. He couldn't use new fees to pay off his old expenses. His giant game of financial musical chairs had come to a stop, and Harrison couldn't find a seat anywhere. But eventually, Harrison realized there was one last chair he could use to win the game. It might not be something that Pru-Bache would approve, but at that point he didn't care. The option of cutting back on his spending was not acceptable.

Harrison rummaged through his desk and found the checkbook for Stamford Hotel LP, a deal that the Direct Investment Group had sold three years earlier. He opened it and picked up a pen. On the first check at the top, he brought the pen down just behind the words "Pay to the Order of" and wrote his own name. He filled the check out for tens of thousands of dollars.

Over the next several months, Harrison would pocket close to half a million dollars from the Stamford Hotel partnership. The man who twenty years earlier embezzled money from a bank to cover his extravagant expenses was simply taking partnership cash that did not belong to him.

Angry brokers and managers drove to the Holiday Inn off Highway 41 near Fort Myers, Florida. After parking in the lot, they traipsed through the lobby to a meeting room. They found seats around a series of long tables set up in a U shape. At the head table sat executives from Graham Resources and the Direct Investment Group. No one in the room was smiling, and for good reason.

This meeting in July 1988 was billed as the first time the Direct Investment Group would tell brokers why the Graham energy partnerships—particularly the growth fund—were unraveling. At that point, no information was more important to the brokers. Every quarter, after the shrinking distribution checks were mailed, they had been forced to spend hours on the telephone trying to explain to clients why all the promises they had made were not coming true. But they didn't know the answer.

As a group, the brokers were angry. Among themselves, they repeatedly said that the firm lied to them. Everything had been described to them as so safe, so assured. Then it all collapsed. None of the brokers understood the details, but many of them felt sure that something slippery had taken place.

All the big brokers in the area had traveled to Fort Myers for the meeting. Up at the center table sat a few senior officers from the Direct Investment Group in New York, including Barron Clancy, Joe DeFur, Joe Quinn, and Russell Labrasca. Jim Parker, the firm's partnership marketer for Florida, was also there. He sat beside Bob Jackson, Graham Resources' marketer for the region.

Clancy stood up and walked to the center of the head table. "We're all here today to talk about what's been happening with some of the Graham partnerships," he said. "We want to lay out all of the events that have been affecting these partnerships so you can understand where everything stands."

The brokers glared at Clancy. They had been hearing the excuses coming out of the Direct Investment Group and Graham Resources for months. They weren't in the mood for another rendition of the explanations that seemed like little more than lies.

"A lot of the things that have happened were simply beyond everyone's control," Clancy said. No one, not even the top executives in the Direct Investment Group, could have possibly predicted the events that had unfolded, he said. The collapse of the price of oil in 1986 wreaked havoc on the early partnerships. Gas prices never came up. Tax reform in 1986 pulled the legs out from under many partnerships. These were all external events. Neither Graham Resources nor the Direct Investment Group was responsible for any of it.

As Clancy spoke, Parker and Jackson glanced around the room. They knew these brokers well enough to tell what was happening. The excuses were driving them absolutely nuts, particularly since a lot of what they were learning made no sense. The marketing materials had said that tax reform would have no impact on the tax benefits of the Graham partnerships. When the price of oil went down, the distributions fell. When the price of oil went up, the distributions fell. Even the distributions from the growth funds, which were created at the bottom of the oil market, were falling.

"Barron, this is just so much bull," one of the brokers called out. "We were told these were safe investments. Are you guys saying you didn't fig-ure out that the price of oil might go down? What, was it safe only as long as prices went up?"

"Now, that's not what I'm saying," Clancy said. He went back, trying to explain again about the unforeseen events. Then he turned to DeFur, who backed him up.

"What are you guys talking about?" another broker barked. "That might explain the trouble in one or two of these partnerships. But all of them? There's got to be something else there."

As the noise of the crowd increased, Clancy and DeFur walked through the same points again. That just made the brokers angrier.

"Face it, you guys lied to us," a manager called out. "Look at the growth funds. We were totally misled about that. How come they stopped buying bank loans, like they were supposed to?"

"Now wait a minute," one of the Direct Investment Group executives said. "Go back and look at the prospectus for the energy growth fund. We never said that we were definitely going to buy those discounted loans. That was just a hypothetical in the marketing material, something we said we might do. We never committed to that."

With that, the room exploded.

"This is bullshit!" a broker called out. "A hypothetical? What are you talking about? You told us they were going to be buying discounted bank loans! It was no goddamned hypothetical!"

"You misled us!" another one shouted. "We're the ones who are pay-ing the price for your dishonesty. We're the ones losing our clients and lis-tening to them accuse us of lying. So what the hell are you going to do about it?"

The meeting broke down completely. Brokers were shouting questions, one after another, without waiting for answers. They were beating Clancy and DeFur badly. It was as if the anger that had built up over the months of deteriorating performance by the partnerships was all pouring out at once in this meeting room at a Holiday Inn.

"You guys have been covering up the facts on the growth fund," one broker shouted. "What the hell happened?"

"The disclosure on the First City loans can't be true," another said. "What's the truth? Stop hiding it from us."

Before they could offer an answer, another broker stood up. "You guys better think fast, because you've got a scandal of big proportions building up here."

The broker stared straight at the senior executives in the front. Solemnly, he uttered one last statement.

"This is Grahamgate."

Al Dempsey hung up the phone after talking with Bob Jackson. What he heard on July 5 about the meeting in Florida disturbed him greatly. Clancy and DeFur had not been prepared to deal with the brokers' rage. Graham Resources itself was facing a deep credibility problem. If the company didn't figure out a way around the problem quickly, its sales of partnerships could rapidly fall off.

Dempsey sat at his desk and wrote a confidential memo to Graham's top marketers. He described some details of the Florida meeting and offered some suggestions about how to handle the energy growth fund, which he labeled EGF, and its deal with First City National Bank, which he called FCNB.

"For a lot of valid reasons, many of the details of our EGF investments, particularly FCNB, have been kept secret," he wrote. "I think the time has come for full disclosure" to the company's regional marketers.

He spelled out a few ideas for crisis management that he wanted adopted immediately.

"I believe this approach will help to solve our EGF credibility problem," he wrote, "and will avoid a 'spill-over' into energy income fund and other products we may introduce in the future."

The strategy would largely succeed. Graham would continue selling its energy partnerships through Prudential-Bache for years to come. Even with all of the damage that had been done, Graham would still find brokers who were willing to believe. Prudential-Bache itself was still tapping into that faith. After all, there was always another high-commission product that could be sold. And Pru-Bache needed the money.

Richard Sichenzio, the second in command to Bob Sherman, almost growled through the telephone in September 1988.

"Why aren't you getting more involved in pushing the Risers?" Sichenzio asked Jim Trice, the regional director for the Southeast. "We're about to do another offering. I want your guys to step up their sales."

Trice just shook his head. Risers was the shorthand name for an enormously complex investment that Prudential-Bache had recently begun pushing. It stood for Residual Income Stream Equity REIT. Risers offered clients a way of purchasing an investment collateralized by residential mortgage loans. They had been marketed as safe investments for conservative clients, but few brokers in the Prudential-Bache system could figure out the concept, and their clients understood even less. But senior executives, and particularly Sichenzio, pushed Risers hard. It was a product manufactured by Pru-Bache. If sales were strong, the firm could make great profits.

But Trice wasn't about to push brokers to sell investments they couldn't explain.

"Look, Rich," he replied. "A lot of brokers and managers don't understand this product. It's very complicated. They don't feel comfortable with it, so they don't understand it."

"Well, that's your job," Sichenzio barked. "Make them understand it so they can sell it."

"Richie, let me tell you, *I* don't understand it in some ways. On top of that, I don't like the way this is being shoved down people's throats."

Trice also mentioned that, even though this product was being sold as safe and secure, the Prudential-Bache analyst who examined Risers had already suggested over the in-house communications system that their outlook was not good. Why on earth would the firm start selling another one, this one called RAC Mortgage, when the analyst seemed so doubtful?

"The analyst didn't know what he was talking about," Sichenzio said. The analyst had already made a revised presentation on the firm's communications system to correct any misimpression.

"So your job is to get behind the effort to sell more of these," Sichenzio said.

The conversation came to an end. Trice said he would see what he could do.

Trice was right to be worried. That same month, Merrill Lynch, which also offered Riser products, distributed a research report to its brokers. It covered the latest Riser being sold by Merrill and Prudential-Bache. But the analysis would only be seen by Merrill brokers. The word "safety" was nowhere to be seen in the report.

Instead, under the bold heading "Merrill Lynch Research Suitability Comment," the report contained this warning: "Research considers the common stock to be suitable only for SPECULATIVE accounts."

At Merrill, only the customers most willing to gamble would be sold the newest Riser product. At Prudential-Bache, the sales focused instead on the elderly and the retired. Merrill was right.

———

Paul Tessler, an executive in the Direct Investment Group, dropped the financial statements for one of the Harrison partnerships on his desk and reached for the telephone. Something in the numbers for the partnership, called Stamford Hotel, didn't make sense. As an asset manager, his job was to review the performance of the partnerships that had already been sold and make sure everything was running correctly. Normally, that involved looking at the numbers, running them through a few times, and signing off. But this time, in the fall of 1988, Tessler couldn't figure out the statements for the Stamford partnership. If he didn't know better, he would have bet that several hundred thousand dollars of the partnership's money was missing.

Still, Tessler wasn't worried. He was sure there was some routine explanation for the apparent discrepancy. He dialed Harrison Freedman Associates and asked for Gayle Gordon, one of the company's accountants. He told her about the document he was examining.

"I'm having a little trouble finding this number," he said. "Could you help me out here?"

Slowly Gordon took him through the numbers, and Tessler followed along. By the time she finished, he was no better off than when she started. He still came up several hundred thousand dollars short. It was too large a discrepancy to shrug off.

"I still don't get it, Gayle," Tessler said. "Could you send me some of the backup on this?"

Gordon said she would send him the supporting documents soon.

About a week later, Tessler was feeling anxious. He still had not heard from Gordon, so he called her again.

"Hi, Gayle," he said. "I still need some help here. Can you send me what I need? I don't understand what these numbers are. I just really need to check."

Again Gordon said she would send the materials soon, and the call ended.

The next morning, Tessler's boss, Joe Quinn, the head of asset management, asked him to come to his office immediately. Tessler walked in and shut the door.

"We've got a real problem, Paul," Quinn said. "Gayle Gordon resigned. Apparently it had something to do with you questioning the numbers on the Stamford partnership."

Tessler was flabbergasted. Until that moment, the questions he had asked had seemed nothing but routine. He had simply been making the workaday demands of his job. But any time an accountant resigns from a company, antennae go up on Wall Street. Gordon must have found something she couldn't tolerate. Before Tessler had another moment to think about it, Quinn answered all his questions.

"Apparently she found out that there's some money missing," Quinn said, his voice completely calm. "We have to move very quickly on this."

Within a few minutes, Tessler and Quinn had Harrison on the line. Slowly, they began to browbeat the man about where the money had gone.

"This is not a problem," Harrison said. "I've just been borrowing some money against future fees."

"Well, how much money are we talking about?" Tessler asked.

"About $200,000."

That amount sounded enormous. Under the terms of the Stamford deal, Harrison had no right to advance himself fees. It wouldn't take too clever a plaintiff's lawyer to argue that he had been embezzling partnership money. Quinn and Tessler told Harrison they would be over to see him immediately.

At ten o'clock in the morning on October 11, 1988, Quinn and Tessler arrived at Harrison's office. When he saw Harrison, Tessler could not believe his eyes. The gregarious, upbeat fellow he knew from the past was gone. In his place was a shaking, downtrodden, highly emotional man. Both he and Quinn had known about Harrison's enormous cash flow problems. Only now did they realize the emotional toll those financial troubles were wreaking on him.

The interrogation made things worse.

"So," Quinn asked, "the full amount you took out was $200,000? We're not going to look at the numbers and find any other surprises?"

Harrison took a deep breath and sighed. "No," he said, shaking his head. "It wasn't just $200,000. It was more."

Over the next few minutes, Harrison admitted that the amount was in fact closer to $500,000. He had been taking the money, a small bit at a time, for much of the year.

Harrison's eyes filled with tears as he said he had always intended to pay the money back once he received his next set of fees.

Quinn stood up. "If you will excuse me, I have to go call the firm's lawyers," he said.

He walked into the other room and dialed the Prudential-Bache law department, telling the lawyers that he had just found out that one of the firm's biggest general partners had been improperly pocketing partnership money. He needed to know what to do.

The changes came quickly. Harrison lost the power to write any more checks out of the partnerships on his own. Control of the partnerships was out of his hands.

It was the last time Clifton Harrison had any major involvement with the partnerships he sold through the Direct Investment Group. Instead, the responsibility for them was largely left with one of his consultants. Harrison simply walked away from the deals. His relationship with Prudential-Bache was essentially over.

In a matter of weeks, the same would be true for Jim Darr.

"Jim, come on in," Ball said as he saw Darr at his doorway. "Let's talk."

Darr stepped slowly into the room, his face a mask of anxiety. He was holding himself together well, particularly for a man who had just been told he was losing his job.

Ball came around his desk and patted Darr's shoulder as they walked toward the couch and chairs on the other side of his office.

It was November 25, 1988, and it had been a day of wild extremes for Darr. It was the first day of the Direct Investment Group's latest quarterly meeting. Darr had opened the meeting with an upbeat speech about the future of direct investments and the new directions he thought the department should take. By the afternoon, he had been told to see Lee Paton, the man who had originally hired him. It was Paton who delivered the bad news. Shortly beforehand, Bob Sherman was also told that he was being let go. Ball wanted to meet with each man after they had heard what was happening and handle any mop-up that was necessary. Ball had met with Sherman first, and the session was short and simple. Then he had waited for Darr to arrive.

The changes had taken a long time to put in place. Ball had finally settled on Richard Sichenzio as the man who should replace Sherman. Even though Sichenzio had never been a broker, Ball thought he had done a fabulous job in a lot of areas, particularly in his recent push to get the Riser products sold. Replacing Darr was much easier. Paul Proscia had been at Darr's side for years. Ball liked Proscia and was fully confident that he could pick up where his old boss left off.

Ball settled into a chair and Darr took the couch. He sat on the very edge, a bundle of nerves.

"I'm terribly sorry about all this, Jim," Ball said. "I know you wanted Sherman's job. You've been lobbying for it very hard. But I decided to give the job to Richie Sichenzio. In view of that, I really think it's better that you leave the firm rather than being a bitter person who potentially might snipe or try to undermine Richie."

The reality of what was happening seemed to be going over Darr's head. Right in the middle of being fired, he launched into a promotion pitch.

"Look, George, I'd be the right person for the retail job," he said. "I know the people here. I know I could run things. I'd be the right guy."

Ball shook his head. "No, Jim," he said. "It's not going to happen."

"Then let me just continue to run the direct investment department."

For the most fleeting of instants, Ball considered bringing up the disquieting Locke Purnell report. But he wanted to keep the conversation strictly on a business level.

"Consciously or unconsciously, you're going to be a critic of Richie," Ball said. "Having somebody who sought a senior position and failed remaining with the company is an invitation to disaster. It's time for you to move on, Jim."

Darr nodded as the reality of what was happening appeared to start crashing down. His career at Prudential-Bache was coming to an end.

About an hour later, a few select executives from the Direct Investment Group gathered for a private meeting in the department's boardroom. Darr had spread the word through Barron Clancy, one of his trusted executives, that he wanted to meet with his top aides. Many of the veterans who worked in New York were there, including Pittman, Proscia, and Quinn. Other longtime marketers in the field were also invited. The men sat around the table quietly, wondering what was happening. They anticipated a big announcement.

Darr stepped into the room and sat down. He was noticeably and uncharacteristically quiet. He stared at the table for a good minute, saying nothing. The gathered executives looked at him and then exchanged confused looks.

What in the world is he going to say?

Finally Darr looked up. "I've been asked to resign from the organization. I just want to tell you how much I appreciate and have enjoyed my association with you."

At that moment, Darr choked up. Tears began to well up in his eyes and

stream down his cheeks. He shook his head slightly and regained his com-
posure, saying, "I'm leaving on good terms with the firm. This is just
something they thought needed to be done."

For the next eight minutes or so, Darr relived his happy memories from
his days building the department. He told stories about several executives
in the room. He mentioned things he considered to be the department's
successes.

"We've been able to get a lot done as a team," he concluded. "I will
never forget you and what we have been able to accomplish."

With that, Darr stood up, and a number of the executives came around
the conference table to shake his hand and thank him for what he had done
for them. They talked for another few minutes before slowly filing out of
the room.

The next day, Curtis Henry was speeding down Interstate 10, heading
from Pensacola, Florida, to Mobile, Alabama. He was scouting out new locations for his video stores. He was in one of those places that seemed like
the end of the earth, with no one in sight and nothing ahead but miles of
empty road.

Suddenly his car telephone rang. It was a former manager from
Prudential-Bache, asking him if he had seen the *Wall Street Journal* that day.
When Henry said no, the former manager read him the story about Darr
and Sherman leaving Prudential-Bache. It quoted Darr saying that he had
resigned. "It was my decision," Darr told the newspaper.

The article went on to say that Darr planned to start his own limited
partnership operation. Ball said that Prudential-Bache expected to be
Darr's biggest customer.

Henry laughed. "Boy, that's a great cover."

Within thirty seconds of hanging up, the car phone rang again. It was
Roy Akers, another former Pru-Bache branch manager.

"Curtis, did you hear about Darr?" he asked. "I know you must have
had something to do with this. Congratulations. You finally got him."

This time, Henry shook his head. "I didn't get him," he said. "I didn't
have anything to do with it."

Akers chuckled. "I'm sure," he said sarcastically.

No, Henry said. He was serious.

"He didn't need me," he said. "Darr got himself."

CHAPTER 15

FEDERAL JUDGE BRUCE VAN SICKLE handed down the decision in *Mc-Nulty* v. *Prudential-Bache* on February 3, 1989, in Minneapolis. It was an all-out win for McNulty and his lawyer, Charles Cox. The secrets of the Harrison partnerships were finally exposed.

Van Sickle ruled that Pru-Bache had failed to tell investors material information about Harrison's 1982 Archives partnership. Some of it involved the Archives' financial condition. But the judge also criticized the firm for not disclosing Harrison's criminal record, a failure that occurred in every partnership he sponsored.

"It seems clear," Van Sickle wrote, "that a reasonable investor would consider information about such a conviction important in making an investment decision."

Van Sickle also dismissed out of hand Prudential-Bache's argument that the pardon Harrison had received from President Ford made his conviction a nonevent.

"The pardon releases Harrison from the effects of his conviction, but it does not have the Orwellian effect of re-writing history to make the fact of the conviction non-existent," he wrote. "The fact stands and the failure to mention it in the offering memorandum constitutes a material omission."

The decision was devastating for Pru-Bache. The ruling was now the precedent. As long as that decision was on the books, the firm could never again argue in court that Harrison's background did not have to be revealed. The judge's finding itself was material and would have to be disclosed to every investor in the Harrison partnerships. Worse for the firm, the finding would be available to every lawyer and in every law library with access to computerized databases. Prudential-Bache would soon be facing hundreds of millions of dollars in lawsuits, with little ability to defend itself.

So the lawyers at Prudential-Bache plotted a strategy. They would make Van Sickle's decision disappear.

Within a few days of the ruling, the firm's lawyers contacted Cox with a proposal. Pru–Bache would not appeal the decision but instead would settle. Even though McNulty won everything back—his entire investment, plus interest, plus legal fees—the firm was willing to pay more. But there was a condition: McNulty had to join Prudential-Bache in a motion to vacate the judgment.

A vacated decision essentially never existed. It does not establish any precedent. It never appears in any legal databases. And it is kept out of the federal records of court decisions. The only way to know it was issued would be to dig through the files at the Minneapolis court, where the only copy of the decision would remain.

Investors and their lawyers would be hard-pressed to figure that out. As a second term of the settlement, McNulty was required to sign a confidentiality agreement. No one would be told about the secret information hidden in Minneapolis. Even though Van Sickle made it clear that Harrison's background was material, Prudential-Bache still would not tell investors. It would not even disclose that Harrison and the firm had just been successfully sued for selling faulty deals.

Deception alone would no longer contain the damage that had grown within the Direct Investment Group for more than ten years. So now Pru–Bache was resorting to the brute force of its law department. With the backing of the giant Prudential Insurance, the firm prepared to use its financial firepower to keep the emerging scandal under wraps.

But soon the problems started popping up faster than the Prudential-Bache lawyers could conceal them.

Brokers throughout Prudential-Bache punched up the results from the first day of trading in the VMS Mortgage Investment Fund on their stock quote machines. After being sold for almost a year, in April 1989 its shares were finally opening on the American Stock Exchange. Shock ripped through the firm on the opening bell. The fund, which had been sold as a safe, guaranteed investment, collapsed in value on the very first trade. Investors had purchased their shares at $10 each. The first share traded at close to $7.50.

Bill Creedon, a broker in Prudential-Bache's Los Angeles office who had sold the fund to his most conservative clients, stared at the Quotron machine on his desk with a rising sense of concern. The fund had a few halfhearted rallies during the day, but it never did—and indeed, never would—recover its original value.

Creedon didn't like what he saw, but he wasn't ready to give up. He still felt safe as long as those guarantees were in place. Whether the shares went up or down, he felt confident that his clients would still get their 12 percent return as well as all of their principal back. But he knew a number of them would be mad when their account statement arrived the next month. The drop in value would bring down the net worth calculation on the front page of their statement. Already, he prepared himself to handle a flood of angry phone calls.

In the middle of the trading day, John Eisle, the Los Angeles branch manager, came out to assure the troops that everything was all right with the mortgage fund.

"Don't worry about VMS," he said. "I've spoken with the people in New York. This is just market action. It'll recover."

Managers around the country made similar assurances to their nervous brokers. Still, a degree of panic was setting in. When the fund price sank below $7.40 a share, one broker decided to bail his clients out. Later the broker told Eisle that he had sold their holdings in VMS. Since they wanted safety, the broker said, he used those proceeds to purchase one of the new energy income partnerships.

Eisle nodded. "That sounds like a viable alternative."

The telephone rang on John Hutchison's desk almost as soon as he hung up from his last call. It was a broker, screaming about his customers' losses in VMS and the falling distributions in the Graham partnerships. The broker wanted to know what the Direct Investment Group was going to do. Hutchison, who marketed both VMS and Graham products for the Direct Investment Group, gave the standard excuses that had been told to him by his superiors. Soon he hung up and rested his head in his hands. The complaints were coming in too fast, at a rate of about 100 a week. And the brokers were angrier than ever.

Everything that the Direct Investment Group had ever touched seemed to be collapsing. Airplane deals with a company called Polaris were unraveling, as were real estate deals with Fogelman Properties. Problems were turning up in the Harrison deals, the Lorimar deals, the Almahurst deals. Hutchison heard brokers complain about another Prudential-Bache deal called Risers that had lost about 80 percent of its value. The list was endless. Nobody could understand what was happening.

Hutchison stood up and headed down the hallway to visit Kathy Eastwick, a friend and fellow product manager. Eastwick had been at the department forever, first as a compliance administrator working for Pittman and then, for the last few years, as a marketer. She was both a straight shooter and Hutchison's best buddy in the department. The two of them viewed each other as kindred souls, strapped to the center mast as the storm blew in around them.

Eastwick was on the telephone when Hutchison walked in. She was speaking to a broker who was complaining about the performance of one of the products she marketed. Hutchison slumped into a chair and listened quietly. Finally Eastwick hung up and looked at Hutchison, exhaustion clouding her face.

"Kathy, this is just awful," Hutchison finally blurted out. "I don't know how much longer I can take this. Everything's erupting at the same time."

Eastwick threw a pen on her desk. "I know." She sighed. "I don't take any phone calls to help place orders anymore. I just listen to brokers all day yelling and screaming. Everybody just keeps asking me what's happening and why aren't we doing anything about it."

The two sat for a moment in silence. Then Eastwick's telephone rang again.

"I wish I knew the answer to that myself," Hutchison said.

Across the country, the answers were slowly starting to emerge.

J. Boyd Page, an Atlanta securities lawyer, sat back in the overstuffed chair in his office and tried to hide his disbelief.

"All right," Page said in a southern drawl. "Walk me through this one more time."

In front of him sat Rick Blass, a Prudential-Bache broker with its Atlanta branch. Blass had asked for this meeting in the spring of 1989 to see about retaining Page. Already Blass had gone through his story once, but he did as Page asked.

"My clients and I have invested in a deal that was sponsored by Prudential-Bache," he said. "The firm told me it was like a CD and that it was safe, secure, and virtually no risk. But everything they said was false. I lost my money, and my clients have all been blown out. I want you to represent all of us against the firm and help us get our money back."

Page leaned toward his desk and picked up a cigarette. "Mind?" he asked. Blass shook his head.

Page took a drag of his cigarette. He had known this broker a long time. Almost ten years before, he had represented him in another case. Still, he had trouble believing him.

"OK, prove it," Page said. "You know, I heard what you're saying, but if I walk into an arbitration and say that, people are going to look at you and laugh. It's a little too convenient for the guy who sold this stuff to blame his firm."

"But it's not just these things," Blass said. "It's not just the Risers. It's everything they push us to sell. They keep telling us that every big product they put together is safe and secure and there's no risk to it. But it's just not happening. Not with any of them."

Page took another puff of his cigarette. "Look, I watch television sometimes on Saturday and Sunday afternoons," he said. "I've seen 'the Rock.' I've seen all these advertisements about the reliability of Prudential. I'm just not too easily inclined to believe that something quite as massive as you're describing has happened at a place like that."

Blass sighed. He said he would go back to his office and look through some of his files for the marketing material that proved he was telling the truth. The meeting came to an end, and the two men shook hands.

Page didn't hold out much hope that the broker was going to persuade him. A native of east Tennessee, Page was the kind of person who needed a lot of evidence to accept the incredible. But the broker had made the right choice by coming to Page. In 1989, Page probably knew more about the internal workings of Prudential-Bache than any lawyer in the country.

His law firm, Page & Bacek, started handling big cases involving Pru-Bache in 1986. The first one that came in the door had helped make his reputation. In that case, Page represented Bill Kane, a former executive with the firm's Atlanta branch. Kane had been fired from his job as an administrative manager. The dismissal came after the firm found out that a broker at the branch had done some improper trades over more than a year. Kane, who had been there just a few weeks, was the only executive punished. From what Page could tell, it looked like Kane had been nothing more than a scapegoat.

The case opened an enormous window for Page on the inner workings of Prudential-Bache. He learned about the sloppy compliance procedures that led to the Capt. Crab settlement. He heard about the heavy pressure exerted on brokers to sell Pru-Bache products. He won the Kane case, but it was not a big economic victory. Kane walked away with about $40,000.

But the case had its benefits. Page earned the reputation among Prudential-Bache brokers and managers as a man willing to take on the firm. His office became a drop-off point for Pru-Bache employees who thought they were being mistreated. Over the years, Page heard numer-

ous horror stories about the way employees were abused and clients' accounts ransacked. Still, with everything he had heard, he was not disposed
to believe the stories that his most recent visitor from the firm had to tell
about massive fraud and deception of clients.

Until a few weeks later. True to his word, Blass returned with his files
in tow. Page met with him in a conference room just off the law firm's entryway. For more than an hour, he reviewed the information. There was
no mistake. The marketing material he sifted through clearly made the
Risers out to be safe and secure investments.

Finally, after reading an array of papers, Page looked at Blass with a
smile.

"Well, sir, congratulations," he said. "We've got ourselves a case."

Loren Schechter walked briskly into the boardroom at Prudential-Bache,
where the firm's executive committee was meeting in 1989. He was there
to make one of his most dire presentations ever. The firm had already been
sued over VMS. It was a small lawsuit, one that normally could be swat-
ted away with a quick settlement. But Schechter believed that the firm's
exposure was enormous. Hundreds of millions of dollars' worth of the
VMS investments appeared to have been sold to elderly, risk-averse investors. Its value was dropping like a rock. The case would be trouble.

Ball glanced up and saw Schechter walking into the room. He had just
finished reporting on some of the events of the day.

"Loren, perhaps you ought to let everybody know about this lawsuit,"
Ball said.

Schechter made a quick presentation, describing the claims of the lawsuit. Then he opened the floor up to questions.

Ted Fowler, the firm's investment banking chief, was the first to speak
up. "Well, Loren, is this just some nut that lost some money, or is this
something prevalent?"

"This is serious," Schechter said. "This is going to be a huge problem.
Huge."

The top sellers of the Graham energy partnerships arrived in June 1989 for
their seven-day sales trip to Costa del Sol, Spain, just a short distance from
the real Rock of Gibraltar. All of the best-known brokers at Prudential-
Bache qualified for the trip. And by now, almost every one of them was
angry.

As always, Graham Resources and the Direct Investment Group planned an awards ceremony, where the top brokers would be honored for their sales. But unlike most years, the awards carried a bitter tinge. By that point, everyone on the trip knew that the brokers who sold the most Graham partnerships in 1988 probably had the most customer complaints in 1989.

The ceremony was going to be led by Joe DeFur from the Direct Investment Group and Al Dempsey from Graham Resources. As DeFur was preparing, he saw Bill Webb, a broker in Pru-Bache's branch in Fort Myers, Florida, heading toward him. Few brokers carried more credibility with the sales force than Webb. He was one of the best-known and most-respected sellers of the Graham products. In years past, Graham Resources had even featured interviews with Webb in the newsletters that the energy company distributed around Prudential-Bache. Webb's opinion carried a lot of weight with his colleagues.

"Hey, Joe," Webb said as he walked over. DeFur returned the greeting.

"Listen, I don't want to sandbag you here," Webb said, "so I want you to know I'm going to stand up during the ceremony and make a few points about the problems with the energy growth fund. The marketing really misrepresented everything. The investments the fund made were nothing like what we were told they were going to be. I really need to say something about it."

DeFur looked Webb in the eyes for a moment. "Good for you," he stated.

As the ceremony began, there was little jovial backslapping or frivolity. This meeting was all business. Eventually Webb stood up.

"Al, Joe, I've got a few things I want to say," Webb said. "I think we all know that there were some serious problems with the energy growth program. We've seen some dismal results. What we were told about the investments the fund was going to make never occurred. This program was clearly misrepresented, both to us and to our customers. So now I want to know what you're going to do about it. What's the answer to this problem?"

The crowd seemed to adopt Webb's statements as the universal opinion. As a group, they turned toward DeFur and Dempsey. The room was silent in expectation.

"We understand, Bill," DeFur said. "We'll just have to get back to you on that."

Webb sat down, feeling proud for speaking up. Even so, he knew that he would never hear back from anyone in the Direct Investment Group.

Bob Jackson, the regional marketer in Florida for Graham Resources, looked at the screen of his personal computer and took a deep breath. Jackson was a family man and was not the kind of person to act irresponsibly. So he had considered his actions carefully before sitting down to write his bosses a letter on the warm afternoon of August 23, 1989. He was sure that once the letter arrived at Graham Resources, he would be fired. After all, it wasn't all that often that an employee accused his superiors of fraud.

Jackson had been struggling for a year with the obvious signs that Graham had deceived everyone in its marketing of the growth fund. Until the prior summer, Jackson could rationalize what was happening. But after the executives in New Orleans decided to let the marketers know some of the truth about the investments that were made by the partnership, Jackson had been unable to stomach it. It was all he could talk about.

Just the week before, Jackson had been speaking with Bill Webb from the Fort Myers branch. Webb was still clearly angry about the growth fund situation. It was obvious to him that the prospectus had been written with enough caveats to provide a cover to Graham Resources and Prudential-Bache but that customers had been told a pack of lies.

"The prospectus may protect Pru-Bache and Graham from any legal liability," Webb had said, "but there is very definitely a moral liability."

For Jackson, that summed up the whole situation. He and all the other marketers had been used in a cynical deception, and he knew it. Regardless of what it meant for his future, he could no longer keep silent about what had happened.

Jackson addressed his letter to Pete Theo, the president of Graham Resources' marketing subsidiary, Graham Securities. He started by saying that, in the past, whenever the marketers had questions about performance, Graham executives became defensive or tried to gloss over the issues with lots of figures and charts. That had always happened with questions about the first Energy Growth Fund, which Jackson called EGF-1. The time had come, he implied, for someone to start talking straight.

"It is still impossible for me to look at the investments in EGF-1 and understand why anyone would have agreed to purchase them," he typed. "We all know only too well that the program ultimately turned out to be totally different from what we were told it was going to be prior to, during and throughout the marketing of the initial growth fund."

There were no heavily discounted, heavily collateralized loans, he wrote. "I do not personally believe that the dismal results we have witnessed in this program would have occurred at all had the investments been made as they were represented."

Without using any names, Jackson recounted his conversation the previous week with Bill Webb and said that he agreed with the broker's sentiments.

"It has been inferred that Jim Darr was the reason that the changes that were taking place in the investment were not communicated to the brokers in the Pru-Bache system," he wrote. "But whether or not he advocated such a policy, it would seem that it would take the cooperation on the part of certain individuals at the senior management level of Graham Resources for our wholesalers not to have been made aware."

This problem, Jackson wrote, had been eating away at him for a year and undercutting his ability to do the job. Making the situation worse was the fact that all of the other partnerships seemed not to be performing anywhere close to how they had been advertised.

"It appears that only a few of the thirty-five Pru-Bache programs formed to date would have the potential to equal the investment results of a CD if they were liquidated today, in spite of the fact that the price of oil is higher," he wrote. After studying the data, "I am considerably more alarmed at the lack of increase in the distributions even if the price goes up."

Jackson wrote that Graham Resources desperately needed to address those concerns, which were shared by his colleagues. If it could not, he wrote, then there was only one option. "I would like to go on record as being in favor of then considering rolling up or consolidating the Pru-Bache energy partnerships in an effort to maximize returns to investors," he typed, "and then withdrawing from the retail marketplace."

Jackson typed his name at the bottom. As he reread the letter, he was frightened. It wasn't every day an employee suggested that his company get out of its most profitable business.

The lunchtime crowd at Houston's restaurant in Fort Lauderdale was large and noisy. Jackson walked through the crowd, looking for Jim Parker, the Florida regional marketer for the Direct Investment Group. Usually the two men met in Parker's office at Prudential-Bache. This time, soon after Jackson wrote his letter to Graham, he had asked for Parker to meet him at Houston's.

Jackson saw Parker at a table and headed over. Parker was smiling, and the two men broke into the easy conversation of good friends. Within a few seconds, Parker could tell that something was wrong. Jackson seemed nervous, almost frightened. He was always a relaxed kind of guy with a level head. Parker didn't want to push, so he waited to hear what the problem was.

Jackson cleared his throat. "I really need to talk to you, Jimmy," he said soberly.

"I can tell. What's wrong?"

"It's about something I'm about to put into the mail."

"What is it?"

Jackson paused. "Jimmy, do you remember when the growth fund first came out? And I told you it was either going to make everybody a lot of money or cause everybody a lot of grief?"

Parker nodded. He'd found the comment amusing when he first heard it.

"Well, it looks like both predictions have come to pass," Jackson said. "It made a lot of money—for the brokers, and Graham and Pru-Bache. But now it's going to cause a lot of grief for everybody who invested in it."

Parker didn't understand. He knew that the growth fund was having troubles but knew none of the details. "Bob, what were you saying about the mail?"

Jackson then told him about his letter. He described how it all but accused the senior management of Graham Resources of conspiring to defraud investors. He said that he ended the letter by suggesting that Graham get out of the retail partnership business.

Parker listened quietly and injected only a few comments. Whatever the truth was about what was happening, he knew it was agonizing for Jackson. His friend made a very good living as a marketer for Graham Resources. For him to risk losing all that, the problems had to be serious.

"So I just want you to know in advance what I'm doing," Jackson said. "Until this gets resolved, one way or the other, I'm not going into the Prudential-Bache branches anymore. I'm not going to represent these products anymore. Not when I don't have any faith in them. And I just hope that you'll support me in this, as a friend."

Parker nodded. "Bob, of course I will. Look, based on what you said, I've already got my own serious doubts. But listen, I don't want to put my job on the line. I'm not going to go to New York and resign. I'm just going to quit selling the Graham products and support your efforts in however you want to go forward from here."

Jackson took a deep breath. "Thanks, Jimmy."

Parker and Jackson discussed what they should do next. Parker suggested that they go up to Gainesville to speak with Ernie Higbee, the biggest seller of the growth funds in all of Florida. Higbee had been so won over with the idea of the growth fund that he had handled some seminars on it. He even sang the praises of the fund at a regional meeting in Virginia. There he had told the brokers to "chuck" the prospectus after they read it.

When Parker and Jackson arrived in Gainesville, Higbee was off at his club, playing tennis. They drove there and wandered around the courts. Finally they spotted Higbee, playing a set with his wife. They waited off court until the game ended. Higbee walked over, mopping his brow with a towel. The three men sat down at a table next to the tennis court.

"Ernie, we're here because we have something we think you deserve to know," Jackson said. "Something has gone terribly wrong with the growth fund."

Higbee listened as Jackson described his concerns and how executives from Graham Resources were unable to answer his questions. He and Parker both said they were going to stop marketing the Graham products. They didn't want any more clients hurt.

Higbee picked up a glass and sipped a cool drink. Then he set it down. "Thank you both for coming forward on this," he said. "I really appreciate it."

"No problem, Ernie," Parker said.

Higbee took another sip. He let out a sigh. "You know, I put all my best customers into the growth fund. Every one of them I could persuade. Every one." He rubbed his fingers across his brow.

"Now it looks like I'm going to lose them all," he said. "Then they'll all probably sue me, too."

Higbee slowly shook his head and took another sip. "This just isn't right," he muttered. "Where was everybody?"

The surviving senior officers of the Direct Investment Group gathered somberly in the thirty-third-floor conference room. Once it had been the place where their victories were mapped out. Now it was the command center where they planned how to handle the sprawling disaster.

Proscia had taken charge after Darr's departure, but there was little he could do as the partnership empire crumbled. Among the other executives in the room were Frank Giordano, a lawyer who had worked for the department for years, and Mark Harper, the regional marketer for the Southwest.

The executives looked at a loss. It seemed as if each week another handful of the almost seven hundred partnerships sold by Prudential-Bache ran into serious problems. Nothing worked anymore. Damage control was the only remaining topic of concern. On this day in 1989, they were running through the latest of the emerging problems.

Harper rubbed his eyes, then looked at the group. "Guys, what we're trying to do here isn't working." He leaned in eagerly.

"Listen, perceived sins are forgiven if the perceived sinner admits fault and vows to do better. We need to think of that."

The others stared back blankly.

"Hey, this whole thing wasn't fraudulent, but there were some serious mistakes made that need to be rectified," Harper insisted.

Specifically, Harper said, it was clear that things had gone terribly wrong with all of the Graham partnerships and VMS, as well. There was no avoiding that liability.

"If we make restitution now, we could save hundreds of millions of dollars down the road," Harper continued. "We need to ask Prudential Insurance to step up to the table with a billion dollars and give the investors their money back with a rate of return. Just the amount of goodwill that would be saved would make it a bargain."

Harper stopped talking. For an instant, no one responded.

"You must be out of your mind," Giordano finally said. "You want us to go ask Prudential for a billion dollars? Just like that?" He snorted a laugh. "Let's get back to work and get serious."

Harper's suggestion was waved away. The senior officers never considered it again.

John Hutchison peeked over his shoulder before he started typing codes into the computer. He had all the necessary passwords to look into brokerage accounts, and today he had decided to satisfy his curiosity once and for all. He was going to call up Darr's account. He didn't care what was already in it. He wanted to know what had just been deposited.

Hutchison knew all about the payments from the partnerships that Darr had arranged for senior executives in the department. They were called "residuals." Every quarter, the checks were distributed. They weren't salary or bonus. Instead, the money was a share of the cash flow from all of the co–general partners, such as Prudential-Bache Energy Production.

Money coming out of the partnerships was going straight into the pockets of the people who put together the deals and sold them. At the same time, the customers who invested their savings in the partnerships saw nothing but losses.

The group that received the money was well known. Proscia and Pittman, of course. A number of marketers, as well. But what left Hutchison agog was the rumor that Darr had made these payments contractual and continued to receive them even though he had left the firm.

The checks had recently gone out, and Darr's would have been deposited in his brokerage account.

Hutchison finally found the account and typed the necessary codes. He watched the screen as the numbers scrolled past.

And then his mouth fell open.

$381,000.

Hutchison sat back, staring at the number flickering on his screen. In one quarter, Darr had received more than a quarter of a million dollars from partnerships he didn't invest a penny in.

The voices of all the screaming brokers ran through Hutchison's mind. So many people were going through anguish for having invested in Darr's partnerships.

And he's getting $381,000.

Hutchison signed off the computer and sat for a moment, staring at it.

If those payments weren't some sort of crime, then he felt sure that somebody needed to write a law.

"New York does the due diligence," Richard Sichenzio said to the crowd of brokers. "New York picks the products. And your job is to sell them. You're not supposed to examine them or ask questions about them. Just sell them."

A number of the brokers who had gathered at Manhattan's Waldorf-Astoria Hotel for a national sales conference shifted uncomfortably in their seats. Ever since taking over for Sherman, Sichenzio often expressed this attitude of "my way or the highway." Still, the brokers gathered for the opening-night event in October 1989 were stunned to hear a senior executive be so blunt. Particularly since so many of the products they had been told to sell blindly had blown clients away.

The event was unlike any other in the history of the Direct Investment Group. The conference focused on a single partnership, the Silver Screen Entertainment Fund. Over the years, Silver Screen Partners, the deal's general partner, had built up a reputation with its partnerships—mostly sold through Hutton and then Shearson—which financed a number of movies, including *Three Men and a Baby* and *Cocktail*. This time, Prudential-Bache had won Silver Screen's business for an ambitious partnership. The deal would invest money with Viacom Inc., the giant entertainment company, to finance programming on its Nickelodeon and MTV cable stations. It would make loans against art with Sotheby's, the art auction company. It would even acquire an interest in the Texas Rangers, the major-league baseball team.

The meeting was loaded with glamour. Executives from Viacom and Silver Screen were there. George W. Bush, the son of the president and one of the owners of the Texas Rangers, also attended to give a booster speech to the brokers selling this partnership for him. Sichenzio took personal charge of the sales meeting, predicting that $50 million worth of the Silver Screen partnership would be sold in a matter of months.

Sichenzio finished his speech to a polite smattering of applause. Whatever else might be said for it, the speech inspired a lot of discussion. But little of it was about Silver Screen. Instead, brokers and managers were still in shock from Sichenzio's insistence that none of them could question the judgments of New York. That one statement became the centerpiece of conversation.

At a table near the front of the room sat Joseph Haick, Sichenzio's top deputy. He was surrounded by a number of retail executives: Roger Parsons, the manager of the Baltimore office; Bill Mitchell, the manager in Washington, D.C.; Marvin Coble, the regional administrative director for the Southeast; and several other managers from Florida and Georgia. All of them discussed the speech, and Haick offered his own thoughts.

Parsons, who had a reputation for being direct, piped up with a question. "In light of what we just heard, is there a place for a manager in Prudential-Bache who just wants to do clean business, stay out of trouble, and keep the profitability up? That's all I want to do, even if it means not selling Prudential packaged products. Is there a place for me?"

Haick looked as if he might jump out of his skin. "What do you mean, is there a place?" he barked, sounding greatly agitated.

Parsons held up his hands. "Whoa, sorry," he said. "Let's talk about something else."

Haick leaned across the table toward Parsons. "No!" he snapped. "What do you mean? I want you to tell me what you mean by 'is there a place for me?' "

Parsons, nervous, started talking with his hands. "All I'm trying to ask, basically, is whether there is a place for someone to think for themselves. If they do what they think is right, can they still keep their job as a manager?"

Everyone at the table started talking. Haick looked furious. Parsons decided to rephrase his question one more time. This time, he would put it in the real context of what was actually happening at the firm.

"We've sold a lot of the packaged products that haven't worked out," he said. "Not only is that wrong, but it's bad business. It hurts the clients. It hurts the office. It hurts the manager. But Sichenzio is saying that we have to sell what New York puts out, no questions asked. So are there going to be any changes to deal with what has happened in the past when we didn't ask enough questions?"

Haick threw up his hands in exasperation. "What happened in the past has nothing to do with anything," he exclaimed. "What does this have to do with doing honest business?"

"Let me take a specific instance," Parsons replied. "If we just settle all the lawsuits on just one of the Riser products we sold, it would wipe out my branch's profitability. Sichenzio says we should sell these products without question. But when they fall apart, is New York going to pay for settling all the lawsuits? If not, it's going to come out of the branch's profits. That's where my bonus comes from. So I'm paying the price for things I'm not supposed to question."

Haick just shook his head in anger. "Why in the hell should we settle?"

Maybe because we sold it as safe at $10, and a few months later it's worth $2, Parsons thought.

"I've spoken to some of the firm's lawyers," he said. "They don't think there's a real defense here. They say we're just going to settle the cases."

Haick glared at him. "I don't want to talk about this. Why don't you just leave the table, and we'll discuss this at some other time?"

Parsons looked relieved. "I need to visit the restroom anyway," he said, standing up and heading out of the room. He took the hint and didn't come back.

The next morning, Parsons woke up early to make sure he would be on time for the sales meeting. He headed down to the hotel lobby, where he waited for transportation to Prudential-Bache headquarters. After a few minutes, Marvin Coble, the regional administrative manager for the Southeast, came down into the lobby and saw him. Coble walked over with a smile on his face.

"Very tactful last night," Coble said with a laugh.

Parsons didn't take it as funny. "Do you think I ought to be catching the early train back to Baltimore?"

"No," Coble said. "I found what you had to say interesting. I don't think it'll cause you any trouble."

Later that day, Parsons was waiting in the firm's auditorium for the sales meeting to begin when he saw Marvin Coble heading toward him.

"Roger, I need you to come with me," Coble said.

Parsons stood up and started to follow Coble.

Coble stopped. "No, Roger," he said. "Bring all your stuff."

Parsons scooped up his belongings and trailed Coble out of the auditorium. Coble escorted Parsons to another room and told him that Michael McClain, the regional administrator for the Southeast, wanted to speak to him.

"Looks like you were wrong about last night," Parsons said.

Coble shook his head. "I don't know what's going on."

In a few minutes, Parsons sat down in front of McClain.

"Joe Haick is very upset about what happened last night," McClain said. "He doesn't want you at the meeting. He wants you to go home and not go back to the office."

Parsons felt his stomach drop. "Mike," he asked softly, "am I being fired?"

"I really don't know, Roger," McClain said. "Joe said to go home and think about it."

Parsons went home. He wasn't allowed back into the office for several weeks. Finally he called McClain and heard the bad news: Haick wanted Parsons removed as a manager.

Parsons hung up the phone in shock. He had lost his job—just for asking if there was a place at Prudential-Bache for an honest manager. Just for implying that New York's due diligence needed to be challenged. Just for suggesting that there were serious problems. The word of what happened spread through the retail branches like wildfire. For many managers, Parsons's fate reinforced New York's theme: *It's my way or the highway.* Either they make sure their brokers sell in-house investment products, or they leave the firm.

A few weeks later, on November 14, 1989, the full truth about the sloppiness of Prudential-Bache's due diligence finally became undeniable.

On that day, VMS, the sponsor of the Mortgage Investment Fund, announced that it was "experiencing liquidity problems" in its operations. It would have to start selling real estate to obtain cash for financing its business. Although senior executives with the company protested that they were not filing for bankruptcy anytime soon, it was apparent that VMS might well go belly-up.

The truth was unmistakable to brokers throughout Prudential-Bache. VMS, whose most recent product had been deemed so safe by the firm that sales were concentrated on retirees and other risk-averse investors, was about to go under. It had been only seven months since the Mortgage Investors Fund started trading. All of these problems had to have been there from the start. The people in New York either missed the problems or, worse, just ignored them.

In Los Angeles, Bill Creedon read the announcement from VMS in dismay. Shares in the fund sank like a rock. In just one trading session after the announcement, they lost close to 20 percent of their remaining value, closing at $5.50.

Like most brokers at Pru-Bache who had been deceived into selling the Mortgage Investment Fund, Creedon was dazed. His telephone started ringing immediately. Customers were demanding to know what was happening with their life savings.

Whatever happened from here, Creedon knew one thing. He was going to fight for his customers to make sure that Prudential-Bache did right by them. He wanted them compensated for the fraud they had suffered. And at that moment, he knew that he would do whatever it took to make sure that happened. Whatever it took.

By December 1989, the problems with the Riser investments had blown up into a full-scale disaster. The potential liability of Prudential-Bache appeared to be in excess of $150 million. The firm's law department analyzed the situation and informed some managers and brokers that they were going to recommend settling the cases with clients. But the senior management of Pru-Bache would hear nothing of it. No one was going to receive a settlement. The firm had to play hardball.

Eugene Boyle, a broker with the Prudential-Bache branch in Wayne, New Jersey, watched the evolution of the Riser situation with great dismay. He had placed about $1.5 million of his clients' savings into the investment. He had believed the firm's assurances about their safety. When the losses mounted, Boyle felt confident that the firm would do the right thing and settle with the defrauded clients. One of the firm's lawyers even told him that the Risers case was virtually indefensible.

Then, early that month, Boyle heard that everything had changed. Carlos Ricca, a Pru-Bache lawyer in New York, told Boyle in a telephone call that the firm's senior management had decided to disregard the department's recommendations and not settle the Riser claims. As Boyle understood it, the firm believed that putting up a fight might discourage some clients from pressing their claims. And the ones who did get a lawyer would be more likely to settle for less if they knew the firm planned to battle them all the way. After all, Prudential-Bache had more money to pay for lawyers than any of its clients did.

Boyle was appalled. The strategy struck him as the most immoral thing he had heard in all his years as a broker.

"Carlos, I wouldn't be able to tolerate that," Boyle said. "If that's the way the firm wants to handle it, then I would have to recommend that my clients find lawyers. Then I'm going to have to cooperate with their lawyers in the cases against the firm. It's my duty to make sure they get back as much money as they're owed."

Ricca paused for an instant. "You do that, Gene, and Pru-Bache will not only fire you," he said, "but then we're going to tie you up in court for seventeen years."[*]

The next day, Boyle wrote a letter to his manager, telling him that the plans Ricca had described were compelling him to resign.

After the conversation, "I was faced with the dilemma of choosing between my firm and my clients," Boyle wrote. "In all good conscience, I cannot stand by passively on the sidelines and watch my clients try to fend for themselves, when I know what the real issues are and I know how indefensible the firm's position really is."

Within a few months, Prudential-Bache appeared to be living up to Ricca's threat. A number of written complaints had been submitted to the firm before Boyle's departure. All of them chastised Pru-Bache, and none made claims against Boyle. In fact, some of the submissions actually praised Boyle for his assistance.

But Prudential-Bache reported the matter somewhat differently on Boyle's permanent record, maintained by the National Association of Securities Dealers. The firm said that the claims were submitted against *Boyle*,

---

[*] Ricca denies making this statement. See Notes and Sources.

who was alleged to have deceived the clients about the Risers. Boyle learned of the firm's false statement when he was informed that he was under investigation by the New York Stock Exchange because of the claims. It would take months for him to be cleared.

To the brokers of Prudential-Bache, the message was clear: Don't take on the firm.

It was a critical message for senior officers to convey. Controversy could smudge the firm's image. A bad image might cut the price Pru-Bache could fetch if it was sold. And at that moment, the firm, in whole and in part, was secretly on the block.

By 1989, the Blackstone Group was one of the most respected of the boutique investment banks sprouting up all over Wall Street. The firm was founded a few years before by Peter G. Peterson, the former chairman of Lehman Brothers, along with one of his Lehman colleagues, Stephen Schwarzman. Whenever a company was being shopped, there was a good chance some information about the proposed deal would pass across the desks at Blackstone.

That year, Schwarzman received a telephone call from one of his fellow investment bankers at Lazard Frères & Company. The Lazard banker had a proposal: Would Blackstone be interested in buying the arbitrage department of Prudential-Bache?

Schwarzman rejected the offer out of hand. He didn't even ask to see any documents on the proposal. He hung up and thought nothing of the call. So Prudential Insurance was trying to sell pieces of its brokerage firm. That came as no surprise. It was Wall Street's worst-kept secret. After seeing Pru-Bache racked by a decade of losses, Prudential Insurance would be remiss if it didn't try something new.

In truth, the attempt to sell pieces of the firm was only the beginning. Prudential Insurance finally was launching a full-scale attempt to turn its huge losses around. It had even set up negotiations with a competitor, Paine Webber, about merging the two brokerage firms. Prudential Insurance wanted out—if not of the whole business, then at least a large part of it.

George Ball set a thirty-seven-page document down on his desk. At that point, in January 1990, it was the most secret set of papers in all of Prudential-Bache. Ball had demanded that the document be written. Only a small handful of his most trusted executives knew about it. Ball was pleased with the results. In a document just an inch thick, every important financial detail about Prudential-Bache was laid out.

Ball thought it was an excellent private investment memorandum. On its cover, the document was simply called an "information package." Regardless of its name, the document meant one thing: George Ball was trying to find new investors for Prudential-Bache. He wanted some financial institutions to take over part of the role being played by Prudential Insurance. After reviewing the potential candidates with his trusted advisers, they decided to send the document to a few German and Swiss banks that would be likely candidates for investing in a brokerage house. If any of the banks were interested, the firm would send them more information. Otherwise, the recipients had to return the document to Prudential-Bache or destroy it. The last thing Ball wanted was to have extra copies floating around.

The information package had high praise for the performance of the firm—it described Prudential-Bache as "the largest sponsor of public limited partnerships in the U.S."—but failed to mention the investor losses. It ignored the monstrous, unrealized liabilities that were washing up relentlessly. In essence, it told nothing of the firm's unfolding disaster.

Ball's attempt to find a new outside investor for Prudential-Bache had all the earmarks of a last-ditch effort to stave off the inevitable. Prudential Insurance had injected well over $1 billion into the firm during his reign. All the Pru had to show for it was the endless stream of losses. Although the Direct Investment Group had pulled in money, overall the firm just seemed to hemorrhage cash. Ball's credibility in Newark was suffering greatly. Some executives believed Ball hoped another investor would lessen the financial pressure on Prudential Insurance. Apparently he was hoping to create a new master and save his job. And the evidence was growing that his time was running out.

Ball had heard rumors that the executives in Newark were trying to sell Prudential-Bache. He even heard that Lazard Frères had been retained for the job. He worried that Prudential Insurance might be getting ready to dump the firm and walk away.

But he felt better after speaking with Garnett Keith and Bob Winters, Prudential's chairman. He told them about the Lazard rumor he had heard and asked if it was true. Both Keith and Winters told Ball not to worry. He still had the full confidence of Prudential. There was nothing to these rumors about Lazard, they told him.

Meanwhile, Lazard continued contacting prospective buyers.

Just four weeks after the information package had been sent to the German and Swiss banks, the whole effort seemed to have been a bust. Not a single positive response came back. After copies of the packet were returned from all over the world, Ball tried a new tack.

On February 7, 1990, he met with Jean-Louis Lalogeais, a respected specialist on the securities industry who worked with Booz, Allen & Hamilton, a consulting firm. The time had come for action, Ball told Lalogeais. Prudential-Bache had to focus on its core businesses. The noncore businesses had to be profitable, or else they would be cut off.

With that, Ball began discussing the entire portfolio of the firm's businesses, labeling each as either "core" or "not core." He listed retail sales, risk arbitrage, merchant banking, and equity underwriting as core businesses. But he also ticked off the names of some businesses that he clearly thought would soon be going by the wayside if they didn't make money: public finance, investment-grade debt, foreign exchange. At one point, Ball made a statement that turned around the attitude of the last decade and signaled the failure of one of his central strategies.

"Direct investments," Ball said. "Not core."

Sichenzio called the emergency meeting of the Direct Investment Group on a February afternoon. No one knew what it was about. The executives in New York were told to meet in a special auditorium that had microphones and a speaker system hooked up to telephone lines. All the marketers in the field were to attend by conference call. They would hear everything through the communications system.

Most of the executives arrived a few minutes early and took seats around a twenty-foot conference table. At the appointed time, Sichenzio walked into the room. He looked angry, but no one thought much of it. Sichenzio usually looked angry.

There were some changes coming in the Direct Investment Group, Sichenzio said. Paul Proscia was out as head of the department. Frank Giordano, the lawyer, was taking over. But the real shocker came next.

"Effective today, the Silver Screen deal is pulled," Sichenzio said. "It's no longer consistent with the firm's marketing plans. It's a difficult sell, and we've got better things to do with our time."

No one knew what to say. Almost the entire department was working on that deal. The firm had a contract to sell it. Under the direction of the Direct Investment Group, Silver Screen had spent $3 million marketing the partnership to the firm's brokers. Then, boom, it was dead. What was going on?

David Wrubel, who had joined the department two years earlier, looked at Sichenzio with contempt. Wrubel was relatively close to Tom Bernstein and Roland Betts, the top principals of Silver Screen. Bernstein had been complaining bitterly to Wrubel about Prudential-Bache. He was used to being treated like a gentleman when he did deals with other firms, Bernstein had told him, but Pru-Bache just treated him like some pocket there to be picked.

I'll bet they don't even know at Silver Screen, Wrubel thought. *I bet you haven't even told them, 'cause you're such chickenshits.*

The meeting ended, and Wrubel raced out of the room. As soon as he found a phone, he called Bernstein at Silver Screen. He told Bernstein's secretary to pull him out of a meeting.

"Listen, I can't talk long," Wrubel said. "We just had a meeting. They pulled the deal. Have they told you?"

"What are you talking about?"

Wrubel explained about the emergency meeting and what Sichenzio had said. "It's a lame excuse," Wrubel said. "Something else is going on. But I can't talk to you now about it."

Bernstein said he would call Wrubel at his home later.

Within a few minutes, sometime after 4:00 P.M., Sichenzio called the senior executives of Silver Screen.

"This offering will not get done at Prudential-Bache," he said.

The Silver Screen executives demanded that Sichenzio tell them how the termination could be justified given their contract.

"You agreed to sell this," one of the executives said. "You signed a binding contract. We spent $3 million to market this based on that assurance. How can you just come along and shut it down?"

Finally Sichenzio offered a new explanation for what was happening.

"We're getting a lot of adverse publicity about what happened with VMS," he said. "And we've heard that *Business Week* is putting together some article criticizing all of our real estate partnerships. We have to pull the deal."

The Silver Screen executives angrily argued that none of this had anything to do with their deal, but Sichenzio could not be budged. It didn't matter if Prudential-Bache had given its word to sell the deal, both morally and legally. Bad publicity was more important. The Direct Investment Group had to take a low profile.

By early 1990, Boyd Page's legal practice in Atlanta was centered largely on suing Prudential-Bache for the Risers problem. Page had found dozens of clients who had lost huge sums of money investing in the mortgage products. Some of them had true horror stories, like Gail and Michael Parks, who lost about $79,000, almost their entire portfolio. About half of that money had been insurance proceeds from the death of Gail's brother, and it had been held in trust for her young niece's education. Now almost all of it was gone.

At first, it seemed as if Prudential-Bache might have been willing to settle some of the cases. Early on, Page had invited lawyers from the firm down to his office so that they could review the documents he had uncovered from months of investigation. He thought the information was damaging enough that the firm would quickly throw in the towel.

After the Pru-Bache lawyers finished their document review, Page gave them two months to respond. They never did. So he began filing his claims.

In February 1990, Page was sitting at his desk when his secretary buzzed in. He had a telephone call.

"It's Chuck Hawkins from *Business Week*," his secretary said.

Page picked up the telephone, and Hawkins identified himself. He was the Atlanta bureau chief of the weekly business magazine. Hawkins told Page that he was working on an article about the huge losses being suffered by investors in real estate deals pushed by Prudential-Bache, from VMS to Risers to others.

"Well, what can I do to help you?" Page asked.

Hawkins asked a number of questions. Page shared all the information he knew about the Risers situation, even telling Hawkins that the firm's own lawyers had predicted the exposure on the mortgage investments alone was $175 million.

"The word we get is that Ball has decided not to address the Risers problem," Page said. "If he takes a hit, it's his job. From what I hear, I think they want to settle this at ten cents on the dollar."

But, Page said, given everything he had learned, the Risers problem paled compared to the troubles in the firm's partnerships. "Long term, the greatest threat to Bache is direct investments."

Hawkins wrapped up his interview with one last question. "Are there any clients that you have who would be willing to talk to me about what they experienced?"

Page thought he knew the perfect people: Gail and Michael Parks. Prudential-Bache had been dragging its feet on their case. Maybe a little publicity would move things along.

"I don't know, but maybe," Page said. "Let me check and I'll get back to you."

The *Business Week* article in late February brought national fame to Boyd Page and his Risers cases. His clients, the Parks, were featured in a photograph looking forlorn above the headline "How Pushing Real Estate Backfired on Pru-Bache." Page was quoted about the $175 million exposure that Prudential-Bache faced on the Risers, a number that Schechter was quoted as calling "completely untrue."

Page liked the way the article turned out. He was now one of the national experts, as far as reporters were concerned, on Risers and Prudential-Bache. Lawyers around the country were contacting him for his advice and assistance in bringing similar cases against the firm.

Weeks after the article appeared, Page received a visit from Joel Bernstein, Sanford Kantor, and Irene Siegel, three New York lawyers who were pursuing Risers cases themselves. Page agreed to share some information with them about his cases. The four lawyers went out to lunch at Trio's, a restaurant next door to Page's office. There they discussed the legal issues of the cases for more than an hour.

As they returned to Page & Bacek, laughing as they stepped into the lobby, Donald Bacek, Page's law partner, emerged from his office looking serious. He hurried toward the group with a small sheaf of papers in his hand.

"You're not going to believe this," Bacek said, handing the papers to Page.

Page looked at the cover sheet, then flipped to the first page. It was a claim that had just been filed in federal court in Atlanta. Page read the caption on the case, then read it again.

"*Prudential-Bache Securities Inc.* v. *Page & Bacek.*"

The lawsuit, which had been approved for filing by Loren Schechter, accused Page of conspiring to subvert Prudential-Bache business by encouraging its customers to sue the firm. It claimed that Page, like some legal Svengali, was single-handedly undermining the confidence of Pru-Bache employees in the firm and encouraging them to steal confidential, proprietary documents that he then used in litigation.

Apparently the *Business Week* story had struck a nerve. Prudential-

Bache was stepping up its legal hardball several notches. Schechter had adopted the strategy that the best defense was a good offense. If clients insisted on suing the firm, then Pru-Bache would bury their lawyers with litigation. The more time Boyd Page spent defending himself in court, the less time he could spend attacking Prudential-Bache.

Page read through each page carefully. "Well, I'll be damned," he said softly.

"This is the most outrageous thing I've ever seen in my life," Bernstein said. "Who do these people think they are?"

Page looked up at the astonished lawyers. "Well, what do we do now?"

Fridays had become tense at the Direct Investment Group ever since word first came out that Giordano would be taking over. Everyone knew the end was coming. Big layoffs would almost certainly occur on the last day of the week, when a pay period closed. The department was loaded with the condemned, all readying themselves for execution. The days of big sales were over. The only question was who would be thrown out, and when.

Giordano took over on March 8. Within a few weeks, he began dismantling virtually the entire department. The layoffs continued for months. The regional marketers heard the news from Giordano by conference call.

"I'm calling to let all of you know that Pru-Bache has decided that direct investments no longer fit into the marketing plans and they are proceeding to dissolve the department," he told the stunned group over the phone. "You are all being terminated."

Before they left, all of the marketers were instructed to pack up the marketing materials and other documents they had collected over the years and ship them to New York, where they were turned over to the firm's lawyers.

The dismissals in New York were swift. Anyone who was fired was barred from returning to the office. Even Bill Pittman, who was fired in the spring of 1990, was listed with the security department as someone to be stopped in the lobby.

David Wrubel heard about his termination directly from Giordano. To a degree, he felt relieved. For months, he had been handling some communication with brokers, and their anguish was beginning to get to him.

Afterward, Wrubel headed out of his office and down the hallway on the thirty-third floor. He saw Russell Labrasca, who months earlier had been named national sales manager of the department. He was sitting in his glass-walled office, tears streaming down his face. He looked as if his world had come to an end.

Wrubel hated Labrasca's public display and thought it was unprofessional. He walked into Labrasca's office.

"Hey, Russ," he said. "What's the matter with you?"

Labrasca sniffled. "This is so sad," Labrasca said as the tears kept pouring out. "This was such a wonderful place, and we accomplished so much. There'll never be anything like it again, with the camaraderie and the teamwork and the spirit."

Wrubel's face wrinkled in disgust. He had been in the department only two years but had seen a lifetime's worth of unprofessionalism and incompetence. He'd seen the wild excesses of spending. He knew how little anyone cared about protecting investors and doing deals properly. He thought everything Labrasca said was a total crock.

"Give me a break, Russ," Wrubel said. "This was bullshit. That's all it ever was."

CHAPTER 16

BY THE SPRING OF 1990, brokers and executives throughout Prudential-Bache were ready to choose sides. Responsible brokers desperately wanted to salvage their customers' floundering finances. The Prudential-Bache law department wanted a united front, with the brokers lined up with the firm against their own clients. There were no recordings of what the brokers had said to the clients when they had persuaded them to buy the partnerships and other failed investments. Just because the marketing material made fraudulent claims didn't mean the sales force used that material, the argument went. Somewhere in the thick prospectuses for the investments were convoluted warnings about risk. That would be the defense. With the prospectus as a shield, Prudential-Bache hoped it could eliminate most of its massive liability.

Throughout the country, brokers were facing the choice of defending Prudential-Bache or risking their careers by fighting on behalf of their clients. A modern-day battle was quietly unfolding with many Davids against a single Goliath.

Bill Creedon felt disgusted as he read a copy of a letter that had been sent to his clients by the Prudential-Bache law department. For months, the Los Angeles stockbroker had followed the recommendations of the firm's lawyers and helped his clients write letters about their VMS investments. The letters laid out what the clients had been told about the guarantees, as well as their investment objectives, their ages, and other relevant information. Creedon thought the letters would be reviewed and then settlements offered. After all, the clients had been sold a supposedly guaranteed investment for $10 a share, and now it was trading for fifty cents. The case was a sure loser.

Starting in late April, his clients began calling him in dismay. They had received letters in response from the law department expressing regret at their dissatisfaction but saying that the firm could not offer certainty on an investment. Creedon fumed—that was exactly what Pru-Bache *had* done with all that talk about viable guarantees.

But it was one of the last paragraphs of the letter that Creedon found most noxious. A class-action suit had been filed in Chicago on behalf of VMS investors. The law department's letter told the investors all about the class action and even provided the case number. Reading it, Creedon felt certain that Prudential-Bache was trying to push everyone it could into the class-action suit.

Although investors might not know what that meant, Creedon was sure that the law department did. It was a despicable move. Anyone who didn't take the class action could sue the firm individually. Those investors not only had the opportunity to get all of their money back, plus interest, but they also could win punitive damages.

On the other hand, too many class-action lawyers in serious securities fraud cases behave in ways that make ambulance chasers look like the backbone of the bar. Few of the lawyers take any class actions to trial. Instead, they almost always settle for a few pennies on the dollar. Investors who lost tens of thousands of dollars usually receive a few hundred back. But the lawyers, who take as much as 35 percent of the total settlement, can walk away with millions for very little work. Creedon knew that the only people who would benefit from a class-action sellout on VMS would be the lawyers and Prudential-Bache itself, which would obliterate its huge liability for a small settlement.

Some brokers and managers around Pru-Bache's office greeted the law department's response as a stroke of genius. It was laughingly called "the fuck-you letter." Some brokers particularly liked the class-action angle. If clients sued individually, those complaints would likely show up on the brokers' permanent records. But class-action settlements never do.

Creedon got up from his desk and headed toward the office of his manager, John Eisle.

"John, I'm really concerned about something here," Creedon said. "I'd been told that all the clients' cases were going to be looked at on an individual basis, but now they're all getting form-letter brush-offs."

"This is how we're going to handle this," Eisle said. "The clients are going to go into the class-action suit. That's how this problem is going to be taken care of."

Creedon started voicing concerns about pushing clients toward the class action, but Eisle cut him off.

"Look, this is how we're dealing with this, and it's none of your business," he said. "You're spending far too much time worrying about this."

"John, it *is* my business. It's my clients that are being hurt."

"Well, then stop being so concerned about these clients and go find some new ones," Eisle replied.

Creedon didn't know how to respond. Apparently the firm was prepared to let elderly investors around the country take the hit for the VMS duplicity. At that moment, his confidence in the integrity of Prudential-Bache evaporated.

"Look, John, I think Prudential is making a big mistake here," he said. "They're handling this all wrong. All they're going to do is piss everybody off. Everybody knows what really happened here. There's a lot to be gained by being upright and standing behind something when you sell it."

"Well, that's because you're focusing too much on this," Eisle said. "Go find new clients. And with your old clients, the only thing you can talk with them about is the class-action suit. Other than that, you should really stop talking to them."

Creedon stared at Eisle for an instant, unsure of what to say. He was hearing the same instructions that were being delivered to brokers around the country: Betray your clients, sell them out, get new ones.* The broker would emerge unscathed, and the firm would be protected.

Within weeks, Creedon began receiving desperate telephone calls from investors asking what to do. As a test, he referred them to Eisle, his manager. Each time, the investors came back saying that Eisle had told them their only option was joining the class action. Creedon quietly told them to check that claim out with their own lawyers.

In the late summer, clients started to call Creedon asking for his advice about the class-action suit and other legal rights they might have. Creedon said he would have to call them back, and walked down the hall again to visit with Eisle.

"John, my clients are very uncomfortable with the class-action idea," he said. "They want to know what other options they have. I want to fully disclose their rights. Let them know they can go to arbitration, or at the very least tell them to talk to a lawyer. I think I have a fiduciary duty to do that."

Eisle pointed his finger at Creedon and began jabbing it as he spoke.

* Prudential Securities denies that it ever attempted to herd investors into class-action suits and denies that Eisle ever suggested that be done. See Notes and Sources.

"If you dare tell your clients about their legal options, you will be fired," he snapped. "Do you understand? You will lose your job and that will be the end of that."

Eisle stood up from his desk and walked up close to Creedon. "And don't think you can sneak around me either. If a bunch of your clients start showing up with attorneys, you'll still be fired. So sit down and keep quiet."

Creedon stared straight at Eisle. "This is wrong, John," he said, "and I can't do it. I think you and the firm are making a big mistake."

Creedon spun around and stormed out of Eisle's office. In his mind, his job was over. If he couldn't help his clients while working at Prudential-Bache, then he would have to quit. It was the same decision Gene Boyle had made over Risers a few months earlier.

The wall of silence was falling, one broker at a time. But the most important defection was yet to come. It was the one that would begin to expose the secrets of Graham Resources.

The Four Seasons Hotel was one of the most popular lunch spots for the brokers in Prudential-Bache's Houston branch. Besides the image of elegance that the name projected, the hotel's restaurant, with its buffet luncheons, was conducive to one-on-one business meetings. Better still, the Four Seasons was directly across the street. Brokers could get there from the branch by walking through an underground tunnel, without going outside. With Houston's blistering summers, that alone would have made it popular.

In August 1990, Joe Siff, a broker in the office, decided that the Four Seasons would be the perfect place for a lunch meeting with one of his clients, Daryl Bristow, a prominent Houston lawyer. Siff hoped to spend the lunch discussing some investment ideas.

Siff arrived at the Four Seasons with anxiety clearly evident on his face. He had sold more Graham partnerships than almost any broker at Prudential-Bache. He had believed everything he had read in the marketing material and thought that the partnerships were safe, secure investments. He had been particularly enamored with the growth funds, and had persuaded many of his clients to purchase those partnerships. But when distributions went down even as oil prices went up, Siff had begun to believe that something had gone terribly wrong. Half of Siff's day was spent answering questions about why the partnerships were not performing as

SERPENT ON THE ROCK

projected. Many of his clients, including some of his most important ones, refused to do business with him anymore.

Bristow arrived shortly after Siff found a table. They chatted for a few minutes and headed for the buffet. Bristow could see that something was disturbing Siff. They returned to their table, plates full, and Siff asked a few questions about Bristow's law practice. The lawyer mentioned with obvious pride some cases he had recently won for plaintiffs. Then he asked Siff how his business was going.

"I'm drowning," Siff said. "A lot of my day is spent taking questions from clients. And I can't get answers for them. They want to know why their partnership investments are doing so badly."

"Well, what do you tell them?" Bristow asked.

"To be honest, I don't have an answer. Every time I try to get one from the people at Prudential-Bache, or from the general partners, all I hear is a lot of double-talk. No one's being straight."

Bristow just listened. Siff could already see the wheels starting to turn.

"And, Daryl, it's not just me," Siff said. "I'm talking to brokers all over the country who are having the exact same experience. My only asset is the time in my working day. And, by not answering my questions, that's being usurped by the very management that's supposed to be supporting me. All they're doing is undermining me."

Siff knew that he sounded as if he were whining. But he didn't care. This was the first chance he'd had to get his frustrations off his chest. After a few minutes, Bristow looked at him with a deadly serious expression.

"Joe, it sounds to me like you need to decide who you work for," Bristow said.

"What do you mean?"

"You need to decide if you work for the firm, or if you work for your clients."

For an instant, Siff felt a little offended. "Well, you're one of my clients," he said. "Who do you think I work for?"

"I know what the answer is, but I don't think you've thought about the question."

"I think about it every waking moment of my business day. I'm working as hard as I can."

"That's right, Joe," Bristow said. "You're working so hard for your clients that you're going to have to leave the firm."

Bristow's words were like a splash of cold water. Until that moment, Siff had always considered himself a loyal company man. He had worked at the firm since 1979, when it was just plain old Bache. He'd ridden through the silver crisis, the Prudential purchase, the Capt. Crab scandal, and he always came out still loving the firm. But Bristow's words made him realize that he had finally reached the end. If he was going to help his clients, he had to leave.

"You know, Daryl, a lot of my clients know that I have a lot of lawyers in my client base," Siff said. "They ask me sometimes if I can recommend a lawyer to them. Would you mind in the future if I gave them your name?"

"Not at all."

Siff looked down at his food and thought for a moment. "One other thing, Daryl."

"Yes?"

"Would you represent me? I think I'm going to need some help. Something really rotten is happening here, and I don't want to get hurt."

Bristow smiled. "Of course I'll represent you, Joe."

The luncheon meeting at the Four Seasons set off a snowball effect. Over the next few weeks, Siff referred a number of his clients who had invested in the Graham partnerships to Bristow. In turn, he showed his new lawyer certain marketing materials the firm had distributed.

Bristow took the information to one of his partners, Stephen Hackerman, a lanky, soft-spoken Texan with a talent for digging through financial records. Based on their conversations with Siff's clients, as well as a review of the documents, they decided to focus their investigation solely on the energy growth funds. Those partnerships seemed like a much clearer case of fraud, and Bristow did not want to bite off more than his firm could chew.

About the same time, Siff received a telephone call from William Webb, another big seller of Graham partnerships. Webb, who worked in the Prudential-Bache branch in Fort Myers, Florida, told Siff that he needed help. For years, ever since the fraud in the growth funds became evident to him, Webb had secretly been telling his clients to seek legal advice from a New Orleans law firm called Adams & Reese. He hoped that the lawyers there would use his clients to launch sweeping litigation that would crack open the secrets of the growth funds. But nothing seemed to be happening. He wanted to find a new law firm.

Webb told Siff that he needed lawyers for his clients and himself. Siff set up a conference call with Bristow. By the end of the call, Webb agreed to recommend the Houston law firm to his clients. He also agreed to retain Bristow himself. After all, by destroying his client base, Prudential-Bache had defrauded him, too.

With Bill Webb, Bristow obtained a critical advantage. Not only did the broker have one of the largest number of clients invested in the growth fund, but he had been collecting documents on the partnerships since he first became suspicious in 1988. He was a walking warehouse of evidence and plaintiffs.

After looking over Webb's evidence, Bristow and Hackerman thought they had a great case on the growth fund. But they needed more information about Prudential-Bache itself. They had heard about a lawyer in Atlanta named Boyd Page who had a reputation as a nemesis of the firm. In mid-1990, Hackerman decided to place a call to Page. Maybe, Hackerman thought, Page might be able to help out. Maybe they could even join forces.

Getting sued by Prudential-Bache was one of the best things that ever happened to Page & Bacek. The news of the lawsuit had been reported in some brokerage industry newsletters. Within a few weeks, the floodgates opened. Scores of Pru-Bache brokers and executives, most of whom would have never heard of the small Atlanta law firm, began contacting Boyd Page. Documents were arriving by the carton. Almost every day, Page had new, previously unknown evidence of wrongdoing at the brokerage firm. It was as if by suing the law firm, Prudential-Bache had placed a stamp of approval on Page & Bacek for the hundreds of bitter, angry brokers and managers who no longer trusted their superiors. Schechter's foolish legal strategy had transformed Page & Bacek from an annoyance into a national clearinghouse for damaging information about Prudential-Bache.

Even better, the lawsuit itself was proving to be a joke. One of its big claims was that Page had damaged Pru-Bache's reputation. But with all the evidence Page had found of crimes and fraud in the Direct Investment Group, it was clear by the fall of 1990 that the firm's reputation deserved to be far worse than it was. Page & Bacek countersued, charging that the original lawsuit was part of a racketeering conspiracy by Prudential-Bache to cover up its dark past.

Prudential-Bache's lawyers spent months trying to find out what Page knew by seeking access to his documents and by deposing members of his firm. It was all largely a waste of time. The lawyers walked away with only a small number of documents, and the depositions provided little helpful information.

Then it was Page's turn to start taking statements. Notices for depositions were delivered to midlevel members of the law department as well as a number of senior officers of the firm, including Schechter and Ball.

On October 9, 1990, Schechter flew down to Atlanta for his deposition. It started at 5:00 P.M. Over the next two and a half hours, as he was questioned by William Sumner, the lawyer representing Page & Bacek, Schechter would learn that Page had uncovered some of the dirtiest secrets of Prudential-Bache.

Sumner produced a document that showed that Pru-Bache was paying someone involved in the case, even though he did not work for the firm. Under questioning, Schechter said that he personally had authorized the payments as part of a consulting agreement. The questions roved through a number of details about Risers and about personnel problems at the firm.

Then the bombshells started dropping, one at a time.

"Who is James J. Darr?" Sumner asked.

Schechter provided some background about Darr. Sumner then moved on to some questions about Sherman. It seemed he was done with that sensitive topic.

Then it came back.

"Have you ever had the occasion to investigate Mr. Darr's business relationship with the First South Savings & Loan of Arkansas?" Sumner asked.

"I believe so," Schechter said. "At one point in time, I directed an inquiry be made into Mr. Darr's relationship with that institution."

Sumner produced certified copies of Darr's first and second mortgages from First South. Schechter looked at them and said he had never seen them before.

"What was the conclusion of your investigation into the relationship between Mr. Darr and First South?"

Schechter said that he had the matter investigated and that nothing improper had been found in the mortgages.*

"Have you ever received any information concerning the payment of

---

* Schechter was referring to the Locke Purnell report. Although the report found nothing improper about the mortgages, it also barely touched on them. It did not mention First South by name and went no further in discussing the mortgages than describing what was said in the anonymous telephone calls engineered by Curtis Henry.

monies to Mr. Darr by First South S&L by virtue of the refinancing of his home?" Sumner asked.

Schechter replied that he only knew that Darr had a mortgage.

"Well, does Prudential-Bache intend to file suit against Mr. Darr or Mr. Sherman?" Sumner asked.

Schechter said no. With that, the deposition came to an end.

A week later, just before the scheduled deposition of George Ball, the case was settled. Page & Bacek walked away with pocketfuls of cash. Prudential-Bache required that the terms of the settlement forever remain secret.

The first picket sign from a partnership investor outside of Prudential-Bache's Manhattan headquarters came in November 1990. Newspaper reporters and television cameramen crowded the sidewalk outside the building as they interviewed the protester, Eloise Burg, a sixty-one-year-old Florida widow. Burg had lost more than $600,000 in limited partnership investments. But unlike some of her fellow investors who suffered their losses quietly, she refused to stay silent. Instead, she walked back and forth on the sidewalk outside the firm, carrying a sign that read "Prudential-Bache has financially and immorally raped me. Investors beware!"

Burg told reporters her story again and again. She had invested the money her husband left her and asked for safety. She had been pushed into limited partnerships and lost most of it. When she made a claim against the firm, an arbitration panel awarded her only $45,000. She complained to the firm, but executives there would hear none of it. As far as they were concerned, the case was closed.

With her protest, Burg accomplished something that few other people had: She forced reporters from a range of newspapers and television stations to finally tell part of the story from the partnership debacle. Her protest was widely covered in the East Coast press, appearing in the *New York Post*, the *Daily News*, and a number of Florida newspapers. The story went national when the *Wall Street Journal* reported it. Investors who might not have seen Burg in the newspaper had the chance to catch her on television after Cable News Network videotaped her protest for its *Moneyline* program. She vowed repeatedly not to rest until Prudential-Bache returned all of her money.

In interviews, Pru-Bache executives attempted to play down the controversy Burg was setting off. Schechter dismissed her as part of a "vocal minority" among the firm's huge number of investors. Still, when executives attempted to persuade her to come inside to talk, she refused.

Instead, she continued her picketing, and the matter became a fight in the press between her and Prudential-Bache. She said that her broker had told her the partnerships were as safe as certificates of deposit. The firm announced that the broker denied saying that.

Eventually the pressure on Prudential-Bache became too great. After several months of protesting, Burg was invited to visit with Schechter personally. He offered her full restitution. The picket in front of the firm immediately disappeared, as did the terrible publicity. It seemed like Prudential-Bache got its money's worth.

Steve Hackerman's decision to call Boyd Page had paid off. The two law firms began swapping documents, helping them both fill in a number of evidentiary holes. By the fall of 1990, Page had teamed up with Hackerman and Daryl Bristow to represent more than two hundred clients in litigation against Prudential Securities. With their combined information, they knew more about the frauds that had emerged from the Direct Investment Group than almost anyone in the country.

At the same time, Bristow and Hackerman pursued the growth fund litigation, filing suit on behalf of a client for access to the partnership investor lists. Even though, under the partnership agreements, the lists had to be turned over on an investor's request, Prudential-Bache refused. The firm knew that with those lists, Bristow and Hackerman could prospect for more clients and increase the firm's liability. But despite a strong fight, Pru-Bache's arguments failed. The court ruled that the firm had to abide by its agreements. It turned over the lists.

The attempt to take the offensive with plaintiffs' lawyers had obviously not worked. The law department went back to attacking the brokers.

Bill Webb picked up the message slip that his secretary had left on his desk. It was marked "urgent" and was from Emerald Johnson, a member of the Prudential-Bache law department. Webb dialed the phone and reached Johnson on the first try. She needed something from him, she said.

"You've got to box up all those sales materials and everything else you have on growth fund one and two and get it up to us right away," she told him.

Webb sighed. Every day of that week in November 1990, he had been getting the same message. With all the lawsuits coming from his clients, the law department seemed eager to dig into the information. But Webb couldn't understand why they needed it so badly from him. It wasn't as if the materials sent to Florida weren't also sent everywhere else in the country. And Webb had simply been too busy.

This time, he thought he had a simple solution.

"Well, I'm meeting with some lawyers from Prudential and Graham on Monday," he said. "I'll just give it to them then."

Johnson agreed and hung up. Webb was getting tired of all the lawyers and all the meetings. The one scheduled for Monday had been arranged by Jane Hewitt, one of Prudential-Bache's lawyers from Davis, Polk & Wardwell, the prestigious New York law firm that was handling the partnership mess. Robert Fiske, one of the firm's senior partners, was the lawyer in charge.* Hewitt had told Webb that she wanted to review with him how the growth fund had been marketed. The whole meeting made no sense to him—just a few months before, the lawyers had interviewed him for several hours on just that topic. He thought the whole thing was a waste of time.

On the night of November 12, a group of lawyers arrived at the Fort Myers office to speak with Webb. He was late for the meeting, and nervous. He quickly realized that the supposed reason for the meeting had been a lie. The lawyers spent only a couple of minutes talking about marketing. Instead, they wanted to ask him about Daryl Bristow and Adams & Reese.

Hewitt was joined by Frank Massengale, a lawyer for Prudential-Bache, and Stephen Kupperman, a lawyer for Graham. As the questioning began, Kupperman pulled out a sheaf of papers that listed Webb's clients.

"Bill," Kupperman said. "All of these clients have filed lawsuits against the firm. I'd like to ask you some questions about them."

"All right."

"Now, five of these clients have all hired the same New Orleans law firm," Kupperman said. "Do you know how that happened?"

Webb's face went red. He felt like he'd been caught.

"Wh-what do you mean?" he stammered.

"How is it that five retirees from Florida all retained the same New Orleans law firm?" Kupperman asked.

Webb took a deep breath. "They asked me for a recommendation. I heard the name of Adams & Reese and passed it on."

Kupperman went through each of the five clients, one at a time. He

---

*Fiske would rise to national fame in early 1994 as the first independent counsel investigating the Whitewater affair.

asked for every piece of information Webb had about how they came to the firm, their financial background, and any other relevant details. Webb began to feel more relaxed. Then Kupperman picked up another, thicker sheaf of papers.

"Now, Bill, these are some of your other clients who have sued the firm," he said. "And all of these people have retained the same Houston law firm, named Miller, Bristow & Brown. Do you know how that happened?"

Webb swallowed hard. He was a terrible liar. But he gave it a shot.

"Some lawyer from the firm called me, looking for clients that needed help," he said. The lie didn't make much sense and didn't help things at all.

Hewitt, the Davis, Polk lawyer, broke in. "Isn't that unethical?" she asked Kupperman.

For the next hour, the lawyers reviewed everything that Webb had done on a case-by-case basis. At one point, one of the lawyers noticed that a number of Webb's family members were among the people filing suit.

"You must have a hell of a family reunion," the lawyer said.

"You have no idea," Webb replied. After all, his family members lost their money in the Graham partnerships, too.

The interview came to an end after almost two hours. Webb gathered his things and headed home.

The next morning, before he had left the house, Webb's telephone rang. It was his secretary, telling him that the branch manager wanted to see him as soon as he got in. Webb agreed, hung up, and headed out to the car. As soon as he reached the branch, he walked to the office of his manager, Richard Hollander.

"Bill, I've got some news I've got to tell you," Hollander said. "I'm going to have to fire you."

Hollander said that he was being fired because Webb's wife had maintained a brokerage account at another firm and he had purchased a stock there. The firm had rules against owning outside accounts.

"That's bullshit," Webb spluttered. It was Webb who had informed the firm of the outside account some time before. Both his manager and a lawyer in the compliance department had told him not to worry about it.

"You know what this is about, and so do I," Webb said. "So don't lie to me."

The manager didn't reply. He ordered Webb to leave the firm immediately. Webb was not allowed to go near his desk or touch any of his paperwork. Even his personal effects had to be left behind. He wasn't worried about being fired, because unknown to Prudential-Bache, he had been hunting for a new job. But that day, two solid offers he had on the table were withdrawn.

The hardball continued for days. A week after his dismissal, Webb received a telephone call from a Prudential-Bache executive, who said that he was passing a message from Loren Schechter: If Webb so much as telephoned any of his former clients ever again, he would have a significant lawsuit on his back.

The bare-knuckle threat worked. Webb, who had been advising so many people how to protect themselves, stopped calling his clients. He heard through the grapevine that Pru-Bache brokers were telling customers to file claims against him. Within weeks, the law department began adding new complaints to Webb's permanent record, all of them related to the growth fund. The complaints alleged that Webb had fraudulently told customers that the growth funds were safe investments that would be buying heavily discounted, overcollateralized bank loans. Prudential-Bache mentioned nothing about the sales material that said exactly that.

A year later, Webb met up with Noah Sorkin, a member of the Prudential-Bache law department. They were both attending an arbitration. Casually, Webb asked Sorkin if he had ever heard why he had been fired.

"Oh, yeah," Sorkin said. "I understand that you were suggesting to your clients that they seek legal counsel."

The damage inflicted on Webb affected brokers and managers throughout the firm. In the days before Webb was fired, a group of about ten brokers had been speaking with him, angry about the losses suffered by their clients. All of them vowed to work with Webb and planned to refer their clients to Daryl Bristow.

Webb's firing ended all that. The brokers never came forward. They left their clients to fend for themselves. Their decision to protect themselves seemed justified a few months later, after Joe Siff left the firm. The law department launched a massive, countrywide effort to find dirt on Siff and to get his securities license pulled. The lawyers let him know it. Brokers were terrified.

By then, Prudential-Bache clients had a new and unlikely ally working for them. In the western town of Boise, Idaho, a securities regulator had heard strange things about Pru-Bache a few months before from a single investor. It wasn't much to go on. But once he started following the trail of evidence, that regulator would prove to be one of the most intractable opponents the firm would ever face.

Wayne Klein, the Idaho securities commissioner, looked up from the portable computer on his desk when he heard a knock at his office door. It was late on a Friday afternoon in September 1990. Wendi Adams, a receptionist for his department, stood in the doorway.

"Wayne," Adams said, "I've got a gentleman here who has come to see Bill Blessing, but he's gone for the day. What should we do?"

Blessing was one of the department's top examiners. Anyone who needed to see him was probably in trouble. Klein saved the files on his computer and pushed back from his desk.

"Let me see if I can help him," he said.

Klein's modest second-floor office in downtown Boise was just off the reception area for the Securities Bureau, a division of the state department of finance. It made Klein the most accessible person in the office other than the receptionist herself. He often spoke to Idaho residents who dropped by with fears that they had been swindled. Many of the bureau's employees worked flexible hours and were out of the office after four o'clock. Anyone who dropped by that late stood a good chance of meeting with the boss.

Klein stepped out into the reception area and saw a casually dressed older man sitting on one of the chairs that lined the wall.

"Hello, sir," Klein said. "I'm Wayne Klein, the chief of the Securities Bureau."

The older man stood up and shook Klein's hand. "My name's Doug Burnett. I've been speaking with Bill Blessing about something and was bringing by some information for him."

"Well, Bill's not here now. But if you'd like, you can come into my office and speak with me."

Burnett agreed, and walked the few steps into Klein's office, where both men sat down. Burnett told Klein that he was retired. Years earlier, he had owned a nursing home and sold it for a profit. With his new nest egg, he went shopping for a broker in Boise. Burnett himself had been an agent with Prudential Insurance many years before and thought the company had high integrity. On that alone, Burnett decided to take his business to Prudential-Bache. He opened an account with Louise Schneider, who was then one of the firm's brokers in its Boise branch.

"I told her I was retired and that I didn't know much of anything about the markets," Burnett said. "I just wanted safe, steady, and secure investments. She assured me that she could do that."

Burnett showed Klein a copy of a document that listed his investment objectives as safety and preservation of capital. Then Burnett handed him some of his account statements.

"They sold me things that they said were safe and conservative," Burnett said. "But they have been performing very poorly. I was supposed to get these great returns, but the checks that come get smaller and smaller every quarter. They're nowhere near what I was told I could expect."

Klein glanced through the account statements. Most of the investments seemed to be limited partnerships, with names that were not familiar. A large number of them were in the oil and gas business. On the statements, they had names like P-B Energy Income and P-B Energy Growth. Klein knew from the names that these were proprietary partnerships that only Prudential-Bache sold.

Burnett said he had a range of other documents, which he handed to Klein. Most of the records pertained to the energy income partnerships, which were cosponsored by Prudential-Bache and a company called Graham Resources. Klein had never heard of the oil company before. But with just a cursory examination of Burnett's material Klein was sure of one thing: There was no way that these risky partnerships could have been properly sold to an investor like Burnett, who wanted his savings preserved.

As he reviewed the documents, Klein also sized up Burnett. The elderly man seemed articulate and sincere. If this case ever went to trial, Klein felt comfortable that a jury would find him a credible witness.

Klein finished thumbing through the material. "Let me make a copy of these documents so we can get something moving here," he said.

He and Burnett walked to the office copying machine. As Klein fed the documents through, Burnett continued to spell out how he felt he had been deceived by his broker on the partnership investments.

Klein nodded. "We're going to want to investigate this and find out if there indeed is a violation here," he said. "Then if there is, we have two desires. We'll want to get your money back, and we want to make sure that the people responsible are reprimanded so that it doesn't happen again. Our job is to ensure that people who are licensed to sell securities do it by the book."

Sometime after five o'clock, more than an hour after Burnett had come into the office, Klein finished his copying and his questioning. He shook Burnett's hand.

"Mr. Burnett, thank you very much," he said. "I'll forward this on to our examiner, and we'll get back to you if we need more information."

He stood up and escorted Burnett out. Then Klein headed back into his office, looked through the documents one more time, and stacked them on his desk. He felt relieved that he was dealing with a firm like Prudential-Bache instead of some bottom feeder. At least, he thought, the firm will be open and cooperative in helping to get to the bottom of this. Probably, he thought, this whole thing could be resolved in a few weeks.

Klein had no idea that he was on the threshold of what would become a three-year war.

When Burnett brought in his complaint, Klein had already established a strong reputation as a no-nonsense securities regulator. He was named the chief of the bureau in 1986, becoming a rare Republican working for Democratic governor Cecil Andrus. An enforcement purist who won the respect of both parties for his success in rooting out fraud, Klein firmly believed that dishonesty in the investment world polluted the free market. It was a conviction he had developed at a young age.

One of twelve children in a devoutly religious Mormon family, Klein grew up poor in Utah. He had always wanted to be a policeman, long after most of his friends began thinking about other jobs. His first exposure to the markets came in sixth grade, when a classmate received fifty shares of stock for a birthday present. It fascinated Klein. Here was a boy his own age who owned a piece of a giant company. Klein recognized that money could be earned from the capitalist system not just through physical labor but also by putting savings to work. The system offered anyone, even him, the chance to step out of poverty.

In high school, a friend of his brother told Klein about some investment ideas. Klein took the little money he had and used it to purchase the inexpensive stocks. Some of the investments fared well, some poorly. But he walked away from the experience with a tidy profit. After working his way through college—including two years spent in Brazil as a Mormon missionary—Klein was accepted by George Washington University law school. In the 1980 school year, he found a job with the Washington office of Fried, Frank, Harris, Shriver & Kampelman. There he worked with Harvey Pitt, a former general counsel with the Securities and Exchange

Commission and one of the most respected securities lawyers in the business.

After graduating from law school, he worked for a year with a Washington, D.C., law firm. But he and his wife wanted to return to the West, and by 1983, Klein was working in the Idaho Securities Bureau. Three years later, he was running it.

As the fast-money days of the 1980s unfolded, Klein was horrified by the number of investment scams that came through Idaho. In his first years on the job, his department uncovered a scheme that raised $1.2 million from Idaho residents. The investment was supposed to offer 120 percent returns after the money was shipped to the Bahamas. But it was all a scam. Klein arranged a complex "sting" that tricked the crooks into returning almost $1 million to Idaho, where it was recovered. The investors got most of their money back.

As bureau chief, Klein committed himself to protecting the financial futures of investors throughout the state. To keep himself focused, he hung two framed stock certificates of ten thousand shares each on the wall of his office. He had purchased the shares in 1972, and now they were largely worthless. The stock was his daily reminder that whenever he reviewed an investment proposal, he wanted Idaho investors to end up with something worth more than wallpaper. That, Klein believed, was the only way to maintain public confidence in the marketplace.

That dedication ensured that Burnett's complaint would be aggressively pursued by Klein's department. The following Monday morning, Klein took the stack of information from Burnett down to Bill Blessing's office and discussed what he thought the documents showed. Blessing said that he would contact the firm in New York for copies of any other necessary records. He also would look into the accounts of some of the other clients of Louise Schneider, Burnett's broker. If inappropriate investments were sold to Burnett, chances were good they were sold to someone else, too.

Klein agreed and headed back down to his office. He felt comfortable that Blessing would easily get to the bottom of this. Big firms didn't want bad brokers in their midst.

"*Eight?*" Klein asked, sounding appalled. "The same thing happened to eight other customers?"

Bill Blessing nodded. "That's what we found when we went through Schneider's accounts."

Blessing had been investigating the Burnett complaint for a few weeks. He had obtained information from New York and had also stopped by the Boise branch unannounced to pore through their records. What Blessing found disturbed Klein deeply. Eight of Louise Schneider's clients had been elderly people who were sold limited partnerships with descriptions of the investments as safe and secure. All claimed to have been told that they could expect a high rate of return on the investments. All had suffered tremendous losses.

Klein knew that even the best of brokerage firms could not help it when a bad broker turned up in its midst. But that was why compliance procedures were supposed to be so tight. That way, when a broker did something wrong, red flags would get raised and the problems would be halted. A few would always get through. But eight customers apparently cheated by the same broker amazed him. Somebody had been slacking off on the job.

"How did the branch manager let it happen to so many people?" Klein asked rhetorically. "For goodness' sake, for that matter, how did New York let it happen?"

"It looks pretty bad," Blessing said.

The two men discussed the investigation for another few minutes and decided that they needed to branch out. If one broker took advantage of the apparent lack of supervision at the branch, Klein said, others might have, as well. The regulators would start checking the records of other brokers in the branch. And perhaps, Klein suggested, the time had come to speak with Louise Schneider.

Blessing and a colleague, Mary Hughes, spent months checking records, calling customers, and interviewing brokers. In early 1991, Blessing updated Klein on what they had found. Other brokers in the branch had also sold a number of limited partnerships, he said. Although none of those brokers had so great a concentration of unsuitable sales as Schneider, their customers still complained. In interviews, most of the clients who purchased limited partnerships said that they, too, had been assured that the risky investments were safe and promised high returns.

Finally Blessing said they had interviewed Schneider herself to find out her side of the story. She no longer worked at Prudential-Bache, having left the year before to take a job at Shearson Lehman Brothers. Blessing seemed ready to laugh out loud.

"And, Wayne, get this, you're going to love her excuse," Blessing said. "She said that all she did was read off the sales material that was created by

Prudential-Bache in New York. So she says we shouldn't blame her for saying what New York told her to say."

Blessing smiled. "That's a new one for me."

Klein looked out his window for a moment, deep in thought. Something about this case had been bothering him from the beginning. When his investigators had called Prudential-Bache in New York, Klein figured they would react in horror that one of their brokers had done something so wrong. Maybe they would launch their own investigation. Perhaps even fire the branch manager. But instead, the lawyers at Pru-Bache didn't seem particularly concerned. It was almost as if this were something the New York executives had heard about before.

Still, Schneider could easily just be trying to shift the blame onto her superiors. Klein had seen a lot of finger-pointing in cases before. There was only one way to find out what was true. He turned back to Blessing.

"Let's find out if there's anything to it," he said. "Let's call Prudential-Bache in New York and get copies of all the sales literature they sent out to the Boise branch. And let's also have them ship along copies of the prospectuses. That'll straighten out who's telling the truth."

Either way, Klein said, they had enough information to pursue a full-scale investigation. If they were going to attempt to prove that New York executives had failed to adequately supervise brokers in Boise, it would take a lot of resources. For a few minutes, Klein thought through his department's caseload, as well as the manpower that would be needed for a full-scale investigation. He appointed five members of the department—Blessing, Hughes, Marilyn Scanlan, Patricia Highley, and Jelean Hale—as investigators in the case. Klein then had an investigative order prepared, which would allow each member of the team to issue subpoenas and administer oaths for sworn statements.

On January 30, 1991, Klein brought the investigative order to his boss, Belton Patty, the director of the Idaho Department of Finance. Patty read through the order and signed it.

The investigation, titled *The State of Idaho* v. *Louise Schneider and Prudential-Bache*, had begun. The timing was perfect. Prudential-Bache was just about to drop its calm facade.

By February 1990, George Ball knew that the game was over. The patience of senior executives at Prudential Insurance had worn thin. Robert Winters, who had been named chairman in 1986, seemed particularly exasperated by the inability of Prudential-Bache to generate any income. In board meetings, Winters frequently commented caustically that he was tired of the brokerage firm consuming cash instead of generating it. Every chance he had, Garnett Keith, the Prudential executive most closely involved in the business of the brokerage, would sharply and publicly distance himself from the decisions made during Ball's tenure. It seemed that Keith rarely made public comments now unless it was to protest that he was not responsible for what had happened at Pru-Bache.

For about six months, Ball's power had been waning. Arthur Burton Jr., a Prudential executive, had been made vice-chairman of the brokerage at Ball's request. Executives could see that Burton was taking over an increasing number of management responsibilities. Ball seemed to be standing by, almost helpless, as the insurance company gradually wrested control away from him. Every few months, Winters would issue a statement in response to press inquiries saying that Ball still had his full support. But every senior executive at the brokerage firm knew that the statement was a lie.

Prudential was also just starting to come to grips with the magnitude of the disaster unfolding at the brokerage firm. To get a fix on the potential liability, it had hired lawyers and investigators to dig through the records of the Direct Investment Group. At that point, things looked ugly. And already, the partnership debacle was causing enormous troubles. An attempt to sell the firm the year before to the Primerica Corporation had flopped because Prudential Insurance refused to limit the liabilities that a buyer would face.

By August, Ball had lost control of his own strategy. Months before, he had been telling consultants to the firm that its merchant banking and arbitrage departments were core parts of the business. The past year had been difficult for both departments, but the future looked strong. Prudential Insurance would hear none of it. Under orders from Winters, Ball cut back the arbitrage department's capital. With only $25 million, the department—which during Ball's tenure had been one of the most profitable divisions in Prudential-Bache—began bleeding. Without the money to run its strategies, the profits from arbitrage dried up. It was like telling a long-distance swimmer to use only one arm.

Finally, on December 20, 1990, with Pru-Bache facing an annual loss of $250 million, Ball sent out a memo describing a massive restructuring of the firm. The assets of the merchant banking department were transferred to Prudential Insurance, officially ending the brokerage firm's four-year effort in that business. The firm's Canadian operations were sold. The arbitrage department was shut down, and its director, Guy Wyser-Pratte, a

Bache veteran of more than twenty years, was immediately locked out of his office.

The last change was in the Direct Investment Group. Even with all the cutbacks the department had already experienced, the new proposal would slim it down even more. It became nothing more than a monitoring division, existing only to find what little could be salvaged out of the wreckage of a decade. James Kelso, an executive who performed the due diligence on the VMS Mortgage Investment Fund, was deemed the best candidate to take charge of that effort.

Even with all the changes, Winters and Keith were too soured on Ball. In February, at his annual performance evaluation by Winters, Ball decided to broach the issue himself.

"Bob, I think this business has been going too badly for too long," he said. "I think the people at the Prudential have lost confidence in me."

Winters stared straight at Ball, looking stern. "George, you're right."

That was that. The time had come for Ball's exit.

"Well, I'd love to stick it out here and see through all the changes that we've made," Ball said, "but the pressure on me is just too intense. I'm not sure that I could still be effective. So perhaps it would be best for me to pursue other options."

"I think that would be best," Winters said. "It would be the most graceful thing for all of us."

A week later, on February 13, 1991, Prudential Insurance announced that Ball was resigning as chairman and chief executive of Prudential-Bache. Robert Beck, the former chairman of the insurance business who spearheaded the merger ten years earlier, was named interim chief executive.

Ball sent his last Ballgram to the employees of Pru-Bache that day. In it, he hinted at the mistakes he had made and the problems they had caused.

"The hubris of what happened to the securities industry in the 80's, and as a result to the firm, led to some bad results in several areas," Ball wrote. "The net of it is that someone who is unencumbered by the aftermath of those past results should lead the firm into the future."

A week later, the brokerage firm announced another significant change. Prudential-Bache was being renamed Prudential Securities. The name change brought the firm closer into the Prudential Insurance fold and marked the death of a Wall Street name dating back to Jules Bache in the 1880s. It was a symbolic break with the firm's sordid history and an attempt to put a shine on the hopes for the brokerage's future.

But a name change couldn't rewrite the past. Within the week, some of the firm's darkest secrets would finally emerge.

Chuck Hawkins, the Atlanta bureau chief of *Business Week*, dialed a long-distance call to Connecticut. It was an afternoon in early 1991, and Hawkins was ready to question Jim Darr. Hawkins had been on the trail of Prudential-Bache ever since writing about its real estate problems almost a year before. The original article had brought in dozens of telephone calls from Pru-Bache brokers and clients, all of whom had tips for him. Hawkins followed up his own hunches, as well, poring through prospectus after prospectus for limited partnerships and digging through court filings for more information.

This time, Hawkins had unearthed the mother lode. He uncovered the criminal record of Clifton Harrison and some of the secret deals between Harrison and Prudential-Bache executives. He knew of the Locke Purnell report and its allegations about Darr's dealings with Watson & Taylor and First South. He had even found evidence that Prudential Insurance executives had questioned Darr's apparent lack of concern about the quality of the investments by the energy income partnerships. Hawkins planned to ask Darr about all of it.

Hawkins finished dialing Darr's number. After a few rings, someone answered the phone.

"Yes?" a man asked, almost as if he were expecting a call.

"Is this Jim Darr?" Hawkins asked.

"Yes."

"This is Chuck Hawkins from *Business Week*."

"Oh, no!" the man blurted out, then quickly composed himself. "Who did you ask for?"

"Jim Darr."

"I'm afraid you have the wrong number."

An instant later, all Hawkins heard was the dial tone.

The Hawkins article appeared as the cover story in the March 4, 1991, issue of *Business Week*. The headline, "The Mess at Pru-Bache," appeared on the cover over a picture of George Ball. The first words of the article set the hard-hitting tone.

"George L. Ball's reign is over at Pru-Bache—but his legacy lives on." The article went on to say that the firm and Prudential Insurance "face legal troubles that could drag down their finances—and images—for years to come."

Hawkins described everything he had found, from the information in the Locke Purnell report to the background of Clifton Harrison. It was a devastating piece of journalism, one that laid bare many of the secrets that Prudential-Bache had kept hidden for so many years.

The story was an earthshaker. After reading it, class-action lawyers throughout the country began filing new lawsuits against the firm. The largest suit, filed in federal court in New Orleans, involved the energy income partnerships.

The enforcement staff of the SEC launched an investigation into Darr, but the inquiry did not receive a particularly high priority. It was not handled by lawyers in the Washington office, as most high-profile cases are. Instead, the SEC investigation into the *Business Week* allegations was conducted by the agency's New York regional office.

The magazine arrived at the offices of the Idaho Department of Finance the week it was published. Belton Patty, the head of the department, read the article quickly and realized that it related to the same matters under investigation in the securities bureau. He walked to Klein's office with a copy of the magazine in his hand.

"Wayne, I think you ought to take a look at this," he said.

Klein read through the article carefully. By then, his investigators had found similar patterns of sales abuses at a number of Pru-Bache branches. He already knew that the problem in Boise was far more widespread than just a few bad brokers.

As he read, Klein was surprised that the story involved many of the same partnerships his team was investigating, as well as many similar allegations. It also astonished him to realize that his bureau probably had one of the most fully developed inquiries into the matter under way.

Klein made a few copies of the article, then took one to Bill Blessing's office.

"Bill, take a look at this," he said. "I think we have some more things we're going to have to look into."

The two men discussed what new documents they would want from Prudential-Bache. In particular, they wanted to see the Locke Purnell report and find out more about this former executive named Jim Darr.

CHAPTER 17

THE LAWYER FROM PRUDENTIAL Securities sat comfortably in a conference room at the Idaho Securities Bureau. Like all of the people Wayne Klein had met from the firm's headquarters, the lawyer, Noah Sorkin, projected a confidence that had long ago crossed the line into arrogance.

"This was not a widespread problem," Sorkin said. "The vast majority of these partnership sales were done right. We had a few renegade brokers, that's all."

Klein stared at Sorkin, not bothering to hide his disbelief. With Klein were two of his investigators, Mary Hughes and James Burns, who had recently joined the inquiry. By the time of this meeting in the spring of 1991, the Idaho regulators had developed enough information to know that they were not dealing with a few bad brokers. The assurances about the safety of the limited partnerships had come straight out of the marketing material sent from New York. The regulators had made some inquiries and found that the same problems existed at a number of Prudential Securities branches in nearby states.

"I'm sorry, Noah, but I don't believe this was renegade brokers," Klein said. "We've seen the sales literature coming out of New York. That's where the problems start."

Sorkin disagreed, again stressing the firm's line that most of the partnership sales had been done properly.

Klein just shook his head. "Now, what makes this worse is, in some of these cases, this broker is making proposals to investors on how to invest their money with a letterhead that says she's a vice-president of Prudential-Bache. She's an officer of the company. Of course they're going to believe what she says."

"Oh, no," Sorkin said. "She's not an officer of the company."

"Sure she is," Klein said, pulling out a copy of the letterhead for Louise Schneider. "It says right here 'vice-president.'"

"But she's not an officer."

Klein took a breath. He was zeroing in on one of the more pervasive deceptions on Wall Street, not only at Prudential Securities. Lowly stockbrokers are often given lofty titles for the purpose of impressing clients. When someone with an officer's title at a national brokerage firm offers advice, investors are more likely to take it. On Wall Street, it's just viewed as good marketing. But Klein saw it for what it was: another deception.

"Well, I'm sorry, I may have gone to the Kmart School of Law, but when I went to law school, a vice-president was an officer," Klein said.

"No, it's just a title," Sorkin said. "She's not an officer."

"Noah, that's ridiculous. Titles have meanings. They certainly mean something to the people out here deciding how to invest their money."

Sorkin smiled. "I'll bet you the coldest beer in Idaho that it wouldn't make any difference to clients whether or not she was just a registered representative or a vice-president."

"I don't drink beer," Klein said, "but I'll take the bet. I'll be happy to go find a hundred people on the street down here and ask them if they would rather buy stock from a vice-president of Prudential-Bache or a registered representative. And I'll take the wager that people are going to be more impressed with someone who has the title of vice-president and more willing to do business with her."

Then it was Klein's turn to smile. "After all, that's why you gave her the title."

The men talked for a bit more. Sorkin asked what would be necessary to resolve the investigation. As Klein understood it, the firm was broaching the idea of reaching a settlement. He quashed the idea immediately.

"We can't resolve anything now," he said. "We need to know the magnitude of what we're dealing with before we settle the case."

The discussion moved on to problems that the Idaho investigators had uncovered at the Boise branch involving the improper trading of options. Late in the afternoon, the meeting came to an end.

A few weeks later, the state of Idaho adopted its first new policy statement coming out of the partnership investigation. Any employee of a brokerage firm with a title that appeared to bestow official authority would be treated as an officer of the company. The marketing deception could continue, but at the cost of increasing a brokerage firm's potential liability for wrongdoing.

———

A secretary buzzed Bill Creedon's intercom and told him that a visitor was waiting in the reception area. Creedon stood up and headed out to the front. He was not looking forward to this meeting.

It was 2:30 on the afternoon of March 9, 1991. Creedon had resigned from his job as a broker at Prudential-Bache several months before because of his refusal to mislead his clients about their legal rights in bringing a suit caused by losses from the VMS Mortgage Investment Fund. Instead, he took a job with a smaller brokerage firm. Still, he could not seem to get Pru-Bache out of his life. Every time a customer filed a complaint, the firm made sure to place it on Creedon's permanent record.

His visitor was Michael Licosati, a lawyer from Keesal, Young & Logan, a California law firm that represented Prudential Securities and specialized in arbitrations. Licosati had set up an appointment with Creedon a few days earlier when he called to tell the broker about a claim that had been filed by one of his former customers.

Creedon greeted Licosati and escorted him to his office. He was a young lawyer and struck Creedon as a friendly type. Once they sat down, Licosati got right down to business.

The former client, Betty Jean Prosser, had filed for an arbitration against Prudential Securities. She had purchased a fair amount of the VMS fund and felt she had been misled.

"She *was* misled," Creedon broke in. "She should get all her money back. All my clients should."

"That's not going to happen," Licosati said. "Your clients are not going to get all their money back."

"Why not?" Creedon asked. "They were defrauded."

"It's not that simple," Licosati replied. "Bill, I want you to know that I'm personally concerned because if too much pressure is put on Prudential, they may declare bankruptcy. We want to settle with the people but we don't want to go too rough on Prudential."

Licosati then explained that Prudential Securities wanted Keesal, Young to represent Creedon in the Prosser case. That way, the defense would be unified.

"It really is in your interest to be represented by Keesal," he said. "If we represent you and we settle these cases, we won't go after you for the money. But if we're not representing you and we settle, we would have every right to go after you in court."

I don't even work for that firm anymore, Creedon thought, *and they're still pressuring me.*

Creedon set down his pen. "Look, I personally don't want to be represented by Keesal on this matter," he said. "Basically, I want to do a laydown and put on no defense. I told her that VMS was safe and guaranteed. And I want to testify that she is entitled to her money back."

"Well, I hope you don't do that," Licosati said.

Too bad, Creedon thought. *You're not going to scare me into cooperating.*

A few months later, in July 1991, Creedon felt reinforced in his decision not to help Prudential Securities. A federal judge approved the first settlement of a class action involving private partnerships sponsored by VMS. After all the assurances to customers that they should look for compensation from the class action, Prudential Securities had cheated them again. In a deal it negotiated with Beigel & Sandler, a small Chicago firm that specialized in class actions, Prudential Securities agreed to pay $25 million to compensate customers who had invested more than $1 billion in ninety-five different VMS partnerships. That worked out to 2.5 cents in compensation—before legal fees—for every dollar that investors had lost.

No reasonable investor would have accepted such a paltry sum. For every $10,000 they invested, they would receive less than $200. But not everyone did so poorly: Beigel & Sandler received $6 million in fees, plus $350,000 in expenses, for minimal work. By all appearances, the law firm was simply selling its clients' legitimate claims to Prudential Securities for the fat fees.

But class actions were the perfect strategy for Prudential Securities. No investor had to accept the settlement. Instead, they received a multipage court notification that described in tiny type the $25 million settlement. It did not say how much investors would receive individually. Under the rules of class actions, only investors who wrote to the court and specifically asked not to participate in the settlement were excluded from it. Investors who did not understand the legalistic document were automatically swept up into the settlement. Even investors who changed addresses and never received the notification were included. Because the essence of the Prudential Securities partnership fraud was that the sales were made to unsophisticated clients, many of the investors did not understand what they were reading and did nothing. As a result, they unknowingly accepted the settlement and waived their rights ever to sue Prudential Securities again. In exchange, they received a payment that was less than they might have obtained for one week on public assistance.

In another few months, a second settlement was reached for the public partnerships. Included in that agreement was the VMS Mortgage Investment Fund, the partnership that had been sold as guaranteed to so many elderly investors. They did not do as badly as the investors in the first settlement.

They received four cents on the dollar—before legal fees.

The word had leaked out days before that Prudential Insurance had found George Ball's successor. Still, when the announcement came out on April 24, some executives in the firm were surprised. Ball was being replaced by Hardwick Simmons, who eleven months before had been eased out as head of retail at Shearson Lehman Hutton in the wake of huge losses there.

Within the firm, the appointment was greeted with mixed emotions. Some executives felt relieved that at least someone was in charge. But others were horrified that the only person Prudential Insurance could find to run the firm was a man who had lost a midlevel management position at a financially troubled competitor.

But Prudential was not giving Simmons as much rope as it had handed to Ball. He was only named president and chief executive. Winters, the insurance company chairman, named himself chairman of the brokerage, as well.

Simmons began making changes quickly, shunting some senior executives aside. He fired Richard Sichenzio, the man who had succeeded Bob Sherman as the head of retail. Instead, he hired George Murray, a senior vice-president at Shearson and the man who gave Simmons his first job as a management trainee on Wall Street. He also brought on board another friend named Howard "Woody" Knight to handle corporate strategy and business development.

Early on, Simmons became aware of the partnership debacle unfolding in the firm. He didn't think much of it. Shearson had sold a wide range of limited partnerships, and many of those were having trouble. Senior executives assured him that the partnerships matter was a problem that could be resolved for, at most, $50 million.

Still, given all the legal troubles the firm was experiencing, Simmons asked for a report on whether Loren Schechter himself should be held accountable in any way for what had occurred. By that time, Schechter was a favorite among the senior executives from Prudential Insurance.

A brief inquiry cleared Schechter of any responsibility for the mess. He had raised all of the appropriate red flags to Ball, Simmons was told. In particular, it was noted that Schechter had immediately informed Ball of the Locke Purnell report. But Ball had, for his own reasons, chosen to wait nine months before doing anything about it.

Simmons liked what he heard. Schechter would continue as the firm's chief legal strategist.

Daryl Bristow carried some files into a room at the Sheraton Hotel in Fort Myers, Florida. Across the room, he saw an elderly man in his late seventies, looking fragile and frightened. The man was Darrell Haney, a former client of Prudential Securities and an investor in the growth fund. Haney was a recent client of Bristow, having retained the lawyer for one of the huge growth fund lawsuits his firm had filed against Prudential Securities and Graham. Bristow had never met Haney personally, and they had only a short time to discuss the case before the lawyers for Prudential and Graham would start taking the elderly man's statement.

Bristow and his partners had already progressed far in their lawsuits over the growth funds. After winning the court order that forced Prudential-Bache to turn over the investor lists for the partnerships, the lawyers had solicited each potential client by mail. Bristow was not filing a class action, so he had to find each of his clients individually. The response was astounding: Thousands of investors, many of them elderly and middle class, sent back a signed contract retaining the lawyers. Bristow had so many clients that, following a disagreement, he was able to split off from his old firm and set up a new one that used the Prudential litigation as its business foundation. The new firm, called Bristow, Hackerman, Wilson & Peterson, opened its doors on May 1.

At about the same time, Bristow had brought another lawyer into the case. With thousands of clients, all of whom had to be kept updated individually, the growth fund litigation was a communications nightmare. Handling it properly would require computer sorting and cataloging of clients' names and sophisticated letter-writing programs. So Bristow contacted another law firm, James R. Moriarty & Associates. Moriarty was a computer whiz who had already used his skills to keep thousands of clients updated in other mass claims. He could easily do the same thing in the growth fund cases. Within weeks, Moriarty had a computer program running that allowed the lawyers to write individualized letters to every one of the growth fund clients. On top of that, the two law firms had put together a slick full-color newsletter called GFL News. Clients began receiving updates on the growth fund litigation in easy-to-read articles, complete with graphics and pictures.

But Prudential Securities was doing everything it could to make the large client base unwieldy. Already one of the firm's lawyers had told Moriarty that they planned to depose all 5,800 of the clients in the growth fund lawsuit. Moriarty understood the threat perfectly: Knowing that the plaintiffs' lawyers were on a contingency fee and were paying expenses out of pocket, Prudential Securities planned to spend the three Texas lawyers into bankruptcy. The brokerage firm seemed ready to make good on its threat, and started with investors in Florida. Haney was the first client who would be deposed.

When Bristow walked into the hotel room, Haney was already speaking with Steve Hackerman, Bristow's partner, and Bill Webb, who had been Haney's broker.

"Mr. Haney, I'm sorry to be meeting you in such unpleasant circumstances," Bristow said, taking the elderly man's hand.

"Oh, no, that's fine," Haney said gently. "We do what we have to do."

Haney apologized for the fact that his wife could not make the meeting. "She's ill, and just can't make it."

Bristow sat down next to Haney and explained what would happen in the deposition the next day. He described how a number of lawyers would be asking him questions. All he needed to do, Bristow said, was stay relaxed and answer to the best of his ability.

"Now, what I'd like you to do, Mr. Haney, is tell me a little bit about your background," Bristow said.

Haney looked down at the coffee table in front of him as he started to speak. He didn't come to Prudential-Bache with a lot of knowledge about investing, he said. With only a grammar school education, Haney had worked his entire life in the steel mills of Pittsburgh. Being handy, he had rebuilt a small unit apartment and sold it for a profit when he retired from the mills. His wife had a job, too, which helped to make ends meet. Because of their hard work, Haney and his wife had a few hundred thousand dollars. It was enough money to let them move to Florida, where they hoped to spend the rest of their lives in comfort. Once they arrived, the couple decided that they couldn't manage their money on their own. They went to Bill Webb, whom they had been told was a serious and religious man who looked out for his clients. Webb sold them a number of partnerships. When the growth fund came out, with its advertised low risk and high returns, Haney invested in it.

"He told us they were buying these discounted loans that would produce a profit and that there was very little risk involved," Haney said.

Haney paused for a moment, closing his eyes and swallowing. "After all those years of hard work and pinching pennies, I had hoped to be able to live a nice life down here," he said. "My wife and I were going to travel a little bit and have the fun we were never able to have when we both were working so hard."

Haney's eyes began to cloud. "Then we lost so much of the money. And then my wife got sick. Now we could never afford to do the things we wanted to do in life. It just doesn't seem right. But there's not a thing we can do about it. We just have to forget all of our dreams."

Haney broke down in deep sobs. For everyone in the room, it was a defining moment. This was what the case was about, this was the reality of the pain Prudential-Bache caused through its lies. At that moment, the lawyers knew that no matter what, this was a case they were going to win.

Bristow reached out and put a hand on Haney's shoulder. "Mr. Haney, I don't think I can appreciate how bad you feel, but I know how bad it is," he said. "And I'll tell you one thing. We're going to get your money back for you. You can count on it."

The deposition of Darrell Haney began early the next day in a room at the Sheraton. When Bristow and Hackerman walked in with Haney, they could not believe what they saw. More than half a dozen lawyers for Prudential Securities and Graham were scurrying about. Video cameras were set up to record what Haney said. The defense lawyers had also brought hundreds of thousands of dollars of electronic equipment—so much that they needed to keep it in an adjoining room—which would allow them to have instant deposition transcripts. They were obviously preparing for an all-day deposition of the elderly man.

Bristow smiled. It was the most comical thing he had ever seen in a deposition. Prudential Securities was obviously trying to send a message. Even with small investors who had little direct evidence to offer, they would do everything possible to run up the man-hours. It seemed they wanted to make the cost of bringing the lawsuit so high that it would serve as a warning to other plaintiffs' lawyers.

There was no question in Bristow's mind that Prudential Securities and Graham fought dirty. From the beginning of the lawsuit, they threw up every barrier and made every accusation possible against the lawyers. Even though the brokerage firm's attempt to sue Boyd Page had had a disastrous outcome, crushing the lawyers was apparently still a central part of its strategy. Already Prudential Securities had tried unsuccessfully to have Bristow's firm removed from the case by filing motions accusing it of every ethical breach. The motions were tossed out. Then, when his firm won access to the client list, Prudential Securities and Graham sent a joint letter attacking the law firm and suggesting that investors should not sue. The letter, from John Graham and James Kelso, the new head of the Direct Investment Group, criticized Bristow's firm by implying that it was not working in the interests of investors.

The letter appeared to be another cynical attempt to use Prudential's good name to trick investors into making decisions that benefited the firm financially. After all, at the same time it was criticizing lawyers willing to fight, Prudential Securities was simultaneously herding tens of thousands of investors into the inadequate VMS settlements.

The Haney deposition dragged on the entire day. The defense lawyers asked questions about every investment decision Haney had ever made. When it seemed there was nothing left to ask, the lawyers came up with another line of questioning. Legal assistants hustled back and forth from the adjoining room, providing the lawyers with the instant transcripts to help them form their next questions.

Finally it was Bristow's turn. He decided to humiliate his opponents for their tactics.

"Well, Mr. Haney," Bristow said, his arm sweeping around the room at the lawyers and equipment, "what do you think about all this?"

"It's amazing," Haney said softly.

"You know, they've got all this electronic equipment over there, and they've already printed your every word," Bristow said. "They can call it back in a flash and stick it right in front of your face. So is there anything you've said that you want to take back?"

"No sir."

"Well, now, Mr. Haney, they've spent something like $300,000 to get all this equipment," Bristow said. "We can all look at what you've said. It's available. So are you sure you don't want to change anything?"

"No sir."

"Would you like them to place some of your words in front of you?"

"No sir."

"You ready to vouch for everything you said?"

"Yes sir."

Bristow dragged on the questioning about the equipment, occasionally fencing with objections from his opponents. By the time he was done, he had made Prudential Securities and Graham Resources look like a bunch of bullies picking on a frightened old man.

After seven and a half hours, the Haney deposition came to an end. Prudential Securities never used the equipment in a deposition again.

A few weeks later, in the late summer of 1991, a letter from Louisiana arrived at Daryl Bristow's law office. The letter was just one of a number sitting in a pile of mail on his desk. Bristow opened it without a second thought. As he skimmed the letter, his face turned red with rage. He jumped up from his desk and ran down the hallway to Hackerman's office.

"Steve," Bristow fumed, thrusting the letter at his partner as he walked in, "look at what these sorry sons of bitches are trying to do now."

Hackerman took the letter and read it, his eyes widening.

The letter was from the securities commissioner in Louisiana, the home state of Graham Resources. It was a notification that the regulators had reason to believe that the Bristow, Hackerman law firm had been offering an investment opportunity without filing an appropriate prospectus. Essentially, it was accusing the law firm of running a securities scam.

But the amazing part was what the regulators said was the "security" that the law firm had been offering: the contract for retainer that Bristow, Hackerman had sent to prospective clients in the growth fund cases. In essence, Louisiana was now questioning whether a contingency fee contract, an everyday product of law firms across the country, was an investment that required registration with securities regulators. A copy of the letter had been forwarded to Texas state regulators and the SEC.

"That's the silliest damned thing I've ever seen," Hackerman said as he finished the letter.

Bristow's mind was reeling. He had heard too many stories about back-scratching in Louisiana state government.

"Surely the Louisiana Securities Commission can't be fixed," he said.

"That's not the problem," Hackerman said. "Look, these guys fight dirty. We should have expected it. They sued Boyd Page, now they're coming after us. They're just a little more sophisticated this time."

Bristow started cursing Prudential Securities and Graham. Never before had he been in a lawsuit where the opposing side spent so much time attacking the lawyers and so little time dealing with the facts of the case. All of the defendants' motions accusing Bristow of unethical conduct had been bad enough, but this one stepped over the line. Bristow wanted to strike back, and hard. He just didn't know how.

Over the next few days, Bristow hired a lawyer from Baton Rouge to represent the firm before the securities commission. A few days later, he and his lawyer traveled to New Orleans to meet with the regulators. The meeting was relatively friendly. The regulators said that they had been obliged to send the letter because some lawyers representing Graham Resources had filed a complaint. The commission seemed to think the complaint was ridiculous, but still suggested that Bristow, Hackerman file a response. Bristow returned to Houston, still seething at the dirty tactics.

That same week, the plaintiffs' lawyer in the growth fund case met in a conference room at Bristow, Hackerman to discuss the case. Bristow was still thundering about the complaint that had been filed in Louisiana.

"These folks have gall to spare," Bristow exclaimed. "Here they're the ones who have committed this huge fraud, but they turn around and try to send a regulator after us!"

Jim Moriarty, the lawyer and computer expert who had been brought into the case a few months before, suddenly jumped up. "Well, goddamnit, they want the regulators involved in this, then let's do it," he said. "Let's get the regulators involved."

"What are you talking about?" Bristow asked.

"We represent five thousand people who were ripped off by these bastards," Moriarty replied. "They're the ones who have the right to file a complaint. So let's find out where they should send their complaints and pass on the information to them."

"Wait a minute, Jim," Bristow said. "We don't have the time to go writing up complaints for five thousand people."

"Daryl, that's the beauty of this," Moriarty said. "We don't write it. All we do is give some information. If they want to write something, it's up to them."

Bristow shook his head. The idea sounded risky. "I'm not going to let one of my clients just haul off and file something without my knowing what they filed."

"Why not?" Moriarty asked, throwing up his hands. "It's their case. It's not ours. They're the ones who know what happened better than anybody. They ought to be able to tell their story their way, without a bunch of lawyers interfering."

Other investors had already shown that it could work, Moriarty said. Just a few months before, in June, regulators in Kansas had filed a complaint against Prudential Securities, charging that it had defrauded customers in seven different partnerships. It was a small case, but it started because customers in Kansas complained.

Bristow still looked doubtful. Moriarty sat down next to him.

"Daryl, you're not seeing what we have here," Moriarty said. "One or two people aren't going to mean spit to most regulators or prosecutors. We've got *five thousand* people. Our clients, together, have power. They can make their voices heard. They can make something happen. All we have to do is give them a little help."

Bristow rubbed his chin for an instant in thought. Then he looked back at Moriarty. "All right," he said. "How would it work?"

Finding the name and address of every securities regulator in the country was the hard part. The computer program was simplicity itself. Like junk mail, it simply substituted different names within a standard text. Investors who lived in Arkansas were told how to write their state regulator, the SEC, and the National Association of Securities Dealers. Florida investors received the same information, but with a different state regulator listed.

The letter, signed by Bristow, was an open invitation to file a complaint with government authorities.

"We have been asked what can be done, besides filing suit, to seek further relief from the deceptive practices of the Prudential companies and their business partners in various failed limited partnerships that our clients were misled about," Bristow wrote. "One very effective measure is to bring these improper sales and management practices to the attention of the proper regulatory authorities."

The letter described what had happened in Kansas. It then said that if clients wished to make similar complaints, they could do so. However, the letter told them not to provide any details of their own personal situation, other than which partnerships they owned.

"Simply invite the authorities to contact us for those details," the letter said. "We will be pleased to provide them with a comprehensive report."

A test batch of the letters was sent out in early September. After a number of positive responses from clients, thousands more were mailed in mid-October.

Bristow, Hackerman, and Moriarty stood back and waited to see what would happen.

The next curve ball in the growth fund litigation was thrown in December 1991. Prudential Securities reached a settlement—but with Stuart Wechsler, a class-action lawyer in New York. The deal with Wechsler would pay the growth fund investors five cents on the dollar, at best. A hearing to review the settlement was called in federal district court in New Orleans, where a class action had been filed.

Bristow, Hackerman, and Moriarty flew to New Orleans for the hearing on December 11. They were bitterly angry. Prudential Securities seemed willing to do anything to limit its liability. The firm had spent months arguing that the Texas lawyers weren't watching out for the clients' interests, but it thought it was just dandy to deal with a lawyer who would settle the claims for pennies on the dollar.

"That firm only likes lawyers who settle on the cheap," Bristow said on the flight to New Orleans.

To a large degree, the class-action settlement being proposed by Wechsler and Prudential Securities was an enormous threat to the Bristow litigation. All of his clients had turned over decision-making power in their cases to a committee of investors. But if this settlement was approved, they would be receiving a complex notice in the mail about it. If they didn't opt out, the clients would get their five cents on the dollar and lose the right to pursue the other lawsuits. Bristow had met enough of his elderly and unsophisticated clients by this time to know that explaining to them how to opt out would be difficult. They would simply be confused. Prudential Securities would wipe out a huge portion of Bristow's client base, making it all the easier for the firm to ignore those people's claims. It was a devious tactic.

The hearing before Federal Judge A. J. McNamara started promptly at 9:00 A.M. The courtroom was packed with lawyers. Wechsler made one of the first presentations. McNamara asked him how many clients he represented, not as a class, but individually, and how much they invested in the growth funds.

"To answer your first question, Your Honor, the number of plaintiffs is twelve," Wechsler said. "I don't have the precise amount of their investments, but they are extremely small."

Big deal, Moriarty thought. Here his group represented 5,800 investors. But this New York class-action lawyer was pretending to speak for all growth fund investors because he had found twelve.

Wechsler described the terms of the settlement. The total value, he said, was $49 million. Prudential Securities and Graham Resources would put up $12 million in cash. The remaining money would be used by Prudential Securities to repurchase the growth fund partnership units, at prices of $200 apiece or less.

"But what are the units worth?" McNamara asked.

"The value of the units may be more," Wechsler said.

The judge looked at Wechsler, puzzled. Most investors didn't clamor to sell assets for less than their actual value. It didn't take much arithmetic to recognize that if Prudential Securities could make a profit on every growth fund unit it purchased, it might be able to finance the settlement with money that belonged to the investors. It didn't sound like that part of the settlement should be counted as a benefit to investors, McNamara said.

Wechsler protested, saying that investors did not know how to sell those partnership units themselves, so at least they would be getting something. A few minutes later, McNamara asked Hackerman how he viewed the buyback proposal.

Prudential Securities was offering clients twenty cents on the dollar to purchase the investments, Hackerman said, even though the firm's own records showed that the units were worth thirty-five to forty-two cents. Essentially, the settlement was structured in such a way that Prudential Securities, one of the authors of the sales fraud, could arguably double its money in profits from the repurchased partnership units.

"They will pay the class members twenty cents, and the class members will give them back something that's worth thirty-five cents and give up all their claims," Hackerman said.

"You're telling me 'Man, this is off the wall,' " McNamara said. "What's on the wall?"

"I think the plaintiffs in the case when we get it to trial will win," Hackerman said. "The damages will be essentially a dollar for each dollar investment. I think an offer that doesn't get these people whole in terms of their investment is woefully inadequate."

The judge circled back to the buyback offer. It would eliminate the risk for the investors in holding the units, he said. Perhaps that made it a better deal for sellers.

As Hackerman listened, an image flashed through his mind of Darrell Haney, the elderly steelworker he represented. He saw Haney, sitting in a room at the Sheraton Hotel in Fort Myers, crying bitterly about his broken dreams.

Hackerman looked up at the judge. Perhaps it wouldn't be a bad deal, he said, as long as the seller knew what he was doing and what the real values were.

"Prudential knows a lot more about these values than Mr. Haney in Fort Myers, Florida," Hackerman said. "Mr. Haney is seventy-eight years old. And when he picks up all this, he won't have any idea what the values are."

As the bickering went back and forth, Moriarty began to scowl. He was sick of the lies, deceptions, and bullying tactics of Prudential Securities and Graham. As far as he was concerned, these two companies were evil.

Hackerman finished his presentation. McNamara looked at Moriarty. "Do you want to be heard now, sir?"

Moriarty stood. "I do, Your Honor."

He identified himself and then set the verbal guns blasting.

"I would like to be the voice from the wilderness, speaking for common sense and fairness and decency," Moriarty said. "The thought that went through my mind as I sat and listened this morning was something was rotten in Denmark. Let me give you a little overview to the threshold question: Is there any reason to believe this is more than a frivolous settlement? The answer is no."

He described the sales pitch the firm had made on the growth funds to "the little old men and little old ladies from one end of this country to the other." He said that the growth funds were supposed to have purchased discounted, overcollateralized bank loans and that investors were told that the deal was virtually guaranteed. Now, Moriarty argued, they wanted to say that a few pennies on the dollar was substantial compensation.

"This is a settlement which is negotiated out of weakness at the wrong time, at the wrong place, and by the wrong parties," he said.

His voice rising, Moriarty pointed toward the table full of lawyers representing Prudential Securities and Graham.

"I would encourage the court to think that the only parties in this room that benefit from this scheme are the defendants who stand the likelihood of extinguishing hundreds of millions of dollars of liability," he said. "When this scheme unfolds, when we try this case a year from now, and when all this evidence is put before a jury, I want to be the one to say, 'I said that five cents on the dollar is ridiculous.'"

Moriarty lowered his arm and paused. "Thank you, Judge," he said, and sat back down.

McNamara smiled for a moment. Moriarty was particularly convincing.

"If this was an ex-parte trial," McNamara said, referring to a situation where only one side in a dispute presents its view to the judge, "you would probably win."

The final weeks of 1991 were upbeat for Bristow, Hackerman, and Moriarty. McNamara refused to approve the class-action settlement proposal.

The lawyers would not have to waste their time trying to inform clients of their need to opt out.

Even better, each day brought new batches of letters to them from securities regulators across the country. Moriarty's computerized mass mailing to clients had hit the target. For weeks, they had been receiving copies of thousands of clients' letters, many in the shaky handwriting of the elderly and infirm. The lawyers loved the letters, in part because the brokerage firm was suffering for having sold partnership after partnership to the same investors. Although Bristow, Hackerman represented the clients only for the growth fund investments, most of them were loaded up with a range of other partnerships. So in addition to the growth fund, the regulators were receiving written complaints about dozens of other partnerships. Each letter instructed the regulators to contact Bristow, Hackerman for more information.

By late December, the regulators had started doing just that. State securities regulators from Florida, Arizona, New Jersey, and a number of other states had requested copies of the documents and records obtained by the law firm. The National Association of Securities Dealers had also asked for information and had begun an investigation of Graham's marketing subsidiary. The New York Stock Exchange and the SEC had opened more than fifty separate informal inquiries into partnership sales practices at the brokerage firm. For every investigation, Prudential Securities had to hire lawyers to respond with voluminous position papers. The Texas lawyers knew that their tactic was costing Pru-Bache a huge amount of time and money.

But the impact of the letters was far greater than that. Finally, more than a decade after the limited partnership fraud began, it was being exposed to law enforcement officials across the country.

Any hope Prudential Securities had of containing the scandal was gone.

Wayne Klein brought a meeting of state securities regulators to order on January 12, 1992. The regulators had gathered for their annual conference that year at the St. Petersburg Hilton in Florida. There they planned to share ideas and discuss emerging trends they were seeing in securities law.

Klein was the chairman of the enforcement meeting in the North Ballroom of the hotel. As the discussion began, it took him only a few minutes to notice the first trend. A number of states reported that in recent weeks, they had been receiving numerous complaints about fraudulent limited partnership sales by the firm now known as Prudential Securities. One at a time, several state regulators laid out what they had heard. Complaints had been filed about fraud in the growth funds, the energy income funds, a number of real estate partnerships, and other deals sold by the firm. It seemed as if suddenly everyone knew where to bring their concerns.

Klein told the assembled regulators that his department had been looking into the partnership problems for some time. After discussion, the assembled regulators decided that they should try to share information in order to speed up their investigations.

By the end of the meeting, Klein had a list of about half a dozen states that wanted to coordinate their efforts. But he also had something more important. Until now, after more than a year of investigating, Klein had felt largely alone in his efforts. At times, lawyers for Prudential Securities subtly played on that, raising doubts in Klein's mind about whether he and his investigators had really found a problem. After all, if they were on the right path, the lawyers suggested, where was everyone else?

All those doubts ended in St. Petersburg. Klein flew back to Idaho relieved. For the first time, he felt certain that his investigation wasn't off base.

The offices of Bristow, Hackerman were packed with lawyers, staff members, and their families over the Memorial Day weekend. They ate pizza, laughed, and stuffed 5,800 envelopes with the notices that Prudential Securities and Graham Resources had agreed to settle the growth fund litigation.

The months of hard battling had paid off. The multiple regulatory investigations appeared to weaken the resolve of the companies to keep fighting the litigation. Already the National Association of Securities Dealers, using information obtained from Bristow, Hackerman, was preparing to bring charges against Graham for improper sales practices. That made victory all the sweeter.

The settlements brought in more than ten times the cash that had been proposed only six months earlier by Prudential Securities and Graham, and would make the investors whole. Clients in the first growth fund would receive fifty cents on the dollar on their investments. Combined with previous distributions, expected future distributions, and the remaining value of the partnerships, a client who invested $1,000 in the first growth fund would receive $1,058. For the second growth fund, the $1,000 investor would receive $1,138.

Under the terms of the agreement, Bristow, Hackerman would not pursue any new claims against Prudential Securities for other investors. The law firm also agreed to give the brokerage firm all of the documents it had obtained. Apparently Prudential hoped to pull the incriminating records out of circulation.

But that condition really didn't matter. By the day that the settlement agreement was signed, the Texas lawyers had copied and boxed up every important document and shipped them all to the Securities and Exchange Commission in Washington, D.C.

Mary Hughes, a securities regulator in Idaho, stepped into Klein's office in the early summer of 1992. She had just been speaking with members of the SEC enforcement staff in Atlanta. The commission was investigating apparent irregularities in Prudential Securities' Atlanta branch that might have violated the terms of the Capt. Crab settlement. The SEC also told her that it was starting to investigate the emerging partnership scandal. That gave Hughes an idea.

Klein looked up as she stepped in.

"Wayne, I've been talking to some people over at the SEC who are looking into the partnership situation at Prudential," she said. "They've been talking with some people in other states who are running their own investigations."

"Yes?"

"I was just thinking that with so many investigations going on, it might be a good idea for everybody working on Prudential to get together and do a little brainstorming. Both the states and the SEC."

Klein smiled. "That's a wonderful idea," he said. "Why don't you call whoever you need to call and encourage it. We'll pay to send you wherever, whenever."

Hughes agreed and headed back to her office. Weeks later, she told Klein that the SEC was thinking about the proposal and might agree to a meeting in a few months. Then the meeting was postponed once, then again and again.

After the joint meeting had been called off for a third time, Klein knew it was no accident. He was sure it was the fault of Richard Breeden, the SEC chairman. Breeden had always made it clear that he thought state regulation of securities was a waste of time. Almost every state regulator had heard the story—perhaps apocryphal—about Breeden saying he would like to have everyone involved in state securities regulation lumped together in a boat, hauled out to sea, and sunk.

"They're not going to meet with us," Klein told Hughes. "As long as Breeden is in charge, it's not going to happen."

Hardwick Simmons, the chief executive of Prudential Securities, came on the firm's internal squawk box in July 1992 to make an important announcement. The proposed settlement of the growth fund litigation with the Texas lawyers had been finalized. Some of the biggest lawsuits the firm faced on its partnerships were all over.

With those headaches out of the way, Simmons told the troops, the time was perfect for Prudential Securities to get back into the partnership business.

As brokers throughout the country listened in disbelief, Simmons said that he wanted to rebuild the Direct Investment Group into a big force in the firm. But this time, the brokerage would make sure that it learned from the mistakes of the past.

"We want everybody to know every aspect" of the new partnerships, Simmons said. No longer would the brokers be ordered to sell the deals blindly, without asking questions. And every one of the new partnerships would be subjected to stringent guidelines.

Few brokers were persuaded. For more than a decade, they had been told that the partnerships had the best due diligence on Wall Street. With their best customers facing huge losses, there was no way they could simply forget the past.

Any chance that the brokers wouldn't revolt was soon eliminated. Within hours of Simmons's announcement, the Dallas district attorney indicted one Prudential Securities broker for fraud in connection with sales of the energy growth fund. Three years before, the broker, Jeffrey Schiller, had given a client a handwritten note promising that the growth funds would perform. The note said, almost verbatim, what Schiller and other brokers had been told by the firm in sales conferences and marketing materials. Apparently the Dallas prosecutors never thought that the fraud may have emanated from the firm itself. Schiller faced the possibility of twenty-five years in jail.*

The symbolic importance of the indictment was lost on no one. Simmons's effort to rebuild the Direct Investment Group died.

---

* Months later, the indictment would be dropped after the prosecutors finally realized that Schiller had only been repeating the lies he heard from Prudential-Bache.

That same summer, a young state prosecutor in Tucson, Arizona, was beginning to see the broad outlines of a criminal case in the partnership scandal. John Evans, an assistant attorney general for Arizona, first heard about troubles at Prudential Securities from a plaintiff's lawyer in Tucson. At first, it seemed only to involve fraudulent partnership sales by a Prudential broker in Arizona named Jay Jablonski. Evans started to pursue the case with the same mentality the Dallas prosecutors had toward Schiller: This was a fraud caused by a bad broker.

As Evans called around to other local lawyers, he learned that Jablonski's major defense was that he, too, had been deceived by the brokerage firm's partnership department. Arizona securities regulators had received dozens of complaints about the firm's partnership sales, most of them involving the energy deals with Graham. The regulators told Evans that they were conducting an investigation into the firm's partnership sales. Many of the complaints referred them to the Bristow, Hackerman firm. Already the regulators had obtained a large number of internal marketing materials from the Houston lawyers.

Intrigued by what he heard, Evans obtained copies of the Bristow, Hackerman records for himself. By the time he finished reviewing them, he had no doubt that he had enough information to justify a criminal investigation. But Evans also knew that a state attorney general's office would need help taking on a firm like Prudential Securities. His department had only three investigators, and alone they could never crack the case. So, in August 1992, Evans picked up the telephone in his office and dialed a number in the Tucson federal building. The telephone rang just a few times before it was answered.

"FBI," a receptionist said.

The first criminal investigation of the partnership scandal had begun.

A group of almost a dozen executives and lawyers with Prudential Securities gathered at the firm's headquarters in the summer of 1992 to debate a single question: Could Prudential Securities finally fire Fred Storaska?

Michael McClain, who had been installed as manager of the Dallas office in late 1990, was demanding the right to get rid of the big-producing broker. As always, the firm was raising hurdles. Storaska already had more than $20 million in claims filed against him by clients. With so much on the line, McClain's regional director, Peter Archbold, was not willing to fire the man without consulting the top executives in retail, as well as Schechter and other lawyers for the firm. Archbold organized the meeting in New York.

Every executive who had contact with Storaska was there, including three men who had worked as his branch managers. Also in the room from the retail group were George Murray, the head of retail, and Joseph Haick, Murray's second in command. Schechter was there with a number of lawyers who worked for him, including Noah Sorkin and James Tricarico.

McClain was given the floor. He said that Storaska refused to allow himself to be supervised. In one case, McClain had ordered Storaska not to do certain business, but the broker just ignored the instructions.

The biggest problem in McClain's mind was something he had found and already shut down. In 1988, Storaska had reached a secret pact with a Prudential Insurance agent named Don Gustovich. Under the agreement, Gustovich would be the agent who would sell Storaska's wealthy clients their multimillion-dollar life insurance policies. But the sales would not be processed through Prudential, which normally would claim half of the commissions. Instead, the sale would go through a shell company called Ambryshell, headed by Storaska's wife, Betty Lou. She was not licensed to sell insurance. Through the scheme, money that should have gone to Prudential went into Storaska's pocket instead.

"I want to fire him," McClain concluded.

"So what's the problem?" Joe Haick blurted out. "Fire the son of a bitch."

The lawyers disagreed. "We're not going to fire him," Schechter said. "We've got millions of dollars in lawsuits from his clients. We need him as a friendly witness."*

Some of the retail executives shrank back. It seemed as if the only way to avoid getting fired at this firm was by angering lots of clients.

"I could force him out, get him to resign," McClain said.

"How could you do that?" Schechter asked.

"You've got to understand this guy," McClain said. "He's an egomaniac. Right now, he's working in his office a floor below the branch. I'll tell him we can't afford the space anymore. We're moving him upstairs to a nice little office next to mine. That we're going to cut his staff in half. Fred'll never stand for it. He'll resign as soon as he can."

---

*Schechter denies using these words. Instead he said he rejected the recommendation to fire Storaska for another reason: He wanted to avoid creating the impression among other brokers that Storaska was being fired because his customers had filed complaints. See Notes and Sources.

Schechter thought about it for a moment. "If you think it will work, give it a try."

The plan was in place. Prudential Securities would force Storaska, a man his bosses believed to be violating any number of securities laws, to resign without a mark on his record. Of course, some other firm would hire him, and he would start doing his business elsewhere. And the problems that led to $20 million worth of lawsuits could start all over again somewhere else.

But nobody at the meeting mentioned that fact. After all, whoever those other clients might be, Prudential Securities wasn't going to be liable for their damages.

The ruse worked. Within days of being told in August of his new restrictions, Storaska resigned to take a job with Bear Stearns & Company. When Bear Stearns asked about Storaska, executives from Prudential Securities gave him a clean bill of health.

Months later, Marvin Coble, the assistant branch manager in Dallas, realized that before leaving, Storaska had opened a series of accounts that charged up-front fees. Storaska had received about $26,000 in those fees before he walked out the door. Afterward, the accounts were canceled and the customers were reimbursed all of their money.

Coble spoke with Peter von Maur, one of the firm's lawyers in New York. He explained what had happened and said that, at this point, the $26,000 repaid to customers was coming out of the branch's profits.

"I want to see if we can go after Fred on this and get him to repay the firm that money," Coble said.

A short time later, von Maur called back and said that the decision had been made to leave things as they were.

"We've decided to let him keep the money," von Maur said. "That will help make sure that we keep Storaska as a friendly witness in all these upcoming arbitrations we have with his former clients."

Coble hung up the telephone, chilled. He couldn't believe that Prudential Securities was willing to walk away from that much money just to make sure it got the testimony it wanted. He was no lawyer, but he knew right from wrong. And this was damned wrong.

Jim Burns, an investigator with the Idaho Securities Bureau, sorted through the latest pile of questionnaires on his desk. Klein had assigned Burns the job of reviewing the answers to the questionnaires that the bureau had recently sent to investors in the Prudential-Bache partnerships. Slightly more than half of the 290 investors who were contacted had responded. For Burns, the questionnaires had started to seem repetitive after the first few weeks, all telling the same story: Safety-conscious investors, including a number of elderly people, were sold the partnerships as conservative and secure investments. Few of the investors ever received a prospectus before they agreed to purchase.

After a while, the responses had stopped coming in, and Burns figured that everyone who wanted to respond had done so. Then something strange had happened. All new batches of filled-out questionnaires had started arriving at the securities bureau. And the story in these new ones was the exact opposite from the earlier responses. Everyone said they knew all about the risks of partnerships before investing in them, had been provided with a prospectus right away, and had been told only truthful statements by their brokers. Burns kept mentioning the differences to Klein. In some ways, the upbeat stories raised some doubts in the regulators' minds.

Today's batch was the same. None of these investors had any complaints. Then Burns noticed something about the answers that bothered him. He was still reading through the new batch when Klein walked in and asked how it was going. All the late arrivals were still telling a story of proper sales, Burns said.

"But, Wayne, there's something about these questionnaires that bothers me," Burns said. "The wording in each one is amazingly similar. It's very suspicious."

Klein looked puzzled. He asked Burns what he was driving at.

"I think some of these positive ones were filled out by the brokers."

On November 5, 1992, Prudential Securities reached a tentative settlement of the largest class-action suit stemming from the partnership debacle. The suit involving the energy income partnerships had been filed by a number of class-action lawyers the year before, immediately after the article in *Business Week* pointed out the problems with the Graham deals.

The latest settlement made all the other class-action sellouts look fabulous. For just $37 million in cash, Prudential Securities wiped out $1.4 billion in potential liability from its eight years of the energy income partnerships. The investors would receive less than two cents for every dollar they put into the partnerships.

The settlement was loaded down with a number of other features, purportedly designed to increase its value to investors. But, in truth, the biggest beneficiaries were Graham and Prudential Securities. Graham made vague assurances that it would reimburse investors for future administrative expenses of the partnerships. That term of the agreement contained the condition that, if any Graham principals stopped acting as managers, the reimbursement was off.

On top of that, Graham would be placed in charge of a publicly traded company that would take over the assets of the partnerships. The investors' partnership units would be exchanged for shares in that new company, called Graham Energy Resources. The limited partners would lose control of the energy assets and turn them over to Graham. And they would cover $13 million of expenses associated with the roll-up.

Analysts were outraged at the deal. The American Association of Limited Partners branded the deal a "scam."

Another partnership publication, called *The Perspective*, was harsher.

"Yes, the champagne will soon be flowing in Covington," an unsigned article in the newsletter said. "And with John J. Graham receiving $375,000 a year as chief executive of this new company, you can bet it won't be the screw-top brands. For Graham, it doesn't get any better than this. As for the 128,000 investors? They lost out the day their partnerships were formed."

Few of the investors would likely figure out how bad the deal really was. For those who did, the chance that they would know to opt out of the settlement was small. The deal was described in a three-hundred-page proxy. The opt-out procedure was spelled out on one page. Investors who didn't follow the tortuous and unusual procedure of writing three separate opt-out letters to three different groups of lawyers would end up in the settlement. In all likelihood, hardly anyone would be able to figure it all out. All Prudential Securities needed was the approval of a federal court in New Orleans, and the deal would be done.

Throughout Prudential Securities, the proposed settlement was treated as a blessing. After the terms were disclosed, Richard Haughey, the manager of the firm's Rancho Bernardo, California, office, called a meeting of some of his top brokers. The branch had been consistently one of the biggest sellers of the energy income partnerships, and it looked like the settlement would bail it out of a lot of potential claims.

As he briefed some of his brokers on the settlement in early January 1993, Haughey smiled. "We're not supposed to give legal advice to clients," he said. "But if your clients go into the energy income class-action settlement, they cannot sue Prudential, and they cannot sue you."

Then Haughey winked at the assembled group of brokers.

James Barrett, one of the branch's biggest sellers of the energy income partnership, stood up and walked out of the meeting. He was incensed. For years after the problems with the partnerships became apparent, he had demanded to know what the firm was going to do for the defrauded clients. Now he knew. It was going to cheat them again.

Barrett headed into his office where his fiancée was waiting for him. As he was describing what had just happened in the meeting, Haughey knocked on his door.

"Jim, I don't like to see you looking so upset," Haughey said. "What's the matter?"

Barrett spun around. "This settlement sounds like a damn screwing, and you know it."

Haughey closed the door. "You know what happens in class-action lawsuits, don't you, Jim?" he asked.

"You tell me."

"The only ones who make out in a settlement are the attorneys and the defendants," Haughey said.

Barrett felt so angry his hands trembled. "Well, what about my clients?"

"The clients always get screwed in a class action, Jim," Haughey said. "They always get screwed."

After a few minutes, Haughey left. The broker sat down at his desk and stewed. He picked up the telephone, dialed the Direct Investment Group in New York, and asked for Jim Kelso, the head of the department. Once Kelso got on the line, Barrett started complaining about the horrible class-action settlement.

"Jim, it's out of our hands," Kelso said. "You need to talk to the law department."

Later that day, Barrett called Carlos Ricca in the law department. He mentioned several concerns he had about partnerships and then got to the settlement.

"What's going on with this settlement for $37 million?" Barrett asked. "Brokers in my office are saying that's like two cents on the dollar. How in the hell can we do this to our clients? I mean, I've got my brother in this crap, I've got my ex-wife in it, I've got myself in it. All my good clients who are my friends are in there. How can we do this to them?"

"It's all being done in New Orleans," Ricca responded calmly. "It's out of our hands, you know."

Barrett was sick of everybody saying it was out of their hands. His anger finally got the better of him.

"Fine, it's out of your hands, it's out of Kelso's hands, nobody is responsible for this bullshit," Barrett said. "What would you do if I called *60 Minutes* or *Business Week* and told them what the hell was going on? Would that be in your hands?"

Ricca's voice stiffened. "I wouldn't do that if I were you."

"Well, I guess you're not me, are you?" Barrett said.

Barrett was angry for the rest of the day. By January 6, two days later, he had calmed down. His statement about going to the media had been an idle threat. Instead, he just went back to work. He began his morning by preparing a mailing of two thousand invitations to an investment seminar. As Barrett was getting them ready, Haughey's secretary dropped by. Haughey wanted to see him.

Barrett walked into his manager's office and babbled for a few seconds about the mailing. Haughey looked on stone-faced.

"Jim, I can't have you do that mailing," Haughey said finally. "I have to terminate you."

Barrett gasped. "Why?"

"This has nothing to do with me," Haughey said, holding up his hands. "I'm just following orders. This comes straight from the law department. Carlos Ricca called and said that we had to fire you. He said that you have an overconcentration of direct investments in your accounts."

"Wait a minute," Barrett said. "I haven't sold one of those things in a long time. Are you telling me they just noticed that I sold a lot of them?"

"Jim, I'm just doing what I was told. I have to terminate you for having an overconcentration of direct investments."

Bullshit, Barrett thought. *You have to fire me because Ricca thought I was going to blow the whistle.*

At that moment, Barrett realized that, even if he bothered to tell any reporters what he knew, Prudential Securities would just dismiss it as the ravings of a disgruntled former employee. He stood up and walked out. It was his last day at the firm. Barrett left convinced that his clients would be tricked into joining the energy income settlement. But he didn't think there was anything he could do. If Prudential Securities fired him for making a hollow threat, Barrett felt sure that the firm would crush anyone it saw as a danger to the settlement. He feared that no one would be able to stop it.

Barrett had no way of knowing that a little-known securities regulator from Idaho was just getting ready to try.

CHAPTER 18

SCORES OF CASUALLY DRESSED state securities regulators milled about the Hibiscus Room at the Brazilian Court Hotel as they hunted for their seats. The meeting about trends in securities law enforcement was scheduled to begin any minute. It was the morning of January 11, 1993, the third day of the winter enforcement conference at the hotel in Palm Beach, Florida.

The group began to quiet down as William McDonald, a regulator from California and the chairman of that day's session, stepped up to the podium. He asked everyone to come to order quickly because they had a packed agenda. The first topic was Prudential Securities. The firm's partnership troubles had first been mentioned at last year's meeting. The number of state investigators had since grown rapidly.

"A number of states have approached me about complaints they have received regarding Prudential in the limited partnership area," McDonald said. "Some states have already progressed far along in their own investigations."

McDonald nodded toward Klein, who was leaning against a wall at the side of the room. "Wayne Klein from Idaho has been looking into this matter for some time. So, Wayne, could you give everyone a sense of what it is that you're finding, and where the investigation might be going?"

Klein spoke for a few minutes about his department's findings. He had expected that McDonald would ask him for a presentation. The previous day, Klein and Joseph Goldstein, a lawyer from the SEC enforcement division who was attending the conference, had spoken with McDonald about setting up a system to coordinate the different state investigations. That would help the SEC, which was receiving dozens of requests for information from regulators across the country, and could give the states more leverage in dealing with Prudential Securities. McDonald had agreed to get it done before the end of the conference.

After Klein finished his presentation, McDonald recognized Don

Saxon, the Florida state securities regulator, and asked for details of his state's investigation of the firm. Saxon's presentation was followed by another from Matthew Neubert, a regulator from Arizona. All of the inquiries were treading on similar ground.

"All right," McDonald said after several presentations. "As you can see, there are a number of states working on the Prudential matter that have expressed interest in getting information from the SEC. Now, the SEC has suggested that a coordinating group would be the best way to funnel information. Which states would be interested in participating?"

A flurry of hands went up. Saxon and Neubert, who had both obtained information from Bristow, Hackerman, were the first to be named. Then Nancy Smith from New Mexico joined up, followed by Lewis Brothers from Virginia.

The last hand was Klein's. He had hesitated for a moment, worried about whether working with the other states might slow his own investigation. But he put aside his doubts in the hopes of gaining access to more information from the SEC. McDonald immediately named Klein chairman of the group.

At 12:15 that same day, the newly formed Prudential Multi-State Task Force met for a buffet lunch at a circular table in the hotel's dining area. They were joined by several members of the SEC enforcement staff.

The regulators quickly established an agenda. They listed the questions Prudential Securities needed to answer and the documents they wanted the firm to turn over. They discussed how, if the partnership matter was going to be resolved, it should be as a global settlement involving both the states and the SEC. That would prevent Prudential Securities lawyers from playing the two sides off each other. The SEC lawyers agreed.

Klein was delighted. Apparently Richard Breeden, the commission's chairman, was no longer an obstacle to cooperation. Then again, Breeden was an appointee of George Bush. Bill Clinton had just won the presidency, so Breeden would be chairman for only another few weeks. Klein felt sure that had at least something to do with the new willingness of the SEC enforcement staff to work with the states.

Near the end of the luncheon, Nancy Smith, the New Mexico securities regulator, raised concerns about the energy income class-action settlement. Smith, a former aide to Congressman Ed Markey of Massachusetts, had investigated the types of partnership roll-ups involved in the settlement for congressional hearings a few years earlier. In her mind, roll-ups

were little more than scams that enriched general partners at the expense
of their investors.

"This is an outrageous settlement," Smith said. "It has such a small
amount of money, then they throw in this roll-up. It's nonsense."

The regulators also knew that the settlement could cause problems for
their investigation. There were 120,000 investors in the energy income
partnerships. Once their claims were resolved—no matter how unfairly—
those investors would be less likely to spend the time and energy to help
the regulators build their case. Not only would the paltry settlement wipe
out valid investor claims, but it would severely hamper any chance regulators had of getting money back for other investors.

"There's a deadline coming up soon," Smith said. "The judge is going
to hold a fairness hearing on the settlement's terms. And I think it's urgent
that we get a letter to him and try to stop it."

The state regulators agreed to write the federal judge in the case, Marcel Livaudais, and asked if the SEC would do the same. Goldstein from the
SEC replied that was not likely. The commission had a policy against getting involved in private litigation.

As the meeting was about to break up, Klein mentioned that he had recently learned an interesting fact: The Brazilian Court, the hotel where the
task force was formed and where its first strategy session was held, was part
of the Prudential-Bache partnership debacle. The hotel had been syndi-
cated in a deal sponsored by one of the firm's biggest general partners,
Clifton Harrison. It was later seized by S&L regulators when it defaulted
on a series of loans. Investors lost everything.

The birthplace of the task force was also the perfect symbol of its cause.

In late January, Pat Conti, a senior counsel with the SEC enforcement staff
in Washington, read over Prudential Securities' five-page response to his
most recent subpoena. Conti was in charge of investigation number HO-
2636, titled "In the Matter of Prudential Securities." When he started
work on the case months before, Conti read through the documents that
had been collected by the New York regional office in its original, aborted
inquiry into the *Business Week* allegations. The material was useful, but
Conti still thought a lot of important documents were not in the file. In
particular, he wanted a copy of the three-volume Locke Purnell report.

A few weeks before, he had subpoenaed Prudential Securities seeking
that report and any other documents relating to investigations of Darr. He

had felt somewhat secure that the firm would turn over the material. In a recent lawsuit, an Alabama court rejected Prudential Securities' argument that the Locke Purnell report was a privileged communication from its lawyers. In essence, the court held that the firm had simply farmed out its legally required responsibilities to oversee its operations. Just because it hired a law firm to handle that job did not mean Prudential Securities could hide the information.

But in its letter responding to the subpoena, Prudential Securities was refusing to turn over the report to Conti. The letter came from Gary Lynch, the former head of enforcement for the SEC who had been in charge when the Capt. Crab case was brought. Lynch was now a lawyer at Davis, Polk and represented the firm.

The letter was blunt: Every document that Conti wanted was an attorney-client product and was exempt from disclosure. The judgment by the Alabama court had no bearing on the situation, Lynch wrote. After failing to reverse the ruling on appeal, Prudential Securities had settled the case on the condition that the former client support having the judgment vacated. The former client accepted, and the judgment was withdrawn. The report was never turned over. As a result, the Alabama decision no longer existed as a precedent. Just as in the McNulty case involving Clifton Harrison, the firm had paid to have an adverse ruling disappear.

Conti finished reading the letter and set it down. The firm was clearly going to fight this one hard. Conti still wanted the Locke Purnell report. But at that moment, he hadn't the faintest idea how he was going to get it.

Klein sat at a desk in the Idaho State Supreme Court's law library, looking for a legal precedent in volume 748 of the *Federal Supplement*. He had returned a few days before from the conference in Palm Beach and was spending every working day in the library, researching class actions. If he was going to write a letter asking Judge Livaudais not to accept the energy income settlement, he wanted his arguments as strong as a legal brief.

The letter to Livaudais had become something of an obsession for Klein from the moment Nancy Smith suggested it. To him, the stakes were enormous. The financial future of thousands of unsophisticated, frightened investors rode on what the judge decided. If nothing else, Klein wanted to be sure that Livaudais had as much information as possible.

For a week, Klein did his research in the law library. Then, at night, he crafted legal arguments on his laptop computer. During his usual family time with his wife and three children, Klein sat alone in a room at his home, perfecting his letter. Sometimes, when his children seemed to really miss him, he carried his laptop into the family room and typed while they played or watched television.

On January 22, the twelve-page bombshell was ready. The letter, which would be placed in the court's public file, disclosed for the first time the existence of the state task force. In careful detail, it described the inadequacies of the class-action settlement. It said the notices of the settlement that had been sent to investors did not disclose all relevant information, including a number of the government investigations. Finally it argued that the settlement could impede the regulators' ability to do anything about any violations they found.

The letter ended with several recommendations, including that Livaudais refuse to approve the settlement or postpone approval until the regulators finished their investigation.

Klein sent the letter by overnight mail to New Orleans. He wasn't confident it would have any effect. At best, he figured, the chances that it would were no better than one in four.

The telephone call from Loren Schechter reached Klein four days later. It was the first time Schechter had called the Idaho Securities Bureau during its two-year investigation.

"I hear you sent a letter about the settlement to Judge Livaudais," Schechter said.

"If you don't have a copy, I'd be happy to send you one," Klein said.

Schechter thanked him, but said he could get a copy himself. "I'd be happy to get together with you and talk about it."

"I'd been thinking about just that," Klein replied. "Let me check with the other members of the task force and get back to you about possibly setting up a time."

Klein hung up, delighted at the turn of events. For the first time, Prudential Securities was reacting swiftly to regulators and offering assistance. It boded well for the chances of cooperation in the task force investigation.

The receptionist told Klein that a judge was on the telephone. She took a swing at pronouncing the name, but it didn't sound like anyone Klein had ever heard of before.

He picked up the telephone. "This is Wayne Klein," he said.

"Mr. Klein, this is Judge Marcel Livaudais from New Orleans."

For an instant, Klein was shocked. But he had no doubt that the deep bass voice with the lilting New Orleans accent belonged to Livaudais himself.

"Yes, Judge Livaudais."

"I've been out of town and just got back today," Livaudais said. "I've read your letter and wanted to thank you for writing it."

"Well, Your Honor, I just wanted to get some information to you that you could have while considering your opinion," Klein said. "I hope it will be helpful."

The two men spoke for another few moments, then Livaudais thanked Klein again and said good-bye.

Klein felt almost a sense of awe as he looked out the window of his second-floor office, gazing at the church next door. For an instant, he closed his eyes. *Maybe,* he thought, *there's a chance this might work after all.*

The Klein letter was the central topic at a meeting on February 1, 1993, between the task force and lawyers for Prudential Securities. The letter had been something of a watershed—now approval of the biggest partnership settlement suddenly did not seem assured. It upended the firm's entire legal strategy. Schechter had told senior executives that the best way to handle the partnership problems was to settle all of the class actions first, then deal with the regulators. The fewer clients with claims against the firm, the easier it would be to settle with the states and the SEC. The firm desperately wanted Klein to take his letter back. The threat to Schechter's strategy was getting bigger each day, as other regulators from around the country wrote Livaudais to support Klein's conclusions.

The meeting between the firm and the task force was held at a hotel in Washington, D.C. All of the task force members were there. A number of lawyers attended representing Prudential, including Schechter; Scott Muller, a lawyer from Davis, Polk who was handling the Graham cases; and Dan Bell, a former North Carolina securities commissioner who had been hired to deal with the state regulators. Bell was given the role of discussing Klein's letter.

"This lawsuit is a private action, involving the parties and Judge Livaudais," Bell said. "State regulation has no role here. It's not your place. You shouldn't be involved in private litigation."

Klein disagreed. He mentioned a class-action suit from years before involving the sale of securities in the bankrupt Baldwin-United Corp. A court held that the brokers who sold those securities were not liable to regulators for any more than was paid to settle the class action. If the state regulators didn't act now, their investigations could be scuttled.

"We have no desire to preclude any enforcement actions," Schechter interjected. Perhaps, the Prudential Securities lawyers suggested, the firm would send a letter to the judge assuring him that it would waive the standard from the Baldwin-United case. If that was done, perhaps Klein would withdraw his letter, Schechter said.

"I'm willing to discuss this," Klein said. "But I meant what I said in that letter."

Bell continued to press Klein to change his mind, without success. Then the floor was turned over to Schechter.

"I want everyone here to understand Prudential Securities," Schechter said. "We want to put this matter behind us. We're not a bad firm, we're not a corrupt firm. We had some serious problems in the past with these partnerships. But it wasn't a firmwide problem. It was a problem with certain brokers."

The explanation got Schechter nowhere. All of the regulators had seen enough information, particularly involving the Graham deals, to know that the problems emanated from New York. Besides, one of the regulators said, the responsibility for what happened could not be sloughed off onto the sales force even if the brokers were responsible. The senior executives in New York were still in charge of supervising those brokers. One way or the other, New York obviously had a problem.

"The people who were responsible are no longer at the firm," Schechter said.

Everyone in the room knew that Schechter was referring to Jim Darr and George Ball.

"Why did they leave?" one of the regulators asked.

"Because the decision was made to put this problem behind us."

"Well, that's fine, put it behind you," said Saxon, the Florida commissioner. "But you're going to have to make people whole to do that."

The firm had been doing precisely that, Schechter said. All told, the settlements or proposed settlements from the firm exceeded $180 million. And the total cost of dealing with the partnership problem, when legal fees were included, reached $300 million.

The regulators listened silently. Several were uncomfortable with Schechter's numbers. Some quick arithmetic told them that the highly criticized class-action settlements made up most of what had been paid to investors. Worse, the firm's legal fees were almost as high as the cost of its settlements. Some regulators concluded that Schechter's own numbers showed that the firm was throwing massive legal resources into fighting the claims of investors who refused to accept the cheap class-action settlements.

The meeting came to an amicable end, with agreements that the firm would voluntarily provide documents to the task force. As everyone headed for the exits, Nancy Smith approached Muller with a question she thought better to ask in private.

"Why aren't you guys going after Darr?" she asked. "You've been pretty derogatory about him and willing to lay blame on him. Why not go after him?"

"After all this is over, we probably will," Muller replied. "But right now, we both have our hands on the grenade, and if either Darr or the firm lets go, we both blow up."

Judge Livaudais's courtroom in downtown New Orleans was packed with lawyers. It was February 9, 1993, the second day of hearings on the fairness of the class-action settlement involving the energy income partnerships. Edward Grossmann, the lead class-action lawyer, and the Davis, Polk lawyers for Prudential Securities had been the chief architects of the settlement. Over two days, they presented witnesses who proclaimed the deal's high quality.

A range of plaintiffs' lawyers had spent the entire hearing attacking the settlement as inadequate and the result of too little digging by Grossmann. Not a single sworn deposition had been taken in the case, they said. How could Grossmann know the value of the case without having questioned witnesses under oath? On top of that, the plaintiffs' lawyers argued that aggressive efforts should be made to sell the partnerships' oil reserves for the benefit of investors rather than just turning them over to a new public company run by Graham. As evidence of the settlement's inadequacy, the lawyers stressed that close to twelve thousand investors had already rejected it—a huge number for a class action. And hanging over the proceedings like a sword was the protest from Klein and the other state regulators.

Grossmann, a heavyset man with an aggressive personality, approached the podium and looked up at the judge. He was ready to present his closing arguments. A lot was at stake; his law firm stood to make millions if the deal was approved.

"This settlement has met with an unusual assault and unprecedented critical press coverage," Grossmann said. "But it has been received with overwhelming approval by the class. All told, 125,000 of the 137,000 investors approved."

The statement reflected the twisted logic of class-action lawyers. No investor had approved the settlement. Instead, 125,000 investors had, for whatever reason, not sent in letters asking to opt out of the deal. The number of investors who had received the settlement notification, read it, understood it, realized that they had to write the court to refuse the deal, and knew that they had to write three separate letters to do so was almost certainly negligible. But in Grossmann's argument, even investors whose notification forms had been mailed to the wrong address had "approved" the settlement by not responding.

"It is irrefutable that 125,000 people believe that this is the best way to resolve their claims," Grossmann said. "If it is not approved, it is not clear that they will get any recovery of any kind."

Grossmann turned to the issue of the state regulators and the concerns raised by Klein's letter. He did little to hide his contempt for their unwanted intrusion.

"Nor should we rely on some state investigator cracking this open with some massive fraud finding that we don't know of," Grossmann said.

The class action should not impede the state investigations, Grossmann said. "But we shouldn't wait for them either. They've shown no evidence, and lots of rhetoric."

Finally Grossmann dismissed the possibility raised by plaintiffs' lawyers of selling the oil reserves for the benefit of investors. The idea, he implied, was ridiculous. The only option, he said, was the roll-up.

"There are no white knights out there to buy limited partnership assets," he said. "I talked to Dillon, Read and Morgan Stanley, in addition to Wasserstein Perella. Each one of these Wall Street firms agreed that it wasn't practical since it would require approval of all of the limited partnership investors."

Grossmann paused. "Nobody could do that."

Livaudais's written opinion on the energy income class-action settlement was filed in the New Orleans Federal Court on February 19 at 3:40 in the afternoon. In eighteen pages, he made it clear that he hadn't bought Grossmann's arguments. Early on, he rejected the idea that the settlement's wide approval was irrefutable.

"There were some 12,000 opt-outs and a large number of silent voices,"

Livaudais wrote. "The court does not feel that mere silence is acquies-
cence. It has a responsibility to those silent voices who will be affected by
this litigation."

Livaudais noted the objections to the settlement by the Idaho regulators,
with support from the other states. This, he wrote, had to be considered
seriously.

"Because there are state administrative and regulatory investigations in
progress," he wrote, "the wisest course and perhaps the most equitable may
be to defer ruling to allow additional information to be amassed."

Livaudais wasn't rejecting the settlement, but he also wasn't approving
it. The settlement was simply being stopped.

The long shot from Idaho had hit the target.

Klein read Livaudais's order carefully. His enormous respect for the judge
grew with each page. The energy income case had to be the largest one
on Livaudais's docket. Most judges simply approved class actions and
cleared them away. Livaudais not only showed enormous guts, Klein
thought, but a clear understanding of the stakes involved for 135,000 retail
investors.

The order also made Klein feel vindicated. For weeks, lawyers for Prudential Securities had kept up their criticism that the regulators were sticking their noses where they didn't belong. Now Livaudais was saying that
the regulators had been right.

Klein finished reading the decision and hustled down the hallway to the
copying machine. Minutes later, he was walking around the office with a
broad smile on his face, handing out copies to his examiners.

"Take a look at this," Klein said as he handed a copy to Mary Hughes.
"It's amazing. The settlement didn't go through."

In the politics of regulatory investigations, the balance of power had just
shifted. The states now had the advantage over Prudential Securities.

That spring, Gary Lynch delivered a demand from Prudential Securities to
the SEC: Prove it. If the enforcement staff was so convinced that they had
the evidence to support a case, then let the lawyers for Prudential Securities see it.

The request was highly unusual, but in this case it seemed like a perfect
idea. Thomas Newkirk, the SEC's associate director of enforcement,
thought that if the firm saw the evidence, it would be forced to settle. And

settling quickly with the firm was the central goal in this case. The elderly investors who suffered horrendous losses needed the money a settlement would give them. The SEC lawyers wanted that done quickly, before too many of the investors died.

Pat Conti and other lawyers working on the case were ordered to put together a notebook of the most damaging evidence, which could then be turned over to Lynch at Davis, Polk.

The idea seemed strange to Conti. The evidence had been subpoenaed from Prudential Securities. All they were doing was handing the same material right back. The firm and its lawyers knew what the documents said. Why go through the exercise?

"This is a waste of time," Conti complained to Newkirk. "Why are we giving them back their own documents?"

"They're testing us," Newkirk responded. "Just because they gave us boxes of documents doesn't mean we found the juicy stuff."

The notebook was finished in a few days. In it were marketing materials about the safety of the VMS Mortgage Investment Fund and the energy growth fund. It also included sales literature advising brokers to stress safety and guarantees to friendly clients, regardless of the partnerships.

When Newkirk finished reviewing the notebook, he had no doubt: The case could not be defended. Prudential Securities could try to fight the commission, but at the end of the day they would lose. No one who saw the evidence could think anything different. Newkirk ordered the notebook boxed up and shipped over to Lynch.

About a week later, the enforcement staff met with Prudential Securities' lawyers in the SEC's fourth-floor conference room. The lawyers representing the firm were Gary Lynch and Arthur Mathews, the Washington lawyer who had represented the firm in the Capt. Crab case. Across from them was William McLucas, who had succeeded Lynch as the SEC enforcement chief, Newkirk, and Pat Conti.

Lynch and Mathews opened up the discussion. Despite everything they had just seen in the notebook, they clung to the firm's line.

"There was nothing systemic here," Lynch said.

"What we had were some isolated cases of bad brokers," Mathews added.

McLucas broke in. "We don't see it that way at all. It's clear that what happened was centrally directed. And we're prepared to establish that if we need to."

It was the last time anyone from Prudential Securities argued the "rogue broker" theory to the SEC. Instead, settlement negotiations soon began in earnest.

The Prudential Securities investigation was taking its toll on the resources of the Idaho Securities Bureau. Other cases were at a standstill. The bureau had spent close to $50,000 hiring experts to help sort through financial material—an enormous sum of money for a single investigation. And there was no end in sight. Without a larger budget, Klein might not be able to see the investigation through.

In March, Klein went to see his boss, Belton Patty. A soft-spoken man with a deep baritone voice, Patty had spent much of his life as a banker in Idaho until Governor Cecil Andrus named him head of the Department of Finance. Patty was a good boss, who believed in letting his people pursue whatever leads they felt were important. All he asked was that he be kept up to date on big cases and consulted on important decisions.

For two years, Klein had been briefing Patty on the Prudential Securities case, and the story seemed to grow more amazing each time. By the end of Klein's briefing in March, Patty felt sickened by what he heard.

"This isn't the kind of conduct I'd expect from a national brokerage firm," Patty said. "It's offensive. If all this is true, then Prudential is no better than a penny-stock firm."

Klein then explained the problem with resources. To finish up the investigation, they would need more money. They didn't have enough lawyers. They might have to bring in an outside firm.

Patty held up his hand. "I'll take care of it, Wayne."

The timing was a little problematic. Because the Idaho state legislature was about to finish its session, it was a terrible time to try to change an agency's appropriation. Patty decided he needed help so he called Governor Andrus to arrange a meeting.

A few days later, in Andrus's office, Patty described the problem. "I've got a serious-sized securities case that might require more money than I had in my appropriation," he said. "I wanted to see if we could do something about that."

Andrus asked no questions. He knew nothing of the details of the case. He didn't even know it involved Prudential. But he trusted the judgment of his appointees.

"Don't worry," Andrus said. "If you need more money, I'll get it for you."

With those words, the only threat to the Idaho investigation was gone.

The bid for the energy income partnerships came out of nowhere.

A group called GBK Acquisition Corp. filed a hostile tender offer on March 22 for thirty-one of the thirty-five partnerships. Livaudais's refusal to rule on the class-action settlement had, in the parlance of Wall Street, put the energy income partnerships in play. Now they were on the block to the highest bidder.

The $173.5 million bid from GBK, a company controlled by George Kaiser, a wealthy oilman from Tulsa, Oklahoma, was quickly criticized on Wall Street as far too low. But it brought other investors out of the woodwork. Soon a bidding war emerged. In less than eight weeks, Parker & Parsley Petroleum of Midland, Texas, agreed to purchase all of the partnerships for $448.3 million. All of that money, more than twelve times the amount of cash that had been in the class-action settlement, would go straight to the partnership investors.

It was the final piece of evidence that the rationale for the proposed class-action settlement had been absurd. After all, the bidding started just forty-one days after Grossmann, the class-action lawyer, proclaimed in New Orleans that such a sale could never occur.

On March 29, sixteen lawyers arrived at a New Orleans law firm to attend the first deposition in the energy income class action. Livaudais's decision had compelled the class-action lawyers to finally begin taking sworn statements of executives from Prudential and Graham. The first witness was Matthew Chanin from Prudential Insurance, the executive who had been most involved in the company's decisions on the energy partnerships.

Most of the lawyers knew each other from the lawsuit. But seated among the crowd was a woman none of the others had seen before. All of the lawyers introduced themselves for the record. Finally it was the unknown woman's turn.

"Marilyn Scanlan," she said. "Representing the state of Idaho."

Klein, who had received a notice from the New Orleans court telling him of the Chanin deposition, had assigned Scanlan to watch and take notes. She was the only regulator in the room.

Klein had good reason to want one of his examiners there. At the beginning of the case, the lawyers from Prudential Securities and Graham Resources had demanded a court order to keep all records and documents confidential, ostensibly to protect corporate secrets. Judge Livaudais had complied, restricting access to thousands of documents.

While the regulators eventually could get hold of those documents, at times Prudential Securities seemed to drag its feet in producing them. Plus, Graham Resources had no offices in Idaho and was largely beyond Klein's reach. If the Idaho investigators heard the testimony personally, there would be no need for a fight to obtain copies.

As soon as Scanlan identified herself, Graham tried to tie her hands. Phillip Wittman, a lawyer for the oil company, said that he wanted her to state for the record that she accepted the terms of the court's protective order. Under that rule, Scanlan could use the information only for the class action and not in the state investigation. She refused.

"I have some statutory considerations here," she said. "I don't know that I can be bound voluntarily by an order like this. I think what I'll propose to do is check with my office."

"You're not really bound voluntarily," said Lawrence Sucharow, one of the class-action lawyers. "It's an order of the court, and you can only participate within the scope of that order."

"Well, I think we certainly have the same power to get the same information without any kind of restriction," Scanlan replied. "So it seems to me that this is a lot of rigmarole. I don't know that the state of Idaho has to abide by this, so let me see how my office wants me to proceed."

Scanlan stood and left the room. Klein had discussed this possibility in advance. They had decided that if the lawyers gave her any problems, she would contact Judge Livaudais's chambers immediately. She walked to a pay telephone, called the judge's clerk, and explained the situation. After Livaudais came on the line, Scanlan told him of the problem.

"Who's objecting to you being there?" he asked.

"I think Prudential and Graham and maybe some others."

"Go back in there and ask who's objecting."

"All right, just a minute."

Scanlan walked back into the deposition room. Chanin was in the middle of answering one of Sucharow's questions.

"Excuse me," Scanlan said. "May I interrupt for a moment?"

"Do you want to go off the record?" Sucharow asked.

"No, I would prefer to stay on the record," Scanlan said. She asked which of the lawyers in the room would object to her attending the deposition if she did not plan on complying with the confidentiality order.

"I would, representing Graham defendants," Wittman said.

A number of the class-action lawyers said they would not object. They actually wanted the evidence to be public. Then the floor was turned over to Frank Massengale, one of Prudential Securities' lawyers. Massengale said that the regulators could not simply ignore the court order.

"So you would not object to my attendance without complying with the order?" Scanlan asked.

"Certainly by agreeing to your presence, we wouldn't waive our position to seek a contempt charge or other remedy if you violate the order," Massengale said. "We believe the order applies to you."

Scanlan left the room for the pay phone, where she spoke with the judge's clerk, Peter Pierce. She explained the positions of Graham and Prudential Securities. As Pierce spoke with Livaudais in the background, Scanlan could hear that he was angered by the companies' attempts to impede the investigation. In a few seconds, Pierce was back on the line.

"The judge wants you to go back and tell everyone that he is revoking the confidentiality order," Pierce said.

Scanlan returned to the deposition and let everyone know what she had been told. The class-action lawyers thought it was hilarious. One said he wanted to start throwing incriminating documents out of the window. The lawyers for Prudential Securities and Graham Resources were apoplectic. They demanded that the other lawyers keep the information confidential, even without the order. Everyone refused.

That afternoon, Livaudais vacated the confidentiality requirement. With the thousands of internal documents suddenly public, an avalanche of bad publicity hit the firm. Articles appeared in the *Wall Street Journal* describing how the documents showed that partnership distributions had been falsely inflated. The *Los Angeles Times*, relying heavily on the newly available documents, splashed a two-part, ten-thousand-word exposé about the energy income partnerships across the front page. Some of the Direct Investment Group's darkest secrets were finally spilling into public view.

The lawyers for Prudential Securities and Graham had overplayed their hand. The regulators from Idaho had outsmarted them again.

An all-new front in Prudential Securities' regulatory war opened up the day after Livaudais's ruling. At 9:53 on the morning of March 30, Ronda Blair, a staff lawyer in the Fort Worth office of the SEC, faxed a two-page document to Prudential Securities' Dallas branch. It was a subpoena, addressed to John Bluher, a lawyer there. The commission wanted records about Fred Storaska.

The enforcement staff had been investigating problems at the Dallas branch for months. They had already obtained copies of managers' memos describing how Storaska could not be controlled. Since then, the commission had met with Douglas Schulz, a former broker and arbitration consultant who represented a number of former Storaska clients. Schulz had conducted his own investigation, and gave the SEC documents he had obtained from former members of Storaska's staff. With the subpoena, the enforcement staff was officially notifying Prudential Securities of formal investigation number MFW-586, titled "In the Matter of J. Frederic Storaska."

SEC inquiries of the firm were sprouting everywhere. The Fort Worth office was investigating Storaska, the Washington, D.C., office was handling the partnership case, and the Atlanta office was looking into apparent violations at the firm's branch offices in Atlanta and Chesterfield, Missouri. All told, nine branches were being investigated.

Within the SEC, the multiple cases were dubbed "Capt. Crab II." Despite the assurances from Schechter during the Capt. Crab settlement negotiations so many years before, Prudential Securities had failed to impose proper compliance procedures. The problems caused by the party atmosphere at the firm during the 1980s were all catching up to it at the same time.

Patrick Finley, the deputy general counsel of Prudential Securities, finished reading a letter from Wayne Klein and reached for the telephone. Finley had assured Klein repeatedly that the firm intended to cooperate with his investigation. But now, in early April, Klein had written that he thought Prudential Securities was stonewalling.

Klein wanted the Locke Purnell report. Prudential Securities was refusing, again arguing that the document was a privileged communication with lawyers. Klein shoved back, sending the firm a letter that asked if their refusal was a sign that they no longer wished to cooperate. To Finley, it sounded like a dangerous breakdown in relations with the Idaho regulator.

Finley called Klein several times, but couldn't reach him. Finally he dictated a letter, assuring Klein that the firm had every intent to continue cooperating. But, he said, that had nothing to do with the Locke Purnell report, which was privileged and would not be turned over.

The letter arrived at the Idaho Securities Bureau a few days later. After reading it, Klein walked to the office of Mary Hughes, one of his investigators. He told her to drop everything else she was doing; he wanted her to review the rules of attorney-client privilege to determine whether the firm's claim was valid.

"What are we going to do if I find out that the firm's position isn't valid?" Hughes asked.

"Simple," Klein said. "We'll sue them."

That same week, on April 20, Prudential Securities sued the National Association of Securities Dealers, the industry's largest self-regulator. The suit demanded that the court overrule an NASD arbitrator's decision requiring the production of the Locke Purnell report to Boyd Page, the Atlanta securities lawyer. Page was representing Donald Smith, a former Storaska client who lost more than $1 million from partnership investments. The arbitrator had accepted Page's argument that the report was essential to prove the conflicts of interest in the partnership department.

The lawsuit against the NASD made news around the country. Not only was it highly unusual for a big brokerage firm to try to strong-arm a regulators group, it also flew in the face of the arbitration code. Under those rules, neither party in an arbitration is allowed to bring a lawsuit over any matters involved in the case until the arbitration is completed. But Prudential Securities just ignored that.

"We are simply looking to make a legal point and make sure we retain this attorney-client privilege," William Ahearn, a spokesman for the firm, told reporters.

State regulators around the country didn't see the matter so simply. Prudential Securities, using millions of dollars in legal might, appeared to be engaged in a cover-up.

Even without the Locke Purnell report, the task force's effort to gather documents from the firm was in full swing. By midspring, Prudential Securities had turned over reams of paper, much of it marketing material and data printouts about investors and employees. Boxes of documents were delivered to Klein in Idaho, and he spent an entire Saturday on his own, dividing up the records for shipment to other states.

The boxes contained few of the due diligence records for the partnerships. The regulators went back and asked for those documents. In a few weeks, Prudential Securities produced a number of thin files. It hardly seemed like enough material to justify selling a car, much less billions of dollars in partnerships. The firm had to be holding back. The regulators demanded to see more.

It took several weeks for the truth to sink in with the task force: The skimpy due diligence files were all that existed. The firm had been selling partnerships without much bothering to find out if they would work.

At the same time, the task force decided it needed proof to counter Prudential Securities' unsupported claims that most partnerships had been sold properly. The overwhelming anecdotal evidence would not be enough in court. Nancy Smith of New Mexico volunteered to put together a questionnaire for tens of thousands of investors around the country. The responses would show how many of the clients were suitable partnership investors and how many of them had been misled.

In April, Smith heard that Jim Moriarty, who had worked with Bristow, Hackerman on the growth fund litigation, had used questionnaires with 5,800 clients. She decided to call him for some tips.

"We hear that you put together a questionnaire for your investors," Smith said. "We're trying to do the same thing on a more national level and could use some advice."

Moriarty said that he had hired an expert on statistics and polling from Rice University for help in writing the questionnaire. He suggested that the regulators hire him, too.

"We don't have the budget for that," Smith said.

"Oh, call the guy," Moriarty replied. "It's not much money. No more than five or ten thousand dollars."

"We don't have that," she said.

Moriarty thought for an instant. At that moment, he was particularly flush. He had just been paid a huge contingency fee for his work on the growth fund cases. The money had come straight out of Prudential Securities' pocket. He broke into a smile.

"How about if I pay for it?" he asked.

"That would be great."

"Well, those boys just sent me some cash for suing them," Moriarty said. "So I'll call this guy from Rice and put their own money back into the cause."

Smith thanked Moriarty. But he just laughed.

"Hey, don't thank me," he said. "I'm going to enjoy this. I love the idea of using Prudential's own money to screw 'em twice."

"Prudential Securities has a lot of concerns about this criminal investigation," protested Patrick Finley, the deputy general counsel. "We don't believe there have been any violations of criminal law."

Finley was sitting across from John Evans, the assistant attorney general in Arizona. Evans had been pursuing the criminal case against the firm for a year. It was June 14, and Finley was meeting with him at the offices of Prudential Securities' lawyers in Phoenix. A number of other lawyers were in the room, including Dan Drake, the head of the general crime section of the federal prosecutor's office there.

Evans had little doubt that the partnership mess at Prudential Securities was a major criminal fraud. Since bringing in the FBI the previous year, he had uncovered boxes of documents showing how the energy income partnerships had been sold. But the investigation had become too large for his office alone. The FBI said it would continue working on the case only if there was federal involvement. Evans was trying to interest the U.S. attorney in the case, and had invited Drake to the meeting to observe.

Finley's presentation was almost old hat. It had been made repeatedly to law enforcement authorities throughout the country.

"We know there were serious problems with the activities of the Direct Investment Group," Finley said. "But the people responsible are no longer at the firm. Now we're dealing with those problems in the civil arena. We're cooperating with all of those investigations the best we can."

He added that the firm also intended to cooperate with the Arizona investigation.

Evans didn't buy it. He had heard the complaints from regulators that the firm was not cooperating as it should. He had also spoken with plaintiffs' lawyers throughout the country who told horror stories about abuses during litigation. He well knew that the firm would claim that certain documents requested in discovery did not exist—until the plaintiffs' lawyer announced that the documents had already been obtained from other sources. Many of the plaintiffs' lawyers felt compelled to request documents they already had to keep Prudential Securities honest.

Even worse were what looked like the firm's deliberate misrepresentations. An Arizona lawyer told Evans about a case where the firm had claimed that a Prudential Securities document used as evidence by the plaintiffs was phony, only to produce the same document itself later in another case to prove a different point. When complaints were filed, the firm often tried to move the case to New York even if the client lived on the other side of the country. It went to the mat with almost any investor who insisted on full compensation.

With all those stories in mind, Evans was not about to take Finley at his word.

"Your statements about cooperation have not been borne out by the comments I have been getting from lawyers across the country," he said. "What I have been told to expect from your company is strategic omission of documents."

Evans leaned forward. "So let me tell you how I'm going to work this," he said. "I've already obtained a large number of documents. Now, some of those documents are going to be covered by my subpoenas. If you don't produce them the first time, I'll make a more specific request. And if your company doesn't produce them the second time, and I know they exist, then I have a pretty good obstruction-of-justice case. Let's all remember that."

The first subpoenas from federal prosecutors in the Southern District of New York went out in the early summer, signaling the start of the second criminal investigation of the partnership fraud.

At Prudential Securities, the new investigation came as a frightening shock. This was not an inquiry by some state. These prosecutors were looking into possible violations of *federal* securities laws. And they were good at it: The Southern District had taken on Michael Milken and Drexel Burnham—and won.

This time, the prosecutors started with an edge. First, they obtained all the information that had been released in the energy income class action. Then they took over the Arizona case from Evans, getting all the documents that he had found during his yearlong investigation.

The federal criminal investigation of Prudential Securities was far down the road from the moment it began.

The negotiations between the SEC enforcement staff and Prudential Securities picked up rapidly over the summer.

Gary Lynch and Arthur Mathews attended every session. Sometimes Loren Schechter appeared as well. A broad range of topics was on the table. With the Capt. Crab settlement having failed to push the firm to clean up its act, the enforcement staff demanded changes in the management structure. Under the setup the SEC wanted, the executives responsible for enforcing security law requirements would be specifically identified. If the firm failed to comply with the law again, those executives would be responsible.

Schechter objected to the proposal.

"The firm's under new management," he said. "They're not responsible for what happened in the past. And new management perceives any requirement like that as a suggestion that they are not operating the firm in compliance with securities laws."

It was the same argument Schechter had presented eight years before when he was negotiating the Capt. Crab settlement. That fact didn't escape the attention of some of the SEC lawyers at the table.

"It may be new management, but it's the same firm," McLucas said.

Even as they haggled over those terms, the basic concept of how the settlement would work was taking shape. The firm would set up a compensation fund for all defrauded investors. Every partnership investor would be allowed to submit a claim to the fund, and each claim would be evaluated individually. For all of the partnerships, Prudential Securities would waive the right to argue that the statute of limitations had expired. Then a cash offer would be made to investors who had been defrauded. The whole process would be supervised by an independent administrator appointed by the SEC.

Numerous questions were still open. In particular, there was no agreement on the amount of money that should be in the fund.

In the opening negotiations, Lynch and Mathews had offered to have the firm pay $50 million, an amount the SEC dismissed as laughable. Over weeks of negotiation, the offer was doubled to $100 million, and then doubled again to $200 million.

The SEC negotiating team rejected the offers. They wanted the firm to pay a minimum in the range of $250 million. But that would be only the start. There would be no cap on the settlement. Instead, the final total would be determined by the damages suffered by investors. Prudential Securities would keep paying valid claims, regardless of the final cost.

"That's nuts," Arthur Mathews said when he heard the proposal. "This is a business. We can't agree to an unfixed liability."

McLucas held firm.

"Look, if we can't reach an agreement on this and you guys hold out for something that's ridiculous from our business analysis point of view, we'll just have to litigate this case," Mathews said.

"That's your decision," McLucas said. "But of course, if we litigate, in addition to litigating for the money, we're going to litigate to pull the firm's license. You know as well as I do that in the circumstances of this case, the firm couldn't tolerate even the threat of that."

Mathews agreed to present the proposal to the firm. But he clearly indicated that he would recommend strongly against it.

Mathews was true to his word. He argued vehemently to Simmons that the firm could not possibly accept an open-ended liability. With such a term, there was no telling how high the final cost might be.

"We've run all the numbers," Simmons replied. "The cost for valid claims is going to be far less than $200 million. Even if it's uncapped, that's all we'll have to pay."

Mathews began arguing again, but Simmons wouldn't bend.

"We have to get this thing behind us," he said.

The lawyers were instructed to tell the SEC that Prudential Securities would accept the uncapped liability for the compensation fund.

Darr's deposition in the energy income class action was scheduled for July. The plaintiffs' lawyers filed a motion with Judge Livaudais asking that Prudential Securities be compelled to produce the Locke Purnell report. Without it, the lawyers argued, they could never properly interview Darr about the suspicious private dealings that had been described in *Business Week* two years before. Judge Livaudais agreed and ordered that the document be turned over.

Prudential Securities rapidly conceded. The months of fighting the SEC, the state regulators, and the NASD were pushed aside. Judge Livaudais was sitting on the case that involved $1.4 billion in potential liability. Schechter had no desire to anger him.

As soon as the decision was made, Schechter rewrote history. All of the battles were forgotten. He reacted as if, to get the Locke Purnell report, all anyone had to have done was ask.

"We're happy to turn over the report," Schechter told reporters. "There was nothing to hide."

Schechter's words destroyed any credibility he had left with the state regulators. All of them knew the statement was laughable. After all, when Schechter made the comment, the Idaho regulators had been putting the finishing touches on their suit against Prudential Securities, demanding the production of the Locke Purnell report. They had been planning to file it in a matter of days. Now they didn't need to.

On Friday, July 16, a voice came across Prudential Securities' internal communications system.

"Hello, everybody, this is Wick Simmons."

It was a critical time for good news. The brokers were horribly demoralized. Every morning brought new headlines and new disclosures. Most of the working day was spent answering the questions of concerned clients. Cold-callers had to tell potential customers that the firm really wasn't a bunch of crooks. Headhunters were calling top brokers, trying to persuade them to leave. Simmons had decided that he needed to do something. A talk with the brokers was his answer.

"I know that many of you are hearing questions about all these news articles that have been giving constant reminders about our mistakes in the eighties," Simmons said. "So I'd like to bring out some points to be sure that everybody knows we are on track here.

"We're at the final stages of what we hope will be an agreement in principle and then a detailed understanding of a global settlement, in which, under the SEC's leadership, we wrap up all of our partnership-related and other regulatory problems." It would be a settlement that would resolve problems with the SEC, the NASD, and many state regulators, he added.

"You should have confidence that we are extraordinarily close," he said.

Simmons did not tell the brokers how much the settlement would cost the firm, but he said that Prudential Securities could afford it. "The settlement will certainly be a large one, but one that wouldn't damage our firm, interrupt our business, or change in any way our ability to serve customers."

Simmons's statement to the troops was big news. Brokers called reporters to let them know what the boss had said. Press reports concluded that a deal was almost wrapped up. After all, the firm's management would deliver such an upbeat message only if they were positive that a deal was at hand. Otherwise, if an agreement collapsed, the demoralizing impact on the sales force would be devastating. No manager would be foolish enough to do that.

The following Monday morning, a group of SEC lawyers gathered around a table in McLucas's corner office. They reviewed the newspaper reports of Simmon's comments to the brokers in disbelief. The anger in the room was almost palpable.

"What the hell is going on here?" McLucas said. "Why are these idiots talking about our settlement discussions in public?"

The SEC lawyers called the firm and demanded a copy of any tapes or transcripts of Simmons's talk. When they finally heard the talk on tape, the SEC lawyers became even angrier. McLucas and Newkirk, the associate director of enforcement, got Prudential Securities' lawyers on the phone in a conference call.

"What are you people doing talking about a settlement before it's ready to announce?" McLucas demanded. "That's not an effective way to deal with us. It puts the deal at risk."

The firm's lawyers tried to explain, saying that the relentless publicity had been causing Prudential Securities to lose some of its best brokers. They felt as if they had to say something to stop the firm from hemorrhaging. After telling them to never do anything like that again, McLucas brought the conversation to a close.

Later that day, the SEC lawyers involved in the Prudential Securities case came into McLucas's office to discuss what Simmons had done. Some laughed about it. His talk had been a blunder of gargantuan proportions. Now that Simmons had announced the settlement, he was going to have to make sure the deal happened. Whatever morale problems existed now would pale in comparison to what would happen if Simmons had to backtrack. That shifted the strategic advantage to the SEC. Now the enforcement staff could be tougher in the negotiations. Prudential Securities would be desperate to settle.

In Boise, Wayne Klein shook his head as he read the newspaper articles about Simmons's pep talk. He thought the message Simmons delivered was divorced from reality. The SEC and Prudential Securities might be close to working out their problems, but not once had the firm discussed settlement with the states. No numbers were on the table. No terms had been mentioned. *Nothing.*

Klein and the other members of the task force had been in constant contact with the SEC and knew they were close to a deal. Klein himself had even sat in on a few of their negotiating sessions. But apparently Simmons was assuming that the states were going to rubber-stamp any deal the firm reached with the federal regulators. Klein knew that wasn't going to happen. He felt he had to get a message to the firm's management that they were blowing it.

About two o'clock that afternoon, the department's receptionist told Klein that Chuck Hawkins from *Business Week* was on the line. Klein thought about it for an instant. If ever there was an opportunity to fire a shot across the bow, this was it. He picked up the telephone.

Hawkins said he was calling about Simmons's comments to the brokers and wanted to know what Klein thought. Klein replied that Simmons appeared to be under pressure from brokers leaving the firm. In Boise alone, Klein said, a branch manager at a competing firm had sent letters to top Prudential Securities brokers inviting them to switch employers.

But, Hawkins asked, was Simmons telling the truth when he said that a global settlement was near?

"We have had no face-to-face negotiations with Prudential," Klein said. "So any talk of a global settlement is just that: talk."

Hawkins scribbled down the words, instantly knowing that he had a story.

Why would the firm pronounce that the deal was almost done if they hadn't even negotiated with the states yet? Hawkins asked.

"It may very well be that they don't think we can stop a freight train," Klein replied.

By Labor Day, the broad outlines of the SEC settlement with Prudential Securities were done. The firm would put less than $300 million down as the floor for the compensation fund. It would consent to findings of massive securities law violations not only in the Direct Investment Group but also in nine branch offices around the country. On top of that, it would accept a finding that it had ignored many of the requirements of the Capt. Crab settlement. This time, a court order would be put in place requiring compliance. If it ignored the terms again, Prudential Securities would face contempt charges. The enforcement staff sent the proposed settlement up the line for approval by the SEC commissioners and its chairman.

In September, the answer came back. The commissioners were rejecting the settlement terms. They wanted the firm to pay more up front: $330 million for the fund plus a $10 million fine. If the amount put into the fund was not needed, the firm would forfeit the money.

McLucas informed the firm's lawyers of the commissioners' demands. The increase in the amount of money wasn't particularly large, but Prudential Securities' management was livid. The firm's lawyers demanded that McLucas and the enforcement staff meet with Woody Knight, the head of corporate strategy and one of the firm's top executives. They agreed, and within days, Knight flew down to Washington. He arrived with a retinue of lawyers.

"The numbers you're talking about are just out of the ballpark," Knight told the SEC lawyers. "They've got no basis in reality. We've done a comprehensive internal risk analysis, and our maximum total exposure here is, at worst, $200 million. This $330 million number is ridiculous."

McLucas just shrugged. It wasn't up to them. Their client was the commission, and the client had demanded $330 million. That was the price.

It wasn't right, Knight complained. All this was doing was taking money out of Prudential Securities and shipping it to the Treasury. This settlement was supposed to be about repaying investors. These numbers had nothing to do with that.

McLucas wouldn't budge. Knight and his lawyers left, saying that they would consider the situation and be back in touch.

Later that week, McLucas heard from them again. Prudential Securities' management didn't like the terms, but they would accept them.

An agreement in principle to settle the SEC charges was complete. Now the firm had to deal with the states.

The five members of the Prudential multistate task force walked out of the SEC's Washington headquarters and headed for lunch at a nearby Chinese restaurant. That morning, they had been meeting at the commission for a final briefing by the enforcement staff on the federal settlement. If the commissioners approved it, the deal would be done. Negotiations between the firm and the states were scheduled to begin in the next few days.

A sense of expectation hung over the table. The task force had maintained a united front for nine months. They just had to keep that up for the next few days. Because of the mammoth size of the fraud, several regulators had found it easier to focus on what their efforts meant for one individual. Nancy Smith, for example, always kept in mind an elderly widow she met in New Mexico who had lost much of her money in the partnerships. During lunch, Smith mentioned that whatever deal they struck, it had to be something that the widow would see as fair.

Throughout the meal, they planned strategy. After they finished, the waiters came and took away the dishes, leaving behind five fortune cookies. Klein picked one up, opened it, and pulled out the fortune. Then he burst out laughing.

"What's so funny?" one of the regulators asked.

Klein passed his fortune around. "Is this an omen?"

One at a time, the regulators read the fortune and laughed. Finally, after circling the table, it came back to Klein. With a smile on his face, he looked at the words on the fortune once more.

"Everything will now come your way."

The final negotiations between Prudential Securities and the multistate task force began the next day in the Grand Canyon Room at the Hyatt Regency in Washington, D.C., just two blocks from the Capitol building.

The mood was somber in the long, narrow meeting room. The states had won several skirmishes, but this was the crucial battle. Without a decent settlement that repaid defrauded investors, their previous victories would be hollow.

Each member of the task force handled a different piece of the negotiations. There were a number of minor terms, such as a demand that Prudential Securities be barred from the partnership business. But the talks became hung up on money very quickly. On top of whatever the firm had agreed to pay for the settlement fund, the regulators wanted fines of $500,000 each for every state, plus Puerto Rico and the District of Columbia. If every state agreed, it would cost the firm $26 million.

Schechter balked. That was too much, he said.

The haggling continued for hours. After a lunch break, Schechter became more resolute. He had contacted executives in New York, he said. They would not accept the fines that the states were demanding. The talks were already approaching a standstill.

"Listen," Schechter said near the end of the day. "Woody Knight is one of our top executives. He's in charge of corporate strategy. He'd like to come down here tomorrow and talk to you about this. He wants to explain the numbers."

The regulators agreed to meet with Knight, and the day's negotiations ended.

Knight came in the next morning. Right away, his cocksure attitude alienated a number of the regulators in the room. An old friend of Wick Simmons, Knight had been at Prudential Securities only a short time. But already he seemed to personify the firm's arrogance and lack of contrition for its fraud. He told the task force that their demands were excessive.

"You just don't understand," Knight said. "You are asking for way too much money. You're out of the ballpark. Now, we've already taken care of all this with the SEC. That should do it. Didn't you all know that when we were talking with them, we had an empty seat at that table representing you?"

"Yes," Schechter interceded. "You were always there with us in an invisible chair. We knew that we had to try to satisfy the things the states were interested in. And we did that."

Invisible chair? The five regulators did their best not to roll their eyes.

"The SEC was negotiating on the issues that they needed to deal with," Klein responded. "They don't speak for us, and can't speak for us. They do not have that authority, and we've made that clear to you from the beginning."

Regardless of whether there was an invisible chair in the room or not, Klein said, clearly the states' concern had not been resolved.

"We're telling you *now* what it's going to take in order to bring the states into this," he said. "Whether you kept us in mind in your talks with the SEC is irrelevant."

"But everything you're asking for we've already negotiated and settled with the SEC," Knight snapped, exasperated. "So now you're trying to take advantage of the best of the SEC's deal and then add your own terms on top of that. That's not fair to Prudential Securities."

The regulators said nothing in reply. After the amount of damage the firm had done, none of them was much concerned about what was fair to Prudential Securities.

Lewis Brothers, the Virginia securities commissioner, brought his hand up to his chin. His face seemed to visibly harden.

"We've given everything we can," Knight continued. "You know, some members of the board and some of the top management already think we have given away far more than we have to."

The room was crackling with anger from the regulators' side. Brothers's face stiffened more.

"You know, a lot of them think we should stop taking our lumps and chuck it all, because you're asking too much," Knight said. "We'd fight the SEC and we'd fight the states. And we'd win. Most of our partnerships were sold properly. Any problems that happened weren't systemic and are behind us. They aren't going to happen again."

As Brothers cleared his throat, everyone turned to look at him.

"Mr. Knight," he said softly, his voice tinged with rage, "I've been in this business for many years, and over that time I've seen lots of frauds and lots of problems."

He stared straight at Knight as his voice began to tremble. "But I have never seen a problem this egregious, or a fraud this massive, with a major brokerage firm lying to its customers. Do you have any idea what this firm has done? Do you know how much damage it's caused? Do you know how many lives it has destroyed? It doesn't give me any solace at all to hear you tell me you won't do this again. I've heard that before from you people. I will not go back to the citizens of Virginia and tell them that they don't need to worry about all the pain they've suffered at the hands of Prudential because the firm says they won't do it again."

No one was moving. No one was talking.

"No, sir," Brothers said. "I cannot go back to my state in good conscience and say that we have accepted anything less than what is on the table right now. This is essential to remedy this problem for the investors in our states and to punish the firm for what it has done. And even still I wonder whether we have gone far enough."

He pointed a finger at Knight.

"Because, Mr. Knight," Brothers said, "given everything that it's done, I question whether or not this firm should be permitted to survive."

The room was silent. Brothers's fellow regulators stared at him in awe.

"I think this is a good time to take a break," Schechter said.

The representatives from Prudential Securities left the room. After an instant, the state regulators converged on Brothers, congratulating him on his eloquence. It was the best statement any of them had heard about the Prudential Securities scandal. For the first time, someone had shot down the firm's breezy dismissal of the fraud's magnitude and, instead, underscored its gravity. Perhaps, one of them suggested, Brothers's speech should be the final point they make in their negotiations.

About twenty minutes later, Schechter returned. Woody Knight was not with him. Schechter said he had left to go home.

"We're at an impasse," Schechter said. "You're just going to have to realize that you're not going to get what you're asking for. You need to make some concessions, so I think you ought to consider that overnight and we'll meet on it again tomorrow."

"No," Klein said. "We've presented our position. You know our bottom line. We don't see any value in meeting tomorrow. We're going home."

"No, no," Schechter said. "Let's get together tomorrow. We can close the distance."

"No," Klein repeated. "We're going home."

The regulators gathered their things and left the room. The talks with Prudential Securities had broken down.

If the firm did not revise its position quickly, it would be too late. In a little more than a week, the state securities regulators' fall conference would be held in Orlando. If nothing changed, Klein would have to inform his colleagues that the task force had been unable to reach an agreement.

Then, one at a time, regulators around the country would start to file their lawsuits against Prudential Securities. Many of them were already prepared to pull its license to do business. This game of brinkmanship was pushing the firm precariously close to disaster.

Klein sat alone in his office on the evening of Tuesday, September 21, typing on his computer. The rest of the securities bureau had gone home long ago. He had stayed behind to finish up a progress report for other states on the negotiations with Prudential Securities. It had been less than a week since the talks with the firm had collapsed, and he had heard nothing since. Already Idaho was preparing to file its enforcement action against Prudential Securities. If nothing changed, the brokerage stood to lose its license in the state within a few months.

Klein was finishing up a section of his report when the telephone rang. It was Schechter. He got right to the point.

"All right, we've got a deal," he said. "It's subject to certain conditions. We want to retain the right to conduct any business we're permitted to under our license. And we want this settlement to be a general release with the states for all prior activity."

"Well, there may be some problems with those conditions," Klein replied. "But we're a lot closer. I think we have room to talk."

They agreed to meet in two days in Atlanta so that the regulators could fly to Orlando for the conference immediately afterward.

Klein hung up, feeling a strange sense of detachment, almost as if it weren't happening. The game of chicken had been tiring. But now it looked like it would all work out.

Maybe this long ordeal is finally over, he thought.

Klein telephoned the other task force members, telling each one to get to Atlanta the next day. On September 23, they gathered in a conference room at the downtown Hilton. They were soon joined by a large team from Prudential Securities, including Schechter, Finley, Mathews, Dan Bell, and Nathalie Maio, the executive who would be in charge of the proposed settlement fund.

The meeting began with Schechter raising all the issues that divided the two sides. After some time, the states agreed to drop the condition that would prevent Prudential Securities from going into the partnership business again. Schechter said that the firm's new management saw that as an unfair criticism of them, since they were not at the firm when the partnership problems occurred.

Both sides were tense, but they gradually made progress. Finally Schechter raised the last issue: Prudential Securities needed a clean slate. The firm wanted the settlement to include every violation from its past. Essentially, the states were being asked to waive their ability to pursue Prudential Securities for any improper activities that they had not yet discovered.

"We don't want to do this settlement and then have you come back and hammer us again on something else that might be hanging out there," Schechter explained.

Some of the regulators wondered if Schechter knew of some other problems at the firm that they hadn't found yet. But others just assumed that Prudential Securities didn't trust the motives of anybody on the other side of the negotiating table.

"We can't possibly sign away our statutory responsibilities like that," one regulator said. "No one gets a walk on everything just for settling one case."

"Well, what other issues are out there that the task force is investigating?" Schechter asked. "What else might be coming down the road?"

"It's not appropriate to get into anything like that," Klein said. "That has nothing to do with this settlement."

"Well, how do we know this isn't just some plan to take one piece out of us and then come back again?" Schechter responded. "We need a general release. Otherwise, we could sit back with a final settlement and then get additional sanctions right after that."

"I'm sorry, but that's ridiculous," Smith said. "That was never on the table in these negotiations. I would have to go back and do an extensive investigation of Prudential Securities for about a year before I could possibly sign off on a general release."

Schechter looked at Smith with fury in his eyes. "You're being disingenuous," he snapped.

"Loren, what are you talking about?" she asked.

"You know!" he exclaimed. "You have an investigation going. You've audited a branch. And now you're just waiting to spring something on us when the settlement is signed."

Smith stared back at him, floored. Her office had conducted an audit of a New Mexico branch of Prudential Securities many months before. But that was just standard regulatory oversight. Nothing had been found, and there was no investigation.

"Loren, I don't know what you're talking about," Smith said. "But I find your comments to be very offensive."

Without warning, Schechter suddenly leaped up from his seat. He went red in the face and began screaming at Smith and the other regulators.

"You're being disingenuous!" he yelled. "You're dealing in bad faith!"

Smith crossed her arms. "So basically, you're saying that I'm lying."

"Well, you know you have this investigation going," Schechter yelled. "You just don't want to include it. Then, after we sign this settlement, you're going to spring it on us and go after our license for this other thing."

Smith tried to control herself. Never before had her honesty been attacked like this. She couldn't believe that Schechter was behaving in such an unprofessional manner. It was almost as if the pressure finally caused him to blow.

"I find your remarks incredibly offensive," she said tersely. "You're questioning my integrity, and you're questioning my good faith. And I won't stand for that."

Don Saxon of Florida broke in. "I don't much like what you're saying either," he said. "I've worked with Nancy a lot, and I have the highest respect for her ethics and integrity. And I'm appalled that you would try and call that into question."

A long, uncomfortable silence followed.

"Maybe this is a good time for a break," Mathews said finally.

The Prudential Securities team stood up and walked out of the room silently. After they were gone, the regulators fumed.

"How dare he talk to us like that!"

"The pressure's getting to him."

"We're too close to agreement, and he wants to push it over the end zone. It was just an eruption of frustration."

But, the regulators agreed, it was another in the firm's long string of tactical errors. Now the Prudential Securities side had to overcome the embarrassment of Schechter's blowup. There would be no more concessions, they decided. They were going to get everything they wanted. That was that.

Within a few minutes, the lawyers and executives from Prudential Securities returned. Schechter looked tired. He sat down in his chair and said, "Nancy, I apologize for getting so agitated. It was inappropriate."

Schechter took a deep breath.

"OK, it's time to bring this to an end," he said. "We'll accept your terms. Let's go through them."

Prudential Securities had finally blinked. For the next half an hour, the regulators laid out the specifics of the settlement. Schechter said he wanted everything in writing. The whole group headed two blocks from the Hilton to Prudential Securities' Atlanta law firm. A secretary had stayed late to type drafts of the agreement.

For more than two hours, drafts were written and reviewed. Finally, at 7:30, the agreement in principle was laid out on the conference room table, ready for signing.

Klein leaned over the table, reading the draft one last time. He picked up a pen and looked up at his fellow regulators.

"Speak now or forever hold your peace," he said.

The other members of the task force nodded. They were in agreement.

Klein looked back down at the document and signed it. Copies were passed around the room. Everyone finally relaxed. Klein took Schechter aside as they shook hands. They walked toward a large window in the conference room. Outside, dusk was changing into night. Workers were walking along the sidewalks, heading home. Cars on the highway were cutting a white ribbon of light past the downtown office buildings. The calm September evening seemed in stark contrast to the tension of the day.

"Loren, I want you to know that now we're moving from opposite sides of the table to the same side of the table," Klein said. "We all now have the same interest in making sure that Prudential Securities operates properly and that this money gets back to investors as quickly and fairly as possible. Now we're here to help you."

Schechter nodded. "I understand. And congratulations. You've negotiated a very good settlement. You've gotten a lot more than the firm ever thought it would give. Investors are going to be a lot better off because of how well you've handled this."

Afterward, Klein and the other regulators headed down to the lobby and out into the Atlanta evening air. Outside, they slapped high fives. Their victory was intoxicating. They walked down the street in search of a restaurant. They hadn't eaten in hours, and all of them were starving. After a few blocks, they found a restaurant called Dailey's and slipped in for dinner.

Until that meal, the regulators had always been frugal at restaurants. The state regulators' association restricted them to spending no more than $35 a day on food or personal items. But now, as part of the settlement, Prudential Securities had agreed to pick up the task force expenses. The regulators unanimously decided that this was the night to ignore the $35 restriction. They'd earned a good dinner, particularly since Prudential Securities was paying for it.

Winding down, they ordered several rounds of drinks. Klein, who didn't drink alcohol, ordered rounds of 7-Ups.

The celebration went long into the night as the regulators laughed and recounted stories from their long battle. They offered numerous toasts. The first was to the task force. The second was to the SEC.

Then Klein rose from the table, 7-Up in hand.

"Now let's have a toast to the people for whom we did this," he said. "The investors."

Without a word, the five state regulators raised their glasses.

EPILOGUE

THE NEXT MORNING, the task force members boarded a plane bound for Orlando, Florida. They were scheduled to brief other state regulators on their negotiations at the fall conference beginning that evening at the Hilton Hotel at Walt Disney World. Now they had some news to tell.

Klein felt restless on the short flight. Ever since returning to his hotel the night before, he had been keyed up. Unable to sleep, he had wandered about the city of Atlanta, haunted by a question: Would the other states accept the settlement? If they didn't, Klein had no doubt that Prudential Securities would walk away from the deal. The next few days would determine whether all the effort had paid off.

The task force made its presentation on September 27, in a meeting room just off the Hilton's grand ballroom. Klein paced nervously in the front as the other regulators found their seats. Security was tight—the room had been searched for recording devices, and everyone was checked at the door to make sure they belonged in the meeting. Klein was terrified of leaks. The last thing the task force needed was outside criticism of the settlement based on sketchy news reports.

Klein began his presentation promptly at 3:15 P.M.

"In coordination with the SEC, we've reached an agreement in principle with Prudential," Klein said, still pacing. "What we want to do now is explain to you the terms of the agreement and get indications whether you think this is acceptable. We'd like to get as many indications as possible right on the spot, at the meeting."

Klein ticked off the terms: the open-ended compensation fund, including the $330 million down payment. The firm's agreement to waive the statute of limitations on claims to the fund. A requirement for stepped-up monitoring of the firm's business by regulators. Another that made the firm responsible for paying the claims administrator selected by the SEC.

There were some downsides to the deal. Investors who had accepted class-action settlements could not file a claim. Since those cases had been resolved by a court, the regulators had no power to reopen them. In essence, Prudential Securities had succeeded in walking away from some of its most egregious frauds for a token amount of money.

After half an hour, Klein was finishing up. He had saved the best news for the end.

"And for the last item," he said, "Prudential has agreed to a fine of $500,000 for each state."

There was an audible gasp. No firm, not even Drexel, had ever paid a fraction of that amount to every state. Some in the audience figured they must have misunderstood.

"Did we hear that right, Wayne?" one regulator called out. "Was that $50,000?"

The members of the task force chuckled.

"No, you heard it wrong," Klein said. "It's $500,000."

For the next half hour, the task force members took questions. A number of regulators stepped forward to congratulate them on a job well done. Even before the questions were finished, Klein could tell that there was enough support in the room to keep the settlement alive. The task force had succeeded.

At 5:00 P.M., Klein checked his watch. He excused himself and turned the floor over to Don Saxon, a fellow task force member. Klein had to leave. His wife and children were scheduled to arrive on a 5:16 flight at the Orlando airport.

After almost two years of nonstop investigation of Prudential Securities, Klein couldn't wait to see his family. He had been working too hard and been out of town too much. Now, with the end of the negotiations and the opening of the fall conference, he could start to make it up to them.

He was taking them to Disney World.

It took three more weeks for the SEC to distill the settlement into a final agreement. By then, forty-nine states, plus the District of Columbia and Puerto Rico, agreed in principle to accept the terms. Only Texas, which was still investigating Fred Storaska's activities, held off.

On the morning of October 21, lawyers for the SEC went to the federal district court for the District of Columbia. They filed a civil complaint against Prudential Securities and the firm's agreement to settle the charges. Afterward, more than a dozen federal and state securities regulators gathered for a press conference in a basement meeting room at the SEC's Washington headquarters. There they listened attentively as Arthur Levitt, the SEC chairman, described the charges against Prudential Securities and the terms of the settlement.

In total, the firm would pay the $330 million down payment plus $41 million in fines, including $5 million for the NASD. It was the largest monetary settlement ever paid by a retail brokerage firm. And, Levitt said, the SEC was continuing to investigate the people responsible for the scandal.

The next morning, an advertisement from Prudential Securities appeared in newspapers across the country. It was an open letter from Hardwick Simmons, explaining the settlements and the firm's commitment to do better. It was a classic example of the doublespeak of Prudential Securities. At no point did Simmons apologize for the firm's centralized fraud that had destroyed the lives of so many trusting clients. Only one grammatically tortured sentence came close to acknowledging the massive wrongdoing: "Certain limited partnerships were sold by our firm to some clients that lacked adequate information or were not suitable for their investment needs," the letter said. "That was wrong."

What Simmons omitted spoke volumes. He mentioned nothing of the fraudulent sales literature pumped out to the branch offices by the Direct Investment Group in New York. He left out that the firm itself had misled clients for years by issuing monthly account statements that showed the plunging partnership values as holding steady. In fact, he disclosed virtually nothing about the widespread fraud that emanated from the firm's New York offices. The words of his statement seemed directed only to failure on the part of certain brokers.

The reasons for that were simple: Despite the mountains of evidence that so many government officials found overwhelming, Simmons still refused to accept that there was a widespread, coordinated effort at the firm to defraud its clients. While trying to portray the firm as reformed, Simmons simultaneously refused to face what it had done. Months later, he summed up that blindness with a single statement:

"I still don't believe that there was a systemic problem."

In Newark, the settlement hit Prudential Insurance hard. After 118 years of seeing its name associated with words like *trustworthy* and *reliable*, Prudential Insurance was being linked to far uglier terms, such as *scandal* and *fraud*. Morale at the company was collapsing. Executives who had once proudly boasted to their friends about the firm now avoided mentioning its name.

On November 23, 1993, the company called a special meeting for employees at Dryden Hall, its auditorium in Newark. Hundreds attended. Thousands of others around the country saw the meeting broadcast live over Prudential television, a closed satellite network. Robert Winters, the chairman, looked somberly out to the crowd as he attempted to soothe their concerns.

Winters implicitly slammed Ball, saying that the management at Prudential-Bache had not lived up to the insurance company's standards. He acknowledged his own failures for not moving quickly enough when the problems started to emerge. Finally he asked Simmons to join him on-stage. Together, Winters said, they would answer written questions that had been submitted from employees anonymously.

Although some questions blamed the press for the company's troubles, most tore away at Prudential Insurance and its management, expressing a deep sense of betrayal:

"Faith has been broken with our employees, with our customers, and with the regulators. Who is accountable?"

"What will it take before the Prudential aggressively disciplines executives and others whose illegal or unethical behavior threatens the company's good name?"

"Since our record on policing ourselves is dubious at best, shouldn't we invite some respected third parties to audit all of our business practices?"

"I think the company is underestimating the damage that has been done to the good name and goodwill that the Prudential once had. Have we considered making a public apology? If not, why not? There are many people who feel an apology is overdue."

"Why should employees want to stay here?"

Winters and Simmons assured the employees that the company had changed. Prudential Insurance would survive, they said. It would rebuild its reputation.

"My job, your job, everyone's job is to safeguard the Prudential's name with more vigilance than ever before," Winters said. "It's not just a question of making sure we follow the letter and spirit of the law. We have to ask ourselves the question: Will this do right by our customers?"

But it was not to be. Instead, over the coming months, Prudential Securities executives pursued a strategy that seemed aimed at a single goal: to pay as little as possible to the investors defrauded by the firm.

Dozens of lawyers sat before Judge Livaudais in his New Orleans court-room in late January 1994. Many were gathered at tables before the bar.

Others, including a federal prosecutor, were sitting in the audience. All were there to hear evidence about the new proposed settlement of the energy income class-action lawsuit.

It had been almost a year since Livaudais had refused to approve the first settlement in the case. Since then, the investors had been paid nearly half a billion dollars for selling their stakes to Parker & Parsley. Now Prudential Securities was offering investors another $120 million in cash in a new class-action settlement. All it needed was Livaudais's approval. The money involved was much more than the $25 million in the first offer. But still, it translated to less than seven cents for each dollar invested.

By this point, the class-action settlement made little sense for anyone except those who had *not* been defrauded. Any of the investors could fill out a form and submit it to the regulatory compensation fund without bothering to hire a lawyer. The fund was required to give them full and fair compensation, not just some penny-ante amount. Based on that alone, some state regulators had asked Livaudais to again postpone approval of any class-action settlement. The only ones who stood to benefit from it were the class-action lawyers, who would receive millions in fees, and Prudential Securities, which would eliminate a huge portion of its liability for a fraction of what it might otherwise cost.

But Livaudais felt the case had to proceed. The states had finished their investigation. Investors who did not want to participate could opt out. The judge had given them two chances to do so. It was time to say "enough" and bring the case to an end.

Livaudais had scheduled hearings for late January, when he would hear arguments about the fairness of the new class-action settlement. After three days of hearing evidence, closing arguments began.

As he had a year before with the first proposed settlement, Edward Grossmann, the lead class-action lawyer, argued that the settlement was the best one possible. Scott Muller, representing Prudential Securities, said that the firm would contest the case if it went forward and believed it could win. It was willing to settle, he said, only out of a desire to put the partnership problem behind it.

The last of the closing arguments was presented by Stuart Goldberg, a lawyer from Austin, Texas. In recent years, Goldberg had turned energy income fraud claims into a virtual cottage industry. He won arbitrations on the partnership for large numbers of investors. To teach other lawyers how to bring those cases, he put together a book and video entitled *Prudential-Bache's $1.3 Billion Energy Income Limited Partnership Oil Scam*. He often bragged that no one had ever bothered to sue him for libel over the title because it was true.

"How many more multibillion-dollar frauds can this country stand?" Goldberg asked. "At what point does our economy get weaker and weaker and weaker? At what point is the message sent to the multibillion-dollar con artists that you can't get away with it? When is it that a court says that a class action isn't going to give you a pass?"

Goldberg finished his plea and thanked the judge. In an instant, Livaudais proceeded with his ruling.

"I'd like to respond to Mr. Muller's statement that Prudential wants to get this behind them by saying, 'Well, Mr. Muller, I will let you get this behind you if you double your offer,' " Livaudais said, sounding torn. "But I can't. My role here is to rule on the fairness of *this* settlement. Take it or leave it."

Livaudais said that many investors had not opted out, despite the chances. All he could assume, he said, was that there were investors out there who, like Prudential Securities, simply wanted this problem behind them.

"I don't think I should stand in the way," he said with a tone of resignation.

Livaudais approved the settlement.

The largest piece of Prudential Securities' liability was gone. Months later, investors would receive less than seven cents for every dollar they invested in the energy income fund. Grossmann and the other class-action lawyers received more than $22 million in fees.

News of Prudential Securities' coup in the class action crackled through law firms and regulators' offices throughout the country. The firm's effort to limit the amount of money it repaid investors seemed back on track. Its executives started getting cocky again.

By early 1994, some state regulators were angry. The firm had been all sackcloth and ashes when it needed them to agree to the regulatory settlement. But now some regulators were wondering whether Prudential Securities had ever meant to do right by its defrauded clients. California regulators in particular wondered whether the firm had tricked them into settling.

Before the state signed on to the agreements, Schechter had sent a letter to Gary Mendoza, California's top securities regulator. It promised that the state's defrauded investors would receive full compensation for their losses. But since the settlement had been announced, the firm had backed away from that commitment.

In particular, Mendoza was incensed to learn that the firm planned to make certain deductions out of every cash award to defrauded investors equal to some appraised value for the partnership stakes still owned by the investors. Never mind that the partnerships could rarely—if ever—be sold. Prudential Securities would simply pretend that the appraised value was the same thing as cash in the investor's pocket. With the partnerships still having some $3 billion in value, Mendoza thought he understood why the firm had been so sure that $330 million would cover its liability. It was planning to use some accounting trick to avoid paying investors the money they were owed.

Mendoza arranged a meeting with executives from the firm to discuss the problem. In early March, several of the firm's lawyers and executives gathered at Mendoza's office in Los Angeles. The chief negotiator was Woody Knight, the man who had so badly mishandled talks with the state task force.

Mendoza offered several suggestions about how to deal with the remaining values of the partnerships. Perhaps, he said, if Prudential was so certain of the appraised values, it should purchase the partnerships back at those prices. Knight waved the idea away, saying it would be too costly and had not been part of the settlement.

Mendoza tried another tack, suggesting that the firm deduct a certain amount from the appraisal values to account for the difficulty in selling the partnerships. These so-called liquidity discounts would be a much better representation of reality, he said.

"Asked and answered," Knight snapped, looking irritated. "That's not part of the deal."

"Fine," Mendoza said as he stood up. "I guess we have nothing more to talk about. I hope you have a pleasant trip back to New York."

With a smirk on his face, Knight shook Mendoza's hand. He and the other representatives from Prudential Securities walked out of the room, apparently confident that they had successfully steamrolled the California regulator.

They had no idea that they had just made another horrible blunder. It was one that would finally humble Prudential Securities.

Two days later, on March 3, a Prudential Securities lawyer telephoned William McDonald, the assistant director of enforcement for California's securities division. The lawyer asked how close California was to signing a final settlement agreement.

"Well," McDonald said, "in fifteen minutes we're going to announce that we intend to suspend you."

The firm's executives had botched it again. Mendoza would not accept their out-of-hand rejections. If Prudential Securities refused to fully compensate the victims of its fraud, then Mendoza would put them out of business in California.

A series of rapid negotiations ensued. The SEC pressed California and Prudential Securities to resolve the problem. Within a week, all the parties met in Washington, D.C., at the office of SEC chairman Arthur Levitt. By the meeting's end, the firm accepted the liquidity discounts. It was going to have to pay far more to investors than it had planned.

With that capitulation, Mendoza agreed to finalize the settlement. He told reporters that the liquidity discounts could as much as double the firm's settlement costs. When told of the statement by a reporter, Knight scoffed, saying that the discounts would cost no more than $25 million. And besides, he added, Prudential Securities had always planned to include them. Mendoza was shocked when he was told of Knight's statement. He could not believe that a senior executive would lie so readily.

Over the next few weeks, scandal after scandal involving multiple divisions of Prudential Insurance emerged in news reports. It was as if the full disclosure of the partnership fraud had ripped aside the company's facade, exposing its dirty secrets.

New York State officials were reported to be investigating Prudential Insurance for illegally selling financial products that had been turned down by insurance regulators. Under pressure from a lawsuit by a whistle-blower, the company also admitted that it had improperly inflated the values of properties in some institutional real estate funds, making it appear that the funds were performing better than they actually were.

The articles were also devastating to Prudential Securities. They disclosed that federal prosecutors were examining the role of the firm's law department in the partnership sales. The government was also reported to be investigating whether the firm had offered misleading legal advice about class actions to its partnership investors. A drug ring was exposed in an Arizona branch, which had been using overnight delivery services to ship illegal narcotics. The firm was forced to repurchase $70 million in recently sold mortgage securities because their true risk had been misrepresented to investors.

Even the firm's advertising led to embarrassment. Prudential Securities

launched a new $22 million campaign just after the settlement in 1993, us-
ing Simmons and some Prudential Securities brokers in television commer-
cials that boasted of the firm's "straight talk." But the talk proved anything
but straight.

In one commercial, a broker named Jeff Daggett told of his desire to ensure the safety of his clients' investments. Within days of its first appearing
on television, the advertisement had to be pulled. An eighty-one-year-old
Roman Catholic priest filed a lawsuit against Daggett, charging that the
broker had sold him inappropriate partnerships, then misled him into joining a class-action settlement.

The most humiliating moment came in July. The senior management of
the firm finally admitted that, despite their months of arrogant assurances,
they had been wrong. The cost of settling valid claims to the compensation fund would be far more than the $330 million down payment. The
firm had to add another $305 million to its cash reserves to pay the claims.
The liquidity discounts and interest on the claims had pushed up the total
cost. All told, the price of the partnership mess to the firm was projected
to exceed $1.1 billion. But even that estimate proved optimistic. The firm's
projections for the cost of cleaning up the partnership debacle would later
rise to more than $1.5 billion. It was the costliest fraud scandal for any in-
vestment house in the history of Wall Street.

In the wake of the July announcement, the cocksure air of the firm's executives melted away. They were left struggling to explain how they could
have been so wrong.

"I wasn't lying" by promising that $330 million would be enough, Sim-
mons later said. "I may have been stupid."

Four months later, the final, crushing blow landed. After three years of
denying that it had broken any law, Prudential Securities was compelled to
admit in public that it committed crimes in its partnership sales.

Federal prosecutors in Manhattan had completed their investigation of
the firm. They had found the mountain of incriminating documents as
persuasive as the regulators had.

On October 27, 1993, the prosecutors filed a criminal complaint against
Prudential Securities charging that the energy income partnership sales had
been laced with fraud. But, in part out of fear that an indictment would
lead to the firm's collapse, they deferred prosecution for three years. If the
firm did not violate the law during that time, the charges would be
dropped. In essence, Prudential Securities was on probation.

In exchange for the deferred prosecution, the firm agreed to pay $330 million more into the compensation fund for investors. In a sign that the prosecutors did not trust executives to police the firm, Prudential Securities was compelled to appoint an independent ombudsman to review future allegations of misconduct. But, most important, lawyers for the firm conceded in a written statement that fraudulent sales literature had been knowingly distributed to brokers by the Direct Investment Group.

That afternoon, Mary Jo White, the U.S. attorney in Manhattan, promised that the criminal investigation of the executives involved in the partnership debacle was continuing. The SEC inquiry of individuals was also still on track.

Long before any of those investigations ended, some of the firm's executives would pay a heavy price.

Jack Graner, the former regional director in the Pacific South, tapped out lines of heroin on the bathroom counter. He was in room 214 at the TraveLodge Hotel in Burbank, California, about a mile up the road from the gates of Warner Brothers studios. It was one o'clock on the morning of January 27, 1994. In the bed a few feet from Graner, a young woman was asleep. The two had met just days before at a hotel in Hollywood. They had been together ever since, smoking crack, snorting heroin, and drinking ethanol.

Graner's life had fallen apart. With the departure of Bob Sherman and George Ball, he had lost his protectors. As the man who had been the regional director in Atlanta during the Capt. Crab fiasco, Graner was marked. His longtime drug problem grew worse. He was forced to leave the firm.

With his finances in shambles, Graner had been trying to get himself back together and kick his drug habit. He had formed a consulting business where, for a fee, he would testify as an expert in investor arbitrations. He specialized in cases involving Prudential Securities, and he always testified against the firm. By late 1993, he was scheduled for at least two arbitrations against the firm. One case involved a former Storaska client. The other was a wrongful termination case brought by Bill Webb, the Florida broker who was fired for helping his clients find lawyers.

Then one day, Graner had called Webb to say he was dropping out of the case. He had just been notified that the SEC planned to file a complaint against him alleging that he had failed to properly supervise his brokers. The charges would destroy him as an expert witness. In a matter of days, Graner had vanished, bouncing from hotel to hotel in a depressed drug spree. After several weeks, he landed at the TraveLodge in Burbank.

Graner leaned over the countertop and snorted several lines of heroin, then stumbled out of the bathroom. Three and a half lines were left on the counter, but Graner had taken enough to accomplish his goal. He staggered past the suicide note he had placed on a bag and fell onto the bed. The woman beside him barely stirred.

Graner closed his eyes and drifted away. He would never wake up.

The death of Jack Graner hit some brokers and executives from Prudential Securities like a bucket of cold water. Suddenly the implications of the multiple government investigations of the firm's current and former employees was all too real; the costs of the scandal in human terms became far more tangible.

About the same time Graner heard from the government, more than a dozen other executives and brokers were informed that the SEC enforcement staff planned to recommend charges against them stemming from trading violations at the firm's branches, particularly in Atlanta. By the spring of 1995, no charges had yet been filed against any individual as the cases wound their way through the administrative process.

The first onetime senior executive to hear that he faced charges was Richard Sichenzio, who had succeeded Sherman as head of retail at Prudential-Bache. He was informed in a letter that the SEC planned to charge him with failing to properly supervise the firm's brokers. Sichenzio had just finished two years of working as a consultant for Prudential Securities for a fee of $1.2 million. He had since taken a job as president of Spencer Trask Securities, a brokerage firm. Within weeks of hearing from the SEC, Sichenzio left Spencer Trask. He now works as an industry consultant.

No matter what decision the SEC makes about Bob Sherman, it will have little effect on his life. After being pushed out of Prudential-Bache, he invested in Nathan's Famous, a hot dog chain, and became its president. In little more than a year, he was out of that job. Sherman now sells heavy equipment in New Jersey. Family members believe that he never intends to join another brokerage firm.

After a decade on Wall Street of dodging the responsibility for scandal, George Ball finally had his Teflon scratched. At the time the regulatory settlement was announced, Ball had been working as a senior executive at Smith Barney, Harris Upham & Co. for a year. But the scandal gave heavy ammunition to his enemies there, who considered Ball an embarrassment and wanted him out of the firm. Within a matter of weeks, he was gone. Afterward, he worked as chairman of Sanders Morris Mundy, a Houston firm run by Don Sanders, one of Ball's top brokers at Hutton.

In December 1994, Ball was notified that the enforcement staff intended to recommend bringing a civil complaint against him for failing to properly supervise Fred Storaska, who in turn also faces charges. Ball said he will contest the case.

Shortly after the regulatory settlement, Loren Schechter was forced out as general counsel of Prudential Securities. Hardwick Simmons asked him to leave following news reports that Schechter had hired a criminal lawyer. Although Schechter was not known to be a target of any criminal investigation, the disclosure made him appear too scarred by the scandals to continue in his job. He remains as a lawyer and adviser to the firm.

By the spring of 1995, the government was finishing the final interviews in its investigation of individuals involved in the partnership scandal. While no action had yet been taken against those men, their lives already seemed to have changed irrevocably.

Graham Resources was purchased by Prudential Securities and was essentially shut down. John Graham decided to largely abandon the energy industry and instead commit his time to raising money for inventions in the medical field. To do that, he opened Graham Partners, a business he started with his old colleague, Mark Files. Tony Rice was also persuaded to participate in some of the new company's ventures. Despite the findings in the criminal case, all three men continue to insist that nothing improper ever occurred in the sale or management of the energy income or energy growth partnerships.

As the partnership scandal unfolded, Clifton Harrison left Dallas for Moscow, the newest and wildest frontier of capitalism. There he linked up with several partners and pursued Russian real estate and film deals. But doing business in Moscow carries risks: One of his partners was killed in what authorities believe was a contract hit by the Russian mob. Still, Harrison has seen success there. "People here know Harrison for what he is," one American in Moscow said. "But it doesn't matter. This is the land of the second chance."

James Darr still lives with his wife and daughter in the Connecticut mansion he purchased with money from First South. He told government investigators that since leaving Prudential-Bache, he has spent his time handling his own investments.

Some of Darr's attempted business strategies have not panned out. A few years ago, he approached Sam Belzberg—once the nemesis of Bache—with a proposal: He and Belzberg would work together buying assets from some of the floundering partnerships. Belzberg turned him down. In 1992, Darr apparently decided to become a lawyer and attended Pace University Law School. He dropped out after one semester.

Darr remains comfortable financially. Each quarter, as provided in the contract he struck in the 1980s, Prudential Securities pays him part of the cash flow out of a huge number of partnerships. In 1994 alone, he received more than $200,000 from the partnerships. And that was a bad year; since 1990, the firm has cut him checks for well over $2 million, cash that could have gone to the investors whose lives he helped to destroy. Those payments will likely remain a steady source of income for a long time. Under his contract, Darr should continue to receive his huge checks, every few months, well into the next century.

AFTERWORD

THE PUBLICATION OF *Serpent on the Rock* in the summer of 1995 brought new troubles to Prudential Securities. In particular, the book's disclosure of Prudential's continued payments to Darr proved a major embarrassment for the firm. Plaintiffs' lawyers who had sued the firm demanded details of Darr's financial deal. More negative publicity hit, with news reports across the country describing Darr's lucrative arrangement. After believing that the cloud of scandal had almost passed, Prudential yet again was being condemned as disreputable.

"It's almost impossible to put into words how that information hits someone," Linda Myers, a partnership investor, said of the payments in an interview with CNN. "It's unconscionable. And for them to continue this charade is just beyond the realm of even discussion."

Prudential executives conceded to reporters that Darr was still being paid but said that the firm was legally obligated to do so.

"Under the contract we had with Jim Darr, he has been receiving residual payments from the limited partnerships," Charles Perkins, a spokesman for the firm, told the *New York Times* in July 1995. "We have no choice but to honor that contract."

Within days, Darr's payments were the subject of numerous discussions at the highest levels of Prudential Securities. The firm's top officers had long been uncomfortable making the payments; Hardwick Simmons, the chief executive, found it particularly distasteful. He had consulted the firm's lawyers, asking if there was any way the payments could be stopped. The lawyers told him that, no matter how unpleasant it was, the firm was contractually obligated to keep paying Darr the money.

But in July, as the time came to approve another payment to Darr, Simmons simply could not stomach it. After talking about it with some of the firm's other senior executives, Simmons made a decision: Prudential was not going to pay. Ever again.

Almost eight years after being forced out of the firm, Darr finally had been cut off. Almost a year later, although his lawyer complained to Prudential about the decision, Darr had not sued for the money.

In August 1995, Prudential was hit by a new setback: For the first time, a broker successfully sued the firm by arguing that Prudential's lies about the partnerships had destroyed her business.

The broker, Betty Allen, had sold more than $12 million worth of partnerships over seven years while working in Orlando, Florida. By 1993, the accounts of her best customers were in ruins. More than forty customers sued, naming Allen in their complaints. The loss of business, coupled with the complaints on her employment record, crippled Allen's job prospects in the securities industry. When she sued, she argued that Prudential was legally responsible for the damage.

An arbitration panel agreed with Allen in August 1995, awarding her more than $327,000. The decision was big news among the firm's brokers who had sold partnerships. Many of them had seen their careers suffer the same fate as Allen's. Some had already filed suit and now believed they could win. Others planned to sue and sought out lawyers.

Even as brokers were readying their cases, another class action came to Prudential's rescue. In August, the same month as the loss in the Allen case, Prudential agreed to pay $110 million to settle the last class action stemming from the partnership debacle. It had been filed months before on behalf of investors who, for whatever reason, had not received money from an individual lawsuit or the regulatory settlement fund. Unlike other Prudential class actions, this one appeared harmless. After all, without it, the investors would never get any of their investment dollars back.

But once again Prudential proved itself to be shrewder than the clients and brokers it had defrauded. The firm negotiated the terms of a long, legalistic notice of settlement that was sent to investors around the country. As in the class actions that came before, anyone who did not want to take part in the settlement had to opt out by notifying the Federal District Court in Manhattan, where the case was filed. The deadline for the opt-outs was October 30. Included in the notice was a little-noticed phrase saying that anyone who did not opt out in the case would have all of their claims stemming from the partnership sales wiped out.

And so the trap was set. With the way the notice was written, even investors and brokers already suing the firm could be forced to accept the class-action settlement as long as they failed to opt out. All Prudential needed was for the arbitrations on those suits to continue past October 30.

In the days leading up to the opt-out deadline, Prudential lawyers moved to extend arbitrations that were hours away from completion. Then when the deadline passed, Prudential declared the case settled and threatened to seek contempt charges against the opposing lawyers if they attempted to proceed with the arbitration.

In numerous cases, Prudential declared the lawsuits settled even if the plaintiffs had never received a copy of the class-action notice telling them of the need to opt-out. At the same time, many brokers with employment claims similar to Betty Allen's case were told that their cases were over as well. Those brokers had invested some of their own money in the partnerships, and Prudential declared that the class-action settlement eliminated all investor claims—even if it was a job-related action.

The tactic was devious but perfectly legal. By outfoxing the clients and brokers it had lied to, the firm saved itself millions. But the plaintiffs' lawyers saw it as another despicable move by the firm to avoid making good to the people it cheated.

"It's absurd and ludicrous," said Phillip J. Duncan, a lawyer trying a case that was tossed out of arbitration because of the tactic just hours before the hearing was to have ended. "It's hitting below the belt, at the eleventh hour, to ensure that people get knocked out of their day in court."

Indeed, for many of the plaintiffs' lawyers, the maneuver showed that, despite all its protestations of being a reformed firm, Prudential had changed very little.

"It's the same scorched-earth tactics they have been using for years," said Seth Lipner, a securities lawyer who brought a number of partnership cases against the firm. "Despite all their talk of being a new Prudential, they still won't deal honorably with the victims of their fraud."

By June of 1996, the final mop-up of the Prudential scandal was under way. The regulatory settlement fund established by the SEC and the states had resolved most of the filed claims. The investors who had been defrauded either had received their settlements or were uncomfortably adjusting to a life with fewer dreams. Many of the brokers had moved on—to other firms, to other careers. Some were still trapped in the past, raging about the wounds inflicted on them by their employer and each day plotting a new and probably hopeless strategy for revenge.

Meanwhile, the federal government continued to move slowly toward bringing actions against those responsible for the scandal. The SEC in particular was actively investigating executives involved in the debacle; a wide number of executives had been informed that the agency intended to bring charges against them. Coordinating the multiple cases proved more complex than investigators had thought, but the first complaints or settlements involving individuals in the Prudential case were expected by the fall.

The investigation by federal prosecutors appeared far less active. One of the main prosecutors in the case had resigned from the United States Attorney's office in 1995 to take a job with a law firm that specialized in class actions. By then, even potential defendants in the case were saying they were not much concerned about the criminal investigation. By all appearances, it was dormant. But, in the spring of 1996, the prosecutors stepped up their interviews of witnesses, offering assurances to some that action would be taken soon. But ultimately no charges would ever be brought against anyone involved in the partnership scandal.

For Prudential Securities and its parent, Prudential Insurance, the final toll from the partnership scandal was still being assessed. Largely as a result of the scandal, the insurance company lost more than $900 million in 1994. The poor earnings pushed Prudential Insurance to announce a massive revamping in the fall of 1995. Businesses that had once run independently would be reined in; the home office in Newark would have far greater involvement in daily operations. As many as two thousand Prudential employees would be fired or transferred for the restructuring.

But Prudential lost something far more valuable in the partnership debacle than all its corporate and financial costs. It is almost impossible to overestimate the value of the reputation once associated with the name "Prudential." Because of its reputation for trustworthiness, doors that would be closed to other names opened widely for Prudential. But in pursuit of short-term profits, Prudential executives abused the name, and the company's once-stellar image was tarnished forever. Once damaged, a reputation, much like a fine piece of crystal, can never be restored to its original brilliance.

Nor, apparently, does it deserve to be. Indeed, in the end, the fast-buck, hard-sell mentality of the firm may have been simply a reflection of the modern ethos of its parent, Prudential Insurance. In July 1996, Prudential Insurance settled charges that it had engaged in a wholly different scheme, frighteningly similar to the partnership fraud: Over many years, its insurance agents had tricked customers—including the elderly—into replacing their life insurance at added cost for no benefit to anyone but Prudential itself.

In its settlement with thirty state insurance regulators, Prudential Insurance agreed to pay a record fine of $35 million and to compensate the victims of the new fraud, whose numbers potentially reach the millions. The total cost is expected to run as high as $500 million.

With a record like that, it is little wonder that across Wall Street, the name "Prudential" became a conversational shorthand for abusive practices and hardball legal tactics. Executives at competing firms often pronounced how they wanted to avoid the missteps that might make them be perceived as similar to Prudential. Indeed, other sellers of limited partnerships, including those with defenses far more credible than Prudential's, moved quickly in 1996 to settle the claims arising from that business. New York Life Insurance Company announced in early 1996 that it would liquidate $396 million worth of limited partnerships it had sold and repay every investor. The company quickly won praise for sidestepping Prudential's strategy. Paine Webber announced that it would pay $230 million to resolve investor claims stemming from its partnership sales; in public comments, the firm expressed deep regret for the past practices and unacceptable behavior that led to improper sales. The settlement and the starkly honest comments, executives with the firm said privately at the time, were a conscious effort to avoid appearing like "another Prudential."

For those not working at Prudential, Wall Street's most destructive scandal contains some seeds of hope. After witnessing the damage Prudential caused itself, and the price that was paid for short-term strategizing, the optimistic believe that Wall Street has learned a painful lesson. But the hope is folly. As long as there is greed, as long as crimes go unpunished, as long as Wall Street can make millions even if clients lose money, the scandal at Prudential will be just another chapter in an ongoing saga of financial fraud. The next chapter will begin without warning, and it will not be about partnerships. Some financial company will offer up another investment that will leave its clients' accounts ravaged and their dreams of the future destroyed. If history is any guide, that is a certainty. The only questions are: Who will do it next time? and When?

ACKNOWLEDGMENTS

ALL BOOKS are collaborative efforts, and this one is no exception. I am grateful to many people who offered me an extraordinary amount of guidance and support in this project, particularly my colleagues at the *New York Times*.

I am indebted to William Stockton, who, as business editor of the *Times* in 1992, recognized the significance of the slowly unfolding scandal at Prudential Securities before I did. After I wrote a few articles on the topic, it was he who suggested I be given the rein to delve into the story full-time. He was unflagging in his support, particularly when I needed it most. Glenn Kramon and Sallie Hofmeister were my primary editors on the Prudential articles for the *Times*, and their commitment and skill were an inspiration. Glenn and another colleague, Douglas Frantz, also offered generous amounts of their time to review parts of the manuscript. Their advice on structure and narrative were invaluable.

I would also like to thank the senior editors at the *Times*, particularly Joseph Lelyveld and Soma Golden Behr, who were generous in allowing me to have the time to do this book. John Geddes, who became business editor while I was on leave, offered his support from almost his first day on the job. For that I am extremely grateful.

Other colleagues, including Dean Baquet, Chris Bockelmann, Robert Pear, Floyd Norris, Adam Liptak, Jonathan Fuerbringer, Adam Bryant, Alison Leigh Cowan, James Sterngold, Bob Candela, and Joan Motyka, offered help at important junctures. Donna Anderson cheerfully helped me dig up news articles. Karen Cetinkaya provided photo research, and Anne Cronin and Patrick Lyons handled graphics.

Every author builds off the journalism of others, and I was fortunate to be standing on the shoulders of giants. The award-winning articles on the Prudential scandal by Scot Paltrow of the *Los Angeles Times* are a must-read for anyone interested in the topic. And of course, the groundbreaking work of Chuck Hawkins brought James Darr to the public eye for the first time and, I believe, is largely responsible for helping many investors get back their money. Both journalists were gracious enough to allow me to pick their brains for suggestions. They are real pros.

In addition, I received important advice on taking my first steps into publishing from Bryan Burrough of *Vanity Fair* and James B. Stewart of *The New Yorker*. Their help made me much more surefooted, and for that I am grateful.

I received help from talented researchers—Lisa Granatstein, Brian Steinberg, and Debra Piehl. And I owe a debt to Diane O'Bara, a hard-working assistant who was always cheerfully ready to help. She saved me from disaster more times than I can count.

I also owe thanks to Zofia Kresa, Lynne and Donell Moor, Carl Moor, Anne Carlson, Errington Thompson, Franz Paasche, and Charles Cleaver. They should all know the reasons why.

My agent, Freya Manston, encouraged me to do this book and was an enthusiastic supporter from the start. She was there for me every step of the way. Thanks are also due to my lawyer, David Glasser, for all his time and energy.

At HarperCollins, I am immensely grateful to Jack McKeown, who acquired this book by dint of his infectious excitement. Adrian Zackheim was tireless in his encouragement. My editor, Suzanne Oaks, never lost her keen eye no matter how late into the night we worked. The talent at HarperCollins ran deep; I am also particularly grateful to Lisa Berkowitz, Marilyn Mazur, Deirdre Walsh, Maureen O'Neill, and Joe McKeown.

Finally, I am thankful to my family and friends, who put up with my endless absences with patience and good cheer. My parents, Heinz and Elva Eichenwald, were always ready with support and suggestions. And when my wife and I had a new baby before the book was finished, my mother stayed with us for weeks to shoulder some of the work and keep me on schedule. While she was here, she gladly reviewed the manuscript and made it better with each suggestion.

Above all, I want to thank my wife, Theresa Eichenwald. Her love and patience were an endless resource for me. When she delivered faster than I did, she assumed extra burdens to allow me to finish. She helped me through many difficult days and many more difficult chapters. She was my keenest adviser, my first editor, and my best friend. Her wisdom and support are reflected on every page.

APPENDIX

In this book, I used a small group of the seven hundred partnerships sold by Prudential-Bache to demonstrate the wanton, reckless nature of the Direct Investment Group. I did that to keep the narrative focused. Readers should not assume that partnerships that were not discussed were properly sold. I have reviewed the marketing material and performance for more than one hundred of the partnerships and, almost without exception, the story is the same. The marketing material stressed safety and targeted retirees, who usually invest in CDs, money markets, municipal bonds, and utility stocks. Then the partnerships collapsed in value. It made no difference whether the partnerships were sold before or after tax reform, or whether they invested in horses, cable television, energy, real estate, airplanes, or high technology. Almost everything the Direct Investment Group touched turned to dross. The following table includes many of the largest partnerships that have not been examined in this book. Their performance speaks volumes.

Partnership	Sales Material Highlights	Change in Value
1. Almahurst Public	Almahurst offers . . . safety	-100.0%
2. First Capital Income & Growth XII	Who should buy: retirees who want to preserve capital . . . CD buyers	-82.0%
3. First Capital Insured	Safety . . . for individual investors	-76.0%
4. Fogelman Mortgage LP	Excellent investment alternative for CDs . . . offers a very high degree of safety	-81.0%
5. Fogelman Secured Equity	Safety . . . guarantees 128% return to investors	-48.5%
6. Fox Strategic Housing	Safety of principal; best prospects: bond buyers, CD purchasers	-72.5%

7. Growth Hotel I	A conservative investment/capital preservation	–81.0%
8. Jones Cable TV Fund 14B	A combination of safety and growth; best prospects: buyers of utilities	–54.0%
9. Lorimar	Safety; a minimum 6% return	–80.0%
10. Metric Income	Highlight: safety	–57.5%
11. Polaris I	Preservation of capital	–89.6%
12. Polaris II	Safety; who should buy: CD	–84.2%
13. Polaris III	buyers, muncipal bond buyers,	–86.4%
14. Polaris IV	money market fund investors	–68.6%
15. Polaris VI	Highlight: safety	–50.0%
16. Prudential Acquisition Fund I	Investment safety	–87.0%
17. Prudential Acquisition Fund II	Low risk; safe . . . safe . . . safe . . . safe	–77.5%
18. Prutech I	Key sales points: safety through diversification	–95.0%
19. Prutech II	Benefits: preservation of capital	–97.5%
20. Prutech III	Reduced risk	–90.1%
21. Spanos Genesis	Structured to provide numerous levels of safety to the investor	–94.7%
22. Spanos Realty	Safety; best prospects: CD buyers	–65.6%
23. Summit Insured Equity I	Safety; best prospects: safety-oriented investors	–57.6%
24. Summit Insured Equity II	100% of investment capital insured against loss	–61.4%
25. Summit Preferred Equity	Safety; subjects . . . CD buyers, utility stock buyers	–65.0%
26. Summit Tax Exempt I	Safety	–43.8%
27. Summit Tax Exempt II	Safety	–39.5%
28. Summit Tax Exempt III	Safety	–35.0%
29. VMS Hotel Investment Trust	High yield, safety	–98.0%
30. VMS Mortgage Investors II	Safety, AAA rated	–100.0%

NOTES AND SOURCES

This book grew out of my coverage of the Prudential scandal for the *New York Times* over more than two years. It is based on more than six hundred interviews, many of which were tape-recorded, as well as hundreds of thousands of pages of documents. The interviews were conducted with a range of people with firsthand knowledge of the events described, including many of the principals. Still, some were not prominent players on Wall Street, and their names might be unknown even to some participants. They were in the position of the cat watching the queen—seeing all, but taking part in nothing.

Nearly all of the interviews for the book were conducted on condition that my sources not be identified. The requests were understandable—many of these sources still feared potential criminal indictments or were subject to investigation by the SEC. A number of others had never been contacted by the government but worried that, if identified, they would be caught up in the ongoing Prudential litigation. Still others work in the securities industry and worried about potential retribution.

The documents included personal diaries, marketing material, internal memos and letters, investigative reports and notes, corporate filings with the Securities and Exchange Commission, police and coroners' records, telephone logs, personal expense files, medical reports, military records, sworn statements and testimony, court filings, video recordings, as well as newspaper and magazine articles and books.

Some executives involved in these events for their own reasons felt compelled to secretly tape-record their colleagues. A number of those audio recordings were obtained for this book. Most references to those recordings in these notes are purposely oblique to protect the confidentiality of sources.

Through Freedom of Information Act requests, I obtained records and testimony from several SEC investigations of Prudential. In some instances, those FOIA requests were denied because the information involved an ongoing investigation. Through other sources, I obtained SEC testimony from those continuing inquiries, including the depositions of James J. Darr, Anton Rice III, William Petty, and others.

Descriptions of individual settings come from interviews, documents, or my personal observation. Most details of weather conditions are taken from the records on file with the National Climatic Data Center.

All dialogue and quotations come from participants or witnesses to the conversations, documents that describe the discussion, or recordings and transcripts of the actual words. In a few rare instances, secondary sources were reliably informed of a conversation by a participant. If these secondary sources agreed on what they were told, the dialogue was used. Such dialogue never amounted to more than a single statement, and was never incriminating. Because of the many sources used in reconstructing dialogue, the reader should not assume that any individual participant in a conversation is the source of the statement, or even among the sources.

Of course, these reconstructions of conversations, taking place over more than a decade, are not a transcript of the event. I do not claim that the statements quoted are the exact words used by the participants. They do, however, represent the best recollections of those words and more accurately reflect reality than mere paraphrase would.

When someone is described as having thought or felt something, the description either comes directly from that individual or from someone to whom the person in question directly described it. Sentences in italics involve thoughts by an individual that were described by that individual to me or to someone else who spoke with me.

As could be expected, disagreements arose about certain details of precise events. Over a decade, memories cloud. People remembering the same event at times would offer conflicting information about things such as dates and locations. In each such case, I endeavored to find documentary evidence that would support one version of events, or use other related interviews to fix time frames and locations.

For an allegation of wrongdoing, denials are cited on the page in which it is described. The documentation that led to the author's conclusion is then described in this section.

Most allegations of wrongdoing come directly from sworn statements and other records of trials, arbitrations, government investigations, and congressional hearings. In those instances where no sworn statements or court records existed, I obtained original documents or other corroborating evidence supporting the descriptions of those events.

PROLOGUE

1–4: Details of Fannie Victor's investments and the circumstances surrounding the loss of her condo were disclosed in the transcript of the November 30, 1993, proceedings in *Victor v. Prudential Securities*, arbitration no. 93–00160.

In January 1994, her broker, Stephen Ziomeck, was censured by the New York Stock Exchange for his inappropriate sales of limited partnerships to his customers. The decision, number 93–156114, involved customers other than Victor. Ziomeck, who agreed to be suspended from the exchange for four weeks, settled the charges.

4–6: The connection between Piscitelli's physical and mental problems—including his thoughts of suicide—and the Prudential partnership scandal comes from interviews and from a series of medical reports. Those documents include a November 10, 1993, report by Dr. Mark S. Lipian, a psychiatrist; a November 10, 1993, report by Dr. Dominick Addario, a psychiatrist; periodic progress reports by Dr. M. Gene Ondrusek, a psychologist; and an April 26, 1993, report by Dr. James R. Nelson, a neurologist.

Dr. Lipian's evaluation was conducted at the request of Prudential Insurance because of Piscitelli's disability claim. In his report, Dr. Lipian summarized the findings of Piscitelli's other health care professionals, saying, "When Mr. Piscitelli attempts to function in his capacity as a Prudential Securities broker, and is confronted with the stress of not only the normal duties involved in this profession but also of the legal entanglements surrounding current government investigations into Prudential's alleged misconduct, the stress becomes overwhelming and Mr. Piscitelli becomes unable to function. . . . The general consensus among these professionals, however, seems to be that removed from the stress of Prudential's current legal entanglement—placed in an equivalent vocational position without the legal hassles and without the bad feelings surrounding his Prudential experience—Mr. Piscitelli would do fine."

5: Many pieces of marketing material for the investment, VMS Mortgage Investors Fund, repeatedly stressed its guarantees and safety. They include the August 15, 1988, DI Sales Action Worksheet from the firm's Direct Investment Group and "Southwest Region DIG Product Snapshot." The guarantees and the stress of safety were also made in undated marketing material by VMS Realty Partners, the fund's general partner. That material includes documents headlined "The Ideal Qualified Plan Investment" and "Let Your Client Be the Banker."

6–9: The magnitude, means, and duration of many elements of the Prudential-Bache fraud are discussed in filings by the Securities and Exchange Commission in the case captioned "In the Matter of Prudential Securities Incorporated," administrative proceeding file no. 3–8209. The agency's findings are included in the Order Instituting Public Proceedings, Making Findings and Imposing Sanctions, release no. 33082, which was filed as case number 93 Civ. 2164 in Federal District Court in Washington, D.C., on October 21, 1993.

Also, see *United States of America v. Prudential Securities Incorporated.* The criminal complaint in that action was submitted to the Honorable Leonard Berkinow, United States Magistrate for the Southern District of New York, on October 27, 1994. Resolution for that case is scheduled for the fourth week of October 1997.

In the criminal case regarding the firm's sale of $1.4 billion of energy partnerships, Prudential's lawyers with the firm of Davis, Polk & Wardwell admit in court filings that the Direct Investment Group knowingly disseminated false information to the brokerage force that was used in the sales of partnerships.

CHAPTER 1

15: The effects of May Day on commission rates are described in "Rate War Rages Among Brokers," *New York Times*, May 30, 1975.

25–27: The description of Darr's encounter with Herb Jacobi comes from a series of secret tape recordings made by an associate of the men and obtained by the author. Further details are provided in "An Early Warning Haunts Prudential," *New York Times*, May 2, 1994.

When first asked about the matter by the author, Darr, through one of his lawyers, denied that he had received any payments. Later, after the author described the checks and deposit slips, his lawyers acknowledged that Darr received money from both First Eastern Corporation and Rothchild Reserve International.

They said a $50,000 check from Rothchild was for personal consulting and a $30,000 payment from First Eastern was a fee for a leveraged lease airplane tax shelter that was never completed. The author notes that the second explanation is the same as the cover story discussed with Jacobi.

In both instances, the lawyers said the payments were approved by Josephthal. Former senior Josephthal executives, including Michael DeMarco, in subsequent on-the-record interviews with the author, denied that they had any prior knowledge of the payments. These executives also said they never would have approved them because of the conflicts of interest they created.

Darr declined to be questioned personally by the author about the payments. In depositions under oath for lawsuits, Darr's lawyers have refused to allow him to answer any questions about his relationships with First Eastern and Rothchild, or about anything involving his time at Josephthal. They also objected to his being questioned about his Josephthal days in testimony to the Securities and Exchange Commission in 1991; the government lawyer dropped that line of inquiry.

The author has interviewed multiple sources who independently said they were questioned by lawyers for the firm about the payments to Darr. Some of these individuals have not had contact with each other in more than a decade; at the time they worked together, they were not close. Yet all of them told stories that are identical in almost every particular. Some said they had personal knowledge that the payments were improper.

In addition, notes from lawyers' interviews quote Barry Trupin as saying Darr requested the payments, which were not paid as part of a consulting arrangement.

25: Darr insists he never did anything improper or questionable during his years at Prudential-Bache. Through his lawyers or in sworn statements, he denies misrepresenting his background or taking any improper gratuity from general partners. He also said that, although he was the man at the top of the limited partnership division, he played little role in the daily running of the division. All partnerships were subjected to rigorous reviews by an investment committee in the department, on which he had a single vote, he said. He also says that all of his investments and outside business activities were approved by superiors.

These statements, however, have been contradicted in interviews with dozens of people who worked with the department and other divisions of the firm and in sworn statements and internal documents. For instance, Darr denies claiming to have served in Vietnam or the CIA—the author has spoken to more than a dozen people who independently say they heard him make such statements. He has denied having conversations that were recorded in contemporaneous notes taken by other participants. He disputes specific events that others have described under oath.

At bottom, the author wishes to stress that almost every allegation about impropriety by Darr comes from sworn statements, including several made to the SEC in records that are still sealed; from contemporaneous documents; or, in a few cases, from multiple interviews with different people making similar claims. Allegations that could not be so supported in that way were not published in this book.

For a succinct description of the allegations involving Darr's department, the Direct Investment Group, the author cites Objection to Settlement and Motion to Intervene, filed October 31, 1994, in *Starr* v. *Graham Energy et al.* in the Superior Court of New Jersey for Middlesex County, docket number MID-L-1165-92. That court document states:

> Darr was actually running a corrupt organization, in which 1) sponsors were either selected for or spontaneously demonstrated their willingness to grant benefits or side deals to Darr rather than chosen on the merits of the particular deal or sponsor; 2) the partnerships were sold to investors on misrepresentations that they were safe, reliable, high-yield and/or tax sheltered alternatives to bank "CDs" (certificates of deposit) when the partnerships were rather among the riskiest of investments, sometimes structured in such a way that they were destined to fail *ab*

initio; 3) the general partners often gouged the partnership with extravagant expenses, excessive "allocated" G&A (general and administrative) charges paid to the general partner on top of the actual direct expense reimbursement; and 4) used manipulative accounting practices to fraudulently conceal the wrongs described above.

Finally, a number of Darr's apparent conflicts of interest and certain questionable activities in the partnerships sold during his tenure were first publicly reported by Chuck Hawkins, with Leah Nathans Spiro, in "The Mess at Pru-Bache," *Business Week*, March 4, 1991.

25: The amount of money given to Darr from First Eastern and Rothchild comes from the checks and deposit slips to his bank account, copies of which were obtained by the author.

27: Some details of Eugene Darr's work history from the *Worcester Telegram & Gazette*, April 20, 1964, and from the *Worcester Sunday Telegram*, October 12, 1975.

27: Darr's high school background from interviews and the West Boylston High School yearbook for 1964. College background from interviews and the Holy Cross yearbook for 1968.

27: A copy of Darr's military service record with the U.S. Air Force was obtained by the author.

28: Dottie Darr's background from interviews, her obituary in the *Worcester Telegram*, May 6, 1992, and a personal letter she wrote in 1975 describing her beliefs.

28–29: Details of Richard and Dottie Bailey's land investments from interviews and documents in the deals. The documents include records pertaining to contract number DN 4449 with the General Mortgage Corporation for the purchase of lot 37 in Deerwood North, as well as to the Manchester Bank's mortgage loan number 06–732–470–5, given to the Baileys for the purchase of the New Hampshire property. In addition, documents from the Richey Company, a real estate concern in Barnstead, New Hampshire, confirm Darr's involvement in the deal.

30–32: Details of Darr's work at Merrill from interviews, with some information provided in the sworn testimony of Anton H. Rice III before the SEC on December 16, 1991, for case number NY-5975, captioned "In the Matter of Certain Limited Partnership Offerings." The testimony, which was obtained by the author, is not publicly available.

31: Description of Barry Trupin's house in Southampton from the *New York Times*, April 1, 1984, and March 31, 1989.

32: The description of Darr's demand for $50,000 based, in part, on notes of lawyers' interviews with Barry Trupin.

The description of Darr's visit to United States Trust Company comes, in part, from the deposit slips of January 30, 1978, which were obtained by the author. The payment to Merrill in the Mattel deal is described in the June 2, 1977, letter from Bertram C. Izant, general counsel of Itel Investment Corporation, to Janet Bascatow of Merrill Lynch Leasing Inc.

33: Darr's statements at the January luncheon meeting are from a letter from him to DeMarco, dated January 16, 1978.

The trail of payments for the $30,000 that eventually went to Darr was reconstructed by the author from copies of the original checks and deposit slips. The price and equity of Darr's house in Stamford, Connecticut, come from the mortgage and deed for the property filed with the Stamford town clerk, reference number 2459–179. The sale closed on April 24, 1978.

36: Darr's transactions with the Josephthal cashier on July 17 is based, in part, on a check he wrote on that date, which was obtained by the author.

37: Darr's proposal to Graham and details about Merrill's investigation of Rice come from Rice's 1991 SEC testimony. In that testimony, Rice said that he believed the lunch occurred in 1981, which would be long after Darr joined Bache. In a subsequent interview, his lawyer, Stephen Kupperman, said that the testimony was wrong and that his client was sure the meeting occurred while Darr was still at Josephthal.

38: The tombstone advertisement announcing Bache's hiring of Darr from the *Wall Street Journal*, November 9, 1979.

CHAPTER 2

40: The date and time of the airport meeting between Jacobs and Belzberg is from "How Bache's Message Angered the Belzbergs, Intensifying the Battle," *Wall Street Journal*, March 11, 1981.

42–43: Details on the death of Jules Bache from the *New York Times*, March 24, 1944, and interviews with people close to the Bache family.

Terms of Jules Bache's will from "Bache Estate Put at $3,000,000 Net," *New York Times*, September 26, 1948, and "Bache Willed Art to Metropolitan," March 30, 1944.

42–48: No history of the firm could be told without reference to the seminal article, "The Botching of Bache," by Chris Welles, published in *Institutional Investor* in September 1980. Many details of Harold Bache's battle for control after his uncle's death, his subsequent political moves, and his personal idiosyncrasies were first disclosed in this account.

43: The financial terms and number of new investors Harold Bache found for the firm after his uncle's death is from *Current Biography*, May 1959.

43–44: The growth of Bache under Harold Bache from the *New York Times*, March 16, 1968.

45–46: Some details of Leslie's time in power from Welles, *Institutional Investor*, September 1980.

The performance of the stock market in 1970 from John Brooks, *The Go-Go Years*.

46: The story of Jacobs's plane crash, and some details of his career, from a September 21, 1994, letter written by him.

47–48: Some details of Jacobs's helicopter ride with Tsai from *The Year They Sold Wall Street* by Tim Carrington.

55–60: Two books that examine the silver crisis are Stephen Fay's *Beyond Greed*, published in 1982, as well as Harry Hurt III's excellent examination of the Hunt family, *Texas Rich*, published in 1981. A number of delicious details about the scandal cited in this book come from those two works.

55: The quote from Jacobs's letter to the Hunts from the statement of facts from the Hunts' 1982 settlement with the SEC of securities law violations charges.

CHAPTER 3

61: Some descriptive details of the Securities Industry/United Way Challenge Race from the *DLJ Confidential*, an internal newsletter of Donaldson Lufkin & Jenrette, for the weeks of October 1, 1980, October 8, 1979, and September 21, 1979.

Background of Bill Pittman from his sworn testimony of February 10, 1992, in the case captioned *In Re: Prudential-Bache Energy Growth Funds*, MDL docket number 867, filed in the U.S. District Court for the Eastern District of Louisiana. This testimony, which is not public, was obtained by the author.

62: D'Elisa's performance in the Securities Industry Race from a 1980 log of racing times.

65: Hutton's performance in tax shelter sales from James Sterngold's *Burning Down the House*, his pathbreaking 1990 book on Hutton's demise.

68: Some details of Trace Management from the August 1, 1991, testimony of James J. Darr before the SEC in case number NY-5975, captioned "In the Matter of Certain Limited Partnership Offerings." The testimony, which was obtained by the author, is not publicly available.

70–71: Some details of the Integrated Energy deal, including the background of its principals, from its prospectus dated March 24, 1981.

77–82: Some information regarding the investment structure of Harrison Freedman Associates and the role of Raymond Freedman in the company, from Freedman's testimony of August 31, 1993, in *First v. Prudential-Bache*, number 91–CV–0047, filed in the U.S. District Court for the Southern District of California.

Harrison's relationship with Phillips N.V. is also described in the Freedman deposition.

78–79: Some details of Harrison's childhood and background from his sworn deposition of April 28, 1994, in *First v. Prudential-Bache*, as well as from his deposition of November 7, 1988, in *McNulty v. Prudential-Bache*, filed with the U.S. District Court for the District of Minnesota, Fourth Division.

79: Some details of Harrison's crimes from a confidential security report dated July 25, 1980, by Cartel Security Consultants, and documents filed in the case *United States of America v. Clifton Stone Harrison,* number CR-3-984, with the U.S. District Court for the Northern District of Texas.

81: In his sworn deposition of April 1994, Harrison would claim that he received recommendations for a pardon from Judge W. M. Taylor Jr., the man who sentenced him to prison, as well as Henry Wade, the legendary district attorney in Dallas who had been scheduled to prosecute Lee Harvey Oswald for the assassination of John F. Kennedy. But an internal memorandum of the U.S. Justice Department, dated October 9, 1974, which lists everyone who provided a recommendation to President Ford for Harrison's pardon, does not list the names of any of those people.

81: The collapse of Harrison's real estate investments and his falling out with his partners is described in Raymond Freedman's deposition of August 31, 1993.

82: Freedman's "hell no" statement from his deposition, cited above.

83: Harrison's purchase of three magnums of Dom Perignon for the Bache lawyers is documented by a receipt for the purchase that was obtained by the author.

89: Paton's promotion of Darr as a regret for the investigation is described by Darr in his testimony before the SEC on January 21, 1992. This testimony was also given in case number NY-5975, captioned "In the Matter of Certain Limited Partnership Offerings."

CHAPTER 4

84: Details of Bache's effort to track down information about Belzberg were first reported in Carrington, *The Year They Sold Wall Street.* Details of the customs report about Hymie Belzberg's contacts with Meyer Lansky in part from Carrington, *The Year They Sold Wall Street,* and the *Wall Street Journal,* March 11, 1981.

94–101: Many of the details of the birth of Prudential Insurance come from two fine histories of the company. They are *The Prudential: A Story of Human Security,* by Earl Chapin May and Will Ousler, published in 1950; and *From Three Cents a Week,* by William H. A. Carr, published in 1975.

Also, see Robert Sheehan, "That Mighty Pump, Prudential," *Fortune,* January 1964, and Robert Bendiner, "The Governor Who Couldn't Stop Stealing," *Real Magazine,* 1956. Also, see the *Wall Street Journal,* August 15, 1960.

101–4: Dates and details of the Prudential negotiations with Bache from interviews and the Schedule 14D-1 describing the deal that was filed with the SEC on March 27, 1981. Also, see *Fortune,* April 20, 1981, and the *New York Times,* March 19, 1981. Also, see "Your Friendly Broker, the Pru," *Fortune,* April 20, 1981.

CHAPTER 5

105: Some details about Bill Pittman's background from his deposition of February 10, 1992.

107: Some details about Paul Proscia's background from his deposition of March 25, 1987, in *McNulty v. Prudential-Bache et al.,* civil number 4–85–765, U.S. District Court for the District of Minnesota, Fourth Division.

115–16: Details of the signing ceremony for the Economic Recovery Tax Act from the *New York Times,* August 14, 1991, as well as *Newsweek,* August 24, 1981, and *Time,* August 24, 1981. Some details of ERTA from the *Congressional Quarterly,* 1981 Chronology.

116: Details of Regulation D from *Inc.,* October 1981, and *The American Banker,* September 17, 1981.

118–23: Some details of the troubles at Bache after the Prudential merger from "After a Year, Prudential's Takeover of Bache Mostly Causing Problems," the *Wall Street Journal,* July 16, 1982. Also, some financial details of the firm's performance at that time from *Fortune,* January 24, 1983.

120–21: Some details of the one-year meeting of Bache and the showing of *Annie* from the *Wall Street Journal,* July 16, 1982.

122: Ball's comments to headhunters from Gregory Miller in "Can George Do It?" *Institutional Investor,* July 1984.

CHAPTER 6

125: The dialogue from Bradford Ryland's conversation with George Ball from Ryland's sworn testimony of March 24, 1987, in the arbitration captioned "In the Matter of the Arbitration Between Christopher Heino and Prudential-Bache Securities."

128: Details of Fomon's battle for control of Hutton and Ball's decision to back the candidate who eventually lost from Sterngold, *Burning Down the House.*

129: The growth of Hutton, in part, from Sterngold, *Burning Down the House.*

130: The financial figures from the Hutton check-kiting scandal are from Sterngold, *Burning Down the House.* Also, see *Sudden Death: The Rise and Fall of E. F. Hutton,* by Mark Stevens.

Ball's use of Monopoly money in bonuses to encourage aggressive efforts to recapture bank float is described in "E. F. Hutton Mail and Wire Fraud," *Report of the Subcommittee on Crime of the House Judiciary Committee,* December 1986.

Ball's May 12, 1981, memo is described in Panel Decision 88–19 of the New York Stock Exchange, April 11, 1988.

133–34: The dialogue between Schechter and bank regulators at the February 10, 1982, meeting in part from Sterngold, *Burning Down the House.*

134: The description of the meeting between Hutton lawyers and Arthur Andersen accountants from two in-house memos to the file at Arthur Andersen, dated March 7, 1980, by Louis T. Lynn and John Tesoro; and February 23, 1982, by John Tesoro and Joel Miller.

135–36: Some details of Franco Della Torre's financial dealings with Merrill and Hutton originally from Ralph Blumenthal, *Last Days of the Sicilians,* 1988.

136: Some details of Al Murray's first steps in investigating the Hutton check-kiting scandal from Barbara Donnelly, "The Man Who Nailed Hutton," *Institutional Investor,* September 1985.

138–39: Mike Fahy's discovery of Della Torre's name was first described in Blumenthal, *Last Days of the Sicilians.*

141–42: Ball's comments to the Bache broker meeting in Phoenix from "Ball Takes Bache and Runs with It," *Fortune,* January 24, 1983. That same article reported his comments about the firm's "second-raters."

141–45: Some details of Ball's first days on the job at Bache from Miller, *Institutional Investor,* July 1984. Also, see "New Bache Chief Pushes a Host of Changes, Including New Name, to Lift Firm's Image," the *Wall Street Journal,* October 29, 1982, and Miller, *Institutional Investor,* July 1984.

144: The residuals program at Bache is described in a memo from Ball to the firm, dated September 16, 1982.

145: The new advertising campaign for Prudential-Bache from the advertising column of the *New York Times,* September 21 and November 1, 1982, and February 10, 1983.

CHAPTER 7

150: Harrison's spending habits are detailed in copies of receipts, checks, credit card bills, and checking account ledgers that were obtained by the author. Details about Harrison's mismanagement of his Diners Club account come from a May 21, 1981, letter to him from B. Singer, the director of collection for Diners Club International. The information about Harrison exceeding his MasterCard spending limit from a 1982 notice from the MasterCard Department.

151: Description of Darr's bank accounts, including the Swiss account in which he had an interest through an investment in another entity, from his testimony before the SEC, August 1 and August 2, 1991. Harrison described the gifts he provided Darr, including the artwork worth $8,000 to $9,000, in his testimony in *First* v. *Prudential-Bache,* cited above.

152: Darr's last-minute changes in fees on a Harrison deal are described in a memo dated June 29, 1981, from Donna Webb of Harrison Freedman to Clifton Harrison.

The Bessemer–Key West deal is described in "Agreement and Certificate of Limited Partnership of Bessemer–Key West Limited Partnership," dated November 15, 1980.

153: The author has obtained copies of the May 20, 1981, letter sent by Clifton Harrison to the investors in Bessemer–Key West.

153: Harrison's net worth or cost basis, as of 1981, is disclosed in "Barbizon New York Ltd. Private Placement Memorandum," dated October 12, 1981. When an estimated value of his properties was included, his net worth was positive. But that number papered over the riskiness of his financial condition: To get into a positive net worth, he would have to sell his properties. That document also describes the details of the Barbizon deal and the fees involved. Bache Properties' participation in the Barbizon cash flow is described in an August 25, 1982, letter to Clifton Harrison from John D'Elisa.

154: The author obtained a copy of Harrison's liquor license application from 1982. Harrison's refusal to sign the document is described in the November 3, 1993, deposition in *First* v. *Prudential-Bache* of Andrew Bene, a former executive with Banque Arabe et Internationale D'Investissement, which lent money to the Barbizon deal.

156–57: The author obtained copies of D'Elisa's memos of April 7, 1982, to Darr and Harrison. The actual impact the document would have in litigation is hard to discern. The firm has not produced the D'Elisa memos in any of the lawsuits involving Harrison that were reviewed by the author.

157–58: Details of the Archives deal from the "Archives Limited Partnership Private Placement Memorandum," undated copy.

The financial problems in the Archives deal are described succinctly in Federal District Judge Bruce M. Van Sickle's opinion, dated February 3, 1989, in *McNulty* v. *Prudential-Bache*, civil action number 3-87-196 in the U.S. District Court for the District of Minnesota, Fourth Division. The opinion was vacated as part of a settlement between McNulty and Prudential-Bache.

164: The proposed Exchange Center deal was described in "Exchange Center Limited Partnership Investment Summary," an internal document of Harrison Freedman Associates.

167: Ball's involvement in the development of the energy income partnership in part from a July 27, 1982, memo from him to Alan Altschuler of Bache.

169–70: The background of Graham Resources, including its deal with St. Paul, is described in the June 1983 prospectus for the Prudential-Bache Energy Income Fund.

176–77: The descriptions of the Graham marketing video come from the 1983 script for the promotion.

The number and total investment of Prudential-Bache clients in P-1 from Stuart Goldberg, *Prudential-Bache's $1.3 Billion Energy Income Limited Partnership Oil Scam*, 3rd ed., June 1993. The document is a published analysis of the energy income deals written to assist lawyers in their suits against the firm.

CHAPTER 8

180: Darr's investment of $4,000 in the first Watson & Taylor public deal is disclosed in his testimony to the Securities and Exchange Commission of August 1, 1991.

180–81: The conversation between Bill Petty and George Watson is described in Petty's deposition of September 26, 1991, to the Securities and Exchange Commission in its investigation captioned "In the Matter of Certain Limited Partnership Offerings," case number NY–5975. This deposition is also part of the ongoing investigation and is not publicly available.

Watson has denied that the conversation took place and also denied that the Stemmons deal, called Lombardi Number Three, was presold. And indeed, the documents in the deal show that the two parcels of land involved were acquired on September 29, 1983, and October 7, 1983. Darr's check for $20,600 was deposited on November 11 of that year. The property was sold on February 21, 1984.

Still, the documents raise odd issues. Darr was not admitted as a joint venturer until March 2, 1984, weeks after the property was sold. However, his admission was given an effective date in the documents of September 29, the date of the first land purchase.

Other former Watson & Taylor executives said that, given the hot Texas real estate market, the dates from the documents could easily show a deal that was presold, particularly if there were rezoning efforts needed for the Stemmons property.

The terms of the Lombardi Number Three deal were also publicly described for the first time in the *Business Week* cover story of February 1991, cited above.

182: The backgrounds of George Watson and A. Starke Taylor III are described in their testimony in *United States of America* v. *Howard J. Wiechern*, case number LR-CR-89-64(1) before the U.S. District Court for the Eastern District of Arkansas. Their testimony took place on October 15 and October 16, 1990. Both men were cooperating with the government in the criminal case against Wiechern, the former head of First South Savings, in exchange for immunity from prosecution.

Also, some details from Watson's background are from a 1994 *Texas Business School Magazine*, the alumni magazine for the University of Texas at Austin, College and Graduate School and Business.

182–83: Information about Prudential-Bache/Watson & Taylor Ltd. 1 is described in the prospectus for that investment, dated January 21, 1983.

183: Taylor recounted his first meeting with Wiechern during his testimony in *United States of America* v. *Howard J. Wiechern*.

183–84: The First South loans to Watson & Taylor are described in the civil complaint captioned *Federal Savings and Loan Insurance Corporation* v. *George S. Watson, A. Starke Taylor 3d, et al.*, case number LRC 87–806, filed in the U.S. District Court for the Eastern District of Arkansas, Eastern Division.

Watson & Taylor subsequently filed suit against its law firm, claiming that the violations in the First South investment were the result of bad legal advice. The suit, *Watson & Taylor Realty Company et al.* v. *Akin, Gump, Strauss, Hauer & Feld et al.*, was filed in the District Court of Dallas County, Texas, as case number 90–12266-A. It was subsequently settled.

184: The performance of Watson & Taylor's private land deals was described by Taylor during his testimony in *United States of America* v. *Howard J. Wiechern*.

Details of Darr's investment in Lombardi Number Three and Trinity Mills from "Final Report Regarding Certain Transactions Among James Darr, George Watson and A. Starke Taylor III," a confidential February 28, 1988, report by Locke Purnell Rain Harrell.

Also, see Darr's deposition of October 18, 1994, in *Griffin* v. *Prudential Securities*, case number 250791 in California State Superior Court in and for the County of San Joaquin. Some details also from Darr's testimony of August 1, 1991, to the SEC.

The author also obtained Darr's Schedule K-1, a federal tax document that lists a limited partner's share of income credits and deductions, from the Lombardi deal for calendar year 1983.

Darr testified that he informed Sherman and Schechter of his investments with Watson & Taylor before they were made on October 18, 1994, in *Griffin* v. *Prudential Securities*. Schechter denies that he was ever told anything meaningful about Darr's investments.

The author obtained certain documents that indicate a degree of Sherman's knowledge. They include a June 14, 1983, memo from Darr to Sherman regarding the Thoner investment and a June 24, 1986, memo from Sherman to Darr relating to some investing material. The second memo says that Darr indicated to Sherman that he had informed Schechter of the investment under discussion.

185: The First South stock purchases of George Watson and Tracy Taylor are described in "FSLIC's Opposition to the Watson & Taylor Defendant's Motion to Dismiss," filed March 11, 1988, in *Federal Savings and Loan Insurance Corporation* v. *George S. Watson, A. Starke Taylor 3d, et al.*

186: Once Darr sold his house in Stamford—the one purchased with money he received at Josephthal from general partners—First South required him to pay down some of the loan. Effectively, the only money he put in his new house came from general partners. Certain terms of Darr's mortgage loan with First South are described in the certified copy of his mortgage, filed with the town clerk in Greenwich, Connecticut, book number 1414, page 247.

188: Petty's discussion about having Watson & Taylor pay for Darr's $1,800 weekend in Dallas with his wife from Petty's testimony to the SEC.

189–90: Information about Prudential-Bache/Watson & Taylor Ltd. 2 from the prospectus for that investment, dated March 2, 1984.

190: Details of Darr's investment in Northwest Highway/California Crossing Joint Venture from the Locke Purnell report, cited above.

190: Sales points on Prudential-Bache/Watson & Taylor Ltd. 2 from an undated fact sheet distributed by the Direct Investment Group to Prudential-Bache brokers throughout the country.

190: The performance of Prudential-Bache/Watson & Taylor Ltd. 2 from *The Perspective*, a publication of Partnership Profiles Inc., April 1993.

192–93: Quinn's telephone call to Barry Breeman is described by Breeman in his deposition of December 2, 1992, in *First* v. *Prudential-Bache.*

Information on 680 Fifth Avenue Associates from the prospectus of that partnership.

193–94: Some details on the Barbizon investment offered to Prudential-Bache executives from the February 1984 brochure on the deal sent to Darr from Michael Walters, a marketer with Harrison Freedman.

193: A copy of Darr's letter of February 27, 1984, to Walters was obtained by the author.

194: Details of Harrison's purchases in 1983 from copies of his receipts and credit card bills, both of which were obtained by the author. Specifically, they include the December 12, 1983, receipt for the satinwood table and mahogany clock from Manheim Galleries of Dallas.

194: Darr's solicitation of Prudential-Bache executives, including George Ball, for investment in the Harrison deal from a March 30, 1984, memo written by Darr and obtained by the author.

The Prudential-Bache executives who invested in the second Barbizon deal and assumed Harrison's debt are named in a December 9, 1985, letter from Carnegie Realty Capital Corporation to Steven B. Lipton. In the end, the loan would prove tortuous. Darr himself skipped payments he owed on the loan, but Carnegie never took action against him. In 1987, Darr paid off the loan and all of his past-due interest payments. That same year, Harrison, who paid nothing back on the loan, was sued by Carnegie for defaulting. The court ruled in favor of Carnegie. Darr's repeated failure to pay his interest on the Carnegie loan is described in an October 17, 1986, letter to him from Carnegie demanding payment. According to the letter, Darr failed to pay interest payments of $13,715.75 and $14,178.08 that were due on May 1, 1986, and August 1, 1986. The letter does not threaten Darr with any action if he fails to pay.

Terms of the Harrison deal for Prudential-Bache executives are described in "Agreement and Certificate of Limited Partnership of CSH-BHP Limited Partnership," a document filed with the Texas secretary of state on November 5, 1984.

195: Walters's "merry men" letter of March 26, 1984, to Howard Feinsand was obtained by the author.

196: Darr's orders to change the Madison Plaza video are described on an invoice to the Direct Investment Group, dated February 7, 1984.

Darr's demands of Ed Devereaux and other regional marketers from the third amended complaint in *First* v. *Prudential-Bache.*

196: Harrison's comment to Barry Breeman regarding his joining the Madison Plaza deal from Breeman's deposition of December 12, 1992, in *First* v. *Prudential-Bache.*

197: Roberts's jet-setting and high spending were described in the August 24, 1993, deposition of James M. Holbrook, a lawyer for Summit Savings, in *First* v. *Prudential-Bache.*

Roberts's illegal purchase of the Gulfstream II jet aircraft is described in *United States of America* v. *John H. Roberts Jr.*, case number CR3-89-154-R, filed on June 8, 1988, in Federal District Court for the Northern District of Texas. He pleaded guilty to two felonies under an agreement filed with the court on July 5, 1989.

197–98: John Roberts's financial dealings are described in detail in personal diaries he kept from 1983 to 1984. The documents were obtained by the author.

198: The transfer of the Summit loan to the Grand Cayman Islands branch of the Republic Bank of New York is disclosed in a wire transfer, dated May 31, 1984, from the New York office of Republic to the branch. Officials with ties to Carnegie were named as the trustees for the account.

Roberts's June 1, 1984, meeting in New York with Darr and John Holmes is described in his personal diaries, cited above.

199: Steven Davis's comments about Harrison's need for new deals to pay for old ones from Holbrook's August 24, 1993, deposition, cited above. Also, Holbrook's disinterest in the performance of Madison Plaza for investors from the same testimony.

199–202: Darr denies having discussed loan swaps between Summit and First South. However, Roberts took contemporaneous notes of the August 30, 1984, conversation in his diary, cited above. Also, Roberts testified under oath that the conversation took place.

Further, Holbrook, the Summit lawyer, testified under oath on August 25, 1993, that Roberts had told him that Darr had requested a loan swap between Summit and First South. In that same testimony,

Holbrook described his own conversation with Darr, in which Darr demanded that the loan swaps be done.

CHAPTER 9

204: Details about the Graham due diligence trip to Cancún from a January 1984 sales sheet to Prudential-Bache brokers, which described what they needed to do in order to qualify. The number of executives who went on the trip was determined by a list of attendees obtained by the author.

212–13: Sherman's actions at the Cancún awards ceremony were described to the author by multiple witnesses.

213: The author spoke to a wide range of people who either witnessed or were subjected to sexual harassment by senior officers of Prudential-Bache.

No executives were the subject of more such accusations of sexual harassment than Bob Sherman and Carrington Clark. One woman sued Prudential Securities, describing situations of sexual harassment that were similar to what the author was told in numerous interviews. The suit, *Kristi Mandt* v. *Prudential Securities*, says:

> Sherman and Clark . . . engaged for many years in wrongful conduct of a sexually harassing nature, in violation of Title VII of the United States Code. . . . Sherman, in his position as head of the retail division of Prudential, insisted and demanded from time to time that Clark, as a regional manager, locate female employees to accompany Sherman on business outings for the sole purpose of gratifying Sherman's sexual desires. . . . Clark himself also insisted from time to time that female employees engage in sexual relations with him as a condition of their continued employment and/or advancement of employment opportunities.

In a sworn affidavit attached to that complaint, one former branch manager, Bruce Biermann, described certain actions by Carrington Clark that were filed to support Mandt's claim. In the affidavit, Biermann said:

> I personally observed [Clark] asking for dates with female employees in my office. While I do not know the results of those overtures by Mr. Clark, I was told by one such employee . . . that she was uncomfortable in Mr. Clark's presence. On more than one occasion, Mr. Clark indicated to me that he would have appreciated my getting him dates. I never did so.

In the case, Prudential Securities, Sherman, and Clark do not address the substance of the allegations. Instead, they successfully argued that the claim was time-barred.

217: The details of the Prudential-Bache Energy Income Partnerships Series II come from a copy of the prospectus, dated March 9, 1984.

218: The sales pitch offered to Prudential-Bache brokers for Series II of the energy income partnerships from an undated fact sheet by Steve Starnes, a marketer in the Direct Investment Group, titled "Prudential-Bache Energy Income Fund II."

Also, similar information was provided in a July 16, 1984, fact sheet from Barron Clancy, head of the Northeast Region of the Direct Investment Group. It is titled "Prudential-Bache Energy Income Partnership II: The Window of Opportunity."

224–25: Ball's experience at Sherwood's retirement party is described in a memo Ball wrote to the firm, dated November 26, 1984—the "losses suck" memo.

The deteriorating financial performance of Prudential-Bache is described in *Business Week*, "Pru-Bache Is Putting Its Parent's Patience to the Test," December 17, 1984.

CHAPTER 10

227–28: Details of the Capt. Crab case from "In the Matter of Prudential-Bache Securities," 34 SEC Docket 1094, Administrative Proceeding number 8–27154, file number 3–6600, brought by the Securities and Exchange Commission, January 1986.

227–29: Saccullo's opinions, and quotes from his SEC testimony, from the transcript of proceedings, "In the Matter of Trading in the Securities of Capt. Crab's Take-Away," investigation HO-1573. The testimony was given on February 20–21, 1985. The documents were obtained by the author under a Freedom of Information Act request.

The quotations cited are the actual statements of the participants in that proceeding. However, at times, the back-and-forth between the investigators and Saccullo—such as questions answered with "I don't recall"—have been edited out for simplicity. None of this editing changes in any material way the meaning of Saccullo's answers or of the investigator's questions.

227–28: Lugo was a cofounder of the Executive Securities Corporation, which went bankrupt in the 1970s. He was barred from the securities industry for one year in 1972 by the SEC because of his participation in a reported stock fraud at Executive Securities. His role in the manipulation of International Diamond won him a suspension for ten days. At the same time he was being investigated for the Capt. Crab manipulation, the SEC was also examining a similar fraud involving Lugo and shares of a company called Creditbank.

Information about the secondary offering of Capt. Crab shares from the July 21, 1983, prospectus for Capt. Crab's Take-Away.

229: Lugo settled the Capt. Crab case with the SEC, and on November 5, 1991, an order was entered against him barring him from further violations of securities laws. At the time, Lugo no longer worked as a licensed stockbroker. See SEC Litigation Release number 130393, dated November 18, 1991.

The performance of the Polaris partnership from *The Perspective*, March/April, 1993.

229–30: Some details of Sam Kalil's sentencing hearing from "Broker Convicted of Theft Ordered to Pay Restitution, Serve Jail Term," *Florida Times Union*, February 9, 1985.

Kalil's crimes from "In the Matter of Prudential-Bache Securities," cited above.

Also, see "Stockbroker Kalil Charged with Theft," *Florida Times Union*, December 30, 1983; "Exbroker Sam Kalil Faces 10 Counts of Stock Fraud," *Jacksonville Journal*, December 29, 1983; and "Troubles Mount for Fired Jacksonville Stockbroker," *Florida Times Union*, December 13, 1983.

232: The quotations from Meese about the Hutton settlement from a copy of his prepared statement.

232–33: Ball's congressional testimony from transcripts of the hearings entitled "E. F. Hutton Mail and Wire Fraud," before the Subcommittee on Crime of the House Committee on the Judiciary, October 31, 1985, pp. 1544–1608.

235: Information about the Capt. Crab/Kalil settlement from 34 SEC Docket 1094 cited above.

Quotes about the settlement from "SEC Censures Bache for Supervisors' Lapses," *New York Times*, January 3, 1986.

235–36: Ball's January 24, 1986, meeting with Storaska is described in part in an internal CES memorandum prepared for Storaska. The confidential document was obtained by the author.

236: The terms of Storaska's employment were described in a memo to Storaska's files, written September 3, 1984.

The author obtained a November 12, 1984, letter to Prudential-Bache from the Chicago Board Options Exchange, saying that the exchange was investigating Storaska for matters that occurred prior to his termination from Kidder.

The letter of complaint against Storaska from Lee Cowen, dated October 31, 1985, was obtained by the author.

240–41: Some details of Jim Trice's discussions with George Ball and Bob Sherman from Trice's sworn testimony in his 1989 arbitration case against Prudential-Bache captioned "James E. Trice vs. Prudential-Bache Securities," NASD number 89–03394. Also, see Trice's testimony of April 14, 1994, in "Alexander and Wanda Belmont v. Prudential Securities," arbitration number 93–02086, before the National Association of Securities Dealers.

241–42: The events surrounding Jim Trice's arrival in Atlanta are described in his sworn testimony in his arbitration case, cited above.

243–44: The author obtained the July 8, 1986, memorandum to the file by Charles Grose, which described his encounter with Storaska about the Heiner account. The author also obtained the letter of complaint from the accountant, Susan Hedegaard.

244–45: The events surrounding the Levine case and its subsequent development were described in fascinating detail in Douglas Frantz's *Levine & Company* and James B. Stewart's *Den of Thieves*.

CHAPTER 11

246: Some descriptions and details about Longleaf Plantation from a series of undated brochures and pamphlets published by the hunting reserve.

Also, for some description of Longleaf, as well as intricate details of the Prudential-Bache Energy Income partnership fraud, see the groundbreaking and award-winning series by Scot Paltrow in the *Los Angeles Times*. Part 1 ran on June 22, 1993, under the headline "Partners in a Troubled Venture." Part 2 ran the following day under the headline "As Energy Funds Stumbled, Companies Reaped Benefits."

Rice's role in teaching Darr how to hunt from Rice's December 16, 1991, testimony before SEC investigators, cited above.

247–49: In a sworn deposition, Graham at first claimed not to remember some of these comments and subsequently denied making them. The deposition was taken on May 25, 1993, in the case *In Re: Prudential-Bache Energy Income Partnerships Securities Litigation*, MDL docket number 888, U.S. District Court for the Eastern District of Louisiana.

However, the conversation was described in detail in a January 9, 1985, memo to Anton Rice III written by Mark Files shortly after it occurred.

247–48: The manipulation of the distributions for the energy income partnerships is described in detail in thousands of internal documents in the case *In Re: Prudential-Bache Energy Income Partnerships Securities Litigation*, cited above. Many of those documents are cited here.

Also, it is described in *State of Idaho* v. *John F. Corbin*, civil complaint number 97964, filed on July 21, 1994, in the District Court of the Fourth Judicial District of the State of Idaho. That complaint, which Corbin, a Graham marketer, later settled, stated in reference to the income partnerships: "Corbin omitted to disclose that the identified rates of return were being manipulated by the general partners, so that the charts did not reflect the actual operating incomes experienced by the prior programs during the relevant time periods."

The author also incorporated information from a series of depositions in the case *In Re: Prudential-Bache Energy Income Partnerships Securities Litigation*, cited above. The 1993 depositions include those of Matthew Chanin, taken March 29–30; Sam Blaize, taken April 14; John Graham, taken May 25–27; Joseph DeFur, taken June 1–3; Mark Files, taken June 4–5; Anton Rice III, taken June 9–11; James Kelso, taken June 14–15; and James Darr, taken July 12–14.

Finally, the inflation of partnership distributions was widely reported in the press. Again, the author refers to the Paltrow series in the *Los Angeles Times*, cited above. Also, see Michael Siconolfi, "Prudential-Bache Inflated Partnership Payouts," *Wall Street Journal*, April 8, 1993.

248: Darr's hardball tactics in negotiating with Graham, and the anger that resulted, are described in Rice's 1991 deposition to the SEC.

250: Dawson's $1.4 million day in selling Prudential-Bache Energy Income partnerships is described in *Energy Digest* for May 1985. The newsletter was published by Graham Resources for distribution to brokers in the Prudential-Bache retail network.

251–54: Descriptions of the May 30, 1985, meeting at Prudential-Bache come in part from a June 3, 1985, memorandum by James C. Sweeney, written for his own files.

254: The marketing video for the Prudential-Bache Energy Income Fund II was obtained by the author.

254–56: The description of Pete Theo's presentation to Prudential-Bache brokers comes from a June 28, 1985, script prepared for those sales lectures. The total marketing misrepresentation is described in Goldberg, *Prudential-Bache's $1.3 Billion Energy Income Limited Partnership Oil Scam*.

256–57: Dempsey's recommendation to puff up the distributions was made in a July 2, 1985, letter to Matthew Chanin at Prudential Insurance. Chanin's acceptance of those terms, and the other requirements he imposed, from a July 16, 1985, letter to Anton Rice.

258: Dempsey's concern about his ability to "finesse" the $500,000 shortfall was described in a July 23,

1985, memo to Files and Rice. Although Dempsey instructed the readers to destroy the memo after reading it, a copy of it was obtained by the author.

Also, see Dempsey's testimony of March 30 and April 1, 1993, in *In Re: Prudential-Bache Energy Income Partnerships Securities Litigation*. The author also referred to Dempsey's November 1991 deposition in *In Re: Prudential-Bache Energy Growth Funds*, cited above. Those records, which are not publicly available, were obtained by the author.

A copy of the July 1985 "$uperbroker" comic book was obtained by the author.

259: Alan Myer's limerick from a 1985 copy of *Energy Digest*.

Barbara Gutherie's letter of complaint to Ball about the "$uperbroker" comic book was described on June 22, 1993, in part 1 of Paltrow's energy income series in the *Los Angeles Times*.

259: The October 17, 1985, meeting between Chanin and executives from the Direct Investment Group is described in handwritten notes from the meeting, as well as a typed record for the files by James C. Sweeney, written on October 30, 1985. Also, see the March 29–30, 1993, deposition of Matthew J. Chanin, cited above.

260: Darr's hunting relationship with Tony Rice as well as his failure to pay for hunting trips and the $900 rifle are in part from Rice's testimony to the SEC. Also, in that testimony, Rice describes some details of his car trip with Darr in which they discussed First South.

261: Details of Darr's second loan from First South and his purchase of First South stock in part from Darr's 1991 testimony to the SEC. Also, the author obtained a copy of the second mortgage, which was publicly recorded in Stamford.

261–62: The $800,000 shortfall in distributions for the fourth quarter of 1985 is described in a January 6, 1986, memorandum from Mark Files to Anton Rice and A. B. Dempsey. Also, see Files's deposition of June 4, 1993, cited above. Details of the oil market collapse from *USA Today*, "Chaos Climbs as Oil Prices Keep Sliding," January 22, 1986; *Time*, February 3, 1986.

262–63: The January 23, 1986, conversation between Sweeney and Chanin is described in a memo of that date from Sweeney to Joe DeFur, Bill Pittman, and Paul Proscia. Also, see the March 29–30, 1993, deposition of Matthew J. Chanin, cited above.

263: Al Dempsey's conversations with Pittman and other Direct Investment Group executives a few days after Chanin's decision is described in a February 4, 1986, memo from Dempsey to Graham, Rice, and Files. That memo quotes certain statements from Pittman directly.

264: The May 1986 fact sheet on Prudential-Bache Energy Income Series III describing the program as "A Proven Producer" was obtained by the author. The statements that the energy income partnerships were ideal replacements for certificates of deposit were made in a wide range of sales materials. In the time frame mentioned in this chapter, the author referred to the February/March edition of *Energy Digest*.

265: The investor numbers as of 1986 in the income funds from Goldberg's *Prudential-Bache's $1.3 Billion Energy Income Limited Partnership Oil Scam*.

The author obtained an internal Prudential-Bache document that listed the expected attendees for the 1986 national sales forum, "A Commitment to Excellence."

268: Darr's expectation that he would be able to take Sherman's and then Ball's job based on a number of confidential interviews and, in part, Darr's testimony to the SEC.

CHAPTER 12

269–70: Darr says he always paid for these expenses out of his pocket. However, the bills from the limousine service suggest otherwise. The author has obtained certain of Harrison Freedman's account statements with Smith Limousine, which describe in detail the passengers, travel time, pickup and drop-off sites, and total cost for various trips. Although Harrison marked the trips of some passengers as personal, Darr's trips were not so marked. The bills were stamped as "paid" by Harrison Freedman Associates. Darr has contended that he used the limousines only for business purposes. The author leaves it to the reader's judgment whether such expenditures, in a city with many inexpensive car services and thousands of taxis, were a reasonable use of partnership money.

270: The trip on the *Queen Elizabeth 2* is described in sales material from 1986 titled "Harrison Freedman Associates and American Capital Partners Invites You to an Atlantic Crossing on the *Queen Elizabeth 2.*"

It was also described in detail by Tillie Tillman, a broker on the trip, in his sworn statement in *First v. Prudential-Bache.*

272–73: The author obtained a copy of Dr. Schieffer's letter to Harrison Freedman, as well as those of more than a dozen other investors in Bessemer–Key West. The author also referred to the 1981 investor list for the deal.

273–75: Tillman's experience with Mike Walters is based, in part, on Tillman's deposition in *First v. Prudential-Bache.*

275–76: Mandt has signed a sworn affidavit, dated August 27, 1992, stating under penalty of perjury that she was compelled out of fear for her job to submit to the requests of Clark and Sherman. Her statement of claim, which she reaffirms in her sworn statement, says that Sherman and/or Clark engaged in sexual relations with her. The statement of claim can be found in the "record on appeal" in the *Mandt* case cited above.

277: The author obtained a copy of Hoffstaedterr's September 24, 1986, cable to Clifton Harrison.

278: The confrontation of Prudential-Bache by the German government was partly described in *Edward M. Strasser et al. v. Prudential Securities et al.* The case is filed under index number 35124/91 in the Supreme Court of the State of New York. Harrison's decision to take a large fee from Bessemer–Key West when there was no cash for distributions from his testimony in *First v. Prudential-Bache*, cited above.

278–79: The signing ceremony and background for the Tax Reform Act of 1986 are described in *Showdown at Gucci Gulch*, by Jeffrey H. Birnbaum and Alan S. Murray. For additional details of the signing ceremony, the author relied on "President Signs New Tax Bill," *New York Times*, October 22, 1986.

The quotes from Reagan's speech are from *Speaking My Mind: Selected Speeches*, by Ronald Reagan.

280–84: The negotiations between Harrison and the Prudential-Bache legal department are described, in part, in Harrison's deposition in *First v. Prudential-Bache*. Also, the author has obtained the correspondence on this matter between Harrison and the legal department from November 1986 until 1988. These include letters to Harrison from Joseph Vallo, assistant general counsel of Prudential-Bache, dated November 13 and 24, 1986, January 2, 1987; from Vallo to Gayle Gordon of Harrison Freedman, dated March 23, April 7, 1987. Also, it includes letters to Vallo from Donna Webb, president of Harrison Freedman Associates, dated December 1, 1986; January 16, March 23, April 1, April 8, 1987; a December 9, 1986 letter to Harrison from Kevin McKay, the firm's deputy general counsel; and letters to Harrison from Joel Davidson, dated November 6 and November 7, 1986, and June 1, 1988. Those are the critical letters among about forty such documents relied on by the author.

282: The failure of Prudential-Bache to obtain the $2 million owed by Harrison, and Schechter's description of that failure as "an administrative oversight," are described, in part, in *Strasser v. Prudential*, cited above.

282–84: The deposition of Harrison by Charles Cox is taken verbatim from the transcript of that encounter in the case *McNulty v. Prudential-Bache*, cited above.

284: Tillman's conversations with Diestel are described, in part, in his deposition referenced above.

CHAPTER 13

285: In this chapter, the author incorporated information from the sworn testimony of a range of individuals in the case *In Re: Prudential-Bache Energy Growth Funds Securities Litigation*, cited above. Charles Patterson, taken February 19–20, 1991; Al Dempsey, taken November 5–8, 1991; Bill Webb, taken December 3–6, 1991; Pete Theo, taken January 14–16, 1992; Bill Pittman, taken February 10–12, 1992; and John Barron Clancy, taken February 14, 1992. Those records, which were obtained by the author, are not publicly available.

285–87: The November 11, 1986, meeting about the growth fund between Rice and the executives in the Direct Investment Group is described in a memo of that date from Rice to Dempsey.

287: The early sales performance of the energy growth fund is from a president's report by John Graham to the board of directors of Graham Resources for 1986.

288: An undated copy of "Harding's Highlights," describing the growth fund, was obtained by the author.

288: A transcript of Higbee's presentation to brokers at the Southeast regional conference was obtained by the author.

A copy of the growth fund sales script for Prudential-Bache brokers in the Southwest was obtained by the author.

289: Patterson's belief that the growth fund paid $10 million more for the First City loans than bidders would have is described in Patterson's February 4, 1987, memorandum to senior officials at First City.

290: Terms of the HRB loan are described in numerous documents, including Patterson's testimony, cited above. Also, see the November 27, 1990, testimony of Chris J. O'Mara, a senior vice-president of First City, in the case *Gallagher et al. v. Graham Energy et al.*, civil action number 89–4296, filed in the U.S. District Court for the Eastern District of Louisiana. Again, the case was settled and the depositions are not publicly available. Also, see the testimony of Al Dempsey in the above-cited case.

Finally, the transaction is described in detail in the December 1991 edition of *GFL News*, a newsletter for growth fund investors suing Prudential-Bache and Graham Resources.

290: A copy of the summer 1987 edition of *Energy Digest* was obtained by the author.

292: Through his lawyer, Storaska denies ever having done anything improper. The author again makes reference to "In the Matter of Prudential Securities," the order instituting public proceedings, making findings, and imposing sanctions. Also, see the above-referenced "The Large Firm Project," a May 1994 report by the SEC. Neither document names Storaska, but his business practices are criticized with enough identifying detail to make it clear that the government is criticizing him. Also, see "Prudential's Firm Within a Firm," *New York Times*, May 25, 1993.

292–93: Storaska's trades on June 12, 1987, are described in the June 17 memo by Grose. The author also obtained confirmation slips for those trades to the accounts in question.

293: Storaska's subsequent purchase of the energy growth fund, which was then canceled, comes from documents in the account of Eddy Phillips, a Storaska customer.

295: The problem with the distributions for the energy income partnerships is demonstrated in the quarterly reports, *Prudential-Bache Energy Income Partnerships Cash Distributions*, which were obtained by the author.

296: Darr's attempts to sell the Prudential-Bache interest in the Graham partnerships for his own personal profit are described in Rice's testimony to the SEC, cited above.

296: The July 23, 1987, instructions from Darr that Graham Resources should structure their deals to ensure that Direct Investment Group personnel received higher pay are described in part in a memo to the files written by Al Dempsey on that date.

296–97: The concern expressed about the distributions by the growth fund is described in the minutes to an October 27, 1987, management committee meeting at Graham Resources.

297: The Maple Gulf Coast deal is described in Al Dempsey's November 6, 1991, deposition in *In Re: Prudential-Bache Energy Growth Funds Securities Litigation*, cited above.

Also, see a March 2, 1988, memorandum from Ed Trahan, a member of the growth fund investment group, to the other members of the committee. That document, in reference to the convertible preferred stock proceeds, says "used fund origination fee prepaid interest and first principal installment on Utah reserve loan on PBEGF." In other words, the proceeds from the preferred stock purchased by the growth fund were used to immediately pay off other obligations to the growth fund.

Terms of the Maple Gulf Coast deal are also described in the December 1991 edition of *GFL News*, a newsletter for energy growth investors suing Prudential-Bache.

302–4: The author has obtained a transcript of Storaska's speech at Vancouver. In certain instances, the transcript is incomplete, and the author relied on the memories of people who heard the speech to fill in the blanks. Storaska's performance and ranking in a branch were discussed in his introduction for that speech.

304: The E. F. Hutton shareholder meeting was described in Carpenter and Feloni, *The Fall of the House of Hutton*.

The amount of partnerships sold by April 25, 1988, comes from the prospectuses for those deals.

304–6: Details of the VMS Mortgage Investors Fund from the prospectus for that deal, filed in March 1988. The author has also obtained a wide range of marketing materials for the investment, all of which tout its safety and describe it as the perfect investment for retirees and CD buyers.

Creedon's original discussions about VMS with Eisle and Macejka are described in part in his April 1, 1992, deposition in *Morris* v. *Prudential-Bache*, number 92K01527, filed in the Municipal Court of the State of California for the County of Los Angeles.

306: The knowledge of due diligence officials about the intended investments by the VMS Mortgage Investors Fund is disclosed in the April 24, 1991, testimony by James Kelso of the Prudential-Bache Direct Investment Group in the case *Miele* v. *Prudential-Bache Securities*, case number 32–136–0357–90-ID before the American Arbitration Association.

306–7: Details of the fraud involving VMS Mortgage Investors Fund from the prospectus, as well as the recently unsealed fourth consolidated and amended complaint in the case *In Re: VMS Securities Litigation*, case number 89 c 9448, in the U.S. District Court for the Northern District of Illinois, Eastern Division.

Also, see "Notice of Intent to Invoke Sanctions under the Kansas Securities Act," in the case *In the Matter of Prudential Securities, a/k/a Prudential-Bache Securities*, docket number 91E127, before the securities commissioner of the state of Kansas.

307: Darr's expenses for the trip to London were obtained by the author, including his itemized bill from the Berkeley, dated May 20–31, 1988.

Details of the Berkeley were provided in interviews with representatives of the hotel. The cost of Darr's Concorde flight was disclosed in the December 1991 issue of *GFL News*.

308: The expenditures for all of the Graham officials and Prudential-Bache brokers were described in a computer printout of expenses by the Wernli Group, the travel agency that handled the trip.

CHAPTER 14

311–13: The encounter between Schechter and Watson was first described in Hawkins's *Business Week* article of March 4, 1991, cited above.

311: The negotiations between Watson and Giordano to change Darr's risk in light of the inquiry into First South are described by Darr in his SEC testimony.

Also, see "Final Report Regarding Certain Transactions Among James Darr, George Watson and A. Starke Taylor III," by Locke Purnell Rain Harrell, cited above.

313–14: The background of Locke Purnell from an undated brochure used by the law firm to describe its services to clients.

316: Colella's conversations with Humphrey, the anonymous caller, from the Locke Purnell report, cited above.

317–18: Some details of Petty's conversation with Bud Berry from a January 28, 1988, letter to Petty from C. F. Allison Jr., a Locke Purnell lawyer.

318–21: Petty's two meetings with Berry are described in the Locke Purnell report cited above.

325: Harrison's removal of money from the Stamford Hotel partnership is described, in part, in an October 11, 1988, memo to the file by Paul Tessler, an executive with Prudential-Bache.

325–28: Some details of the contentious July 1988 meeting in Florida from handwritten notes about the meeting and Dempsey's July 5, 1988, memorandum to Pete Theo and Leo Cailleteau.

328–29: Sichenzio's conversation with Trice in September 1988 was described in Trice's testimony in his arbitration, cited above.

329: A copy of the 1988 Risers brochure distributed to Prudential-Bache brokers was obtained by the author.

The evidence of the firm's soft sell of the risks with Risers is based on the author's review of certain sales material. In addition, the author relied on the sworn affidavits of former Prudential-Bache brokers and branch managers. Many of those affidavits were filed in the case *In Re: RAC Mortgage Investment Corporation Securities Litigation*, file number K–89–1796, filed in the U.S. District Court for the District of Maryland.

The affidavits are from Robert Leacox, a former branch office manager from Denver; A. James Whitney, the former branch manager in the firm's Poughkeepsie, New York, office; Richard McCrea, the former branch manager in Wooster, Ohio; Peter A. Dwan, the former branch manager from Syracuse, New York; James A. Laurick, the former branch manager for the Oklahoma City office; John E. Bayum, the former branch manager of the Richmond, Virginia, office; and William Hutchins Smith, a broker with the firm's midtown Atlanta branch office.

CHAPTER 15

335: Van Sickle's ruling is filed as case number 3–87–196 at the U.S. District Court for the District of Minnesota, Fourth Division.

336–37: The trading performance of VMS Mortgage Investors Fund from the class-action lawsuit, cited above. Creedon described his reaction to the situation in his deposition, cited above.

339: Apparently Page was right about Kane being a scapegoat. Jim Trice, the regional director in Atlanta at the time, testified in his own arbitration against Prudential-Bache that he had been ordered by the legal department to have Kane fired to make the firm's response look good to the SEC. Page's case with Kane is described in the June 12, 1987, statement of claim in "Kane v. Prudential-Bache," filed with the director of arbitration with the New York Stock Exchange.

The Kane matter is also described in the June 12, 1987, statement of claim from "In the Matter of the Arbitration Between William A. Kane vs. Prudential-Bache Securities, Michael McClain and Patrick Finley."

341: The details of Webb's statements in Spain about the growth fund come in part from his December 3, 1991, deposition in *Kaminsky v. Graham Energy*, number 91–017196, filed in the District Court of Harris County, Texas, 55th Judicial District. That deposition has since been sealed as part of a settlement in the case.

Also, see Webb's June 10, 1993, deposition in *Robertson and Sitter v. Prudential Securities*, case number 33–136–00114–92 before the American Arbitration Association.

342–43: A copy of Jackson's August 23, 1989, letter was obtained by the author.

347–48: Some details of Sichenzio's speech at the October 1989 national sales meeting dinner in New York from Roger Parsons's sworn testimony in the Trice arbitration, cited above.

348: Some details of the Silver Screen deal from the complaint in *Silver Screen Entertainment Management v. Prudential-Bache*, index number 25683, filed in the Supreme Court of the State of New York for the County of New York.

348–50: Parsons's run-in with Haick and subsequent removal as a branch manager from his sworn testimony, cited above.

351: Details of the announcement by VMS from the company's 10-Q, filed with the SEC in November 1989. The subsequent stock action from the fourth consolidated and amended class action and derivative complaint in *In Re: VMS Securities Litigation*, cited above.

351: Creedon's experiences after the collapse of VMS Mortgage Investors Fund are described in part in his deposition, cited above.

351–52: Some information about Eugene Boyle's experience with Risers from his September 13, 1990, supplement to the statement of answer in "Prudential-Bache v. Eugene Boyle 3d" before the National Association of Securities Dealers. Also, see Boyle's testimony in that case and his sworn affidavit of July 9, 1990, in the case *Prudential-Bache Securities v. Page & Bacek*, civil action number 1:90-CV-1300-GET in the U.S. District Court for the Northern District of Georgia.

352: Boyle described his conversation with Ricca in a sworn statement dated June 4, 1990, cited above. He elaborated on that statement in his own arbitration case.

In sworn testimony on October 10, 1990, Ricca denied ever making the "seventeen years" statement. In his testimony in *Prudential-Bache* v. *Page & Bacek*, Ricca labeled the claim by Boyle "a complete fabrication."

After examining the information, the author has concluded that the facts surrounding the case more closely support Boyle's version of events. Boyle immediately wrote a letter laying out the nature of the conversation with Ricca. That letter, which was obtained by the author, was fully consistent with his subsequent claims, although it did not specifically mention the "seventeen years" comment. Second, once Boyle left the firm to assist his clients, Prudential-Bache did indeed bring litigation against him, seeking a return of up-front money he had been paid to leave Merrill Lynch for Prudential-Bache. Third, and most disturbing, after Boyle left the firm, Prudential-Bache filed a false form with the National Association of Securities Dealers claiming that Boyle, rather than Prudential-Bache itself, had been the subject of customer complaints for misrepresentation. But those complaints, which were obtained by the author, do not allege impropriety by Boyle but rather by Prudential-Bache. The firm settled those cases. Boyle, on the other hand, was investigated by the New York Stock Exchange because of the form submitted by Prudential-Bache. He was cleared. Subsequently Prudential-Bache was ordered by an arbitration panel to revise its false submission to the NASD. Finally, the author notes that a similar event transpired subsequently, involving James Barrett and described in chapter 17.

353: Schwarzman's telephone conversation with Lazard was described in an April 16, 1992, letter by Mark Kenyon, a vice-president of finance at Blackstone, to Larry Jacobs, a lawyer with Kramer, Levin, Nessen, Kamin & Frankel.

The negotiations between Prudential and Paine Webber were disclosed by Sarah Bartlett in her article "It's Deadline Time for George Ball," in the *New York Times*, January 14, 1990. Some of the figures on performance also come from that article.

353–54: The author obtained a copy of the confidential information package on Prudential-Bache, dated January 1990, and assembled under Ball's direction for distribution to German and Swiss banks.

355: Ball's meeting with Jean-Louis Lalogeais on February 7, 1990, is described in a memo by Lalogeais to his colleagues at Booz Allen. The memo, dated February 9, 1990, was obtained by the author.

355–56: The emergency meeting called by Sichenzio is described, in part, in *Silver Screen Entertainment Management* v. *Prudential-Bache*, cited above.

358: The first big Prudential-Bache article in *Business Week* appeared in the February 26, 1990, issue of the magazine, under the bylines of Chuck Hawkins, Jon Friedman, and David Greising.

358–59: A copy of Prudential-Bache's lawsuit against Page & Bacek and the service papers were obtained by the author. The case, under the caption *Prudential-Bache* v. *Page & Bacek*, is cited above.

359: The timing of the replacement of Proscia by Giordano from *Wall Street Letter*, March 12, 1990.

CHAPTER 16

361–64: Creedon's experiences come, in part, from his sworn testimony cited above.

362: The author obtained multiple copies of the law department's form response—the so-called fuck-you letter—to the client VMS letters.

363: Although the firm denies it ever attempted to push investors into the class-action suits, the evidence against Prudential-Bache is overwhelming. The author has interviewed brokers from across the country who tell substantially the same story as Bill Creedon. Some have stated that they personally heard Jack Graner, a regional director to the VMS task force established by Ball, state that brokers were to tell investors to join the class action. Similar claims have been made about every major class action involved here. Moreover, the author has obtained notes written by Pru-Bache brokers instructing their clients to wait for the class action, as well as a number of tape recordings that clearly document the nature of what was occurring. With John Eisle, several clients—including Charles Vallas, Mary Lee Griswold, David Hendry, Robert Blondeel Timmerman, Charles Limmer, and Salvatore Russo—filed complaints against him personally, claiming that he fraudulently instructed them that the class action was their only option for compensation. The only court case involving Mr. Vallas's claim was dismissed because Mr. Vallas had signed a general release.

The other complaints about Eisle were sent to the NASD. The organization took no action, saying it could not find enough supporting documentation. An NASD official said that the group did not consider the various claims as supporting each other because the clients all had the same lawyer. However, the author has spoken to other brokers who confirmed the clients' version of events. In addition, a series of secret tape recordings obtained by the author also substantiate it.

The author would note that the basis of the denials being issued by Prudential Securities is that the firm steadfastly avoided ever giving legal advice to clients. That statement is a bald-faced lie.

When the firm faced the growth fund litigation from Bristow, Hackerman, it sent a letter in June 1991 advising clients *not* to participate in the lawsuit. The author notes that this was not a typical class action, which might be settled for pennies on the dollar. Indeed, Prudential-Bache was pushing for a class action, and Bristow, Hackerman was resisting. The potential for huge losses for the firm was apparent.

It was in that atmosphere that the firm sent out its legal recommendations to every investor in Growth Fund 2. The letter criticized the fee structure of the lawsuit and then said: "The soliciting lawyers further ask that you turn over virtually total control of a lawsuit brought in your name to them and to a committee composed of a few of their clients, people whom you probably do not know. The committee has the right to make almost every decision about your lawsuit without your prior notice or input."

Finally, the growth fund letter states: "We would prefer that you not file suit. We recommend that you consult your professional advisor and consider all factors before deciding whether to accept the proposal of the lawyers soliciting you."

A number of the recipients of this letter interpreted the "professional advisor" statement to mean they should ask their stockbrokers. After all, if they had a lawyer to consult, they didn't need another one to take the case. In each instance, the author found, the stockbrokers advised the clients against proceeding with the growth fund litigation.

This letter is legal advice. Prudential Securities' statements that it has never done such a thing are not true.

364–66: Some details regarding Joseph Siff from his affidavit and other documents from the arbitration case, *Prudential Securities* v. *Joseph Siff*, number 91–01262 before the National Association of Securities Dealers.

367: Details of Webb's conference call with Bristow from Webb's June 10, 1993, deposition in *Robertson and Sitter* v. *Prudential Securities*, cited above.

368: The dialogue from Schechter's deposition from a transcript in the *Prudential-Bache* v. *Page & Bacek* case, cited above. Some statements were edited out by the author for clarity's sake. No material information was omitted.

369–70: Eloise Burg's experiences were chronicled in a number of publications. See "Broken Trust," *Palm Beach County Sun-Sentinel*, November 18, 1990; "Prudential Unit Faces Woes in Unloading Partnerships," the *Wall Street Journal*, September 20, 1990; "Investors Advised to Read Prospectuses, Learn Risks," the *Tribune Review* of Ligonier, Pennsylvania, October 29, 1990; "Taking It to the Street," *New York Post*, September 27, 1990; "Prudential to Pay Investor $680,000," *Palm Beach Post*, May 4, 1991; and "Brokerage Opts to Cover Widow's Loss," *New York Newsday*, April 18, 1991.

370–73: Webb's experiences in his termination were described by him in part in his June 10, 1993, arbitration, cited above. Also see his December 1991 testimony in *Sondock* v. *Graham Energy*, number 91–020404, filed in the District Court of Harris County, Texas, 281st Judicial District.

377: The cases pursued by the Idaho Securities Bureau under Wayne Klein are described in the annual reports for the state's Department of Finance, filed each year with the office of the governor.

378: Some background on the Schneider investigation from the investigative order *State of Idaho* v. *Louise Schneider and Prudential-Bache*, docket number 1991-7-3, before the director of the Department of Finance of the state of Idaho.

379–81: The details of Ball's last months from a series of internal Prudential-Bache documents. They include internal notes by bankers, dated November 1990, discussing the options for the firm, including its sale; a November 1990 annual review of Prudential-Bache by its bankers; and a series of confidential memos between Burton, Ball, and Winters from the fall of 1990.

380–81: Details of the restructuring were announced in a December 20, 1990, memo from Ball entitled "Restructuring and Strategy." Also, see a memo from Winters to all employees of Prudential from that same date.

382: The Hawkins article, "The Mess at Pru-Bache," is cited above.

CHAPTER 17

386–87: A copy of contemporaneous notes from Bill Creedon's meeting with Michael Licosati was obtained by the author.

387: The VMS private partnership class-action settlement was described in a July 1991 analysis by First Winthrop Corporation.

Beigel & Sandler, which handled many of the Prudential-Bache class actions, has been widely criticized in the profession for settling cases without performing sufficient investigation. The settlement style of Beigel & Sandler was described in "Millions for Us, Pennies for You," the *New York Times*, December 19, 1993.

The criticisms of Beigel & Sandler's work by judges include an April 1992 opinion by Judge Thomas P. Griesa in the case *Kushner v. DBG Properties*, a limited partnership sold by another firm. The judge dismissed twenty-seven complaints, calling them "equally frivolous," and saying that "it appears to the court as if the complaints were spun out of a word-processed original, with little attention to the details of each partnership and its private placement memorandum."

In 1994, the firm was sued in a class action on behalf of investors in other cases. That litigation accused the firm of legal malpractice, fraud, and misrepresentation. The class action against the firm is captioned *Adelstein et al. v. Beigel & Sandler*, case number BC104597, filed on May 11, 1994, in the Superior Court of the State of California for the County of Los Angeles. The case involves a Beigel & Sandler settlement of a lawsuit involving a limited partnership called Mayer Warner Center, which was sold by Shearson.

The VMS public partnership class-action settlement was described in an October 1991 analysis by Page & Bacek.

388: The appointment of Hardwick Simmons was described in "Prudential Names Simmons to Head Brokerage Unit," the *Wall Street Journal*, April 25, 1991. Also, see "Prudential Securities Reorganizes at the Top," in the *New York Times* on the same date.

The firing of Richard Sichenzio is described in "Prudential Unit Fires Sichenzio as Brokers' Chief," the *Wall Street Journal*, June 10, 1991.

The hiring of George Murray is described in "Prudential Names Head of Retail Securities Unit," *New York Times*, July 31, 1991.

The hiring of Woody Knight is described in "Prudential Securities Taps Woody Knight for New Position," the *Wall Street Journal*, May 20, 1991.

391–92: The deposition of Darrell Haney was described in "Plaintiff's Motion for Sanctions" of February 11, 1992, in the case *Hitchcock v. Prudential-Bache*, cited above.

394: The Kansas complaint is described in "Notice of Intent to Invoke Sanctions under the Kansas Securities Act," cited above.

395: Copies of some of the Bristow letters to clients regarding regulatory complaints were obtained by the author.

395: Wechsler's history in the growth fund litigation is described in "Objection to Settlement," in *Starr and Lipton v. Graham Energy*, cited above.

396–98: The dialogue regarding the proposed class-action settlement on the growth funds from a transcript of the proceedings before Judge McNamara on December 11, 1991, in the case *In Re: Prudential-Bache Energy Growth Funds Securities Litigation*, docket number cv-91-md-867-d.

399: Copies of dozens of letters both to regulators and from regulators in response to the Bristow, Hackerman mass mailing were obtained by the author.

400: Terms of the growth fund litigation settlement are described in *GFL News*, June 1992.

402: Simmons's announcement about the rebirth of the Direct Investment Group from *Wall Street Letter*, July 20, 1992.

402: A copy of Schiller's letter to his client was obtained by the author.

Also, see "True Bill of Indictment" against Jeffrey A. Schiller, number GJR F92-02923, filed in July 1992 with the 194th Judicial District Court in Dallas. The case was subsequently dismissed.

404: Copies of the corporate records for Ambryshell were obtained by the author.

405: Peter von Maur's instructions that Storaska be allowed to keep $26,000 in fees to ensure he remained a friendly witness in part from a December 3, 1992, memorandum from Michael McClain to branch administration in New York.

407–8: The terms of the energy income settlement are described in "Memorandum, Opinion and Order" by Judge Marcel Livaudais, dated February 19, 1993, and filed in the case *In Re: Prudential-Bache Energy Income Partnerships Securities Litigation.*

Analysis of the energy income settlement in part from a January 19, 1993, examination of the deal by the American Association of Limited Partners. Also, see "Prudential Makes Settlement-Rollup Offer," *The Perspective*, November/December 1992.

408–10: Barrett's experiences in part from his complaint filed before the National Association of Securities Dealers. Also, see Barrett's April 14, 1994, sworn testimony in "Belmont and Belmont v. Prudential Securities," case number 93–02086 before the NASD.

CHAPTER 18

412: A sixth regulator, Burnet Maybank III, the securities commissioner of South Carolina, also joined the task force during the meeting at the Brazilian Court Hotel. Shortly afterward, he stepped down from his job with the state and resigned from the task force.

414: A copy of the January 14, 1993, letter to Pat Conti from Gary Lynch was obtained by the author.

414–15: A copy of Klein's January 22, 1993, letter to Livaudais was obtained by the author.

418–19: The details of Grossmann's closing argument from contemporaneous notes taken of the presentation.

419–20: Livaudais's "Memorandum, Opinion and Order" of February 19, 1993, was filed in the case *In Re: Prudential-Bache Energy Income Partnerships Securities Litigation*, cited above.

423: Details of the GBK bid from tombstone advertisement that appeared in the *New York Times* and the *Wall Street Journal* on March 22, 1993.

Details of the Parker & Parsley bid from a news release issued by the energy company on May 10, 1993.

423–25: Some details of Scanlan's discussions during the Chanin deposition from the transcript, dated March 29, 1993. The case number is cited above.

425: A copy of the subpoena to Prudential Securities involving Fred Storaska was obtained by the author. The timing of the issuance of the subpoena comes from the fax "telltale" imprinted on the document.

426: A copy of Finley's April 13, 1993, letter to Klein regarding the Locke Purnell report was obtained by the author.

427: An unnumbered copy of the statement of claim in "J. Donald Smith v. Prudential Securities and J. Frederic Storaska" before the NASD was obtained by the author.

Ahearn's statements regarding Pru-Bache's decision to sue the NASD over the ordered release of the Locke Purnell report from the *Wall Street Journal*, April 21, 1993.

428: Copies of the questionnaire distributed by the task force were obtained by the author.

432: Schechter made his statement about being "happy" to turn over the Locke Purnell report in the *Wall Street Journal*, July 13, 1993.

434–35: Klein's shot across the bow that he delivered through Hawkins was printed in *Business Week*, August 2, 1993.

EPILOGUE

446–47: The author attended the press conference where the settlements were announced.

447: A copy of the Prudential Securities advertisement ran in the *New York Times* on October 22, 1993.

The method of preparation for the advertisement and Simmons's state of mind about it are described in a series of interrogatories he answered in the case *Ashmore, Brown and Brown* v. *Prudential Securities*, case number 663808, filed in the Superior Court of California for the County of San Diego. In those interrogatories, Simmons is asked specifically what he meant in the letter advertisements when he described what went wrong with the partnership sales. All he refers to in those answers are failures on the part of brokers. He never refers to the fraudulent marketing material disseminated from New York.

Simmons made his statement about there being no systemic problem at the firm in "Fixing a Piece of the Rock," *Newsweek*, August 8, 1994.

448: The author obtained a copy of the videotape of the November 23, 1993, meeting in Dryden Hall. It is not publicly available.

448–50: The dialogue from the energy income fairness hearing of January 1994 from notes taken by the author and an official recording of the hearing.

451–52: The author obtained a copy of the never-used March 3, 1994, press release announcing California's decision to launch an enforcement action against Prudential Securities, with the intention of suspending the firm's license to do business in the state.

453: The troubles with the "straight talk" campaign are described in "Prudential Image Mending Stumbles," *New York Times*, February 17, 1994.

453: Simmons's statement that he wasn't lying when he told the public that $330 million would be enough to pay defrauded investors from Siconolfi, "Prudential Securities Escapes an Indictment, but Firm Is Still Shaky," *Wall Street Journal*, October 12, 1994.

454–55: Details of Jack Graner's death from the report by the Los Angeles medical examiner of January 28, 1994, and police reports of January 27, 1994. The medical examiner at first ruled the death an accidental overdose, apparently overlooking the fact that police had found the suicide note. When contacted by the author about the apparent discrepancy, an official from the medical examiner's department said that the original finding had been in error and that Graner had indeed committed suicide.

455: Some details of Sherman's life after Pru-Bache from his testimony in the Trice arbitration, cited above.

457: The amount of money obtained by Darr in recent years from his residual participations is described in his sworn testimony in *Griffin* v. *Prudential Securities*, cited above.

AFTERWORD

458: The statement from Linda Myers from a report by Steve Young for the July 20, 1995, broadcast of *Moneyline* on the Cable News Network.

458: The quote from Charles Perkins on Darr's contract from "Book Says Prudential Continues to Pay a Former Executive," *New York Times*, July 21, 1995.

459: Details of Betty Allen's case from "Prudential Told to Pay Broker in Fraud Case," *New York Times*, August 8, 1995.

459–60: Details of the last Prudential partnership class action settlement from "Prudential Pact: $110 Million to Settle Suit," *New York Times*, December 11, 1995.

461: Details of the Prudential Insurance reorganization from "Prudential to Shift 1,110 Jobs to Newark," *Bloomberg Business News*, February 29, 1996.

461–62: Details of the Prudential Insurance settlement with state insurance regulators from "Prudential to Pay $35 Million Fine, Make Restitution," *Bloomberg Business News*, July 9, 1996.

462: The decision of New York Life Insurance Company to repay its partnership investors was described in "New York Life in Partnership Liquidations," *New York Times*, April 2, 1996.

462: The Paine Webber settlement was described in "Paine Webber Is Settling Fraud Counts," *New York Times*, January 19, 1996.

INDEX